'History books should give us insight and information, surprise and entertainment, and allow us to see the world, an incident or a character differently. *Six Minutes in May* delivers in abundance'
Observer Books of the Year

'An eloquent study in how quickly the political landscape can change – and history with it'
The Economist Books of the Year

'Of the abundant new books on the Second World War, *Six Minutes in May* takes the prize. The familiar story of how Churchill unexpectedly became prime minister in 1940 has never been told so amusingly, nor in such detail'
Daily Telegraph Books of the Year

'Unputdownable... Using new evidence with a novelist's feeling for personality and atmosphere, *Six Minutes in May* tells how a military disaster, parliamentary intrigues, a hidden love affair and a six-minute meeting enabled Winston Churchill to come to power'
John Gray, *Guardian* Books of the Year

'Enthralling... Shakespeare has written a book that will captivate readers and fill professional historians with envy at how far he outclasses them'
Peter Craven, *The Australian* Books of the Year

'Far and away the best account of the moment which changed our national life and the world'
John Simpson

'Magnificent'
Times Literary Supplement

NICHOLAS SHAKESPEARE

Nicholas Shakespeare was born in Worcester in 1957 and grew up in the Far East and Latin America. He is the author of *The Vision of Elena Silves*, winner of the Somerset Maugham and Betty Trask awards; *The High Flyer*, for which he was nominated as one of Granta's Best of Young British Novelists; *The Dancer Upstairs* and most recently *Inheritance*. His non-fiction includes *In Tasmania* and *Priscilla* and an acclaimed biography of Bruce Chatwin. He is a fellow of the Royal Society of Literature, and in 2016 was a Visiting Fellow of All Souls.

NICHOLAS SHAKESPEARE

Six Minutes in May

How Churchill Unexpectedly
Became Prime Minister

VINTAGE

3 5 7 9 10 8 6 4

Vintage
20 Vauxhall Bridge Road,
London SW1V 2SA

Vintage is part of the Penguin Random House group of companies
whose addresses can be found at global.penguinrandomhouse.com

Map of the Norway Campaign by William Donohoe

The author and publisher have made every effort to trace the holders
of copyright in quotations and images reproduced in this book. Any
inadvertent omissions or errors may be corrected in future editions.

First published in Vintage in 2018
First published in hardback by Harvill Secker in 2017

penguin.co.uk/vintage

A CIP catalogue record for this book is available from the British Library

ISBN 9781784701000

Printed and bound by Clays Ltd, Elcograf S.p.A.

Penguin Random House is committed to a sustainable future
for our business, our readers and our planet. This book is made
from Forest Stewardship Council® certified paper.

TO JOHN HATT

'Strange that we do not fully realise men's characters
while they are alive.'
NEVILLE CHAMBERLAIN, 27 February 1918

CONTENTS

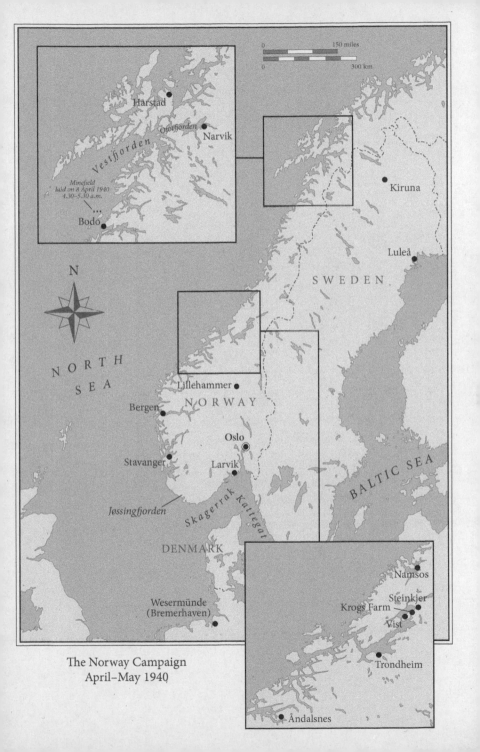

The Norway Campaign
April–May 1940

LIST OF ILLUSTRATIONS

Endpapers: Neville Chamberlain speaking in the Norway Debate, 7 May 1940; uniformed MPs on the Opposition benches – John Moore-Brabazon © RAF Museum

DRAMATIS PERSONAE ON 7 MAY 1940

War Cabinet

Neville Chamberlain – Prime Minister

Edward Wood, Lord Halifax – Foreign Secretary

Sir John Simon (Liberal National) – Chancellor of the Exchequer

Winston Churchill – First Lord of the Admiralty

Sir Samuel Hoare – Secretary of State for Air

Oliver Stanley – Secretary of State for War

Sir Kingsley Wood – Lord Privy Seal

Maurice Hankey, 1st Baron Hankey – Minister without Portfolio

Sir Edward Bridges – Secretary to the War Cabinet

Lieutenant General Sir Ian Jacob – Military Assistant to the War Cabinet

Chiefs of Staff

General Sir Edmund Ironside – Chief of the Imperial General Staff (CIGS)

Admiral of the Fleet Sir Dudley Pound – First Sea Lord

Air Marshal Cyril Newall – Chief of the Air Staff

Major General Hastings Ismay – Churchill's Chief of Staff (since 1 May)

Ministers

Anthony Eden – Secretary of State for Dominions

Sir John Reith (Independent) – Secretary of State for Information

Euan Wallace – Secretary of State for Transport

Frederick Marquis, Lord Woolton – Secretary of State for Food

Harry Crookshank – Financial Secretary to the Treasury

Robert Bernays (National Liberal) – Parliamentary Secretary, Transport

Geoffrey Shakespeare (National Liberal) – Parliamentary Secretary, Dominions (since 2 April)

House of Commons

Captain Edward FitzRoy – Speaker
Sir Dennis Herbert – Deputy Speaker

No. 10

Sir Horace Wilson – Permanent Secretary to the Treasury
Captain David Margesson – Government Chief Whip
Sir Arthur Rucker – Principal Private Secretary to Chamberlain
John Colville – Junior Private Secretary to Chamberlain
Alec Douglas-Home, Lord Dunglass – Parliamentary Private Secretary to Chamberlain
Sir Joseph Ball – political adviser to Chamberlain

Foreign Office

Sir Alexander Cadogan – Permanent Under-Secretary
Richard ('Rab') Butler – Parliamentary Under-Secretary
Henry ('Chips') Channon – Parliamentary Private Secretary to Butler
Valentine Lawford – Private Secretary to Halifax (until December 1940)
Charles Peake – Head of News Department (and Private Secretary to Halifax from 1941)

Buckingham Palace

Sir Alexander Hardinge – Private Secretary to George VI

Rebel Conservative MPs

Leo Amery
Nancy Astor, Viscountess Astor
Brendan Bracken
Bob Boothby
Harold Macmillan
Alfred Duff Cooper
Paul Emrys-Evans

Admiral of the Fleet Sir Roger Keyes
Major General Sir Edward Louis Spears
Ronald Tree

Other rebel MPs

Harold Nicolson – National Labour
Clement Davies – Independent Liberal
Leslie Hore-Belisha – National Liberal

Labour Opposition MPs

Clement Attlee – leader
Arthur Greenwood – deputy leader
Hugh Dalton – Shadow Foreign Secretary
Herbert Morrison – Shadow Home Secretary

Liberal Opposition MPs

Sir Archibald Sinclair – leader, Liberal Parliamentary Party
Sir Percy Harris – Chief Whip, Liberal Parliamentary Party
Dingle Foot – Liberal Parliamentary Party
David Lloyd George – Liberal Opposition Party

Norway Campaign: Namsos

Captain Peter Fleming – i/c No. 10 Military Mission
Captain Martin Lindsay – No. 10 Military Mission
Private Tom Fowler – 146ᵗʰ Infantry Brigade
Private Frank Lodge – 146ᵗʰ Infantry Brigade, Intelligence
Major General Adrian Carton de Wiart – Army commander, 'Maurice Force'
Storm and Birger Evensen – drivers

Norway Campaign: Narvik

Giles Romilly – correspondent, Daily Express
Major General Pierse Mackesy – Army commander, 'Rupert Force'

Admiral of the Fleet William Boyle, Earl of Cork and Orrery – Naval commander, 'Rupert Force'

Miscellaneous

Ivan Maisky – Soviet Ambassador

Joseph Kennedy – American Ambassador

Max Aitken, Lord Beaverbrook – owner, Daily and Sunday Express

Geoffrey Dawson – editor, The Times

William Berry, Viscount Camrose – owner/editor-in-chief, Daily Telegraph

Albert James Sylvester – Principal Private Secretary to Lloyd George

Basil Liddell Hart – military correspondent, The Times

Lady Alexandra 'Baba' Metcalfe – George Curzon's youngest daughter

Irene Curzon, Baroness Ravensdale – George Curzon's eldest daughter

Nicholas Mosley – son of Oswald Mosley; nephew of Baba Metcalfe

Violet Bonham Carter – Liberal activist; daughter of Herbert Asquith

Margot Asquith, Countess of Oxford – widow of Herbert Asquith; stepmother of Violet

Blanche 'Baffy' Dugdale – niece and biographer of Arthur Balfour

Nancy Dugdale – wife of former Deputy Chief Whip, Sir Thomas Dugdale

Anne Chamberlain – wife of Prime Minister

Valerie Cole – niece of Prime Minister

Dorothy Wood, Viscountess Halifax – wife of Foreign Secretary

Clementine Churchill – wife of First Lord

Mary Churchill – youngest daughter of First Lord

Nellie Romilly – sister of Clementine; mother of Giles

Colonel Bertram Romilly – father of Giles

PROLOGUE

On the one and only occasion that he visited Norway, Winston Churchill was received like a great hero. In May 1948, a fortnight before publication of *The Gathering Storm*, his first volume of memoirs of the Second World War, he flew with his wife Clementine to Oslo to receive an honorary Doctorate of Philosophy. While accepting the award in the University Aula, Churchill spoke with emotion about Hitler's invasion of neutral Norway eight years earlier, that 'foul and treacherous outrage' which ranked with the Sicilian Vespers and the massacre of Glencoe 'as one of the black deeds of history'. He told the hall into which more than 1,500 students had once been packed for transportation to concentration camps in Germany: 'We have emerged from the most terrible of wars which has yet been fought in the world.'

Yet many in his audience felt that Churchill – 'known all over the globe as "the Architect of Victory"' – had omitted something of immense significance. It fell to the governor of the Bank of Norway, Gunnar Jahn, to point this out. At a banquet in Churchill's honour, after tens of thousands of Norwegians had waved him through the streets as he passed in an open motor-car, Jahn spoke of an argument he had had in 1942 with a depressed countryman who believed that the Germans would win the war. Jahn had said to him: 'Oh no, the Germans lost the war when they invaded Norway.'

He then explained. 'It had this effect, that Winston Churchill took over the leadership of Great Britain.'

PART ONE

SIX MINUTES IN MAY

1
PERFECT BLACKOUT

'Is there any MP who doesn't want to be Prime Minister?'
LESLIE HORE-BELISHA MP, 4 January 1940

A year to the day after Churchill became Prime Minister, the House of Commons was 'blown to pieces' by a Luftwaffe bomb. On 10 May 1941, the Speaker's Chair and the front and opposition benches were crushed beneath a steep hill of smoking rubble. The MP Vernon Bartlett met Churchill clambering over it, 'his face covered with dust, through which the tears that ran down his cheeks had made two miniature river beds'. All that remained of Churchill's cherished Chamber – which, he was to tell the Norwegian Storting, 'we pride ourselves is the cradle and also the citadel of parliamentary government throughout the nations' – was a mass of broken masonry, ashes, and the tangled remains of metal railings. An historic stage stood obliterated. Reliable records of the dramas and rituals enacted upon it seemed, at that moment, irretrievable.

Then, in the 1960s, a tin of photographic negatives was discovered which were to give a tantalising glimpse into a vanished past. The twenty-nine images are the only known record of the old House of Commons during a sitting. More than that, they captured a seismic moment: what A. J. P. Taylor called the 'splendid upheaval' of the Chamberlain government.

These unique photographs were taken illegally on two of the hottest afternoons of the unbelievably warm spring of 1940, during the Norway Debate of 7 and 8 May. It was a breach of privilege to take pictures inside Parliament. If discovered by the Serjeant at Arms or one of his Doorkeepers, Conservative backbencher John Moore-Brabazon risked confiscation of his negatives, and suspension. Not in the eighty-eight years of Sir Charles Barry's Chamber had a Member violated this rule.

Moore-Brabazon had pioneered the art of snapping photographs from behind enemy lines. He was the first Englishman to fly. In 1914, he established a photographic unit for the Royal Flying Corps, and following the first gas attack at Ypres made a map of the German trenches, diving low enough to identify the uniforms. At that time, he knew more about aerial photography than anyone in the world. Twenty-five years on, startling developments in a new world war compelled him to pick up his camera again. He used a special Minox as issued to Intelligence staffs. Purchased from Latvia and nicknamed 'the spy camera', this was small, light, easy to hide.

What became known as the Norway Debate, and was to be so significant to the fortunes of the British government and the Second World War, began with a routine adjournment motion on Tuesday 7 May. The Prime Minister appeared in the Commons to defend the conduct of Britain's armed forces in Narvik, Namsos and Åndalsnes, and to answer some far-reaching questions about a calamitous military campaign that had been obscured by rumour, secrecy and hopelessly optimistic press reports.

After an ominous respite lasting seven months, following Germany's annexation of Poland, the British army in its first land battle of the war had engaged the Nazi enemy – and been routed. The navy, which had been fighting unrelentingly at sea from September 1939, had had to evacuate 11,300 troops from central Norway, with the eventual loss of 4,396 men.

This stunning news had been delivered to Parliament by Chamberlain on 2 May. In the fearful words of Vernon Bartlett, the German invasion of Britain seemed at this point 'almost inevitable', with foreign troops predicted to land in large numbers on British soil for the first time since the Norman Conquest.

It is important to emphasise that there was no expectation of a vote. The Conservative leader enjoyed a huge majority of 213 for his National government, and the opposition Labour Party under Clement Attlee was reluctant to divide the House at this precarious moment. Even though less popular with an increasingly anxious public, Chamberlain still appeared unassailable within Parliament. On 7 May, the reality for the majority of Conservative MPs was that there was no clear alternative to Chamberlain as Prime Minister; neither was there any formal procedure whereby the party could dispense with its leader.

The House was packed. A Conservative backbencher conveyed the mood. 'We are meeting to-day at a time of danger, the gravest danger that our nation has ever faced, danger not only to our material prosperity, but to the spiritual things which we value even more highly.' The former Prime Minister, David Lloyd George, judged the debate that followed to be 'the most momentous in the history of Parliament', and he would make a devastating contribution on the second afternoon. A future Prime Minister, Harold Macmillan, also present, believed that the two-day debate 'altered the history of Britain and the Empire, and perhaps of the world'.

Moore-Brabazon caught the debate at several key moments, in rapid, surreptitious shots – standing behind the Serjeant at Arms's chair; at the Bar of the House; resting his camera on a rail.

One close-up shows uniformed Members who had been summoned back from their regiments. Wedged in the half-gloom on dark green leather seats, they listen, arms folded, to a short, squat figure who addresses the House from the government benches.

Moore-Brabazon stopped snapping only when one of the Doorkeepers seemed to get 'a little suspicious' of the movement of his left hand. Observing him approach, Moore-Brabazon pocketed the Minox, and produced a silver cigarette-lighter that resembled it. Casually, he rubbed the lighter down the side of his nose. The Doorkeeper withdrew.

The negatives lay in their original Riga tin until 1992 when the Clerk of the Records had the prints made up. Blurred, underexposed, snatched in poor lighting, the images might have been photographed 'sitting on a jelly in a strong draught', as Moore-Brabazon described his first experience of flying.

'In vain we look for a glimmer of light. It is a perfect blackout.' A private memorandum circulated a month earlier to opposition and rebel Conservative MPs reflected a growing despondency at the record of the Chamberlain administration.

A comparable darkness prevails in Moore-Brabazon's photographs. We see Barry's gloomy, badly ventilated Chamber – the sandbagged windows and doors, the blacked-out rooms and corridors, giving the neo-Gothic hall, according to Chamberlain, who hated it, the appearance of the aquarium at London Zoo. It was in underwater terms that the National Labour MP Harold Nicolson described the Commons to one of the shapes craning forward on the upper level, the diminutive but politically agile Soviet Ambassador, Ivan Maisky. Nicolson reminded Maisky how he used to look down from the Diplomatic Gallery with benevolent interest, 'rather like a biologist examines the habits of newts in a tank'.

Packed in alongside Maisky, in the Distinguished Strangers' Gallery, the Peers' Gallery, the Press Gallery and the Speaker's personal Gallery, were diplomats, journalists, civil servants, plus friends and relatives of the MPs below. These included the Prime Minister's wife, Anne, dressed in black and with a buttonhole of violets gathered that morning from the garden at No. 10. Also seated on the padded benches were Winston Churchill's seventeen-year-old daughter Mary; and thirty-six-year-old Lady Alexandra 'Baba' Metcalfe, whose father was Lord Curzon, a former Foreign Secretary.

The dark-haired and sternly attractive Baba, separated from her husband, was acting as the eyes and ears of the Foreign Secretary, Lord Halifax, whose peerage barred him from sitting in the Commons. Were the Prime Minister to step down as the rebel faction demanded, Halifax, universally respected, would have been their outstanding favourite to succeed.

But resignation was not on Chamberlain's mind when he stood up at 3.48 p.m. to present the government's case for what, in private, his War Cabinet considered to be a spectacular disaster largely of Churchill's making.

In an essay on Curzon, Churchill made this aside about the Commons: 'It was then, as now, the most complete and comprehending judge of a man' – a sentiment with which Halifax concurred, reflecting in the diary that he dictated to his secretary every morning: 'Curious what a good judge of character the House of Commons generally is.'

A fugitive from the same regime that three weeks earlier had occupied Norway, the future Nobel Laureate Elias Canetti had the Norway Debate in mind when he wrote in his notebook: 'Whenever the English go through bad times, I am wonder-struck by their Parliament . . . There is a possibility here of attacking the rulers, a possibility that has no equal anywhere in the world. And they are no less rulers for it . . . Six hundred ambitious men watch one another with hawks' eyes; weaknesses cannot remain concealed, strengths make a difference as long as they are strengths. Everything takes place out in the open.' Canetti concluded: 'There is nothing more remarkable than this nation doing its most important business in a ritual, sporting way, and not deviating even when the water is up to its neck.'

And that, on the afternoon of 7 May, is where the level had risen.

A surprised Rab Butler, shown Moore-Brabazon's pictures three decades on, recognised himself in the second row, where he sat as Halifax's spokesman in the Commons. After hesitating, Butler picked out other members of the War Cabinet:

Sir John Simon, Chancellor of the Exchequer.

Sir Samuel Hoare, Air Minister.

Sir Kingsley Wood, Lord Privy Seal.

Even though blurred from camera shake, Neville Chamberlain can be seen standing at the Despatch Box. And seated to the Prime Minister's right, the First Lord of the Admiralty – in one of the only images that survive of Winston Churchill in this House of Commons. As the Minister most closely involved in the military expedition to Norway, Churchill had consented to wind up for the government.

These figures, how familiar they are. Looking at them seated in the hot, dark Chamber, dressed in their formal clothes and uniforms, it all seems inevitable. We know what will happen, even if they do not. We know that Chamberlain is delivering his last statement as Prime Minister. We know that in three days' time Germany will pounce again, in France. We know that Churchill will take over.

The broad story still holds. Churchill is safe on his 'pinnacle of deathless glory', as he wrote of Alfred the Great round about this time. In proposing a toast to Churchill's health in Moscow four years later, Joseph Stalin was unable to cite any other instance in history where the future of the world had depended on the courage of one person. The historian Philip Ziegler says: 'If ever there was a man who happened to be in the right place at the right time, it was Churchill.' Without Churchill in control, the future of our country would have taken a radically different path, believed Lord Halifax's biographer Alan Campbell-Johnson, another watcher in the Chamber. 'Six more weeks of the tentative technique of the Chamberlain Administration and the Allied cause might have been engulfed in total defeat.' Here, in Churchill's phrase, lay the 'hinge of fate'.

But the weight of the Churchill legend has suppressed knowledge of other possibilities that were available and seemed more probable at the time. In the extremely unlikely event that Chamberlain were to step aside, Churchill was merely one among several contenders, on both sides of the House, who had spent their political careers jostling for such an opening.

The Lord Privy Seal, Kingsley Wood, admitted that 'the number of people who think they are the future Prime Minister of this country is quite amazing'. Wood was a long-standing confidant of Chamberlain, and a demon for preferment. From his position on the front bench, Wood had reason to believe that his moment was approaching – something confirmed by Rab Butler's Parliamentary Private Secretary, the Conservative MP Henry 'Chips' Channon, who wrote in his diary: 'I think that Kingsley Wood might easily become our next P.M., and that is now the P.M.'s intention . . . Halifax would only be a stop-gap.'

Even if this view of his prospects came from the realms of fantasy, Wood was not alone in considering himself stuffed with the material of leadership. Ranged behind the favourite, Lord Halifax, sat a pack of politicians straining to become premier should the office all of a sudden fall vacant, plus one candidate who had held the title. Four days earlier, Harold Nicolson had written in his diary: 'People are saying that Lloyd George should come in.' Memories of his victory in 1918 suddenly made the Father of the House an attractive proposition once more.

Also in the frame at various moments during the months and weeks leading up to the debate, and in the febrile days following it, either touted by others or considering themselves ripe for the premiership: Samuel Hoare, John Simon, Anthony Eden, Max Beaverbrook, Roger Keyes, John Reith, Duff Cooper, Oliver Stanley, Walter Elliot, John Anderson, Stafford Cripps, Lord Woolton, Clement Attlee, Nancy Astor, Lady Rhondda and even Marie Stopes, who told Halifax that 'in the light of her special knowledge of Germany, Japan, Norway, birth control and science, she ought to be in the Cabinet'. This was a time when, as one Labour frontbencher observed in his diary, 'History goes past at the gallop.'

There was also, fleetingly, the vision of Chamberlain's fellow Member from Birmingham, Leo Amery, taking over as Prime Minister. It is likely that Amery is the squat figure, reduced by Moore-Brabazon's distorting lens to a spiky circle of light, who speaks to a riveted House from the government benches. If correct, the image catches Amery in the act of delivering his tirade against Chamberlain, triggering the sequence of events that within seventy-two hours were to sweep him away.

Corresponding with Amery after the war, another recent contender for the premiership was reminded of how unlikely a prospect Churchill's accession appeared at this moment. Leslie Hore-Belisha was the former Minister unexpectedly moved from the War Office back in January. In October 1954, Hore-Belisha wrote to Amery: 'What you tell me of your opinion that if it had come to a vote in the House of Commons it would have been Halifax is most interesting, and likewise what you tell me of Max [Beaverbrook]'s opinion that no debate in Parliament could possibly overthrow Neville. These statements show how difficult it is to predict the fate of men and how uncertain the outcome was at the time.'

Observers do not share the same perspective as participants. There is a natural impatience, in reading about the momentous events of May 1940, to press forward to the evening of 10 May when Churchill was invited by a reluctant George VI to form an administration. In this dominant narrative, the Norway Debate marks but one step in an orderly, inevitable and unavoidable transfer, before the real fight.

This interpretation assumes much and misses a lot.

The overwhelming cataclysm of the next six weeks, which saw the fall of the Netherlands, Belgium and France, has tended to submerge the dramatic processes which brought Churchill into Downing Street. How Churchill landed there at the last moment, with much greater odds stacked against him than is commonly supposed, is every bit as interesting a story.

In May 2015, Britain celebrated the seventy-fifth anniversary of the evacuation from Dunkirk. Lost in all the attention paid to Churchill's speeches about fighting Germans on the beaches was his assumption of the premiership only a few days earlier – a handover which passed virtually unnoticed. Yet what we take for granted so nearly did not happen.

Baba Metcalfe's father knew from humiliating experience 'upon what small vicissitudes great events may turn'. In May 1923, Lord Curzon had been prevented from becoming Prime Minister when an outsider (Stanley Baldwin) shot past. When the Norway Debate began on 7 May 1940, there was no realistic expectation that Churchill would step into Chamberlain's shoes, and potent reasons why he should not. Speaking at Martin Gilbert's memorial service in 2015, former Prime Minister Gordon Brown recalled asking Gilbert to sum up what he had learned after writing his thirty-eight volumes on Churchill.

'I learned,' Gilbert said, 'what a close thing it was.'

Of course, to many afterwards it did seem like divine intervention. Interviewed on *Desert Island Discs*, Lord Hailsham (who participated in the Norway Debate as Quintin Hogg) spoke of his belief that 'the one time in which I think I can see the finger of God in contemporary history is Churchill's arrival at the precise moment of 1940'. Churchill famously convinced himself that he was walking with destiny. Dining with him a few months later, Lady Halifax confessed that she 'got slightly confused as to his meaning when he said with some emotion: "That old man up there intended me to be where I am at this time."' Was he alluding to her husband? Not so. Pointing a finger at the ceiling, he went on: 'It's all destiny.'

However, Neville Chamberlain was an obdurate believer in his own star no less than Churchill. Ambassador Maisky gained the impression after speaking with Chamberlain that 'the P.M. considers himself a "man of destiny". He was born into this world to perform a "sacred mission".'

If, when reading about the Norway Debate and its tumultuous aftermath, one gains an overriding sense that 'things were "written"' – as Churchill told the Chief of the Imperial General Staff, General Sir Edmund Ironside, with whom he had been a subaltern in the Boer War – then this may be because Churchill wrote them. Viscount Stuart's version is as reliable as any. 'I heard Churchill say in the House once, in reply to a questioner who was pressing for further details on some awkward point, "Only history can relate the full story"; and then he added, after exactly the right pause, "And I shall write the history."'

Chamberlain's biographer, David Dilks, believes that of all the books written in the twentieth century the one that has exercised most influence on the general view is *The Gathering Storm*, the opening volume of Churchill's war memoirs, which was published in June 1948, selling an astronomical 530,000 hardback copies. 'Churchill wrote of his experience with a persuasive power which no other leader of the twentieth century has matched.'

So persuasive was Churchill's narrative that a more recent authority, David Reynolds, considers that this 'extended essay in retrospective wisdom' has guided the writing of history ever since. Yet as Reynolds, Dilks, Ziegler and others have shown, *The Gathering Storm* is a highly selective interpretation, and 'something of a distortion'.

Leo Amery had known Churchill since school. A censor of Churchill's earliest articles for the *Harrovian*, Amery detected the continuation of a boyhood tic after reading Churchill's account of the First World War, *The World Crisis*. 'It is a pity he should think it necessary to spoil so much good history in order to have the satisfaction of writing it up and vindicating himself afterwards.'

Few possessed sharper insights into Churchill's vindications and distortions than Admiral John Godfrey, Director of Naval Intelligence, who sat long hours with him at the Admiralty Operational Intelligence Centre throughout the Norway Campaign. In an unpublished memoir, Godfrey wrote that 'the public of our generation will never know the malignant influence he exerted on the early strategy of the war because he will probably be the first person to write a popular history which, like *The World Crisis*, will show that everything that went well was due to his inspiration and that when things went badly it was someone else's fault.'

Supported by Churchill, a lot of legends risk passing out of history and memoir into unbudgeable myth. That is why it is worth pausing to re-examine the highly personal nature of Churchill's relationship to the historic events of April and May 1940.

Churchill was once walking through the Commons Lobby when he halted, 'raising his hand rather like a policeman on night duty', and declaimed to a fellow MP about Napoleon. 'The great night of time descends, but the glow of the emperor's personality remains. And those who were his friends are gilded by it and those who were his foes are clouded.'

Little in Churchill's account of the war proves more clouded than his

portrait of Chamberlain, whose death inspired one of Churchill's most eloquent tributes, to a man whose conduct 'ought to be a model for us
all' – though he told his secretary after he dictated it: 'Of course, I could
have done it the other way round.' In *The Gathering Storm* he did exactly
that. Having clashed with Chamberlain during eleven wilderness years
when he was excluded from office, Churchill would freeze him out in posterity as 'this narrow, obstinate man'.

It was an unfair contest. 'I myself can claim no literary gifts,' Chamberlain admitted, in the only book he ever wrote – about his cousin Norman,
machine-gunned to death on a French battlefield – and he died before he
was able to provide an alternative version. It fell to Halifax to defend him,
and to insist that Chamberlain, a reserved, complex man, had been 'consistently misjudged', and that Churchill did Chamberlain 'less than justice
in his War history'.

David Dilks was the last person to interview Halifax, in December 1959.
Dilks says: 'For a long time, Halifax knew that a great deal written and said
about Chamberlain was nonsense, and he took great pains to tell me.' Halifax's discreet autobiography *Fulness of Days*, published two years earlier,
had corrected a few of Churchill's 'unwittingly inaccurate' perceptions and
errors, but, says Ziegler: 'Halifax felt it rather undignified to fight his own
corner, argue his case' – with the consequence that Halifax's reputation has
likewise suffered. *Fulness of Days*, says Dilks, did little to overturn 'the still-
prevailing fashionable notions of Halifax as somebody who wished to sell
out to the Nazis or grovel to everybody, which is how Churchill was sometimes inclined to regard him'.

What this boils down to is that our picture of the disastrous Norway
Campaign which led to the debate, and of Chamberlain and Halifax as
well, is mainly thanks to Churchill, who wrote the history and who had all
the best lines. For most readers, his is the received version, the last word on
the subject; a closed book in which Chamberlain's name has been passed
down in ignominy, and the Norway Campaign dismissed as a pathetic prelude to what Churchill's friend, Conservative MP Major General Sir Edward
Louis Spears, called 'the real thing'.

At his fine valediction to Chamberlain, made in this Chamber, Churchill had likened history to a flickering lamp that stumbles along the trail of

the past, 'trying to reconstruct its scenes, to revive its echoes and kindle with pale gleams the passion of former days'. In point of fact, Ziegler says: 'Churchill's writing of history was totally dishonest. He would admit as much. It was a propaganda exercise.' Although aided by a team of extremely able and experienced researchers, he was putting his own case, as only he knew how to do.

The relationship between history and propaganda was whisky and soda to Churchill. He immersed himself in his *History of the English-Speaking Peoples* right up to the Norwegian expedition. Before that, he had published four volumes on his seventeenth-century military ancestor, the first Duke of Marlborough – the Churchill equivalent, as it were, of Norman Chamberlain.

The horrible circumstances of Norman's death had moved Chamberlain with every particle of his being to prevent another war. The reverse was true of Churchill. Having spent four years and 2,128 pages on vindicating Marlborough's reputation, he strove when at the Admiralty to emulate his military victories. As someone remarked who worked with him during this period: 'He sees himself as another Marlborough.'

Churchill staked out his partisan purpose in a letter to Professor Lewis Namier: 'to defend effectively Marlborough's early career . . . by contrasting the true facts with the odious accusations which have so long reigned'. In the same letter, Churchill described his method:

'One of the misleading factors in history is the practice of historians to build a story exclusively out of the records which have come down to them. These records in many cases are a very small part of what took place, and to fill in the picture one has to visualise the daily life – the constant discussions between Ministers, the friendly dinners, the many days when nothing happened worthy of record, but during which events were nevertheless proceeding.'

Applied to his own biography, Churchill's call 'to visualise the daily life' is not always easy to achieve, especially when examining the days leading up to his accession. Anyone wanting to build a story that deviates from Churchill's own will discover that important records are missing, like the memorandum which tilted Attlee into calling for a division; or consumed by the incendiary bomb that hit the House of Commons on 10 May 1941; or deliberately destroyed, as were the papers of Brendan Bracken, Churchill's main promoter in the leadership stakes, which Bracken instructed his chauffeur to burn; or simply not written. Churchill never kept a daily diary, fearing, in Dilks's words, that 'it would reveal his frequent changes of opinion and, when published, make him look foolish'. Many conversations have escaped the record, particularly on topics which Ministers felt unable to discuss in public, and where these exchanges are reported it is often hard to judge their context. Compiled in secret and afterwards adjusted, Ivan Maisky's London journals catch familiar faces at bracing, fresh angles, yet it must be remembered that the Soviet Ambassador, a clever and charming but sometimes unreliable witness, penned each entry in fear that it might be discovered by the NKVD, who had already rooted out two of Maisky's staff for execution.

Even when something is written down uncensored, the essential point can be overlooked. Diaries are not infallible. A frustrated Leo Amery admitted: 'They often get written up in a hurry a day or two later, and what turns out of the first importance twenty or thirty years afterwards gets left out.'

Nor is being present at an occasion any guarantee that it will be remembered with fidelity. In Churchill's own description of the meeting at No. 10 Downing Street on 9 May 1940 at which Providence stretched out its hand to offer him the premiership, written eight years after the event, he mistakes the date, the time of day, even the identities of those in the room.

Halifax *was* in the room. Yet his account, probably dictated the following morning, differs from the one that he gave at the time to his Permanent Under-Secretary, Sir Alexander Cadogan, and also from the version which he offered up a year later to his Private Secretary, Charles Peake.

As for Halifax's relationship with Baba Metcalfe, this is scarcely mentioned in contemporary narratives, any more than is the extent to which Chamberlain used the Intelligence Services to monitor the telephone conversations of his political adversaries.

There are other significant absences. Supremely hard to judge, and therefore to use judiciously in an historical account, is the emotional frame of mind of political figures like Churchill. 'He is a very emotional man,' Lloyd George told Maisky. Fatigue, infatuation, grief, hurt – these are some of the feelings that governed not only Churchill's behaviour but the actions of his closest Cabinet colleagues during this all-important span of days. Even so, emotion is a factor that too often is left out of the picture, by historians as well as by diarists, so that Chamberlain, Halifax and Churchill can appear to operate as if they reached important decisions inside an isolated bubble in which the circumstances of their personal lives were irrelevant to a degree that is unrealistic.

For example, the puzzle over why Churchill continued to be obsessed with Narvik only begins to make sense when one takes into account that his nephew Giles Romilly was captured there. Yet the impact of Romilly's arrest on Churchill, and on Clementine and her family, is rarely given attention by historians, any more than is the absence from Churchill's side of his chief adviser and confidante – that is to say, Clementine – during the three critical days of 8, 9 and 10 May.

Last but not least is the danger to anyone contemplating a rival narrative. Three months after Churchill took over as Prime Minister, Leo Amery wrote to a friend in a state of anxiety about the plight of Stuart Hodgson, a former editor of the Liberal campaigning newspaper the *Daily News*, and author of *The Man Who Made the Peace: Neville Chamberlain* (1938). The sixty-three-year-old Hodgson was well known to Amery: a 'good anti-Nazi who after writing a sympathetic life of Chamberlain has suddenly found himself interned while completing a life of Halifax, on which he cannot continue while in prison, incidentally, too, leaving newly married wife expecting child and completely stranded'. Not much else has come to light about this dramatic and intriguing incarceration of a good-tempered, trenchant biographer who liked chess and cricket and was famous for never having lost his temper. Still, it is tempting to draw the inference: when dealing with Churchill, 'who wrote history, lived history, and made history', then woe betide any competitor – even one blessed with Hodgson's 'keen sense of justice, tolerance and humanity'.

Brief though Hodgson's internment seems to have been, since he went on, in 1941, to publish his portrait of Halifax, it is an illustration of why old assumptions, assertions and fashionable opinions need to be constantly tested. David Dilks does well to remind us that we should not accept without deep reflection any version of the past, no matter how secure it appears – and further, that 'the irrational or the unpredictable elements . . . are crucial'.

Regarding the Norway Debate, there is a popular narrative about how events unfolded, in large measure established by Churchill, which is unsatisfactory and which, when tested, is clearly found wanting. Hold the picture to the light and another outline emerges.

In this competing tableau, Churchill, an ex-Liberal who had twice crossed the floor, assumes the shape of a divisive outsider, tainted by the Tonypandy riots of 1910 when he sent troops to South Wales to resolve a mining dispute, the Dardanelles, his opposition to the General Strike and the India Bill, his support for Edward VIII, and, more immediately, by the capitulation in Norway, one of the great failures of his career, and a campaign in which he alienated every Cabinet colleague. The likelihood of Churchill's political advancement from First Lord of the Admiralty was negligible; nor did he appear to do anything to promote it, remaining steadfast in his loyalty to Chamberlain. Indeed, he rounded angrily on supporters like Bracken who plotted without Churchill's knowledge on his behalf.

Lord Halifax's contours are no less divergent. Once it had become obvious that Chamberlain would resign, Halifax was the most favoured candidate for the premiership, supported by Chamberlain, the War Cabinet, a majority of Conservative and Labour MPs, the press, and George VI, who had given Halifax the unique privilege of a key to the garden of Buckingham Palace. Even at the eleventh hour, King, Prime Minister and Rab Butler were pressing 'the Holy Fox' to accept. Why did he not? Historians and biographers do not tally in their speculations. Then there is his secretive relationship with Baba Metcalfe, referred to in his surprisingly passionate letters as 'my dearest Baba' and 'my darling one'.

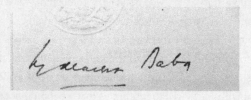

History has cast Chamberlain as a feeble and colourless prevaricator with 'a lust for peace', yet there are moments when he reveals himself to be a ruthless schemer, determined to use his majority, the Whips' Office and the Intelligence Services to cling on to power 'like a limpet'. Tight-furled in public like his umbrella, he expands in private as a cigar-smoker, a wine connoisseur, a brilliant mimic and a generous-hearted family man. On top of everything, he gets on remarkably well with Churchill.

Under closer scrutiny, no one behaves true to type.

The Norway Debate is an improbable example of the darkest spot being under the lamp. A very interesting transfer of power occurred within a short time, but how this occurred remains unresolved. What happened and what is thought to have happened turn out not to be the same thing.

'When the clamour of the guns dies away, the clamour of the history writer begins,' noted the Finnish historian C. L. Lundin. Three quarters of a century has passed, and an untold number of books repeat the story, yet there are wide discrepancies in the memoirs of contemporaries, and in the accounts of historians. As one historian puts it, no two of them agree 'on the precise order in which events happened, on the reliability of the sources, or on which were the decisive moments'. This is a week of incalculable historical significance, but in spite of the vast literature on it, the leading players remain hazy, still tantalisingly out of focus.

Instead of being ejected from the Commons for his illicit snapshots, Moore-Brabazon was made a Minister in the next administration. If anyone might have lent his expertise at interpreting 'barbed-wire, holes and paths and camouflage', and used it to decipher the faces that reach us today as small blobs of light, then it would have been this tall and ponderous ex-aviator, who once flew with a pig at his side to illustrate a popular saying.

In vain, I scan his inadequate photographs for other players in this compelling drama. Clement Davies, the Independent Liberal MP who, with Amery, galvanised the rebels. Lloyd George, whom Davies had to drag out of his room to make one of his most effective speeches. Nowhere do I find the face of my great-uncle, the National Liberal MP Geoffrey Shakespeare. A friend of the Chamberlains, Uncle Geoffrey had served as Lloyd George's Private Secretary in the 1920s; and in 1937 was appointed Parliamentary Secretary to the Admiralty where he was the official to greet Churchill on the outbreak of war, 'so as to introduce to him the members of the Board'. Churchill was reoccupying the position that he had left in disgrace twenty-four years earlier, following the catastrophe of Gallipoli. It was to Geoffrey, his 'indefatigable second in command', that he gave his first order on that Sunday evening in September 1939 – asking for a bottle of whisky.

PRIVATE SECRETARY

As a child, I knew that Uncle Geoffrey had mixed with senior politicians. He did not talk about it a lot. I would have asked, and he would have told me, but I was not interested then; not even in how he secretly 'saved from the waste-paper basket' pencilled notes which Lloyd George had flung away. These personalities had little bearing on a boy growing up in the tropics. They were as remote and anonymous-sounding as the voice on the tannoy above a Singapore swimming pool which one humid afternoon announced the death of Sir Winston Churchill. Only later on have I felt the pull to read their memoirs, diaries and letters; to go back through the records, and speak to historians and to descendants of the politicians involved, as well as to combatants who fought in Norway, in an attempt to answer a simple, but still baffling question: how did a Minister who advocated, planned and directed one of the most disastrous campaigns since the Crimean War become Prime Minister?

A glint of light in one of Moore-Brabazon's photographs is not the face of an MP, but represents the Victorian sandglass on the Table of the House in front of the Speaker's Chair. At about 5 p.m. on 8 May, it had become clear that the opposition would, in fact, vote on the motion for the

Whitsun adjournment as a means of – as Churchill described it in his winding-up speech – having a vote of censure on the conduct of the government. At 11 p.m., the Speaker, Captain Edward FitzRoy, put the question: 'That this House do now adjourn'. The division began, the sandglass was flipped over by one of the Clerks at the Table, and the fine grey granules started trickling down through the wasp-waist. Out of a possible total of 615 MPs, more than 550 were present in the Chamber on that Wednesday evening. They had six minutes to file into the Aye or the No Lobbies before the oak doors were locked. The government had begun the debate the previous afternoon in a reasonably confident mood. Now, no one could be certain of the outcome.

PART TWO

THE CAMPAIGN

2
'NAR-VIK'

'My eye has always been fixed on Narvik.'
WINSTON CHURCHILL, 8 May 1940

'Who will want to know about Giles Romilly?'
GEORGE WEIDENFELD

The Norway Debate was about a military campaign. For a few intense weeks in the spring of 1940, the attention of everyone in Britain was fixed on a snow-bound coastline 1,300 miles away across the North Sea. After months of aggravating inactivity, during which an assumption formed that some important move to frustrate the enemy was being put into action, British forces were fighting for the first time in a land battle with the Nazis, and winning.

My nine-year-old father was one of millions who listened up to four times a day to a brown Bakelite wireless – 'the focal point of the room as the TV is now' – and followed reports of successful landings in Norway to oust the Nazi invaders. 'It was a ray of hope. We'd had seven months of Phoney War, there'd been nothing. I remember thinking, "Jolly good, first action of the war and it's been a success." Most vividly, I recall the names. Narvik, Trondheim, Namsos . . .'

Between 8 April and 10 May, these names were repeated on the lunch-time and evening bulletins, in newspaper headlines, on people's lips, in the air they breathed. On the Wiltshire Downs, the writer Frances Partridge thought that even the plovers seemed to be shrieking 'NAR-vik' into her ears.

'And then,' my father says, 'it all went dead for a few days and it never really came back.' As April wore on, so did the sinister lull in the news. Fewer victories were announced. There were rumours that something had

25

gone wrong, but no details. A strange anxiety took hold. Looking back a year later, after the names Dunkirk, Boulogne and Saint-Malo had been added to the roster of Allied defeats, Partridge believed that 'no time has been harder to bear, it seems to me, than the Norwegian campaign', because of the uncertainty of not knowing what was happening and 'the struggle to maintain hope'.

My father says, 'We didn't know it had been a disaster.'

Everyone knows what happened next, when Hitler invaded Holland, Belgium and France in the early hours of 10 May. Yet how many of us can repeat with certainty a fraction of what occurred before that fatal Friday, at Narvik, Trondheim, Namsos, Åndalsnes, Lillehammer, Bergen, Harstad, Stavanger? Those names on the map, which my father is able to recite seventy-five years on, were more than mere fjords and fishing villages and ore-towns. These were the places where Neville Chamberlain was toppled, out of which Winston Churchill became Prime Minister.

April in Narvik, a cold, unsung outpost hidden away up in the Arctic. The small north Norwegian port – population, 10,000 – lay forty miles inland from the Norwegian Sea at the end of Ofotfjorden, below Fagernes mountain. In winter months, the sun never climbed above Fagernes. Narvik's pine houses and dark streets banked high with snow were lit by bronze lamp posts purchased second-hand from a town in the south. In February, the sun returned, and now – early spring – it gave twenty hours of daylight, even if the dominant colours remained white and grey. Twice the distance from Westminster as Chamberlain's faraway example of Czechoslovakia, Narvik was, one historian observed, an outlandish place in which to wind up an era.

The town's name was taken from a remote homestead enclosed in the half-moon bay. Before Narvik, it was called Victoria Harbour, the creation of a British company, Pen & Miller, which built a railway to exploit iron-ore deposits from the Swedish mines at Kiruna, over a hundred miles away. Iron, of which the Nazis could not get enough, was the continued reason for Narvik.

The trains trundled every few hours down to the raised loading quay, and tipped their high-grade cargoes into the holds of up to thirty waiting merchant ships, most of them flying German or British flags.

Until the outbreak of war, 4.5 million tons of this crushed ore had sailed every year to Germany – providing two thirds of the iron essential for Hitler's armaments. The Swedish ore was of cardinal importance also for Britain's war effort: since September, more of it had sailed to Britain (798,000 tons) than to Germany (763,000 tons). Giles Romilly, a twenty-three-year-old journalist sent there by the *Daily Express*, wrote that 'a battleship could be made out of one day's work in Narvik'.

It is customary to see the Phoney War ending when Hitler launched his Western Offensive on 10 May. In fact, it ended one month earlier, on 9 April, a Tuesday, with the unprovoked invasion of Denmark and Norway. 'That day lightning struck and our world broke into pieces,' remembered Narvik's mayor, Theodore Broch.

At 4.37 a.m., Broch was woken by a terrific blast, followed by another. His small daughter appeared barefoot in the doorway. 'Is it Christmas?' Broch thought that it might be the Ore Company, dynamiting.

At the Royal Hotel, two 'abominable, insulting bangs' also woke Romilly who had been chatting with Broch in the lobby a few hours before. 'I was going to Bergen that morning and fretting a bit because I knew I had to get up early to catch the boat; an 8-inch gun was my alarm-clock – three hours too early.'

The person who leapt out of bed was five foot six, dark-haired, and rather pugnacious-looking, says his son. 'What he did next was very stupid of him, and it banged him up for five years.'

Romilly pulled open the burgundy curtains, but all he could see in the leaden half-light was snow and driving sleet. He called the hall clerk, who stammered: 'Yes. Yes. It is trouble in the river.' Romilly laced on his boots and ran downstairs, into the lounge where he had drunk beer with young officers from the Norwegian coastal vessel *Norge*. Unbeknownst to him, the *Norge* had just been sunk by the German destroyer *Bernd von Arnim* in the first explosion, with the loss of 105 men; a second coastal vessel *Eidsvold* had been sunk by the destroyer *Wilhelm Heidkamp*, with the loss of 177.

Now crowding the lounge were officers of the Norwegian garrison 'buttoning shirts over hairy chests, fumbling with boots, buckling belts . . . picking sleep off their eyelids'. Romilly followed them outside, rifles clutched, down the slippery slope leading to the quay. The dawn fog pulsed with flames. Then out of the mist there emerged several shapes, kneeling on one knee and with rifles at the shoulder, 'as close, straight, and fixed as altar rails'. The German troops wore white camouflage tunics, and had wrapped white towels around their helmets. The Norwegian soldiers whispered amongst themselves. Their orders had been to fight any invader who threatened their country's neutrality, but one of them pulled a handkerchief from his pocket and waved it in surrender.

'I dashed back,' Romilly wrote in the diary that he lent to Churchill after the war, 'but they were already on my heels. They went in brandishing pistols, shouting for "papers!" and for the British Consul. They were screaming for him. A posse was rushed up to his room. He was gone.'

Romilly's hotel swarmed with German officers, grenades dangling from belts. Their claret-collared commander, Lieutenant General Eduard Dietl of 139th Mountain Regiment, arrived by taxi; tall, with a narrow sharp face and a slight stoop, he was followed indoors by the cab driver, who complained that the general had not paid his fare from the pier. Dietl issued a polite declaration explaining his mission. 'I want to make it clear from the start that we have come as friends, to protect your country against any further British breaks of your neutrality . . . Norway is now occupied peacefully in the name of Der Führer.'

The British Consul, George Gibbs, a sixty-year-old former naval captain, had fled the hotel to a tool-shed on the outskirts of Narvik, where he lived out the next three weeks posing as a deaf mute. Romilly was not so lucky. He wrote to his parents three weeks later: 'I got captured through being too interested in the "story"!' An armed guard escorted Romilly into the hotel reception office where the flaxen-haired proprietress 'fluttered around crazily ... She barely understood my request to settle my bill.' Romilly's British passport was confiscated. His first wife Mary remembers: 'He was upset that he hadn't thrown it away. He could have posed as a Swede.' He was locked in his room. The German soldier posted outside his door commiserated. '*Das ist Pech für Sie.*' This is bad luck for you.

At 9 p.m., dressed in a Swedish fur hat and carrying a brown suitcase, Romilly was marched downstairs and across the railway line, through the snow, to the Villaveien school, an austere, four-storey building next to a black stone church. A light was switched on, bodies stirred. Romilly stood in a classroom, desks pushed together – and lying on the wooden floor dozens of men covered with blankets, sailors from five British ore ships.

'What ship are you off, brother?'

Romilly replied that he was a journalist.

'Room for you here, journy!'

The light was switched off.

Romilly had lived in the East End, distributing copies of the *Daily Worker*, before he went to fight for the Communists in Spain. He felt a kinship with these sailors. Mary says: 'When I read his account of him in the schoolroom, I thought: "This is the real Giles."'

At 4.30 a.m. on 10 April there were explosions, gunfire, sirens. Out in the harbour, a naval battle was going on. The prolonged bombardment rattled the windows.

Later that morning, German soldiers moved the prisoners to a classroom on the floor above. Beyond the church spire, the harbour lay in sunshine. Thick black smoke rose from the oily water which was now 'a forest of mast tops of sunken ships'. Of the twenty-seven merchant ships anchored there the night before, only half remained afloat following what Romilly learned had been a counter-attack by the Royal Navy.

Major Alfred Haussels, a 'dominating and brutal' Nazi, was in charge of the British prisoners. He ordered that new quarters be procured for them. The rooms did not need to be good.

At 4 p.m., the British merchant seamen plus Romilly walked with their gear in a ragged column down the hill to a café on the corner of the main square where they joined fourteen survivors of the destroyer HMS *Hunter* who sat in blankets 'without a stitch of clothing between them'. The *Hunter* had gone down in the dawn engagement, her sailors having to plug a shell hole in the engine room with towels. Fished out of the middle of the icy fjord, the men were still shivering.

The 109 prisoners were jammed in tight in the long narrow Café Iris. Some stretched themselves out on glass-topped tables placed end to end, which cracked. Romilly elbowed himself space on the brown lino floor and used the woollen dressing gown that he had managed to bring with him as a blanket.

The enormous café windows had a panorama of all that was going on in town. Romilly could see the harbour and watch the ships steam in and out. From the British sailors, from an Austrian guard and from Mayor Broch, who visited the prisoners, he was able to scribble out a 'very rapid survey of first few days as prisoner . . . Stiff toilet roll only writing paper available.'

Romilly had arrived in Narvik on 5 April from Sweden after receiving a midnight call from the *Daily Express* to go and report 'on the general situation there and also on any possible developments arising out of it, should there be any'. There had been whispers all winter that the British Navy planned to halt Germany's iron supply by laying mines at the southern approaches to Vestfjorden, the wide fjord that formed the entrance to Ofotfjorden and to Narvik harbour. The Narvik operation, codenamed 'Wilfred', had remained Churchill's 'pet project' throughout the Phoney War. Only on 5 April had the Supreme War Council given it the go-ahead. 'Wilfred' was fixed for 8 April.

Before taking part in the British counter-attack on 10 April, HMS *Hunter* had been one of the destroyers accompanying the minelayers. The last man overboard succeeded in rescuing the *Hunter*'s log, which Romilly transcribed. 'Monday April 8, 3 a.m. entered Norwegian waters. Minelaying. Armed Norwegian trawler asked what we were doing. He said: 'F . . . off.' He was informed that there was a minefield ahead of him . . .'

A total of 234 Mark 17 contact mines, each containing 1,210 kilograms of TNT, were laid at a depth of twelve feet in the approaches to Vestfjorden, in a triangular shape 'from shore to seven miles out'. Half an hour later, a broadcast made to the world explained the necessity for this action in Norwegian territorial waters.

But the Germans had outmanoeuvred the Allies. Even as the Admiralty congratulated itself for seizing the initiative, military planners in London and Paris failed to recognise that they were on the back foot already. At the same time as the minelaying was taking place, unsuspected by the British and French, despite no shortage of warning signs, the largest invasion fleet that Germany had put to sea in twenty years was converging at twenty-two knots on the Norwegian coast.

One of Romilly's Austrian guards told him: 'In war, speed is everything!' The guard revealed how ten German destroyers had left Wesermünde on 6 April, and had taken a little over two days to reach Narvik, 1,240 miles away. Bad weather had allowed the convoy to slip past the British fleet into Vestfjorden. The British minefield was too near the coast to be in the way of the German ships.

The German destroyers each carried up to 200 mountain troops, all able to ski. The diary of a young Alpine soldier from Steiermark, Klaus Herman Klaushauser, dated 7 April 1940, and later found by Mayor Broch in the abandoned German quarters at the Seamen's Home, described a parade in Bremen on 6 April and speeches by officers who assured Klaushauser that he was about to fight for the Führer in one of the most audacious military expeditions in history. Their destination was not disclosed. Chatting in their hammocks, the men guessed Scotland, Iceland or the French Channel ports. Not till 8 April were they informed that it was Norway. Klaushauser wrote: 'We did not know very much about the country or about the people we were going to visit,' but one of his officers explained it over a beer. 'We were to protect our racial brethren and bring the New Order to the Land of the Midnight Sun.'

The explosions that woke Romilly in the Royal Hotel were part of a meticulous surprise attack across Norway that had been planned since February. Oslo, 900 miles south of Narvik, was occupied at 2 p.m. by a few hundred lightly armed troops flown in by Ju-52 transport aircraft. Leland Stowe, a reporter for the *Chicago Daily News*, stood on his hotel balcony and watched them marching three abreast down the main street while a military band played 'Schön blüh'n die Heckenrosen' – *How beautiful bloom the wild roses.* 'Six mounted Norwegian policemen led the way. We could scarcely believe our eyes.' Behind the police ambled a pouchy-eyed general – the invasion force commander Nikolaus von Falkenhorst – and then came the German regulars with machine guns on their shoulders. 'They were hard muscled and they had lots of iron in their faces, the coolest cucumbers I have ever seen in uniform anywhere.' With the same ruthless speed and suddenness, German troops had seized Bergen, Trondheim, and – in the first offensive use of parachutists in history – the airport at Stavanger. Locked up in the Café Iris, Giles Romilly was prevented from reporting what Stowe was excitedly telling himself was maybe 'the most important and constructive story you have ever filed for a newspaper at any time in your life'. It fell to Stowe from his restricted and not well-informed vantage point to reveal to the world how 'an unbelievable Nazi plot' had been perpetrated 'almost without a hitch and with amazing boldness and efficiency . . . within the incredible space of 12 staggering fantastic hours'.

More than a week had passed when a German lieutenant in a forage cap ordered Romilly to pack and come with him back to the hotel. It was Romilly's first exercise in nine days, during which he had lived 'practically on starvation ration'. The soles of his boots slid about on the thawing uphill road, and he felt weak. What he remembered afterwards was 'the snow, snow, snow and terrible gauntness of Narvik'. He wrote to his parents: 'You can't imagine how mortally sick of snow one gets – really a painful feeling.' It returned him to a Christmas at Chartwell when he had built an igloo with his brother and cousins.

The lieutenant led the way into the lounge. There was blackout paper on the windows. Romilly watched the carcasses of eleven pigs file past on the shoulders of German marines.

'Well, Mr Romilly, how do you feel now?' the lieutenant asked.

A black beard had grown over Romilly's face. He had no clean underpants and had a racking headache after surviving on dry bread and coffee in sub-zero temperatures. In Kiruna, which he had visited prior to Narvik, the trams which carried the miners up the side of the iron mountain were centrally heated for ten months of the year. In the Café Iris, there had been no insulation against the cold.

'Fairly well, thank you.'

'What will your uncle say when he hears what has happened to you?'

'I don't suppose I shall be a consideration of policy.'

'You have an uncle who is a high personality in English politics, haven't you?'

'Yes, Churchill.'

A proclamation by General von Falkenhorst had singled out Romilly's uncle as the British politician responsible for the presence of German troops in Norway. 'Winston Churchill, the greatest warmonger of the century, who already during the First World War was a disaster for all mankind, has openly declared that legal factors will not stop him. He has prepared the attack on the Norwegian and Danish coasts. Days ago he was appointed Commander-in-Chief of the British armed forces.'

Early on 23 April, Romilly was removed from Narvik by flying boat. His last diary entry read: 'The Nazis are taking me to Germany. I was only able to write this because one of the plane's engines failing to fire and so they have dumped me in the Café Iris again to await completion of repairs. I am leaving these notes behind me in the hope that they will somehow be delivered in England.'

The *Daily Express* had reported Romilly's arrest under the headline: 'Nephew of Churchill Held.' Churchill tried to make light of the news at the 11.30 a.m. War Cabinet on 12 April. He told Halifax that it 'caused him no concern at all; the Nazis were welcome to him'.

Yet Churchill had been a young journalist held by the enemy – as a prisoner of the Boers – and there are signs that he was affected by his nephew's capture. While his concern for Romilly did not govern his strategy, it haunted Churchill for a substantial part of the ensuing Norway Campaign; not in the forefront of his mind, but in the sense that he was constantly thinking about it.

Time and again in the Norway Debate, politicians stood up to ask why Churchill had attached 'undue importance' to this ore-town and to question his indestructible enthusiasm for seizing it. Narvik was a dead end – geographically and from most military and political aspects. Once the Germans had taken Narvik, the sensible thing would have been to leave them there, says Geirr Haarr, Norway's foremost authority on the campaign. 'The British have stopped the iron ore. The Germans can't be reinforced by sea, and their airlift capacity is minuscule. But Churchill is hooked on the north, obsessed. He uses all arguments for an attack, and shelves all those against. Narvik becomes a slogan. Why is he hooked?'

No satisfying answer is found in the records.

When speculating about Romilly's role in Churchill's motivations for focusing on Narvik, it is interesting to note the rumours concerning Romilly's younger brother Esmond. Esmond's wife, Jessica Mitford, learned the story of Esmond's paternity from her sister Nancy. ' "Everyone knows he's Winston's son." I pressed for details and she told me about a Mediterranean cruise on which the Romillys and the Churchills went some months before Esmond's birth and during which Churchill had an affair with his sister-in-law ... I don't think I took the story too seriously. Nancy had a wonderfully active imagination.'

There is no disputing that Winston and Romilly's mother, Clementine's sister Nellie, were close. Churchill called her 'La Nellinita'. Nellie, in a letter to Churchill four weeks after Romilly's capture, called him 'my dearest love'. John Colville once caught them together on a sofa in Chequers, where Churchill was 'reading telegrams, dictating manuscript comments, and carrying on a conversation with Mrs Romilly (who was most outrageously reading the telegrams too) all at the same time'. In order to unpick the puzzle of Churchill's stubborn attachment to Narvik during the two weeks when Giles Romilly was held prisoner there, Churchill's emotional ties with Giles and his mother have to be considered.

Nellie divided her life between a cottage on the Chartwell estate, where she helped Clementine with household chores, and Huntington Park in Herefordshire, looking after her sick husband, who battled with throat cancer.

Giles's father was Colonel Bertram Romilly, described in *Misdeal*, a self-pitying novel that Nellie wrote under a pseudonym, as 'a stern-looking man with an expression of permanent sorrow on his face ...' In 1915, while fighting with the Scots Guards in France, Bertram had suffered a head wound which for the rest of his life made him sensitive to noise and stress. Invalided home from Neuve Chapelle, he had fallen in love with Nellie, then working as a nurse, who accepted his second proposal only after a doctor said that much depended on her, even though a voice seemed to whisper: 'No, no. Escape while there is yet time.' Her sister Clementine wrote to Churchill: 'I don't believe she loves him at all, but is simply marrying him out of pity.'

It was a difficult marriage. Giles and Esmond knew their father as a semi-invalid in constant pain who sat stiffly upright and said little, hoping only that they would join the Brigade of Guards. He was absent during much of their childhood – 'a perambulating vacuum' in Stephen Spender's phrase – first as Military Governor of Galilee, then as Chief Instructor of the Military School in Cairo. Inevitably, the boys viewed their famous uncle as a more effective paternal figure. Like Bertram, Churchill had seen action in South Africa, the Sudan, and in France, where the family legend was that he had worn Colonel Romilly's uniform while waiting at St Omer for an offer of higher military employment. Giles's wife Mary was told the story of how Churchill had squeezed into his brother-in-law's much smaller uniform when, after Gallipoli, he had quitted politics and returned to his first career of soldiering.

Now retired, Bertram lived at Huntington Park, the family's 400-acre estate near Kington, in a gloomy mid-Georgian country house which Giles later bulldozed, considering it 'a big-shouldered structure of decent brick, though architecturally a heap of luggage'. Giles was much fonder of his uncle's house in Kent, which became a second home. He and Esmond spent their holidays and Christmases at Chartwell, where Churchill nicknamed them 'the Lambs' – after Nellie's habit of leaving table 'to see how the lambs were'. They were staying there when Churchill was working on the second volume of *Marlborough*. He impressed both brothers with the way that he concentrated on his work, and was willing to ask an expert about some particular technical problem. For the first part of the morning, Esmond recalled, the expert delivered a lecture to their uncle. 'For the latter part, my uncle delivered the same lecture to the expert!'

At Christmas, there was always a play in which the Lambs acted for the benefit of guests and staff, Giles once performing the part of a boot-boy in a drama called 'The Bathroom Door'. Churchill considered it a huge joke when in 1932 Giles hotly defended his adopted creed of Communism. From then on, Giles became 'the Red Rose'. Yet whatever their political differences, it did not colour their affections. In T. C. Worsley's autobiographical novel *Fellow Travellers*, Gavin Blair Summers is based on Giles, 'a very tough character' who 'always defends that old arch-Liberal uncle of his if anyone else attacks him'. Giles's wife Mary was present when the *Daily Express* got through to Giles after Churchill had had a stroke, and recalls the intensity of his response. She says: 'Giles turned around. "Something's happened to Uncle Winston" – and looked shaken. They were a very united family.'

After Giles went to Spain to train with the International Brigade in Albacete, Nellie predicted that 'it would kill his father if anything were to happen to him'. At the end of her tether, she had turned to Churchill, 'who was inclined to send a battleship out', to bring his nephew home; this failing, Churchill had intervened with the International Brigade to keep Giles away from the front.

Three years on, the news of Giles's capture in Narvik – the first British civilian to be taken prisoner by the Germans – was a 'hideous blow' to his parents and brother. Beyond the bald detail of his arrest, Nellie had no idea what had happened to 'Gilo', as she called her elder and favourite son. Once more she turned to Churchill for assistance, but he was equally in the dark – he did not know if the Norwegians or the Germans had taken Giles. Meanwhile, all that the family had to go on were 'ghastly stories' in the German and Italian press 'of how he had whipped out a revolver & tried to shoot down his captors'.

Dramatic as ever, Nellie remembered her own experiences as a POW of the Germans in November 1914. After the evacuation at Mons, she had worked as a nurse in Lady Angela Manners's ambulance unit when a Prussian officer arrested her, shouting: 'You shall not return to England and we will make you suffer as you are making our German hospital nurses suffer.' She was locked in a cell in a large Belgian prison, with one bed, one blanket, and a pewter jug with some brown malt liquid tasting of mud, which she flung through the bars into the garden below. She survived for four days on a potato that was pushed through the bars, and by reading aloud from the *Oxford Book of English Verse*. On the fifth morning she was released and put on a train to Aachen, the first part of a journey that saw her locked up in waiting rooms in Köln, Osnabruck, Bremen and Hamburg, before she arrived at the Danish town of Vandrup. She remembered a conversation with a German NCO who pointed to an enormous picture of the Kaiser, and sliced his hand across his throat, saying: 'Of course for him we would all lose our heads.' His great joy was to tell Nellie how easily Germany's four million soldiers would cross the Channel on their conquering march to England, as Hitler now promised to do.

On learning of Giles's capture, Nellie wrote to his brother Esmond: 'I needn't tell you the hours of agony I have lived through . . . I was knocked out for 3 days & knew nothing of anything.' Aside from her own 'dreadful sorrow and pain', she worried about the effect on her husband. She held out for three days before informing Bertram. He was pierced to the heart.

The impact on Churchill was less obvious, but behind his posturing he was a family man as much as Chamberlain. Despite his offhand remark to Halifax, Churchill was sensitive to his nephew's predicament and to its effect on Clementine and her sister. John Colville observed that Churchill's 'sympathy for people in distress was immediate, whatever he might have felt about them in the past . . . Perhaps because his own youth had been unhappy, he went out of his way to be kind to young people.' Harold Nicolson's perception that Churchill was rather 'sentimental about people' was nowhere truer than in the case of the elder 'Lamb'. Giles Romilly was an errant son in Churchill's mould who had spent each Christmas from 1924 to 1933 at Chartwell, once reducing the housemaids to tears with his grand finale of Kipling's 'You're a better man than I am, Gunga Din!'

Churchill had quoted Kipling when he inaugurated the Kipling Memorial in November 1937: 'What stands if Freedom fall? Who dies if England live?' Three years on, the answer to this 'supreme question', which governed Churchill's life quite as much as it had Kipling's, seemed personified suddenly by his nephew.

Romilly had gone to Narvik to report for the *Daily Express* on a military action which had been Churchill's idea. Now the Nazis had captured him in a brilliantly executed operation. The drama of the next four weeks played out against the backdrop of Colonel Bertram Romilly's struggle to keep alive, and of his son's uncertain fate.

Was this to be Britain's fate too?

3
OPERATION 'WILFRED'

'A lot of nonsense has been written about Norway.'
ADMIRAL J. H. GODFREY

'I have read that in the high mountains there are sometimes
conditions to be found when an incautious move or even
a sudden loud exclamation may start an avalanche.'
NEVILLE CHAMBERLAIN in his first speech as
Prime Minister, 25 June 1937

For the British, the military expedition sent to Norway in response to the German invasion was a spectacular cock-up, with no one quite sure who was in charge in London, and on-the-spot generals and admirals fighting each other in the blizzards of Narvik. Seven months in the preparation, the eight-week campaign became a byword for bungling; a tragedy of bad organisation, missed opportunity and divided command, with interferences by the Admiralty, and with Churchill going behind the backs of the Chiefs of Staff and the War Office, even his own admirals, and in spite of his loyalty to Chamberlain, still playing his own game.

Churchill had not been to Narvik, nor ever would. It existed for him in the shape of an outsized chart on his wall. Yet this remote trading port became Churchill's mesmerising obsession during his second short stint at the Admiralty. In that turbulent time, there was a multitude of pressing factors for him to consider. He could never say: 'For the next three days I shall concentrate on Narvik.' But if his eye did swivel back to one spot, then it was to this small town at the head of Vestfjorden, 200 miles north of the Arctic circle.

The initiative to mine Narvik had been Churchill's. The Scandinavian operation was one of the first conceived and put into action by him after a sizeable period of inactivity. To understand his obsession, Churchill's fellow Ministers needed to wind back to May 1915 and the humiliation of his forced departure from office after Gallipoli. 'I can't help longing for the power to give those wide directions which occupied my Admiralty days,' Churchill wrote to his wife in January 1916. 'The damnable mismanagement wh has ruined the Dardanelles enterprise & squandered vainly so much life & opportunity cries aloud for retribution: & if I survive, the day will come when I will claim it publicly.' Dogged by the shambles – the senseless bloodshed, the ill-executed naval attack against shore-based targets, the lack of experienced troops – he hankered to eradicate its memory. In the opinion of Halifax's normally unruffled Permanent Under-Secretary, Sir Alexander Cadogan: 'This so called Scandinavian "plan" is not a plan: it's a hang-over.'

Churchill initially promoted to the War Cabinet 'the importance of stopping the Norwegian transport of Swedish ore from Narvik' a fortnight after his return to the Admiralty in September 1939. The First Sea Lord and Chief of the Naval Staff, Admiral Sir Dudley Pound, had suggested the idea on 18 September, reminding Churchill that the navy had laid a minefield up to the Norwegian three-mile limit in 1918, and had planned to establish a British base near Stavanger. A proposal to use the Royal Navy's unchallengeable command of the sea to resuscitate this operation – 'doing Narvik' Cadogan called it – would be argued indecisively back and forth, agreed and hesitated over, at innumerable War Cabinet and Supreme War Council meetings in London and Paris until the end of March 1940.

In London, the arguments took place at a long rectangular table behind the double doors of the Cabinet Room at No. 10. The War Cabinet of nine was made up of a hard core of Chamberlain, Halifax, Hoare and Simon, supplemented by Lord Chatfield (Minister for the Coordination of Defence until April 1940), and the three forces Ministers – Churchill (Navy), Wood (Air), Hore-Belisha (Army, replaced after January 1940 by Oliver Stanley) – and with Lord Hankey brought back from retirement as Minister without Portfolio. Its morning meetings were often attended for particular items of the agenda by the Chiefs of Staff – Admiral Pound, General Ironside and Air Marshal Sir Cyril Newall – as well as by Major General Hastings Ismay (Secretary of the Committee of Imperial Defence), Sir John Anderson

(Home Secretary), Sir Anthony Eden (Dominions Secretary), Sir Edward Bridges (Cabinet Secretary), Cadogan, and Chamberlain's special adviser, the senior civil servant Sir Horace Wilson. On the outbreak of war, Chamberlain had invited the Labour leaders to join what was tenuously still called a National government, but they had declined. From January 1940, the Chancellor John Simon, a National Liberal, was the only non-Conservative politician in the War Cabinet.

Not all these people normally sat around the table, but all did so from time to time. Churchill had to persuade each and every one that a minefield off Narvik would force enemy merchant ships out into the open sea where the navy could legally sink or seize them.

The Chiefs of Staff were immediately opposed. In General Ironside's view, it smacked alarmingly of the Gallipoli plan and was likely to accelerate any contemplated German action in Scandinavia. 'It is like putting a stick inside a hornet's nest without having provided yourself with a proper veil.'

Halifax was opposed, on the grounds that an attack against a neutral country risked alienating other neutrals, as well as American public opinion. The key to a stoppage of ore was surely at Luleå in Sweden, on the Gulf of Bothnia; most convenient for eight months of the year, but usually frozen from January to April, when Narvik took over. Halifax pointed out that there had been no iron-ore traffic from Narvik to Germany since the start of the war; between 3 September and 25 October, not one ship was sent from Germany.

Chamberlain was opposed because he did not want to provoke Germany into retaliating. Contrary to his posthumous image, he was more alert to the supremacy of the Luftwaffe than Churchill. Chamberlain had written to Churchill on 16 September, saying that he felt the lesson of the Polish campaign was 'the power of the Air Force when it has obtained complete mastery in the air to paralyse the operations of land forces . . . and as a result, it seems to me to be above all things vital that we should not allow ourselves to get into the same position vis à vis Germany as the unfortunate Poles.'

The arguments over appeasement and the country's unpreparedness for war scarcely need to be recapitulated. What is worth repeating is that

Chamberlain's obsession with a German bombardment of London was shared by the majority of his War Cabinet. Chamberlain feared that a violation of Norwegian neutrality risked bringing about that knock-out bolt from the blue – from '900 bombers at Mannheim ready to take off immediately' – which his planners had predicted might result in one million casualties in the first week, 'with the possible destruction of our means of communication'.*

In any case, Chamberlain was convinced that his economic blockade of German ports by the Royal Navy was working, and that Hitler's strange silence was explained by his 'abject depression'. He wrote to his sister Ida on 8 October: 'However much the Nazis may brag and threaten, I don't believe they feel sufficiently confident to venture on the great war unless they are forced into it by action on our part. It is my aim to see that that action is not taken.'

Churchill took precisely the opposite view. 'Winston, of course, is in favour of immediate action,' wrote Chamberlain's Junior Private Secretary, John Colville – who shared a large room, adjacent to the Cabinet Room, with Chamberlain's typist Miss Edith Watson, a spinster in her late fifties, and his Parliamentary Private Secretary (and future Prime Minister) Alec Dunglass. For them, as for senior Downing Street staff like Chamberlain's Principal Private Secretary Sir Arthur Rucker, Churchill was a disturbing presence who 'needed a diet consisting of the carcases of abortive and wild cat operations' and whose military enthusiasms had to be treated with extreme caution. Unlike their wary Prime Minister, Churchill relished the idea of provoking Germany into reacting. If Hitler did attempt an invasion of Norway, 'it would give us the opportunity to take what we wanted, and this, with our sea power, we could do'.

Mad to start something, not least to prevent the French from controlling British strategy, as they had in the First World War, Churchill's impatience to tempt Germany 'into an imprudent action which would open the door for us' was never balanced by a clear assessment of what he

---

* His Air Intelligence was weak. There was scarcely one bomber in the Luftwaffe capable of reaching London from Mannheim, over 500 miles away. The real air threat did not develop until after the fall of France.

wanted or what form a German reaction might take. In spite of the fact that he had flown himself – 'I can manage a machine with ease in the air, even with high winds' – and had become Air Minister at what was in effect the beginning of the aerial age, Churchill was still slow to learn the lesson of the impact of air power on naval operations. That was perhaps inevitable to some degree, for there was no solid experience upon which to base a judgement. The Fleet Air Arm had gone to the Royal Navy early in 1938 with no history of fighting in the air. Churchill was surrounded by many senior battle-hardened people who were singularly reluctant to accept the revolutionary change which air power had made.

The Royal Navy was the only major navy with a modern A.A. system. Its exposure to the Luftwaffe in the confined waters of the Norwegian fjords was not yet a risk that troubled Churchill. First, there were at that time no German aircraft within range of Narvik or central Norway. Secondly, Churchill was confident that his ships could defeat air attack, meaning high-level bombing, which was virtually the only method known to major air forces. 'A modern fleet was unassailable from the air,' he had informed Ironside two years before. 'A curtain of fire could be put up which would make it impossible for aeroplanes to come.' Admiral Godfrey worked alongside him at the Admiralty, and observed that Churchill was 'obsessed with the idea that a fleet of ships could provide complete aerial protection with its own A.A. guns'. The Norway Campaign would show how out of date were some of Churchill's most firmly held ideas, and how right Chamberlain had been to express concern.

Over the next three months, Churchill was the one Cabinet member consistently to press for some drastic offensive action to seize back the initiative from Germany. 'The search for a naval offensive must be incessant.' Once Churchill had presented his case on 19 September, he dug in his heels. 'And when he digs his heels in,' the Soviet Ambassador observed in his diary, 'nobody can budge him.'

Churchill's aims were set out in a memorandum that he circulated to the War Cabinet on 16 December. He had interrupted his proofreading of *A History of the English-Speaking Peoples* to compose it. 'If Germany can be cut off from all Swedish ore supplies from now onwards till the end of 1940, a blow will have been struck at her war-making capacity equal to a first class victory in the field or from the air, and without any serious sacrifice of life. It might, indeed, be immediately decisive . . .' Churchill did not accept Halifax's objections – being himself half-American, Churchill needed no one to tell him how the Americans might react. Besides, what did arguments over neutrality matter when at stake was the ruin of civilisation? The Allies were fighting to re-establish the reign of law and to protect the liberties of small countries. 'Our defeat would mean an age of barbaric violence, and would be fatal not only to ourselves, but to the independent life of every small country in Europe . . . Humanity, rather than legality, must be our guide.'

Churchill calculated that the cutting of the iron-ore traffic from Narvik was worth more than all the rest of the blockade, and would shorten the war and save thousands of lives. Plus, President Roosevelt had given the go-ahead. Churchill had asked the American Ambassador, Joseph Kennedy, to canvass the President's opinion. Roosevelt had sent back a coded message: 'My wife doesn't express an opinion.' If he had objected, the message would have read: 'Eunice had better not go to the party.'

But in January – 'much to the disgust of Winston', according to Ironside – the Cabinet decided 'to turn down Narvik'. A deciding factor was the objection of the Norwegian King. Haakon VII had issued an appeal to George VI, his nephew, who used his influence on the Foreign Secretary. Halifax 'now convinced that W. S. C. on wrong track,' Cadogan wrote on 11 January. 'Heard later P.M. shares his view. Fear this will produce something like a Cabinet split.'

Halifax sent an emollient letter to Churchill two days later. 'I have felt very unhappy at finding myself taking a different line to you on the Narvik project: not only because I realise all the force of the argument you deployed, and appreciate how disastrous it may be to refrain from positive action in such a struggle as this, but also because I have too great a respect for you and for all that you bring to this business of saving civilisation to feel other than uncomfortable when my mind does not go with yours.'

Churchill believed that the mining of Narvik amounted to no more than a 'technical infringement' and that the Cabinet should not let itself be bound by judicial scruples which their enemies had thrown to the winds. Never still, his need to act consumed him. Admiral Godfrey had close contact with Churchill up to May 1940. In his unpublished 'worm's eye view', Godfrey wrote that if the First Lord had a bright idea, 'he wanted to <u>do</u> something about it straight away', and, to get his own way, 'brought the <u>whole</u> battery of his ingenious, tireless and highly political mind to bear on the point at issue. His battery of weapons included persuasion, real or simulated anger, mockery, vituperation, tantrums, ridicule, derision, abuse and tears, which he would aim at anyone who opposed him.'

Churchill directed this arsenal to wear down Halifax. He attacked the position of the neutrals in a broadcast which angered the Foreign Office and set back the work of the Ministry of Information 'by a full three months'. At the Paris Embassy, Churchill burst into Halifax's adjoining bedroom in his dressing gown as Halifax was about to turn out the lights, and held forth for two hours, saying it was 'very seldom that two intelligent people got the chance of a nice uninterrupted talk'. He continued to deluge the War Cabinet with memorandums urging action. It was very painful, he repeated, to watch, during the last two months, 'the endless procession of German ore-ships down the Norwegian territorial waters carrying to Germany the material out of which will be made the shells to kill our young men ... when all the time the simplest and easiest of motions would bring it to an end'.

Then, in the middle of February, a black tanker with a grey funnel steamed into Jøssingfjorden and snapped everyone's attention back to Norway.

Late on 15 February, an Admiralty signal reported that a suspected armed German supply ship with 299 British POWs on board had passed Trondheim at noon. The prisoners were gathered from merchant ships sunk in the South Atlantic by the German raider *Admiral Graf Spee*. The supply ship was thought to be the *Altmark*, making a run for Germany within the protection of Norway's three-mile limit, a long narrow band of water known as the Leads. But there was no clear information about her appearance until Captain Vian on board HMS *Cossack* identified her from a wardroom copy of the *Illustrated London News*.

When, next day, the British caught up with the *Altmark*, they signalled for the supply ship to proceed on a course which would take her out to sea. The signal ignored, the destroyers HMS *Ivanhoe* and HMS *Intrepid* entered the Leads, and the *Intrepid* fired a warning shot.

Two Norwegian torpedo boats escorted the *Altmark*. Lieutenant Halvorsen, commander of the *Kjell*, came aboard the *Cossack*, which had also sailed inside the Leads, to assure Vian that Norwegian authorities had already boarded the *Altmark* four times to check the ship's papers, and no prisoners had been found. Halvorsen was unaware that the German captain had on each occasion refused the Norwegian request to inspect the hold, claiming that the *Altmark* was a 'state ship' and therefore enjoyed diplomatic immunity. The commanding Norwegian admiral in Oslo had overruled the local commander in Bergen – who, due to the refusal, wished to send the German ship out of Norwegian sovereign waters – and he had given instructions for the *Altmark* to proceed.

Halvorsen said that his orders were to resist the entry of British warships into the Leads.

When Churchill telephoned Halifax at 6.30 p.m. from the Admiralty, he sounded as if he were on the *Cossack*'s bridge. 'We are sitting opposite the *Altmark* and there are two Norwegian gun boats facing us with their torpedo tubes trained on our boats. These are the instructions we propose to send and I want your approval.' The Foreign Secretary asked for ten minutes to decide, and made 'one or two suggestions' about the order which

Churchill accepted, 'and so the thing went ahead'. The amended order read: 'You should board the *Altmark*, liberate the prisoners and take possession of the ship pending further instructions.'

The following day, wrote Halifax, 'Winston rang me up at 7 o'clock in the morning to tell me that they had got the *Altmark* prisoners . . . It had been a very fine performance, and quite in the Elizabethan style.'

With the same triumphant 'tang' in his voice, Churchill contacted the Prime Minister at Chequers, where there had been a heavy snowfall. Chamberlain wrote to his sisters: 'At 7.45 before I had got up Winston rang me up "urgently". Luckily I have a telephone at my bedside so I didn't have to go and sit half dressed in the cold but I took up the instrument with some misgiving.'

Churchill's call reassured him.

At 11.12 p.m., a boarding party of British petty officers and ratings had leapt over the tanker's rail after the *Altmark* tried to ram the *Cossack* and blind the bridge with searchlights. In steel helmets and holding fixed bayonets, they made fast the *Altmark* with a hemp hawser. Eight Germans were killed, three of them while trying to lower a boat, and the rest as they fled across the ice.

The climactic moment came when the leader of the boarding party unlocked a hatch and peered down at scores of upraised faces.

'Come on up. The Navy's here!'

The news reached Churchill at 3 a.m. 'You must have had a very thrilling & anxious night on Friday,' wrote his daughter-in-law Pamela, who travelled to Leith to welcome back the sailors. 'It's comforting to know we can be ferocious.'

Geoffrey Shakespeare helped to organise a reception for the men at the Guildhall. The brunt of the Phoney War had fallen on Britain's mariners, Churchill told them. Their rescue by the *Cossack* 'under the noses of the enemy and amid the tangles of one-sided neutrality' was a glorious epilogue to the scuttling of the *Graf Spee* off Montevideo in December. 'The warrior heroes of the past may look down, as Nelson's monument looks down upon us now . . . And to Nelson's immortal signal of 135 years ago, "England expects that every man will do his duty," there may now be added last week's not less profound reply, "The Navy is here." '

Within two months, this phrase was to rebound on Churchill with stinging force.

The Conservative MP Ronald Tree expressed the general mood when he wrote that the '*Altmark* – drawn cutlasses etc.' was 'almost the first important bit of news to come our way' since the start of the war. This heroic rescue of British sailors, with no casualties, elevated Churchill's position in the public eye, but also within the War Cabinet. It meant that Chamberlain and Halifax now had to listen to him when Churchill put Narvik back on the agenda.

Germany's misuse of Norwegian territorial waters was, Churchill insisted, 'the most flagrant breach of neutrality of a technical character which could be imagined'. In Leith, Pamela Churchill had talked to the liberated seamen. 'Most of them would only say "It was the Norwegians that done us in, they knew all about us."' The *Altmark*'s transgression persuaded Halifax of the 'complete subservience of Norway to German pressure', and it caused Chamberlain to consider a riposte.

At the War Cabinet on 23 February, Churchill 'pleaded earnestly for action to be taken immediately. Such action would be more than a naval foray; it might well prove to be one of the main fulcra on which the whole course of the war would turn'. In yet another memorandum, he enjoined his colleagues: 'Strike while the iron is hot! In three days from the moment of sanction by Cabinet the minefield can be laid.' He had a name for the minefield, after a long-eared young rabbit in a cartoon in the *Daily Mail*. 'The operation being minor and innocent may be called "Wilfred"'.

The *Altmark* incident, a 'medieval story of rescue from dragons', wrenched Germany's attention back towards Norway.

Churchill's opposite number in Berlin was Grand Admiral Erich Raeder. Head of the Kriegsmarine and veteran of the Battle of Jutland, Raeder sponsored a plan which in broad outline mirrored Churchill's.

Raeder's memoirs were written by a committee and cannot be trusted, but they contain the salient facts. Ten days after Churchill first suggested laying the mines in September 1939, alarming news reached Raeder from Admiral Wilhelm Canaris, the head of the Abwehr (German Military Intelligence), of 'certain indications that Britain intended to seize a foothold in

Norway . . . With growing anxiety we now realised the full scope of the danger.' On 10 October, Raeder went with his notes to see Hitler, declaring that the only way to forestall the British was 'by ourselves establishing bases at decisive points on Norwegian territory'. Hitler was interested – he had apparently told Raeder back in November 1934 that 'the war could not be carried on at all if the navy did not protect the ore elements from Scandinavia' – but he was preoccupied with Operation 'Gelb', the single 'all-destroying blow' in the West, which kept being postponed because of bad weather, among other reasons. Hitler asked Raeder to leave his notes behind.

There matters rested until 10 December, when a Norwegian right-wing politician and former Defence Minister, Vidkun Quisling, arrived in Berlin by train.

Quisling was a mathematician who had graduated top of his military academy, yet the Norway Campaign made his name synonymous with treason, and it would be freely invoked by Chamberlain to damn his Conservative critics, and by those same critics to insult Chamberlain's supporters.

The son of a country priest, with prominent blue eyes, a doughy face and no sense of humour, Quisling was known as the Pepper Minister, following an alleged nocturnal attack when alone in the Defence Ministry. Ground pepper was flung into his face and he was hit on the head with a blunt instrument; he then fainted. His assailant was not caught, and the incident was never proven to have taken place, but it consolidated Quisling's image with his many critics as a fanatic prone to seeing non-existent enemies. He abominated Communists, and was suspicious of the French and the English. On 11 December, he met with Raeder and told him that 'if Germany were defeated as a result of Allied landings in Norway then a vital threat to the whole of Western civilisation would result'.

Raeder's naval aspirations dovetailed with Quisling's political ambitions as head of the small minority nationalist party, Nasjonal Samling. Next day, Raeder told Hitler about their meeting, saying that he had formed 'a trustworthy impression' of the Norwegian. Intrigued, Hitler received Quisling at 3 p.m. on 13 December, and again on 18 December. What did Quisling know about British plans for establishing bases in Norway? Not much, it turned out – beyond a rumoured alliance between Britain's Jewish

Secretary of State for War, Leslie Hore-Belisha, and the President of the Norwegian Parliament, who had Jewish great-grandparents. Quisling's suspicion of a Jewish plot to occupy Norway caused Hitler to lean forward for the first time. Quisling was gratified to observe that 'upon mentioning the eventuality of a violation of neutrality, Hitler worked himself into a frenzy, culminating in a sort of ecstasy.' In Quisling's account, Hitler said that 'if he ever detected the slightest British intention of entering Norway, he would be sure to intervene in good time' – with six, eight, twelve divisions.

No sooner had Quisling left the Chancellery than Hitler summoned Major General Alfred Jodl, Chief of Operations at the Armed Forces High Command, the Oberkommando der Wehrmacht (OKW), who that night wrote in his diary: 'Führer orders investigation, with smallest possible staff, of how occupation in Norway can be carried out.'

Studie Nord was the code name for Jodl's preliminary investigation. Hitler received his assessment on 20 January and acted on it next day, tasking General Keitel to put together a small team from within the OKW, of which Hitler was head, and emphasising that the 'issue of Norway should not leave the hands of the OKW'. A chief feature of the German operation was that the plans did not have to be shuttled back and forth, and debated over by obstructive layers of democratic decision-making – what Churchill lamented to Halifax were 'the awful difficulties which our machinery of war conduct presents to positive action'.

On 5 February 1940, Keitel assembled his Special Staff and told them that the German government had learned of a plan to give 'a decisive blow' against the Reich. To prevent this, Germany needed to prepare for an important operation in Norway. In contrast to its British counterpart, which fragmented into a dozen confusing and mutating code words, the German operation was known henceforth by a single name, 'Weserübung'. Preparations were to go ahead in total secrecy, with no civilian personnel involved, not even the German Foreign Secretary, Joachim von Ribbentrop. All other political and military authorities were to be kept 'in complete ignorance of the investigation of this matter'. Hitler trusted nobody.

Even at this stage, Hitler intended for Operation 'Weserübung' to be planned 'on a theoretical basis', as a contingency. Operation 'Gelb' remained the priority. But the situation was 'electrified', wrote Raeder, by the *Cossack*'s attack on the *Altmark*. 'This incident put the whole problem in a new light, for now it was quite clear that the Norwegian Government was not in a position to defend Norwegian neutrality.'

For Hitler, the *Altmark*'s capture and the death of German sailors was a stab in the gut. 'No opposition, no British losses!' he spluttered to Jodl. Enraged, he saw himself in a duel with Churchill, casting him as Public Enemy Number One. In their first clash of cutlasses, Churchill had come out on top. Hitler resolved to thrust back sharply.

After witnessing Hitler's reaction, Alfred Rosenberg, head of the Foreign Policy Office, wrote in his diary: 'Really stupid initiative on Churchill's part. It confirms Quisling's views and his warnings.' Fearful of losing momentum, Hitler was receptive to an operation in the north that might add to his legend of invincibility at a moment when this risked being tarnished because of his failure to attack in the west. The postponement of Operation 'Gelb' had freed up powerful air forces for deployment elsewhere.

If one motive for the invasion of Norway was to safeguard the source of Germany's iron ore, then another was Raeder's desire for a base with access to the North Sea and Atlantic. Rosenberg, too, thought Norway would be invaluable in a 'siege of Great Britain' and as a launch pad for an invasion. And a further lure: Norway played to Hitler's ambition for a Greater Germany. Hitler believed that Norwegians were Aryans who had fallen asleep, but could be reawakened by National Socialism. The invasion of Norway represented an important step towards the aim that he would outline to his Propaganda Minister, Joseph Goebbels, on 10 April: 'a north-Germanic confederation'. When celebrating his fifty-first birthday ten days later, Hitler announced that he looked forward to Norway sending back to Germany its 'human material' for the 'upbreeding of men'.

On 19 February, Hitler had ordered Keitel to speed up preparations. Abandoning any determination to uphold Norwegian neutrality, Hitler no longer viewed Operation 'Weserübung' as theoretical, but as a blueprint for imminent action. He told General Nikolaus von Falkenhorst, whom he summoned on 21 February at Keitel's recommendation, that 'the boarding of the *Altmark* had dispelled all ambiguity as to British intentions'.

One of the attractions of fifty-five-year-old von Falkenhorst, Commander of XXI Army Corps, was that he had served in Finland in 1918. Hitler questioned him about how the German army then had coordinated with the navy, explaining that he intended 'to launch a similar operation in order to occupy Norway'. Quickly deciding that von Falkenhorst possessed the necessary qualities, Hitler appointed him Commander-in-Chief of 'Weserübung', placed five divisions at his disposal, and told him to report back that same afternoon, with plans for how he might deploy them.

Von Falkenhorst knew no more about Norway than did the British War Cabinet. 'Once outside, I went to town and bought a Baedeker, a tourist guide, in order to find out what Norway was like . . . I had no idea . . .' He pored over the Baedeker's maps in his room at the Kaiserhof Hotel, opposite the Chancellery, and returned at 5 p.m. His suggestions satisfied Hitler, who told him that there was no time to lose and it was imperative to get there ahead of the Allies. 'I cannot and I will not begin the offensive in the West before this affair has been settled.'

As with Churchill, the Norwegian Campaign took the shape of a private war that Hitler imposed on the Kriegsmarine, the Wehrmacht and the Luftwaffe. The success of 'Weserübung' owed much to Hitler's insistence that his armed forces overcome inter-service squabbling, and cooperate. Raeder wrote: 'It was remarkable as being the first occasion on which the three arms of the Wehrmacht had worked in such close tactical connection on a large scale.' In contrast, Britain's position had been laid out by General Ironside on 28 December. 'We have no war policy whatever. There is no plan to use the Navy, Army and Air Force together.'

Von Falkenhorst's team began work behind an unmarked door in Bendlerstrasse, in Berlin. To help form a rapid picture of the country, German Intelligence traced some of the hundreds of orphans who in the 1920s had been sent to Norway and billeted with families there; they were interviewed for information, and several would serve on the invasion fleet as guides and translators. Priority was laid on secrecy, speed, maximum surprise. Hitler ordered von Falkenhorst to report back every two days, and on 1 March he again stressed the 'utmost importance' that 'the Allies be caught unawares by this operation'.

On 3 March, Hitler commanded that Operation 'Weserübung' precede Operation 'Gelb', sending Goering 'into a rage'. On 20 March, von Falkenhorst announced that his men were ready to land by air and sea at seven places in Norway. Six divisions had been assigned: 3rd Mountain Division, which had fought in Poland; and 69th, 163rd, 181st, 196th and 214th Infantry Divisions. Up to 8,850 men would land in the first attack from ships; a further 3,500 from the air. A total of 1,500 planes – He-111 and Ju-88 bombers, Ju-87 Stuka dive-bombers, twin-engined Me-110 fighters, and three-engined Ju-52 transport planes – had been temporarily put at von Falkenhorst's disposal under X Fliegerkorps.

Hitler, according to the Naval War Diary, 'expressed his complete satisfaction with the way the war preparation had been made ... The whole history of warfare taught that carefully prepared operations usually succeeded with relatively insignificant losses.'

On 1 April, after a 1 p.m. 'breakfast', von Falkenhorst introduced Hitler personally to the admirals and generals who were to take part in the landings. Hitler 'cross-examined every single general, who was to explain very precisely the nature of the task he was to carry out. He even discussed with the ship commanders whether they would land their men on the right or the left of a given objective. He left nothing to chance.' As with Churchill's plan for Narvik: 'It was his idea, it was his plan, it was his war.'

On 2 April, Hitler signed the order for the invasion. At 7.17 p.m., a message was sent out to the fleet and to the U-boats: '*Wesertag ist der 9. April.*' The time was set for 5.15 a.m. Cut out of the decision-making process, the German Foreign Ministry was informed only the following day.

On 6 April, General Dietl and 139 Regiment, with Edelweiss symbols on their caps and sleeves, arrived at Wesermünde, and in the evening embarked on the ten destroyers waiting for them. By 11 p.m., Group 1 convoy bound for Narvik was moving down the channel towards the German Bight. The Germans hoped that the movements of their ships would be interpreted by the Admiralty – as they were – as an attempt to break out of the naval blockade and find a passage into the Atlantic to menace British shipping.

On 8 April, the date when the British laid their mines off Narvik, Hitler summoned Goebbels to discuss the German reaction to the news of 'Wilfred'. It was a hot day, and in a walk around the Chancellery gardens, Hitler informed his Propaganda Minister of the operation that was due to take place within the next few hours. The club-footed Goebbels, a former novelist, listened in silent admiration to his Führer's imaginative plan. 'Everything has been prepared down to the last detail. The action will involve around 250,000 men. Most of the guns and ammunition have already been transported concealed in ships.' At a late stage, Denmark had been included in 'Weserübung'. Hitler was confident there would be no resistance. 'First we will keep quiet for a short time once we have both countries, and then England will be plastered.'

'A hundred incidents should have prepared us,' wrote the American Minister to Norway, Florence Harriman. In the run-up to that 'fatal daybreak', few in Oslo, Stockholm, Paris or London had taken seriously the 'abundantly available' evidence of a German invasion.

The warning signs had been there to read since before the war, and in Hitler's own words. On 9 February 1940, Chamberlain asked his sister Hilda: 'Have you read *Hitler Speaks* by Rauschning? It is illuminating.' The English edition had appeared in December, and extracts were circulated to the War Cabinet. The conversations with Hitler had taken place in 1933 and 1934, and jotted down by Dr Rauschning – 'a very pleasant quiet man, an East Prussian landowner', according to Leo Amery. Hitler might have been describing 'Weserübung'. 'When I wage war . . . in the midst of peace . . . troops will suddenly appear, let us say in Paris. They will wear French uniforms. They will march through the streets in broad daylight. No one will stop them. Everything has been thought out, prepared to the last detail . . .' Hitler even indicated where his 'gigantic, all-destroying blow' might land. ' "We need space," he almost shrieked, "to make us independent of every possible political grouping and alliance . . . I shall have . . . a Northern Union of Denmark, Sweden and Norway." '

Hitler's ambition for his Northern Union was given impetus by a book published in 1929: *Die See Strategie des Weltkrieges*, by Admiral Wolfgang Wegener. In May 1939, Cadogan's predecessor at the Foreign Office, Robert Vansittart, drew the First Sea Lord's attention to Wegener's book, from which it seemed probable: '1. that Denmark and part of Norway may be seized as a jumping off ground. 2. that the trade routes will be attacked with all available naval and air power working from such shore bases as can be seized and held, or can be concealed, and from supply ships.'

Then, in January 1940, Maurice Hankey, Lloyd George's Secretary to the War Cabinet who had been brought back from retirement by Chamberlain, received an anxious letter from a Norwegian friend, a former schoolmistress with good contacts in government circles in Oslo. On 5 January, she had met the new German Minister to Norway, Curt Bräuer, on a train to Oslo, and in the course of a long conversation the diplomat had told her that 'the danger came from England who threatened to take possession of Stavanger and Bergen *and in that case we go directly to Oslo*'.

A month after Hankey had passed on her letter to Halifax, the American journalist William Shirer was told 'a fantastic story' in Berlin. 'A plan is afoot to hide S.S. shock troops in the bottom of a lot of freighters, have them put in at ports in Scandinavia, Belgium and Africa, and seize the places . . . I suspect this story is a plant that the Nazis would like us to put out as part of their nerve war.' Yet the stories kept coming which suggested that Germany was up to something. On 17 March, the British Military attaché in Stockholm reported that German officers had told Swedish colleagues how Norway 'would be taken care of in a very short time'. On 30 March, the French Naval Minister wrote to both the new French Prime Minister, Paul Reynaud, and to the Commander-in-Chief of France's armed forces, General Maurice Gamelin. 'Recent information reveals that [Germany] has gathered the material for an expedition against bases in south Norway.' On 1 April, the head of the Swedish Foreign Office informed the *Daily Telegraph*'s correspondent in Stockholm, who instantly passed it on to the British Minister, that 'the Germans were going to attack Norway'.

Made aware of these rumours, British Intelligence dismissed them. As late as 8 April, Military Intelligence issued a paper, 'The Possibilities of German Action against Scandinavia', which 'did not support any probability of a Scandinavian invasion'. At the Admiralty, Captain Ralph Edwards, the new Deputy Director of Operations (Home), recorded in his diary the opinion of British Intelligence that the German military chiefs would never allow such 'a mad expedition to sail'. A note pencilled by General Ismay during a meeting of the War Cabinet on 26 April betrayed a retrospective exasperation. 'Information reached us many months ago that the Germans had collected and prepared transports for an operation of this character and were training their troops.'

So why was nothing done?

Where German preparations for 'Weserübung' were conducted in conditions of pain-of-death secrecy, with single-minded focus, British plans were characterised by stalls, hiccups and shilly-shallying; or as Churchill put it, 'vain boggling, hesitation, changes of policy, arguments between good and worthy people unending'.

Between February and April, the race for Norway was between two leaders with competing strategies and temperaments. On one side was Hitler, who, unconcerned at offending Norwegian goodwill or neutrality, wished to gamble everything on what he boasted to von Falkenhorst was 'one of the most daring operations in the history of modern warfare'. Agonising on the other side over whether to mine a neutral country's territorial waters was Chamberlain, who did not want to take risks without being sure of the result, long believing that 'you should never menace unless you are in a position to carry out your threats'.

Against this cautious mindset, Churchill's renewed championing of 'Wilfred' made juddering headway. Cadogan wrote in his diary on 23 February: 'Apparently Cabinet still undecided about minefield in Norwegian waters. Of course, it is really only a Winston stunt, and ill-conceived.'

Increasingly, Chamberlain felt ground down by his First Lord who took a broad view of his responsibilities, and made his weight felt outside the Admiralty, as often as not despatching Geoffrey Shakespeare to be his errand boy. 'I am concerned about the shortage of fish,' Churchill told Shakespeare. 'We must have a policy of utmost fish.' Shakespeare several times had to send a message to a Minister 'that Mr Churchill intended to raise the matter in question at the next War Cabinet unless it was settled forthwith'. Another of Shakespeare's tasks was to prepare the Prime Minister's weekly naval statement on the progress of the war. Included in the confidential list of telegrams ('so I might be aware of losses and sinkings'), Shakespeare could not fail to be aware that Operation 'Wilfred' was a project, as Chamberlain put it, 'on which Winston was particularly & fiercely keen'. For Uncle Geoffrey no less than for Chamberlain, 'Wilfred' represented each and every one of Churchill's plans and interferences to which he had relentlessly subjected Ministers since joining the War Cabinet.

For six months now, Chamberlain had resisted Churchill's 'rash suggestions'. Even so, he was 'conscious that Winston would like very much to become Minister for Defence with authority over the War Office and Air Ministry, and that just won't do'. On 2 March, Chamberlain felt obliged to remind Churchill who was in charge. 'I said that for once & contrary to my usual practice I would speak first and that I did not anticipate any serious trouble with Winston for the simple reason that if I put my foot down he must either accept my decision or resign. Now he would just <u>hate</u> to resign . . . he is thoroughly enjoying life.'

Instead, it was under pressure from his chief ally, the French premier Edouard Daladier – 'a bull with snails horns', Chamberlain called him – that the Prime Minister consented on 11 March to send a more ambitious expedition to Narvik.

Since November, a beleaguered Finnish army had fought a valiant rearguard battle against a brutal invasion by 450,000 Russian forces and 1,000 tanks. 'Avonmouth' was a proactive Allied plan to bring assistance to the Finns, and Narvik was to serve as its base. Had the plan gone ahead, it would have meant the Allies breaching Norwegian neutrality on the mainland before the Germans. The operation was quite distinct from 'Wilfred', though Chamberlain believed that he could 'kill two birds with one stone' by also occupying the Swedish ore-fields. Churchill's support was immediate and enthusiastic. 'We had everything to gain and nothing to lose by the drawing of Norway and Sweden into the war.'

After much toing and froing, the Anglo-French force of 20,000 men, gathered from two British brigades and a brigade of French Chasseurs Alpins, had been assembled to embark by mid-March. When Air Marshal Cyril Newall learned the details on 11 March, he muttered to Major General John Kennedy, the operation's designated Chief of Staff: 'I think the whole thing is hare-brained.' Kennedy agreed – as did Major General Ismay. Cadogan, too, considered the plan 'amateurish and half-hatched by a half-baked staff'.

Next morning, 12 March, General Ironside swelled their number. 'We had a dreadful Cabinet . . . A more unmilitary show I have never seen. The Prime Minister began peering at a chart of Narvik, and when he had finished he asked me what scale it was on. He asked what effect an eight-inch shell would have on a transport and finished up by saying that he was prepared to risk a four-inch shell but not an eight-inch shell. He then asked what the weight of the shells were.' Ironside had since come round to the plan for this 'northern sideshow', but he was scornful of the politicians whose job was to give the operation sinew and muscle. 'The Cabinet presented the picture of a bewildered flock of sheep faced by a problem they have consistently refused to consider.'

At 6.30 p.m., General Kennedy walked over to No. 10 where a 'tired and lugubrious' Chamberlain shook hands with the military commander of 'Avonmouth', Major General Pierse Mackesy. Chamberlain 'half-listened in grave silence' and 'looked more and more horrified' as Admiral Edward Evans, the navy commander, gave an excited exposé. Chamberlain's jumbled instructions differed radically from those issued by Hitler to von Falkenhorst. 'It is not the intention of the Government that the force should fight its way through either Norway or Sweden. None the less should you find your way barred by Swedish forces you should demand passage from the Swedish Commander with the utmost energy.' Halifax advocated a position even less confrontational. 'Well, if we can't get out except at the cost of a lot of Norwegian lives, I am not for it – ore or no ore.' Kennedy could only wince. 'The meeting ended with Neville Chamberlain shaking hands with us as we filed out of the room, saying, "Goodbye, and good luck to you – if you go."'

Newall put the odds at three to one against; Mackesy at a hundred to one. To their secret relief, 'Avonmouth' was cancelled next afternoon on 13 March, on news that the Finns had signed a peace treaty with Russia.

On 14 March, Churchill wrote a private letter to Halifax summing up his frustrations since he had first presented his Narvik plan to the War Cabinet six months before:

'My dear Edward,

'I feel I ought to let you know that I am vy deeply concerned about the way the war is going. It is not less deadly because it is silent . . . All has now fallen to the ground; because so cumbrous are our processes that we were too late.

'Now the ice will melt; & the Germans are masters of the North . . . Excuse me writing like this – wch I so seldom do – but I am bound to tell you that we have sustained a major disaster in the North: & that this has put the Germans more at their ease than they have ever been. Whether they have some positive plan of their own wh will open upon us I cannot tell. It w'd seem to me astonishing if they have not.'

Churchill had emphasised to his First Sea Lord Pound on 6 March: 'The first step is the one that counts.' In the days following the Russian–Finnish cease-fire, Chamberlain became sensitive to the need 'to do something spectacular' to keep public morale high. On 19 March, the Liberal leader Archie Sinclair goaded him in the Commons. 'It is time we stopped saying: what is Hitler going to do? It is about time we asked: what is Chamberlain going to do?'

Recently back from Finland, Harold Macmillan criticised 'the delay, the vacillation, change of front, standing on one foot one day and on the other the next before a decision is given'. Chamberlain merely had to glance across the Channel to recognise the dangers posed by a policy of continued inaction. Hard on the dispersal of the Anglo-French forces assembled for Operation 'Avonmouth', the French premier Edouard Daladier had been replaced in poisonous circumstances by his rival Paul Reynaud, a friend of Churchill. This was one day after *The Times* had written: 'Great Britain and France are fortunate in having Prime Ministers whose resilience is exceptional.'

If Daladier was a snail-horned bull, then Reynaud, reckoned Chamberlain, had 'a foxy expression which causes me to wonder if his real name is not Reynard instead of Reynaud'. The new premier, surviving on just one vote, reiterated a demand made by the French government on the day after 'Avonmouth' was cancelled: for the British to launch Operation 'Wilfred' without further delay. Reynaud wanted action, like Churchill, who had immediately written to him: 'I rejoice that you are at the helm.' Anxious to consolidate his precarious position, Reynaud decided that it was essential to win 'the battle of iron', and on 27 March he flew to London for a meeting of the Supreme War Council at which the decision was taken to sow mines at the entrance to Narvik, and also in the Rhine. The twin operation was planned for 5 April.

To Rab Butler, the decision to go ahead with 'Wilfred' meant that the 'Winston' policy on Norway had triumphed over the 'Halifax' policy,

Halifax only agreeing 'because of his loyalty to the P.M.' The Foreign Secretary had never been all that keen on Churchill's Narvik plan 'as I believe its practical value is overrated, but psychologically – and this war seems to be largely one of psychology – it will make the Germans wonder a bit'. Chamberlain remained to be convinced, according to Colville, while believing in 'the necessity of throwing occasional sops to public opinion'.

In fact, the Prime Minister seemed unusually upbeat. He still clung to his hunch that the war would be over 'by the spring'. The longer its phoney phase continued, the deeper grew his confidence that his strategy to strangle Germany by an economic blockade had been the correct one. Opinion polls supported him: 56 per cent of the population approved of his leadership, a figure unchanged since January. In contrast, only 30 per cent preferred Churchill as an alternative. It cheered Chamberlain to think that Labour politicians previously obstructive as well as bitterly hostile to him might have fallen in with his way of thinking. 'Attlee actually looks me in the face sometimes . . .'

Ambassador Maisky had been a close observer of Chamberlain since he replaced Baldwin as leader. On 4 April 1940, Maisky was reminded of Chamberlain's first speech as Prime Minister in 1937. On that occasion, recalled Maisky, Chamberlain had spoken 'of the gathering thunderclouds, the tense international situation, and the need to keep a *cool head* so as not to provoke a catastrophe with an incautious step. The P.M. employed a metaphor in this connection: he spoke of avalanches of snow in the mountains which had sometimes been caused by movements in the air from a human voice.' Three years on, an incautious remark from Chamberlain lent fatal weight to his earlier metaphor.

On the same day that Maisky made this entry in his journal, Chamberlain climbed on stage at Westminster Hall to deliver a lunchtime speech to the National Union of the Conservative Party. Halifax wrote in his diary: 'This I heard later he did very successfully, assuring them that, by having allowed nothing to happen for the last six months Hitler had missed the bus.' Chamberlain, too, thought his speech was 'very warmly received, and the informality and "jauntiness" of "Hitler missed the bus" seems to have given peculiar satisfaction.' Churchill would take issue with Chamberlain's phrase in *The Gathering Storm*, and no doubt was reacting to it the following day when he said to Louis Spears in Paris that 'we showed a lamentable tendency to miss the bus (Nous allons perdre l'omnibus)', though as Lord Normanbrook later pointed out: 'I doubt if he had ever travelled on a bus.' The phrase was used a third time – by General Ironside, in an interview given to the *Daily Express* in which he downplayed the Nazi threat. 'We are ready for anything they may start, as a matter of fact we would welcome a go at them . . . I think it is right to say that the British Army is the finest equipped army in the world . . . Thank goodness Hitler missed the bus.'

Chamberlain's speech was well received and widely reported. The change in the French Cabinet had inspired him 'to speak more like Winston', observed Lord Salisbury. Especially uplifting were Chamberlain's remarks to the Free Church Council on 6 April that he was now ten times more confident of victory than at the beginning of the war, despite the unnatural calm of the last few weeks. On the same day, he wrote to his sister Hilda: 'There is a curious and some would say ominous lull in war activities . . . one wonders what the Boche is up to . . . we are getting the usual information from "reliable sources" that something prodigious is imminent, but I remain sceptical . . . But by the time you get this we should have accomplished a little surprise of our own.'

After the cancellation of 'Avonmouth', Churchill had written to France's sixty-eight-year-old Commander-in-Chief, General Gamelin. 'When an operation set for a particular day is postponed, the risks of leakage are, as you know so well, augmented.'

In contrast to the total secrecy demanded and achieved by Hitler, Allied security was, in David Dilks's phrase, 'deplorably insecure'. The trouble with the French, Chamberlain joked, was they could not keep a government for six months or a secret for half an hour. In Paris on 27 March, John Colville was shown 'an alarming communiqué to the effect that the French had "leaked" about the project of laying a minefield in Norwegian waters and stopping the iron ore trade'. Next day, as Chamberlain was leaving No. 10 for the Supreme War Council meeting at the French Embassy, his attention was drawn to an article in *Le Temps* which 'indicated a decision not to respect neutral territorial waters in view of their violation by Germany.' Chamberlain pointed the passage out to Premier Reynaud, who professed dismay. A denial was issued. But as the Swedish military attaché in London told General Ironside, after revealing that he too had heard that an Allied Force intended to land at Narvik: 'You cannot keep anything secret with so many people with a finger in the pie.'

Gamelin on his visit to London that Thursday would accidentally leave behind Supreme War Council secrets in the foyer of a hotel owned by Italians. Yet British commanders were just as porous. A paragraph deleted from the final draft of *The Gathering Storm* describes the alleged state in which Major General Mackesy left for Narvik. The young female driver who conveyed Mackesy to his port of embarkation came immediately afterwards to the War Office 'and stated it her duty to say that the General with 3 other officers on his staff had been heavily under the influence of liquor and she had heard their whole plan talked out as they went down in the car'. This was on 12 April, but the American General Raymond E. Lee, in Britain at the time, recorded that the Norway operations 'were talked about so much that everyone in London had heard of them and the Germans knew all about them a considerable time before they started'.

Churchill had warned Geoffrey Shakespeare against discussing confidential information outside the Admiralty. 'If anyone starts asking questions, change the subject and talk about the breeding of pigs.' Yet Churchill was not always obedient to his own instructions. On 2 February, he had dropped hints of British intentions at a secret conference with neutral press attachés. These remarks were noted in Germany. As was the row of Green Line buses waiting outside the Chelsea barracks of 1st Battalion Scots Guards. Written for anyone to read in large chalked letters on the side of the coaches: 'See the midnight sun', 'North Pole Express', 'To Norway'.

A French spanner in the works delayed 'Wilfred' by a further three days. Out of the blue, Daladier, who remained in charge of France's defence, announced his concern about reprisals for the Rhine operation, 'Royal Marine'. This was to have been conducted simultaneously to 'Wilfred', sending floating mines down the river. With set jaw, Daladier insisted that 'Royal Marine' be postponed by three months. The French War Committee agreed. Churchill flew over to Paris to break this 'tragic impasse', and to impress on both Reynaud and the divisive Daladier the folly of further delay.

On 5 April, after seven months of prevaricating, 'Wilfred' was given the green light to proceed by itself, on 8 April. But the consequences of the three lost days would be incalculable, as Hitler later acknowledged. 'Thanks to our gaining a few hours' advantage over the enemy, Britain's most dangerous attempt failed; the attempt to strike us to the very heart in the North.'

The last-minute hiccup had coincided with Churchill's promotion in a Cabinet reshuffle on 2 April,* putting him in charge of the Military Coordination Committee (MCC). The coordination of the fighting services had long been Churchill's dream – 'Winston has hankered after this all his life,' Leo Amery had told Chamberlain eleven years earlier. In the calculation of the Lord Chancellor, Thomas Inskip, '1st L now becomes almost equal in power to the P.M. In fact, he is Lord Haldane's Minister of Defence.' This was how Maisky interpreted the news – as did General von Falkenhorst, after hearing of Churchill's boast that every German ship using the Skagerrak and Kattegat straits would now be sunk. It was, wrote Maisky, nothing less than 'putting Churchill in charge of the armed forces of Great Britain', which may have been how Churchill also perceived his promotion.

As it was, Chamberlain could report to his sister, 'Winston is in seventh heaven . . . there is no misunderstanding between us. He has told me that he deeply appreciates the confidence I have given him and that he will endeavour to respond to it, and I know from various colleagues and others that he invariably speaks of me in the warmest & most loyal terms.'

On the eve of Operation 'Wilfred', Churchill still failed to envisage the German response. At the War Cabinet on 3 April, confirmed in his new position, he 'personally doubted whether the Germans would land a force in Scandinavia'. Lord Chatfield, whom Churchill had replaced as chair of the MCC, remarked that Churchill 'always rather pooh-poohed the idea that Germany could do anything in Norway'.

At the same time, Churchill rather hoped that Germany *would* react to his innocent, rabbit-eared bait, and 'commit some overt act upon the soil of

---

* Eden wrote in his diary that it was less a reshuffle than 'a game of musical chairs'. Wood and Hoare swapped Ministries, prompting Peter Fleming to ask: 'Why take the trouble to change places when it would have been simpler just to change names?'

Norway'. In the event of German counter-measures to 'Wilfred', Ironside and Gamelin had agreed to send British and French forces to occupy Narvik, Stavanger, Bergen and Trondheim. Troops hastily reassembled from the aborted 'Avonmouth' expedition to Finland were to make up the force, now renamed 'R.4'. They would sail in three convoys from Rosyth 'the moment the Germans set foot on Norwegian soil or there was clear evidence they intend to do so'.

Why Churchill failed to act on the mass of evidence that was brought to his attention remains unclear. He may have believed that the inferior Kriegsmarine would never risk a confrontation with the Royal Navy. Or he may have wished to minimise to the War Cabinet any cause for concern that, once raised, might again have postponed 'Wilfred'. But the signs were there, and flashing, as Leo Amery told the House of Commons on 7 May. 'It was known everywhere that Hitler had designs on Scandinavia.'

In early April, there were reports of ships loaded with troops leaving Stettin; of bars and restaurants crowded with 'new officers of all kinds'. Amery heard that RAF planes returning from leaflet drops on 6 April had flown over the Baltic ports 'and found forts, docks, everywhere, brilliantly illuminated in order to enable the work of embarkation to proceed at full speed. What an opportunity for damaging the German expedition at the outset!' But the accuracy of the intelligence was matched only by the Admiralty's failure to interpret it correctly.

The first signs of any movement reached the Admiralty at 6.37 a.m. on Sunday 7 April. A large unidentified German ship had been spotted the night before steaming north of Heligoland. Admiral Pound was salmonfishing at Broadlands, and it was not thought necessary to disturb him. Then at 2.35 p.m., the Admiralty received a message from the British naval attaché in Denmark who that morning had driven south of Copenhagen to investigate rumours of German minesweepers. He observed 'German warships *Gneisenau* or *Blücher* with two cruisers and three destroyers', and remarked on 'their probable Norwegian destination'. Ralph Edwards, duty captain at the Admiralty that evening, took this message straight to a 'well dined' Churchill who looked at it and said: 'I don't think so.'

Nor had Churchill been perturbed earlier in the day by news that a German force of '100 Ships' was reported passing through the Great Belt at

2 a.m. and that RAF Hudsons had sighted 'one cruiser and six destroyers escorted by aircraft' steering west of Horns Reef at 8.48 a.m. The suggestion that this unusual movement of enemy ships 100 miles from the German coast might signal a break-out from the Royal Navy's blockade of German ports, and even form 'some operation against southern Scandinavia', as Vice Admiral Tom Phillips, Deputy Chief of the Naval Staff, had advised Churchill, was dismissed as 'in principle fantastic'. At that moment, it remained inconceivable that Germany would try to invade Western Norway, let alone Narvik, across 1,300 inhospitable miles of the North Sea. These ships were 'evidently doing [an] exercise'.

At 2 p.m. in Scapa, Admiral Sir Charles Forbes, Commander-in-Chief Home Fleet, received a telegram from the Admiralty which bore Churchill's imprint. 'All these reports are of doubtful value and may well be only a further move in the war of nerves.'

On that afternoon of 7 April, Churchill still only had eyes for his imminent operation near Narvik.

In the early hours of Monday 8 April, Captain Bernard Warburton-Lee on HMS *Hardy* escorted four destroyers of 20th Minelaying Flotilla inside Norwegian territorial waters to mine the approaches to the Leads south of Vestfjorden, in a severe violation of Norwegian neutrality. 'The war is going to start quite soon,' he wrote to his wife. 'I am going to start it.'

The Swedish Foreign Secretary was in London that morning. When he learned that the Royal Navy had laid mines off the north Norwegian coast, he told Cadogan that the British had done 'the silliest thing in history'.

The First Lord was elated, though. A combination of his recent new powers to direct the policy of the fighting services, and the opportunity to take charge of his first serious offensive naval action since Gallipoli, made him more cheerful than his colleagues had seen him in months. To General Ironside, 'he was like a boy this morning describing what he had done to meet the Germans'. Churchill had telephoned Halifax at breakfast to tell him that the operation had 'all gone without a hitch'. He was still buoyant when Halifax saw him at Cabinet, and he continued to be in a state of barely suppressed euphoria when he dined that evening with two members of the War Cabinet: Oliver Stanley, Secretary of State for War, and Samuel Hoare, the new Secretary of State for Air. 'Winston very optimistic,' Hoare wrote in his diary. 'Delighted with minelaying, and sure that he had scored off the Germans. He went off completely confident and happy at 10.30.'

Churchill's pleasure was shared by a public famished for signs that the navy was there, and that Herr Hitler had indeed missed the bus. At 5.30 p.m. Pam Ashford, a secretary in Glasgow, was travelling home from work. 'The man who sat next to me on the bus spread his paper out very wide, and said to me, "the battle has begun". He beamed. In all my 22 years in Scotland, never has a stranger spoken to me on a vehicle.'

4
THE FIRST CRUNCH

'Faultless timing,' said Basil cheerfully. 'That's always been Hitler's strong point.'
EVELYN WAUGH, *Put Out More Flags*

The Phoney War ended for General Ismay with a telephone call that woke him from a profound sleep in the early hours of 9 April. 'It was the Duty Officer at the War Cabinet office. I could not make head or tail of what he was saying, in spite of frequent requests for repetition; so suspecting the trouble, I suggested that he should draw the black-out curtains, switch on the lights, find his false teeth and say it all over again. My diagnosis was evidently correct, because after a pause he started speaking again and was perfectly intelligible. His report was brutal in its simplicity. The Germans had seized Copenhagen, Oslo and the main ports of Norway. As I hurried into my clothes, I realised, for the first time in my life, the devastating and demoralising effect of surprise.'

Cadogan was telephoned at the Foreign Office at 8 a.m. 'No news from the Fleet – "wireless silence" – rather ominous. Germans seem to have got in to Narvik! How?!'

Thirty minutes later, General Ironside denied reports that Narvik had been taken. 'Our information was that the Germans were not in occupation there,' he advised the War Cabinet, at which it was agreed that 'R.4', the forces assembled at Rosyth, should depart at once for Narvik, Bergen and Trondheim.

The silence of the Fleet – a standard security measure – gave Colville and the No. 10 staff nothing to go on. 'We listened to the news which was derived almost entirely from German sources: scarcely a word from our own.' Pious statements from Berlin announced that Germany had occupied Denmark and Norway 'to protect their freedom and independence'. At 11 a.m., von Ribbentrop held a press conference. 'The German Government has the proof that French and British General Staff officers were already on Scandinavian soil, preparing the way for an Allied landing.' He boasted that no Englishman or Frenchman would be able to set foot in Norway till the war was over. The government-controlled press was ecstatic – 'One of the most brilliant feats of all time' (*Angriff*); 'Germany saves Scandinavia!' (*Völkischer Beobachter*). Meanwhile, Hitler celebrated with a group of his closest collaborators. 'In the same way as from the year 1866 Bismarck's Reich evolved, the greater Germanic Reich will come into being from to-day.'

The Ambassador in London who represented Nazi Germany's new Soviet ally had had no forewarning. 'What a sharp and unexpected turn of events!' Maisky wrote in his diary. 'Only yesterday the British were planning for a lengthy *Sitz-Krieg*; today, the Germans have made *Blitz-Krieg* the order of the day.'

Louis Spears compared the impact to live shells exploding at a picnic. 'Little girls could not be more taken aback had they found some of their dolls developing genuine whooping cough and going blue in the face.' Incredulity was a common response. Lunching at the Beefsteak, Harold Nicolson was assured by another member that there was 'no chance of Narvik having been occupied'. It was a misreading. This seemed confirmed at 4 p.m. by a hesitant Prime Minister in the Commons. When asked whether German troops were in Narvik, Chamberlain replied that he was 'very doubtful', and that it was 'very possible' they had landed in a port with 'a very similar name' 800 miles to the south, Larvik.*

Equal confusion reigned in Paris, where General Gamelin arrived at the Quai d'Orsay to find Premier Reynaud 'despatches in hand, trying to locate on the map the names which appeared in the telegrams'. Reynaud asked Gamelin what he thought they should do, and said it was a cruel surprise for the Allies to find themselves anticipated in 'an operation we had devised

---

* The War Cabinet did not know much about Norway. On 3 January, Leslie Hore-Belisha had asked 'if Bergen was the capital'. General Ironside still viewed the country through the prism of his memories with the Allied Expedition to Archangel in 1918. He assured Chamberlain's wife that you could hear the Aurora Borealis 'crackling in the forests', and 'you seemed literally to see the flowers growing'. Halifax mistook a railway line for the Norwegian frontier; while Churchill invested the Norwegians with the fierce military characteristics of their Viking forebears, about whom he had recently been writing – 'beyond all challenge the most formidable and daring race in the world'. He was dumbfounded when, in Halifax's words, they 'totally failed to blow up any railway line or obstruct the German advance anywhere'.

for our convenience'. Unmoved, Gamelin answered: 'War consists of the unexpected.'

The confusion in London and Paris was nothing to that felt in Norway, which had battled so hard to remain neutral. When the Norwegian King – shortly to become a symbol of national resistance – was told that Norway was at war with Germany, he badly wanted to know whether 'Norway was against Germany or with her'. At 7.32 p.m., Quisling removed all doubt after he entered the national radio station in Oslo, and created outrage in the general population by giving a five-minute broadcast in which he announced that he was taking over as Prime Minister and Foreign Minister to form a national government, and then read out a list of eight ministers none of whom were known.

The Allied governments knew no more than they were able to sift from Leland Stowe, who told the story of Quisling in a way that made people suspicious thereafter of any Norwegian. The details amazed. Hitler was turning out to be the Bonaparte of a mad wonderland, thought Spears. 'Judging by the way the Germans descended on Norway, it was quite obvious the walrus was right – pigs had wings!' The Chancellor, John Simon, could not disguise his admiration for the Nazis' 'clock-like precision'. It was very clever, he told colleagues, 'and we were ninnies, we were ninnies!'

How the Germans had taken Norway from under the teeth of the British Navy was the mystery. 'The Navy is here!' had been Churchill's war cry. Yet Ambassador Maisky, listening to Chamberlain's statement in Parliament, reported that 'all had one and the same question on their minds: where the devil was our navy? . . . in the corridors of the House, the navy's miraculous disappearance was the only subject of conversation.'

Somewhere out in the North Sea, trying to block exits into the Atlantic, the much superior forces of the Home Fleet continued to scan the blurred horizon, with the penny only now beginning to drop that Norway and not the Atlantic was the enemy's destination, and that the movements reported forty-eight hours earlier formed no part of any nautical exercise. Not since the *Dreadnought* hoax of 1910, when, led by Neville Chamberlain's brother-in-law, a group of fake African princes inspected the fleet and bestowed invented honours, had the Royal Navy provoked such derision. Ironside was scathing. 'We have bungled badly . . . a frightful piece of carelessness on the part of the Navy.' He feared that Hitler's move on Norway was a curtain-raiser for an attack nearer home.

Impatient, Churchill awaited signals from the North Sea, where a violent storm was now raging. He telegraphed Admiral Forbes, the Home Fleet's Commander-in-Chief, asking him to break radio silence. 'It is sometimes difficult to understand what you are doing and why.' The difficulty of communicating in order to mount a counter-attack was exacerbated by a damaged wireless aerial on Vice Admiral William 'Jock' Whitworth's flagship HMS *Renown*, and a failure to supply some destroyers with the correct signalling instructions. In atrocious weather, which prevented their execution and in some instances their reception, orders and counter-orders streamed out from the Admiralty into the fog.

Without news, and prone to mood swings, Churchill vacillated between thinking that the German assault presaged the much anticipated onslaught on the west, and elation that Hitler had overstepped himself like Napoleon when in 1807 the French Emperor invaded Portugal and Spain. Churchill signalled to Admiral Forbes: 'I consider Germans have made strategic error in incurring commitments on Norwegian coast which we can probably wipe out in a short time.'

Churchill was observed in his upbeat mood by Colville. 'The First Lord (who at last sees a chance of action) is jubilant and maintains that our failure to destroy the German fleet up to the present is only due to the bad visibility and very rough water in the North Sea.' According to the military expert Basil Liddell Hart, Churchill was 'even more exultantly confident when news first came', and talked of how it provided an opportunity to attack Germany from air bases in Denmark, 'not then aware that Denmark had been overrun in a few hours'. Others might have been stunned, but Churchill was caught up in the moment's heat, exercising his full capacities, and revelling in it. Infected by his enthusiasm, Lloyd George's Private Secretary, A. J. Sylvester, believed in certain whispers he had heard, 'that something very considerable is happening at sea and that good news is on the way'. Sylvester's private information was that an elaborate trap had been laid for the Germans and they had fallen into it.

In fact, Churchill was depending for his local knowledge on the last report that Giles Romilly had telephoned through to the *Express*. At noon,

Churchill still believed that there might be 'only one enemy ship' in Narvik: the German transport *Jan Wellem*. Then through the fog there started to filter reports which presented 'an entirely different situation'. George VI visited the Admiralty War Room in the afternoon. Churchill was proudly showing the King the position of the fleet off Norway when the 'gloomy news' came in that German forces were in possession not merely of Narvik, and therefore of Giles, but all the main ports. The King later wrote in his diary: 'I have spent a bad day.'

A frantic edge had crept into Churchill's behaviour by the time that he chaired the second Military Coordination Committee meeting at 9.30 p.m. in General Ismay's room in Richmond Terrace. A new report that Narvik was in fact held by six German destroyers and one submarine had been received by the First Lord, Ironside grumbled, 'with monkeyish humour'. At the same time, Churchill annoyed the Air Minister Samuel Hoare by 'nagging at everybody'. Churchill offloaded his frustration on Admiral Forbes who, from his position further south, had proposed for parts of the Home Fleet to attack Bergen and Trondheim with dispositions that Forbes insisted were 'excellent'. Churchill had been all in favour of this plan a little earlier. He now flatly rejected it, and argued instead for the 'paramount necessity' to capture Narvik 'with the utmost expedition'. He refused to wait just a few more hours for reinforcements to come up, and announced that he intended to rush in a destroyer flotilla the following dawn. Despite the 'lack of information', he assured Halifax that German forces at Narvik stood to be mowed down 'like cut flowers'.

Narvik was situated in a 'very large, wild, mountainous country', Churchill told the House of Commons two days later – and 'freedom, it is said, dwells in the mountains'. All of a sudden, a small town in Norway had come to represent that freedom. In the days ahead, Narvik continued to hold a unique place in Churchill's duel against Hitler. When the editor of the *Manchester Guardian* visited the Admiralty on 1 May, Churchill drew him to his desk 'and said "Look at it! It's quite clear, isn't it – except for this document." There was one lying on the top of the top drawer and he picked it up and said "Narvik!"'

From 9 April, Churchill bent his energies to seizing this snowbound peninsula, where his nephew was held captive. For everyone else, Narvik was little more than 'a sideshow in the Arctic', in Peter Fleming's phrase. But for Churchill it remained his 'first love', his 'pet', 'the trophy at which all Europe is looking' – in which Norway would play a liberating role, freeing Europe from Hitler as the Iberian Peninsula had brought down Napoleon.

At 7.04 p.m. on 10 April, the Admiralty sent another message to Forbes, summoning him north. 'As enemy is now established at Narvik recapture of that place takes priority over operations against Bergen and Trondheim.'

The bombardment that Giles Romilly heard in Narvik early on 10 April was the first of the Royal Navy's two counter-attacks.

The assault was led by Captain Warburton-Lee on HMS *Hardy* who had commanded the escort force of five destroyers for the minelayers in Operation 'Wilfred'. At noon on 9 April, when there was still believed to be a single German ship in Narvik, Warburton-Lee had received an encouraging signal from the Admiralty. 'It is at your discretion to land forces if you think you can recapture Narvik from number of enemy present.' The signal was relayed to Warburton-Lee's superiors, Admiral Forbes and Vice Admiral Whitworth, and had the effect of disempowering each of them and of isolating Warburton-Lee, a reserved, thoughtful Welshman known as 'Wash', who took himself off for half an hour to brood on the implications. Confused by the signal, Forbes was reluctant to break radio silence to seek clarification. An infuriated Whitworth later regretted 'that I did not intervene and order Warburton-Lee to postpone his attack' – an attack, Whitworth went on, which had resulted from 'the Admiralty's intolerable action in communicating direct to ships under my command and entirely ignoring my presence'. Had Whitworth discussed the situation with Churchill, says Geirr Haarr, he would most likely have advised for Warburton-Lee to wait a few hours until his back-up arrived, and meanwhile plug the entrance to the fjord. 'There was no reason to go into Narvik, since whatever was in there had to come out.'

Without anyone to turn to, Warburton-Lee had to decide on his own. At 4.20 a.m. the next day he led his destroyers through a snowstorm into Narvik harbour, where he found not one enemy transport ship but ten German destroyers. At the cost of his life and his ship, he engaged them.

On 10 April, Frances Partridge wrote in her diary: '8 a.m. news. In a battle off Narvik described as "wholly successful" we lost two destroyers and a third damaged.' First reports suggested a trouncing victory for the Allies, with the Norwegian government announcing the recapture of Narvik. The *Daily Express* trumpeted: 'It ranks with Cadiz where we singed the King of Spain's beard.' The *New Statesman* was ululatory. 'A miraculous change took place as news began to filter through of the greatest naval action of the century.' In the Essex village of Tolleshunt D'Arcy, the novelist Margery Allingham had interpreted the uncanny inactivity of the Phoney War to mean that 'something considerable was being done very quietly indeed'. Now, after months of preparation, Britain had gone into battle and won a great victory, apparently.

In his statement to the Commons on 10 April, Chamberlain said that he could not tell the House about ongoing operations, but he confirmed that five British destroyers had steamed up the fjord and engaged six German destroyers, sinking one and heavily hitting three others, plus sinking 'six merchant ships'. This much at least was accurate, and the information was joyfully received by the old lady who served tea in the Lobby bar. 'There's something about a naval action that stirs the blood as nothing can do on land or in the air.' But the day brought more uplifting news, concerning all of Norway. At 9.30 p.m., the not always easy Canadian Prime Minister, William Mackenzie King, received word that 'the British had effected the landing of troops at Bergen and Trondheim and had captured both places. Also that British troops had landed at Oslo and were fighting the Germans there ... If this is true it will have a considerable effect on the whole war.'

With reports that the Fleet was involved there was a palpable stiffening of morale, noted the editor of the *Sunday Despatch*, Collin Brooks. 'Everywhere, in the streets and in office lifts, there was a new satisfaction in this strange war.' One London charlady was overheard telling another London charlady: 'You can take it from me, while one bloody brick stands on another old Churchill will never let us give in.' In Glasgow, a man on Pam Ashford's tram home kept exclaiming: '"We have the Germans bottled up, bottled up!!!" ... For myself, the strongest feelings are pride in the Navy and satisfaction that we have emerged from that detestable calm we called the War of Nerves.' Hitler's defeat seemed imminent. A soldier on the Clyde about to embark for Narvik had heard that 'the shores of Norway are clogged with drowned Germans'.

Studying the headlines on 11 April, the Transport Minister Euan Wallace found himself questioning the optimistic exaggeration behind the claims. 'The papers were full of the most glowing accounts of British naval victories up and down the coast of Norway, but, reading them through carefully, they were qualified by reference to reports received from outside sources; and before I went to the War Cabinet at 12.30 we had already learned that the situation was not as depicted in the Press.'

After lunching with the travel writer Peter Fleming, who was now working as an Intelligence officer, Geoffrey Dawson, editor of *The Times*, hurried to the Commons to hear Churchill's statement. 'The world was all agog for news from the North Sea . . . everything was saved up for Winston's speech at 3.45.'

Churchill's much anticipated first statement to Parliament about the news from Norway was broadcast around the world, and later cited by Labour's deputy leader Arthur Greenwood as evidence that the First Lord had raised expectations that were not only false but downright dangerous. 'In that speech he led this House, the country and the neutrals to believe that victory, swift, certain, was bound to come.' The left-wing MP Stafford Cripps was even more critical, telling the Commons during the Norway

Debate that it was largely Churchill's speech on 11 April that had had 'such a damaging effect on our prestige'.

Even so, Churchill's bombastic message was in strange contrast to his collapsed appearance and tired delivery which startled everyone who witnessed it.

Churchill's deplorable performance in the Chamber must be seen in the context of this private admission to Admiral Pound the previous day: 'We have been completely outwitted.' However combative his public image, behind the scenes he was wobbling. Reports that the Germans had got to Narvik had made everyone at the Admiralty 'terribly despondent', according to Eric Seal, his personal Private Secretary. Seal was with Churchill when the news of the invasion arrived, and he confided to his wife: 'I was very worried . . . about Winston, who was knocked right out.' On top of that, there was the blow of Giles Romilly's inevitable capture.

Churchill's closest political confidant, his Parliamentary Private Secretary Brendan Bracken, was a sponge for his master's moods, and it is possible that Bracken was fantasising about Giles's fate at the hands of the Nazis when he movingly reduced Ronald Tree's son, on leave from the army, to tears, by describing in great detail the 'entirely fictitious' death of Bracken's allegedly combatant brother in Narvik.

In the dearth of news, it was natural for Churchill to imagine that something terrible had happened to his nephew. Seal went on: 'I had to manoeuvre him to bed.'

When Anthony Eden called in at the Admiralty War Room after dinner on 10 April, he was surprised to find Churchill in so vulnerable a state. Churchill had bitter things to say about the ambitious Air Minister, Samuel Hoare, of whom one source in Parliament wrote in his diary: 'It is said of Sam Hoare that he is so slippery and so INTENT that he would do anything and anybody – to be made Prime Minister.' Eden also disliked Hoare, nicknaming him 'Aunt Tabitha', and he registered Churchill's alarm that Hoare was taking advantage of the evident turmoil within the Admiralty to promote himself: 'He is indignant with Sam whom he suspects of being eager to score off him . . . "A snake" and some stronger epithets.'

Uncharacteristically late for Cabinet on the morning of his speech,

Churchill wrote an abject note to Chamberlain. 'I must apologise for not having sufficiently gripped this issue in my mind this morning, but I only came in after the discussion had begun.'

A few hours later, at 3.48 p.m., showing 'obvious signs of strain' according to the Independent Liberal MP Clement Davies, Churchill stood up to give the House the 'fullest possible information' about the situation in Norway.

Churchill's shambolic and lacklustre appearance is not the Churchill who has been handed down to us. Halifax wrote in his diary: 'His speech in the House does not seem to have gone too well.' Harold Nicolson was appalled. 'He hesitates, gets his notes in the wrong order, puts on the wrong pair of spectacles, fumbles for the right pair, keeps on saying "Sweden" when he means "Denmark", and one way and another makes a lamentable performance.'

Another disconcerted diarist was the Soviet Ambassador. 'I had never seen him in such a state. He clearly hadn't slept for several nights. He was pale, couldn't find the right words, stumbled and kept getting mixed up. There was not a trace of his usual parliamentary brilliance.'

Churchill produced lame arguments to explain the German break-through: bad weather, the vastness of the sea, the impossibility of controlling it all, and so on. For Dawson, it was a dreadful anti-climax. 'As I listened to his long and rather laboured narrative, I kept hoping for some dramatic revelation. But there was none.'

The First Lord admitted that British forces were yet to take Narvik or Trondheim, contrary to what Members might have heard. He claimed not to be dismayed, though. 'I must declare to the House that I feel greatly advantaged by what has occurred.' He concluded: 'We have probably arrived now at the first main crunch of the war,' and he called on the need for 'unceasing and increasing vigour to turn to the utmost profit the strategic blunder into which our mortal enemy has been provoked'.

His message was unconvincing. Maisky noted that the audience was visibly disappointed. 'The prevailing mood was one of growing irritation and concern for the future. But Chamberlain, sitting on the front bench next to Churchill, was clearly pleased. No wonder: Churchill's failure is Chamberlain's success.'

After his speech, Churchill stood by the outer doors to the Chamber talking to Admiral Keyes, while he took snuff from the Doorkeeper. A reporter watched him move in slow steps across the Lobby, 'looking bent and tired, and like a man who was getting no sleep – but smiling . . .' General Ironside who had seen more of Churchill than most in the past few days remarked that 'his physique must be marvellous but I cannot think he would make a good Prime Minister. He has not got the necessary stability for guiding the others.'

5
IN GREAT STRENGTH

'Everyone said "Lyne made nonsense of the embarkation."'
EVELYN WAUGH, *Put Out More Flags*

'Norway was a disaster from beginning to end.'
ROBERT BLAKE

If Operation 'Weserübung' was perceived as a masterpiece of tactical improvisation, then the opposite was true of the British response, in which Churchill played a controlling part. Admiral Keyes, an old friend from the Gallipoli Campaign, put to Churchill five days later what he saw as the essence of the problem. 'You provoked action by declaring you would break the Narvik iron ore trade and were not ready for every conceivable counter stroke (however unlikely) which the enemy might make . . .'

Lack of preparation was one thing, but other difficulties sprang from the impossibility of stopping Churchill 'running riot', as one anonymous senior officer complained in a letter to Admiral Godfrey. Now that battle was joined, the First Lord's 'zest for taking charge' became a source of muddle and chaos. The widespread public assumption that Churchill was an effective war leader was not shared by those who served under Churchill at the Admiralty between September and May, or sat with him in the War Cabinet and on the Military Coordination Committee. A 'stimulating martyrdom' was how General Alan Brooke later described the experience of working with a chief who was 'constitutionally incapable of not interfering with his entire heart, soul and mind in any operation, great or small, of which he had cognizance, whether strategical, tactical or technical'. Admiral Godfrey was especially damning about the efficacy of Churchill's interferences in the Norway Campaign. 'The tragedy of Churchill was that the thing he loved most he did least well, i.e. strategy. Early on in the war his decisions were invariably wrong and caused us to lose ships, men etc. unnecessarily and to have the stuff at the wrong place. If you didn't agree with him you were axed . . .' As for what Admiral Cunningham called the First Lord's 'tormenting telegraphic prods', Godfrey went on: 'Mr Churchill would resort to any subterfuge to get his way, and not the least tantalising procedure was his trick of drafting telegrams as if they originated in the Admiralty.' General Sir John Dill, who succeeded Ironside as CIGS, found Churchill's work methods worryingly reminiscent of an earlier campaign. 'All the careful teachings of the Staff College were ignored, the chain of command disrupted and . . . every military sin perpetrated at the Dardanelles repeated on a more extended scale.'

Churchill viewed his position differently. He blamed the failures in Norway on the impediments thrown up by official machinery, and afterwards claimed that he had had 'an exceptional measure of responsibility but no power of effective direction'. His Private Secretary defended him, saying that it was 'almost malicious' to infer that Churchill had ever assumed control: he sat at a table where everyone had a voice, and if anything it was Chamberlain's dominating influence which was the key to understanding the whole campaign. But seated at the same table had been Geoffrey Shakespeare – who observed 'how firmly Churchill has his finger on the Admiralty's pulse' – and Captain Ralph Edwards, whose frustrations on 29 April boiled over into his diary. 'Winston entered the fray and decided against the recommendation of the Naval staff. This interference is appalling and we don't appear strong enough to stand up to it.' Even an ardent supporter like Bob Boothby dismissed as absurd the notion that Churchill never interfered in Admiralty decisions. 'The exact opposite is true. He never stopped.'

Churchill tends to be an obvious scapegoat for his rivals and for those who did not like him, so that when his colleagues wrote their memoirs they clung to his faults. A recent study of his stewardship of the military expedition to Norway has pointed out that virtually 'every misstep and miscalculation during this campaign has been attributed directly to Churchill at one time or another'.

Even now, it is not possible to explain how much of the defeat of the Allied counter-attack against the German invasion can be laid at

Churchill's door. For one thing, a lot of material is missing. When Stephen Roskill went to work in the Cabinet Office's History Section in 1949, he discovered that the Admiralty's War Diary had been destroyed, plus 'all the daily signals'.

From the picture that can be obtained from surviving records, it is unfair to blame Churchill for all that went wrong, as it is disingenuous to maintain, as Churchill did, that he had 'no power to take and enforce decisions', being merely one voice in a War Cabinet of nine. The truth is not found in the middle, but rather in a zigzag between impetuous decisions based on sudden intuitions which Churchill forced through, and then, when things did not go according to his plan, his willingness to retreat behind the shelter of collective responsibility. As far as Chamberlain was concerned, up until 27 April when the order was given to evacuate all Allied troops from Namsos and Åndalsnes, 'no decision over Norway has been taken against his advice'. On the other hand, vital decisions were made by Churchill without the knowledge or agreement of the War Cabinet, starting on 8 April, the day of Operation 'Wilfred'.

At the 11.30 a.m. War Cabinet on Monday 8 April, Churchill had given details of the minefield that had been laid six hours earlier in Vestfjorden.

Next, Churchill responded to the proliferation of Intelligence reports which indicated that a considerable force of heavy German ships had entered the North Sea, sailing northwards. He revealed that Admiral Forbes had left Scapa the previous evening at 8.30 with three battleships, two cruisers and ten destroyers to intercept them. Churchill admitted to Ministers that he had initially found it 'hard to believe' that Narvik 'could possibly be' the target for this sudden activity. The obvious presumption, based on a reading of Wegener's book on German strategy, was that the enemy vessels – believed to include two of Germany's biggest battleships – were heading for the North Atlantic to attack British convoys, as they had hoped to do for twenty years. Information received during the last three hours, however, had now convinced Churchill that the German force was 'undoubtedly making towards Narvik', but they would 'no doubt be engaged' by the Royal Navy.

'He sounded optimistic,' Halifax wrote in his diary. 'I hope he is right.'

Obscured from Halifax in the friction of war, and from the habit that Chamberlain shared with Churchill of keeping his Cabinet colleagues in the dark, was that an amphibious operation had become a purely naval one, but without any Minister at the Cabinet table registering the consequences. Bundled up in a list of measures announced by the First Lord was an important decision that the Cabinet had not discussed. Four cruisers of Admiral Cunningham's First Cruiser Squadron at Rosyth, which had been on the point of sailing as part of 'R.4' for the purpose of forestalling the Germans at Stavanger and Bergen, in the event of a German reaction to 'Wilfred', were instead departing imminently to join Forbes and the Home Fleet in the North Sea. General Sir Ian Jacob, Military Assistant Secretary to the War Cabinet, had 'the clearest possible memory' of Chamberlain asking Churchill whether the cruisers had sailed, or could sail, to put troops ashore in Norway, as intended, and Churchill looking 'decidedly sheepish', before replying that the troops had already disembarked in Rosyth so that the cruisers could leave to follow the Fleet. 'The Prime Minister said "Oh," and there was a distinct silence.' Without regard to the broader requirements of Allied aims, and without a word to anyone in the War Cabinet, Churchill had unilaterally cancelled 'R.4', so ensuring that any landing operations could not be carried out in the near future. Nearly every setback experienced thereafter in the Norway Campaign flowed from this decision.

In the North Sea at the time, and maintaining radio silence, Admiral Forbes only later that afternoon and 'much to my surprise' heard about the instructions to disembark, confounding Churchill's claim that 'all these decisive steps were concerted with the Commander-in-Chief'. Nor was Churchill accurate in saying that the troops had already been marched ashore. Admiral Pound telephoned the order to Rosyth at 11.30 a.m., as the War Cabinet prepared to meet. It was confirmed by an Admiralty order at 12.16 p.m., and probably did not reach Admiral Cunningham until 12.30 p.m. at the earliest – that is to say, after the Cabinet was over. Had Chamberlain known the true situation – i.e. that troops were still on board – he might have chosen to countermand Churchill's order.

Was Churchill free to make this decision without expecting Cabinet approval? The question is left unclear by the way that Chamberlain had set up his government. Chamberlain did not want anything in the nature of a small War Cabinet, because he was confident that he could do the job himself. He was a strong Prime Minister who brooked no brother near the throne, and he did not wish to have any Chief of Staff or Minister interfering. What this meant in practice was that there was no regulated system. Churchill was filling power in a vacuum created by the lack of central machinery, which the Admiralty was better equipped to fill than the two other services. Such a situation inevitably led to the Admiralty taking command, and Churchill was not reluctant to accept the implications.

The peremptory unloading of battalions earmarked for western Norway proved to be a tactical error of the first magnitude. There is no argument that the responsibility lay with Churchill, who had been caught with his pants down. In struggling to haul them up, he proceeded to commit blunder after strategic blunder. As the colonel in Evelyn Waugh's novel *Put out More Flags* told Cedric Lyne, the unfortunate officer in charge of embarking his regiment for Norway: 'You seem to have made a pretty good muck-up.'

Churchill's intervention was to have huge repercussions. We can never know what would have happened if the 'R.4' troops had been sent to Bergen, Stavanger and Trondheim on 9 April with adequate naval support, and had Sola airport been recaptured. Norway might well have resisted a British landing. But the war might also have followed a different course. Geirr Haarr has spent seventeen years studying the Norwegian Campaign. 'Though I generally do not like to speculate too much, it would have meant hard fighting and probably more destruction in Norway than what was eventually experienced, but it may also have meant no attack on the Western Front on 10 May.'

Instead, Churchill's order to disembark, made on his own initiative at the outset, laid the unstable foundation for a campaign in which, Harold Macmillan observed, 'everything went wrong from start'.

By chasing a naval victory, the Admiralty lost the initiative. Churchill and Pound had perceived that a naval operation was developing – possibly another battle of Jutland – and made a naval response, freeing up as many ships as they could. A quarter of a century after Jutland, Churchill was still reacting in the old tradition. Entrenched in Admiralty thinking that an unusual movement of heavy German ships meant a break-out into the Atlantic, he had failed to recognise that 'Weserübung' was an operation, according to the War Diary of the German Naval Staff, which 'violated all the rules of naval warfare'.

In the Admiralty Map Room, Churchill had kept his eyes trained north-west on the seas between the Shetlands and Iceland, and south towards the Skagerrak. In spite of ample warnings, he failed to look north-north-east, on which of all places he should have focused: Narvik. As a former First Lord, Leo Amery, told the Commons three weeks later: 'Rarely in history can a feint have been more successful.'

Someone directly touched by Churchill's order was a twenty-one-year-old private in 4th Battalion Lincolnshire Regiment. Today, Tom Fowler is ninety-seven and one of the very last survivors of the Norway Campaign. It was the experience of Territorials like Fowler, raw, half-trained, poorly equipped, hopelessly led, which provided the ammunition for the opposition's assault on the government in the Norway Debate.

Fowler was a milk-delivery boy in Spalding when he was called up. He learned how to use a rifle, and on 8 April, with kitbag packed, got on a train to the Royal Naval dockyard at Rosyth and there, in the morning, boarded the heavy cruiser HMS *Berwick*. In the event of a German counter-measure, the *Berwick* was destined for Bergen. Fowler says: 'We hadn't been on deck more than a few minutes before the captain spoke on the siren: "You have two hours to get off this boat with your kit or I'll dump it overboard." We learned she was going out to meet a German battleship that had just left Denmark.'

At 2.15 p.m. the cruisers departed in a hurry, leaving four battalions on the quay, but with their machine guns, mortars and equipment still on board.

Fowler carried his gear back to Camp 4 near Dunfermline: battledress, respirator, pouch, water bottle, and a 1914 Lee Enfield rifle. Four days later, he boarded a pre-war cruise ship, *Empress of Australia,* and was told to go down to the second deck for his new kit. The issue was the same as for winter in Tientsin, coldest of the army stations. Part of it was left over from the aborted Finnish Campaign: Marks & Spencer overalls for snow warfare, and an old stock of badges from the Non-Intervention Committee, with the NI turned upside down, Amery recalled, 'so that it stands as IN for "International"'. Fowler was given a leather jacket, a pair of heavy boots, eight pairs of socks, three pairs of gloves, and a sleeping bag.

His ship sailed at 10 p.m. on 11 April in a convoy of twenty-five vessels that included four other liners, a battleship, two cruisers and twelve destroyers. For many of these young men it was their first trip at sea. There were high buffeting waves, and kippers for breakfast. Travelling also on the *Empress of Australia* in one of three Territorial Battalions of 146th Infantry Brigade was Frank Lodge, a nineteen-year-old Intelligence private with 4th Battalion King's Own Yorkshire Light Infantry (KOYLI). Lodge wrote in an unpublished memoir: 'I, along with the majority, went to the side of the ship and deposited the fish back to the fish.'

On the *Monarch of Bermuda* was forty-two-year-old Lieutenant Colonel Walter Faulkner of 1st Battalion Irish Guards who would be buried in Narvik. He summoned his officers to the liner's stateroom to reveal to them the orders that he had received in London. They were to land in Narvik, and occupy the peninsula. Maps would be issued. Then, hours later: 'Gentlemen, I have just heard that neither of these is possible. The maps are in another ship and the Germans are in Narvik. H.Q.s are now trying to choose another base.'

Without warning on the evening of 14 April the convoy split in half. The *Empress of Australia* and two other liners dropped behind, veering south. There had been a further change of plan.

Tom Fowler says: 'I didn't know where we were going.'

On 12 April, a pressing message had come from Britain's phlegmatic Minister to Oslo, Sir Cecil Dormer. He had handed the keys of the British Legation to Florence Harriman, and then joined the fugitive Norwegian King and government near the Swedish border. Dormer managed to wire a telegram to the Foreign Office. 'Military assistance at Trondheim is first necessity. Seizure of Narvik of little assistance to Norwegian government.'

Trondheim – the ancient capital, where new kings were blessed – controlled the central and narrowest part of Norway, and was considered by almost every authority except Churchill of greater strategic significance than Narvik, 400 miles north. It possessed a deep harbour with extensive quays, an airfield, and a railway line, and in the view adopted by the War Office it was 'the only base from which effective military action can be undertaken'. A force in occupation of Trondheim would be able to cut off the north of Norway from the south.

Blame has fallen on Churchill for diverting limited military resources away from Narvik before the town was captured. In fact, Halifax was behind the premature move to shoot Trondheim up the strategic scale. Only after the complete failure of the operation would Halifax admit that he had not been competent from a military point of view to judge whether Trondheim should have been the target. 'It really is the devil having to express opinions on what is often such speculative knowledge.'

A rumour leaked out from high in the Foreign Office that Lord Halifax had 'threatened to resign unless Trondheim was attacked' – even if such was not his habit; nor did the nature of his friendly, respectful relations with Chamberlain suggest anything of the kind. Still, it was rare for the Foreign Secretary to adopt a firm position on military matters. When he did so on 12 April, the War Cabinet took note. Halifax had been briefed by his Deputy Under-Secretary, Sir Orme Sargent, who wrote in a memo that 'for all practical purposes, Norway ends at Trondheim' – Narvik, Churchill's baby, was no more important than John o' Groats. Cadogan, too, emphasised that Trondheim was 'the only thing that matters in Scandinavian eyes'.

The situation was fast-moving. The Foreign Office had not known until a few hours earlier who was the head of the Norwegian army, or if it had surrendered. Halifax quickly measured the political implications, and he now insisted that securing Trondheim was 'imperative from the political point of view'. The operation to take Narvik could wait if necessary.

In the grip of his Narvik obsession, Churchill was not in a mood to wait. His recommendation made only the day before, and accepted by the War Cabinet and the Supreme War Council, was that the capture of Narvik might take two weeks, and until then 'no serious operations' could be undertaken against Bergen or Trondheim. Halifax's move threatened to undermine everything that he had been working towards. Churchill

pointed out that an opposed landing in Trondheim would be a very difficult operation, and might 'lead to a bloody repulse'. Preparations for
another attack on Narvik by Admiral Whitworth were well advanced. This
followed Captain Warburton-Lee's action two days earlier, which would
earn him a posthumous VC – the first of the war. On 10 April, Warburton-
Lee, having sunk two and damaged three of the enemy's ten destroyers, was
mortally injured by a shell that exploded in the bridge of the *Hardy* shortly
after he had sent the signal: 'Keep on engaging the enemy'. No one was
more susceptible than Churchill to the orders of a heroic sailor who had
died on a nearby beach, and he wanted to ensure that 'Wash' Lee's last
instruction was obeyed.

Whitworth had sought permission to lead the attack, and Churchill was
apprehensive of any proposal which might 'mar its integrity or delay its
speed'. He promised Halifax: 'Once Narvik is cleared up, and we are established there, very good forces will be available for other enterprises.'

But Churchill was unable to budge the Foreign Secretary, who had the
support of the War Cabinet.

Bowing to the majority, Churchill only with great reluctance accepted
the 'very important political factor'. He revealed that he was already, in fact,
investigating the landing of a small force at Namsos, a timber port a hundred miles north-east of Trondheim. Perhaps Namsos could operate as a
forward base from which British troops might advance on Trondheim once
the operation in Narvik was wound up.

At the 11.30 a.m. War Cabinet next day, Churchill's hopes of keeping
Narvik the priority suffered a further setback when the Prime Minister

sided with Halifax in favour of shifting operations to support the Norwegian army in central Norway. Chamberlain was swayed not only by his Foreign Secretary, but by Admiral Evans who had telegrammed from Stockholm: 'Most urgent that Trondheim be captured forthwith'; and by Prime Minister Reynaud from Paris: 'Trondheim is now the vital point.'

Chamberlain's resolve was further strengthened that afternoon by a series of frantic appeals transmitted to the mountains of Scotland from a portable wireless rigged to a hotel flagstaff near Hamar. These requested 'immediate military and aerial assistance' and culminated in a personal message to the Prime Minister.

The ciphered telegram had been sent by MI6 officer Frank Foley, using an emergency code based on a copy of John Ruskin's *Sesame and Lilies*. It was composed by Major General Otto Ruge, the new Commander-in-Chief of Norway's armed forces, who told Chamberlain that 'we began this war in the belief that the British Government would act at once', and if Ruge did not receive assistance 'today or tomorrow', then the war would end in a few days. In separate messages, Foley added that Ruge was 'a very level-headed man' and that his troops were 'fighting almost with bare fists . . . unless Trondheim is captured at once by a ruthless attack, there will be a first class disaster from which the Allies will find it hard to recover.'

Ruge's appeal reached London at 5 p.m. Chamberlain was still framing his response when a signal arrived from Admiral Whitworth in the Norwegian Sea which determined the course that the Allies would take.

Propped up on pillows at Huntington Park and avid for news of his son, Colonel Romilly was revived to read in the *Hereford Times* how on 13 April Whitworth had sailed up Vestfjorden in the battleship *Warspite* with nine destroyers, and sunk all eight remaining German destroyers which had carried German troops to Narvik.

In the overcrowded Café Iris, Giles Romilly and the other British prisoners ran to the windows and watched ten biplanes swoop overhead – Swordfish from the carrier *Furious*. 'One plane in diffys – disappeared very low over house, pilot waving from cockpit.' There was the muffled throb of faraway guns and the louder thump of bombs in the harbour. Romilly's diary catches the chaos: fires on the quayside; German sailors straggling ashore in clinging soaked uniforms, gold buttons hanging loose; the wounded heaved up into lorries. 'Three black horses careered over the bridge. Red X cars dashed down towards harbour.' One of the makeshift ambulances, with tasselled curtains, was the iron-ore director's car. 'The window panes were misted with our breath.'

Romilly wrote that Whitworth's bombardment had left German forces in Narvik 'without a single ship, almost munitionless and almost foodless, and without communications except by air'. Out in Vestfjorden, Whitworth recognised that if there was a moment to strike then it was now. He signalled to Admiral Forbes at 10.10 p.m. that the German garrison was 'thoroughly frightened' and he recommended that 'the town be occupied without delay'.

The hope which flared for Romilly's parents that Giles would soon be rescued was echoed within the Admiralty by his uncle. What had been considered a major obstacle – 'for which long and severe fighting will be required,' Churchill had warned Pound – was suddenly no more than a mopping-up operation. In the afterglow of Whitworth's victory, Churchill regarded Narvik as taken. Bounding ahead of himself, he saw no reason why the navy might not repeat a similar 'deed of fame' in central Norway to satisfy the ambitions of his Prime Minister and Foreign Secretary. Some of the reinforcements destined for Narvik could without detriment to that operation, now called 'Rupert Force', be sent 400 miles south to Trondheim.

At 2 a.m. Churchill went to see an exhausted and irritable General Ironside in his room at the War Office. It was the second time in two days that Churchill had interrupted Ironside in the early hours. At 1 a.m. on 12 April, he had already floated to Ironside the idea of despatching part of 'Rupert Force' to Namsos with a view to 'staking out a claim' for Trondheim. On that first occasion, Ralph Edwards had judged Churchill to be 'half-cocked as usual'. Edwards reported that the meeting was going well 'when Winston lost his temper and spoiled the whole show'.

Ironside's reaction had been hardly less stable. 'Maddening,' he barked back. He admitted in his diary: 'I am afraid I lost my temper and banged on the table.' He then snapped at Churchill to wait until the troops had taken

Narvik. 'A convoy packed for one place is not suitable for landing at another.'

Yet barely forty-eight hours later, Ironside's concern was rendered trifling to Churchill in the glare of Whitworth's 'brilliant operation'. Brimming with the latest naval action at Narvik, and under renewed pressure from Chamberlain – already the Prime Minister envisaged 'a direct attack with warships up the fjord "a la Narvik"' – Churchill again confronted Ironside. 'Tiny, we are going for the wrong place. We should go for Trondheim.'

Ironside protested 'with some heat' that if part of the force approaching Narvik were detached, it stood to imperil both operations. But flexing his new authority as Chairman of the MCC, which gave him more influence over strategy, Churchill 'on his own', according to Admiral Godfrey, insisted that the rear half of the convoy, carrying the three Territorial Battalions of 146th Infantry Brigade, plus 'the administrative services and much of the supplies for the troops in the front half', should be diverted to Namsos. He tasked Ironside with landing forces further south at Åndalsnes as well. 'This unexpected disruption,' wrote Godfrey, 'surpassed in futility the loading, unloading and reloading of the Dardanelles convoy at Alexandria in 1915.'

By way of illustrating the point that 'bright ideas in the middle of the night are not always very bright in the morning', Churchill once told Major General Kennedy, Chief of Staff of the original operation to capture Narvik, of a dream in which a philosopher saw the secret of the universe revealed. He wrote it down on a piece of paper, and when he woke in the morning found that he had written: 'A strong smell of turpentine pervades the whole.'

Churchill's idea for seizing Trondheim carried the same whiff. 'Left to myself I would have stuck to my first love, Narvik, but serving as I did a loyal chief and friendly Cabinet, I now looked forward to the exciting enterprise to which so many staid and cautious Ministers had given their strong adherence . . .'

The signal from the Admiralty reached the Narvik convoy at 7.28 p.m. on 14 April. Shortly afterwards, the *Empress of Australia* – with Fowler and Lodge on board, who had originally been loaded and prepared for Bergen, then unloaded and reloaded for Narvik – changed course again, this time for Namsos, as part of Churchill's latest plan to take Trondheim. That same evening a message was sent from No. 10 via Wick in Scotland to Major General Ruge in Norway. Chamberlain had used a passage of Ruskin for his cipher. 'WE ARE COMING AS FAST AS POSSIBLE AND IN GREAT STRENGTH'.

6
FLEA AND LOUSE

'We disembarked, our odd little party being the first British
troops to land in Norway.'

MARTIN LINDSAY, 17 May 1940

'No single action of mine had done anybody in Namsos any good.'

PETER FLEMING, 16 May 1970

The War Cabinet's vacillations infuriated France's new Prime Minister Paul Reynaud. 'While the Germans were disembarking a division each week in Norway, we still had not a man there.'

This changed on 14 April when two Intelligence officers, Captain Peter Fleming of the Grenadier Guards and Captain Martin Lindsay of the Royal Scots Fusiliers, landed in a flying boat in Namsenfjorden, 'wounding the still dark surface of the water with that wonderful arrogant swish which a Sunderland makes'.

Fleming, code-named 'Flea', and Lindsay, code-named 'Louse', were the vanguard of a new operation, 'Henry'. Their mission: to prepare the path for Tribal-class destroyers to land the first Allied troops in central Norway. 'A better pair never existed,' said their commanding officer Major General Carton de Wiart, 'my idea of the perfect staff officers, dispensing entirely with paper.' It is no exaggeration to say that the information which 'Flea' and 'Louse' carried in their heads back to London three weeks later altered the course of the Norway Debate, and assisted in Chamberlain's removal from office.

Fleming was the self-deprecating elder brother of the novelist Ian; Lindsay, a fellow travel writer who had crossed Greenland by sledge (twice), and trekked on foot through the Congo. At the time of the German invasion of Norway, Lindsay was the prospective Conservative candidate for the Lincolnshire constituency of Brigg.

Intrinsically modest, Fleming never spoke of his role in the Norwegian Campaign. His biographer Duff Hart-Davis knew him from the age of twelve, and says: 'He was taciturn to a fault, and talked less and less as he got older.' Already well regarded for his books about the Amazon and China, and tipped as a future editor of *The Times,* Fleming had, according to Anthony Powell, 'a preoccupation, almost an obsession, with not appearing to "show off"'. Joan Bright Astley worked in the same office at Military Intelligence Research on the day that Fleming walked out 'imperturbably' for Namsos. 'He was a four-square, basic, solitary sort of person immune to luxury, to heat or to cold, with a brick-like quality which made him the most staunch of friends and a kindness which made him the least vindictive of enemies. He was in a way a famous figure not only because of his early and romantic success as explorer and writer and his marriage to one of our best actresses Celia Johnson, but also because he kept his own brand of personality intact and dignified, dealt with all men as equals and used his pen honestly and well.'

Fleming had lost his father early, and was a friend to men of his father's age, like the editor of *The Times* and the Foreign Secretary. He wrote in his diary on the day of the Russian–Nazi pact in August 1939: 'Should have been shooting grouse with G. Dawson and Halifax, but the crisis is on us and one almost saves a cartridge for the Germans.'

Another of Fleming's father figures was Churchill, who knew Fleming as 'my dear Peter'. Fleming's habit of speaking 'terribly slowly' caused Churchill to complain that he was 'a slow-motion picture'. But Fleming was also a film that spooled Churchill back to the First War, and to his friendship with Peter's father, Major Valentine Fleming, MP for Henley, 'for whom I had a deep affection'. Hart-Davis says: 'Churchill carried over his affection from Valentine to Peter.'

Churchill was in the same regiment as Valentine Fleming, the Oxfordshire Hussars, and had written his obituary in *The Times* after he was killed instantaneously by a shell in France in May 1917. Churchill's eulogy included this moving line: 'As the war lengthens and intensifies and the extending lists appear, it seems as if one watched at night a well-loved city whose lights, which burn so bright, which burn so true, are extinguished in the distance in the darkness one by one.'

Alert, methodical, resolute, Valentine Fleming had died a hero's death in the front line, serving in the first Yeomanry regiment to come under fire. A similar desire to prove himself consumed his eldest son, something noticed by W. H. Auden and Christopher Isherwood, who met Peter Fleming in China. After abandoning their defensive attitude, 'a blend of anti-Etonianism and professional jealousy', Isherwood wrote that 'Auden and I recited passages from an imaginary travel book called *With Fleming to the Front*'.

Fleming's opportunity to emulate his father came at 5 p.m. on 12 April, when he received the order 'to proceed by air to the Namsos area with a small party in order to carry out reconnaissance, and to take any necessary measures to conceal and facilitate the landing of an Allied Expeditionary Force'. He telephoned Martin Lindsay, with whom he had planned a mission to China, recently aborted. 'Come to Norway.' The Director of Military Intelligence, seeing them off three hours later, advised Fleming to keep a diary – 'which I am doing'.

Peter Fleming's team of six was known as 'No. 10 Military Mission'. It comprised Fleming, Lindsay, two signals sergeants – with two Marconi wireless sets 'to communicate with the fleet' – and two Norwegian-speaking officers. On the flight to the Orkneys, Fleming wrote to a friend: 'Nobody, even in the War Office, knows what the job is.'

He discovered this on a morning of squalls and sleet as a Sunderland carried the party to Namsos. During the flight, Fleming received a signal for him to 'ascertain whether the town was held by Norwegians, and – if it was – to land and cover the disembarkation of a naval party that night'. The message ended 'ESSENTIAL OBSERVE SECRECY' – a pious hope,

Fleming remarked, as the four-engined flying boat roared up a fjord and flew for thirteen miles between white jagged cliffs.

'Suddenly, swinging round a bend, we saw Namsos ahead of us.'

The plane circled low over a little wooden town tucked under a rocky outcrop. Peering down through field glasses, Fleming saw smoke rise from one or two chimneys. The only sign of life was a ginger cat picking its way along a street of trampled snow. 'We had no more idea than Mr Neville Chamberlain whether the Germans were in the town or not.'

Gunners at the alert, the plane touched down near the small village of Bangsund on the other side of the fjord at 3.30 p.m.

An agitated Norwegian rowed out to meet them. No Germans were in the area, he assured Fleming. But the British were fortunate: this was the first afternoon when there had not been a Luftwaffe reconnaissance seaplane flying backwards and forwards overhead – searching the ground, in Evelyn Waugh's image, 'like an old woman after a lost coin'.

Fleming sent one of his Norwegian-speaking officers ashore to ring the police at Namsos to stop outgoing telephone calls and to prevent cars from leaving town. The Sunderland then flew the short distance back to Namsos and taxied up to the wooden quay, evoking from the assembled populace 'a susurrus which we chose to interpret as a cheer'.

Storm Evensen, now ninety-seven, was part of the welcoming crowd. He says: 'I was there when the Sunderland flew in and the English officer came ashore. I couldn't see the pilot or passengers for the mist on the windows.'

Fleming climbed up onto the wharf, followed by his team. Twelve days later, he wrote in a secret report to the War Office: 'It is perhaps of interest to record my belief (which I cannot confirm here) that we were the first British troops to land in Norway.'* In a short speech, he told the crowd that with their assistance they would kill every German in the land, 'and once more there would be peace in Norway.'

The Sunderland flew off at 4.30 p.m., with instructions to send a 'coast clear' message. Fleming made a quick reconnaissance, 'buying up all the white cloth in the town for camouflage, arranging for billets and air raid warnings'. He then persuaded the harbourmaster to produce four Norwegian sailors to help pilot in the destroyers waiting at the mouth of the fjord. The suspicion that Fleming might be a German officer in disguise was resolved that night as the *Mashona*, *Matabele* and *Somali* appeared, and landed 341 marines.

The marines had disembarked when, at 2 a.m., Fleming received a signal that Major General Carton de Wiart was to arrive in a Sunderland at dawn.

With eyepatch and sling, Adrian Carton de Wiart, VC, looked like a pirate. He was one of several First World War heroes whom Churchill revered, as he had Fleming's father, and who were brought back into service for the Norwegian Campaign. Carton de Wiart recalled the circumstances of his appointment. 'In the middle of one night there was a telephone message for me to report to the War Office. It dawned on me the reason might be Norway, especially as I had never been there and knew nothing about it. Norway it was, and I was ordered to go there immediately to take command of the Central Norwegian Expeditionary Force.'

Like Fleming, Carton de Wiart was brave and modest, never mentioning in his autobiography that he had won a VC. Like Fleming, he had lost a

---

* On the mainland. On 9 April at 4 p.m., Lieutenant George Stanning and torpedo officer George Heppel had visited the pilot station at Tranøy to seek information on German forces in Narvik.

parent young. The two men got on from the start. It was the experience of serving under Carton de Wiart in Norway that motivated Fleming to write the General's biography after the war. In notes for this unfinished project, Fleming located the source of Carton de Wiart's bravery and the 'cocoon of self-sufficiency into which he was always ready to retire' in the desertion by and total disappearance of his mother Ernestine immediately after he was born. 'He believed and occasionally confided to intimate friends that she was a Circassian, bought by his father in a Turkish slave-market from at least partly chivalrous motives.'

A tall, wiry man of great physical strength, with abnormally slender wrists and legs, and skin that tanned easily, Carton de Wiart was the model for Evelyn Waugh's Brigadier Ben Ritchie-Hook, who once came back from a raid across no man's land 'with the dripping head of a German sentry in either hand'. He also happened to be, as Fleming wrote in his diary four days after meeting him, 'a damn nice man'.

Born in Brussels, Carton de Wiart was brought up in Cairo and educated at Balliol, from which he ran away under an assumed name to join Paget's Horse to fight the Boers. An 'absolute non-ducker' who held that consequences were meant to be damned and risks to be taken, he lost his left eye in Somalia in a fight against 'the mad Mullah', Haji Mohammed bin Abdullah Hassan. In the Dervish fort at Shimber Berris, Carton de Wiart leapt in, 'swatting the muzzles of the defenders' muskets with the broken shaft of a polo stick', and sustained a glancing blow. 'I've lost my bloody eye!' he complained to his friend Hastings Ismay who found him in a trench near the fort, his face bandaged in a blood-soaked handkerchief.

Carton de Wiart lost his left hand in the second battle of Ypres. A machine-gunner remarked: 'My godfather, he must have had a large spare-parts box.' It did not prevent Carton de Wiart from hurling grenades at the enemy with his remaining hand after tearing out the safety pins with his teeth. He sustained in action 'between 20 and 30 wounds', calculated Fleming, his wounds healing 'in the sort of swift, sure uncomplicated way that is more characteristic of a primitive race'. He refused to wear wound stripes. 'Any damn fool can see that I have been wounded.' Of his injuries, none cut deeper than his mother's desertion. Forty years after she abandoned her son, Ernestine wrote him an affectionate letter upon reading about his exploits.

'She said she was married to a Frenchman in Bordeaux by whom she had several children.' Carton de Wiart sent a courteous reply, but they never met.

Fleming regarded Carton de Wiart as 'a rather cool, sensible, experienced officer who because of these attributes has consistently been called on to handle unusual and generally unorthodox situations'. On paper, he was the ideal commander to sort out the mess in Norway. Yet as Carton de Wiart swiftly found out, the Norway operation was 'a campaign for which the book does not cater'. Six days after Carton de Wiart landed in Namsos, Churchill was forced to admit 'that no operation of this character had ever been carried out in similar circumstances before'. By then Namsos had become, in the words of a Swedish reporter, 'the most thoroughly bombed city in the world', after German planes had reduced the wooden houses to their foundations and added a fresh verb to Churchill's vocabulary: to be 'Namsosed'.

Delayed by a blizzard, Carton de Wiart's flying boat was strafed by a German fighter as it landed at the mouth of Namsenfjorden, wounding his staff officer in the knee – he had to return to England in the same plane. Carton de Wiart wrote: 'We did not seem set for victory from the start.' He refused to get into the Sunderland's wobbly rubber dinghy, and waited until the Me-110 had fired all its ammunition and flown off.

Fleming went out to meet him in a launch. Their first encounter took place on board HMS *Afridi*, commanded by Captain Vian who had seized the *Altmark*. Fleming gave Carton de Wiart the local information he had collected 'which would be of assistance to the forces going ashore'. But Carton de Wiart had counted sixty bombs aimed at the destroyer HMS *Somali*, which was acting as his communications link to London, and his solitary ferocious eye saw what was needed. He sent a signal to the War Office registering 'the difficulties presented by the enemy air activity whereas we have no planes at all'. Vian identified in a sentence the outstanding characteristic of the Norway Campaign: 'The cards were held by the aircraft.' Everyone in the War Office had banked on open skies in Norway, but in the steep narrow fjords it was hard to spot the enemy planes. They came over the mountains without warning.

Slow and vulnerable to air attack, the *Empress of Australia* and the *Chobry* were approaching the coast after separating from the Narvik convoy the night before; each carried up to 1,700 men. Carton de Wiart ordered both liners to remain out at sea until dark. In the early hours of 16 April, they anchored off Lillesjona, 100 miles north of Namsos.

Black against the snow, six German planes appeared in the afternoon while Fowler, Lodge and their equipment were being transferred onto faster destroyers. The howling of the bombs falling and the deafening explosions as they hit the water tested the nerves of the young Territorials of 146th Infantry Brigade. The curving white streaks were from Heinkel exhaust pipes, but Fowler and Lodge were soon exposed to the menace of Stuka dive-bombers. Fleming remembered how 'a special attachment caused them, as they lunged almost vertically downwards, to emit a shrill deafening scream, and this, superimposed on the roar of their engines and the rattle of their guns, heightened the demoralising effect of their attacks'.

Their approach screened by rock walls, the Heinkels flew over repeatedly, their bombs narrowly missing the *Empress of Australia*. Frank Lodge had a clear memory of 'naval lads tossing coins and betting which side of the ship the next bomb would fall!' Tom Fowler marvels that none of the bombs struck home. 'Our skipper guided the ship between them. Then two small naval boats tied up on each side, and we unloaded all our kit.'

Ladders and chutes were propped up, the soldiers scrambled down, but many personal belongings and equipment fell into the fjord, later to be recovered by the Germans. Lodge wrote: 'The names on the equipment, one of which was mine, were read out on German radio as being lost at sea.'

With the Territorials safely reboarded onto the faster ships, the destroyers left at full speed for Namsos, 'in a flurry of frothing stern wash, curving bow waves and the tall thudding splashes of bomb burst'. In a freezing blizzard and four feet of snow, the greater part of two battalions were landed that night, taking advantage of the four hours of darkness. At midnight, Carton de Wiart sent a message to the War Office: 'Have brought 1000 men to Namsos today . . . Enemy aircaft still bombing at leisure.' The crackle on Fleming's wireless transmitter was 'not dissimilar', thought Lindsay, to the noise of 'our rear gunner firing'.

On 18 April, Fleming watched the remainder of 146th Infantry Brigade disembark from the *Chobry*, 'cumbered with enormous fur coats but short of transport and totally devoid of any supporting arms'. Anxious to get away before the quick dawn came, the *Chobry* sailed off with 130 tons of vital equipment, adding to the 170 tons of supplies and ammunition still on board the *Empress of Australia*.

When Fowler and Lodge stepped ashore at Namsos, they found none of the normal apparatus of a base, merely Fleming and Lindsay, who swept the trampled snow on the jetty and directed the troops to grab their equipment and hide everything. It was up to 'Flea' and 'Louse', with such volunteer help as they could scrounge, to restore the status quo – 'to put the gangways and the coils of rope and all the other stage-properties back where they had been the day before, so that the Luftwaffe's first, early-morning emissary would take back to Trondheim the same mise-en-scène that his cameras had recorded yesterday'.

German reconnaissance planes flew over three times a day. On 19 April, Fleming interrogated a pilot who had made a forced landing and been taken prisoner: he revealed that right up to noon on 18 April 'German Intelligence did <u>not</u> know that a British force had landed at Namsos'.

For five nights, Fleming and Lindsay won their game of hide-and-seek, but on the evening of 19 April, the first French soldiers came ashore. The Chasseurs Alpins were regarded romantically by Churchill as 'probably the best troops in the world'. Watching them disembark in their broad flopping berets, Fleming had doubts. 'Chattering, overloaded, making noise for its own sake, they might have been Chinese.' Storm Evensen recalls that 'everything the French couldn't carry, they left on the docks.' More provocative than the tall stacks of stores piled high on the wharf, the Chasseurs Alpins did not bother to keep undercover during the day, and they would ignore Carton de Wiart's instructions not to fire on enemy planes.

The Major General landed ashore in a whaler that night. He had recruited Fleming to act as his Staff Officer. Fleming wrote in his diary: 'Took Carton de W back to our pleasant billet.'

The wooden house that Fleming had secured as Carton de Wiart's HQ still stands on the top of a steep grass bank below the Klompen rock face, overlooking the town. It is one of the few buildings in Namsos to have survived the Luftwaffe's blanket bombing. Their 'elfin-like' cook was Fanny Fahsing, a pregnant twenty-six-year-old who had au-paired for a couple in Wimbledon, and spoke English. Her daughter describes the night that

Fanny met Carton de Wiart. 'She thought it was a ghost because he came into the hallway in a white nightshirt and a black eyepatch and one arm and wearing a nightcap. "Oh my God!" she said. He wanted water for his bath.'

For the brief span of the Namsos campaign, Fleming served as the General's batman, driver, chief of staff and cook.

Carton de Wiart's written instructions had been issued when 146th Infantry Brigade was at sea, on the way to Narvik as part of 'Rupert Force'. His ever-shifting responsibilities as Allied commander of what was now 'Maurice Force' were shaped to a single purpose: the recapture of Trondheim, 134 miles south. 'My orders were to take Trondheim whenever a naval attack took place.'

The plan for a 'pincer movement' which Churchill had proposed to Ironside had evolved. On 13 April, Churchill sketched out 'a new conception for Operation "Maurice"', landing the troops directly at Trondheim. This plan had since altered again. 'Maurice Force' was to disembark at Namsos and strike southwards down the road to Trondheim. Meanwhile, a second Allied contingent, 'Sickle Force', would push north along the railway from Åndalsnes, at the end of Romsdalsfjord 180 miles south-west of Trondheim.

Subordinated to the main prong, 'Maurice Force' and 'Sickle Force' were to act as diversions – 'to confuse and distract the enemy in order that the blow may be delivered with full surprise and force at the centre'.

Churchill explained this tridentine operation in signals to Admiral Forbes, whom he had earlier ordered north to Narvik. The middle and main thrust – the hammer blow – was to be delivered by Forbes, who would sail south again for a full-scale direct naval assault on Trondheim. Rather along the lines of Churchill's attempt to force the Dardanelles, the battleships of the Home Fleet would attack the coastal batteries. Then cruisers and destroyers with troop transports would advance thirty miles up the Trondheim fjord and cover the landing. This was to take place on 22 or 23 April, and Forbes, who at once expressed objections, saying that he had no high explosive shells for a bombardment, was instructed by Churchill to consider 'this important project further'. The Operation was to be called 'Hammer'.

Carton de Wiart's immediate priority was to find vehicles to carry his troops towards Trondheim. Most civilians in Namsos had taken the precaution of driving their cars out of town. With Fleming, Carton de Wiart called at the home of Storm Evensen, whose father was the local head of General Motors and whose elder brother Birger worked for Shell and had access to petrol supplies. Evensen was present at the meeting during which Birger agreed to chauffeur Carton de Wiart in the family's 1937 dark blue Chevrolet.

The bulk of the remaining vehicles in Namsos were milk-lorries. Evensen's father telephoned the local dairy to make these available. Evensen, aged eighteen, volunteered as a driver. He says: 'I myself ferried British troops to the front line in a 1934 milk-truck.'

German Intelligence had intercepted Carton de Wiart's signals to London. Hitler's suspicion that something was going on was confirmed by a Reuter's report at 10 p.m. on 19 April that British soldiers had landed at Namsos. On the same day, Hitler ordered the Luftwaffe 'to destroy places outside the German-occupied coastal cities occupied by the English, or announced to be occupied, without consideration for the local population'. The fig leaf that Germany was coming to assist the beleaguered Norwegians was about to be blasted off.

At first light on 20 April, a German seaplane flew over. By now, British troops were accustomed to reconnaissance aircraft, giving them nicknames like 'Sammy' and 'George' and 'Faithful Freddie'. The Chasseurs Alpins, instead of hiding, stood up and fired their machine guns.

Later that morning, church bells rang out – a warning that enemy aircraft had been spotted. Storm Evensen was on the quay. He had performed a U-turn, so that the Scottish soldiers he was taking to the front line at Steinkjer could jump straight from the trawler HMS *Rutlandshire* into the back of his milk-lorry. Just then, another reconnaissance plane glided silently past, engines off. Evensen says: 'There was a roaring sound as the engines switched on, and the plane went directly over our heads.' The soldiers scrambled back on board ship and opened fire with a Lewis gun while the *Rutlandshire* prepared to cast off. Evensen was accelerating away when a wave of German bombers flew high overhead.

The police log recorded that the first bomb fell at 10.11 a.m. near the railhead. From then on, bombs fell every one or two minutes, the planes coming in lower and lower after their pilots realised that Namsos was not defended by A.A. guns. It was Hitler's birthday, and there are people still alive in Namsos who will tell you that they read 'AH' written in the sky with smoke trails. As a birthday present to the Führer three years before, allegedly, Goering had bombed Guernica.

Fleming saw the station explode in successive gouts of black, and timber flying through the air. '"Dispersons!" cried the French, and took to the rocks like rabbits, annoying C de W who lounged about in his red hat and refused the disguise of a naval balaclava.' In black eyepatch and empty sleeve, Carton de Wiart lit a cigarette with his only hand. 'Damned Frogs – they're all the same. One bang and they're off.'

Martin Lindsay was breakfasting at the Grand Hotel near the quay. He ran outside, and succeeded in getting clear of the town by stages, but a British naval officer, Captain Blake, who had taken shelter in the cellar was fatally wounded when the hotel received a direct hit. Worried about Lindsay, in a quieter moment Fleming went to the hotel and saw Blake lying under a table, 'almost certainly dead'.

The bombing stopped at 1.08 p.m. and the German planes flew on to Trondheim to refuel. A total of fifty-three He-111 and Ju-88 bombers had set off at 7.30 a.m. from airfields in Denmark. In the afternoon, they attacked the remainder of the town, dropping incendiary bombs and 'making even thinking virtually impossible', according to a journalist. Lindsay reported: 'Huge fires were soon blazing everywhere. In the middle of the fiery furnace one man took shelter in a refrigerator and froze to death.' Another fugitive hid in a waterlogged open grave in the churchyard. 'Most people huddled under trees and rocks just outside the town, crouching under any cover available, holding their breath during the whistle of each falling bomb, and shuddering as it detonated; several grazed their faces trying to get closer into the rocks in their anxiety to avoid that rain of death.'

Evensen's milk-lorry was still packed with guns and ammunition from the *Rutlandshire*. He says: 'I felt I had to move the truck before it blew up.' He drove down Harbour Street past Jakob Agesen's shoe shop, a wooden building that had been blown apart. 'There were piles of white shoe-boxes scattered in the street. I tried to be careful, to drive round the new shoes, then I remembered this was war, so I drove straight through.' Evensen parked the lorry by the hospital, left the key in the ignition and raced home. He was running across the Namsen bridge when a German plane released its bombs into the water. 'The column of water shooting up was like a waterfall upside down.' But the image Evensen recalls most vividly was of zigzagging for his life down an avenue of trees – 'looking for thicker trees to hide behind' – while a Heinkel shot at him. Even Carton de Wiart was prepared to admit that 'it is a most unnerving and unpleasant sensation to be peppered at from a plane bearing straight down on one, and takes a lot of getting used to'.

German planes flew low, machine-gunning people as they ran up the streets or into the woods. Fleming wrote: 'They went for our trawlers in the fjord and eventually sank one (*Rutlandshire*) with more casualties.' Evensen watched the *Rutlandshire* going down – the same ship from which he had picked up the Scottish soldiers – two He-111s circling and shooting, and a huge explosion. He says: 'I saw the bridge thrown up in the air and hitting the water.' Next day, he found parts of the bridge on the beach: the wooden wheel with two spokes, and a triangular piece of metal with a big porthole that he carried home and used for the next forty years as a table.

Led by Carton de Wiart and Fleming in the Evensen family Chevrolet, a line of milk-trucks had set off at 12.30 p.m. for the two-hour drive to Steinkjer. The convoy had left Namsos, according to Fleming, before the Luftwaffe 'blew the town to hell with incendiaries'. He and Carton de Wiart got back around 7 p.m., when Namsos was 'nothing but a loud fire', with the church gutted and the hours on the clock face showing like a skeleton.

At 9.30 p.m. HMS *Nubian* arrived, guided by a red glow in the cold night sky. Commander Ravenhill rounded the last promontory and saw a mass of flames from end to end, 'and the glare on the snows of the surrounding mountains produced an unforgettable spectacle'.

In the early hours of 21 April, Birger Evensen drove Carton de Wiart down to the fjord to board the *Nubian*. He waited while the General sent an urgent signal to the War Office. 'Enemy aircraft have almost completely destroyed Namsos . . . I see little chance of carrying out decisive, or indeed, any operation, unless enemy air activity is considerably restricted.'

7
THE FIRST LAND BATTLE

'People say Churchill is tactless, that his judgement is erratic, that
he flies off at a tangent, that he has a burning desire to trespass
upon the domain of the naval strategist.'
DAVID LINDSAY, diary February 1940

'What we are entitled to ask is a very serious question: By
whom and on whose authority was the indispensable hammer
blow at Trondheim itself countermanded?'
LEO AMERY MP, House of Commons, 7 May 1940

'Wild horses will not drag from me whose hand it was. All I can say
is that it was a dead hand and came from above.'
COMMANDER ROBERT BOWER MP,
House of Commons, 8 May 1940

In the freezing cold and dark, travelling only by night, Privates Tom Fowler and Frank Lodge had pressed on south towards the front line at Steinkjer. It was now that they realised how badly prepared they were. General Ironside had boasted that the occupation force was the finest equipped in the world. Yet their artillery and heavy weapons had been left on board the transport ships, and other essential equipment was still in the holds of HMS *Berwick* and HMS *York*. Fowler slipped and slithered into battle clutching his .303 rifle; Lodge, a revolver and ten rounds of ammunition.

Progress was unwieldy and slow. From Namsos, they had to tramp their way through dense-packed snow without skis, without sledges, without snowshoes, without even the correct maps. Lodge had been given a fifty-year-old map for Bergen hundreds of miles away, 'so I had to go and find out where we were'. One of his officers tore a map off a classroom wall showing the towns that they were supposed to be recapturing. The coordinates proved even harder to establish for French troops coming ashore at Namsos: they were furnished with maps of Berlin.

The Territorials of B Company 4th Lincolnshire Regiment reached Steinkjer on 19 April and billeted for two nights in a school. Fowler says: 'That's where I had a cooked meal.' At 4.05 a.m. on Sunday 21 April, he was woken with news that a lookout had spotted 'a 300-tons' ship in the supposedly frozen narrows leading from Trondheimsfjorden to Steinkjer. At 6.25 a.m., an Intelligence report suggested that up to 400 enemy troops had landed on the ice with motorbikes and were advancing towards Vist four miles from Steinkjer.

Under the command of Captain Reggie Tweed, a Horncastle solicitor, B Company headed to Vist in a convoy of lorries and buses provided by locals. They arrived at 9 a.m., climbed out, and began marching west towards Korsen, but because of an inaccurate map took a wrong turning. Instead of proceeding to Korsen, they walked down a narrow track, five-foot banks of snow on either side, through a wood, towards Krogs Farm. They had travelled two miles when scouts from No. 10 Platoon came under fire. A junior officer yelled out: 'Fix bayonets!' The men rolled into the snow, and waited while Tweed brought Fowler's Platoon up into Krogs. It was here, in a Norwegian farmyard beside a pine wood, that the first land battle in the Second World War took place between British and German troops.

The farmer's daughter who witnessed it still lives at Krogs. Torlaug Werstad points at the red barn across the yard, and she is twelve again, and the telephone is ringing with news that the Germans have landed from a big ship, and all at once incendiary bombs are exploding in the barn where she has locked up her horses and cattle, and through the flames she can hear the animals' cries and tracer bullets from a machine gun concealed in the pine trees, and she watches a British soldier leap down from the barn into the snow and disappear in the smoke.

Tom Fowler was that soldier. He says: 'We were in a farm building full of hay, looking through a crack in the wood. We were supposed to be looking for Germans.' But the enemy was hard to make out against the snow. 'They were white shadows in the distance. They'd got sledges, and machine guns and white coats. We had nothing. Just what we stood in – not even a kitbag. We had left our kitbags behind which lorries were to bring up later.'

The last living member of 'Maurice Force', Fowler sits beside his gas fire in Spalding and hammers it out. 'We had not one aeroplane. We had no ammunition. We had no mortar of any description.' Against the Luftwaffe's incendiaries, four-inch mortars, and the unending barrage of five-inch naval artillery from the German destroyer *Paul Jacobi*, Fowler had his 1914 Lee Enfield rifle and a satchel containing four dozen cartridges.

Incredibly, Fowler's company held Krogs Farm for several hours. From his observation point in the loft, Fowler heard German orders being shouted in the woods. Enemy planes flew constantly overhead. Around 6 p.m., they attacked the farm buildings.

Fowler says: 'Suddenly incendiary bullets were coming through the walls of the barn and setting fire to the straw. Captain Tweed, who had a stutter, ordered us to evacuate. Lance-Corporal Jacklin said: "Fowler, you take my Bren gun, I've got something in me eye." A piece of shrapnel had blinded him. The private beside Jacklin had a bullet in his leg. I took them both down to the steps at the back of the house where the first-aid men were. Then I knocked my way out of the woodwork and dropped the Bren through the hole and jumped out and followed it. I was crawling along the old cart track leading to Vist when a voice from the other side called: "All right, Tommy, keep buggering on." It was my old school pal Tommy Jinks in C Company, telling me to keep going.'

The enemy in the woods were Austrian Alpine troops from 138 Gebirgs-jäger Regiment, well trained, well equipped, fitter, with light field guns, MG-34 machine guns, machine pistols, and trench mortars that they fired from the side of half-track motorcycles. These were veterans from the Polish campaign, and the raw Territorials in their khaki uniforms made easy targets: untrained civilians until very recently – milkmen, wool-millers, solicitors – whose movements stood out against the snow and who lacked the materiel, skill and experience to defend themselves. The American journalist Leland Stowe arrived from Oslo in time to witness their rout. 'Beside those German veterans, these fellows looked like boy scouts.'

Churchill had described his 1898 experience at Omdurman, the last great cavalry charge in history, as a battle where 'ancient and modern confronted one another'. At Krogs Farm, and at Steinkjer, which high-level German bombers razed that afternoon, the situation was reversed. French officers complained about the lack of defensive weapons in the Namsos area, in a conversation that reached Colville in Downing Street. 'The British have planned this campaign on the lines of a punitive expedition against the Zulus, but unhappily we and the British are in the position of the Zulus, armed with bows and arrows against the onslaught of scientific warfare.'

A lack of specialist knowledge was rumoured to have compromised the expedition even before it had set sail. George Orwell heard that the War Office was 'so ill-informed' as not to know that Norwegian nights were short, imagining that troops which had to disembark in broad daylight 'would have the cover of darkness'. The Minister of Supply, Leslie Burgin, boasted to journalists that he did not know 'of any force which had been so splendidly equipped in so short a time'. But in a measured attack on the opening afternoon of the Norway Debate, the Liberal leader Archie Sinclair, who less than twelve months before had led the Liberals to vote against conscription, reminded MPs how Burgin had appeared in a press picture in a becoming white coat, while the troops at Namsos had no white coats at all. 'Apparently he had the only one.'

Once ashore, the soldiers were exposed without camouflage. An officer complained: 'The Jerries could see us everywhere in the snow. They just mowed our men down.'

Churchill's interferences compounded the mess. Owing to the chaos of loading and unloading at Rosyth on 8 April, and the dividing of the convoy on 14 April, 146th Infantry Brigade had arrived in Namsos with anti-aircraft guns but without predictors, so that the ship's carpenter had to contrive sights out of string and wood. One company was provided with magazines loaded with anti-aircraft rounds, which at once betrayed the men's positions to German snipers. None of the correct shells for the three-inch mortars arrived, only smoke shells. When a corporal in the Sherwood Foresters fired off his first two rounds, 'there was no explosion – oh no, just this bloody cloud of smoke'. Junior NCOs frequently did not have the requisite training to handle the Bren light machine guns. Field telephones were separated from their cables, and wireless equipment was rationed to two sets per battalion. 'Even more important,' said Martin Lindsay, 'all the ground was covered in snow, and the only way to operate in it was with ski troops and we hadn't got ski troops and therefore the troops were confined to the road.' The situation was no more satisfactory for the skiers of the French Chasseurs, who had landed without mules to pull their sledges, and, worse, without binding straps – making their skis unusable. A young Norwegian soldier later told Theodore Broch: 'There seemed to be no order to anything.' The only rule was confusion. 'We could hear our wounded crying in the woods, but we couldn't get to them,' reported one soldier. Joseph Kynoch would remember to his last breath the hellish din on St George's Day: '. . . men shouting orders, wounded men screaming in pain, the horrendous shriek of the dive bombers and the explosion and dust of their bombs and the deadly song of flying shrapnel'.

Carton de Wiart wrote: 'I felt in my bones the campaign was unlikely to be either long or successful.' The totality of the confusion can be measured by his reaction when he first heard the German destroyer *Paul Jacobi* open fire on Krogs Farm. He told Admiral Keyes on his return to London that he thought it was the British navy.

Leland Stowe recorded this 'catastrophic British defeat' for the *Chicago Daily News*. Everyone told the same bitter story. 'It's the planes. We've got no planes. The Jerries have been bombing us all afternoon – and shelling us on our right flank from the fjord. It's been bloody awful.' 'What we need are planes, and planes as fast as we can get them.' 'I'm glad you're a reporter. For God's sake, tell them we've got to have airplanes and anti-aircraft guns.' 'For God's sake, why don't they give us planes?'

In Somaliland in November 1914, Carton de Wiart had watched British DH9 bombers dropping 460-pound bombs on the Dervishes, and muttered: 'Damned unfair!' The planes were under the control of the Admiralty in London, of which Churchill was then chief. Twenty-six years on, Churchill was again in charge, and Carton de Wiart had never been more in need of air cover. 'Still I waited for news of our naval attack which was to be my signal to take Trondheim, but still it did not come.'

On 17 April, the War Office fixed the combined attack on Trondheim for the 22nd and briefed Major General Frederick Hotblack who was to command the landing force, impressing on him the 'paramount need for speed'. Hotblack – nicknamed 'Boots' – was hurrying home from the Athenaeum Club shortly after midnight when, in an accident that seemed of a shape with the campaign, he slipped down the Duke of York Steps and seriously injured himself. He was picked up unconscious and taken to Millbank hospital. One of his brigade commanders, Brigadier Horatio Pettus Berney-Ficklin, was next day appointed to replace him, but his plane crashed on landing at Kirkwall, leaving Berney-Ficklin unconscious. Ironside questioned in his diary whether the operation was jinxed. 'A peculiar fatality over this wretched Trondheim attack. Two of our best commanders knocked out as they had just got the plans.'

At 5.15 p.m. on 19 April, a third commander, Major General Bernard Paget, a large-nosed, sharp-tongued martinet, who had been wounded four times, rendering his left arm as useless as Carton de Wiart's, received a call saying that he was to catch a train for Scotland at 10.15 p.m. 'The only clue as to my task was that I should bring warm clothing with me.' An hour later, Paget was telephoned again. Plans had changed. He was now to report at the War Office in London at 10.30 next morning, 20 April. There, Ironside told him that he was to assume command of 148th Infantry Brigade, the second of 49th (West Riding) Division's three Territorial Army brigades, which under the name of 'Sickle Force' had landed two nights before at the small port of Åndalsnes. Paget's orders were to organise the base at Åndalsnes, and 'to co-operate with the Norwegian Army in preventing the Northward advance of the German army based in Southern Norway.' Oddly, no mention was made of a major direct assault on Trondheim, even though this was the priority of Lieutenant General Hugh Massy who the day before had been appointed Commander of the North-Western Expeditionary Force, in charge both of Paget and Carton de Wiart. Massy wrote: 'My instructions, as I understood them, were to capture Trondheim.'

With little intelligence information available, Paget had to create his headquarters from scratch. His Chief of Staff, Lieutenant Colonel Cameron Nicholson, recalled that everything was in a state of constant improvisation. Once again, the men lacked maps. 'We had to tear them out of geography books and send the ADC to the Norwegian Travel Agency to buy a Baedeker and collect any brochures he could find.'

Von Falkenhorst had had two months to prepare; Paget five days. One of Paget's three infantry brigades was left in Rosyth, with sappers and medical equipment. Most of the A.A. guns and transport sank off Bergen on 21

April with the torpedoing of the supply ship *Cedarbank*. The materiel that did eventually make its way to Norway proved useless.

'Sickle Force' was composed of units that had been destined for an unopposed landing at Stavanger as part of 'R.4'; hastily unloaded at Rosyth on 8 April, reloaded on 13 April for Namsos on the liner *Orion* as 'Maurice Force'; and at the last moment ordered to Åndalsnes on the night of 16 April.

The result of equipment not being stowed tactically was tremendous confusion – with stores slung ashore in short order and carried off into the holds of five different ships with no method or inventory. There was never a chance of sorting them in the blackout, wrote Lieutenant Colonel Dudley Clarke, assigned to the Brigade from the War Office. 'The scene below decks had become a sort of Storeman's Inferno, with shadowy figures burrowing about in the semi-darkness of shaded lamps and torches.' Colonel Beckwith, Commanding Officer of the Sherwood Foresters, peered down into the hold, appalled. At the bottom was 'a vast pyramid of stores of every description, with men of a number of units climbing over it like flies searching for anything with their unit's markings'.

On 21 April, the nine o'clock news announced that General Paget was at Lillehammer and that all was going well in Norway. Paget had not yet left Rosyth. When he arrived at a smouldering Åndalsnes on 25 April and received his first grim briefing, he learned that 'Sickle Force' had landed 1,750 men a week before, but with no artillery, no tanks, no armoured cars, no transport, no medical services, no signals equipment, and four anti-aircraft guns – though Nicholson had noticed 'several fishing rods and many sporting guns'.

This was the force that Chamberlain had promised to send in 'great strength' to fight 'in full association' with Major General Ruge, and for which the Norwegian Commander-in-Chief had been waiting in a state of impatience and desperation since 14 April.

In response to persistent appeals from Ruge and 2nd Norwegian Division, instead of marching north on Trondheim, 148th Infantry Brigade had moved south-east to Lillehammer to ward off a German advance from Oslo. The newly appointed British military attaché had confirmed that the situation there was so critical that unless reinforcements arrived within twenty-four hours the front was unlikely to hold. Against tanks, artillery and overwhelming air power, the British had suffered 700 casualties, and the commander of 1/5th Battalion Leicestershire Regiment, Lieutenant Colonel Guy German, was taken prisoner with several officers. Paget had assumed control of a brigade that was reduced to six officers and 300 men, and had ceased to function as a military unit.

The situation disappointed more than surprised the local Norwegian commander in Åndalsnes. Oberst Thue had watched the British forces file ashore, young, small, skinny and pale, and he considered them to be 'little more than children and riff raff – the only thing they were good at was insulting women and stealing whatever they came across in shops and private homes.'

The Germans had swept clean through in armoured cars and lorries full of troops, covered by planes operating from Norwegian airfields. By 26 April, the bombers and fighters still available to Luftflotte V had established what Peter Fleming called 'the Luftwaffe's almost unchallenged supremacy in the air'. The key German advantage was that the Luftwaffe could seize aerodromes like Stavanger with airborne troops, fly in supplies, and commence operations at once. In sad contrast, the RAF's hopelessly outmatched force of 240 aircraft, of which only two thirds were in service, proved unable to intervene from distant bases in Lincolnshire and Scotland until the army could secure a local airfield with railway access. A frustrated Halifax wrote in his diary that 'with no aerodromes our fighters cannot get there'.

The difficulties for the bombers were considerable. The Wellingtons, Whitleys and Hampdens had to fly enormous distances in shortening nights over great stretches of sea in often abysmal conditions. After flying up to 750 miles – the extreme range of bombers – attacks were then based on 'information necessarily some hours out of date', and the targets were easy to miss, having to be located from torn-out town plans from Baedeker guides. Another restriction was the Allied order for air activity: in the first three days of the Norway Campaign, German-held airfields could only be attacked by machine guns and not by bombs. Between 7 April and 10 May, Bomber Command lost 31 aircraft in 782 sorties.

Namsos was out of range, so Allied air support took the flimsy shape of sixty-minute patrols over Åndalsnes. For the rest of the time, Dudley Clarke observed, German pilots flew 'just as they liked'. Major Desmond

Fitzgerald had lain in the fjords around Åndalsnes, being bombed hourly day after day – a scene which Evelyn Waugh wove into *Put out More Flags*. Meeting Waugh on his return, Fitzgerald criticised the pitiful response of the RAF which 'constantly flew without their distinguishing signs and neglected to give answering signals; were constantly fired on and sometimes brought down'. On 23 April, three Coastal Command Hudsons from 224 Squadron approached Åndalsnes, one of which was shot into the fjord by batteries from the cruiser HMS *Curacoa*; the two others were damaged, but managed to return to base.

Less than twenty-four hours after arriving in Norway, Paget sent a message to General Massy. His troops could not endure more than another four days unless 'adequate air support was forthcoming'.

In London, Massy had promised Paget sixty fighter aircraft. On 24 April, eighteen Gladiator Mark II fighters were flown ashore from the carrier HMS *Glorious* and landed on an iced-over lake thirty-five miles from Åndalsnes. Maps issued to Wing Commander Victor McClure had persuaded him that he was headed for the Middle East. 'We saw ourselves in singlets and shorts under a burning desert sun . . .' Exposed on the unsheltered lake at Lesjaskog, McClure's carburettor froze overnight, and his out-of-date biplane was unable to take off – 'plumb at the mercy of anything that buzzed along' – when the Luftwaffe appeared at 7.45 the next morning. He-111s and Ju-88s attacked in V-formations throughout the day, leaving 132 craters in the ice. By nightfall, there were five Gladiators left, and these were in danger of sinking into the lake. The last Gladiator was destroyed the following evening.

A small force of Whitley bombers did attempt to bomb Trondheim airfield on 22 and 23 April, but failed to locate it.

Paget never spoke to his son Julian about what he had experienced in Norway, save to suggest that it was 'a scenario that even the most sadistic of instructors at the Staff College would not have dared to devise for his students'. And the situation was about to get worse. Operation 'Hammer' was in the balance.

Churchill had sent Chamberlain a note clamping together 'the various & changing plans wh are now afoot'. The complicated progress of the Norway

Campaign proved hard for the Prime Minister to hold in one hand. Even today Churchill's initiatives resist easy summary, and nowhere more so than in the seaborne assault on Trondheim.

Chamberlain complained to his sister that 'Winston changed his mind <u>four</u> times over Trondheim'. Churchill was initially against it, ordering Forbes and the Home Fleet back up to Narvik on 10 April; then grudgingly in favour, under pressure from Halifax and Chamberlain; then fully in favour; then, under pressure from the Chiefs of Staff and the Admiralty, reluctantly against it; finally in favour again on 25 April, before resigning himself to evacuation.

At first opposed to 'Hammer' because it might prejudice 'Rupert', Churchill had swiftly become its chief champion – to such a degree that his account in *The Gathering Storm*, according to Admiral Godfrey, 'gave no idea of the fervour and relentless determination with which Churchill . . . advocated the assault on Trondheim'. On 15 April, Churchill wrote to George VI. 'We are aiming at Trondheim wh will be an even greater prize than Narvik.' He told the Military Coordination Committee that nothing should 'prejudice the effectiveness of the central thrust'. The assault would be fraught with risks – but, if successful, another 'brilliant' operation, offering 'the opportunity for a deed of fame'.

The ferocity of German air power had sobered Admiral Forbes, though. The navy Commander-in-Chief had considered Churchill's important project, and announced that he was 'not . . . very keen on forcing his way into Trondheim because of the risk of air attack'. Forbes told Churchill that the operation was not feasible 'unless you are prepared to face very heavy losses in troops and transports'.

To Churchill's annoyance, Forbes's misgivings were shared by the Chiefs of Staff at a moment when Churchill's relations with them had deteriorated further. Less than a fortnight had passed since Chamberlain had entrusted Churchill with the chairmanship of the Military Coordination Committee. In that brief time, the First Lord appeared to have descended the rungs from 'seventh heaven' to the deck of a ship simmering with mutiny.

The MCC had a pet name: 'The Crazy Gang'. Lieutenant General Henry Pownall, Chief of Staff for the British Expeditionary Force, predicted that 'with Winston as chairman they are likely to be extremely volatile'. Within days, General Jacob, the War Cabinet's Military Assistant, had come to recognise that Churchill was 'unpredictable and meddlesome, and quite unsuited to handle his colleagues in a team'. In Lloyd George's office in the Commons, A. J. Sylvester heard a joke. 'They may not be fighting in France; but they are in the War Office!'

After seven days in the MCC chair, Colville reported that Churchill had been 'talking a lot and getting nothing done'. Churchill was one of few in Cabinet who had fought in a war; he was accustomed to people deferring to his experiences in Cuba, the Sudan, India, South Africa and France. His high-handed behaviour suggested to Ralph Edwards that he was still on his charger at Omdurman, riding roughshod over the opinions of his military and political advisers. 'Everyone is very indignant about the conduct of affairs and Winston appears to be the chief target. He will try and be a naval strategist if not an actual tactician.' Geoffrey Shakespeare had observed during the *Altmark* incident how it was not enough for Churchill to conceive and direct operations himself: he had to be there in the thick of it. When Churchill niggled about the disposition of the Expeditionary Force to Norway, he behaved to General Ironside as though he was 'a company commander running a small operation to cross a bridge'. His interest glided quickest to where the prospect of action seemed most imminent. Pownall felt that 'great as are his uses, he is also a real danger, always tempted by the objective, never counting his resources to see if the objective is attainable'. Churchill's colleagues in the War Cabinet were especially critical. The Chancellor John Simon believed that 'his judgement is at its worst when things go badly'. 'A farce' was how Kingsley Wood described to John Reith the MCC meeting on 14 April, as a result of the 'dreadful state Churchill had gotten himself and everyone else into. Admiralty in a state of jitters from top to bottom.'

Rarely would things go so badly for Churchill than in Norway. Samuel Hoare was reduced to a state of hair-tugging despair by Churchill's 'meddling' and 'complete wobbles' over tactics and strategy. In one estimate described as 'conservative', Churchill changed his mind about the military objectives fourteen times in three weeks. These tensions bubbled away as the date approached for Operation 'Hammer', and on Tuesday 16 April they erupted.

Early that morning Churchill summoned an astounded General Ismay to tell him that he 'disagreed entirely' with the Chiefs of Staff's plan for the attack on Trondheim. Ismay feared that 'a first-class row' might develop into 'a first-class political crisis' if Churchill then went ahead and chaired the MCC meeting to discuss 'Hammer'. Ismay tackled the Chiefs of Staff directly, imploring them not to lose their tempers. Churchill seems to have recognised the mutinous atmosphere. He requested that Chamberlain take the meeting at noon and get him 'out of a hole'.

Chamberlain chaired all MCC meetings from that day forth. 'The result was magical. We were always unanimous,' he wrote in relief to his sister. 'Oh dear!' Ida wrote back. 'What a state of affairs when the P.M. cannot depend on those who ought to be his chief support and continually has to take over the most important jobs himself. You do indeed have to pay for your Winston.' His other sister Hilda was equally sympathetic. 'You do manage Winston wonderfully & he is clever enough to know when he must give way gracefully, although doubtless his brilliant ideas are stored somewhere to be brought out in book form later to show how much better he could have done than you.' She was spot on. Here is Churchill, the self-proclaimed skilled strategist and bold dynamic leader, reflecting eight years later on the disasters in Norway: 'Had I been allowed to act with freedom and design when I first demanded permission, a far more agreeable conclusion might have been reached in this key theatre, with favourable consequences in every direction.'

Chamberlain had spent his twenties in the Caribbean, where his native workmen had a saying: *'You can't buy meat without getting some bone.'* He confided to his sisters that Churchill's presence in the Cabinet was 'just the price we have to pay for the asset we have in his personality and popularity'. Still, the cost continued to escalate. Under Churchill's chairmanship, the MCC had been 'getting into a sad mess, quarrelling and sulking, with everyone feeling irritable and strained and with a general conviction that Winston had smashed the machine we had so carefully built up . . . He does enjoy planning a campaign or an operation himself so much and he believes so earnestly in all his own ideas (for the moment) that he puts intenser pressure on his staff than he realises. The result is apt to be that they are bullied into a sulky silence – a most dangerous position in war.'

With Chamberlain once again in charge of the machine, it was decided on 16 April to go directly for Trondheim 'with the least possible delay'. The War Cabinet was united. Churchill appeared delighted. Chamberlain wrote that the First Lord was 'in the best of humour & tells his friends that he and the P.M. are working admirably together'.

But three days later Churchill claimed to have faced 'a vehement and decisive change in the opinion of the Chiefs of Staff and of the Admiralty'.

A critical draft memorandum by the Joint Planning Staff had already been circulated on 15 April. Then at the morning MCC meeting on 19 April, the Chiefs of Staff presented a new paper strongly opposing 'Hammer'. A naval bombardment of Trondheim was too risky. The Germans had had ample time to fortify the entrance to the harbour. If the British lost a cruiser in a German air attack, as suddenly seemed likely, then Italy might declare war. The paper recommended a 'complete alteration of emphasis', placing the entire onus on the pincer movements.

In a striking departure that was based on what Peter Fleming called 'a blithe disregard for the realities of the situation', Churchill's senior military advisers suggested that 'Maurice Force' and 'Sickle Force' ought no longer to be diversionary operations – given the 'considerable advance' made by Carton de Wiart and the 'unexpected success' in landing Paget's forces at Åndalsnes without a casualty. Although separated from each other by 200 miles of snow-covered mountains, birch forests and wide expanses of frozen water, the two forces should form the main attack on Trondheim, which it was still thought essential to seize for a base.

At a loss to know what to commend, Chamberlain, now back in the MCC chair, looked for answer to the First Sea Lord, having, in General Alan Brooke's account, a deep respect for Admiral Pound and his judgement. At the other end of the table, Pound responded with one of his enigmatic silences until it was realised that he had begun to doze, as he often did in these long MCC meetings.* 'But at the mention of the Fleet,'

---

* No autopsy was performed when Pound died in October 1943. It was clear that he had died of a brain tumour, though how long he had been suffering from this is not known. Stories of him falling asleep at meetings went back several years, but his staff defended him, explaining that he was

Brooke wrote, 'the old man, to whom the security, traditions and transmitted wisdom of his Service were life itself, awoke to full activity and shook his head vigorously.'

Churchill was said to have lost his temper when Pound assured him that 'there was no need to risk ships', and that the military were confident of the success of their pincer attacks. 'You admirals all the same . . . agree on plans . . . when it comes to fighting you're yellow.' This was the story put around by Brendan Bracken to defend his master from rumours that Churchill had developed cold feet. In the Bracken–Churchill version, Churchill only with immense reluctance agreed finally that evening to Pound's proposals.

Churchill's other colleagues in the War Cabinet, however, felt that the First Lord was not quite so reluctant or angry about his advisers' volte-face as later he maintained, and that Churchill had been all in favour of cancelling 'Hammer'. The Chancellor, John Simon, was emphatic about this in his diary. 'Churchill never for one moment urged a different course.' Simon's understanding was shared by Halifax. 'Great efforts are being made to represent the Norwegian business as the result of timid colleagues restraining the bold, courageous and dashing Winston. As a matter of fact the exact opposite would be at least as near the truth, and on Winston certainly rests the main responsibility for the abandonment of the naval attack on Trondheim.'

Simon and Halifax are supported in their accounts by Chamberlain, who described to his sisters how, with no advance notice, Churchill had called the Chiefs of Staff to the Admiralty 'which he had then no authority to do' and bullied them into agreeing 'with a course which they disapproved'. Churchill had next telephoned Chamberlain and asked for the Prime Minister's authority to drop the direct blow on Trondheim, saying that the Admiralty advised it and all the Chiefs of Staff concurred. Chamberlain wrote: 'I said that if that were so, I would be guided by their opinion and the necessary orders were taken at once.'

Chamberlain was merely doing what Churchill had asked, even if

---

concentrating with his eyes closed. Godfrey wrote: 'That he used to doze was common knowledge, but what I find hard to believe is that he was mentally awake the whole time.'

Churchill tilted it somewhat differently in *The Gathering Storm*, saying that he had no option but to agree to a paper that represented the collective view of the military chiefs. Yet as General Percy Groves had observed six years earlier: 'There are few paradoxes more striking than that to be found between Mr Churchill's deeds as a Minister and his words as an historian.'

On 20 April, Churchill signalled Forbes to cancel 'Hammer'. Cadogan was disgusted. 'All Trondheim plans upset. "Frontal attack" given up, and we can't expect anything for a month! This was recommendation of Cs of Staff, approved by P.M. and Winston. But it seems to me awful!'

To compound the awfulness, the War Office had yet to inform the British or Norwegian commanders on the ground that the seaborne assault on Trondheim had been aborted, in Pownall's words, as 'a dud plan'.

In the burning ruins of Namsos, Carton de Wiart fretted for 'Hammer' to begin, unaware that his Territorials and not the navy now constituted the main attack force on Trondheim. At 11.35 p.m. on 21 April, he sent another signal marked Urgent. 'Enemy aircraft again very active and dominating situation . . . Fear our position becomes untenable . . . Only three small store houses standing . . . All civilians left Namsos. No cars left.'

Back in the Admiralty Map Room, Churchill's mercurial focus had swivelled northwards – much to the dismay of Ironside. 'He is so like a child in many ways. He tires of a thing and then he wants to hear no more of it. He was mad to divert the brigade from Narvik to Namsos and would hear of no reason. Now he is bored with the Namsos operation and is all for Narvik again.'

8
WORST OF ALL EXPERIENCES

'Ah, it is all very difficult, we are used to travelling on camels across the desert and here you give us boats, and we have to go across water.'
FRENCH FOREIGN LEGIONNAIRE, Narvik, April 1940

'Chamberlain was destroyed not in the West End but in the fjords of Norway.'
SIMON BALL, *The Guardsmen*

While Carton de Wiart waited in vain for the Royal Navy to hammer Trondheim, 300 miles north a separate naval offensive was about to get under way.

Vice Admiral Whitworth had sent another excited signal to the Admiralty after sinking the remaining eight German destroyers on 13 April. 'I am convinced that Narvik can be taken by direct assault without fear of meeting serious opposition on landing. I consider that the main landing force need only be small.' Churchill's deduction that Narvik was there for the taking prepared the ground for the fiasco which followed.

Flushed with the news of Whitworth's easy victory, Churchill continued to be magnetised by the iron-ore town. Whatever his public commitment to seizing Trondheim, behind the scenes Narvik was his false north; a place that interfered with his ability to orient his attention properly elsewhere. He never ceased to regard its capture as the 'primary strategic objective', and he telegraphed the naval commander, Admiral Cork: 'Once this is achieved we have the trophy at which all Europe is looking. We must get into Narvik or its ruins as soon as possible.'

Yet the same combination of heavy snow, lack of men, equipment and air cover which had proved lethal to Operations 'Sickle' and 'Maurice' now bogged down Operation 'Rupert' in ways that rivalled the routs at Namsos and Åndalsnes. When General Auchinleck arrived in Narvik on 12 May, he had one word for the farcical situation that he found there: 'Gilbertian'. Even the town's German commander was at a loss to understand why Churchill had not seized Narvik in April. General Dietl said that it remained 'a mystery which only the British leaders could explain'.

On 15 April, the day after Peter Fleming landed in Namsos, the cruiser HMS *Southampton* steamed into Vägsfjord off Harstad, a small town on an island forty miles north of Narvik. On board and recovering from seasickness was the military commander of Operation 'Rupert', Major General Pierse Mackesy, the original land-force commander of 'Avonmouth' and 'R.4'. Mackesy had asked to rendezvous with Admiral Cork, on board the cruiser HMS *Aurora*. Their brittle meeting was to shape the battle for Narvik.

Mackesy had changed operations as many times as ships in the previous week, having to transfer with his staff from the *Aurora* to the liner *Batory*, and then on 11 April to the *Southampton*, after receiving fresh Cabinet orders. The revised convoy was to be known as 'NP1'. Long before he reached Narvik, Mackesy felt that he had stepped up onto a stage of 'plans by impulsiveness and out of ignorance' in which – and of this he had not an ounce of doubt – the First Lord was a leading player. 'Mr Winston Churchill had almost supreme personal responsibility for the direction of the Imperial war effort.' The questionable strategic value of Mackesy's latest destination did nothing to deepen his confidence. 'Narvik was really a name on the map, the place itself of little use to anyone.'

Sailing ahead, the *Southampton* had arrived at Harstad the day before, on 14 April. Finding no German forces on the island, Mackesy disembarked his troops – two companies of Scots Guards and a detachment of Royal Engineers: twenty-two officers and three hundred and thirty-five men, who would establish headquarters in cooperation with the Norwegians. Mackesy described his men as 'a typical advance party, chiefly administrative personnel loaded for a peaceful and orderly landing at an organised friendly port'. The remainder of his force, four more battalions from 'R.4', were scheduled to arrive the following day; and a demi-brigade of Chasseurs Alpins five days after that.

His men were already ashore when at around 3 p.m. Mackesy received a radio message from Admiral Cork. Because of the mountains, the signal was garbled, but its gist was clear. The navy commander had read

Whitworth's first signal about the 'thoroughly frightened' enemy in Narvik, and he suggested to Mackesy that 'we take every advantage of this before enemy has recovered' – by landing Mackesy's troops in Narvik at daybreak the following morning. Faced with the prospect of one more hasty re-embarkation, Mackesy 'disliked the suggestion enormously'. He wired back that it would be better to wait for the rest of 24th Guards Brigade, expected shortly on 'NP1', and meanwhile reconnoitre the area, which according to an old pilot on the lighthouse at Tranøy, was 'very strongly held': he had advised the British not to attack until they had twice as many ships.

Mackesy proposed that he and Cork get together the following day, 15 April, to discuss the next step.

Admiral of the Fleet the Earl of Cork and Orrery greeted Mackesy on the *Aurora* that afternoon by chucking up his monocle and catching it in his eye. He was someone the army commander had not met before, a short, impetuous Irish peer, known as 'Ginger' for his red hair and 'Cork-n-horrible' for his temper, and another First World War veteran hauled out of retirement in order to command the naval forces that would assist in the amphibious capture of Narvik. Cork was Mackesy's senior in age and rank, even though Mackesy remained the operation's overall commander. The 'ridiculous appointment of Cork', as the anonymous senior officer wrote to Godfrey, coming on top of 'the side-tracking of the C-in-C Home Fleet', was the next most serious criticism of Churchill's conduct of the Norway Campaign. It was felt that the First Lord had injected unnecessary confusion into the chain of command.

A veteran of the Murmansk Campaign, Mackesy, according to his son Piers, was not a conciliatory man, 'and he did not gladly accommodate himself to those in high places with whom he disagreed. He had sailed for Narvik already convinced that the plan was inept and the expedition badly mounted. And at Harstad he was confronted by a total stranger sent by the statesman whom he knew to be chiefly responsible for the Scandinavian adventure and its disastrous organisation. Many witnesses of that first encounter in the *Aurora* were to recall the intense antagonism of the two commanders.'

Aside from not getting on, each commander carried contradictory orders. Cork's instructions from Churchill had been delivered orally on 10 April, and not shared with the War Office or with Mackesy, at a late-night meeting of Churchill's Military Coordination Committee, during which it was made clear to Cork that the government desired 'to turn the enemy out of Narvik at the earliest possible moment'. Churchill reiterated his impatience for bold and prompt action the following afternoon, 11 April, during a brief car trip from the Admiralty to the House of Commons, where Churchill was to deliver his first statement on Norway. 'The crowd lining the streets gave him a great ovation,' Cork recalled, 'and attending to this and the fact of other people being in the car precluded any serious attention to the matter in which I was interested.'

Mackesy, meanwhile, had arrived in the theatre of operations 'with diametrically opposite views' from those of the navy commander. According to the official account in the *London Gazette*, 'not only was his force embarked as for a peaceful landing . . . and unready for immediate operations but . . . the orders he had received . . . ruled out any idea of attempting an opposed landing'. Mackesy's written instructions from General Ironside were specific and cautious, issued in a totally different situation, and intended to avoid fighting with Norwegian troops if the Allies were to land in Narvik prior to a German response to 'Wilfred'. Orders issued earlier on 5 April had been even less combative, recommending that 'fire in retaliation is only to be opened as a last resort'.

The result was that Mackesy, the intellectually intolerant engineer, and Cork, the monocled fiery Irish peer, were pitched into an instant stand-off, reflected by the fact that Mackesy established his HQ ashore while Cork remained on board his flagship. There was little prospect of laughing it off to reach a rapprochement – a pilot who had dealings with Cork observed: 'If there was one thing the Admiral detested it was the humouring approach.' To illustrate the bristling tension between them, Cork flew from the *Southampton* to *Aurora* in an old Walrus which was attacked by his own side's Bren gun, fired by Lance Corporal Ludlow, who was reprimanded for 'missing a low-flying admiral'.

Reduced to a convoy of fourteen ships after the sudden detachment of the rear half, 'NP1' arrived off Harstad on 15 April. The troops disembarked in fishing boats onto a slippery pier, slowly edging closer to Narvik while Force HQ made up their minds. The Norwegian Chief of Staff, Major Lindback Larsen, seeing men with bare knees puffing on bagpipes, reported gloomily back to his commander, Major General Carl Fleischer, that nothing could be expected of them. In contrast to the young German mountain troops who had been gathered on the afterdecks of their destroyers and shown maps and been told where they were heading and why, none of the British officers had a clear idea of the mission, and hardly any of the soldiers spoke Norwegian – there were fewer than two interpreters to every thousand men. Instead of going into action, 1st Irish Guards hunkered down in cramped accommodation in freezing temperatures, in a landscape foreign to anything they had known. The men's despondency was registered by their Quartermaster who opened the *Daily Mirror* and read the headline 'Narvik in Allied Hands'. 'What the – hell do they think we are?' In his official history of the regiment, Major Desmond Fitzgerald wrote that 'all the battles in Africa, Italy, France, Holland and Germany, longer and bloodier though they were, could not efface the memory of the Norwegian campaign as the worst of all experiences'.

Cork was said to have boasted that in the first twenty-four hours he could have seized Narvik with his bare hands. Against his impatience to take immediate advantage of Whitworth's attack, Mackesy counselled caution. Mackesy's strength had been halved the night before by the sudden diversion of 146th Infantry Brigade to Namsos. In his soldier's view, it was the height of folly to attempt any landing at Narvik until he had received his promised reinforcements of men and equipment, plus intelligence concerning the enemy's strength. Each hour brought fresh rumours which made an accurate assessment impossible. A Norwegian coastguard telephoned that five enemy submarines were moving at full speed towards Narvik. A flurry of flashes passed between the Battalion HQ and the *Aurora*, followed by more signal activity. 'For submarines, please read whales.' In fact, there *were* five U-boats in the vicinity.

A warning of the risk to Mackesy's troops even from limited shore defences was the example of Germany's newest heavy cruiser *Blücher*, sunk in Oslo on 9 April with the assistance of two nineteenth-century shore guns. Narvik's beaches were believed to be mined and covered by machine guns that had already wounded eleven British servicemen. The harbour was clogged with wrecks and still-burning debris. Because of the botched unloading at Rosyth, Mackesy had no landing craft or maps, other than poor reproductions of a 1906 Norwegian survey; and his anti-aircraft defences were 'quite inadequate' to cope with the 140 raids which took place on Harstad during the eight weeks of operations. Mackesy cabled the War Office: 'I must point out that I have not even one field gun and I have not even one anti-aircraft gun. I have practically no Mortar ammunition. My force is probably inferior to the enemy . . . Offensive operation without artillery must be ruled out.'

On top of everything, the weather was atrocious. The War Office had assured Mackesy that there would be no snow in Narvik after mid-April. Yet the snow lay five feet thick to the waterline, and continuous blizzards rendered visibility 'seldom greater than two cables'. As at Namsos, the occupying force lacked skis, sledges, snowshoes. On 16 April, Mackesy agreed with a reluctant Cork to send a joint communiqué to the War Office. 'Until snow melts about end of April, operations on any scale across country cannot take place.'

This was not what Churchill wished to hear. He sent back a 'most urgent' message addressed to both commanders, asking them to give their full consideration for 'an assault on Narvik', and emphasising that the capture of the port 'would be an important success'. In a separate message to Admiral Forbes, Churchill placed scornful blame on Mackesy for wanting 'to sit down in front of Narvik and convert the operation into a kind of siege'.

Churchill expressed his unshakeable belief that 'failure to take Narvik will be a major disaster', and a long delay 'disastrous both for military and psychological reasons'. Yet the psychological reasons were mostly Churchill's. General Mackesy was far from being the only authority to question Narvik's strategic worth. At home, Leo Amery wanted to know 'why we are wasting men on Narvik where the Germans have been isolated and helpless from the moment their ships were sunk instead of concentrating every possible man on the immediate capture of Trondheim'. In Amery's decided opinion, 'Here Winston was all wrong.' This was the opinion, too, of more or less every military adviser aside from Cork, and also of the press. The *Spectator*'s correspondent wrote: 'There was no apparent reason why British warships should have devoted their attention to Narvik alone.'

But Narvik had taken on extra resonance with the capture of Churchill's twenty-three-year-old nephew. Quite apart from having to deal with the anxiety of Romilly's parents, there was the First Lord's own position. He had been the chief advocate of the minelaying operation, not least in a bid to wipe clean the Gallipoli slate. After the German invasion, the taking of the ore-town was supposed to be his masterstroke, up there with one of Marlborough's conquests. Maisky wrote of Churchill's ambitions: 'He always imagined himself in the role of a great military leader who flung armies from one end of Europe to another, conquered kingdoms and won brilliant victories . . .' Now Narvik risked turning into an Arctic Dardanelles.

The two campaigns bore similarities in their conception – the wish to break a stalemate by deploying British sea power – but also in their bungled planning and execution: the sending in of the navy before troops were ready, the diversion to another port, the failure of ships to suppress land targets, even down to the wild confusion over transporting equipment – horses in one ship, harnesses in another . . . The baffling command structure was a further unwelcome echo: Admiral Godfrey had landed on Y beach at Gallipoli on 24 April 1915. 'The question of who was in local command was not clear, even to some of the senior officers on the spot.'

Tormented by the parallels, Churchill claimed to have 'pondered a good deal upon the lessons of the Dardanelles'. He flinched at whispers that the 'iron of the Dardanelles had entered into my soul'; that it was the iron ore of Narvik now affecting his judgement and quite possibly his nerve.

Typical was the reaction of General Pownall when informed of the scheme for Norway. 'Of all the harebrained projects I have heard this is the most foolish – its inception smacks all too alarmingly of Gallipoli.' The dread words 'harebrained' and 'Gallipoli' bobbed up again and again. In March, Lord Gort, head of the British Expeditionary Force in France, expressed his fear that the Scandinavian expedition 'might . . . prove a Gallipoli'. On 17 April, Colville was taken aside by Lord Hankey who hinted that he was 'a little worried by Winston's determination to direct the war: he remembers, he says, the operations at the Dardanelles all too clearly. He is going to warn the P.M.'

Obvious to Lloyd George was that Churchill had been 'bruised' by the

Dardanelles, and had 'some sort of *inferiority complex* when it comes to offensive operations'. 'Bruised' was an understatement. When describing the events of 1915, Clementine said: 'I thought he would die of grief.'

Churchill admitted in his memoirs that there was no compelling strategic reason to desire quick success at Narvik, but Piers Mackesy argued in his father's defence that 'there were political ones; and Churchill himself had a personal reason to desire one'. By late April, A. J. Sylvester was hearing from various sources 'that Winston is worried for purely political reasons – he has got a "Dardanelles complex"'. To Admiral Godfrey, nothing could be plainer. Churchill had anticipated redeeming himself in Norway, and he was 'determined that he would not leave the Admiralty a second time under a cloud of failure'.

Twenty-five years earlier, Churchill had found a scapegoat in General Stopford. He now piled on General Mackesy the failure to exploit Whitworth's golden opportunity. Impatient to resolve 'the damaging deadlock and the neutralisation of one of our best brigades', and ignoring Ironside's efforts to get him to understand that it was fatal 'to start monkeying about from here with the General on the spot', Churchill cast the army commander as the villain and the reason for a situation 'at once unexpected and disagreeable'.

Chamberlain had noted how Churchill intimidated his staff so that they were afraid to speak out, dismissing those who disagreed with him. Churchill's unflattering portrait of Mackesy in *The Gathering Storm* was a further example. Its vindictiveness mystified Mackesy's son Piers. 'How can one explain the bitterness with which Churchill pursued the little Narvik operation in later years?' Piers Mackesy objected that Churchill's contentious narrative was cast in a framework of 'factual inaccuracy, of careful innuendo and of inconsistencies which can only be explained by the author's profound emotional involvement in the operation'.

Mackesy, the general on the spot, did not consider Churchill's plan worth the 'sheer bloody murder' which it would entail. He asked Cork to pass on the following message: 'So far as I am concerned, I will not have the snows of Narvik substituted for the mud of Passchendaele in public opinion.' After making a reconnaissance on 20 April, Mackesy – now 'in a thoroughly disgruntled state', according to Ironside – reported that the chances of a successful landing from destroyers were 'non-existent', and from open boats would involve 'NOT the neutralisation but the destruction of 24th Guards Brigade'.

As at Gallipoli, Churchill professed not to care too much about casualties, believing that his orders 'so evidently contemplated heavy losses, that they should have been obeyed'. He had been 'taken aback' by Mackesy's unwillingness to engage with the enemy, and now tried to sideline him. Days earlier, he had bypassed Admiral Forbes and Vice Admiral Whitworth. In the same spirit, and behind everyone's backs, he signalled the navy commander directly.

Geoffrey Shakespeare was at the Admiralty at 3 a.m. one night when Churchill asked his yawning secretary, 'Where is the oil?'

'What oil, sir?'

'Wake up,' said Churchill, 'I want the oil [Earl of Cork and Orrery].'

On 18 April, Churchill telegraphed Cork. 'Should you consider the situation is being mishandled it is your duty to report either to me personally or to Admiralty upon it.' In a startling instruction, Churchill gave Cork the authority to detain Mackesy. 'If this Officer appears to be spreading a bad spirit through the higher ranks of the land force, do not hesitate to relieve him or place him under arrest.' Then on 21 April, Churchill used 'the apparent lack of harmony' between the two commanders as the excuse to put Cork in supreme charge of 'this crucial operation'.

With his own man now in position, the seizure of Narvik appeared closer than it had ever been. But Churchill's eager hopes were dashed almost immediately. On going ashore personally to 'test the snow' with a party of Royal Marines, the diminutive Cork sank in up to his waist and had to be pulled out after losing his monocle. 'To make any progress was exhausting,' he reported to the Admiralty that night. And he had a request. 'What is really our one pressing need is fighters, we are so over matched in the air.'

Whether by design or not, Cork set the operation for 24 April – an indelible date in the Churchill calendar. Preceded by a heavy naval bombardment, the battalion was to land on Narvik's north side at the subsidiary harbour of Vasvik. 'It is a curious fact,' Lieutenant Colonel Faulkner told his company commanders on 22 April, 'that the 24th is the anniversary of Gallipoli. On that date, the day after tomorrow, the Battalion is going to make an assault landing and capture Narvik. There is only one assault landing craft available.'

When Mackesy heard of Cork's plan to pummel the town and its civilian population into surrender, he cabled a formal protest to the War Office, saying that the shelling was likely to achieve nothing militarily, but stood gravely to impair good relations with Norway, and he demanded that his views be represented to the government. 'There is not one officer or man under my command who will not feel shame for himself and his country if the thousands of Norwegian men, women and children in Narvik are subjected to the bombardment proposed.'

One of those standing in the direct line of Cork's contemplated attrition was Churchill's nephew. When the Germans picked up a radio warning from Tromsø, General Dietl decided to evacuate the town. Shortly after 3 a.m. on 23 April, Giles Romilly was woken in the Café Iris and driven to Beisfjord where a seaplane was moored. This is the last entry in a log kept by the mate of the steamer *Blythmoor*: '3.30 Romilly taken away. Guards say he is to be flown to Germany. Poor beggar.'

The naval bombardment of Narvik began in a heavy snowfall at 7.05 next morning, twenty-five years to the day of the Gallipoli landings. It was a bitingly cold dawn. A howling gale flung snow into the faces of 1st Battalion Irish Guards, muffled up to the eyes and waiting to land from the repair ship *Vindictive*. At 8.30 a.m., the last guardsman had been heaved up the rope ladder from a fishing boat used to transfer the troops, when the *Aurora* flashed the message 'Negative embarkation'. The bombardment had not been satisfactory. But the main reason, wrote Major Desmond Fitzgerald, who passed the details on to Evelyn Waugh, was that the naval staff 'could not guarantee that the landing craft would ever reach the shore'.

'We want a bit of luck,' General Ironside had written when the Norway Campaign was at the planning stage. General Pownall ascribed the muddles in Narvik and Namsos to Churchill's bad luck – 'he is *unlucky*, he was throughout the last war; and that is a real thing and a bad and dangerous failing'. Lord Gort was another who reckoned that Churchill had 'an unlucky star' and that the Scandinavian expedition was 'a mistake' from the beginning.

Yet Churchill's outrageous good fortune must not be overlooked either.

Churchill's kismet seems to have smiled on him when he waved on Vice Admiral Whitworth to engage with the German fleet on 13 April, as he had urged Captain Warburton-Lee three days earlier. ('Attack at dawn, all good luck.') A further fluke was the success of Churchill's convoy in avoiding the multitude of torpedoes aimed at it from German submarines.

Churchill had greatly underestimated the risk to his navy from above water. But he ignored as well the dangers from below the sea. Trond Kristiansen is a Narvik publisher specialising in the Norway Campaign. He says: 'It was suicidal and insanely dangerous to bring the navy into Vestfjorden, because five U-boats were waiting for them.'

U47 was commanded by Günther Prien who six months earlier had sunk HMS *Royal Oak* in Scapa Flow with the loss of 833 men. On the evening of 15 April, Prien came upon the Narvik convoy 'NP1' at anchorage fifteen miles east of Harstad, waiting to disembark. Prien was amazed to see through his periscope 'a wall of ships', including 'three large transports, three small and two cruisers' – the destruction of which, believes Geirr Haarr, could have influenced the entire Allied campaign in Norway. The weather was good, the target impossible to miss. At 10.42 p.m., Prien fired four torpedoes at two cruisers and two large transports. The distance: 700 yards. He waited for the certain explosion – but nothing. He reloaded, navigated closer, and three hours later fired another four torpedoes. Again, nothing happened, except that *U47* became grounded on an uncharted reef, and Prien had to send his crew out on deck to run up and down in order to rock the submarine free.

In what became part of the ongoing Torpedo Crisis or *Versager* (failure), Prien fired a total of ten torpedoes at sitting ducks like HMS *Warspite* and HMS *Hotspur* – all of which malfunctioned, either exploding prematurely or failing to detonate. The same failures were reported by the captains of *U48*, *U46*, *U38*, *U49* and *U65*. The reasons were never explained satisfactorily. The high iron-ore content in the soil may have affected the magnetically activated pistols, and caused the gyro-magnets to make the torpedoes run deeper. Nicholas Rodger, one of Britain's foremost naval historians, points out that before the war the German navy had practised firing torpedoes in a freshwater lake in Schleswig, and he conjectures that

Prien's torpedo officers might have neglected to make adjustments for the heavier salt water. At any rate, a disgusted Prien complained to Admiral Karl Dönitz that he had been sent to war with the equivalent of 'wooden rifles'. In a few hours at Gallipoli, three of the largest vessels in the British fleet had gone to the bottom. Operation 'Rupert' might have been over and done with in a day at Harstad if Prien's torpedoes had detonated on 15 April. Kristiansen says: 'If the German torpedoes had functioned, Gallipoli would have looked like a children's birthday party.' For Churchill, it would have been a career-stopper.

War is supremely the domain of accident, and great flukes often decide great events. Although some scepticism is in order when introducing any speculation, Gunnar Hojem, head of Namsos's History Society, predicts an outcome even more dramatic had Churchill's army and navy commanders in Norway carried out his orders. 'If Churchill had done what he meant to do, it would have been a catastrophe. Maybe we'd all be wearing brown shirts still today.'

9
THE WINSTON IMPASSE

'He was all for instant recognition: he wanted the people to throw up their sweaty nightcaps and shout "Vive Winston!"'
STANLEY BALDWIN to NEVILLE CHAMBERLAIN, October 1940

'An ill fate . . . followed every step of the project.'
PHILIP JOUBERT DE LA FERTÉ, planner for the
operation to retake Trondheim

The Dardanelles, Jutland, the Peninsula, 1066. Churchill was sensitive to historical analogies. Cork's failure to capture Narvik on the anniversary of Churchill's most humiliating defeat hit hard in the wake of the cancellation of 'Hammer'. It also coincided with another anniversary: the seizure of the German submarine pens at Zeebrugge on St George's Day, 1918.

Churchill had barely received Cork's disappointing message when he was given further cause to brood on the historic battle of Zeebrugge.

The 'hero of Zeebrugge' was the Conservative MP for Portsmouth, Admiral of the Fleet Sir Roger Keyes – put back on the active list by Churchill two months earlier, in February, and described as someone not 'overburdened with a sense of proceeding through the normal channels'. When rumours reached Keyes of a prospective naval attack on Trondheim, the sixty-seven-year-old Admiral had sought a meeting with Churchill. Once upon a time, he had hastened to London to plead personally with Kitchener for permission to attack the Dardanelles. On 16 April, he turned up at the Admiralty to press a case for broaching Trondheimsfjorden.

If ever there was a person to outstrip Churchill in his desire for 'immediate offensive action' of the boldest possible nature, then it was Roger Keyes. In Operation 'Workshop', a plan that he prepared eight months later to seize the rocky Italian islet of Pantelleria, Keyes intended to crouch in the first assault boat, and when it was pointed out to him that he would be killed instantaneously, he replied: 'What better way to die!' In the words of his loyal wife Eva, he had a 'genius for making war'. As a lieutenant in China, Keyes had captured a fort which Russian and German generals judged too dangerous to attack. In the Boxer Rebellion, his short, compact figure had been the first to squeeze through the narrow sluice gate into the British Legation after he had scaled Peking's thirty-foot perimeter wall 'with his Union Jack in his teeth'. And on 23 April 1918, he had planned and led the Zeebrugge raid, blocking German shipping and submarines inside the Belgian ports of Zeebrugge and Ostend, an action which Churchill ranked 'as the finest feat of arms in the Great War, and certainly as an episode unsurpassed in the history of the Royal Navy'.

In Churchill's sentimental estimation, Keyes seemed 'to revive in our own generation the vivid personality and unconquerable spirit of Nelson'. On the day after Churchill returned to the Admiralty in September 1939, he promised the heroic veteran, or so Keyes had understood, 'that as soon as he has looked round he will find a "mission" for me, so I live in hope . . . I have faith in my Star.'

Keyes interpreted the attack on Trondheim in this providential light. He had heard rumours of difficulties, but, not permitted to know any details, he submitted a plan of his own, which involved using superannuated battleships and other 'oddments' to 'smash up the Norwegian ports'. Such an attack, Keyes believed, was divinely crafted for his talents, and he begged to be allowed to lead the mission. 'Some of the great Sea-Captains of old, who were left unemployed for many years, emerged while older even than I am, and struck a resounding blow at sea, and so would I.'

The interview with Churchill on 16 April failed to satisfy Keyes. Immediately it was over, Keyes despatched an indignant letter to his wife. 'He rang the bell half way through and said he was sorry he was tired and must rest,' and 'tried to dismiss me like an importunate beggar.'

Keyes sent Churchill another letter the next day, one of a salvo of fourteen marked 'secret and personal' that landed on the First Lord's desk during this period. 'Let me organise it . . . Pity we can't be ready on St George's Day. Why not? . . . It *can't* and won't fail if you let me do it, and be responsible for it. Back my good fortune . . . Our stars are linked.' He appealed to his exploits at Zeebrugge, to their joint support for the Dardanelles campaign. 'I know I represent the fighting spirit of the Navy. If my advice had been followed in 1915, when I fought almost single-handedly to be allowed to force the Dardanelles (which is now accepted as having been a feasible operation) the flower of the Turkish Army would have been cut off and decisively defeated, and we would have been spared the Palestine, Salonika and Mesopotamia campaigns . . . Give me the small force I asked for and the Royal Navy and its Sea Soldiers will show the world that they can stand up to any German air attack.' The operation that Keyes had in mind was 'a combination of Wolfe and Saunders in the St Lawrence; of what might have been done in the Dardanelles and Gallipoli . . . it runs through the books you inspired me to write, but can never have had time to read, or you would not have hesitated to listen to me.'

Churchill was in a difficult position. He had come to share Keyes's enthusiasm for a naval assault on Trondheim, and he had circulated Keyes's plans 'to hammer a way' into Trondheim harbour with R-class battleships. But as he wrote to his 'very devoted' friend, 'I have to be guided by my responsible Naval advisers,' most of whom, like Dudley Pound, confessed to a history of impatience in their dealings with the Admiral. When Churchill was forced to turn Keyes down, using the excuse that he was too old, Keyes's wife responded with ferocity.

On 23 April, the anniversary of the Zeebrugge raid, Eva Keyes wrote a private letter to Churchill admonishing him for his treatment of 'the universally recognised best man for the job of winning the war'. In the First World War, Clementine had gone behind her husband to the then Prime Minister, Herbert Asquith, writing him, he said, 'the letter of a maniac', in which she acknowledged that Churchill had his faults, 'but he has the supreme quality which I venture to say very few of your present or future Cabinet possesses – the power, the imagination, the deadliness to fight Germany'. Eva now wrote to Churchill, defending Keyes in the same chastising terms. 'It was a nasty shock for him to be told by you that he was too old for a command! although you did not consider Lord Cork too old for one.' She said of her husband, in words probably dictated by him: 'He has more ideas of war in his little finger than the whole Admiralty Staff put together, and he would not have let you be caught napping as you were in

Norway – even if the Navy has saved the situation for you since.' Her husband, Eva went on, had not simply 'saved your reputation over the Dardanelles'. He had done a colossal amount more to salvage Churchill's standing. 'I wonder if you realise how much you owe your present position to him? . . . for years, when many people were against you, he has been going round the country and in the House of Commons singing your praises . . . Many people told him that you were not to be trusted, that you were only out for yourself, but he assured them that they did not know you as he did, and he converted many. I begin to wonder if they were not right after all?'

It was only when Churchill repudiated him a second time, on 25 April, that Keyes learned from his former staff officer Pound, known to Keyes as 'Do-Nothing Dudley', that the proposed naval attack on Trondheim had been set aside as too risky – a whole week earlier.

On receiving this news, Keyes became, according to Alec Dunglass, 'so excited as to be almost incoherent, and apparently heading for a brainstorm'. Keyes fumed that Carton de Wiart, the army and the navy had been 'damnably' let down by the 'inexplicable ineptitude' of the Admiralty, whose refusal to attack Trondheim was 'deplorably pusillanimous and short-sighted'. He wrote to Churchill: 'Steinkjer will stink in the nostrils of the Navy until this disgrace is wiped out,' and in a separate letter urged Churchill not to delay: 'The Military situation is extremely critical and needs a bold stroke to save it.' Then in his twelfth letter, Keyes gave an ominous warning. 'If the scuttle is persisted in the Government will have to go and I shall do my damnedest to speed them.' Leo Amery visited Keyes on the morning of 29 April, and he heard him rage that Churchill had been 'the chief author of the scuttle, over-riding the Sea Lords, as well as the WO'. His blood up, Keyes made this promise to his wife. 'I don't think he will ever ring his bell to dismiss me again.'

On the night of 17 April, when General Hotblack fell down the Duke of York Steps, General Ironside dined with Churchill at the Admiralty. Ironside reflected of his host: 'He was very human' – as though it were Churchill who had taken the tumble. Ironside admitted to finding him 'a curious creature of ups and downs. Very difficult to deal with when in his downs.'

In his ups, Churchill enthralled and inspired. One of his researchers for the *History of the English-Speaking Peoples* recalled conversations at this time in Churchill's room about the Norman invasion. 'I still see the map on the wall, with dispositions of the British Fleet off Norway, and hear the voice of the First Lord as he grasped with his usual insight the strategic position in 1066 ... The distant episodes were as close and real as the mighty events on hand.'

Yet Churchill in his downs could be impossible, and there was no hiding the darkness or direction of his mood as the situation in Norway spiralled from his control.

Churchill had not really expected a German attack on Norway, despite going along with preparations for that possibility. Then when it came, he expected a quick victory. He had not achieved this. What he faced instead was an obscure and extraordinarily confusing situation which changed every moment, with people reacting to events that had happened some time before, and with no fast means of knowing the true state of affairs, because of his warships' radio silence, other than intercepts from southern Norway.

In this vacuum, only what he could follow with his finger on a map took on importance. When he looked at the charts pinned to the Admiralty wall, he was confronted by no Narvik, no Trondheim, and no good news from Åndalsnes, Namsos or Steinkjer – Peter Fleming had been in touch with the Norwegians at Steinkjer 'and had reported that they were in very low spirits'. Churchill's nephew Giles was a prisoner of the Nazis, and rumoured to be interned on a small island south of Denmark. Trusted dugouts like Cork and Carton de Wiart had proved disappointing; and however much the idea appealed to him, he dared not, in the teeth of opposition from his Chiefs of Staff, entrust Roger Keyes with a comparable command. Churchill's stewardship of the Norway Campaign was once again bringing into question his fitness as a leader. At No. 10, Colville wrote in his diary: 'The Norwegian Minister in Brussels gloomily prophesies a second Gallipoli in Norway.'

In its 1917 investigation into the Gallipoli Campaign, the Dardanelles Commission was struck 'by the atmosphere of vagueness and want of precision which seems to have characterised the proceedings of the War

Council'. In the second half of April 1940, the stress on the government's multi-layered decision-making machinery became intolerable for many similar reasons, and on Churchill in particular.

On 23 April, Ironside noted that 'Winston was a bit wild at the Cabinet . . . railing'. At the MCC meeting that day, Colville heard how Churchill was 'being maddening, declaring that we had failed at Namsos, and making the most unreasonable proposals'. It was plain to Colville that 'his verbosity and recklessness make a great deal of unnecessary work, prevent any real practical planning from being done and generally cause friction'. Churchill's volatile behaviour was also taking its toll on Chamberlain. 'The P.M. is depressed – more by Winston's rampages than by the inherent strategical difficulties with which we are confronted in Norway.' To Lady Halifax, the Prime Minister looked smaller and smaller each time she saw him, 'in fact he seems to shrivel before one's eyes'.

Chamberlain confessed to his sister that it had been 'one of the worst, if not the worst, weeks of the war, and for once I feel really tired'. He was having to take a tablet of Someral to sleep his usual five and a half hours, and he admitted to frayed nerves and 'constant gnawing anxiety'. He credited his exhaustion to Churchill's 'most difficult' attitude, 'challenging everything the Chfs of Staff suggested and generally behaving like a spoiled & sulky child. This was the committee over which he is supposed to preside but which he had got into an almost mutinous position. Next morning he wasn't much better in Cabinet and I heard from a friend who lunched with him [probably Kingsley Wood] that he had been complaining bitterly of being "thwarted" and not having sufficient powers.'

The Prime Minister believed strongly that 'the public must not think there are any differences in the Cabinet'. The following day, 24 April, he sent Churchill a handwritten note marked 'secret' asking him to come to Downing Street after dinner. 'I have been thinking over the Scandinavian situation and the rather unsatisfactory position in which it stands. I don't feel that I get your whole mind in Committee and should very much like to discuss it all with you in private.'

Colville led Churchill into the Prime Minister's room. The talk did not go well. 'He is proving a difficult colleague.'

Later that evening, Churchill sketched out his concerns in a letter that he appears not to have sent. 'My dear Neville,' he began. 'Being anxious to sustain you to the best of my ability, I must warn you that you are approaching a head-on smash in Norway.' The same finger that Churchill had stabbed at General Mackesy he now raised towards Chamberlain. 'No one is responsible for the creation & direction of military policy except yourself.' The MCC Chair which Churchill had accepted with eagerness three weeks before had become a chalice overspilling with poison, and having relinquished it to Chamberlain he was not willing to receive it back 'without the necessary powers . . . If you do not feel you can head it, with all your other duties, you will have to delegate your powers to a Deputy who can concert & direct the general movement of our war action.'

Churchill was making a pitch to be Chamberlain's deputy.

Colville understood that if the Prime Minister refused to acquiesce, Churchill threatened to go to the House and say he could take no responsibility for what was happening. And 'there would then be a first-class political crisis, because the country believes that Winston is the man of action who is winning the war and little realises how ineffective, and indeed harmful, much of his energy is proving itself to be'.

Chamberlain remained, as he admitted to Colville, 'at a loss how to solve the Winston impasse'. Meanwhile, Churchill's restless focus had switched once more, from Narvik back to central Norway where 'Maurice Force' and 'Sickle Force' were disintegrating. Inspired by Keyes's call for a bold stroke, Churchill made a final appeal for 'a revival in some form or other of Hammer'. But this was rejected on 26 April. Talk in the War Office was of evacuation, not attack. That evening came further shocking news.

Peter Fleming was reported dead, killed in a raid on Namsos.

10
EVACUATION

'The evacuation of Namsos has been referred to as a disaster like that of the evacuation of Gallipoli.'
FIELD MARSHAL LORD BIRDWOOD, House of Lords, 8 May 1940

'Norway was the dullest campaign in which I had taken part.'
MAJOR GENERAL CARTON DE WIART

In Namsos, the non-appearance of the navy had put a stop to any idea of attacking Trondheim. On the evening of 22 April, Birger Evensen drove General Carton de Wiart to a suitable place from which to send a signal for a British destroyer to pass on. At 8.29 p.m., a message transmitted on Fleming's portable H6a wireless reached the War Office. 'Steinkjer has been bombed and completely destroyed. Our men cannot fight off road owing to deep snow, this does not handicap the enemy who is using snow shoes . . . if a heavy raid on Trondheim had taken place I might have made a dash for Trondheim but now I clearly cannot do this.'

Burdened by his lack of equipment, Carton de Wiart saw little point in 'sitting out like rabbits in the snow'. He shared the same rule of attack as his fictional counterpart, Brigadier Ritchie-Hook – 'Never reinforce failure . . . In plain English that means: if you see some silly asses getting into a mess, don't get mixed up with 'em.'

The reply from the War Office did not make Carton de Wiart any more optimistic. 'For political reasons they would be glad if I would maintain my positions. I agreed, but said it was about all I could do. They were so relieved that they actually wired me their thanks.'

On Friday 26 April, Carton de Wiart sent Peter Fleming back to London to establish what was going on. At noon, a Sunderland flew Fleming to Scotland where he was delayed by fog, and he eventually reached London on Sunday morning by chartering a special train from Inverness. He wrote in his diary: 'Many congratulations at the Station Hotel as I had been reported killed the night before.'

Leland Stowe was the unreliable source. A Norwegian soldier had mistaken for Fleming the dead naval officer in the cellar of the bombed Grand Hotel in Namsos, who Fleming had worried was Martin Lindsay. The news was printed in the *Daily Sketch* beneath the headline 'AUTHOR KILLED IN NORWAY'. Fleming's mother reported to Geoffrey Dawson that Peter's brother Ian 'had a ghastly time until he found it was not true'.

Early on Sunday 28 April, Fleming delivered to the War Office the nine-page report that he had written while on the Sunderland. He then had an interview with Churchill 'in silk combinations & a cigar'. After asking if Churchill minded him lighting a pipe – 'Yes, I bloody well do!' – Fleming summarised the situation in Namsos, and enquired on Carton de Wiart's behalf about 'future plans'.

No minutes survive of the meeting. Relieved though Churchill would have been to see 'dear Peter' alive, he could not divulge a word to him about the Cabinet's latest plan – to withdraw from all parts of Norway except Narvik. This decision had been reached two days before, following another desk-thump from Ironside. 'Communications with "Sickle Force" have all gone to hell. Somebody will have to go and get the troops out of Åndalsnes before it's too late.'

'Pretty awful!' had been Cadogan's assessment of the War Cabinet on 26 April. Concern about the blow to Britain's prestige and the psychological effect on the public had led Ministers to order preparations for a withdrawal to go ahead 'in the greatest secrecy' – not even their French or Norwegian allies were to know. At the same time, the government hoped to postpone the evacuation until after the seizure of Narvik. Late in the day, Churchill's first love had become everyone else's *beau idéal* too.

Anticipating success in Narvik, Samuel Hoare, the new Secretary of State for Air – the Ministry which had contributed perhaps least to the campaign – gave a broadcast in which he strove to outsoar Churchill for uplifting rhetoric. 'Today our wings are spread over the Arctic. They are sheathed in ice. Tomorrow the sun of victory will touch them with its golden light, and the wings that flashed over the great waters of the north will bear us homewards once more to the "peace with honour" of a free people and the victory of a noble race.'

The capture of Narvik, Chamberlain now decided, would mitigate the effects of the withdrawal from central Norway, and give the public something to celebrate. 'We should then be able to claim it was a strategical triumph and emphasise that it was all part of our plan for concentrating our efforts on Narvik.'

As if these plans were not convoluted enough, Churchill had begun distancing himself from the rest of the Cabinet, pressing for a guerrilla force under Colonel Colin Gubbins to be left in the mountains behind Trondheim. Peter Fleming flew back to Namsos carrying a brown-paper bag stuffed with detonators for blowing up bridges and petrol dumps, and with orders to carry out 'a secret, complicated and as it turned out impossible task'.

Fleming reported to Carton de Wiart on 30 April: 'You can really do what you like, for they don't know what they want done.' Carton de Wiart had reached the same conclusion on receiving a signal from General Massy on 27 April. 'Evacuation decided in principle. Plan in your case gradual but rapid.' His instructions from the War Office over the next five days reflected London's continuing disarray. 'First to evacuate, then to hold on, then to evacuate.' When Carton de Wiart remonstrated with Massy, saying that he considered an evacuation from Namsos 'unsound in every way', Massy replied in panic: 'There is no, repeat no, question of any British or French troops being left behind at Namsos.'

The French were not told until 29 April. Through Fleming and Lindsay, instructions reached Frank Lodge in Steinkjer to pass on an oral message to the Chasseurs Alpins. 'Orders have been received from the War Office that you should rejoin the main force and return to the point of embarkation.' After half a day's trudge through the snow, Lodge came across the Chasseurs firing at a German reconnaissance plane that he recognised as 'Sammy'. He delivered Fleming's message, and asked the Chasseurs to follow him back to Namsos. For their retreat at least, the French troops possessed the proper equipment, recently arrived from Scotland. Without his own snowshoes or skis, Lodge was confined to a narrow path over the mountains, trekking single file in wet boots and socks through eighty miles of deep snow that froze at night to minus 30 degrees Fahrenheit.

Tom Fowler and B Company 4ᵗʰ Battalion Lincolnshire Regiment retreated from Steinkjer on the evening of 22 April. Fowler says: 'The Germans had bombed Steinkjer flat.' This was not the news that was broadcast on the BBC. Soldiers assembled around a farmhouse radio heard the announcer say in heartening tones that 'British expeditionary forces are pressing forward steadily from all points where they have landed in Norway . . . In the Namsos sector British and French are advancing successfully towards Trondheim, where German forces may soon be isolated.'

Listening to this, Stowe's Swedish photographer shook his head. 'What's the matter with those mugs? Are they crazy?'

The German bombing had destroyed B Company's kitbags of Arctic clothing, fur coats, special boots and socks, though this was not the setback it seemed. Carton de Wiart had observed that if his men 'wore all these things they were scarcely able to move at all, and looked like paralysed bears'.

Fowler grabbed dry clothing from the ruins. Major Stokes was wearing pyjamas under his battledress. Private Turner, also from B Company, had on a dinner jacket and a ski cap.

'We got moving,' Fowler says. 'Nobody had any food, nobody had any cigarettes, and we marched for two days like that, with nothing.'

It was snowing hard as they slithered northwards through the mud slush and the trees. They began to tear off and throw away their respirators, haversacks, overcoats, even their helmets – the pine branches scraping against the steel made too much noise. Fowler's hands were puffy and red with chilblains. At night, his feet and legs were too cold to feel. After stumbling through Asp, Namdalseid, Rodhammer and Skage, Fowler's platoon reached Namsos, and boarded the French merchant ship *El Kantara* on 2 May. Lieutenant Colonel Walter Hingston of 1/4 King's Own Yorkshire Light was one of those who threaded their way in the half-light between the remains of wooden houses, with only their brick chimneys standing 'like blackened totem poles', to the wharf. Looking back on that day, Hingston doubted 'whether British troops have ever been forced to retire with so little effort on the part of the enemy. On the other hand, it is also doubtful if a British force have ever before been asked to do so much with so little.'

As at Gallipoli, the evacuation from Norway was the only decently organised part of the campaign. The night before, 5,084 troops of Paget's

'Sickle Force' had been successfully extricated from Åndalsnes. That left Carton de Wiart, as he bleakly saw it, 'the only unenvied pebble on the beach. Alone against the might of Germany.'

Operation 'Klaxon', the evacuation of Carton de Wiart's 6,200 men from Namsos, was scheduled for the night of 1 May. But a dense sea mist prevented Captain Louis Mountbatten and his 5th Destroyer Flotilla from running up the fjord. Under the cover of fog, Mountbatten had turned back and passed the night at sea.

On 'that last, endless day' as Carton de Wiart called it, there was time enough for Fowler, Lodge, Fleming and Lindsay to absorb the devastation. According to a *Times* correspondent in Namsos, three days of incessant German bombing raids had resulted in an 'absolute destruction such as has never been witnessed in any war before. It is impossible to see where the streets used to run. All is just one knee-deep amorphous mass of charred and blackened debris.'

In the town's razed centre, Lindsay was reminded of pictures of Ypres. The thick snow did nothing to muffle the crackle of burning timber, like odd rifle shots, and banging and hammering from suspended pieces of steel. 'It sounded as if the dead were trying to force their way up through the ruins.'

Hjørdis Mikalsen, then aged twelve, went looking for her cat in the ruins, until someone told her that there was no point, the French would have eaten Nusse. 'Our house was pulverised,' she says. 'There was nothing left, not even a mug. Only a ghastly burnt smell that lingered for months and months.'

What had occurred at Namsos gave birth to a new word. Churchill wrote in a passage that he cut from the final manuscript of *The Gathering Storm*: 'The expression which I certainly used long afterwards, 'We mustn't get Namsosed', embodied that feeling of dread for this experience.' The word 'Namsosed' was to flash across Churchill's mind the following month at Dunkirk, during the North African landings, and in Sicily – to remind him of the 'perils and horrors of landing, or of evacuation, without the command of the air'.

Chamberlain had warned Churchill at the outset of the danger from the Luftwaffe. Norway had proved the Prime Minister right. He wrote to his sister that 'this brief campaign has taught our people, many of whom were much in need of teaching, the importance of the air factor'. The navy in particular, observed Peter Fleming, who had served in the frontmost line, had formed 'for the first time, a just and most disturbing appreciation of its limits in the face of air power'.

The ships came in through the sea mist. After a campaign lasting sixteen days, 'Maurice Force' was evacuated in the course of a few hours on the night of 2 May. 'It was the fog which saved them,' wrote Ironside.

On HMS *Afridi*, Captain Vian waited for thirty-five men from the Hallamshire Battalion of the York and Lancaster Regiment who had covered the retreat. At 3.15 a.m. with the rearguard safely on board, the *Afridi* cast off. In his final action before sailing, Vian ordered his pom-pom guns to open fire on the vehicles, now massed on the quay, which had arrived a few days earlier, and which, Fleming wrote, 'had made possible our withdrawal'. There was no time to load all the equipment that Carton de Wiart had requested. Six of the Chasseurs' newly delivered A.A. guns had had to be pushed into the fjord.

Fleming's instructions to embark on the *Afridi* with his men were changed as they waited to board. He came away with Lindsay and Carton de Wiart on HMS *York*. Fleming watched the last stragglers clatter onto the wharf through 'a sour, charred, flat mass of rubble, eerily and dangerously illuminated by a huge dump of inextinguishably burning coal'.

Conspicuous in his soft red hat, Carton de Wiart had not informed the Norwegians until the last moment that the Allies were deserting them. At 10.40 p.m., as the first Allied soldiers embarked, he entrusted his driver, Birger Evensen, with 'a very important task'. Birger was to take a letter from Carton de Wiart to Colonel Ole Getz at the Norwegian 5th Brigade HQ. 'It is with the deepest regret that I must let you know that we must evacuate this area . . . Our one hope is that we may return and help you bring your campaign to a successful conclusion. Believe us.'

In Wiltshire, it had been a beautiful May day, with the sun belting down on the sycamores under a blue sky. Frances Partridge felt 'physically sick' when she heard on the evening news about the complete withdrawal of British troops from central Norway. 'What I'm suffering from is the crushing of a hope, built on stronger foundations than I knew, of the war being ended quickly through the Norwegian campaign, and the realisation again of the immense strength of Germany.'

The German High Command issued a statement. 'In unresting pursuit of the wildly retreating English, German troops reached Åndalsnes and raised the Reich war flag there at 3 p.m. today.' William Shirer in Berlin witnessed Hitler's crowing. 'It would be hard to exaggerate the feeling of triumph in the Third Reich today . . . Germany has at last met the great British Empire in a straight fight and won hands down.'

In Ottawa, an apprehensive Canadian Prime Minister wrote in his diary: 'Hitler claims complete victory, has given the German Commander decoration of "Iron Cross".'

Medals and badges were also distributed to von Falkenhorst's troops. Awarded to all airmen, sailors and Alpenjägers, the 'Narvik Spange' entwined a propeller, an anchor and an edelweiss to mark the first occasion when Germany's three armed services had fought together. To strengthen his depleted Kriegsmarine, Admiral Raeder introduced a new Type-36A destroyer, unofficially named 'the Narvik class'.

Few attempts in Britain were made to celebrate the 'Norway veterans', and no specific Norway Campaign medal was struck. Frank Lodge was given a temporary medal ribbon, and later ordered to remove it and hand it back. Towards the end of his life he visited the Imperial War Museum with his wife Elaine. She says: 'There was a whole wall celebrating the battles of the Second World War, and he couldn't find Norway. "They've forgotten us, they don't want to know."' Lodge felt that he had been obliterated once already. On his return from Namsos, he learned that his parents had held a special service, believing him to have drowned in the icy waters off Lillesjona.

Some 1,896 British servicemen were killed, severely wounded or went missing in Norway, roughly the same number as Germans; and another 2,500 at sea. Of the 1,896, an estimated 150 died in battle. Tom Fowler's battalion lost eight men in and around Steinkjer. It took another seventy years to establish most of their graves. Two of the Lincolnshire Regiment's dead, Harry Prike and Ronald Smith, were wrongly named on a war memorial at Verdal, twenty miles from their actual burial places. These two young Lincolnshire territorials were the first British soldiers to fall in direct combat with the enemy in the Second World War. A third grave carried the name of stretcher-bearer Private Joseph Croft, from Woolwich. In fact, Croft was taken prisoner on 22 April, and ended up in a POW camp in Poland. After the war, he returned to Woolwich, for the rest of his life unaware that he was presumed buried at Skei church, five miles east of Steinjker. The body in the pine woods undisturbed in the snow for seven weeks was that of someone else.

In Britain, moves to bury the Norway Campaign commenced almost at once. Tom Fowler went on leave as soon as he got home, and was told by senior officers not to talk about Norway. On a visit to a friend in Lincoln Barracks, he was stopped by the sergeant who asked where his cap badge was. 'I said: "I lost it." "Where's your rifle?" "I lost it." "Your respirator?" "Lost it." "Where did you manage to lose all this stuff?" "In Norway, sarge." "Oh, you are one of them," he said with a bit of disgust, as though it was a crime we'd committed.'

Since returning to Krogs Farm in 2010, Fowler has not stopped talking about what he witnessed there in April 1940. 'Seven days a week,' grumbles his wife Gwen. 'That's why I take my hearing aid out.' Ignoring her, he repeats: 'We were the first ones into action. I say so, but nobody takes an interest. You never hear of Norway.'

'The whole thing is so damned silly.' That was the last thought of Evelyn Waugh's dandy-aesthete Cedric Lyne, before a bullet killed him instantly in the mountains above Åndalsnes. In this respect, Hitler was right about the British invasion. 'From the military point of view, it can only be described as frivolous dilettantism.' The campaign had been such a 'lamentable, footling, butter-fingered' shambles that the Labour MP Ellen Wilkinson suggested that from now on the Women's Auxiliary should be entrusted to hold the Western Front.

German losses at sea were considerable, but so were Germany's gains. She had safeguarded her principal supply of iron ore, in the same stroke denying export of Swedish ore to Britain from Narvik. She also had bases which were much nearer to ports in the north of England and Scotland. No one regarded Hitler's advantage with more trepidation than General Ironside. 'We are on the defensive and the Germans have the initiative. He can do what he likes. Where will he go next?'

In Oslo, on the eve of the German attack, Curt Bräuer, the Nazi Minister, had invited 220 guests at short notice to his Embassy to watch a documentary 'peace' film *Feuertaufe*, about the invasion of Poland. In the final scene, a map of Britain went up in flames to the music of Wagner, fulfilling the promise that Hitler had made six years before in his interviews with Dr Rauschning: 'Today there is no such thing as an island. I shall land on the shores of Britain. I shall destroy her towns from the mainland.'

In Ottawa, Canada's Prime Minister believed that he was witnessing the overshadowing of the British Empire by the most devilish powers the world had ever seen. 'It must be a dark and sombre night in the British isles.'

Harold Nicolson learned of the evacuation at Lord Salisbury's house in Arlington Street, where he found a downcast crowd of government critics, including Louis Spears who thought that 'we were heading for complete disaster'. If the Germans could invade Norway with impunity, why not Scotland? 'The general impression is that we may lose the war,' wrote Nicolson. 'We part in gloom.'

Sprawled out on a big red armchair in Halifax's room at the Foreign Office, the American Ambassador Joseph Kennedy reported in his bluff Boston voice that a meeting of US attachés had agreed that England 'would be beaten' in the war.

In her Wiltshire farmhouse on that grilling hot evening, Frances Partridge watched a friend, looking pale and ill, turn to her husband Ralph.

'You don't think it's possible we might lose the war?'

'Certainly it's possible.'

A German invasion looked likeliest to those who had fought her soldiers, sailors and pilots in Norway. The fear of it preoccupied Peter Fleming as the convoy steamed home from Namsos. In an unpublished novel that he began to write shortly after arriving back in England, he imagined the worst. 'For hundreds, perhaps thousands of years, 1940 will be part of the ABC of history like 1066 before it: the year in which England was conquered.'

With his own candid eyes, Fleming had seen the capabilities of the German war machine. The Luftwaffe delivered its final punch to 'Maurice

Force' as the Allied ships entered the open sea, after having disembarked from Namsos without leaving a man behind. At 8.45 a.m., German dive-bombers attacked the French destroyer *Bison* and HMS *Afridi*, sinking both vessels. Fleming and Lindsay felt that they should have been among the 105 dead. Ordered home on the *Afridi*, they would not easily forget how they had been switched to HMS *York* at the very last moment.

Fleming wrote of his experience: 'When men escape from mortal danger, the mere act of survival has a curiously moving and even exhilarating effect upon them.' At the same time, he knew that 'however daringly executed, a military evacuation is an ignoble proceeding . . . it leaves behind it bitterness and a squalid havoc'. Reprieved, both Fleming and Lindsay resolved, as soon as they got back, to expose the deficiencies in Britain's armed forces and political leadership; the former through his contacts on *The Times*, the latter by using his political connections in the House of Commons.

In the secret report that he had prepared for Churchill three days earlier, Fleming wrote of Martin Lindsay that he had been nothing but 'untiring, resourceful and cool'. As the *York* pitched home through the heavy swell, and the tired soldiers slept or sang or vomited on the crowded decks, Lindsay gave vent to raw anger. His daughter says: 'My father was direct. He was very determined and convincing, and made as many enemies as friends, but if he thought someone should know something, he would tell them, definitely.'

Lindsay believed that his expeditions across Greenland had owed their success to two factors: 'the skilful arrangement of the smallest details', and 'the efficiency of the equipment' – since the penalty for an error leading to 'the breakdown of an article on a journey may be death by cold or hunger.'

In Norway, a disregard for details and equipment had risked the lives of British servicemen and their French and Polish allies. Among the returning soldiers on deck were 'a very high percentage of shock cases . . . due to unremitting bombing with nobody replying'. In this, as in other aspects – 'vital parts left behind or on wrong boats, no transport, no medical equipment and very little food' – the planners of 'Maurice Force' had demonstrated a negligence that was beyond forgiveness, Lindsay felt.

Before crossing Greenland on his 1,200-mile sledge journey, Lindsay had visited Smithfield market to be taught how to kill and skin a dog – a lesson that he drew on after he was obliged to shoot his huskies. With the training that he had perfected in the Arctic, Lindsay set about flaying the authorities whose responsibility it had been to transport, equip and protect him.

On board HMS *York*, with the battle for Norway as hard to erase from his mind as the mud and ash on his uniform, Lindsay began writing a 'memorandum', as he described it, which encapsulated what he and Fleming had witnessed from the moment that they touched down in Namsenfjorden on 14 April.

A strict radio silence was observed for the next three days as the convoy zigzagged back across the North Sea. It was during this time that MPs and the public were made aware that the expedition to Norway had not been the 'gallant picnic' which the press and the Admiralty had led them to believe it would be, but a military catastrophe to rank alongside Gallipoli, Black Week in the Boer War, and the Crimea.

On the afternoon of Thursday 2 May, Chamberlain made his first statement about the Norwegian Campaign, breaking the news to a House which for three weeks had been willing to go along with Churchill's claim that Hitler's occupation of Norway and Denmark was a blunder. A lobby journalist registered the gigantic shock that was given to the House by the Prime Minister's announcement of the withdrawal of our Forces from Southern Norway. 'This was a rushing disappointment after great expectations had been raised.'

A member of the government told Ronald Tree that he had 'never seen the House in such a disgruntled and sullen mood. He also said that while our own side were prepared for what was coming, the Socialists were taken entirely by surprise & were stunned.' Even so, the government was still 'very shaken', the Conservative MP Paul Emrys-Evans wrote to Lord Cranborne, 'and I am told that they actually thought of sending for L[loyd] G[eorge], so they must have been almost in extremis.'

Chamberlain struggled manfully to camouflage the defeat. He insisted that the Royal Navy had successfully withdrawn Allied troops from Åndalsnes 'under the very noses of the German aeroplanes', and that 'the balance of advantage' rested with the Allies. His reference to the fact that German naval losses now enabled Britain to reinforce the Mediterranean Fleet was received by his front bench with cheers. A. J. Sylvester listened in disbelief. 'He might have been announcing a great victory rather than a defeat.' Any setback was blamed on fifth columnists and their 'long-planned, carefully-elaborated treachery', and 'almost unarmed' Norwegian troops. Maisky, seated in the Diplomatic Gallery, gained the impression that 'Chamberlain is clearly bankrupt'.

The Prime Minister ended by asking the House not to discuss the situation, as it risked endangering men's lives because 'certain operations are still in progress', suggesting that the navy was still withdrawing troops from Namsos.* When he concluded his speech, Ed Murrow noted, 'there was a flat, dead silence'. In response to a demand by the Liberal leader Archie Sinclair 'to have more than one day's Debate' on the failure of the expedition, Chamberlain promised a full statement on the following Tuesday by both himself and the First Lord, with an extra day if necessary.

That night, a despairing Harry Crookshank, Financial Secretary to the

* Some would blame this premature announcement for the sinking of the *Afridi*.

Treasury, wrote in his diary: 'What a Govt. What a P.M. They must go soon.'

Outside the House of Commons, the shock to a hitherto tolerant population was dramatic. Up until this moment, the news that things had not gone well had failed to spill out, despite a deep thirst for information. 'The campaign in Norway is our main interest,' Frances Partridge admitted. 'While these sensational events are happening, all other interests are submerged in intense painful excitement.' Yet as A. J. Sylvester noted in his diary, 'on the pretext of not giving information to the enemy (about things on which he is obviously well informed)', the government had shown 'a curious lack of touch with public opinion'.

In the Essex village of Tolleshunt D'Arcy, the great lid of secrecy and silence had meant that it had been impossible for Margery Allingham to obtain a clear picture. Petrol rationing limited travel. Practically no one used the telephone. Instead, everyone absorbed in the drama of Norway had to follow it, either by listening to BBC bulletins – it was at this time that 'the tremendous importance of the wireless to us ordinary country people first became so very obvious' – or else by reading newspapers that were censored and drastically reduced in size: the *Observer* soon shrank to eight pages after the German invasion cut off Norwegian newsprint.

The most alarming aspect to Allingham was the complete absence of anything but 'medicated news'. It would have further distressed her to learn how the owner of the *Daily Express*, Max Beaverbrook, had inserted fabricated reports in the closing stages of the Norway Campaign. On 1 May, Beaverbrook gleefully told Leo Amery of 'the false news he has been putting in to cover our withdrawal'. In Canada, Prime Minister Mackenzie King suspected earlier than most British politicians the degree to which 'we have been given much too one-sided accounts in all our papers . . .' In Downing Street, Colville watched the faces at the Cabinet table grow longer and longer – and suddenly realised that even Ministers had been 'partially misled by the extravagant optimism of the press.' The Information Minister John Reith had to admit that he knew 'no more about what was happening in Norway than the man in the street'.

Already, the paucity of good news had begun to sap the confidence of those who recalled Churchill's invigorating promise to sink every German ship in the Skagerrak. As Evelyn Waugh noted in *Men at Arms*, 'the smell of failure had been borne to them from Norway on the East wind'. The numbers of people carrying gas masks in Piccadilly Circus trebled. To Frances Partridge, her Wiltshire Downs looked dried out and colourless beneath a heavy, battleship-coloured cloud. Round and round in her head went the possibility of air raids on London.

Scales tumbled from eyes with Chamberlain's interim statement in the Commons, with the return of 'Maurice Force' and 'Sickle Force', and with Leland Stowe's syndicated and unvarnished reports on the fall of Steinkjer.

When Violet Bonham Carter learned of the evacuation on 2 May, she felt 'completely "winded" with horror & amazement – for we had heard nothing from Govt. spokesmen but the most optimistic forecasts & reports'. After all the talk of victory, Britain's armed forces turned out to have nothing to show for their opening clash with the German war machine, other than what Stowe headlined as a 'catastrophic defeat' in central Norway and a 'stalemate' at Narvik – where that unhappy pair Mackesy and Cork sat in furious impotence waiting for the Arctic snow to thaw.

The effect of this discovery on Margery Allingham was 'almost indescribable'. It was, she wrote, like suddenly noticing that the man driving the charabanc in which you were careering down an S-bend mountain road was slightly tight and not a brilliant driver. 'I thought the Government was working like a fiend to get ready for a smashing spring offensive, probably in the north, and I thought we were incomparably better equipped, especially in the air, than we turned out to be . . . It never occurred to me that we were in such danger.'

On his arrival back in London, Peter Fleming observed behaviour that was 'scarcely capable of rational explanation' – people's complete failure, until this moment, to take the possibility of invasion into account, 'as though a kind of black-out had expunged from their minds, and even from their instincts, the lessons of history'.

In Poland, we were not there; we had not seen it. Norway made tangible for the first time the disastrous picture of what happened when Hitler succeeded. It reminded everyone that the British Isles were not unconquerable after all. At the Soviet Ambassador's residence in Mayfair, Maisky asked Moscow for instructions how to conduct himself 'if the Germans were to occupy the district in London in which our Embassy is situated'. The American Embassy prepared to advise all 4,000 US citizens in Britain to return home by way of Éire. Baba Metcalfe's sister watched the new 'Irene' barrage balloon, which had been named after her, float in the sky above Regent's Park like a great silver elephant. 'Each day and night we have been expecting the German bombers and tanks to arrive.'*

A captive of the Nazis, Giles Romilly could not inform British readers about the circumstances in which unsupported and insufficiently equipped British battalions had been badly cut up in Norway. In effect, Leland Stowe filed for him. 'Everything was very clear now. It was not only a defeat; it was a rout, and behind the rout lay a colossal, almost unbelievable blunder.'

The reports by 'one of America's most respected newspapermen', as A. J. Sylvester called Stowe, spread consternation not just in Whitehall. On 3 May, the social research organisation Mass Observation noted two marked tendencies. A soaring distrust of news channels, and a rapid increase in pessimism. The journalist Kingsley Martin paced up and down the terrace of the House of Commons with Conservative MP Sir Ralph Glyn. 'He told me the Home Guard had really nothing to fight with except garden tools, because the only rifles we had were on the high seas coming from the United States.' Frances Campbell-Preston was a friend both of Giles Romilly and Peter Fleming, and a future lady-in-waiting to the Queen Mother. She was living in Scotland when she heard about the evacuation from Namsos. She says: 'We talked about how we would go into caves, Bonnie Prince Charlie and all that.'

How would Britain escape the Blitzkrieg? How could these disasters have happened? Who was responsible? Mingled with the panic and fear came demands for 'unmedicated' explanations – and for heads. Margery Allingham's villagers represented the nation in wanting to hear about the causes of the failure, what had gone wrong with the timing, 'who had muffed it'.

---

* An indication of the utter lack of readiness was Walter Monckton's suggestion at the Ministry of Information to decide 'immediately on a pass-word, an English word with a "W" and an "R" in it preferably. But such a word that every German (with very rare exceptions) will be known to mispronounce.' This password should be demanded of 'any suspicious-looking people in various disguises who might be dropped from parachutes . . . these parachutists might find themselves in difficulties if they were unable to pronounce the pass-word to the satisfaction of the challenger. There seems to be quite a lot in this idea.' Yet at least two of the War Cabinet, Halifax and Churchill, could not pronounce their 'r's or 's's.

For the first time in the war, Allingham noticed an odd phenomenon. Public life became melodramatic, and private life formal and ordinary. Living in Tolleshunt D'Arcy 'was like following a quiet domestic film which had been accidentally photographed on the negative of a sensational thriller'.

The setting for that thriller was Westminster. Once Chamberlain had responded to Attlee's call and committed himself to a debate in the Commons, promising fuller information about the planning of the Norwegian military expedition, he exposed his leadership to every sort of rival and would-be assassin. Allingham sensed the fear and tension rising in her village. Tolleshunt D'Arcy – or Auburn as she fictionalised it – had 'something far more serious to worry about than even the loss of the Norseland coast. Auburn was worrying about the Prime Minister.'

Five years as Viceroy of India had taught Halifax about civilian unrest, and he smelled the gunpowder in the air. The Foreign Secretary recognised that 'the debate is likely to range over wider ground than Norway alone'. He had 'no doubt the affair will do the Govt. and the Allies a great deal of mischief'.

Potentially more damaging than 'the fiasco in Norway', as Labour's garrulous spokesman Hugh Dalton publicly referred to it, was the battlefront that Colville saw opening up in the House of Commons. 'What disgusts me is that everybody is concentrating their energies on an internal political crisis (à la française) instead of taking thought for the morrow about Hitler's next move.' When MPs learned further details about the reasons for the awful reverse, then it was bound to bring to a head the accumulated discontent of the past three years.

The Conservative MP Chips Channon viewed the coming storm with a churning stomach. 'A Westminster war added to a German one is really too much.' General Ironside regarded the fallout among his colleagues with the same revulsion. The War Cabinet, he wrote in his diary, 'were thinking more of public opinion than of the military disaster', and he noted how every Minister, 'including the P.M.', was beginning to make up stories they could tell the public.

The stories needed to be exceptional. On 3 May, Ironside heard that 'there is a first-class row commencing in the House and there is a strong movement to get rid of the P.M.' A young Conservative backbencher had told Leland Stowe on the eve of his departure for Norway that it would take nothing short of a major disaster to remove Neville Chamberlain. 'Well, Steinkjer was a disaster,' Stowe now pointed out. 'Maybe there is enough dynamite here even to rock 10 Downing Street?'

Leo Amery felt so. 'It is all terrible, and must mean the end of the Government and perhaps of Winston as well.'

These impassioned conversations continued as the convoys from Namsos and Åndalsnes steamed towards Scapa Flow on Saturday 4 May and Sunday 5 May. General Ironside had considered it nothing less than his duty to remain in London that weekend – unlike two thirds of the War Cabinet. He could not damp down his contempt for his political masters as he prepared to travel north to welcome back the troops. 'Most of the Ministers are away for the Sunday and they are all employed making up the speeches which they will have to make to excuse their operations. A miserable state of affairs.'

PART THREE

THE WEEKEND BEFORE

11
MONSIEUR J'AIMEBERLIN

'Chamberlain. What a man. With a face like a nutcracker and a soul like a weasel.
How long are the English going to put up with the bastards who run the country?'
MARTHA GELLHORN to H. G. WELLS, 13 June 1938

'He seemed the reincarnation of St. George . . . I don't know what this country has
done to deserve him.'
CHIPS CHANNON MP, 28 September 1938

'When the perspective of time has lengthened, all stands in a different setting. There
is a new proportion. There is another scale of values.'
WINSTON CHURCHILL, from his valediction on NEVILLE CHAMBERLAIN,
12 November 1940

As HMS *York* carried Fleming and Lindsay back from Norway, the Prime
Minister's chauffeur drove Neville Chamberlain and his wife to Chequers
for a 'much needed rest'.

The War Cabinet had a scheme in which three out of the nine Ministers
remained in London on Sunday. A new rota system meant that when it was
his turn off Chamberlain could leave town on Friday. He planned to use the
weekend to prepare his statement for the debate on Norway.

In those days, the Prime Minister had to provide his own car and chauffeur out of his salary. In the back of his Armstrong Siddeley – upon buying
which he had remarked cheerfully: 'One may as well reach the Bankruptcy
Court in comfort!' – Chamberlain's mood was 'light-hearted'. The evacuation had been successful; the political situation at home had improved. He
was aware that various MPs were scheming to overthrow the government,
but he thought that the situation was not so serious as his Minister of Information maintained. Chamberlain consoled himself that the press and
'the good British public', in spite of their anxieties, remained broadly

supportive of his leadership. His spirits lifted further on arriving at Chequers, shortly after 6.30 p.m., to see that the new summer house had been erected. The wild cherries were in bloom, and three willow tits sat in the bird boxes.

Chamberlain hated to be disturbed at weekends. He never took a Private Secretary with him to Chequers, or his typist Miss Watson. Until the outbreak of war, he had communicated with the world from a single telephone in the pantry, to be used for emergencies.

One of very few regular guests invited to the Prime Minister's country retreat in Buckinghamshire was his twenty-one-year-old niece Valerie Cole, who lived with the Chamberlains in London. She said: 'When they went to Chequers, I went. He had a chauffeur called Card who used to drive me mad. He would never drive over twenty miles per hour. Nothing would make him go quicker.' In this last respect, the devoted and long-serving Mr Card was not unlike his employer.

Valerie had a room on the top floor at No. 10, and was accustomed to what his critics saw as her uncle's unsociableness. The only time her aunt scolded her was when Valerie invited back an Irish Guards officer to Downing Street. 'She was very protective of Uncle Neville. She didn't want people to bother him.' The result of this tight shield around the Prime Minister, wrote one of his earliest biographers, Derek Walker-Smith, whose unauthorised study of Chamberlain had come out a few weeks before, was 'an almost complete ignorance . . . as to his tastes and habits in private life'.

No word got into the press, for instance, about the close family connection between the Prime Minister – whose public persona was characterised by a reputation for humourless sobriety coupled with a fastidiousness in his business dealings – and the bankrupt remittance man who had earned the title of 'the biggest practical joker in England'. Valerie's spendthrift father – Anne Chamberlain's brother – was Horace de Vere Cole, known by Augustus John as 'the God of Mischief'.*

* His pranks included challenging athletes to midnight races in the streets, and yelling out 'Stop thief!' when they were well ahead. Another involved him sharing a taxi up Piccadilly with a tailor's dummy. As he passed a policeman, de Vere Cole halted the taxi, opened the door and started banging the dummy's head on the pavement, shouting 'Ungrateful hussy!' For his most enduring hoax, he blackened the faces of a group of friends, including the young Virginia Woolf, and inspected the

Mischief produced no income, though. By the 1930s, Chamberlain was having to pay his brother-in-law a weekly stipend of £3. De Vere Cole died destitute in France in 1936, the year before Chamberlain took over from Stanley Baldwin, but he had always considered Neville 'incurably modest and un-selfassertive' – and far too old to be Prime Minister. At first glance, no two men could have been more opposite in character or led more different lives.

With no one to provide for Valerie, the Chamberlains extricated de Vere Cole's teenage daughter from a French convent and brought her to stay in Downing Street. Valerie helped her aunt to decorate the upstairs quarters, and acted as a hostess when she was away, causing Chamberlain to note with amusement that the presence of his very attractive and vivacious niece had a powerfully concentrating effect upon some of his other guests. Right up to her death in 2011, Valerie spoke of Uncle Neville almost as though he had been the victim of one of her father's crueller tricks. 'He had a reputation for being cold. He wasn't at all cold. He was amusing and he was interesting and he was kind. What more can you have?'

Neville Chamberlain once wrote to his sister Hilda: 'I often think to myself that it's not I but someone else who is P.M.' Cold. Aloof. Weak. Vain. Stubborn. A dupe. A radio-set tuned to Midland Regional. Above all, a failure. This is the Chamberlain that persists. During a dinner at Geoffrey Shakespeare's house in 1933, Lloyd George's son Gwilym described Chamberlain as 'the sort of man who would make an efficient Mayor of Birmingham in a lean year'. Yet these attributes were not always encountered in the flesh, and they did not describe the whole man.

On a wet moonless night in the second week of October 1939, Churchill invited the Chamberlains to dinner in his private apartment at Admiralty House. Incredibly, this was the first occasion on which the two men and their wives had dined together socially, despite having known each other

---

battleship HMS *Dreadnought* at Weymouth, having persuaded Admiral May, who greeted the party in full dress uniform, that the distinguished foreign visitors were Prince Makalen of Abyssinia and his suite. The incident became a moment of unsurpassed embarrassment for the Royal Navy, as painful in its way as the failure of Churchill's fleet to prevent German destroyers from reaching Narvik. Little boys pursued the humiliated May in the street for months afterwards, calling out 'Bonga Bonga'.

politically since 1900, when Chamberlain's statesman father, the famous 'Joe', had canvassed for Churchill in Oldham. Joseph Chamberlain had driven with Churchill in an open carriage to a meeting where he had spoken for over an hour, and so helped secure Churchill's first election victory by a margin of 230 votes.

An appreciative Churchill had come to view Joseph Chamberlain, 'this extraordinary man' – perhaps the only man Churchill was frightened of – as a paternal figure. 'I must have had a great many more real talks with him than I ever had with my own father.' No comparable warm fraternal feelings had developed between himself and Joe's youngest son. Neville Chamberlain was speaking for both of them when he wrote of Churchill, who was five years younger: 'There is too deep a difference between our natures for me to feel at home with him or to regard him with affection.' Quoted in the *Birmingham Daily Post* in January 1907, Chamberlain suggested that the sooner the bumptious Churchill 'was sent as Ambassador to Timbuctoo, the better it would be for the country and the Empire'.

Within No. 10 Downing Street, Churchill was known as 'the wild man'. In her diary entry for the evening of the dinner party, Churchill's seventeen-year-old daughter Mary revealed the pet name by which their guests were known in the Churchill household. 'Hectic preparations all p.m. for Les "J'aimeberlins". I wish Mummie wouldn't fuss so hectically over everything. The dinner went off quite satisfactorily . . . I think Mrs Chamberlain is lovely & v. sweet, but she asks "cuckoo" questions . . . Mr Chamberlain seems very nice.'

The Churchills had telephoned the Chamberlains beforehand to ask if they liked oysters and champagne. Anne wrote in her account of the evening: 'I said no oysters as we were rather afraid of them in view of the fish regulations. No champagne, as we were rather humble and as Neville never liked it. At dinner, however, there was champagne, upon which I remarked, and Winston said he drank a pint of champagne every night of his life and had done so for years. I said "How awkward, because then if you want to feel a little extra happy as I hope to do tonight . . ." He replied: "I take a little more." '

The evening was an eye-opener for Churchill. Perhaps because of the champagne, Chamberlain unwound at the small round table in what his wife thought was a 'very dingy' dining room converted from the day nursery. The Prime Minister talked not about the war or politics or Birmingham. Instead, he spoke of his life as a young man struggling to survive in the Bahamas. Mary Churchill observed that 'my father was gripped'.

Churchill, amazingly, had no knowledge of this aspect of Chamberlain's past, but from then on he formed a more substantial opinion of his 'chief', even if he did not communicate this in *The Gathering Storm*, other than to say: 'What a pity Hitler did not know when he met this sober English politician with his umbrella at Berchtesgaden, Godesberg and Munich that he was actually talking to a hard-bitten pioneer from the outer marches of the British Empire!'

In what Churchill later described as 'really the only intimate social conversation that I can remember with Neville Chamberlain amid all the business we did together over nearly twenty years', the Prime Minister spoke of the six years that he had lived on his own on the island of Andros, endeavouring to grow sisal for his father. As Churchill had done, but two years before him, Chamberlain had visited Cuba, riding through thick forests where sunlight never penetrated. On a sugar plantation in Guantanamo

Bay, Chamberlain had discovered 'the finest cigars in the world'. The cigars were a defence against the horseflies known as '*hard to dead*'. Chamberlain smoked them from sunup to dusk.

The First Lord, it turned out, was not the only member of the War Cabinet who enjoyed Havana cigars, possessed a nose for Chateau Montbrun, had not been to university, had a relative whom he revered and an American mother (Chamberlain's stepmother was the daughter of a US Secretary of War), and built walls with his bare hands. On a rise near Mastic Point, the twenty-two-year-old Chamberlain had constructed a five-foot stone wall and a thatched dwelling with a wine cellar. The Umbrella Man in pince-nez and wing collar, who had arrived back from Munich fluttering a barren sheet of paper, had dived for conches in nine feet of water. He had caught native octopuses from the deck of his schooner *Pride*, and an eleven-foot shark that took six men to haul onto the beach. He had grown whiskers and a beard, and worn dirty cotton trousers, which he tied around the leg with string when he walked. '*Then he ain't look heah nor dah, but he go right off*,' his labourers muttered, unable to catch up. '*It want one horse to follow him.*'

On the 100-mile-long island, there was a white population of three. Days passed, ten at a time, when Chamberlain did not set eyes on another white face. His closest companions were a pet iguana, five foot long, that he fed on bread; a praying mantis which he housed in a glass-topped box; and a Cuban bloodhound, Don Juan.

It was on Andros that his biographers first detected a trait: how every dog 'spontaneously attached itself' to him.

Followed at heel by Don Juan, Chamberlain strode out at five each morning to oversee a workforce of 250 black Bahamians, labouring alongside them with a machete while they sang, '*Work away boys, work away*,' and the chorus, '*Oh Mr Chimblin lumbah!*' With a gift for mimicry that he had succeeded in hiding from Churchill for forty years, Chamberlain recalled his men's patois.

In his six years on Andros, 'Mr Chimblin' cleared 7,000 acres to grow sisal for rope. He planted cotton between the sisal rows to choke the weeds. He built a railway – and almost blew himself to smithereens when blasting a two-mile track through the coral. At night, he sat round the campfire with his workers, some of whom baptised their sons after him.

Chamberlain was an enthusiastic amateur naturalist. On Andros, he studied the local birds and learned their calls. He shot and messily skinned the rarer species, scraping away the flesh and hanging them to dry from the rafters out of the reach of rats. Then, following the example of W. H. Hudson who from the Argentine pampas had sent the skins of 500 shot birds to the Smithsonian Institution, Chamberlain presented his Bahamian skins to the British Museum, including a Northrop's Oriole that had not been found anywhere else.

For six years, Chamberlain stuck it out, obedient to the family motto, *Je Tiens Ferme*, as his father enjoined him. But what he had assured his father was 'the best site available in the Bahamas' turned out to be 'seven thousand acres of worthless land'. The shed burnt down, with a loss of thirty-two bales. The price of sisal collapsed – a result of Neville growing it so successfully, joked his sisters. In fact, American buyers had rejected his first plants as too stiff. His mature plants turned yellow and shrivelled, the thin layer of soil an exhausted rehearsal for his policy with Hitler. In 1897, he put down his machete and wrote to his family:

I'm goin' 'ome! I'm goin' 'ome.
My ship is at the shore

I'm goin' to pack my 'aversack
I ain't goin' back anymore!

The failure of the Andros Fibre Company lost his father £50,000 (£6 million in today's prices), but 'in spite of all the disappointments it was a great experience, and I know that I am much the better and stronger for it'. It had taught Chamberlain the politician's virtues of independence, resilience and self-sufficiency, and planted in him the same 'very tough fibre', as Churchill said approvingly and accurately, that Chamberlain had struggled to bring forth in his *agave rigida sisalana* leaves, and made him refuse to admit defeat. He told his sisters more than thirty years later: 'All the time there was a hard core in me that only appeared when circumstance for the time cut away the covering.' But he hated to be 'in a position that reminds me of the Bahamas when the plants didn't grow'.

In 1921, Chamberlain had sold his 7,000 acres to his agent's son Neville for £200, and bought an antique French cabinet. All that survives of the Andros Fibre Company are some chimney remains and the foundations of a shed. Plus the skins of forty-nine birds that he donated to the Natural History Museum 'which had but a poor collection from the Bahamas Islands'.

Neville Chamberlain's bird collection is today stored in Tring. It has received only one enquiry in the last twenty-five years, for a species of loggerhead shrike hitherto unrecorded in the Bahamas. The Dutch curator in charge, Hein van Grouw, admits: 'I'd never heard of Chamberlain.' From a cardboard box, he takes out and examines a black-and-white merlin, and is unimpressed by its taxidermist's skills. 'The head is not supported, the beak should point straight forward,' and demonstrates how Chamberlain would have had to tie the twine over the depressed beak, make an incision in the throat with a scalpel, and peel off the skin like an orange; then rub the insides with arsenical soap to stop moths from eating the feathers. 'He knew how to skin, but not how to stuff.' Chamberlain had filled the merlin's eye-sockets with white cotton gathered from his cotton plants, and padded out the belly with a curious brown woolly material. Van Grouw flips open the unstitched skin, pokes a finger inside.

'That looks like sisal,' he says.

It takes a moment to absorb what we are staring at – the fruit of six years' hard labour in the Caribbean. A few bales were sold for a mixture to make straw hats. Otherwise, the only use of Chamberlain's sisal was to stuff forty-nine dead birds which have never been put on display.

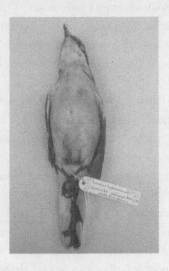

Messily dissected and hidden away, Chamberlain has suffered the fate of his bird collection. A yellow-and-mauve dahlia named for him in September 1939 was never registered. There is a blue plaque outside his house at 37 Eaton Square, which Chamberlain rented for a while to the Nazi Ambassador, Joachim von Ribbentrop, but he has no public statue in London, nor in Birmingham, the city identified with his name; or anywhere else in Britain. A Lord Mayor with an outstanding record of public service, one of our most successful Chancellors and Ministers of Health, Prime Minister for three of the most vital years in our history, and leader of the Conservative Party – Neville Chamberlain has been erased from the picture like the Russian Ambassador Ivan Maisky on his return to Moscow.

Only in Lisbon was a large monument to him commissioned, to stand in front of the Palácio das Necessidades and to be entitled 'To Chamberlain, from Thankful Mothers'. By December 1938, the project had raised the considerable sum of £13,420 (worth £830,000 in today's money), and a local sculptor, Diogo de Macedo, was appointed to commemorate in lasting stone that brief but still-astonishing moment when Chamberlain was regarded as 'the world's life-buoy'. Chamberlain's niece remembered how he became, then, an international hero. 'The house was full of presents from all over the world, including a television, one of the world's first.' After Munich, which Quintin Hogg hailed as 'the greatest miracle of modern times performed by a single man', *Sunday Express* columnist Godfrey Winn did not consider it blasphemous to mention Chamberlain in the same breath as the Almighty. 'Praise be to God and to Mr. Chamberlain. I find no sacrilege, no bathos, in coupling those two names.' Even President Roosevelt was impressed, saying to Halifax: 'Did you ever see the telegram I sent to Chamberlain at the time of Munich? . . . The shortest telegram I ever sent. Two words: "Good man."'

Yet the same event which had inspired grateful Portuguese mothers to pay for his marble effigy, a million readers of *Paris-Soir* to subscribe to buy him a house in France near a fishing resort 'since he loves to fish', and roused the Poet Laureate John Masefield to liken a 'divinely led' Chamberlain to the Greek hero Priam, soon became the source of his vilification. On the evening that he resigned, Chamberlain told Herbert Asquith's widow, Margot Oxford: 'The day may come when my much cursed visit to Munich will be <u>understood</u>.'

That moment has been excruciatingly slow to arrive. When, nine years after Chamberlain's death, Geoffrey Shakespeare wrote about 'the precious breathing space' which he believed that the Munich Agreement had earned for Britain, he feared that 'my defence of Neville Chamberlain will no doubt bring a hornet's nest around my ears'.* Lord Maugham, Lord Chancellor at

---

* Anne Chamberlain wrote to Geoffrey Shakespeare in January 1950, after reading his account in *Let Candles Be Brought In*: 'Nowhere have I seen so clear and convincing a statement published as to what you say about Neville's policy at that time . . . I think you would be interested to know that Neville regretted immediately afterwards his words from Downing Street "Peace in our time" – uttered on the spur of the moment when he suddenly found himself in a time of great emotion called upon to make a speech from that window where Disraeli made his "Peace in our Time" speech. How doubtful Neville felt that Hitler would stick to his words can be proved by his action and speech almost immediately afterwards in pressing forward the increase in the Armed Forces and the preparations for Defence. Having myself listened to the criticisms in the House, I asked him whether he could not give some explanation of the doubt which I knew he held in

the time, was stung by the reviews of a short book that he wrote about the Munich Agreement, and 'appalled' by the letters he received. The certainty of his correspondents that Britain should have gone to war in 1938 against the advice of her military chiefs represented a 'species of insanity which precludes a sane judgement'. So fatal was it to express sympathy for Chamberlain, even as late as 1961, that Iain Macleod believed he wrecked his chances of becoming Prime Minister by publishing a favourable study.

In view of the lofty line taken by many of the Labour and Liberal leaders, and indeed by Churchill himself, there was always one cardinal point insufficiently stressed in most assessments of Chamberlain: that the programme of rearmament after the General Election of 1935 was carried through on an enormous scale. David Dilks says: 'If you want to provoke reactions of incredulity, even among people generally well-informed, ask the question: "Did you know that while Chamberlain was still Prime Minister, Britain was spending between 40 and 50 per cent of GDP on defence?" You then have to explain that this isn't a misprint; you really do mean 45 per cent or more, not 4.5 per cent.' Whether measured as a proportion of GDP or as an absolute sum, it far exceeded anything that had ever been spent by any British government in peacetime.

It is true that the effort was made late, and if it could have begun in earnest even twelve months before, this would have made a very significant difference. Whether that was possible, given the politics of the time, is an open question. Churchill after the war told Attlee 'and his friends' in the Commons that 'the whole effort of their party was designed to make every preparation for defence of the country and resistance to Hitler so unpopular, that it was politically impossible'. The same became true of any defence of Chamberlain. As one reviewer commented of David Dilks's admirable 1984 biography, the first part of a projected two-volume work which Dilks has still to complete: 'The task of rehabilitating Chamberlain will inevitably be the work of Sisyphus.'

The Chamberlains, meantime, kept their heads low.

Elias Canetti wrote in his notebooks how one family may imperil a

---

regard to Hitler's good faith, but he felt that to do this might well wreck any chance there might be of a better understanding with Germany.'

name. 'It can ingest the name completely, make so much use of it that for others it becomes empty and bloodless.' At prep school in the 1960s, Chamberlain's great-nephew Arthur Chamberlain denied that he was related – 'No, just the same name.' Married to my Latin master at Winchester, Anne Stow never talked about what it was like to be Chamberlain's granddaughter, and she waited stoically for the tide of popular opinion to turn. The stigma against him continued on into the 1970s, when Chamberlain's only grandson was at Marlborough. 'Neville's my name. I found it awkward to use at school. I changed it to Francis.' Francis had been the name of his father, Chamberlain's only son. 'My father was a great mimic, funny, charming, but I've never seen a Prime Minister's son with a lower profile. Put his name on the Internet – there's nothing there. Unlike Randolph.'

As it turns out, Chamberlain does not even have a statue in Lisbon. The project was abandoned on his death, after which he was skinned for posterity – with Churchill's assistance – as 'the most disastrous Prime Minister in British history'. Another of his biographers, Keith Feiling, privately expressed what many professional historians have come to believe, but which the public imagination is reluctant to accept: Chamberlain was 'a man ill-timed, who therefore went astray, but has since been made, unduly, the scapegoat for many peoples and individuals'.

In *Put Out More Flags*, Cedric Lyne's wife was rarely spoken of by her friends without the epithet 'Poor' Angela Lyne. The same is true of Neville Chamberlain. On the eve of the Norway Debate, the journalist Collin Brooks wrote in his diary: 'Poor Chamberlain has had more of "Hosanna today; crucify him tomorrow" than anybody since Christ I should imagine – not that he is a particularly Christ-like person.'

Opinions vary over what he was like. His Parliamentary Private Secretary Alec Dunglass was said to know his words and actions by heart, yet even Dunglass conceded: 'He was by no means easy to get to know.' Dunglass found Chamberlain an essentially solitary figure, but fascinating when he did unbend. 'This attractive and endearing side of his personality was almost deliberately concealed, and the public saw only the forbidding exterior, the dark clothes, the stick-up collar, and the black hat and umbrella of the Whitehall world.' Violet Bonham Carter called him 'Ombrello'.

Like an air-raid warden, Chamberlain worked hard to ensure that no chink of light escaped his windows. Harold Nicolson wrote: 'His intimates assure me that never has there been a man who so successfully conceals his charm.' Within No. 10, his favourite topic was the weather. He had no time for gossip. When Dunglass went into his room for a general talk to convey the Party's feeling, Chamberlain looked up, pen poised. 'What do you want?' His abrupt manner was not rudeness, Dunglass decided, but what Chamberlain acknowledged to be his 'accursed shyness', which made him reticent to the point of being secretive, and was easily misinterpreted. The Conservative MP George Harvie-Watt considered Chamberlain the shyest man he had ever met. 'I never knew it to be so hard to converse with any man.' The only time that he sparkled was when some Member knew something about fishing. 'A gleam would come to Chamberlain's eye . . .' He had fished for salmon and trout since the First World War, on the Dee, on Loch Rannoch, on the Test, and at Chequers by moonlight in Silver Spring, and he wrote in 1931: 'I can't really consent to die until they arrange some fishing in the next world.' Some fishing is what he looked forward to after the Norway Debate.

Most MPs who failed to penetrate the Prime Minister's reserve gave up. To Members like Nicolson, Chamberlain had 'the mind and manner of a clothes-brush'. In public, he came across as stiff and prickly like his sisal plants. A disappointed supporter in his Birmingham constituency complained that 'if the b—— was cut in half, neither part would bleed'. Even Chamberlain's half-brother Austen recognised the problem. 'Boiled down, it all comes to this. N's manner freezes people.' But not all people. Margot Oxford adored him. 'What a good, wise, misunderstood creature he is, though he can't look a blind man straight in the face.' Her positive view was shared by those who worked for him like Dunglass, or who had regular dealings with him, like Alexander Cadogan. 'Many people who did not know Chamberlain personally had the impression that he was a gullible and obstinate old man . . . I will say, from my observation of him, that nothing could be further from the truth.' When Ellen Wilkinson made a violent tirade against Chamberlain, Halifax corrected the Labour MP. 'She had got him dead wrong and was just miles away from the truth.' Halifax worked 'as closely with him as anyone' and wrote that the kind of picture drawn of Chamberlain by his Labour opponents – 'of a rigid bureaucrat in domestic administration, and in foreign affairs of a man too ready to be half-hearted in his condemnation of totalitarian governments' – was a total misreading of character. Chamberlain himself was pleased to see how his former Labour adversaries changed their tune, as had Churchill, once they worked with him. He wrote to his sisters: 'I have increasing evidence that my Labour colleagues like Greenwood & Alexander are finding that I am a very different person from what they supposed.'

Chamberlain's niece Valerie never once altered her opinion that 'his reputation is at odds with his personality'. The man beneath the painfully reserved exterior was funny, warm and interested, even if it required one to be in the same room to appreciate his qualities. His sister Hilda wrote to him on 2 May, after a Supreme War Council meeting with Chamberlain's French allies: 'You have a wonderful faculty for winning their confidence as well as that of your own people but it seems only to hold if you can have them with you in the flesh.'

'Why look at our boss, he never dress like dat for we to see.' Chamberlain's misfortune is that he was unable to expose the appealing sides of his character to all except his workmen on Andros, one or two fly fishers, and his family. Family was everything to him, says his grandson Francis. 'The Chamberlains were great family people. Our toast is "To the Clique" – meaning "To the family".'

It was a family that had drawn together around a tragedy. His mother had died in childbirth when Chamberlain was seven. His sister Ida wrote: 'Papa could not bear to have her mentioned and so no one ever spoke to us about her.' His mother's place was filled by Chamberlain's spinster sisters Ida and Hilda, who lived together in a large house in Odiham in Hampshire. For most of his adult life, he wrote to them every week.

Not surprisingly, Chamberlain's closest friend was a cousin – after whom he would name an Andros butterfly, the *Terias Chamberlainii*. He could have been describing himself when he wrote of Norman Chamberlain, a fervent educationalist killed by German machine-gun fire outside the village of Fontaine in December 1917: 'Naturally reserved, shut and sensitive, he did not wear his heart upon his sleeves and it was only to his intimates that he showed all that there was in him.'

N. G. C. AT WOODHAY.
1917.

Chamberlain had felt Norman's death terribly. 'I was counting and depending on him more than I realised and he was in fact the most intimate friend I had.' Anxious for future generations to realise 'how greatly Norman had contributed to the family fame', Chamberlain wrote his one and only book about him, a memoir published in 1923, and today almost impossible to get hold of, in which Chamberlain revealed his commitment to continue where Norman had abruptly left off – above all, to be 'the statesman in him'. Norman's powerful posthumous influence can be traced in Neville's ideas on tariff reform, education and political economy; and in his reluctance to see repeated the carnage in which his cousin had been slaughtered.

Chamberlain was too old to fight in the trenches, but in editing Norman's letters he gained a paralysing insight. 'The terror I suffered can't be imagined,' Norman wrote. 'I know now what fear – naked and absolute – means, and it isn't pleasant . . .' He continued: 'Everything is mud, sticky mud . . . I can't reconcile myself to such waste, and such <u>blind</u> striking down right and left . . . and it's going on in hundreds and thousands of families throughout the world . . . Nothing but immeasurable improvements will ever justify all the damnable waste and unfairness of this war – I only hope those who are left will <u>never</u> <u>never</u> forget at what sacrifice those improvements have been won.' Chamberlain made it his duty not to forget. Before Norman was killed, he had written a message to be given to his mother in case he fell, expressing his conviction that a new and better England would arise after the war. Chamberlain would take these farewell words, and he would do everything in his power to secure that new England.

No one came to admire Neville Chamberlain's strengths more than his son. Francis Chamberlain shows me the last letter that his father Frank wrote to Chamberlain, in October 1940. 'I do want to say this, Papa. I shall always see you, and always have seen you, as far away above any other person I've ever known or read about in all the qualities which are worth while and all the principles which are worth striving for. I shall always try to be like you . . . I know that is the feeling of all decent people and it's some pride to me to think that it was my father who saved England and that so many people love and admire him. You have been a marvellous Papa and it is a shame that you should be ill now and have to hand on all your plans and ideas to those small-minded men who are out for their names. But it does all come out in the end and it's really what you know you've done that matters.'

To his last breath, Neville Chamberlain never doubted the rightness of what he had done, yet outside the Clique, he remains largely unrehabilitated, his good qualities unsuspected as his years on Andros.

Everyone knows what he looks like, how he sounded. His dry voice announcing that we were at war reminded Peter Fleming of 'stale digestive biscuits'. With his piercing dark eyes, hooked nose, and awkwardly angled small head, he resembled one of his Bahamian marlins. 'Look at his head,' jeered his unforgiving enemy Lloyd George, who prided himself on his ability to judge skull shapes. 'The worst thing Neville Chamberlain ever did was to meet Hitler and let Hitler see him.' Umbrella thin, unsmiling, wearing the same business suit every day – black swallow-tailed coat, striped trousers, laced boots – Neville Chamberlain advanced towards other Members in the Lobbies like a provincial undertaker, his face set in a kind of permanent wariness, never looking at them.

Brendan Bracken called him the Coroner.

But this appearance was deceptive, too. His grandson says: 'He looked like what he was not.'

At seventy-one, he was young for his years, with plenty of hair and very little grey around the temples. 'He looks well and does not trouble, as he might, to invest himself with a faded air,' observed Peter Fleming, who had been shooting with him in December. ('He is slow and tends to let birds past him before he fires . . .') Celebrating Chamberlain's birthday in March, *The Times* reported that his 'whole appearance and manner refuted any suggestion of staleness in himself'. Chamberlain had taken an eye test in January, and boasted to his sisters that his sight would enable him to pass into Churchill's navy, and was better than that of eleven out of twelve schoolchildren. 'Not unsatisfactory for an old 'un.'

The oldest member of his government, his only ailment was gout, which had flared up since September, and required him to wear a 'snowshoe' over a thick sock. That and nettle rash. 'Every night I have to anoint my hands with Vaseline and cover them with linen gloves which makes them itch and tingle very uncomfortably.' Otherwise, according his doctor, Thomas Horder, Chamberlain had the constitution of a man at least thirty years younger.

He needed only five and a half hours of sleep, and still felt 'surprisingly well', with no outward signs of the cancer that had begun to invade his body.

From his diary, from notes made by his wife and sisters, and from a taped interview with Valerie recorded a year before her death, it is possible to visualise Chamberlain's last weekend before the Norway Debate.

He woke on Saturday 4 May to a glorious hot day and the sound of blackcaps – his favourite birdsong, which never failed to produce in him a sensation of 'pure ecstasy'. He had not lost interest in ornithology, and kept a pair of binoculars beside his bed. As Churchill tossed worms to his carp, so Chamberlain fed bacon rind to blue tits. In Downing Street, to attract them, he opened up the dining-room window and left out pieces of toast. He knew the bird calls in Westminster, and claimed to have detected an impostor, though Peter Fleming was unpersuaded. 'He told us of a starling in St

James's Park which by whistling like a kestrel scares the sparrows. I am inclined to disbelieve in this bird. Kestrels rarely whistle . . .'

Chamberlain rose at eight and took a cold bath. He was spartan about cold, wrote Hilda. Nothing would induce him to have a hot-water bottle. Once, when he caught a bad cold, Hilda surreptitiously introduced one. 'He gave a most humorous account next morning of the awful thing he found in his bed – a large soft body – and how he sprang onto the floor before he discovered what it was.'

At 8.30 a.m., he sat down to a 'good cooked breakfast' prepared by Anne. Colville always found her breakfasts inedible at No. 10. The coffee tasted of 'strong burnt chicory', even though the Chamberlains believed it to be 'unique in its excellence'.

He was at his desk early. Churchill said of himself that long as he worked, Chamberlain worked longer, 'his years in the Bahamas having made him a "tough buccaneer"'. Yet the war never succeeded in consuming his whole day. 'I have occasionally times, perhaps an hour or even more, when there has been nothing for me to do.' If he stayed in London, after finishing his correspondence, he walked with Anne around the lake in St James's Park (followed by a single detective twenty yards behind), and wearing an old summer coat that his wife complained was 'green and shapeless' – Chamberlain's retort: Lord Halifax's coat was 'much worse than mine'. Sundays were for taking Valerie to Kew Gardens; or to London Zoo, to look at the tropical fish and the gorillas Mock and Maina, while doing his best to acknowledge passers-by. Plagued by autograph hunters, he disguised himself by putting on a grey hat instead of a black one. 'Even walking near Chequers in plus fours doesn't save me from recognition.'

He no longer walked as fast as on Andros, but at Chequers he managed up to twenty miles a day. He frequently took Valerie with him, always his sheepdog Spot. He liked to climb to the top of Coombe Hill and sit in the sun by the Boer War memorial, gazing down on the Vale of Aylesbury. His favourite path was through the woods which he had arranged to hand over to the Forestry Commission – 'I must remain P.M. a little longer to see the scheme well under way.' He had planted twenty-six new trees in November, and was impatient to see how they were doing. This Saturday morning, it relieved him to discover 'no young trees lost this year'. Stalin's chief recreation was playing the pianola; Churchill's bricklaying. Chamberlain's was planting trees. The wood from his trees, until September used for clarinets and tennis rackets, had become a source for rifle butts.

Leaving the woods behind him, he checked on the white peach tree in the orchard. Out of habit, he inspected the unsatisfactory squirrel trap that he had copied from Lord Halifax – as soon as the trap had appeared, the squirrels had vanished. Counting rook's nests, he strode back through the gardens.

Chamberlain was not a clubbable man. The Royal Horticultural Society was one of few organisations to which he belonged. Punctiliously in pencil, he recorded its Tuesday meetings in his diary, noting down simply 'RHS'. On this hot cloudless Saturday morning, it was the flowers that dazzled. Not only the cherry blossom. The path all the way to the gate was bordered by a mass of poet's narcissus. The first bloom of German iris had opened, and the tulip tree which he had planted in the east forecourt was fully out.

To Maisky, Chequers was merely a collection of 'dark halls, old paintings, strange staircases . . .' But to Chamberlain, it was the place he loved most – the only spot, his sister recognised, 'always there in the background . . . where you could get free even for a moment to breathe the fresh air & peace of the country'. His wife felt the same pull. Chequers, Anne wrote, was a haven 'where one can be oneself, and do things upside down if one likes all day long'.

Everywhere Chamberlain's sharp eyes fell, he saw evidence of his handiwork. With Valerie, he had planted magnolias on the north lawn; propped up the laburnum trees, trimmed the elders in Crows Close with his woodsaw. Whenever he was missing, Anne wrote, she found him there with his saw. 'It was his saw he wanted to fetch when we went down one evening to say goodbye to Chequers.'

He never smoked before lunch – a light meal consisting of fish and cheese ('They never ate meat,' Valerie said), with a glass of cider, or very occasionally Hock, such as the vintage he offered Kenneth Clark, saying with his curious defensive vanity: 'It was given me by the wine growers of Germany for having saved the peace of the world.' He did not bother with afternoon tea. He had a pipe in the evening and a glass of claret at dinner, and smoked a large cigar over coffee. After dinner, he no longer played the piano as he used to – Mendelssohn and Beethoven mainly; Chamberlain could not be wicked, said a friend of Frances Partridge, because he had a passion for Beethoven's last quartets – though he loved it when others played in his presence; especially when the pianist was his daughter Dorothy who reached professional standard. He personally knew Vaughan Williams and Bartók, and had helped to found the Birmingham Chamber Orchestra. He was a member of the National Art Collections Fund, and up until the war he liked to dash into the National Gallery in his lunch breaks to gaze for half an hour at Dutch masters. To Lord Salisbury, his artistic tastes were as 'bourgeois' as the Carl Spitzweg canvas which Hitler had presented to Chamberlain, after the two leaders discovered a shared interest in German romanticism. He had treated Hitler as President Obama was later said by critics to have treated the Iranian President, as 'a logical actor', never completely convinced of the Führer's true feelings, which the British diplomat Ivone Kirkpatrick was unable to resist jotting down: 'If ever that silly old man comes interfering here again with his umbrella, I'll kick him downstairs and jump on his stomach in front of photographers.'

He played patience until late to clear his mind, and usually read for twenty minutes, between midnight and 12.30 a.m., before going up to bed. 'One must have something to take one's mind off these perpetual war problems.' Since September, he had worked his way through Shakespeare's comedies, a biography of his half-brother Austen, and Derek Walker-Smith's unauthorised biography of himself, *Man of Peace*. When he first began this, Chamberlain found it 'full, as was to be expected, of grotesque inaccuracies culled from journalistic sources. Of course, the man had no business to write it. He has no qualifications for it, neither personal acquaintance with me nor knowledge of the political, industrial or social history of the period.' But as Chamberlain read on, 'I find it is a good deal better than I thought. There are mistakes . . . but there is a more adequate account of many things.'

Chamberlain woke on Sunday to 'one of the loveliest spring days I remember'. The sky was clear, almost too brilliant, with no sign of Luftwaffe formations or parachutes – the fear expressed in the weekend newspapers, and not without grounds: 5 May was the date fixed by Hitler for his most recent aborted plan to invade Britain. The German leader liked to attack his victims on Sundays, Stafford Cripps told Maisky. 'It gives him a small advantage: the enemy is somewhat less prepared on Sundays than usual.'

The assault on Chamberlain came from the press. In the *Sunday Pictorial*, Chamberlain's steadfast foe Lloyd George lambasted the government for their 'feeble, fatuous and futile' conduct of the war. At a barnstorming speech in Southampton, the Labour frontbencher Herbert Morrison expressed the widely reported hope that 'a bad British Prime Minister' would not remain in office. In Cambridge, another Labour frontbencher, big, bluff, hearty Hugh Dalton, demanded Chamberlain's resignation. 'Then an encouraging notice-board could be put up in Downing Street. "*War Against Hitler; under New Management.*" '

Unease stirred as well in the Conservative camp. In Belgrave Square, Chips Channon leafed through the 'storm of abuse', and calculated that 'Rothermere has come out against the Government: Kemsley is pro it: the "Telegraph" and Beaverbrook are mildly critical, but stay their hand.'

Lord Rothermere's defection was a disappointment. Only two days earlier, Chamberlain had received a letter of endorsement from the *Daily Mail*'s proprietor. 'Your endurance and courage under great difficulties will rally behind you all the women voters and most of the men voters in this country. They have not lost faith in their leader or belief in victory.'

As he was to flattery, Chamberlain was sensitive to criticism: 'Chamberlain hates criticism,' said Brendan Bracken, 'he can't stand it, he gets hurt and angry at the sound of it.' All at once, Chamberlain felt 'very down and depressed' after digesting the newspapers and the results of the latest BIPO poll: 60 per cent of the population against him, in contrast to the BIPO survey on 26 April when 57 per cent had approved of him as Prime Minister.

It further riled him to read speculation about who might take over. Halifax and Lloyd George cropped up as candidates, but Churchill's was the name which rankled. The government was having to take the rap over Norway for something that Chamberlain could not reveal to the public. As Chips Channon, one of Chamberlain's most faithful supporters, put it: 'Our failure in Norway is largely Winston's fault, and yet he would profit by it. I am appalled.'

Inevitably, when Chamberlain felt the need to unstitch, he turned to his sisters. His correspondence with Ida and Hilda was the closest that he came to a diary or autobiography. He relied on their unstinting support, keeping their replies in his jacket to bring out and reread when he was fishing or shooting. Once, he was staying with Alec Dunglass in Scotland when Dunglass pulled from Chamberlain's pocket a letter from Ida 'covered in blood and feathers'.

This weekend, Chamberlain was the quarry. He went into his study, and though he disliked using a fountain pen because of his nettle rash, he sat at his writing table and completed the long letter that he had begun on Saturday to Hilda, knowing that she would share it with Ida. His grandson says: 'It was a massive security breach, and not very healthy – his sisters were completely uncritical – but he could say whatever he liked.'

A backlog had built up of the confidences which he wanted to share. Most sprang from his recent impasse with Churchill.

In his unpretentious handwriting that was uniformly slanted at ten past two, Chamberlain revealed the full catalogue of Churchill's shortcomings since the start of the Norway Campaign: how Churchill had changed his mind repeatedly over Trondheim, how he had bullied the Chiefs of Staff into agreeing with a course of which they disapproved, how Stanley and Hoare had said they would resign if Churchill was appointed Defence Minister, how Chamberlain had threatened to resign if they did, and how Churchill's vacillations and alterations did not 'square with the picture the gutter press & W.C.'s "friends" try to paint of the supreme War Lord'. Churchill was 'too apt to look the other way while his friends exalt him as the War Genius & hint that if only he had not been thwarted things would have gone very differently. How thankful I must be that the good British public does not know that truth & persists in ideas which recall the Kitchener legend.'

The First Lord had in point of fact given him 'more trouble than all the rest of my colleagues put together.' So much so that Chamberlain had been mulling over whether to promote Churchill or sack him; or even step aside himself.

The temperature on Sunday afternoon rose to 88 degrees Fahrenheit. At the Old Vic, John Gielgud had been playing since early April to a full house, standing room only, in a drama about an autocratic leader who finds it difficult to relinquish power. Geoffrey Dawson wrote in his diary after seeing Gielgud's King Lear: 'It was a shattering performance.'

Like Lear, Chamberlain had a 'strong inclination to take my head out of the collar & let someone else do the donkey work'. But he resisted handing over his reins in the absence of an obvious replacement – and Churchill was not that; his behaviour had been such that the Service Ministers, whether right or wrong in their opinions, were often in the same state of open revolt as the rest of the War Cabinet. Chamberlain confided to the American Ambassador, Joseph Kennedy, that 'he didn't think there was one man in his Cabinet who would vote for him for Prime Minister'.

A week after the outbreak of war, Chamberlain had estimated that 'half a dozen people could take my place'. Now when he darted his eye about, 'I don't see that other to whom I could hand over with any confidence . . . who would be better than I.' In certain respects, he felt stronger than before, more in control; and it encouraged him to know that his political opponents believed this. A mournful Attlee reported that Chamberlain's authority in Cabinet, which he continued only too easily to dominate, was absolute.

The rumours about Chamberlain's domination of the War Cabinet are easy to exaggerate. He was orderly, persuasive, open to consultation with individual ministers, seldom spoke early in the discussion, and allowed all the members to have their say. On the other hand, it is quite true that he kept a sharp watch over both colleagues and rivals.

He was assisted in his scrutiny by the press. Despite his reputation for shyness and aloofness, and his distaste for the telephone, Chamberlain was a ruthless pioneer of the dark arts that we now take for granted. He held weekly meetings with leading journalists; he maintained intermittent contacts of a friendly kind with Beaverbrook; he had close relations with Camrose, Iliffe and others, not least in the provincial press. Inside the House of Commons, he counted on a small team to manipulate lobby correspondents and MPs with aggressive briefings. Chief among his henchmen were the 'ubiquitous' and 'cadaverous-looking' Horace Wilson, and the government Chief Whip, Captain David Margesson, who ruled the Whips' Office, in the phrase of one Conservative backbencher, 'like a teak-faced Red Indian and secured a very wide measure of subordination'.

The press was not the Prime Minister's sole lens. In maintaining a tighter surveillance of the Conservative Party and the Commons than is commonly realized, Chamberlain used methods that today seem modern. He told his sisters: 'Our Secret Service doesn't spend all its time looking out of the window.' In 1932, Chamberlain had been staying in Ottawa when he discovered that his conversation was being tapped by the Canadians. On becoming Prime Minister, Chamberlain adopted their practice of eavesdropping on political opponents; as Robert Vansittart noted, 'he had a devious mind in this field'.

Two examples suffice from this period. On 7 March 1940, Gladwyn Jebb reported that the Claridge's apartment of the American Under-Secretary of State, Sumner Welles, who was on a visit to London, 'had been fixed up with microphones'. Intelligence officer Guy Liddell in his diary for 9 March 1940 gave further proof of MI5's monitoring habits. 'The telephone check on Rickatson-Hatt, editor in chief of Reuters, shows that he is hard up, has many women friends, and that he talks indiscreetly on the telephone.'

Chamberlain depended for much of his snooping on a shadowy intermediary who was said to have taught him fly fishing: Sir Joseph Ball, head of the Conservative Research Department, and one of a handful of people outside the Clique with whom Chamberlain spent time – they were fishing together when Hitler invaded Prague.

Born in Luton, a trained lawyer and a talented footballer, Ball had worked in MI5 during the First World War, and developed a substantial working knowledge of 'the seamy side of life and the handling of crooks' – according to the Conservative Party Chairman J. C. C. Davidson, who recruited Ball as director of publicity, and with whom he was soon running 'a little intelligence service of our own, quite separate from the Party organisation'. An excellent judge of domestic politics, Ball inserted former Intelligence colleagues into the Labour Party headquarters, but also engaged them to spy on members of his own party, like rebel Conservative MP Ronald Tree who all through the Norway Campaign hosted meetings with fellow dissidents at his house in Queen Anne's Gate. Tree was incensed when Ball 'had the gall to tell me that he himself had been responsible for having my phone tapped'. Tree anyway had grounds for suspicion. On 2 May, following Chamberlain's statement on the evacuation from Norway,

Tree wrote to Lord Cranborne that he was off to his country house, Ditchley Park. 'Ring me there if you want to talk . . . but I am advised that one should be careful about telephone <u>talks</u>.'

In 1936, Ball increased his capacity to subvert and smear when he bought the weekly magazine *Truth* and deployed it to demolish the reputation of anyone who impeded Chamberlain's path, such as Leslie Hore-Belisha, the pushy Minister of War who had got into a state of open friction with the commanders in the field. Samuel Hoare, the tight-lipped Air Minister known as 'Slippery Sam', was another victim – as Baba Metcalfe recorded in her diary. 'Hoare's star is definitely on the descendant, I think. The *Truth* articles seem to have done the trick.' Ball's besmirching hand was probably behind the story of how Hoare, a passionate ice skater, would invite colleagues in the Cabinet to watch him skating in black tights.

Yet another target was Churchill. On 23 July 1939, Chamberlain noted gleefully that 'Winston himself is very depressed and . . . distressed by a couple of witty articles making fun of the suggestion that he would help matters in the Cabinet which appeared in *Truth*.'

Joseph Ball burnt all his papers, and a convincing account of the exact nature of his relationship with MI5 or MI6 is still to be written, but few public figures exchanged confidences beyond the range of his telephone tap – and these did not include former kings. One of Baba Metcalfe's suitors at this time, Walter Monckton, was the Duke of Windsor's solicitor. Writing to the Duke in Paris in November 1939, about his wish to fly over to London by plane and have an interview with his younger brother, George VI, Monckton warned: 'It is very difficult to discuss this matter on the telephone where we are overheard.' In his reply, the Duke enclosed a note typed out in red: 'To WHOMSOEVER steams this letter open! I hope you are as edified at the contents of this letter as I am over having to write them!!' Monckton clarified his own position on surveillance in a secret memorandum that he wrote when he became Director General of the Ministry of Information in May 1940. 'What we really want is an English variation of Herr Himmler. MI5, MI6 and possibly also the Special Branch of Scotland Yard should be brought together and a responsible head given proper executive powers . . . They should be allowed to develop on a large scale the two obvious methods of finding out what a person is doing, namely to read his correspondence and to listen to what he says on the telephone in such a way that he does not know that it is being done.'

The Prime Minister had known what Churchill was doing since the time of the Munich Debate. On 9 October 1938, Chamberlain complained of Churchill 'carrying on a regular conspiracy against me with the aid of Masaryk the Czech Minister. They of course are totally unaware of my knowledge of their proceedings. I had continual information of their doings and sayings.' But Churchill may have suspected as much when he speculated in the House the following April 'whether there is not some hand which intervenes and filters down or withholds intelligence from Ministers'.

Another filterer was Colville's predecessor as Chamberlain's Junior Private Secretary: Jasper Rootham, a civil-servant-cum-Intelligence-agent who had worked in Downing Street as a French and German interpreter. Rootham admitted to Andrew Roberts that Chamberlain regularly taped Churchill's private conversations after Munich, 'and that his job was to take transcripts of the tapes to the Prime Minister'. There is no reason to suppose that this practice stopped when Churchill joined the Cabinet in September. Or that Churchill would have been exempt from the type of surveillance to which MI5 had recently subjected one of Churchill's oldest friends: the leader of the Liberal Party, Sir Archie Sinclair.

Tall, handsome, charming, with Churchill's slight stammer, Sinclair was one more protégé, like Giles Romilly and Peter Fleming, whom Churchill had treated almost as a son. Before the First World War, Sinclair was considered a suitable husband for Romilly's mother, Nellie. During it, he had served as Churchill's adjutant; they had arrived together on black chargers at the regiment's HQ in Moolemacher, hours before a German shell passed through their shared bedroom. Churchill wrote to him: 'You have been a great comfort to me and I shall always be on the qui vive where your interests are concerned.' After the war, Sinclair worked as Churchill's personal secretary at the Colonial Office, enjoying the same close contact with him as Chamberlain had with Dunglass and Colville, and causing Churchill to say of Sinclair: 'Archie knows or guesses what I feel.' In 1935, Sinclair became leader of the Liberals, a party of seventeen MPs on the edge of extinction, as he himself sometimes could appear. One MP who had known Sinclair at Eton said that he 'used to play football with his hands in his pockets. The fellow was always a complete skug.' In Colville's opinion, Sinclair's feelings were more powerful than his brains, and he was 'blinded by prejudiced hatred' of Chamberlain.

Sinclair had made a critical speech in Edinburgh on 30 April, cautioning Chamberlain not to 'scuttle away' from Norway. A livid Chamberlain summoned Sinclair the following afternoon, suspecting him of disclosing secret information gained in his capacity as a Privy Counsellor. He then revealed that Sinclair's telephone at his home in Caithness was tapped, and that his conversations with the political journalist Harcourt Johnstone had been recorded. The Liberal Chief Whip Percy Harris accompanied Sinclair to the interview. 'We had the impression that the P.M. had read the notes.'

Chamberlain was extremely suspicious of Sinclair's 'close relations' with Churchill. He had taken an even keener interest in their activities since Chips Channon tipped him off that Churchill – 'this brilliant, puffing old charlatan' – had been intriguing again, with none other than Sinclair. 'Chagrined by his failure at the Admiralty, he has now thrown off his mask, and is plotting against Neville, whom up to now he has served loyally; he wants to run the show himself.' To this end, Churchill 'has had secret conversations and meetings with Archie Sinclair, A. V. Alexander and Mr Attlee and they are drawing up an alternative government, with the idea of succeeding at the first favourable moment'. That was on 25 April. Six days later, Channon stumbled upon the alleged conspirators a second time. 'Tonight Churchill sat joking and drinking in the smoking room, surrounded by A. V. Alexander and Archie Sinclair, the new Shadow Cabinet.'

The rumour that Churchill was 'playing politics' reached the ears of A. J. Sylvester, who passed it on instantly to Lloyd George. 'I am told that Winston met a number of The Old Guard in a private house somewhere at some time last night. Where it was I do not know. It is stated that Winston is double-crossing everybody.'

Chamberlain reacted strongly to what he perceived as Churchill's treachery. On 30 April, he complained to the King, who wrote in his diary: 'Winston still seems to be causing a good deal of trouble . . . The P.M. is having another talk with W. tonight, laying down what he can & cannot do without the War Cabinet's sanction.' George VI depended on a separate source, his Private Secretary Sir Alexander Hardinge, to advise him of the reason for Churchill's behaviour. Hardinge had been told by Stanley and Hoare 'that Winston's attitude over all of them is part of an intrigue for him to oust Mr Chamberlain . . .'

Chamberlain's mood was unforgiving when he suspected that the opposition parties intended to support a Conservative revolt to install Churchill. He had told Churchill after the Munich Debate: 'You cannot expect me to allow you to do all the hitting and never hit back.' Outraged and 'full of fight still', Chamberlain despatched Dunglass to sound out the feelings of Conservative MPs in preparation for a possible counter-strike. Chamberlain's faithful bloodhound Chips Channon was 'pumped' by Dunglass. 'Did I think that Winston, the man who has never been right, should be deflated, was the moment ripe to begin to sell him? Ought he to leave the Admiralty? Evidently these thoughts are in Neville's head.'

On 1 May, Chamberlain discussed Churchill's 'inflated' reputation with his Information Minister John Reith, leaving Reith in 'no doubt' how he felt about Churchill. Still suspecting treachery, Chamberlain's instinct was to hang the First Lord out to dry – and on his Norwegian petard. Cecil King learned on the same day that 'there is a movement on foot to foist the blame for the failure in Norway onto Churchill'. The Conservative MP Paul Emrys-Evans was attending a dinner of the Watching Committee, a new group of Conservative critics of the government, when the Chief Whip David Margesson appeared unexpectedly. Emrys-Evans wrote: 'The Government was obviously very unhappy about the Norwegian expedition, and it looked as if they were trying to throw the responsibility on Winston.' Harold Nicolson was told the same story, 'that the whole Norwegian episode is due to Winston'. Gossip about Churchill that was 'exceptionally slanderous, even for the intriguers' circulated to Labour MP Emanuel Shinwell on the party's Parliamentary Committee. 'It was said that he drank too much; he was prematurely aged; he was the real culprit of the Norwegian catastrophe, which was a repetition of his ill-starred Gallipoli campaign; he could not be trusted . . .'

Yet this smear campaign was no sooner launched than it was abruptly called off. Why? We still do not know all the reasons. But given the Prime

Minister's 'devious mind' and his track record in this area, it is reasonable to suppose that further intercepted conversations procured by Ball and Rootham had presented Chamberlain with a different picture of the First Lord's behaviour, and revealed that Churchill, far from plotting against Chamberlain, was supporting the Prime Minister.

'I am no good as a conspirator,' Churchill would say in old age. 'I talk too much.' At a lunch for lobby journalists in February, he had pledged himself loyally to stand by his 'captain' for the duration of the voyage, 'till we bring this ship of ours however battered she may be through all the gales that blow into the harbour of our heart's desire'. Chamberlain had bowed his thanks. In the same month, Cadogan and Halifax witnessed Churchill saying to Chamberlain with tears in his eyes: 'I'm proud to follow you!' His loyalty was confirmed by one of his supposed co-plotters, Labour's former First Lord A. V. Alexander, who spoke with Churchill on 29 April – when 'Winston had made it quite clear that Chamberlain was behind Winston and Winston was behind Chamberlain'. Lord Camrose had the definite impression after meeting Churchill on 3 May, that despite toxic stories to the contrary, 'Churchill was on excellent terms with the P.M., better than ever before'.

Their rapprochement had taken more than a decade to mature. Chamberlain and Churchill had first worked together in Cabinet in 1924, when Churchill, to everyone's astonishment including his own, became Baldwin's Chancellor. This was largely thanks to Chamberlain passing up the job for the Ministry of Health – to achieve the social reforms which had engrossed his cousin Norman.

Ever since, Chamberlain had regarded Churchill through his pince-nez with mingled admiration and horror. 'What a brilliant creature he is! . . . But not for all the joys of Paradise would I be a member of his staff! Mercurial! A much abused word, but it is the literal description of his temperament.' Churchill was a man of multiple talents, but no judgement. Working with him was 'like arguing with a Brass band'. He reminded Chamberlain of Hore-Belisha, another *mauvais coucheur*. 'Winston is very amusing but a d——d uncomfortable bedfellow.' In 1928, Chamberlain declared to Sir Douglas Hogg his disinclination to 'see W. Chu Prime

Minister', and in 1936 he opposed his half-brother Austen's view that Churchill be made Minister of Defence. Churchill always backed the wrong horse, had a new idea every hour, floundered in the details, and did not stand by his decisions, which were 'never founded on exact knowledge nor on careful or prolonged consideration of the pros and cons'. On top of everything, there was his intolerable verbosity. If Chamberlain took Churchill into the Cabinet, then he would dominate it. 'He won't give others a chance of even talking.'

Chamberlain's mind was hard to change once made up. Yet in respect of Churchill, his distrust was a fluctuating, petulant thing. After Hitler's invasion of Poland compelled him to bring Churchill into the Cabinet, there is evidence that as the war progressed a solid and genuine trust did spring up between the two men, much to the surprise of them both.

Lord Beaverbrook later told Halifax that Churchill 'had behaved with complete wisdom when the time came for him to replace Chamberlain, and no-one could find any fault with his comportment!' Beaverbrook's explanation for Churchill's success was simple. 'If you want to supplant the Prime Minister, you must always be on the most friendly and loyal terms.'

Too much has been made of their blatant differences, not least by the protagonists themselves. Not sung enough is how well Churchill got on with Chamberlain. On the day after the Norway Debate, the Chancellor John Simon wrote this in his diary about Chamberlain: 'He has throughout got on very well with both Winston and Halifax.'

Not long after the Chamberlains dined at Admiralty House in the autumn of 1939, the American journalist Virginia Cowles had lunch at the same table, and was startled by Churchill's reaction when his children attempted a mild jest at Chamberlain's expense. A scowl appeared on his face. 'With enormous solemnity he said: "If you are going to make offensive remarks about my chief you will have to leave the table. We are united in a great and common cause. I am not prepared to tolerate such language about the Prime Minister."'

Churchill had favourably revised his opinion of 'Monsieur J'aimeberlin' after learning about his past on Andros. Five months on, there is evidence that a naturally inflexible Chamberlain had shifted in his attitude towards 'the wild man'. Chamberlain wrote to Ida on 30 March: 'To me personally he is absolutely loyal and I am continually hearing from others of the admiration he expresses for the P.M.' Inhaling Churchill's cigar-scented flattery, Chamberlain suspended the misgivings that he had expressed earlier, writing on 27 April about how the First Lord 'was profuse in his protestations (which I believe to be quite genuine) of his desire to help and his complete loyalty to me'. A grudging Hilda accepted her brother's statement with a caveat. 'I do believe that Churchill was loyal to you – up to the standard of Churchill loyalty, but that is not & never has been the Chamberlain standard.'

Reassured for whatever reason that Churchill stood solidly behind him after all, Chamberlain calculated that it was in no one's interest to advertise the First Lord's prominent role in the Norwegian debacle. In the long confessional which he wrote to Hilda over the weekend, Chamberlain emphasised: 'I am extremely anxious not to have any breach with him for that would be disastrous to the Allied cause and I am sure he does not want one.' Instead of hanging Churchill out to dry, Chamberlain now planned to keep Churchill firmly within the Conservative camp, and take shelter behind him. The survival of each man had come to depend on the survival of the other.

To break his impasse with Churchill, and also to neutralise him, Chamberlain had decided not to move him from the Admiralty, but instead to give the First Lord further responsibilities – more rope. At the end of April, under the guise of a major reconstruction, he had made Churchill responsible for the Chiefs of Staff Committee, in effect appointing him Minister of Defence, with the right to direct and guide the Chiefs of Staff without consultation with the Military Coordination Committee. Churchill was thrilled. He jumped up and down before the editor of the *Manchester Guardian*: 'Now I've got more power – I've got more powers!'

Yet Channon suspected the Prime Minister of 'playing a deep game'. Aside from the advantage to be gained from a satisfied Churchill, Chamberlain's move was designed to spike the guns of those Conservative dissidents like Tree, Emrys-Evans, Cooper and Macmillan who might have looked to a disaffected Churchill as a leader. Chamberlain told Hilda how he had drafted a paper which 'set out & defined Winston's new functions', and that Churchill had 'accepted the whole thing at once . . . and thanked me very warmly for the efforts I had made to meet him'. The new measures were to be announced on Monday 6 May.

As a final precaution, Chamberlain had asked Churchill to defend the government in the debate on Tuesday. 'I shall have to lead off & leave Winston to wind up.'

One of Chamberlain's strongest Conservative critics, Lord Cranborne, thought that the Prime Minister was 'quite convinced that, like the Pope, he is infallible'. Chamberlain's character was to believe what he wanted and ignore the rest. He wrote in a diary that he had started in December 1939: 'My reasoning power is too strong to allow of my being seriously disturbed by worried thoughts'. Adverse press reports, opinion polls and rumours of cabals were to be swatted away like horseflies on Andros. He had learned from his stableman on the island that '*it no use to wex w'en tings humbug you, cos' if you wex dey on'y humbug you worser!*'

On Andros, Mr Chimblin's men had called him '*strong as de debble*'. When he finally did speak in Cabinet, Chamberlain generally knew his own mind, and he tended to treat bothersome colleagues as he had his sisal planters ('I keep tightening the rein of discipline on the people and though they grumble a good deal to each new rule they begin to understand that they have got to work according to my ideas and not according to theirs.'). Leo Amery perceived Chamberlain to be 'a much stronger man than any of them, rightly or wrongly', and that 'where he is interested in anything, it moves'. To another rebel MP, Ronald Cartland, Chamberlain's often dictatorial habits had made him 'a Führer now in the Conservative party'. When push came to shove, complained Macmillan, it was Chamberlain's word that counted. 'If Chamberlain says that black is white, the Tories applaud his brilliance. If a week later he says that black is after all black, they applaud his realism. Never has there been such servility.'

Black at the end of April, Churchill's standing with Chamberlain had whitened as the Norway Debate approached. If not yet the hue of the snow around Narvik, then it ensured that the two men would work together to defeat the government's critics. These critics, Chamberlain told his sister, were 'not malevolent at all, but merely not very intelligent, and it should be possible to answer them effectively'.

After the debate, Chamberlain proposed 'to try and get a week himself at Whitsuntide' and go fishing, 'and forget the war'. At Whitsun the year before, he had fished the Great Weir at Alresford. 'More & more I am convinced that much of the art of statesmanship lies in accurate timing, as the fisherman knows when he is trying to get a long cast out.'

Chamberlain had had to reel out extra line to keep Churchill on the hook, but he maintained his providential belief in what he once described to Hilda as 'the Chamberlain touch'. He dismissed the anecdote in Walker-Smith's book, how someone remarked after Chamberlain had landed an exceptional fish: 'Yes, it must be nice to catch something after having been caught himself so often.' On that sunny Sunday afternoon in May, despite being momentarily cast down by the newspapers, Neville Chamberlain gathered strength from the fresh colours and scents of the garden that he could see from his writing desk, and he believed that the government would survive the debate.

He ended his letter to his sister: 'It is a vile world, but I don't think my enemies will get me down this time. I should be sorry if they did because I should then have to leave this lovely place. You couldn't imagine anything more perfect than it is today. But I must work at my speech.'

12

THE MASTER OF GARROWBY

'*We human beings are the creatures and the subjects of personal relationships.*'
LORD WOOLTON, handwritten note, 1940

'*What a different world it would have been if Hitler and Goering had been to Oxford.*' LORD HALIFAX, quoted by STUART HODGSON

'*I have a stomach ache. I have had it for a week and nobody has asked after it.*'
LORD HALIFAX to CHARLES PEAKE, 28 June 1941

On Saturday, Lord Halifax cancelled an early-morning appointment at the Dorchester with the editor of *The Times* and 'motored off' with his wife Dorothy and their dachshund Max to Baba Metcalfe's new home in the country – 'which, thanks to her description, we found quite easily about six miles the other side of Chipping Norton. A most delightful house of regular Cotswold stone. We were the only guests, and had a thoroughly peaceful evening, seeing ponies, garden etc.'

This was Halifax's first visit to Baba's Tudor mansion in Little Compton. Her recently acquired estate, with its horse paddocks, croquet lawn and deer park, had belonged in the seventeenth century to Bishop William Juxon who accompanied King Charles I to the scaffold, not to die but to pray. Over the next five days, Baba performed a comparable role for the Foreign Secretary.

Dining alone with Baba at the Dorchester two nights earlier, Halifax had paused over a meal of rabbit and carrots to tell her that the withdrawal from Namsos was to be announced the next day. 'It was no good going on,' he said, 'the Norwegians offered no co-operation and did not want to fight.' This was privileged information. In her diary that night, Baba wrote of Halifax's fears about Hitler's next move. 'A landing by Germans is seriously considered a possibility.'

Shrugging off any pressure to remain in London, Halifax had brought his red boxes with him to Little Compton, in order to compose his speech for the Norway Debate. He had looked forward to seeing Baba's manor house since the previous July. A collector of ghost stories, Halifax was intrigued by the legend that Bishop Juxon's spirit continued to haunt an oak staircase on the ground floor, causing Baba's corgis to bark every time they saw it.

Baba's daughter Davina was ten years old at the time, and remembers Halifax coming to stay. She says: 'He should have been knees under the desk.'

The weekend flight of Ministers from London appalled at least one Junior Minister, Robert Bernays. 'There still seems to be a most unfortunate, indeed lamentable, failure on the part of the Cabinet to grapple adequately with the situation. This is Friday afternoon and they have all disappeared to their country houses.'

Halifax was more culpable than Chamberlain in wanting to leave Westminster behind him. His Private Secretary Valentine Lawford wrote in an unpublished memoir that 'Halifax might sometimes have to put in weekend appearances at Chequers. But he would happily escape into the Chilterns for an afternoon alone with Lady Halifax . . . and I doubt whether he was anything but relieved to hear on returning that his absence in the hills had coincided with a number of telephone calls from his Private Secretary in London.'

However dangerous the situation confronting Britain, a weekend in the country was, for Halifax, an institution as sacrosanct in its way as his Anglo-Catholic Church. He once wrote to his friend Geoffrey Dawson, editor of *The Times*, who owned Langliffe Hall in North Riding: 'There is nothing I should like so much as a weekend at Langcliffe if it was possible.' Cadogan complained that 'even in times of crisis, H goes off to Yorkshire on a Friday afternoon'.

Halifax in his memoirs had only praise for 'the well-assorted week-end party in pleasant surroundings and with plenty of scope for easy conversation'. He abominated any disturbance. Staying at Garrowby, Halifax's Yorkshire estate, Baba's oldest sister Irene had found the telephone system 'inconceivably incompetent for a Foreign Secretary. A private phone rings in the Tower, which is seldom heard, or Halifax is too bored to go up to it, and suggests when he talks on the phone that he fears it is being tapped.' It was Halifax's bugbear that 'the material of the historian is shrinking all the time, as telephones destroy with ruthless thoroughness all value but their own'. In this, as in other respects, Halifax shared the prejudice of Baba's father, who did not wish to be contacted unless for an exceptional reason. When informed at Kedleston by telephone – 'a disastrous invention' – that a foreign statesman of the first rank had died, Lord Curzon snorted: 'Do you realise that, to convey to me this trivial information, you have brought me the length of a mansion not far removed from the dimensions of Windsor Castle!'

At Garrowby, Halifax preferred nothing more than to button on his oldest clothes, lie out on a rug in the garden, or help with the haymaking. Fox hunting was another obsession: Halifax was Master of the Middleton Hounds. When a mere MP, he had tried with his brother-in-law, George Lane-Fox, 'to order my life as to reconcile the claims of the House of Commons with as much hunting as we could fit in'. In India, Halifax had hunted with the Delhi Hounds whatever the level of political turmoil, and he had not tailored his habits since returning to England. As acting Foreign Secretary when Parliament went into recess, he proposed, according to an incredulous *Times* journalist, 'to direct affairs from Yorkshire'. Once the war started, Halifax's weekend absences were manna to Nazi propagandists, who broadcast on German radio how 'he was wasting time on his Yorkshire moors'.

Over a Whitsun bank holiday weekend, while cutting his lawns in his shirtsleeves, Lord Curzon, Baba's father, believing his succession inevitable, had waited for a telephone call to ask him to take over the premiership from Bonar Law. Seventeen years on, Halifax braced himself for a similar summons. Chamberlain was known to view the impeccably credentialled Halifax as his natural heir. Halifax 'was now generally trusted and would be thought of if anything happened to me', Chamberlain wrote to Ida. 'I would rather have Halifax succeed me than Winston.' This was the opinion of most of the 416 Conservative Members of Parliament, a majority of the 169 Labour Members, and the powerful preference of the King and Queen.

The Prime Minister had not broached the subject to his Foreign Secretary, but Halifax was aware of the clamour. His friend Geoffrey Dawson had used his position on *The Times* to argue since March for a reorganised government, but he doubted 'if Halifax would make a suitable P.M. even if he would take it'. Neither man trusting the telephone, Dawson had hoped to learn more of Halifax's intentions early on that morning of 4 May. They had arranged to meet at the Dorchester for a walk in the park.

The editor of *The Times* was an All Souls confrère and shooting companion, whose Langcliffe estate lay eighty miles from Garrowby. Although not the Foreign Secretary's poodle to the extent that he has been painted, Dawson was in regular touch with Halifax during the Norway Campaign. In the course of a single week, Halifax took the influential journalist to Grosvenor Chapel, walked with him to the Foreign Office, lunched with him at the Dorchester, and they had gone together to 'a roaring farce' called *Good Men Sleep at Home*.

That Saturday, Dawson was anxious to alert Halifax to a development in the drama to supplant Chamberlain: a letter, which Dawson had rejected for publication, from 'a leading member of the House of Commons', in which an alternative Cabinet was proposed, listing Halifax as Prime Minister. Dawson had learned that this letter, written by Stafford Cripps, was to be printed on Monday on the front page of the *Mail*. He hoped in the course of their early-morning stroll to discover Halifax's response.

Halifax had cancelled at the last moment.

By now, the Foreign Secretary knew that Cripps was not the only advocate for a small, Halifax-led War Cabinet. Cripps's letter would be followed by one from A. L. Rowse, sponsored by the Labour Party, which Dawson did decide to print. Both letters came on the heels of an approach to Halifax from the former leader of the House of Lords, the Marquess of Salisbury.

Salisbury and his son Lord Cranborne had recently formed 'a small Committee of influential Members of both Houses ... to watch the conduct of the War' and to give expression to growing dissatisfaction with the government, which presented, Salisbury complained to Halifax, 'an appearance of doing nothing'. On 27 March, Salisbury had distributed a memorandum to the twenty members of his group, which included several ex-Cabinet Ministers. 'The question which all the world is asking is: Have H.M.G. got a plan? Presumably yes, but if so what is it?' Cranborne summarised their chief gripe: 'The economic war is a very slow process & in the meantime Hitler continues to register spectacular successes elsewhere.' With his father, Cranborne had argued since September for a smaller War

Cabinet and retaliatory action. They both shared the view of the architect of the RAF, Lord Trenchard, who had joined their informal discussions, 'of the necessity of hitting at Germany by air in Germany'. They had named their group the Watching Committee.

Father and son had held the first meeting on 4 April at Salisbury's London home in Arlington Street. The decision was taken to organise 'very respectable Conservatives' – in other words, not Churchill nor anyone from his disreputable circle of 'inefficient and talkative people' – and 'keep the Government up to the scratch' – in other words, agitate for Chamberlain to be replaced by a more aggressive Conservative leader. Salisbury dismissed Chamberlain's approach to international disasters as 'Birmingham politics'. 'Personally I was no longer in favour of Neville.'

The Watching Committee did not reconvene in full force until 16 April owing to a mix-up over addresses. Invitations sent by Salisbury failed to reach either its new Honorary Secretary, Conservative MP Paul Emrys-Evans ('as my house, 2 Lowndes Street, is now occupied by the Red Cross') or Lord Trenchard ('Your last letter telling me of a meeting was sent to Dancers Hill House, Barnet, which I left two months ago'). Thereafter, Salisbury encouraged members to call at 21 Arlington Street 'at 9.30 any morning that they felt so disposed'.

Initially, the Salisburys thought to champion Anthony Eden: Cranborne had worked as Under-Secretary to the 'glamour boy' Eden, and hoped to be rewarded with the Foreign Secretaryship. But Eden had returned to government, and Emrys-Evans had started to look elsewhere. His preferred candidate was Halifax. Emrys-Evans explained to Cranborne: 'An interim Government under Halifax would allow a possible leader to come to the surface . . . The war could not be won by him, but he may find the man.' The fact that Halifax was in the Lords was not considered an impediment. Salisbury's father had been a Prime Minister peer.

Halifax could scarcely refuse the seventy-eight-year-old Salisbury's request for an audience; besides having been his chief in the Lords, 'Jem' was one of very few men whom the Foreign Secretary addressed by his Christian name. But Halifax was irritated when, on 24 April, Salisbury limped into the Foreign Office in a top hat and billowing frock coat and gave Halifax his frank opinion that the neutrals would take as 'a sign of softness and funk' the government's lack of retaliation against Germany. Halifax 'told him very politely that I wished he was sitting where I was: that my experience was that in a war everybody who was not running it thought that they could run it better than the people who were.'

Even so, Halifax grudgingly agreed to be 'cross-examined' by Salisbury's committee. Among the group of nineteen who came to see him on 29 April were Leo Amery, who thought Halifax 'diffuse and unimpressive', and Harold Macmillan, who was reminded of 'a dinner at All Souls'. In the judgement of the All Souls historian S. J. D. Green: 'In effect they were offering him the Premiership. The meeting was a disaster.'

Salisbury sent a summary of their discussion to his son, who was too ill to attend: 'It is not encouraging.' Halifax had blamed the French (for being 'the great difficulty') and the Norwegians (for their 'profound apathy'), but he had himself no solution to offer. 'Upon the general question he was not able to throw any light upon the final method of winning the War.' Salisbury had concluded the meeting by saying, 'Lord Halifax, we are not satisfied.' Emrys-Evans, who had championed the Foreign Secretary, felt let down. 'Halifax had a most depressing effect on me.'

For his part, Halifax found this garrulous group of senior Conservative politicians 'in thoroughly critical mood, and nothing I said had the least effect upon them'. To crown it all, his punctilious Private Secretary Valentine Lawford had then ordered tea for Salisbury's deputation, which detained them for a further half-hour. 'I told him that if he ever did it again he would be murdered!'

On that brilliant Saturday, as his motor-car curved around St Denys's church and passed through her gates, Halifax looked forward to discussing this and other matters with Baba, as he talked to her about everything else.

The person who stepped out of the car was six foot five, a tall, gaunt figure dressed in a black office coat, with a long vent up the back that shone with a greenish tinge in the strong sunlight. Up the short drive his hostess came to welcome him, leading her twin daughters and two dogs, Rex the labrador and Tim the corgi.

In a photograph taken of that weekend, a small girl approaches Halifax.

'That's me!' Davina says. 'We had ghastly middle partings, like Mummy. You remember everything when you're a child. I can remember as if today.'

Their guest stood to his full lanky height to greet them.

When Halifax moved, Lawford wrote in his unpublished memoir, he could be graceful and shy simultaneously, like a waterbird wading in the shallows. 'Architecturally, the upper half of Halifax's head resembled a dome, which, since it rested on rather more than usually jutting ears, appeared illusively to taper towards the apex. It was a fine head, though. When he walked it fell very slightly forwards; and as he sat reading at his desk he would cup the weight of it in the palm of his right hand . . . Yet his was by no means the neglected body of a dreamer. His back and legs were magnificently straight and he looked his best astride a horse.'

Lawford used to ride with him in the early mornings on Wimbledon Common, after which Halifax walked through St James's Park to the Foreign Office. One morning, Halifax arrived in rubber boots 'almost three foot six high' which had to be pulled off by an office keeper. 'He had bare feet underneath.'

Not all that he was togged up to be? A minority always thought so.

Christened Edward Frederick Lindley Wood, and known from 1924 to 1935 as Lord Irwin, and since then as Viscount Halifax, he had been born in 1881 with a withered left hand which he covered with a black leather glove, but he never referred to his deformity in his memoirs, or in public; nor was it mentioned in Stuart Hodgson's 1941 biography. 'One couldn't say anything to him, he would have minded beyond all belief,' says his daughter-in-law, Diana Holderness. 'I did see it once. There was almost nothing there but a little thumb. I went into his room by mistake, and he put his other hand over it. He used his other hand tremendously.'

Once in America, Halifax went out sea-fishing with his Private Secretary Charles Peake, and he caught four big barracuda. 'He had landed the lot single-handed, managing both his rod & reel with his one arm, a feat which the boatman said he could not have believed if he had not seen it.' But Halifax's agility and economy of movement could not protect him every time. When an American photographer 'tried to get hold of his left hand and "arrange" it,' Peake glanced at Halifax's face 'which remained immobile, but I knew he had been touched to the raw . . . he was still quivering inside like a nerve.'

That quivering nerve remained gloved from the world, which was how Halifax preferred it, quoting Dryden: *'Anything, though ever so little, which a man speaks of himself – in my opinion is still too much.'* Naturally reticent and discreet, Halifax confessed to Charles Peake: 'It is so terribly difficult to talk of oneself.' In 1931, Gandhi had sought an interview with Halifax to meet 'not so much the Viceroy as the man in you'. Yet the man within Halifax, who by a whisker did not become our wartime Prime Minister, was elusive to a remarkable degree.

'Queer bird, Halifax,' said Clement Attlee, 'very humorous, all hunting and Holy Communion.' David Dilks found Halifax 'singularly inscrutable' when, as a twenty-one-year-old, he interviewed him in December 1959, three weeks before he died. 'He had a grave, measured style of speech. There was nothing gushing about him. He didn't use two words if one would do.' In part, this may have been due to a speech impediment; rather as Curzon pronounced his 'a's short (so that colleagues called him Alabasster), and Churchill had trouble with his 's's, so Halifax had difficulty in saying his 'r's.

Labour MPs dubbed him Lord Dullard, Conservative MPs 'the Master of Garrowby'. But to Harold Nicolson, writing to Baba on Halifax's death, Halifax was a man 'who possessed both grandeur and simplicity. I know what a close friend he was of yours and what a gap he will leave . . .'

When Baba attempted to pin down Halifax's character, she considered that he was above all things a statesman, not a politician. 'His strong point is his balanced detachment, with no pettiness or personal ambition rearing its head.' Diffident, modest, unpompous, Halifax was, in Lawford's view, a man who led 'a life of unselfish public service' and was 'an impressive survival from England's more decorous past: the sort of statesman to whom it was in no way inhibiting to begin a letter: "Lord Halifax with his humble duty to Your Majesty."' In fact, he was a friend both of the King (who 'liked Halifax's telegrams') and the Queen (Dorothy was one of her ladies-in-waiting). Halifax would invite them to dine in his London house at 88 Eaton Square. The King had given him a key to the gardens at Buckingham Palace, through which Halifax walked with his dachshund on his way to the Foreign Office. He wrote in his diary: 'The Queen has repeatedly exhorted me to use their garden-house, where are chairs and a telephone! I have never been able to yet. One of these days, if I am kept in London for the week-end, I might settle in there on Sunday.'

It was impossible to imagine Halifax misbehaving. To the vast majority, he was a man of immense prestige and probity, above politics, a type of 'statesman that only this country can produce', wrote Geoffrey Shakespeare. At the same time he was capable of the unexpected, suddenly breaking 'into broad Yorkshire'. He once took his daughter-in-law Diana to an all-in wrestling match, dressed in striped trousers, bowler hat, stiff collar and watch-chain. She says: 'He spat on the pavement while waiting for a bus. "That's revolting," I said. He replied, "My father's generation did it."'

Allegedly a saint, he was considered by a small group to be hard as nails, and not one hundred per cent truthful. His religious faith was offputting to the Soviet Ambassador who viewed him as a 'pious old fool'. Maisky nicknamed Halifax 'the Bishop' who 'retires to pray and comes out a worse hypocrite than before', after saying to Rab Butler at the beginning of each working day: 'Mind, Butler, we mustn't sacrifice a single principle today!' Amused at the great interest which Halifax took in Rasputin, Maisky believed that beneath the Foreign Secretary's appeal to exalted feelings and noble principles, he had 'a landlord's heart' and was 'always mindful of his own interests'. Chips Channon was another diarist suspicious of the way that Halifax 'fascinates and bamboozles everyone'. In observing Halifax's 'extraordinary character, his high principles, his engaging charm and grand manner', Channon could not help noticing as well 'his power to frighten people into fits . . . his snobbishness . . . his eel-like qualities and, above all, his sublime treachery which is never deliberate and, always to him, a necessity dictated by a situation. Means are nothing to him, only ends.'

Halifax's real end, whatever it was, remained an enigma to almost everyone.

'How mistaken one can be about people.' Over the course of a single year, Charles Peake wrote an unpublished diary, recently rediscovered, in which he set out to describe Halifax's character, 'which has constantly eluded his other friends'.

Peake considered that 'if greatness means anything, he probably has it; but I wish he wouldn't be so sensitive . . . With all his tiresomeness, his wings cleave the upper air, and are strong enough to bear one up with him, and strong too to keep one there . . .'

At the same time, Peake's master could easily be yanked back to earth by, for example, his dachshund. Halifax talked 'the most appalling dog drivel I have ever heard in my life,' Peake wrote, after watching him cuddle the dog in the course of a discussion about death, judgement, hell and heaven. 'Oh look at that little waggetty, waggetty tail oh let daddy kiss his popsy little nose again – Dowothea! your dog's gone and wee-weed again.'

As for Halifax's flaws, Peake felt that 'his attitude is too inhuman (but then he is a little inhuman)'. Talking one night about the use of Christian names, Halifax shocked Peake by saying that they should be confined to the smallest possible circle of a man's friends. 'I always make Ruth, my daughter-in-law, address me as "Lord Halifax". I am certainly not going to become "Popsy" or anything like that, and as I have often to speak to her for her good it would be highly inconvenient to let her call me Edward.'

Like Chamberlain, Halifax had only a few intimate friends with whom he found it possible to relax his guard. One of a minuscule number who called him Edward, or 'Edouard' as she pronounced it, was Baba. What would have astonished those for whom Halifax stood as a pillar of unimpeachable detachment is that in his letters to this married woman, marked 'Very Private', he called Baba 'my beloved'.

*

No other woman in England was better placed to appreciate Edward Halifax's predicament that weekend than his thirty-six-year-old hostess, Lady Alexandra Naldera 'Baba' Metcalfe. Her father, like him, had been Viceroy of India, Prize Fellow of All Souls, Chancellor of Oxford University and Foreign Secretary, and a front runner for the premiership. Unique in having occupied the same offices as Lord Curzon, Halifax was the only survivor of 'the Curzon Cabinet' of the 1920s. If there was anyone to whom he could turn in safety for frank advice, then it was to Curzon's youngest daughter.

Davina says of her mother: 'She's not Curzon's daughter for nothing. She loved being in the thick of it, oh yes. Mummy always wanted to be part of the action.'

Socially Halifax's equal, Baba was someone who had no influence over government and yet knew what was going on and was not a burden to his wife. She had been at the hub a long time, and savoured her position there. As he stretched out in his chair on the lawn at Little Compton, poring over the same red boxes as Baba's father, and reading the weekend's 'excited' press calling for a reconstruction of the government, Lord Halifax might have been Lord Curzon waiting for the summons at Montacute House on that Whitsun weekend in 1923; and Baba one of those young women like Venetia Stanley, whom Duff Cooper in December 1916 had found seated beside Prime Minister Asquith's fire, warming herself, 'while under their feet the fate of the Empire was being decided'.

*

Baba in those days captivated every eye that gazed on her. Her beauty had the power to waken sensations long dormant. Slim, with smooth white hands, in a low-cut grey organza dress, she was exquisite, says her nephew Nicholas Mosley, then sixteen, who stayed at Little Compton that summer, and for whom 'Aunt Baba' acted as a surrogate mother. 'Very chic, but exquisite is the word.'

Yet not a cosy mother. Even though possessed of a powerful libido, 'she never told you the facts of life', says her daughter, who cannot recall once being kissed or hugged by Baba. 'She was extremely bossy, a serious put-downer.'

Every inch a Viceroy's daughter, Baba was accustomed to positioning herself at the head of any queue. Nancy Astor ticked her off, writing that 'I never hear from you unless you want something – Never – and I resent it very much.' Not even when Baba's son David had a temperature of 102 did it deter Baba from her evening plans. Her sister Irene was always complaining about her. 'Gosh! She is selfish.'

Women were frightened of Baba. She might be immaculate, but she scared people, said Halifax's granddaughter. 'She was cold and promiscuous, not a woman's woman.' Men, though, responded in droves. Diana Mosley said of Baba that she had the slight touch of the governess which a lot of men find attractive. One of her beaux was Walter Monckton, head of the Press and Censorship Bureau, who complained that 'you keep me tantalisingly suspended between frying pan & fire,' leaving him 'to sizzle – with cool detachment . . . I do love you.'

James Lees-Milne was a friend. 'I like her, although she is, if not exigent, taxing, in that her presence is demanding of constant attention. She is *très grande dame* . . . Proffers in that truly womanly way a contribution towards the fare, diffidently, and determinedly, yet knowing all the time that the proffer will be rejected.' Amused by her 'deliberate action, her careful loud diction, her proud, self assured manner', he found Baba handsome, energetic – and terrifying; and saluted how she simply got her way by 'quietly bulldozing'.

Her parents' wealth enabled Baba to call the shots in her marriage, family, home. Her son David said: 'She ran the show,' and he admitted to being 'extremely careful' around her. 'She had the money. She was the one who was there. Her personality dominated the whole thing.'

On this Saturday afternoon that irresistible and seductive force was directed at the tall, bald figure who had come to stay, whom Monckton called 'my hated rival'. Baba's daughter says: 'To use old-fashioned words, she was horns in.'

They had first met in Simla in 1926. Halifax was Viceroy, living in the house where Baba had been conceived twenty-three years before – it was either there, Viceregal Lodge, or under the deodar trees at Naldera, the golf course that Curzon built for himself, just below Simla, and from which Baba took her middle name. Her nickname 'Baba' was derived from Curzon's Punjabi servants who baptised her 'Baba Sahib', the Viceroy's baby. 'We wanted a boy,' said Irene, eight years older, who was jealous of Baba and always joking at her own expense about her bosoms, comparing herself to her beautiful slim sister. Much more recently, Baba had become maliciously known as 'Ba-ba-Black-Shirt', following a liaison with her Fascist brother-in-law, Oswald 'Tom' Mosley.

Her upbringing had been sumptuous. At Simla's Viceregal Lodge, there were said to be as many native servants as days in the year. One man brought the bathwater, another heated it, a third poured it into the tub, a fourth emptied it. A dairy cow shipped out from England provided her with milk.

Baba's mother, the Vicereine, died when Baba was two. Mary Curzon had been a singularly gentle and kindly woman. She had none of the head-strong imperiousness of her youngest daughter, who would turn down a proposal from the Duke of Kent in favour of the son of an Irish prison inspector, a charming but penniless polo player seventeen years her senior, Major Edward Metcalfe, popularly known as 'Fruity'.

Louis Mountbatten was best man at their wedding at the Chapel Royal in 1925. Soon after, Baba returned to live in India, where Fruity had been appointed to General Birdwood's staff. Invited to stay at her old home by Lord Irwin, as Halifax then was, Baba was disappointed not to find her childhood kingdom intact. On 5 September 1926, she wrote in her diary: 'We left Simla this evening by the rail motor. I hadn't one pang about leaving. It is an odious place, the people not too good and the weather past description.' She came to feel the same about Fruity, who jovially admitted: 'I have no money and I've got no brain,' and who set her neat white teeth on edge with his daily request: 'Which tie shall it be this morning, Babs darling? D'ye think it should be the blue? Or would you say the red?'

Another ten years passed before an intellectually starved Baba stayed again with Halifax, in Berlin. In November 1937, Irene wrote in her diary: 'Baba rang up full of news. She had a great time staying with Nevile Henderson with Lord Halifax there.'

This was the weekend when Halifax met Hitler, ostensibly in Halifax's capacity as a Master of Foxhounds during a visit to an International Hunting Exhibition. The German for 'Tally-ho!' being 'Halali!', Halifax was nicknamed 'Lord Halalifax' as he posed beside antlers while a gramophone played the roar of a stag. Poland won first prize with a giant stuffed panda. Asked to broadcast a few words on air, Halifax could think of nothing to say 'except how wonderful it was'. He then went off in a special train provided by Hitler, with white-coated attendants, to Berchtesgaden.

Baba was in Berlin as a guest of the British Ambassador, Nevile Henderson, who had wanted to marry Irene, and was present at the Residence on Wilhelmstrasse when Halifax returned. She was one of the first to learn how, as his car drew up at Berchtesgaden, Halifax had observed through the car window a pair of black-trousered legs, finishing up in silk socks and pumps, and was poised to hand his coat to the helpful servant 'when I heard von Neurath or somebody throwing a hoarse whisper at my ear of "Der Führer, der Führer", and then it dawned upon me that the legs were not the legs of a footman, but of Hitler'.

Halifax told Baba about his three-hour lunch at which Hitler ate vegetable soup and walnuts, while drinking a hot concoction out of a glass in a silver holder; how Der Führer liked to watch two films a night, preferably featuring Greta Garbo; how one of his favourite films was *The Lives of a Bengal Lancer*; and how, speaking through an interpreter, since Hitler did not understand more than a few words of English, he had chastised Halifax over the failings of British policy in India. Hitler's solution was to 'Shoot Gandhi' and to go on shooting the Congress leaders until peace was restored.

Baba was also at the British Residence when Halifax returned from his meeting with Goering, 'a great schoolboy' dressed in brown breeches, a green leather jerkin and a green hat with a chamois tuft. Goering's tame elks had eaten out of his hand. Halifax's wife was patron of the Elk Hounds Club.

And Baba was present for the tea party next afternoon with Joseph Goebbels, when the Nazi Propaganda Minister tried to persuade Halifax to order the cartoonist Low to tone down his anti-Hitler rhetoric. Baba introduced Halifax to Low's employer on their return to London, the first of several instances when Baba – 'that indefatigable young lady' Herbert Morrison called her – acted as a conduit.

Baba was in touch with Halifax at important moments over the next two years. On St Valentine's Day 1938, she wrote to congratulate him on becoming Foreign Secretary. In his answer, there was the reluctance of a man who accepts promotion, but only after initially turning it down – as he had declined the Viceroyalty when first offered it in 1925, and the Foreign Secretaryship once before, in 1931. 'My dear Baba, Thank you so much. At this moment I am not actually FS, but I fear I shall be tomorrow! It's not a very pleasant thing to look forward to: but I couldn't well help myself! And I think it's the biggest thing to have a shot at all!'

On 1 October 1938, Baba drove with Irene to Heston airfield to see Halifax welcome back Chamberlain from Munich; and when news broke of the Soviet–Nazi pact on 22 August 1939, it was with Baba that Halifax elected to dine. She wrote in her diary: 'Edward entrancing and charming, might have no cares, after politics we discussed every kind of ordinary subject.' In the same month, Baba served as intermediary between Halifax and the Duke of Windsor, to whom Fruity had been best man.

Looking back on their summer evenings of 1939, when they had dined in the Dorchester's Spanish-decorated Grill Room or 'in the big window of the Hyde Park Hotel', Halifax confessed that 'I was rather frightened of you in those days . . .'

Once war was declared, Halifax learned to master his fear.

The signature tune of the Dorchester hotel band was 'The Sweetest Music This Side of Heaven'. Baba's diary entry for 6 October read: 'Dined with Edward tête-à-tête. My idea of a perfect evening.' Nothing was off the table, from her marriage troubles with Fruity to Halifax's reservations about becoming Prime Minister – which he had first aired to her in August. On that occasion, she had written: 'The Eden, Churchill type is the politician devoured with ambition for power. Edward totally devoid of the wish for power and always more and more amazed at finding himself caught up in the machine doing the job he is doing. Would gladly forsake it all for a country life of sport and reading with a few intelligent friends.'

Two months on, the subject of power still preyed on him, and it occupied much of their dinner conversation. 'Edward said he would not take on the Premiership if offered, his reasons being that not being in the Commons makes the position too difficult. The leader of the House of Commons, say Winston, would have the difficult job of being the leader without the cachet of P.M. Situations would be bound to arise in which the P.M. in the Lords got irritated by what was being said in the Commons. The question of posts to be filled would have to be done by Edward without knowledge of the proper men available, therefore he would be dependent on other men's advice, and if those difficulties were surmounted by an act giving him a safe seat in the Commons he felt he was too tired to start that racket again.'

A paragon of self-abnegation, Halifax appeared yet again to be positioning himself in order to turn down an important promotion. 'He thought Kingsley Wood would do better!' And if not the Air Minister, there were other willing candidates. Deflectingly, Halifax told Baba of a friend recently back from Harvard where a group of highbrows had asked who would be Prime Minister if Chamberlain went, to which he had replied, without hesitation: 'Lady Astor.'

The more serious question: would Halifax accept if pressed, as had happened before over the Viceroyalty, and also the Foreign Office?

In October 1939, Halifax closed his large house in Eaton Square and went with Dorothy to live in a suite on the sixth floor of the Dorchester hotel, newly constructed, according to the brochure, out of 'almost indestructible concrete' – and equipped to resist air and gas attacks. 'No disturbance can penetrate through the walls. Below every floor is a thick layer of dried seaweed such as is used by the BBC for deadening sound.' Here the Halifaxes established themselves 'in a flat with a good deal of our own furniture and some of our own pictures'. 'Dowothea', as Halifax called his wife, whom he had first met in the refreshment room at Berwick-on-Tweed station, was often away at Garrowby. In her absences, Halifax begged Baba 'to come &

cheer my solitude'. They were soon dining together two or three times a week.

EIGHT FLOORS OF HEAVILY REINFORCED CONCRETE, EACH ONE FOOT THICK

The Dorchester Air Raid Shelter is protected by 12 feet of almost indestructible concrete. Experts agree that the Shelter is absolutely safe against even a direct hit.

RESTAURANT AND OTHER PUBLIC ROOMS

THREE-FOOT RAFT OF HEAVILY REINFORCED CONCRETE

GAS-PROOF SHELTER

Ida and Hilda Chamberlain were sibling repositories for what the Prime Minister felt unable to share with anyone else. The unhappily married Baba provided an outlet for Halifax's confidences and frustrations as Churchill continued to pester Halifax to mine the entrance to the waters off Narvik.

Over a 5-shilling war economy dinner at the Dorchester, Halifax described how he had complained to Chamberlain about Churchill's broadcast on 20 January against the position taken by neutral countries, all hoping, said Churchill, to be the last one eaten by the crocodile. 'Really, it is intolerable that Winston should come floundering into my department. What would he say if I made similar excursions into his?' Baba felt it 'incredible that a man in his position should make such gaffes. His bragging about the war at sea is followed every time by some appalling loss . . . and his voice oozes with port, brandy and the chewed cigar.' Churchill 'terrified' Baba, despite his flattering comment at her father's funeral, at which he had been a pallbearer: 'What better monument can a famous man leave behind him than a beautiful daughter.' Another entry in her diary reads: 'Winston is causing endless trouble as he absolutely refuses to disgorge even the most essential facts till hours too late.'

At their intimate dinners and in letters, Halifax discarded his chilly aloofness. 'Baba dearest. I can't tell you what your letters mean. Do take every care of yourself for you are very precious to me . . .' In case of their correspondence being steamed open by one of Joseph Ball's agents, they concocted private nicknames. Lloyd George was 'Corgi', Anthony Eden was 'Draughty Mouth', Churchill was 'Pooh'. Emphasising that she must 'for heaven's sake keep all this to yourself', Halifax wrote to Baba about 'the Pooh': 'With all his faults of egocentricity, total lack of the right sort of humility and utter inconsiderateness for anybody but himself, I do take my hat off to the sheer confidence, vitality and vigour of the man.'

Through Halifax, Baba had prior secret knowledge of the evacuation from Namsos. But the Foreign Secretary's transgressions passed beyond oral confidences. She wrote on the same night, 2 May: 'I saw a letter to Winston from Roger Keyes in which he blamed Dudley Pound and said that the handling of the situation had been lamentable and the Navy disgraced etc., and when was he going to be given the chance of leading the Navy to victory etc.' This was not the first occasion when Baba had been privy to Halifax's 'FO papers', which at night he handed to the hotel manager to put in the safe. 'He showed me his day to day, in fact hourly account of the weeks previous to the declaration of war.' In another diary entry, Baba writes of 'an evening of sheer delight reading bits of Ed's speeches, telegrams from the FO . . .' When Halifax gave a speech at the Sheldonian in February – 'by far the best speech he has ever made', Stuart Hodgson wrote – it was Baba who read the first draft. Her response: 'It lacks strength and firmness. I told him this and he said, "You mean I'm floppy and you want me to be more virile"!!'

Baba summarised her feelings for Halifax after a drizzly morning during which she had first walked with him to 'early church', then sat with him while he worked, and then walked two further miles with him in the rain. 'Ed unbelievably sweet – our companionship is perfection, he seems to get as much enjoyment and happiness from me as I do him. We discussed the reason and strangeness of our friendship for ages. He never tires of asking why I like him and I answered "because you make me feel sunny all through". I asked him why and what he liked about me and he said "I can't put it into any crisp phrase as that, but I love you very much."' In another letter, he struggled to explain. 'It is perfect being with someone like you who shares everything and with whom one has not reserves or lack of understanding. A very perfect companion, you are.'

It was during the Norway Campaign that their relationship broke surface, thanks to Charles Peake, at the time head of the Foreign Office News Department. During the Supreme War Council Meeting on 28 March, Peake had needed to see Halifax at short notice, following the leak by the French agency Havas that the Royal Navy was about to mine Norwegian waters. Peake had telephoned the Dorchester and requested that they should dine together. Halifax refused. 'I have to go to the French Embassy at nine and have to say something, so must have time to think. Come round at 8.30 p.m. and I'll give you a quarter of an hour then.' Peake, now being hounded by journalists, went up to Halifax's suite at 8.15 p.m. and rang the bell. Halifax came to the door. 'You've come too early.' Peake explained. Then Halifax took him in. There was Baba, who winked at Peake. Halifax said: 'Talk away, Lady Alexandra is one of us.' While Peake was talking, the telephone rang. It was Lady Halifax. Peake could hear every word. 'Edward, haven't heard from you for two weeks.' Halifax replied: 'Been very busy.' Lady Halifax: 'Oh nonsense, I'm sure you have that charming Baba with you at this very moment.' Baba winked at Peake again, according to Peake.

This account in Robert Bruce Lockhart's diary is virtually unique, even though Halifax's extremely close relations with Baba Metcalfe were common knowledge, says David Dilks. 'Everyone knew, but in those restrained days most diaries would not have recorded such material.' Neither Cadogan nor Lawford, Halifax's closest assistants during these months, make any mention of Baba in their diaries (but then nor does Lawford mention his own homosexual life); and Peake's diary contains but a single reference to Baba, in which Dorothy wonders whether Baba might be tight. ' "Not tight, but perhaps tiddley," Edward corrected.'

A valuable exception is the journal kept by Baba's sister Irene, 'a large buxom woman with an obsession for hunting and a voice like a foghorn', according to their nephew Nicholas Mosley. At the Dorchester, Baba moved into Irene's room, leaving Irene to witness with stupefied amazement the way in which Britain's enamoured Foreign Secretary, one floor below, could behave in time of war. Once the Blitz was on, Baba and Halifax would regularly shuffle downstairs in their dressing gowns and pyjamas, and sleep in the Turkish baths on beds laid out in little cubicles. Irene wrote with some bitterness in her diary: 'Lord Halifax can seldom keep off Baba.'

Rumours of Lord Halifax's crush on Lady Alexandra Metcalfe spread beyond the reinforced walls of 'the Dorch'. At a lunch with Churchill, Harvard University's President caused a roar of laughter when he said that since Claridge's was not of steel construction, he was thinking of moving to the Dorchester. It was then explained that though his life might be in greater danger at Claridge's, his reputation would be in greater danger at the Dorchester. On an occasion that became notorious, Churchill telephoned Halifax late at night at the hotel – only to be put through to Baba.

A friend of Irene's muttered how 'unfortunate' it was for Baba to telephone Halifax 'in the middle of dinner with others present who might talk'. When Baba started accompanying the Foreign Secretary to Mass at the Grosvenor Chapel, Irene cautioned her sister that 'it was not fair on him to be seen going to early service with him, people in the hotel could so easily put the wrong construction on it'. Baba retorted that 'it was Lrd H. who had given her a faith and belief and everything was on the highest plane.'

An embarrassed Irene raked over the matter with Bessie Hyslop, nanny to Baba's nephews and nieces – 'We could not fathom the Halifax–Baba thing. Baba was in a secret glow of delight.' Irene pored over it with another of her suitors, Victor Cazalet, Conservative MP and director of the Dorchester, who had offered Irene the use of the twin room on the seventh floor. 'Discussed with Victor Cazalet Baba's extraordinary power over Lord H and that she rang him at any moment over minor things and that he always responded and that it was always Baba first and then his family. That Dorothy Halifax was the saint, not him.'

Mary Curzon, mother to Baba and Irene, had felt the same amorous passion for their father. 'The sweet test of affection is not if you can live with a person, but if you cannot live without him, and if you feel that when Mr X comes into a room, that the room is glowing with pink light, and thrills are running up and down your back with pure joy, then it is all right.' This described Baba's behaviour – and it captured Halifax's mesmerised state. 'I can't tell you, darling one, what a great relief your letter was . . . You know, I think, my dearest, how much love surrounds you as a kind of moral armour plate protection, and there is as much more to be called into service as you need . . . you are really never out of my thoughts.' When Halifax left for America in January 1941, with her gift of a miniature dachshund in his pocket, he was as stricken as Baba. 'All I have had of you since then is your photograph kept on my desk which looks at me as I write, and your last note which I keep locked up but look at from time to time.' Whatever messages her letters contained, they were too incendiary to be read by others. 'I am keeping your last note for a little longer until I know it all by heart. Then it shall be destroyed.'

The inevitable moment came when Irene grew sick and tired of finding Baba's clothes strewn over her room, Baba dressed in a 'lace brassiere and black chiffon drawers', Baba always on the telephone to her 'beau'. 'I said she loved comfort and ease and was very selfish and that if it had not been for one or two friends to protect her, her name would be mud over Edward Halifax. She hit me savagely in the face.'

Nanny Hyslop reported the sisters' terrible row to their teenage nephew, Nicholas Mosley, who was still able to recall the conversation seven decades on. 'Irene said to Baba: "You really must stop this business with Lord Halifax because everyone's going yackety yak." Baba said: "I don't know what you're talking about. Lord Halifax and I are very good friends and I'm very good friends with Dorothy." Irene said: "I've never heard such rubbish, of course you're carrying on" – which was the term – "with Lord Halifax." Baba said: "I've just got a very good friendship," and then they didn't speak. As a sixteen-year-old, I thought this was very interesting.'

Violet Bonham Carter was the daughter of Prime Minister Herbert Asquith, who in 1914 at a time of national peril had formed an intense attachment to Violet's best friend, Venetia Stanley. The mystery of that romance remains unresolved – most of Asquith's letters from Venetia are missing, as are Baba's to Halifax – but when the riddle of sex came up in later life, recalls her daughter-in-law Leslie Bonham Carter, and speculation was invited, Violet would put a hand to her throat and enquire, 'My dear, was it *thorough-going*?'

Even as the Germans were driving our troops out of Norway, this question was being asked of the Foreign Secretary and his relationship with the estranged wife of Major Metcalfe. Forty years on, the question was still being posed. On 18 December 1991, James Lees-Milne wrote in his diary after meeting Halifax's biographer, Andrew Roberts: 'Asked me if I thought Lord Halifax went to bed with Lady Alexandra Metcalfe.'

On the night that the French Chasseurs came ashore in Namsos, Baba had gone with Irene to the opening of *Gone with the Wind*. Mass Observation reported a new fashion among young couples of having 'intercourse in shop doorways on the fringe of passing crowds'. Baba's friend Nancy Astor wanted 'a girl curfew' to counteract immorality in parks, with the banning of make-up and short skirts. Thoroughgoing love was in the air that spring. But between Halifax and Baba?

Lees-Milne was doubtful, telling Roberts: 'I shouldn't think so somehow.' David Cecil also thought not. 'Edward was purely Edwardian in his love of purely decorous flirtations in which he played the part of instructor and adviser.' Yet Churchill had believed that the romance between the Duke of Windsor and Wallis Simpson was 'psychical rather than sexual' and a most 'natural' companionship completely free 'from impropriety or grossness' – even if the King's Private Secretary found it as easy to believe in the innocence of that relationship as in 'a herd of unicorns grazing in Hyde Park', where since November Halifax and Baba had taken to strolling.

'They seem to be walking in Hyde Park. Then she sleeps in the next bunk at the Dorchester. It must have been perfectly maddening for Dorothy that he had this crush on Baba.' Seventy-five years on, Baba's daughter Davina continues to be puzzled by 'this extraordinary relationship', which had made her father so jealous – Irene's diary records how Fruity, whom Irene likened to 'some large wounded animal hitting its head against granite or an iceberg (Baba)' gave 'a v ugly diatribe on Baba's selfishness . . . spending all her time with Ld H.'

Davina did not muster the courage to question her mother. She says of Baba: 'She was part of a generation who never showed feeling, ever. If I'd asked her about Edward, I'll tell you exactly what she always said: "I really can't go into that now."'

Diana Holderness was married to Halifax's son Richard. 'Was the relationship sexual? We argued, all in this small circle, Richard and his sister, and Charles Peake, who had been his PPS, and his wife Catherine. We argued ad infinitum. Most of us said no. My own thought is yes. I just do believe it. Roman Catholics sleep with everyone. I don't think religion stops one. Let's be honest, people can say their prayers, but they still have sex.'

On meeting Halifax that summer, the journalist George Ward Price could not help noticing Halifax's deprecating smile 'almost as if he had a guilty secret'. Valentine Lawford wrote that out of all the political leaders for whom he worked, Halifax 'was perhaps the most susceptible to the charm of clever women'. Roy Jenkins definitely formed the impression that Halifax was 'a bit of a "gwoper"'. If so, it ran in the family. Halifax told Charles Peake how his great-great-grandfather had fallen madly in love with Georgiana, the Duchess of Devonshire, who had had a daughter by him.

In his diary, Halifax noted how the French Minister Georges Mandel had asked whether he could come to London, for a Supreme War Council meeting, with '*des bagages*', which the British Ambassador interpreted as his mistress. That Daladier and Reynaud had mistresses was widely known, to the extent that Madame de Portes sent messages to Reynaud even while the War Council was in session. Baba may or may not have achieved '*bagages*' status with Halifax, but she had form. Lord Curzon had sinned on a tiger-skin with Elinor Glyn, and Baba was her father's daughter.

A previous lover was a friend of Halifax, the Italian Ambassador Count Dino Grandi. 'Naldera, darling, my sweet friend, I am yours,' Grandi had written from Rome the previous May.

Then there was her brother-in-law, Tom Mosley. Baba had gone to bed with Mosley two months after his wife, her sister Cimmie, died in May 1933. After the war, Baba went to Mosley and suggested this arrangement should continue as before, says Nicholas Mosley. 'My father told me he had felt obliged to say no.' Instead, Baba took up with Sim Feversham, who, though married to Halifax's daughter Anne, went on to build Baba a cottage at Pennyholme three miles across the moor from where he had his home in Yorkshire. 'Baba never left anyone alone,' says someone who knew both her and Halifax reasonably well. 'If you sleep with your brother-in-law, why wouldn't you like to sleep with the Foreign Secretary? After all, she went on to sleep with his son-in-law.'

The last word on this subject must go to Halifax's biographer Andrew Roberts, who believes that even if their relationship was not thoroughgoing 'then it was as good as'. Roberts says: 'They were emotionally bound in a way that contrasts with the public image.'

Whatever the nature of their relationship, it was of consuming importance to Halifax. Possibly, it was even more important to him at this critical moment than being Prime Minister. If that was the case, then his weekend with Baba Metcalfe at Little Compton served to confirm what he already knew.

Everyone praised how Baba had spruced up the house. She had brought a walnut wing-chair and table lamps from Kedleston; from another Curzon country house, Montacute, pieces of lacquered furniture. She had mingled Regency and Victorian with Oriental, and pinned up a Bedouin-style tent over her bed in the main bedroom. Wallis Simpson wrote to Baba from the South of France: 'Everyone tells me that your house is a <u>dream</u> and that you have done it all too beautifully.' Wallis was 'still struggling with the butler question – we have an ape at present'. At Little Compton, Baba had a butler called Simpson, May the parlourmaid, two housemaids, and a chef.

The guest room looked over the back garden. Halifax wrote to Baba: 'I can't conceive how you ever tear yourself away from such a concentration of tranquillity.' It could have been a weekend at Naldera, eating cherries from the trees after a long walk through the deodar woods, only in this case through Baba's small deer park. And in the evening, playing charades ('Baba doing the Immaculate Conception was a scream,' Irene wrote on another occasion) and reading aloud from his father's ghost book, *A Collection of Stories of Haunted Houses, Apparitions, and Supernatural Occurrences* which Halifax had published in October, with an introduction by him.

The reluctance of Bishop Juxon's phantom to materialise did nothing to dent Halifax's enjoyment. Afterwards, as though 'still living in the "sun" of that pleasant weekend', Halifax came to stay often, sometimes on his own, sometimes with Dorothy. 'We could count upon a standing welcome from Alexandra Metcalfe at her home in Little Compton,' he wrote in one of two spare references to Baba in his memoirs. 'It was always agreeable and stimulating so that the weekend never failed to send us back to work refreshed in body and soul.'

After yet another 'rare weekend', Charles Peake wrote to Baba that 'it was lovely to see Edward so blissfully happy and to feel he deserved to be happy – for he has been hard hit and has never thought of himself.' Dorothy expressed her gratitude in similar ecstatic terms. She had not seen her husband 'so light-hearted since the war, no indeed, not since 1938 when he took over the FO! & it was very good to see him giggling!'

Halifax's levity on that first weekend masked the fear that he shared with the nation. 'There was no shadow of doubt about the fact of the public expectation of invasion.' An Intelligence report from Prague indicated that the Germans had completed their preparations, and had divided London into several administrative districts. Even the King was taking precautions, telling Halifax that he was going to carry a rifle in his car, and intended to do rifle practice in the gardens of Buckingham Palace. Churchill informed Halifax that if the Germans came to London, 'I shall take a rifle (I'm not a bad shot with a rifle) and put myself in the pillbox at the bottom of Downing Street and shoot till I've no more ammunition, and then they can damned well shoot me.'

At 8.30 on Sunday morning Halifax walked with Baba to the local church. The bells still rang out – not until 13 June were church bells silenced, 'to ring only in case of invasion alarm'. Even so, the atmosphere inside St Denys's church reinforced the nervous expectation felt in congregations up and down the country. 'Is it possible that the Prussian jackboot will force its way into this countryside to tread and trample it at will?' The idea outraged Halifax, 'much as if anyone were to be condemned to watch his mother, wife, or daughter being raped'.

Over breakfast outside in the sun, Halifax discussed the Norwegian Campaign with Baba. She wrote in her diary: 'Edward is absolutely sure the Government did right in going to the aid of Norway and also in withdrawing when we did.'

There is no evidence for this, but Halifax may also have told her about Peter Fleming's escape from Namsos under Louis Mountbatten's protection. In the light of Halifax's other disclosures, there was little reason for him to keep this secret – given, also, the fond references to Fleming in his letters to Baba (Halifax wrote to her concerning the Viceroyalty of India: 'If I were dictator I might try someone like Peter Fleming') and that Mountbatten had been best man at her wedding.

What is known is that Halifax revealed to Baba classified information about the Norway Campaign which otherwise remained secret to all but the War Cabinet. Among the details she learned was that its failure had been due to 'a series of unexpected happenings' of which the gravest was Churchill's intervention at the outset on 8 April. 'There were troops actually on board one of the battleships ready to sail at the time of our mine-laying, but when it was heard that Germany had sent 2 of her biggest ships, the troops had to be disembarked in order for the ship to go after the German battleships. This caused delay.' In Chips Channon's reckoning, 'the delay in sending the fleet on that fatal 9 April may well cost us the War'.

Yet none of Churchill's interventions or gaffes might be mentioned in the Norway Debate, said Halifax. 'It is very difficult having public debates, and risking revealing to the Germans how our minds are working. That we obviously cannot do.'

Breakfast over, Halifax sprawled in a garden chair, hat on, left hand hanging limp and black out of his sleeve, and 'tried to make up a speech for Wednesday'. This he found 'very ticklish' to compose, but he finished it in time for lunch.

'A most perfect day,' he wrote in his diary, 'and after a comparatively idle afternoon we motored back to London, where I found piles of boxes, which I knew was the price of having to be away.' When thanking Baba for this heavenly weekend, he wrote that he was pulling strings for her to watch the debate in both Houses. 'The world is foul, isn't it! And I shall think it fouler on Wednesday in the H/L. Not that that matters tuppence. I will cast a glance in yr direction. Hope to get you seat in H/C tomorrow.' His mood was positive. Neither he nor Chamberlain would be ascending any scaffold. 'There is considerable political clamour but I doubt whether this, at present at all events, will amount to much.' He told Baba that he was sure the Prime Minister 'will remain in power for a long time'.

13
THE WILD MAN

'I don't know what to make of him.' Conservative MP to LADY ASTOR
'How about a nice rug?'

'I wonder whether any historian of the future will ever be able to paint Winston in his true colours.'
FIELD MARSHAL LORD ALANBROOKE

'He was still playing a solitary game, and with the cards stacked against him, in those spring days of 1940.'
EMANUEL SHINWELL MP

A strange peace had descended on Namsos following the departure of the Allied ships early on 3 May. With no one to put out the flames, the long line of vehicles continued to burn away on the quay.

Singly at first, then in stumbling groups, the town's starved inhabitants who had taken refuge in the Namdal valley flocked back through the ruins of their homes to help themselves to the food and drink that the Chasseurs Alpins had left behind. All codes of behaviour disappeared as famished men and women tore open the boxes and sated themselves on corned beef, biscuits and rum, and afterwards, groggily, on each other. This period of debauchery before the arrival of the Germans became known as the Rum Weekend.

On Sunday 5 May, the local Norwegian commander Colonel Getz, recognising that the Allies had abandoned him, was forced to sign a ceasefire with Oberst Krätzner of 181st Infantry Division. A tall column of dark smoke pointed the way to Namsos. Wary of the booby traps which Fleming and Lindsay had concealed under bridges, German troops advanced with care through a chill white landscape of narrow lanes choked with overturned milk-carts and broken-down cars. In the outlying streets, they found a dazed population meandering between the bomb-blasted trees.

In London, the obliteration of Namsos portended the destruction of Church-ill's political career: this too, it was felt, had been 'Namsosed'. Supportive MPs like Louis Spears voiced concern that 'the Norwegian fiasco had diminished his chances of assuming the leadership'. The Labour MP Josiah Wedgwood feared that the evacuation 'would only reflect injuriously on Churchill ... word passed round everywhere in the House – "Churchill is to blame."'

On 26 April, captured British troops from 148th Infantry Brigade had been flown to Berlin and paraded before Hitler, who made a vain attempt to crush their anti-tank ammunition between his fingers. 'This war was not necessary. You can thank your Government for it,' Hitler told the British POWs, and left.

Churchill's nephew was not among the prisoners. A German float-plane had removed him from Narvik, and Churchill was trying to find out where he was being held. An unconfirmed report from Amsterdam stated that Romilly had been interned on the Danish island of Bogø. Beaverbrook, his employer, had written to Nellie about Giles, whom she had always regarded as 'her heart's delight', and he implied that 'American sources have been tapped to help him', yet the family had heard 'no whisper of news'.

In Herefordshire, Nellie was at Huntington Park looking after Giles's critically ill father, and 'in a terrible state'. Bertram Romilly's condition had been exacerbated by his son's arrest, then imminent rescue, and now disap-pearance. The colonel's cancer had spread over his lungs, and on 23 April the doctor began to give him morphine. 'He had reached the highest peak of human suffering,' a stricken Nellie wrote to Churchill, who had sent a cheque – which Bertram resisted cashing, telling Nellie: 'I am only struggling to live as I don't want to waste Winston's 100 guineas for my operation.'

Inevitably, Giles Romilly's uncertain fate cast Churchill back forty years to his own experiences as a captive young war correspondent. Churchill admitted to Leo Amery that he had never felt so lonely as the morning after he escaped his prison building in Pretoria – climbing over a paling at the back of the lavatory – and found himself on his own in the veld. Much the same sense of isolation took hold as report after report of successive defeats streamed in from across the North Sea.

'*The beaten general is disqualified . . .*' Churchill the military historian was familiar with Marshal Foch's quotation which the Paris newspaper *Le Journal* printed that week, calling it 'a profound true remark which holds good for all defeats and for all in authority'. In the opinion of a correspondent to *The Times*, the military expedition to Norway was 'a disaster as great as that of Gallipoli.' In Westminster, its failure rebounded hardest on the Minister most identified with the campaign. Clementine later told her husband that had it not been for his repeated warnings about Germany, 'Norway might have ruined you.'

Outside the Commons and Downing Street, Churchill was still popularly regarded as a man of action and courage who had stood up to Hitler. Yet his 'unassailable' position in the country, as John Colville described it without huge conviction, was not replicated in Cabinet. On 1 May, Colville had watched Churchill gaze out of the window and say, as if looking at the sudden blight which had descended on the face of the earth, 'If I were the first of May, I should be ashamed of myself.' Colville was unsympathetic. 'Personally I think he ought to be ashamed of himself in any case.' A beaten general was how Colville and the No. 10 staff viewed Churchill.

Withheld from the public was Churchill's part in the messes of Narvik, Namsos and Åndalsnes. A majority in the War Cabinet shared the perception of Chancellor John Simon that Churchill 'is more directly responsible for recent defeats and strategy in Norway than any of his colleagues'. In 1914, Simon had written to Asquith urging him to sack Churchill as First Lord. Were Chamberlain to have canvassed Simon's opinion in May 1940, there is no reason to suppose that Simon would not have urged the same course. If any commander deserved to be disqualified, it was the First Lord.

On 5 May, General Pownall wrote in his diary that Churchill 'is probably more to blame than anyone for the various muddles which have taken place (and certainly for the general mix up in affairs generally)'. His assessment was shared by the military expert Basil Liddell Hart. 'The prime responsibility for this fiasco rested on Churchill, who from September on had pressed for drastic action to cut off Germany's supply of Swedish iron ore.' Beaverbrook was so disturbed by Churchill's 'harebrained' operation, which had resulted in the arrest of the *Express*'s 'star war correspondent' – Giles Romilly's name had 'figured enormous at the top of his brilliant despatches', wrote Nellie – that the newspaper owner allegedly said to one of his associates: 'Churchill? He's the man who let the Germans into Norway.'

Churchill's conduct over the previous three weeks had strengthened opinions in Westminster that not only was he not to be trusted at the helm, but that to hand him command risked inviting the same fate as had befallen HMS *Afridi*, which had sunk in twenty minutes. Colville famously summed it up: 'The mere thought of Churchill as Prime Minister sent a cold shiver down the spines of staff at 10 Downing Street . . . Our feelings . . . were widely shared in the Cabinet Offices, the Treasury, and throughout Whitehall.' The same trembling affected Admiral Godfrey in the Admiralty Intelligence Room. 'We all felt very uneasy that Mr Churchill . . . was leading us into a strategical adventure that might culminate in the defeat of the Allies.'

To many well-intentioned people who had worked with Churchill since the first mines were dropped into the Norwegian Sea on 8 April, his repeated interferences and changes of mind, his idiosyncratic and exhausting working methods, his failure to foresee or to parry the supremacy of the Luftwaffe, made him more culpable, operationally, than at Gallipoli. The War Minister Oliver Stanley told Halifax that, after the experience of sitting with Churchill in Cabinet, 'he could not serve Winston loyally having seen so much of him in the last two months'. Concerned, Clementine would be driven by her husband's behaviour to write him a letter shortly afterwards, then tear it up and write it out again, in which she referred to 'your being generally disliked by your colleagues & subordinates because of your rough sarcastic & overbearing manner'.

Despite Chamberlain's agreement to cede him more responsibility, which would be confirmed on Monday 6 May, there were signs that Churchill suddenly felt beleaguered – and not empowered, as he had earlier claimed to the *Manchester Guardian*'s editor, William Crozier. Lord Camrose saw Churchill on 3 May and felt that 'he was not quite the master of himself or cool politician that the P.M. is'.

For one thing, he was drinking too much.

The bottle of whisky fetched by Geoffrey Shakespeare on Churchill's first night back at the Admiralty had been followed by crates. After Operation 'Hammer' was called off, a disappointed President Roosevelt confided to the Canadian Prime Minister that Churchill 'was tight most of the time'. Hitler's view of Churchill as a 'superannuated drunkard' was supported by the journalist Cecil King who in April had watched Churchill having difficulty finishing a speech in the Commons and needing to be led away. 'It is at times like these that age and excessive brandy drinking tell.'

Churchill's scientific adviser Professor Lindemann calculated that if all the brandy Churchill had drunk was poured into the very large dining room at Chartwell, the level would rise $5/8^{th}$ of an inch up the wall. But brandy was merely one of his tipples. Churchill's intake of other alcoholic beverages intensified during this period.

Since September, Churchill's personal consumption of wine had been costing him £30 a month (£1,800 in today's prices). General Jacob observed that Churchill began the day by drinking 'white wine on occasion' at breakfast. He proceeded to take a glass of dry sherry at mid-morning, and a small bottle of claret or burgundy at lunch. Churchill's secretary Phyllis Moir told readers of *Life Magazine*: 'To Mr Churchill a meal without wine is not a meal at all. When he is in England he sometimes takes port after lunch, and always after dinner.' She continued in her merry vein: 'In the late afternoon he calls for his first whisky and soda of the day . . . He likes a bottle of champagne at dinner. After the ritual of port he sips the very finest Napoleon brandy. He may have a highball in the course of the evening.'

Churchill's excessive drinking had become damaging to his constitution as well as to his judgement. Cranborne was so concerned that he wrote to his father on 18 April about 'a real risk of his cracking up altogether'. When Lord Salisbury visited Churchill two nights later, their hour's conversation was taken up with an elaborate discussion of the statistics which covered the walls. 'Frankly, I was disappointed . . . he seemed to me rather to have lost his grip on the broad aspects of the War.'

Plagued by 'very deadly' thoughts, Churchill's conversation was no longer so brilliant. A dull look had entered his once prominent aquamarine eyes as he rushed from meeting to meeting. His bodyguard Walter Thompson noticed Churchill's 'rumpled slump', which made Thompson feel a foot taller than he really was. His deportment alarmed Admiral Keyes, who had known him for longer than Thompson. Keyes reported to his wife that he found Churchill incredibly 'jumpy' at their curtailed meeting to discuss Trondheim: 'He was very tired he said 2 or 3 times, so I said too tired to listen to me.'

As ever when he was exhausted, Churchill's lisp became more pronounced. In 1899, the Pretoria police had circulated a description after his escape: 'pale features, reddish brown hair, speaks through his nose and cannot pronounce letter S'. Forty-one years on, his Principal Private Secretary reported that 'the chief difficulty is understanding what he says, and great skill is required in interpreting inarticulate grunts or single words thrown out without explanation'. He misplaced more than words. Jaspar Rootham recalled having to take Churchill's dentures into a Cabinet meeting in order for him to carry on talking.

By early May, even parliamentary reporters had started to comment on how tired Churchill looked – and when Churchill was tired, said Lord Woolton, he 'never bothered about being polite to anyone'. The French Prime Minister was on the receiving end of barks which 'made the telephone vibrate'. Clementine wrote in her letter admonishing him: 'I must confess that I have noticed a deterioration in your manner.'

How jittery Churchill had become towards the end of the Norwegian Campaign can be seen in an extraordinary incident that occurred during the morning Cabinet meeting on 6 May, when his 'slightly bloodshot and watery eye' rotated in a rage on the Foreign Secretary – and accused him of treason. Churchill turned a deep shade of red, 'as always happens to him when he is very angry', after the latter's suggestion that they try and gain time by deluding the Germans with peace talks. Halifax replied that his irresponsible ideas 'may be silly, are certainly dangerous, but are not high treason'.

Churchill afterwards apologised. 'I had a spasm of fear,' he confessed, placing the blame for his rudeness on 'the present atmosphere of frustration'.

Alarmed by Churchill's erratic behaviour, *Times* journalist Leo Kennedy wrote in his diary that what was really needed was for Churchill to be ordered to rest. 'He is overdoing himself and taking the strain by stoking himself unduly with champagne, liqueurs etc. Dines out & dines well almost every night. Sleeps after luncheon then to the House of Commons, then a good & long dinner, & doesn't resume work at the Admiralty till after 10 p.m., & goes on till 1 or 2 a.m. He has got into the habit of calling conferences & subordinates after 1 a.m., which naturally upsets some of the Admirals, who are men of sound habits. So there is a general atmosphere of strain at the Admiralty which is all wrong. Yet Winston is such a popular hero & so much the war leader that he cannot be dropped. But he ought somehow to be rested.'

On the same day, 4 May, General Ironside registered concern at Churchill's lack of sleep and concentration at what should have been a triumphant moment for the First Lord in his expanded new role. 'We had yesterday for two hours our first meeting with Winston as Chairman of the Co-ordination Committee and found him very tired and sleepy and we hardly did anything at all. He took quietly what we said without demur. The lull after the storm.'

An official Humber conveyed Churchill the short distance from the Cabinet Room back to his official residence. He eschewed buses and public transport, and had ventured only once onto the London Underground. On that occasion, he needed to be retrieved after making several circuits without knowing how or where to get off.

On his arrival at the Admiralty, the car door was opened by his bodyguard, who sat in the front seat next to the chauffeur. It was noticeable to Walter Thompson that Churchill moved with less vitality than in February, when the journalist Charles Eade had accompanied him into Admiralty House. Eade had been 'amazed at the speed with which this man of 65 walked along passages and up steep staircases'.

Three weeks after Operation 'Wilfred', Churchill looked all of his years. He had lost most of the hair which had caused him to be known as the Red Terror. His cheeks were pouchy, and he walked with a stoop, his right shoulder lower than the left after he injured it falling onto the Bombay dockside more than forty years before. Mildly deaf when he wanted to be, he carried his seventeen stone with his large head thrust forward, scowling at the ground, in his doctor's description, with 'the sombre countenance clouded, the features set and resolute, the jowl clamped down as if he had something between his teeth and did not mean to let go'.

Unlike Chamberlain and Halifax, Churchill had chosen to remain in London for the weekend. His address was a Palladian-style building once occupied by Leo Amery, Samuel Hoare and Duff Cooper, and entered by a door in the Mall behind the statue of Captain Cook. Here Churchill had lived since September with his wife, their youngest daughter Mary, whose oldest sister had been born here, and a black cat called Nelson that slept at the foot of his narrow bed. His pregnant daughter-in-law Pamela, married to his son Randolph since October, also had rooms here while Randolph was stationed with the Fourth Hussars at a training camp in Kettering.

A 'fairy-tale fortress' was how the First Lord's residence struck the Soviet Ambassador. Churchill acknowledged that the Admiralty 'leaves its mark on everyone who has been in it'. It never bored him to show off the cast-iron stove commemorating a naval victory in the Punic War; or John Webber's paintings of Cook's voyages; or the Board Room into which Lieutenant Lapenotière had staggered in the early hours of a November morning, his uniform splashed with mud, crying: 'Sir, we have gained a great victory, but we have lost Lord Nelson!'

For Duff Cooper, who had lived here until his resignation in 1938, Admiralty House, with its views through tall windows over Horse Guards Parade, 10 Downing Street and St James's Park, was the most romantic address in Whitehall – an image sustained by Cooper's wife who commissioned Rex Whistler to install a bed that rose sixteen feet high 'from a shoal of gold dolphins and tridents'.

In March, Diana Cooper revisited the Churchills' top-floor apartment, which back in September had been converted from her former nurseries and attics. She reported on the sea change. Clementine had retained Diana's chintz curtains, but the dolphins were stored away, 'and on a narrow curtainless pallet-bed sleeps the exhausted First Lord. My gigantic gold-and-white armoire holds his uniform. The walls are charts.'

The library, state bedroom and boudoir had been turned into secret map rooms. On the walls hung duplicates of maps in the basement War Room. These were covered with black cloth to hide from unauthorised personnel the day-to-day progress of hostilities.

At their dinner in October, the Chamberlains had eaten in what had been the Coopers' nursery, where their son John Julius had kept a large fish tank full of sea horses that he fed on fleas. After the meal, Churchill had escorted the Prime Minister and his wife down in a lift to see the staff at work on two floors, in rooms strengthened by iron girders against air raids. Anne Chamberlain toured, in turn, the Result Room, 'where all the results came through to a Staff News Commander'; the Code Room; and the Typists' Room, in which secretaries typed out codes. 'Everyone appears to do 12 hrs on, then 24 or 36 hrs off. There is of course no fresh air, but simply air pumped in and out, and all the work has to be done by artificial light.'

On a visit down stuffy half-lit passages to Churchill's office, Maisky observed a lamp with a broad dark shade hanging from the ceiling. Churchill nodded to it, and pouring whisky said with satisfaction: 'The lamp was here 25 years ago, when I was naval minister for the first time. Then it was removed. Now they've put it up again.' Churchill led Maisky to a folding door in the wall, where in a deep niche the Soviet Ambassador saw a map of Europe with faded small flags pinned onto it in various places, including the Dardanelles. Churchill said: 'It's a map of the movements of the German navy in the last war . . . Now we will need it again.'

Anne Chamberlain had recently refurbished No. 10 with her niece. She approved of Churchill's cosy-looking office, with its red leather chairs and sofa, 'and a very tidy pair of brown leather slippers which Mrs Churchill pointed out to me with some relish, showing how comfortably the first Lord tucks himself in when he gets back there to work in the evening'.

Churchill had a large desk in the corner, where he sat with his back to the room, with the light on his left side. His chair, made out of fragile wood, was an old chair which had belonged to his father. His spotted blue-and-white bow-tie was another homage to his father, who had worn one. Immaculate in his dress, Churchill normally wore striped trousers, pearl-buttoned boots which he would kick off, and a white shirt under a loose-fitting black jacket.

His shirts were silk, as were his socks and his pale pink underwear which he ordered from the Army & Navy store at an annual cost of £80

(£4,700 in today's prices). 'I have a very delicate and sensitive cuticle.' Of special sensitivity was the patch on his right forearm where he had sacrificed a 'bit of pelt' to help out a fellow officer wounded in the Sudan Campaign. Churchill liked to show off the scar left by the Irish doctor who had scalpelled out a piece of flesh 'about the size of a shilling' to graft onto the arm of Lieutenant Richard Molyneaux. It tickled Churchill to think that someone else might be walking around in his skin.

Aside from a patch of eczema on his jaw, Churchill's skin was remarkably smooth. Journalists who came to interview him at this time were struck by the pallor of his face, which seemed bloodless and clean (owing to Churchill's use of a Beecham's skin cream, Lait Larola). To one visitor, he gave the impression that 'he had just dressed after a bath and had used talcum powder with liberality'.

His unconventional working habits are well known:

The fifteen Havana cigars he smoked a day – sometimes throwing the lit end into his waste-paper basket, which moments later needed to be doused with a soda-syphon.

His afternoon siesta – a custom adopted, like the cigars, following his 1895 visit to Cuba, where he was impressed by the practice of government troops and rebels of suspending their war for an hour during the heat of the day. 'That,' wrote Geoffrey Shakespeare, 'is why he could start again at nine p.m. looking as rosy as a baby back from a pram ride in park.'

His elaborate bathing rituals – with the water at exactly the right temperature. 'I had to test it carefully with my elbow,' said his valet Norman McGowen, who once overheard Churchill muttering, and asked: 'Do you want me?' The reply: 'I wasn't talking to you, Norman, I was addressing the House of Commons.'

His dictation – while parading up and down in a dressing gown embroidered with green and gold dragons, and underneath, a long silk nightshirt restrained by a woolly tummy-band. Geoffrey Shakespeare was frequently summoned to be in attendance to answer questions about the navy. 'He wanted me there as I was versed in current Naval practice whereas he had been the First Lord twenty-five years ago.'

Uncle Geoffrey's description still holds good for the statement which Chamberlain had asked Churchill to prepare in order to wind up the Norway Debate. 'Usually after dinner he held a Naval conference from 9 to 11 p.m.'

There is, among Uncle Geoffrey's papers, a prized photograph of one such meeting in the Admiralty Board Room, and beneath it he has written 'the only photograph of the Board of Admiralty ever taken': it shows my great-uncle seated at the end of a long table, eyes closed, possibly with exhaustion, or else conserving his energies for the night ahead; and Churchill at the other end, hands on the table as if poised to spring up. Uncle Geoffrey continued: 'But after 11 p.m. he devoted himself to speech making. Having been closely associated with Lloyd George in the preparation of his speeches, I was interested to observe Churchill's technique. He used no notes or headlines giving the sequence of his points. He dictated directly and firmly to an expert typist who used a silent machine. One night he remarked: "Are you all ready? I'm feeling very fertile tonight." . . . As he dictated he padded up and down in soft bedroom slippers, arms behind his back, head thrust forward, a cigar protruding from his mouth. The argument flowed in smooth logical sequence. Now and again he paused to ask me a question or I made a suggestion and he replenished his glass from a whisky decanter on the table. On he went . . .'

Once Churchill had corrected and polished what he had to say, he asked Clementine to sit in a chair and he practised aloud in front of her. His valet revealed: 'His speeches must first be tried out in her presence.' Churchill's speech to wind up the Norway Debate on Wednesday was one of the most difficult that he had been called upon to make since his arrival in the Commons forty years before. Clementine's input was vital. 'I tell her everything,' Churchill confided to Maisky. 'But she knows how to keep mum. She won't spill a secret.' The historian David Cannadine says that there was no one he trusted more to give him hard truths and offer political judgement. 'He always needed to be managed, and she was his great manager.' The extent of Churchill's dependence on his wife may even have reached Narvik, where Giles Romilly's Austrian guard told him: 'England – old statesmen! Young Führer is good! And not married! Also good! A wife plays too big a role!'

There was no danger of any Halifax-like infatuation. In his mid-sixties, Churchill unconsciously likened his sexual appetites to those of Chamberlain's sisal-stuffed merlins. When another MP whispered to him that his flies were undone, Churchill replied: 'It makes no difference. The dead bird doesn't leave the nest.'

On the other hand, he was strangely bereft during Clementine's sometimes not-so-brief flights from home. During one of these, she formed an attachment to a London art dealer, Terence Philip, bringing back a dove in a wicker cage, and after the bird died burying it beneath the sundial at Chartwell. When she wanted to go off again, Churchill refused. 'Mr Pug is very sweet but now he says NO.'

In the days leading up to the Norway Debate, he counted on Clementine's support. But the absence of a military victory threatened to make redundant even her management and advice. In Admiral Godfrey's stark judgement, 'Churchill needed a victory.'

If Churchill finished dictating by 2 a.m., Uncle Geoffrey recalled, he was wider awake than ever. 'What about a visit to the War Room?'

Inside the War Room, Narvik had risen again to the top of the agenda. The Chiefs of Staff were receiving daily reports, though there had been no further progress since Admiral Cork's aborted attempt to put troops ashore on 24 April. Maddened at the stagnation, Labour's Hugh Dalton complained to the new Air Minister Samuel Hoare: 'We have nothing at all to show on land.' Fidgety and defensive, Hoare blamed the impasse on recurrent blizzards that mantled the town, so that scouts could not distinguish a single enemy target. 'The trouble at Narvik is that there is a continual snow storm. You can't see your hand more than a few inches in front of your face.'

Early in May, the snowstorm abated. By the weekend of 4/5 May, a thaw had set in. As rising temperatures melted the five-foot drifts into slush, Churchill's attention roved back to the chart of Narvik pinned to his wall. This was the victory he required. There must be no excuses.

Stung by criticism of its optimistic press releases, the Ministry of Information decided on Saturday not to draw special attention to Narvik 'until it was clear that our task there was going to be accomplished'. The War Office communiqué on Sunday night was deliberately downbeat. 'There is nothing of importance to report from Narvik.'

Behind the scenes, though, despite competing claims from France, Holland and Alexandria, Narvik was Churchill's priority. In message after message, he urged Admiral Cork to get on and seize the town, emphasising the danger of delay, and reiterating that the government was prepared to accept heavy losses and that a defeat would have serious repercussions. 'It would show that our will to win and our fighting capacity were less than those of the enemy.' Plus it would have a devastating effect on world opinion. In an assessment that proved correct, though not in the way he anticipated, Churchill sent Cork another signal. 'I must regard the next six or seven days as possibly decisive.' As if that was not enough, 'I shall be glad to share your responsibilities.' Once again, he stood on the bridge.

Adding to Churchill's frustrations, the news from Narvik continued to be dismal. Early on Saturday, the Polish destroyer *Grom* was bombed by a Heinkel 111, suffering a direct hit on her torpedo tubes, and sank in two minutes with the loss of sixty-five men. Three battalions of Chasseurs Alpins had arrived, but their mules had disappeared like Cork's monocle into the snow. After ten days, French troops had advanced less than five miles, and were suffering from frostbite and snow-blindness. An Intelligence report received on 4 May warned that 120 troop-carrying German aircraft were about to leave Denmark, probably to reinforce General Dietl's garrison. And most troubling: even though weather conditions had improved, no commensurate thaw had occurred between the British army and navy commanders. In a boiling communication to the War Office,

General Mackesy wrote that Admiral Cork's military knowledge was 'exactly NIL' and the situation was 'simple lunacy'.

General Ironside was compelled to agree with Churchill that Mackesy had not provided bold enough leadership. With Ironside's blessing, Churchill decided to send out Lieutenant General Claude Auchinleck to investigate the cause of the failure and take over command on his arrival. But that would not be until 12 May.

With Mackesy suffering from flu, his acting Brigade commander was ordered to conduct an immediate reconnaissance with the French commander, to identify suitable landing spots on the Narvik peninsula, and to prepare an airfield which could counter the growing number of German bombers flying up from Trondheim now that the Allies had left the area. Their findings would dictate Cork's next move. Churchill waited to learn the result, in Geoffrey Shakespeare's phrase, 'like a caged lion'.

Churchill's appointments book is missing, but not his wife's. The Chief Whip David Margesson came to dinner with Churchill on Saturday while Clementine and Mary attended a ball in Bryanston Square. On Sunday, Clementine travelled to their three-roomed cottage at Chartwell. Whether or not Churchill accompanied her, and the likelihood is that he did not, he was back at the Admiralty by late afternoon.

Sunday was another abnormally warm day in London. In the park, the band of the Coldstream Guards played until 7 p.m. Blossom was on the chestnut trees, and the paths were thronged with strollers who had been forced to stay in town because of petrol rationing.

Churchill still had heard nothing from Admiral Cork when, at 7 p.m., he received Colonel Birger Ljungberg, the Norwegian Defence Minister. Ljungberg had arrived directly from the war area with his Foreign Minister, Halvdan Koht. In a broadcast from London made on that Sunday, in words which Churchill was to paraphrase eight years later in Oslo, Koht stated that the German attack on Norway would go down in history as 'one of the worst criminal acts ever known'.

Both Koht and Ljungberg still smarted at the peremptory and secretive manner in which the Allies had deserted the Norwegian forces at Trondheim – they, like Ruge and Getz, had been informed only after the evacuation had taken place. It smacked of the Allies' 'skedaddling habits of the last war'. A measure of their anger was the Norwegian government's refusal to grant permission, three weeks later, for two new motor torpedo boats owned and crewed by the Norwegian navy, but then stationed in a British port on the south coast, to help retrieve troops from Dunkirk. Nonetheless, Ljungberg provided Churchill with information on the terrain outside Narvik, and he advised him that the aerodrome at Bardufoss fifty miles from Harstad could be ready by 12 May.

After Ljungberg departed, Churchill continued to pad up and down, now and then striding over to examine the large map which showed the disposition of every Allied company surrounding Narvik. General Ironside, on the point of leaving for Gourock in north-west Scotland to welcome back the Namsos convoy, worried that he was abandoning Churchill at a vulnerable moment. 'Winston seems to me to be a little weighed down by the cares of being solely responsible for Narvik. He wants it taken and yet doesn't dare to give any direct order to Cork.'

Cork's signal from Narvik finally reached Churchill in the early hours of Monday, bringing further unwelcome news. The reconnaissance had revealed only one small beach, 150 yards long. This was bordered by steep inclines over which it was unlikely that troops could 'clamber let alone assault'. The lack of darkness made a surprise attack impossible – the men would be in sight of the enemy for ninety minutes. Plus, there were only four landing craft. General Mackesy was supported by the unanimous verdict of his senior officers that an opposed landing in these conditions was 'absolutely unjustified'. Cork had with 'great reluctance' submitted Mackesy's report to the War Office.

Not satisfied, Churchill pressed Cork to reveal his own opinion about a frontal attack. Cork replied that while he did not think success certain, he strongly believed that there was a good chance of it, and he proposed anchoring HMS *Resolution* within fifty yards of Narvik pier. 'Her bulk at that range would scare enemy troops while her guns would blast them to Hades.' Cork planned the operation for 8 May, the day on which Churchill was due to speak in the Commons. A successful assault on Narvik would supply the tonic that everybody was looking towards Churchill to provide.

As the snowstorms abated which had reduced visibility to a few feet, and contours began to appear, General Mackesy perceived one thing with increased clarity. Churchill's keenness to capture Narvik had less to do with the town's strategic value than with the First Lord's survival in Westminster. Mackesy explained to his French counterpart, Brigadier General Antoine Béthouart, why he had behaved with such belligerence in standing his ground: he was unwilling 'to provoke a hecatomb to save the political fortunes of Mr Churchill'.

This, then, was Churchill's position on the eve of the Norway Debate – isolated, defeated, tired; not holding his drink; frustrated by the command structure, yet, on the instances when he had overruled it, unable to brandish a victory; unpopular in Cabinet; and hanging on by the extra rope that Chamberlain had reeled out for him to use, either to save the situation, or, as Chips Channon speculated, to hang himself from.

One other factor must be taken into account when trying to visualise Churchill's daily life at this time. It is contained in a bleak record in Clementine's appointments book, her last entry for Monday 6 May, the single word, 'Bertram'. Her sister Nellie had telephoned that evening from Huntington Park to say that Giles's father had died. His funeral was to be held later in the week. Right at the moment when Churchill needed her most, his wife would be in Herefordshire.

14
THE REBELS

*'Oh! the excitement, the thrills, the atmosphere of ill-concealed nervousness,
the self-interest, which comes over the House of Commons when
there is a political crisis on.'*
CHIPS CHANNON MP, 1 May 1940

In corridors and committee rooms, in bars and clubs, in nearby drawing rooms and restaurants, a political crisis was brewing which tracked the tussle taking place in the Arctic. In the blizzard of rumours and counter-rumours swirling through Westminster, it proved no easier than in Narvik to make out the disposition of the enemy; to establish who was an ally of whom, and what, if anything, might result from the approaching clash on Tuesday 7 May.

Members had gone away for the weekend and listened to their constituents, and returned with the same question: why after seven months of preparation was the government not in a position to strike back when Hitler invaded Norway? Inflammatory speeches by opposition leaders on Saturday and Sunday revealed how events in Norway had disturbed the political waters. Suspicion was rising that the results of Chamberlain's economic blockade were not all that they were claimed to be. Britain's humiliating defeat in the first serious encounter with Nazi Germany was, for many MPs, the final straw.

Beyond providing a fuller and franker account, the Whitsun Adjournment Debate offered one of the few chances since September for opposition MPs and dissident Conservatives to close in on Chamberlain. Up to now, opposition to the Prime Minister had taken the shape of shifting allegiances that had failed to cohere into a genuine threat. Here was an opportunity for these competing factions to combine forces and pin responsibility for the disaster on a single target; and – though the likelihood of this was remote – bring about a revolt among backbenchers, and create a coalition government drawn from all parties.

Yet how this coup was to be achieved remained as obscure as the person who might lead it.

'In vain we look for a glimmer of light. It is a perfect blackout.' A secret memorandum by the Welsh Liberal peer Lord Davies reminded an all-party group of rebellious-minded MPs that there was a precedent for the change of leadership they sought: when, in the middle of the First World War, Lloyd George had taken over from Asquith with the assistance of the House of Commons. 'Many of us are now passing through the same phase of doubt and fear of divided counsel which we experienced during those far off days of 1916.'

Aged seventy-seven, Lloyd George was still an MP, and on 20 April he had celebrated a milestone: a dinner was held at the Commons in tribute to his fifty years in Parliament. Not only that, but several figures were still around who had helped him into power, like Leo Amery and Max Beaverbrook. Lord Davies, who as David Davies had supported Lloyd George in 1916, was eager to champion him again. Why not summon back 'Corgi' as leader?

Churchill's star might have sunk to its lowest in eight months, but that of Lloyd George had rocketed over the weekend to astronomical heights. On Saturday, Harold Nicolson wrote in his diary: 'People are so distressed by the whole thing that they are talking of Lloyd George as a possible P.M.' Basil Liddell Hart heard 'on all sides' a growing volume of support voiced for the recall of the man who had 'triumphantly ridden the storm' in the First War. A letter to *The Times* posed the question: 'What would quicken the momentum, both spiritual and material, of our people most effectually? The answer is, Lloyd George as British Prime Minister . . . he is the man for the job.'

But was he the man for the job – and would he agree? With a mane of white hair thicker than ever, Lloyd George continued to be as devious and divisive in his political machinations as in his private life. In the opinion of his Private Secretary, he was 'as artful as a cartload of monkeys'.

A disappointed majority in the Commons felt that Lloyd George had entered his defeatist dotage after suggesting in October that Britain should seek peace terms with Hitler, whom he once rather embarrassingly had lauded as 'the greatest German of the age'. Lloyd George was generally perceived as a big beast all on his own, having fractured the Liberal Party into three disunited factions, and been reduced to sitting in a family rump with his son Gwilym and daughter Megan. Yet for a small, passionate group of supporters, he remained the architect of a victory that the country was in supreme need of seeing repeated. Churchill had once written to him saying that he would 'never forget the fearful days through which you led us to safety'. Two decades on, Lloyd George behaved as though he were not too old to head another coalition, though this was unlikely to happen unless Chamberlain, whom Lloyd George abominated for having kept him out of power, was eliminated from the picture. Striding up and down, Lloyd George fulminated to Leo Amery: 'To think that I who saved the country should be allowed into the Cabinet by the gracious permission of that pinhead.'

Lloyd George's most strident champion was the first female MP, the volatile Nancy Astor, who had spent the weekend at Cliveden talking up his prospects with the editor of the *Observer*, J. L. Garvin. Like Astor, Garvin believed that Lloyd George should come back as the leader of a coalition. To the argument that Lloyd George was too physically frail to do even a full day's work in peacetime, Garvin countered that 'he was quite capable of working for six hours a day, and that six hours would be better worth having than anyone else's eighteen!'

A. J. Sylvester had succeeded Geoffrey Shakespeare as Lloyd George's Private Secretary, and he kept an alert eye on the 'Old Goat', as he preferred to call him. 'I am always amused as he walks down the corridors. He just flies. That is all stage-managed to make people say what remarkable energy he has.' Only a few weeks earlier, Lloyd George had confided to Sylvester, 'I have a great part to play in this war yet.'

Precisely what part remained unclear. Down on his Surrey farm, Lloyd George kept his ambitions buttoned up beneath his blue waistcoat. When Geoffrey Shakespeare on a visit to Churt asked if he ever hankered after the days of his power, the former Prime Minister stooped to pick a dandelion. 'Well, there was a time when I conducted a great war-r-r-r-r. Now all I can do is pick dandelions for my secretary's rabbits.'

But Operation 'Wilfred' had begun life as a rabbit, and Lloyd George's secretary – Frances Stevenson, with whom he lived at Churt – went on to become his second wife. Might the 'Old Goat' be persuaded to toss his hat into the political ring a second time?

No one could have been more unsuitable as Prime Minister in 1940, yet Sylvester observed how Lloyd George's head was 'literally turned' by the bags of adulatory letters that he received from the public – 'Every day he is crazy about the letters – not what is in them but "How many are there?"' Feeding his master's vanity, Sylvester kept Lloyd George abreast of the Westminster gossip, writing to him on 1 May: 'I heard men talk about your return who in the past have been most unfriendlily disposed towards you.' Sylvester had bumped into an 'important member' of the Labour Party – probably Willie Henderson, head of the Labour Press and Publicity department – who confided that there were only two people whom he could see as Prime Minister. 'One was Lloyd George and the other was Winston, and he said that the Labour Party would never serve under Winston's Premiership.' Sylvester's next titbit was calculated to tantalise. What was required, said Sylvester's authoritative informant, was drive from the top, 'and he envisaged you as Prime Minister . . . You were the one man who could do that . . . The only man was yourself.'

Lloyd George was 'much interested' to learn this, but he was not yet prepared to commit himself.

On Tuesday 7 May, a mere three hours before the Norway Debate, a last-minute lunch party was held by Nancy Astor and Garvin to 'sound' out Lloyd George to see if he would 'play'. A former civil servant, Tom Jones, who could talk in Welsh with him, was present at the gathering in 4 St James's Square. 'Nancy welcomed the Grand Old Man with his flowing white locks and told him in her blunt way that he had been produced for inspection and to be tested for his fitness to return to the helm of ship of state.' But even at this late stage, Lloyd George prevaricated, saying that they should not count on him . . . His forty-year friendship with Churchill made him hesitant to speak out in the debate . . . It would be very difficult to do so without castigating Churchill for the navy's part in the withdrawal. Jones wrote: 'We were left to infer that Lloyd George preferred to wait his country's summons a little longer.'

Two other significant figures emerged out of the political snowstorm that from Monday battered Westminster. One was a pedantic ex-Minister, the author of copious diaries, memoirs and letters, who had helped to bring down Lloyd George's coalition in 1922 – and before that had been the 'very soul' of 'the horrible intrigues against Asquith'. The other was an Independent Liberal MP, a strong-minded and fearless Welsh-speaking lawyer with a brilliant brain, once described by another barrister as having 'more presence than anyone I've ever known', but who remains strangely absent from popular accounts of this period.

Since September this pair had worked tirelessly to press the government into taking a more aggressive approach to the war. When Chamberlain failed to act, they decided to mount an assault on his leadership should the opening present itself. Convening in secret, they recruited supporters from all parties. Composition was fluid. Members from one group attended meetings of the other, and in April they merged with a third band of dissident Parliamentarians, Lord Salisbury's Watching Committee, made up of senior Conservatives from both Houses. All three groups sought the same end: to organise the discontent that was spreading, and force a change in government as had occurred six weeks earlier in France.

Leo Amery was the ex-Minister and the leader of the first group.

Just how wounding was Amery's subsequent betrayal must be understood in the light of his enormous debt to Chamberlain. The sixty-seven-year-old Conservative MP for Birmingham Sparkbrook had for thirty years been a colleague of the Prime Minister, whose constituency of Ladywood was adjacent to his. Largely thanks to Chamberlain, Amery had been elected to Parliament in 1911. Amery wrote to his wife of a year: 'I gather I owe it nearly all to Neville Chamberlain who saw and persuaded a number of people . . .'

Since then, how many times had Amery and Chamberlain walked home together to their respective houses in Eaton Square, dined at the Carlton Club, sat beside each other on the train to Birmingham? When his only son Francis was born, Chamberlain asked Amery to be godfather. Yet Leo Amery's relationship with Neville never grew beyond a certain level. When Amery boasted of 'knowing my Neville', it was not from any knowledge founded on intimacy. They were good friends who gradually over the course of working together had become old friends, with less and less faith in each other's judgement. Since the outbreak of war, their relationship had cooled further. By May 1940, they regarded each other with positive distrust.

Amery's strongest feeling of connection towards 'poor Neville' lay, as did Churchill's, in his admiration for Chamberlain's father Joseph, who had filled a father-shaped gap in Amery's political development. Amery was one of thirty members of the Chamberlain Club, which dined annually at the Mayfair Hotel on Joseph Chamberlain's birthday. In 1936, Amery created the Chamberlain Centenary Movement – laying a wreath on Chamberlain's grave, and giving a talk at the Albert Hall to 8,000 disciples of 'old Joe'. One of several things that irked Neville Chamberlain about Amery was the way that he adopted Joseph Chamberlain's protectionist principles as though Leo Amery were his true heir and not his sons.

Amery was cranky and pugnacious because he had had to fight his way up. His own father had been an English forestry conservator in north-west India who disappeared with his mistress after Amery was born, and died penniless prospecting for gold in British Guiana, leaving Amery's mother, a Hungarian Jew, to bring him up. She took Amery first to Cologne, where his teachers beat him, then to England. To hide his Jewish ancestry, Amery changed his middle name from Moritz to Maurice. Boys at school called him 'Pocket Hercules'. One of these boys was W. S. Churchill.

The House of Commons benches were crammed with MPs who had attended the same school and university. A disproportionate number went to Harrow – like Margesson and Hoare – but by no means all. Lloyd George once took Geoffrey Shakespeare back to his school near Criccieth, where they came across an elderly red-faced tramp with a bulbous nose. Lloyd George produced a pound note from his wallet and said to Shakespeare: 'Give this to that poor fellow. He used to be an old school friend of mine.'

At Harrow, Amery was a year ahead of Churchill, standing out from him as much cleverer, routinely coming first in exams; and as a prize-winning athlete and gymnast. But neither Amery's brain nor his muscular physique was what drew him to Churchill's attention. Rather, it was down to Amery's small size – never growing beyond five foot four – that he received from Churchill, then a new boy, his bullying baptism.

What occurred in the summer of 1889 became a dinner party story that was recounted by Churchill with glee, and set the template for their long, tense, always complicated relationship. Amery was 'standing in a meditative posture' on the edge of the school swimming pond when a 'red-haired, freckled urchin' mistook him for a fellow new boy and pushed him in. Churchill afterwards explained: 'How could I tell his rank when he was in a bath towel and so small?'* A furious Amery got out, hared after Churchill, seized him 'in a ferocious grip' and hurled him into the deepest part of the pool. They made up, but the incident was not forgotten, and was on Amery's mind forty-five years later when he humiliated Churchill in the Commons during the India Bill, giving him 'the best ducking he has had since he first pushed me into Ducker in 1889'.

The prize-winning prefect in Amery never fully accepted being overtaken by his cheeky, opportunistic junior. After Ducker, there was an incident in Natal when as war correspondents together they shared a tent on the rain-sodden veld near Estcourt. Amery asked Churchill to wake him up if the armoured train was sent down the line next morning to conduct a reconnoitre inside Boer territory, and then fell into a deep sleep. When he woke, Churchill had gone – the train, too. Amery heard firing in the distance as the Boers galloped down to ambush it. Churchill liked to tease Amery that had he accompanied Churchill that morning, Amery would have been taken prisoner as well, and so shared in the scoop without which Churchill would never have had the materials 'for lectures and a book which brought me in enough money to get into Parliament in 1900 – ten years before you!'

When, twenty-five years later, Churchill re-crossed the floor to join the Conservative front benches, Amery detected a pattern in which Ducker, Natal, and the circumstances of Churchill's escape from the Boer prison

---

* In another version, Amery was 'fully-clothed'.

camp all fitted together. Churchill's behaviour was that of a man out for himself, happy 'to desert his Liberal colleagues with the same swift decision that led him to climb over the railings at Pretoria'. If Amery felt a residual gratitude to Chamberlain, then towards Churchill he never relinquished his earlier feelings of suspicion, envy, irritation and resentment. Almost to the last, Amery was 'at sixes and sevens' over whether he wanted Halifax to succeed Chamberlain, or Churchill.

A loquacious perfectionist, Amery spent the next decade before he entered Parliament in editing the seven-volume *Times History of the South African War*. He brought with him into politics the same attention to detail, plus some fairly mountainous ambitions. He mused about his political future on the day that Chamberlain arranged for him to stand as an MP, in the seat that he went on to represent until 1945. 'What I shall achieve in it, I cannot tell. I know I have great weaknesses, but also great strength, and if I really grow in inner and outer stature during the next five years, and if fortune is not unkind, I may really play my part in getting big things done.'

As to achieving those 'big things', Amery trusted in a characteristic that he appeared to have shared with Chamberlain: his near-clairvoyant ability to read a situation correctly where others might not. It was 'an immense advantage', he wrote to his wife, to have 'the absolute conviction of being in the right'. To be right for Amery was even more necessary than to be liked. Decades passed before he intuited that what he understood as his divine gift was also, politically, a mortal flaw. By the time of the Norway Debate, thirty years on, he had discovered that 'being right, and still more having been right, are tremendous obstacles to securing the places where it really matters being right!'

Not that Amery was on the ball every time. Rather as Churchill had been impressed enough to commend Mussolini as 'the greatest law-giver among living men', so, after meeting Adolf Hitler at Rosenheim, Amery had found the Führer 'a bigger man, on the whole, than I had expected . . . We got on well together, I think, owing to the fundamental similarity of many of our ideas.'

A passionate skier and mountaineer, there was something Sisyphean about Amery; always plummeting down slopes and anxious to scale the next peak, yet for all his 'alpinising energy' never satisfied with the summit conquered. Even when he made the first ascent of a 10,940-foot mountain in the Canadian Rockies that had been named after him – 'a steep snow-crowned tower soaring gracefully into the the the sky' – a blizzard prevented him from taking in the view.

His wife Bryddie was Canadian. When someone once asked her Amery's whereabouts, she replied: 'Oh, Leo's on the executive.' If the position of chief executive eluded him – the only presidency he achieved was President of the Alpine Club – then he had form as a kingmaker, and in the 1920s was an active participant at two turning points in the nation's political life.

Amery was instrumental in preventing Baba Metcalfe's father from assuming the leadership from Bonar Law, ensuring that Baldwin did: 'I . . . made him P.M. in 1923.' A year before that, Amery had taken part in 'the revolt of the Under-Secretaries' which overthrew Lloyd George's coalition and brought in Bonar Law.

At the time, Amery occupied Geoffrey Shakespeare's position as Financial Secretary to the Admiralty. Bonar Law rewarded Amery with the Admiralty itself, to the outrage of Chamberlain and of Churchill, who thundered unselfreflectingly that it was 'a reward of successful mutiny which is certainly an unwholesome spectacle'. Almost Amery's first act on becoming First Lord was to march over to the mark on the Board Room wall which recorded Nelson's height, and measure himself. Amery was pleased to discover that though shorter than Nelson he stood taller than Napoleon.

Chamberlain's half-brother Austen remarked of Amery that 'if only he were half as big again he would before now have reached a much higher place'. It was not his height alone that held him back. Amery's ponderous and long-winded manner was a compelling restraint, his earnest sub-editorial pedantry earning him a reputation in the Commons as one of its two or three most boring speakers. In the crisis of 1931 Chamberlain wrote to Halifax in Simla to say that Amery was 'listened to with undisguised impatience and in the House he does not seem to carry much weight. Why? No doubt if he were bigger 'twould be better. But lots of little men have been impressive enough . . . I think it is because he has no sense of proportion and insists on little points with the same exasperating pertinacity as on big ones.' In Cabinet, Amery's fellow Ministers were constantly looking round for someone to 'pull his coat' and stop him talking.

It became a tedious refrain: were Amery a half a head taller and his speeches half an hour shorter he would have become Prime Minister by now. His diaries show that he never renounced that possibility. Since the 'moral collapse' of the party leadership, he wrote in December 1931, 'I have been much freer and have increasingly asserted my authority and been increasingly looked to as a leader.' Seven years on, he listened to a speech by Violet Bonham Carter, and thought that 'with such gifts of eloquence I might easily have been Prime Minister long ago . . .' Meanwhile, he pawed the ground, believing that '*I shall be justified one of these days*'.

Yet when Neville Chamberlain, his former patron, took over in May 1937, the new Prime Minister declined to invite Amery into his Cabinet, giving as excuse that 'there are always more horses than oats'. Amery was despondent. 'What a difference I would have made to his Government both in fact and in public estimation.' In July 1939, Amery reported that the *Manchester Guardian* 'spoke of my "persistent exclusion" as one of the minor mysteries of politics'.

It mystified Amery, though not many others. Balfour described him as 'the cleverest bloody fool alive' who was 'frequently most devastatingly right, but never knew how to play his cards in the game of politics'. His biographer David Faber says: 'He had the most incredible thick skin, never letting friendship get in the way of speaking his mind.' What Amery discovered to his political cost was that whenever he spoke his mind it got in the way of friendships. Colleagues perceived him in not quite human terms. To Hankey, he was 'a scheming little devil'. To Macmillan, he was 'combative and persistent, like a well trained terrier'. To Spears, he resembled 'a wise and benevolent beetle'. Even to Field Marshal Wavell, as reported by Amery, 'I had the best brains in the country and the heart of a lion.' Such a combination was not congenial to Chamberlain. The Prime Minister preferred merlins to griffins.

Amery had the highest hopes that the war would give him a chance, but when the idea of including Amery in the Cabinet was put to Chamberlain he dismissed it with an 'irritated snort'. Amery had been a truculent critic of some of his policies, and on 2 September 1939 had caused Chamberlain to turn around 'as if stung' when, following Chamberlain's statement, the deputy Labour leader Arthur Greenwood rose, saying that he spoke for his party – whereupon, to loud cheers, Amery shouted: 'Speak for England!' implying that Chamberlain had not. Amery was correct to predict that his 'most insulting' intervention, as Chamberlain afterwards called it, though not recorded in

Hansard (and sometimes remembered as 'Speak for Britain!'), 'killed off all chances of Neville asking me to join his Government'. Chamberlain perceived Amery from now on as one of 'the smaller fry' who, disappointed at not getting office, were 'really traitors just as much as Quisling'.

Out of office for so long, Amery found it 'very hard not to be critical or contemptuous of the brains and courage of the crowd in office'. With dismay, he had watched the promotion of men like Inskip and Stanhope and Stanley ('he has not been a success in any office that he has held hitherto') – even Churchill. They had disagreed on many aspects, and not only over tariff reform which had caused Churchill to leave the Conservative party in 1904. Amery was Churchill's most constant opponent intellectually in the 1920s, and in the 1930s he took opposite positions over India, the League of Nations, and the Abdication, and had little sympathy for Churchill's proposal of a Grand Alliance with Russia. While Amery was 'just senior to Winston in actual years, I am, I think, a good deal his junior in body, and not yet fossilised in mind'. Still convinced that his contribution 'would make a real difference to the winning of the war', he wrote to Geoffrey Dawson: 'It is absurd that I should not be being made use of today.' Hurt and frustrated, Amery lapsed back into the role of fearless prophet, the self-appointed Cassandra who told unpalatable truths, regardless of the consequences, 'always seeing further ahead or deeper into problems than my colleagues and contemporaries'.

On a shelf in his Eaton Square library where he had plotted Lloyd George's downfall, intrigued against Asquith, and scuppered Curzon, among the novels of Proust and histories of the English Civil War, was a thin volume entitled *Notes on Forestry*. Written by Amery's father before he absconded, the book offered advice on the best way to fell 'distorted or damaged trees which although they may dominate, will not make good timber'. Fretting for a role to justify his ambitions, Amery dedicated himself to toppling Chamberlain according to the tenets of his forester father. 'Every tree threatening to interfere with the healthful development of trees of the more valuable classes should be remorselessly cleared off.'

A tree-felling team was in place already – an informal group of dissident Conservative backbenchers who had congregated around Anthony Eden after his stunning resignation as Foreign Secretary in 1938 in protest at appeasement. When Chamberlain drew their sting by bringing Eden and Churchill into the government, Amery took over as leader. Originally nicknamed 'the Glamour Boys', the twenty or so members included Harold Macmillan, Louis Spears, Duff Cooper, Paul Emrys-Evans and Ronald Tree. Another member was the National Labour MP Harold Nicolson.

The Amery Group, as it now became known, dined every Wednesday at a round table in a back room of the Carlton Hotel's restaurant in Pall Mall, and made it their aim 'to harass the Government until it conducted the war as though it meant it'. Out of them all, Amery was the most suspicious about the War Cabinet's resolve. His father had visited forests in Germany and had written instructively about their 'yield of fuel'. When Amery tackled Kingsley Wood, then the Air Minister, about bombing the Black Forest to spark off a huge conflagration, Wood's stuffy reply made Amery incandescent: 'Are you aware it is private property? . . . Why, you will be asking me to bomb Essen next.' Wood's 'insane ban', Amery later railed, would prevent 'our airmen even bombing German aeroplanes on Norwegian aerodromes during the first days of the invasion of Norway'.

Amery had been at this miserable point before. With Churchill in Natal, he witnessed the same picture of 'helplessness and vacillation' – which he had then written about in the second volume of his Boer War history. Forty years on, not much had changed.

With the Boer War in mind, Amery outlined his group's revolutionary motives to South Africa's Prime Minister, Jan Smuts. Amery wrote that he wanted 'not merely to upset the Government, but to make possible a National Government including all Parties. I have pleaded for this ever since Munich, as well as for a small War Department free of departmental duties.' What was essential was a proper structure of government – which Chamberlain did not have.

At a group dinner on 11 January at the Reform Club, a resolution was passed to fight for a coalition government, 'Neville giving place to Halifax with Winston leading in the House'. The evening was significant for one other reason. Also present was the Independent Liberal MP Clement Davies.

In an article headlined 'Clem the Giant Killer', Beaverbrook's *Sunday Express* went on to describe Davies as 'a pale-faced Welsh lawyer of fifty-six with thin, sandy hair smeared flat to his scalp, and an everlasting expression of gloom'. Broad-shouldered, with huge physical energy, never sleeping more than four hours a night, and blessed and cursed with a photographic memory, Davies was an unlikely David. Because he was not self-promoting, never spoke on the two main days of the Norway Debate, and failed to leave behind any memoirs or journals, he remains a little-known backbencher. His most dedicated supporter, Bob Boothby, felt that Davies was too modest to tell the story himself, but one day it would be told. 'I have no doubt myself that Clement Davies played the principal part in making Churchill Prime Minister.' When a Beaverbrook employee ejaculated: 'Thank God' – after Beaverbrook told him: 'We've got a new Prime Minister'– the press lord allegedly replied: 'Don't thank God, thank Clem Davies.'

Even to the two leading players, the narrative of what they were about to achieve was less than straightforward. Davies wrote to Amery fourteen years later, when they were both puzzling out the chronology: 'I do deplore the fact that I did not keep a diary.' But Amery did keep a journal. With the help of this, plus Davies's commanding memory and the input of Emrys-Evans, Halifax, Reith, Attlee, Hore-Belisha and Bracken, they pieced together their putsch.

One of his ancestors had voted for the Reform Bill, but Davies, a director of Unilever, was more at ease with margarine and soap than with plotting a revolt against a Prime Minister cemented in power by a majority of 213. A Welsh farm boy who had won a scholarship to Cambridge, where he gained the best first-class degree in law that Trinity Hall then had on record, Davies's gift was for friendship and not subversion. Originally a National Liberal, Davies had been a loyal supporter of the government for eight years. Then, on 29 September 1939 his son David was found dead in the office where he worked as a solicitor's clerk, after an epileptic seizure – one of three of Davies's four children who would die young, all at the age of twenty-four. The shock numbed Davies, who had earlier struggled with a drink problem. Alcohol made him forgetful, but also aggressive, and when roused, said his wife, the good-natured Davies had a 'devil of a temper'. He had been dry for two years at the time of his son's death. He coped with this immense family tragedy, not by retreating into alcoholic binges, but by turning his fighting spirit and fury against the government. His chosen vessel: the All Party Action Group that he had founded a fortnight before.

Sometimes also known as the Vigilantes, this 'ginger group', as Amery called it, gathered for the first time in a committee room in the Commons on 13 September. Thereafter, it met on Tuesday evenings, usually at the Reform Club. A Conservative MP – Boothby – was its secretary, and members of Amery's group attended, as well as the Labour leader Clement Attlee and his deputy Arthur Greenwood.

Amery viewed Davies as 'a very live wire and very anxious to get a move on'. The Welsh-speaking radical supplied what Amery outstandingly lacked: the ability to befriend and cajole MPs irrespective of their political make-up. By way of a character reference, Lord Wolmer wrote to Lord Salisbury that Davies was 'an able and successful businessman. Any statement of fact that he makes should be treated with respect.' A definitive list of membership is hard to compile, but by Christmas, Davies's All Party Action Group numbered about sixty MPs.

Clement Davies's blazing temper found a target in the Prime Minister – who in turn came to regard Davies as a 'treacherous Welshman'. On 14 December, Davies crossed the floor to the opposition benches, the decision forced on him, he wrote scornfully to Chamberlain, by so many instances of failure 'to take the measures necessary for the vigorous prosecution of the war'. Davies likened Chamberlain's 'lethargic', 'complacent', 'smug' administration to 'an orchestra without a conductor', and he argued that 'the country could not be properly organised until the Government went'.

If only Davies and Amery between them could persuade sixty supporters of the government to abstain or better still to vote against it, then the pair believed that they might inflict irreparable damage on the leadership. Chamberlain's shocking interim statement on 2 May about the withdrawal from central Norway gave them their chance. Norway, Amery wrote to Smuts, 'brought things to a head with a rush'.

The House adjourned at 8.35 p.m. Immediately, Amery telephoned Hoare. 'The Government must go.' He then hurried off to join an emergency conclave convened by Davies to discuss the line for the promised debate.

Davies wanted to table a motion to stop the House dissolving for the ten-day Whitsun break: it was 'almost criminal' that the government should adjourn in such a time of crisis for a holiday. Boothby was confident that forty Conservative MPs would vote against the government, which might then collapse. Using 'big words', he 'built new Cabinets' with Lloyd George as Prime Minister, and a War Cabinet formed of Lloyd George's son Gwilym, Harry Crookshank, Duff Cooper and Amery.

Although flattered, Amery advised caution. He chafed no less than did Davies and Boothby 'at the complacent methods of the little governing circle'. But Amery warned that a confidence motion risked playing into Chamberlain's hands. It might even reunite the Conservatives, and herd wavering backbenchers to the Prime Minister's side, giving him a renewed mandate (not unlike that which the Labour leader Jeremy Corbyn received in September 2016). Already, Amery had learned that Margesson was plotting to isolate the government's critics and put down such a motion in order 'to scotch the Opposition'.

Amery's priority was to present a united front in order to gain a change of government, and not become mired in premature discussions about who might lead it. He pleaded for both groups to bang their heads together and combine with Lord Salisbury's Watching Committee and, 'without bothering for personalities', press for the Lloyd George model of a National government and a small War Cabinet – and no Whitsun holiday. Once more, he cited his experiences in the Boer War. 'I urged that the essential thing was change and if necessary change and change again till the right men emerged – "always swap mokes [donkeys] crossing a river till you find one that won't founder."'

This plan was too cautious for Davies. In full gallop, he hurried off to see Attlee later that evening, and begged the Labour leader to force a division and turn a bland procedural motion into a vote of no confidence.

The leader of the Labour Party was a small, slight, undemonstrative man of few words, known by his colleagues as 'Clam Attlee' – 'and worthily he sustained the reputation', said one. Even a loyal MP like George Strauss admitted that it was difficult to get Attlee to open up on any subject other than bishops and cricket. Although Attlee and Chamberlain did not get on, they were hobbled by the same reticence. After Attlee became Prime Minister in 1945, he told a Junior Minister: 'If I pass you in the corridor and don't acknowledge you, remember it's only because I'm shy.'

In May 1940, Attlee had only recently returned to Westminster after recuperating in North Wales from two prostate operations, and he was not in good health. A full-on fight with the government at this dangerous time for the country would strike the public as unpatriotic, he felt. England required its political classes to continue the electoral truce that they had made on the first day of the war, or unite – not to divide further.

Attlee's response to Davies that night was identical to the response given to George Orwell, at about the same time, by two of Attlee's MPs. George Strauss and Aneurin Bevan had just come from hearing Chamberlain's statement on the evacuation from Namsos when they met Orwell, who asked them what hope there was of 'unseating Chamberlain'.

'None at all,' they replied.

The Labour leader liked Davies. He had attended what Chamberlain later called Davies's 'sordid gatherings at the Reform Club'. But he did not believe in his figures. Attlee was on the side of Violet Bonham Carter who had rolled her eyes at Boothby's claim of forty Conservative No-voters – 'He has told us that so often & up to now it has usually resulted in 3 abstentions.' Not one Conservative had voted against Munich. Experience told Attlee that Tory dissidents huffed and puffed, but scampered back into the fold as soon as Margesson and his 'Iron Guard' of Conservative Whips lashed them with the threat of deselection or exposure in *Truth* magazine. 'Again and again they will vote against what I believe in their hearts they desire.'

As well, Attlee was not much encouraged by Davies's mutating choice as to who should succeed Chamberlain. In the event that his 'dear chief' Lloyd George could not be persuaded, Davies had opted for Halifax, writing to Lord Salisbury on 15 April: 'To my mind the man who would command the respect and confidence of the nation is Lord Halifax, and I fully expect that if he were Prime Minister he would change the team and reorganise the Government of the nation so as to put it on a virile, thrusting war footing.' But a fortnight on, Davies had changed his mind again: he now wanted Churchill for PM. Attlee was against Churchill for a host of reasons which he did not need to enumerate to Davies, the politest being his age. 'Not Winston,' Attlee had told Harold Wilson at a recent dinner in Balliol. '65. Too old for a Churchill.'

Unless Attlee could be convinced that a division would be followed by action, he was not going to press for one. Out of government for so long, since 1931, he lacked information on the specific causes of the misdirected military expedition. In his clipped sentences, he told Davies that it was really quite impossible to arrive at any trustworthy judgement until Parliament had had the opportunity of hearing what the government had to say. Everything depended on how the House took the Prime Minister's opening statement.

Rebuffed, Davies did not give up. The following morning, he visited the ringleader of the 1916 revolt against Asquith.

When Clement Davies turned up at Stornoway House on 3 May, Max Beaverbrook half expected him. The owner of the *Express*, a man described by a rival proprietor as a 'gollywog itching with vitality', had that morning received a letter from the Liberal peer Lord Davies, most likely written at Clement Davies's request. The letter was an appeal for Beaverbrook to 'plump for Winston', and it invoked the fall of Asquith and the rise of Lloyd George in which Beaverbrook had played a significant role. 'Dear Kingmaker, Why have you given up your job? You did the trick in 1916 and, by getting rid of old Squiff at the right moment, you enabled us to win the war which we should probably have lost if he had remained in office. Now, even more than in 1916, we are up against it . . . My dear Kingmaker, come forth from your tent and put an end to the drifting, muddle and tom foolery of the present crowd.'

But Beaverbrook refused to intercede for two reasons. First, he did not share the appetite of the Davies' for Churchill, towards whom Beaverbrook expressed an attitude that was also 'very changeable', as Ivan Maisky had noticed. 'One day he might praise him as Britain's greatest statesman, on another he might call him a "swindler", "turncoat" or "political prostitute".' Second, much as Beaverbrook deprecated Chamberlain, and looked on Halifax with 'a mixture of scorn and envy', he did not believe that the Prime Minister could be unseated from outside his own party. He told Clement Davies what he had told Leo Amery two days before, and what he wrote in reply to Lord Davies. 'In every case the revolt that broke the Government came from within. The same applies this time. Those who try to do it from without are simply wasting their ammunition.' No. It would have to be a 'palace revolution', or no revolution at all.

Signals from within the 'palace' indicated a united front for the Norway Debate. 'We have this situation in hand,' the Chancellor John Simon declared in a bullish address on Saturday. 'You may dismiss from your minds the idea that this is going to be material for some exciting political controversy or combat.' When the facts were laid before the public, these would show that the action in Norway had been taken on the best advice. Simon repeated his message of solidarity on Monday. It was no good looking for culprits. The Cabinet were collectively responsible. 'We'll all swing together.'

Inside No. 10, Colville recorded that Margesson, Dunglass and Butler felt that the position was 'good politically' and that Chamberlain, though 'very depressed' by the hostile press coverage, would carry the House. 'Obviously the Government will win through tomorrow.'

Chamberlain believed this – the *Daily Herald* reporting that he had been 'assured by the intelligence service of the whips department that defection in his ranks has not gone far enough to be dangerous'. Halifax believed this – his chief source of news, Charles Peake, told Baba Metcalfe on Monday evening that 'no one expected anything to happen'. So, too, did Churchill, who 'thought they would get through the Debate all right'. By Tuesday morning, the same view had come to be held, grimly, by all three groups of dissenters and by the opposition Labour and Liberal Parties. The government was impregnable, even if it did not mean that MPs were satisfied.

After the lunch to vet Lloyd George, Tom Jones made his way with Lloyd George and Nancy Astor to the Commons where MPs were gathering to hear Chamberlain's statement. Jones believed that the 'P.M. is expected to survive this crisis', and he held out little hope for a Lloyd George intervention. A. J. Sylvester had made a final plea, writing to Lloyd George: 'I think there is only one thing that is likely to upset the P.M. And I think you can do that. That one thing is to make him lose his temper. When he loses his temper he does and says foolish things. He loses his poise.' Yet even Sylvester felt that the chances of Lloyd George stirring himself to goad Chamberlain had faded. 'P.M. expects to have a rough time, but both he and his friends think they will weather the storm.'

One of few observers to scent which way the storm winds were blowing was a political and cultural outsider, Ivan Maisky. The wily Soviet Ambassador belonged to no English group, cabal or set. On that memorable Tuesday, Beaverbrook was having lunch with Maisky at the Soviet Embassy. Before they left to watch the debate, Maisky closely questioned Beaverbrook on the state of the government.

'Should one expect any changes?'

With a dismissive wave of his arms, Beaverbrook confidently asserted that the government would of course be criticised during the debate, but no serious consequences would follow. 'Chamberlain's position is secure. The Cabinet will be unchanged . . . the P.M. is not in danger.'

Beaverbrook's certainty surprised Maisky. Brendan Bracken had spoken to him the day before in equally confident terms, convinced that nothing much would happen. Maisky wrote: 'And he, after all, is Churchill's *alter ego*, with an excellent knowledge of all the goings-on in the kitchen of politics. It's strange. Beaverbrook and Bracken are by all appearances exceptionally well-informed individuals. And yet, I have the feeling that England has approached a crucial boundary; that these debates ought to yield something; that change is in the air . . .

'We'll see.'

*

The three-day cocoon of radio silence in which Fleming and Lindsay had lived since their departure from Namsos was broken when HMS *York* berthed at Gourock. The dazed survivors of 'Maurice Force' were welcomed back by General Ironside inside the transit shed. Ironside read out a message from the Secretary of State for War, Oliver Stanley, who praised the withdrawal as an operation worthy of the British army's 'highest traditions'. Then, in a speech that was listened to with mute astonishment, Ironside commended the Infantry Brigades for their achievement in getting away. 'Remember the good things: how you beat these people when they came at you – you with none of the implements that they had.' He urged them to take pride in all that they had achieved. 'Don't think you were driven out of Norway: you were ordered out of Norway, and the great thing is that your discipline brought you out.'

Underpinning Ironside's instructions for Tom Fowler and Frank Lodge to keep their heads up and tell people how well they had fought was panic that the Territorials might pass on a different message. Churchill took the line that returning troops had to be regarded 'as heroes', yet should not be permitted contact with soldiers embarking for further operations. Reith pressed for action 'to prevent all sorts of stories emanating from uncontrolled interviews in Gourock', and the question was raised of forbidding members of the armed forces to board trains over the Whitsun weekend. It was vital that these heroic 'Norway veterans' did not lend substance to the claim of the *Daily Mirror* columnist 'Cassandra' that it was the Germans who had ordered them out of Norway.

News that the Norway Campaign was to be discussed in Parliament had a galvanising effect on 'Flea' and 'Louse'. As Fowler and Lodge dispersed to their homes only to talk about the bright side, the two Intelligence captains headed for London, ferocious in their determination to cause maximum irritation to the body politic. The errors which they had witnessed had to be communicated and acted upon – or else Britain was never going to win the war.

On 6 May, Fleming called on Geoffrey Dawson at *The Times*. The editor had only days earlier recovered from the 'shattering rumour' that Fleming was dead. Elated to see him, Dawson invited Fleming home to lunch. In private, they discussed the military situation, Dawson hearing the details for the first time. He wrote that Fleming was 'v interesting and v depressing about the muddles of the Norway expedition'. Afterwards, Dawson asked him to come back to the office and 'look over' the *Times* leader before it went to bed. Fleming's contribution was to nudge the government into the cross hairs. The paper's leading article next morning emphasised how Carton de Wiart's lack of success at Namsos, and Paget's failure at Åndalsnes, 'was not their fault or that of their troops'.

While Peter Fleming laid mines in Fleet Street, Martin Lindsay was having his memorandum typed out to show whose fault it was.

Not enough is known about the Lindsay Memorandum and its contribution to the Norway Debate. Although the conditions to remove Chamberlain were in place, Lindsay's three-page manuscript acted as 'the sudden loud exclamation' which started the avalanche that carried the Prime Minister away. This was the argument advanced by Laurence Thompson, who in 1965 interviewed Lindsay for his book *1940*. Martin Lindsay repeated the claim on Thames Television for the 1973 *World At War* series. Yet because his memorandum vanished in the hiatus that it had helped to create, historians have had only Lindsay's word to go on. Without the hard text, it has remained one more mystery in a period full of them.

The day after delivering the first draft of this book to my publisher, I visited Hatfield House, home of the Salisburys, to read correspondence relating to the Watching Committee. I had lost hope of finding Lindsay's missing document. My intention was to check quotes that I had taken from other accounts against their original sources, alert for omissions or errors of transcription which can creep into any text, as the experience of twenty-five years of working in archives has taught me. Then, in a folder of letters from Lord Salisbury to his son, I came upon an undated typescript. Underlined in red at the top of the first page were the words 'Private & Confidential'.

The anonymous author was a British officer who had 'just returned from the Southern front in Norway after serving in a very humble position on the Staff'. He was aware that to write as he did was against the regulations, 'but I consider that the truth should be made known in the public interest and not buried'. In the interests of serving his country, he was bringing 'the facts as observed by myself and my comrades . . . to the notice of responsible persons so that those responsible are not able to cover up their misdeeds next week in Parliament'.

Already, I had a premonition that this was Lindsay's long-lost 'memorandum', which proceeded to outline in sombre detail 'the whole story of muddle and incompetence which has resulted in one of the most complete disasters in our military history'. By the time I reached the excoriating conclusion, I was convinced. But how to prove it?

Although unsigned, the typed manuscript contained four handwritten words: *no, known, subjected, continuous* – corrections which the unknown author had inserted in blue ink using a thick-nibbed fountain pen. The only way to confirm my hunch was to determine if this handwriting was Lindsay's. In the Bodleian Library in Oxford I juxtaposed the insertions against a letter that Lindsay had penned to Attlee in 1946. I next compared the words to a 1948 letter from Lindsay to Churchill, thanking him for signing *The Gathering Storm*. The script in both instances displayed the same 'e', 's', 'c' and 't'. As a last resort, I scanned the four words to Lindsay's daughter. She emailed back: 'Yes, I'm 99.9 per cent sure it's my father's writing.'

That being the case, then it is virtually certain that Peter Fleming looked over Martin Lindsay's memorandum, as he had the *Times* leader, because Lindsay alludes to eyewitnesses who 'have seen this letter and state that, in their opinion, it does not fully disclose the extent of the disorganisation and incompetence exhibited'.

Lindsay was adamant that 'if the lessons of this disaster are not learned, and the people responsible weeded out, the prospects of our winning this war are slender'. In short, he hoped that his exposé of the British military expedition to Norway, placed in the right hands, could be the dynamite with which Leland Stowe had sought 'to rock 10 Downing Street'.

In a letter in the same folder, dated 2 May, Lord Salisbury wrote to his son that 'the whole look' of Chamberlain's Cabinet was of a 'tottering' government. 'My spot, however, is that Neville . . . will not survive fuller information.'

It was against this background that Lindsay now approached the Watching Committee. He needed the help of its 'responsible' Conservative critics to find the right hands. Shorthand notes on the back of his memorandum point to the Committee's Honorary Secretary Paul Emrys-Evans as the member who effected the crucial introduction.

May I use a private friendship to bring a public matter to your
notice in the hope that it may be of some service to the country?   I have just
returned from the Southern front in Norway after serving in a very humble position
on the Staff.   Now that all those who will ever get back have got over, I
think that the facts as observed by myself and my comrades should be brought to
the notice of responsible persons so that those responsible are not able to
cover up their misdeeds next week in Parliament.   The facts as regards the
front itself come from eye witnesses, some of whom have seen this letter and
state that, in their opinion, it does not fully disclose the extent of the
disorganisation and incompetence exhibited.

PART FOUR

THE DEBATE

15
TUESDAY 7 MAY

'The dead columns of Hansard cannot reproduce it. They can only provide those who were present with the necessary aids to memory.'
ALFRED DUFF COOPER MP

'The doped somnambulists have been jerked back to consciousness.'
Daily Mirror, 9 May 1940

No matter how often the story is told, nothing seems predestined about the upheaval that took place in the House of Commons on Tuesday 7 May 1940. As in the Dardanelles, hardly anyone behaved on that day as expected. When Giles Romilly's fellow war correspondent on the *Express*, Alan Moorehead, looked back at Gallipoli, he felt in a curious way that the battle 'might still lie before us in the future; that there is still time to make other plans and bring it to a different ending'. The same is true of the Norway Debate, with the Chamber on the opening afternoon packed to capacity, and Members jammed in at the Bar to watch a piece of parliamentary theatre that for dramatic tension vied with Gielgud's performance in *King Lear* at the Old Vic.

The Commons assembled at 2.45 p.m. The Speaker and Chaplain walked up the Chamber, turned and knelt at the Table. The Members lining the green benches bowed their heads as the Chaplain prayed for them. 'May they never lead the nation wrongly through love of power, desire to please, or unworthy ideals, but laying aside all private interests and prejudices keep in mind their responsibility to seek to improve the condition of all mankind.'

The sources available to historians are punishingly similar, yet there is a contemporary account which has been overlooked, written by Harold Nicolson in the pressure of the moment, and cabled to the now defunct *Montreal Standard*. Not cited before, Nicolson's words describe the scene as it unfolded, without the blemish of over-familiarity or hindsight, capturing the picture and the mood from the perspective of someone who was present throughout. This is how it begins: 'The general opinion on that first day of the debate was that the Opposition would not press for a vote, but that the Commons would be able to indicate that the country as a whole, not content with the present administration, would expect an early strengthening of the Cabinet. No unusual dramatic developments were foreseen.'

At 3.45 p.m. the Serjeant at Arms advanced to the desk, bowed to the Speaker, and lifted the Mace from the top of the Table to the rack below. The House transformed itself for a few moments into a Committee of Supply. Nicolson informed his Canadian readers: 'The House never allows procedure to be altered by historic events since that procedure is even more historic.'

A proposal was made that 'a sum not exceeding £319,655' should be granted His Majesty the King for salaries and expenses of the House of Commons, including a grant in aid of the Kitchen Committee.

The Speaker in charge of the Norway Debate was a tall, crusty cattle-farmer who had been wounded at Ypres. A taciturn ex-soldier, Captain Edward FitzRoy was famously ineffusive, though not always. Nancy Astor accosted him once during a garden party at Cliveden, saying in her Virginia twang: 'Listening to the bores in the House you must often, Captain FitzRoy, wish you were dead.'

'On the contrary, I have often wished _you_ were.'

FitzRoy was said to be as sharp a judge of a politician as of a shorthorn bull. He liked brief speeches, and to remind Ministers that a lot could be said in fifteen minutes. During long speeches, his leg, encased in its stockings and breeches, had the habit of moving up and down with rhythmic annoyance.

Overhead, the Galleries had filled almost to overflowing, with Ambassadors and High Commissioners stepping over each other to reach their reserved seats. Baffy Dugdale joined Dorothy Macmillan in the Distinguished Strangers' Gallery. 'I never saw the House so packed, even for the Munich debate. But what a change.' Looking down, she was surprised to see Dorothy's husband Harold sitting below the gangway on the opposition benches. These seats had been allocated to the Conservatives owing to the large turnout.

The Question on the Supply Motion was put and agreed to without debate.

The Serjeant at Arms advanced and lifted the Mace from the rack to its normal position on the Table.

The Chief Whip moved: 'That this House do now adjourn.'

'The Prime Minister,' called the Speaker in a calm voice.

Chamberlain rose, to be greeted by loud cheers from some of his supporters, and on the opposition side by a few cries of: 'Who missed the bus?' and a shout directed at the Chief Whip: 'Well staged, David, well staged!'

'I confess that the House of Commons depresses me,' Chamberlain had written to Ida in January. Sensitive to heckling, it made him 'sick to see such personal prejudice & such partisanship when I am doing my best to avoid any Party provocation in the national interest'. He shared Cadogan's low opinion of MPs: 'Silly bladders! Self-advertising, irresponsible nincompoops. How I <u>hate</u> Members of Parliament!'

Most speakers suffered from nerves. The Chancellor John Simon confessed to Geoffrey Shakespeare that before a speech: 'I feel just like a man sentenced to death, who is to be hanged shortly.' The Prime Minister was more nervous this afternoon than he let on. After writing out his speech at Chequers, he had shown a draft to Halifax and Churchill. Whatever their input, it could do little to alter Chamberlain's inescapable handicap: although an extremely accomplished debater, he tended to speak like the chairman of a Chamber of Commerce. In 'a candid portrait' that Duff Cooper had published four months earlier in the *American Mercury*, Cooper wrote: 'He has no charm of manner or command of rhetoric. The unexpected epithet, the telling metaphor, the burst of eloquence – all those qualities that render the speeches of Winston Churchill an unending source of delight are utterly foreign to the oratory and the character of Chamberlain . . .' His voice was thin, his prose unimaginative, his delivery uninspiring. 'When he said the fine true thing,' lamented the Independent MP A. P. Herbert, 'it was like a faint air played on a pipe and lost on the wind at once.' His unofficial biographer Derek Walker-Smith cautiously accepted that 'there is little or no poetry in Mr Chamberlain'. A Labour MP compared listening to a speech by Chamberlain to paying a visit to Woolworth's – everything in its place and nothing above sixpence.

The motion before the House that afternoon was one for the adjournment – purely a vehicle for debate, without the possibility of an expression of substantive opinion or amendment – and so the Deputy Speaker, Sir Dennis Herbert, did not expect Labour to demand a vote. 'No one anticipated that there would be any division.' Members waited in attentive silence to take their cue from Chamberlain's opening statement. In common with Attlee, A. J. Sylvester believed that 'if he rallies his supporters and satisfies them, the present political crisis may blow over . . .'

Where the Prime Minister stood was once a stinking mud flat referred to as a 'terrible place' in early Saxon chronicles. A charged occasion like this returned him to a boiling evening in Andros when he stood behind the counter of his primitive store selling biscuits and rice and 'everything mahn want' to a demanding crowd of sisal planters. He rested a compact little sheaf of pages on the despatch box scarred by Gladstone's signet ring, and started speaking in a composed, unemotional tone, glancing from time to time at his neatly written notes. Nicolson observed how Chamberlain emphasised his points 'by allowing the back of his left hand to fall into the outstretched palm of his right hand, and at moments whipping off his pince-nez between his thumb and finger and turning around to his supporters below the gangway'.

When he last addressed the House, Chamberlain began, he had been anxious to say nothing which might involve risk to the troops. To expressions of 'Hear, hear', he commended their magnificent gallantry. He then said that he proposed to examine the causes of the failure which had created profound shock in the House and country.

'All over the world!' came a Labour shout.

More shouts of 'missed the bus' forced Chamberlain to break off, sit down on the front bench and wait for an angry Speaker to restore quiet and order. Harold Macmillan was one of Chamberlain's severest critics, but he felt that the Prime Minister was rudely and unfairly interrupted. Heckled again moments later, Chamberlain reacted with what Nicolson described as a 'rather feminine' gesture of irritation.

'A great many times some hon. Members have repeated the phrase "Hitler missed the bus"—'

'You said it,' voices shouted.

'Yes, I said it, and I will now explain the circumstances in which I said it . . .'

But it was no good. The flop might have been heard in Birmingham, a lobby reporter told Leo Amery. Feeble, faltering, without his customary self-assurance, Chamberlain 'looked a shattered man', decided the Liberal MP Henry Morris-Jones.

Chamberlain had hoped to narrow the scope of criticism to the actions taken by the government since the German invasion. In this scenario, evacuation was not only inevitable, it was sensible. He resisted any comparison to the withdrawal at Gallipoli. No large forces were involved. The Germans had suffered heavy losses. The 'balance of advantage lay on our side'. The Liberal MP Dingle Foot could not believe what he was hearing. 'No one listening to his speech would have supposed that Britain had suffered a major defeat.'

A spoof of Chamberlain's speech was printed in the *New Statesman*. 'Germany has invaded Aberdeen. The Army is to be congratulated on a brilliant achievement in withdrawing from the Highlands under the very noses of the German aeroplanes. Not one man was lost in the evacuation . . . My impression is that on balance the Allies have gained . . . no one has ever got very much out of Aberdeen anyway . . . I am more confident than ever of Allied victory.'

It did not surprise Chips Channon, glancing up, to see the Egyptian Ambassador asleep.

Chamberlain's most important announcement concerned the new powers that he had granted Churchill. Herbert Morrison leapt up from the Labour front bench to demand if this new arrangement covered the period of the Norwegian operations – or had it been made since they commenced?

Chamberlain admitted: 'It has only been made recently.'

For the first time, Amery took heart. 'That Churchill had not been responsible under this lop-sided arrangement was at any rate some relief to those of us who looked to him as a future leader.'

The Prime Minister had spoken for fifty-seven minutes. He looked pale, sounded tired. At times fumbling his words, he closed with a call for unity, warning the House of further German attacks, even an attempt to invade, and sat down 'thin and burning-eyed'.

His statement had left the House bored, restive, and depressed at what Amery called 'his obvious satisfaction with things as they stood', but not mutinous. If Maisky felt that his speech 'was simply rot,' then Colville reflected the more positive mood from within the Chamberlain camp 'that the Government was going "to get away with it"'.

Colville sustained his optimism through the next two speeches by the main opposition leaders.

Chamberlain was followed at 4.45 p.m. by Clement Attlee for Labour. Quiet, prim, schoolmasterly, bald-headed, Attlee tended to come across, in Hugh Dalton's phrase, as 'a little mouse'. In a low-key delivery, only rarely looking at his notes, Attlee blamed recent speeches by Chamberlain and Churchill for being 'far too optimistic'. The government had made no provision for the inevitable German counter-stroke, and had not appreciated 'the vital importance of protection from the air'. And what was to become a repeatedly gnawed bone of contention: the government was 'too much fixed on Narvik'.

Lobby correspondents considered it significant that Attlee was not interrupted when he escalated his attack. Attlee's statement – 'Everywhere the story is "Too late"' – was received by a rumble of Labour cheers, but no challenging shouts from the Conservative back bench. 'The Prime Minister talked about missing buses. What about all the buses which he and his associates have missed since 1931? They missed all the peace buses but caught the war bus.'

The correspondent of the *Daily Worker* was among the first to register that Attlee's uninterrupted censure had injected a fresh note. 'When a Premier and a Party leader is attacked in Parliament and the attack is received in silence by his supporters the writing is already on the wall.'

Clement Davies considered Attlee's speech 'direct', Amery 'pretty good', and Nicolson 'feeble', while Reith thought it did 'no damage'. Of more consequence than his criticisms was Attlee's restraint in not calling for a division. This, believed Amery, 'made it much easier for Conservatives to be influenced by the opening day's debate'.

Halifax had organised a ticket to the Peers' Gallery for Baba Metcalfe. She missed the first two speeches, but arrived in time to hear Archie Sinclair. Baba was not impressed – 'a bad speaker'. Colville, on the other hand, felt that the Liberal leader was 'eloquent and venomous', revealing 'as usual, a remarkable store of inside information'. There were shocked noises as Sinclair itemised the shambolic state of the expedition. The men at Namsos had no snowshoes or white coats. The anti-aircraft guns were 'utterly useless'. One transport had sailed without a chronometer, with no international code book and, therefore, no means of communicating with other vessels. Sinclair mocked John Simon's recent claim that 'the action decided on was wisely taken on the best advice'. The Chancellor reminded Sinclair of Lord Galway and his campaign of 1707. 'He drew up his troops according to the methods prescribed by the best writers, and in a few hours lost 18,000 men, 120 standards, all his baggage and all his artillery.' Sinclair, in concentrating his venom on Simon, a National Liberal, was targeting the most unpopular member of the War Cabinet, and not launching an all-out assault on the Conservatives. 'Violent attacks always disconcert them,' he had written to Salisbury's brother, Lord Cecil, 'but if we sing in a low key they are more likely to sing out.' Sinclair's speech was good, thought Baffy Dugdale, 'but not devastatingly so'.

The House remained in a state of suspense, uncertain if any dramatic developments would follow. Harold Nicolson felt the initiative inching back towards the government. 'Up to that moment there was no indication that the debate was likely to become critical.'

A deflated Bob Boothby took Baffy Dugdale to tea, gloomily predicting that there would be no change of government, that Lloyd George and the Labour leaders were 'determined not to take charge of affairs at this juncture, that the mess is so great, and the disasters to be expected in the next six weeks so terrible, let those who have sown the wind, reap the whirlwind. That was Bob's story about 5.30 p.m.'

Nicolson recorded the first sign of tension at 5.43 p.m. when the Speaker called on a diehard Chamberlain yes-man, Brigadier General Sir Henry Page Croft. 'This active and high-minded Baronet is not popular with the Labour Party. Protests which they emitted when he caught the Speaker's eye indicated that their blood was up.' Page Croft stood to a loud moan from the opposition benches.

Leo Amery had also leapt up, after two hours of 'agonised discomfort', but the Speaker ignored him. Earlier, Amery had talked to Captain FitzRoy when he met with his secretary to decide on a rough running order, and Amery has to be the leading candidate for the 'very distinguished ex-Cabinet Minister' accused by the Deputy Speaker of delaying the Speaker's procession by a few minutes – FitzRoy had to march at double-pace to catch up. A Privy Counsellor since 1922, Amery, though a backbencher, had 'a certain customary right to be called'. Yet the Speaker gave no hint when this might be. Amery then realised 'that he meant to postpone me to the dinner hour – deliberately, I suspected, because he knew that I was out to make trouble'.

Amery's suspicion that the Speaker was trying 'to kill the debate' by calling on Page Croft – who proceeded to deliver what Baba Metcalfe called 'a dreary and not impressive tirade in favour of the Government' – was shared by Labour MPs. The following afternoon Aneurin Bevan stood up and voiced the 'great resentment' felt in the House concerning 'the absence of impartiality from the Chair'.

Page Croft was followed by Josiah Wedgwood, 'a veteran Socialist, much loved by the House', wrote Nicolson. Wedgwood's speech was provocative, indiscreet and rambling. One of the lessons of Norway, he suggested, was that 'an army of the future must always move by night'.

At one moment, Wedgwood asked whether the government had prepared any plan to prevent the invasion of the country.

Vice Admiral Ernest Taylor, Conservative MP for Paddington South, rose to interrupt with the remark that the navy would see to that.

Wedgwood countered immediately by saying that the navy had gone to the other end of the Mediterranean 'to keep itself safe from bombing'.

Nicolson believed that it was this 'incidental, impulsive, excitable rejoinder which marked the point where the debate ceased to be an ordinary debate and began to be a tremendous conflict of wills'.

Moments after Wedgwood made his remark, the short, stocky figure of Admiral Sir Roger Keyes strolled into the House, causing a stir. He was dressed in the gold-braided uniform of an Admiral of the Fleet. He wore six rows of medal ribbons, and the Grand Cross of Bath, with neck badges for his KCVO and his CMG. 'Questionable taste,' thought Chips Channon, 'but it lent him dignity.'

Nicolson seized a piece of paper, scribbled on it the remark Wedgwood had just made, and handed it to Keyes who had squeezed onto the bench behind him.

Keyes at once left his place and went behind the Speaker's Chair. He begged Captain FitzRoy to call him next, as the honour of the navy had been placed in question.

Wedgwood sat down shortly afterwards. The Admiral rose, clutching his order paper in which he had concealed his speech.

'Sir Roger Keyes,' said the Speaker.

The Hero of Zeebrugge had shaved that morning with a copy of Kipling's poem 'If' propped up before him. He had put on his ostentatious uniform after consulting with a former First Lord, Duff Cooper, who strongly advised him to wear it.* He had written out what he intended to say on the recommendation of Harold Macmillan, who had been given the same tip by Lloyd George in 1923. Keyes had a reputation second only to Leo Amery for his lack of parliamentary charisma – 'I am not very quick with my tongue,' he admitted to Churchill. To overcome this, Macmillan told Keyes to ignore the etiquette that he speak from notes, and to read out his speech once he had rehearsed it thoroughly.

A meeting with General Carton de Wiart a few hours after his return from Namsos had steeled Keyes in his determination to criticise 'the whole campaign'. He was aware that this meant attacking the Admiralty and his long-standing friend, the First Lord. Yet Keyes felt that he had no choice after learning about the situation in Namsos from the mouth of the commander in charge, who had not minced his words. Carton de Wiart was furious at the evacuation – and 'very disappointed' by the 'non-appearance of the Navy', which had 'knocked out all idea' of attacking Trondheim. When Keyes rose to his feet at 7.09 p.m., he was ready to defend the navy's traduced reputation against what he perceived as the cowardice of Whitehall.

---

* There was (and still is) a prohibition on wearing military uniform in the Chamber, but this was suspended from 1939 to 1945 for those on active service. Oddly, Keyes, as an Admiral of the Fleet, was *on the active list* but not *on active service*.

Seated on the bench immediately below him, Nicolson had a ringside view of Keyes's performance, which he had in part provoked. 'Now the Admiral, although the bravest man in England, is usually a nervous speaker. It is his diffidence and modesty coupled with his heroic qualities that endear him to the House. But in his opening phrases he forgot that diffidence, since at that moment he was enraged.'

Keyes referred to Wedgwood's remarks and said that they constituted a 'damned insult'.

The House roared its applause.

Lloyd George, who had just come in, 'slapped his little thighs in ecstasy and roared louder than anyone else'.

Nicolson detected that a feeling of intense drama had suddenly entered the already tropical atmosphere. 'The temperature of the House rose from 99 to 101.'

In the Diplomatic Gallery, bunched in alongside the newly evacuated Norwegian Foreign Minister and the French and American Ambassadors, Maisky watched Keyes lumberingly read out his lines. 'He stumbled, got confused and agitated, and for precisely those reasons produced a very moving speech.' This was the first time that Keyes had worn his Admiral's regalia in the House, yet not even Duff Cooper who had encouraged him could have anticipated the effect which his uniform produced. 'The sincerity that lay behind his words gave them life,' Cooper wrote. 'Those who listened knew that here was no scheming politician, no seeker after office, no captious critic and, although all his principles were Conservative, no party hack. The loyalest of men, he could no longer offer his loyalty to the Prime Minister. He knew that it was no little thing that he was doing, and in order that others might understand what it meant to him he put on for the occasion the uniform that he had so nobly earned the right to wear – the livery of glory.'

In a low voice, Keyes began to tell the story of how he had offered to seize Trondheim if only he could be placed in command of a few old ships. 'The capture of Trondheim was essential, imperative and vital.' But his suggestions were not welcome at the Admiralty. There were whistles of shocked surprise when Keyes revealed that the Admiralty had told him that it was not necessary to go into Trondheimsfjorden 'as the Army was making good progress'. This story 'made a deep impression', wrote Nicolson.

In salvo after salvo – so it seemed to his audience – Keyes blasted the government with the firepower that he had hoped to deploy on Trondheim. To Maisky, 'Keyes's words had the effect of shells fired from 16-inch guns.' Baffy Dugdale was mesmerised by his broadside. 'It knocked the House in the very pit of its stomach. Impossible to say what the reaction will be, but never have I seen the speech of a back-bencher change history, as I think this must.'

Keyes stumbled on, his every phrase devoured by a silent, engrossed Chamber. Baba Metcalfe realised that she had read many of these phrases before – with Halifax at the Dorchester. She reported back to the Foreign Secretary that the Admiral spoke 'on the lines of his letter to Winston. He had the riveted interest of a packed House and obviously a lot of sympathy.'

The result of not using our sea power vigorously had been little short of catastrophic. 'The Gallipoli tragedy has been followed step by step.' The lack of naval cooperation had doomed the Namsos force to failure. General Carton de Wiart had advanced from Steinkjer in the hope of finding British ships to assist him. He had found, instead, two German destroyers which opened fire on his flank and defeated the whole expedition. 'It is a shocking story of ineptitude, which I assure the House ought never to have been allowed to happen.'

Keyes concluded his address with a warm tribute to Churchill – 'I am longing to see a proper use made of his great ability' – and expressing his fear that he might never be forgiven by his dear admired friend. Churchill, who had sat throughout his speech with bowed head, turned around in his seat and gave Keyes a broad grin of affection, wrote Nicolson. 'The House notices these things. It is Churchill's generosity of mind which stills petty animosities.'

But Keyes was not done. In a stirring final barrage, the Admiral assured MPs that there were 'hundreds of young officers who are waiting eagerly to seize Warburton-Lee's torch, or emulate the deeds of Vian of the *Cossack*. One hundred and forty years ago, Nelson said, "I am of the opinion that the boldest measures are the safest," and that still holds good to-day.'

For a flashing, glorious moment, the House had an image of Nelson parading up and down his deck with gold braid and epaulettes. The contrast with the absent Chamberlain, at that moment in audience with the King at Buckingham Palace, but seen earlier shrinking on the front bench in his black morning clothes and wing collar, could not have been wider.

It was 7.30 p.m. when Keyes finished. Nicolson wrote: 'There is a great gasp of astonishment. It is by far the most dramatic speech I have ever heard and when Keyes sits down there is thunderous applause.' From then onwards, it became evident to Nicolson that the debate would be not merely an investigation of the Norway Campaign, 'but a criticism of the Government's whole war effort'.

The Chamber thinned out as Members departed to chew over Keyes's speech, and to eat. In the third row below the gangway, Amery tried to catch the Speaker's eye, but this time the Speaker called Lewis Jones. Ten minutes later, Jones sat down. Amery scrambled to his feet, but the Speaker called Captain Bellenger.

It was now 7.41 p.m. Amery had sat in the same seat for more than four hours, 'divided between perfunctory listening to unimportant speeches which never seem to end, and vainly trying to remember the all-important points of the all-important speech one hopes to make oneself.' He glumly watched as Members 'steadily dribbled out' of the Chamber. 'The whole effect of what I had to say depended on the response of a live House and not on those who might care to read my speech in Hansard.'

Bellenger finished speaking at 8.03 p.m. It now being the dinner hour, the Deputy Speaker, Dennis Herbert, was in the Chair. With some hesitation Amery got up. This time he heard: 'Mr Amery.'

Amery remained standing. Even so, he was disheartened when he cast his eye over the deserted benches. There were fewer MPs – 'barely a dozen' – than for his maiden speech in May 1911. Not even his ally Clement Davies, with whom Amery had gone through his talk, had come to listen. If Amery sat down now, he was confident of being called early the next afternoon. 'I nearly decided to leave the reasoned criticism of the Government to another day.'

Amery had spent the morning preparing his speech in his library in Eaton Square. The business of writing still came hard. Decades of practice had failed to animate the soporific impact of his prose. In 1932, he had bumped into a friend 'cherubically asleep' with Amery's latest book *A Plan for Action* 'open on his tummy'. It took Amery back to the scene on deck sailing home from South Africa in 1902 'when I saw ten officers simultaneously asleep over Vol II of my S. African history'.

A slumber-inducing prose style was not Amery's only drawback. He was a lamentable orator, as Chamberlain's brother once tried to explain. 'Austen told me that I put too much material into my speeches, not enough scene-painting and rather too fine work, the result of the habit of writing. He also told me that I was too fond of dropping my voice to a mysterious whisper.' To overcome these shortcomings, Amery had taken lessons on the art of public speaking from a lecturer at Queen's College London who taught him to vary his pitch and pace, and to use his diaphragm. Amery sent him a postcard after one by-election: 'Very rowdy meeting last night – diaphragm won.' But such occasions were infrequent, and Amery's prolix speeches in Parliament, delivered with 'a curious sing-song, parsonical intonation', rarely rose to the same triumphant pitch. Almost Amery's first speech in the Commons had been on the treatment of syphilis in the natives of Uganda. 'Spoke with considerable hesitation and awkwardness in view of the difficulty of the subject.' Thirty years on, the hesitation and awkwardness remained, and the subject had not grown any easier.

To inject spice into his speech on the Norway Campaign, Amery had looked up 'my favourite old quotation of Cromwell's' when Prince Rupert's cavalry was beating the Commons' troops as Hitler's pilots had pursued their successors out of Norway. Cromwell had chastised the leading Parliamentarian: 'Your troops are most of them old decayed serving-men, and tapsters, and such kind of fellows . . . We are fighting to-day for our life, for our liberty, for our all; we cannot go on being led as we are.' Amery then remembered Cromwell's other quotation when he dissolved the Rump Parliament in 1653 after it had been in power for thirteen years. Amery wondered if this was not 'too strong meat', but he decided to keep it up his sleeve 'in case the spirit should move me to use it as the climax to my speech, otherwise preparing a somewhat milder finish'.

When finally called upon to speak, Amery was 'doubtful whether I should make the whole speech I had prepared . . . I did not feel like talking for more than a few minutes.'

Nicolson watched him stand up. 'The temperature continued to rise,' he wrote. 'Amery's speech raised it far beyond the fever point.'

The Chamber which Amery addressed was almost empty, but it was loaded with the elements which were to produce what Andrew Roberts has called 'a case of parliamentary spontaneous combustion'.

If Keyes had supplied the first spark, then Clement Davies provided the second. In a letter to Amery in October 1954, Davies's recollection was that Lloyd George had asked Davies to dine with him, 'and naturally I accepted his invitation, but I told him that the moment that I knew you were up I would be leaving him. I knew that you would be called only by Dennis Herbert and you would have to wait until he was in the chair. I then heard the annunciator and saw that you were up and told LG that I was off and asked him to come in. I ran to the House, came behind you and urged you to make your full speech and then crossed the floor to the other side.'

In Amery's recollection, Davies 'murmured in my ear that I must at all costs state the whole case against the Government, and went off to collect an audience from the Smoking Room and Library'.

Davies's letter continued: 'In the meantime, the House was filling and, as you say, Lloyd George came in within a few minutes and sat at his usual corner on the Front Bench, leaning forward with great interest. Though it was the dinner hour, the House was filling rapidly.'

David Faber was a Conservative MP before he wrote Amery's biography. 'I've seen it happen. Members start drifting in from the dining room, the Members' bar, the Strangers' bar. Members who've eaten might be in the Library or entertaining guests, or rush across from Lord North Street or their clubs.'

It became one of the most famous speeches in parliamentary history. From the moment that he opened his mouth, Amery was 'far beyond his usual form'. He ceased to be an ambitious backbencher with a grudge. In the crucible of the Commons, he transformed into his forester father, standing before an ancient tree which had crumbled to decay.

He began slowly, talking in a quiet, clear, level tone, his small figure growing imperceptibly in stature with every indignant phrase and with the appearance of each new Member who streamed in to listen, 'a tribute less perhaps to my eloquence than to the thought that I might be saying something of moment' – until, as Ronald Blythe put it, 'a squashed little man with the minimum of presence, suddenly seemed, to the hallucinated eyes and strung-up nerves of the House, to loom over Parliament like a monolith'.

Amery claimed to have no loyalties 'except to the common cause.' He played for time, glancing up from his notes to assess the mood and extent of his audience. He had wanted Chamberlain to be there, but the Prime Minister was still at the Palace. 'I fully understand the good reason for his absence.'

With the first strokes of his axe, Amery laid into the government for its woeful deficiencies in the initiative, planning and execution of the Norway Campaign. Encouraged by the murmurs of approval from the steadily fill-ing Conservative benches, Amery directed attention away from Norway and towards the absent Prime Minister, who this afternoon had once again 'expressed himself as satisfied that the balance of advantage lay on our side'.

Chamberlain's complacency was a danger to the nation. To illustrate how dangerous, Amery took himself back to Africa, telling the story of a friend who had gone lion-hunting and spent the night asleep in a railway carriage, dreaming of hunting his lion in the morning – but in the night the lion 'clambered on to the rear of the car, scrabbled open the sliding door, and ate my friend. That is in brief the story of our initiative over Norway.'

Those baying their approval were ready to perceive a connection between Amery's devoured friend and Amery's fellow Conservative MP from Birmingham – his colleague of thirty years, the man who had got him into Parliament, whose father and brother had been Amery's mentors, whose son was Amery's godson – and they had a thrilling presentiment that Amery was about to savage him. Blythe wrote: 'There are few sights more quelling – a cannibal banquet perhaps – than one Tory slaying a fellow Tory for the good of the country in the parliamentary arena at Westminster.' Geoffrey Howe's assault on Margaret Thatcher is a recent example of a rare species. Yet even that assassination pales before Amery's attack on Chamberlain.

Amery had addressed the Chamber on numerous occasions since 1911. He knew how hard it was to gain what he called the 'ear of the House'. 'All that can be said is that there is no satisfaction equal to that feeling that you are carrying the House with you on some subject about which you care deeply. For no other audience has such power to influence the mainsprings of action.'

On hardly any other previous occasion had Amery enjoyed the House's ear, but he had it now. As he warmed to his speech, and his audience with him, 'I found myself going on to an increasing crescendo of applause.'

Members remained still and strained as they witnessed for the second time that day a well-known tedious speaker metamorphose into an eloquent hatchet man. Louis Spears felt as if Amery were hurling stones as large as himself at the government glasshouse. 'The crash of glass could not be heard, but the effect was that of a series of deafening explosions.'

In an increasingly tense atmosphere, Amery arrived at his conclusion. His implacable sentences, Spears noted, gave 'the impression of volleys fired into sandbags'. Amery said: 'We cannot go on as we are. There must be a change.' This was war, not peace. The time had come for 'a real National Government'. Amery still refused to be drawn into 'a discussion on personalities', but he felt that victory required a new leader with 'vision, daring, swiftness and consistency of decision'.

At this point, Amery hesitated. 'I could only dare to go as far as I carried the House with me.' To go beyond would be a fatal error of judgement. 'In no little doubt, I had left it open to the inspiration of the moment. Now I felt myself swept forward by the surge of feeling which my speech had worked up on the benches round me.' So evident was this feeling 'that I cast prudence to the winds and ended full out with my Cromwellian injunction'.

Oliver Cromwell had directed his injunction at Parliament, not at one individual. In Amery's case, it is generally assumed that he was looking at Chamberlain when, at 8.43 p.m., after speaking for forty-one minutes, he delivered his peroration. But a curious aspect of Amery's speech is that no one seems to know whether the Prime Minister was present on the front bench to hear it. This uncertainty is the more astonishing given the sheer number of interested witnesses, not only in the House and the Galleries, but in the country beyond. Margery Allingham wrote: 'The debate in the House was followed by everyone.'

If the claims for Moore-Brabazon's illicit photograph of Amery are true, and his image does capture Amery in the act of making his speech – and not, say, Duff Cooper – then Chamberlain can be seen glancing up from the bench with a taut expression. But what is odd, considering the near-universal focus on him, is that no one mentions the Prime Minister's reaction, not even Amery. In this respect, Amery's onslaught departs from Howe's savaging of Thatcher, when a number of memoirists recorded their impressions. The only documentary evidence to survive is a letter that Chamberlain wrote to Amery one month before he died, addressing him as 'My dear Leo' and admitting that 'I have been deeply hurt by some of the things you have done and said which cut just because they came from an old friend.'

Amery would have been intensely conscious of the blow that he was about to deliver. Up until recently, he had regarded himself as someone 'so consistently helpful to the Government and so old a personal friend' of the Prime Minister that it is impossible to believe that he would be so vague about his target. Yet when thinking about it afterwards, Amery could not swear whether the colleague he was about to fell, and 'not without real distress', was in the Chamber. Amery did recall 'the pained faces of the front bench and even more vividly the look of amazed admiration on L[loyd] G[eorge]'s face', but as he wrote to Clement Davies: 'I cannot remember myself whether Neville was actually there.'

Cecil King in his diary next day reported that 'both Chamberlain and

Churchill looked all-in last night . . . Chamberlain fidgeting his right foot nervously' – but King gave no indication of the timing. Martin Gilbert has Amery looking towards Chamberlain when he made his attack, but historians like Laurence Thompson believe that Chamberlain was still absent from the Chamber, and that the Prime Minister was informed of it by the Chief Whip. This is the view of Amery's biographer. David Faber says: 'Chamberlain would have had to come back in especially (as the rest of the crowd did, into an initially empty Chamber) from the bar/dining room/ Palace (who knows), and it seems incredible that he would have consciously done so knowing he was almost certainly in for a hammering.'

Harold Nicolson was one of a tiny handful who claimed to have witnessed Chamberlain receiving Amery's final blow. In his article for the *Montreal Standard*, Nicolson has the Prime Minister sitting on the 'glum and anxious' front bench when Amery turned to address the government, encouraged to go on by the gusts of laughter that had greeted his quotation about old serving-men and tapsters.

Amery continued: 'I have quoted certain words of Oliver Cromwell. I will quote certain other words. I do it with great reluctance, because I am speaking of those who are old friends and associates of mine, but they are words which, I think, are applicable to the present situation. This is what Cromwell said to the Long Parliament when he thought it was no longer fit to conduct the affairs of the nation: "You have sat too long here for any good you have been doing. Depart, I say, and let us have done with you."'

Amery's concluding note struck a gong, Nicolson wrote. 'His last words were highly dramatic. In almost a whisper he said, pointing at Chamberlain: "In the name of God, go."*

'The Opposition broke out into violent cheering.'

If Chamberlain was present to hear Amery whispering his terrible words for him to go, then it was at the King's suggestion.

Chamberlain had entered Buckingham Palace at 6.30 p.m. in the belief

---

* Even the whisper is debatable. 'I have witnessed few scenes so dramatic and emotional as that when straight-hitting Amery cried "In God's name Go!", Alexander Mackintosh, *Echoes of Big Ben*.

that he had more or less got away with the debate. This impression was shared by Alexander Hardinge, the King's Private Secretary, who advised George VI: 'There is little doubt that the Government will get through the debate on the Norwegian campaign without much trouble . . .'

Chamberlain smiled to the King that he was not coming to offer his resignation. Moreover, he had not given up hope of reorganising his government along the lines of a National coalition, as Hardinge had advised 'for some time past'. Chamberlain revealed how he had seen Attlee and Greenwood that morning 'and had asked them about their coming into the Govt'. He admitted that their response was disappointing. 'They had said nothing.' At this, George VI offered to intercede with Attlee, who had dined at Buckingham Palace the night before, when the King 'had found him easier to talk to'. Chamberlain was grateful for his offer, but suggested that a royal appeal for Labour to 'pull their weight and join the National Government' might be much more effective coming after the Labour Party conference, convening in Bournemouth on Friday. Attlee would be unable to give any definite answer before then, said Chamberlain, as he was unsure of his party's feelings. The King accepted this. He and his wife got on well with Chamberlain. The Queen's future lady-in-waiting Frances Campbell-Preston says: 'Neville Chamberlain had sort of protected them. They were very young, and to them Chamberlain was like a godfather' – a feeling which Chamberlain reciprocated, confessing to Halifax on his deathbed that 'he felt he had been in a sense their Godfather'.

The King then told Chamberlain that he did not like the way in which, with all his worries and responsibilities, the Prime Minister 'was always subject to a stab in the back from both the House of Commons and the Press', and he encouraged him to return to the debate, which drifted on for another three hours.

Whether Chamberlain's government was savaged beyond rescue when the House adjourned that night at 11.30 p.m., or merely mauled, depends on which memoir or diary is consulted. The Transport Minister Euan Wallace registered the gamut of moods. 'Harold Macmillan and his friends were jubilant over what they regarded as the certain overthrow of "the worst Government which this country has seen since the war and probably for

100 years." The Chief Whip on the other hand thought we had had a reasonably good first day in an admittedly difficult situation.'

Many were tempted when they raked over Amery's speech, like the Liberal MP Dingle Foot, to suggest that it marked the pivotal point of the debate. 'Members began seriously to consider the possibility that the Government might be overthrown.' Afterwards, Macmillan was convinced that Amery's speech 'effectively destroyed the Chamberlain Government'. This was Amery's opinion. 'It settled the fate of the Government, for apparently it seems to have impressed our Members who read it in Hansard quite as much as those who heard it.' General Smuts wrote to him from Pretoria: 'Your great speech in the Commons at the final inquest made me literally sit up.' Six months later, Amery was already commemorating it as the speech 'which tipped the scale against Neville'.

In fact, the issue was not decided when Amery sat down. What was evident to the *Daily Telegraph*'s correspondent J. E. Sewell was that 'the Government had undergone the most damaging assault since before the war, but it was still far from clear that the inner defences had actually been penetrated.' Harold Nicolson remained to be convinced when he joined Baffy Dugdale for dinner in the Strangers' Dining Room, telling her that he did 'not want a change of Government now, but gradually'. Still, he admitted to feeling apprehensive. 'There is no doubt that the Government is very rocky and anything may happen tomorrow.'

Amery went on to a combined late-night meeting of his Conservative Group with Clement Davies's All Party Group. He and Davies agreed on MPs to speak in the debate next day. In a significant move, they decided not to press for a division, Amery having gathered from Davies, after the latter's non-committal interview with Attlee, that 'the Labour leaders themselves were doubtful of its advisability'.

Amery's speech had raised the temperature to beyond fever point, but it is important to bear in mind that it was one of several combustible elements. There could be no explosion, no avalanche, without Labour's participation. Maisky, gauging the atmosphere in the Smoking Room, reported that it 'was still unclear whether Labour was going to request a vote of no confidence'. Harold Macmillan urged the Labour leaders to do so, but in vain. 'Even the usually militant Hugh Dalton was doubtful.' A vote might benefit the government, worried Dalton, a Cambridge-educated barrister, with party discipline ensuring a massive majority. Or else, if Chamberlain used the pretext of a vote to call an election, 'the Old Man would win hands down and we would be wiped out further than in 1931'.

A large, bald, clerical-looking figure, Dalton was on good terms with Macmillan – both had been to Eton. Dalton told him that the Labour Executive would meet in the morning to decide their course. But most lobby correspondents left the Commons that night convinced that the opposition had already decided against dividing the House. Collin Brooks wrote in his diary: 'Labour is not to press for a vote of confidence,' and the political correspondents of the *Daily Herald* and the *Star,* each of whom had close links with Dalton and Morrison, were of the same opinion.

In the darkness, MPs, journalists and diplomats picked their way past the sandbags and plane trees, past the lifeless buildings which Maisky likened to menacing cliffs, through the blacked-out streets, to catch the last trains home.

The American war correspondent Webb Miller had covered the debate for the United Press. There was international speculation about Miller's mysteriously fractured skull when his body was found next morning beside the tracks at Clapham Junction. A coroner eventually concluded that the forty-nine-year-old journalist – who had seen 'more death and destruction than almost any man alive' – had stepped out when his train stopped in a tunnel and not at a platform, but the German press detected the sinister silhouette of 'Sir Joe Ball', and reported that Miller had been murdered by the British Secret Service 'on account of his report about Mr Chamberlain in the Commons'.

16
WEDNESDAY 8 MAY

*'If it's piracy you want, with broadsides, boarding parties, walking the plank and
blood on the deck, this is the place.'*
DAVID LLOYD GEORGE MP

*'If Lady Alexandra Metcalfe cannot get a place in the box of Peers' Married
Daughters could another seat be kindly found for her?'*
Pencilled note from LORD HALIFAX

*'I accept this challenge, I welcome it indeed. At least I shall see who is with us and
who is against us and I call on my friends to support us in the Lobby tonight.'*
NEVILLE CHAMBERLAIN, 8 May 1940

'I was the first person from this Force to reach London.' Captain Martin
Lindsay strode into the House on Wednesday morning, the second day of
the debate, and briefed Clement Attlee while still in his 'battle-stained service dress'. The government might reasonably have expected the prospective
Conservative candidate for Brigg to call in at the Chief Whip's office, but
instead Lindsay had contacted Paul Emrys-Evans, using his 'private friendship' with the dissident Conservative MP to effect an introduction to the
Labour leader, 'and I gave him a memorandum about the appalling improvisation and deficiencies in Norway because I was quite convinced that we
should lose the war if we went on like that'.

Peter Fleming's last act in Namsos had been to type out a message and
half-burn it, to suggest that the Namsen bridge had been wired up with
dynamite. Fleming never knew if his ruse had worked, but there was no con-
cealing the repercussion of Lindsay's document on Attlee. In a short history
of the House of Commons which Lindsay published after the war, he
described how Guy Fawkes had planted twenty barrels of powder in the
House of Lords' cellars. His son Colonel Oliver Lindsay attributed to

Lindsay's three-page memorandum a punch scarcely less explosive. 'His first-hand information helped to bring down the Chamberlain Administration.'

Up until that morning, David Margesson believed that he had an understanding with the Labour Chief Whip Sir Charles Edwards that if either party planned to vote, the other would be informed. Margesson had noted the critical undercurrent of Peter Fleming's leader in Tuesday's *Times*, but the coverage of the debate in Wednesday's newspapers, though unfavourable, had set off no further alarm bells. Labour frontbenchers Morrison and Dalton had given their assurance that there would not be a division to Maurice Webb of the *Daily Herald*, the mouthpiece of the Labour Party. Webb had written in his column on 8 May that it would be 'an unwise tactic' for the Labour Party to put down a vote of censure. 'The view taken by the most experienced critics of the Government is that the debate should be allowed to end without any direct challenge.' But Webb had not spoken to Attlee.

The Labour leader had listened with great care to the speeches of Keyes and Amery the night before. These revealed 'that discontent had gone far deeper than we thought'. A deciding factor was the arrival in Attlee's office of one more disgruntled Conservative – a combatant, moreover, who had served as General Carton de Wiart's staff officer. For melodramatic impact, Martin Lindsay in the soiled uniform of a 'Maurice Force' veteran eclipsed even the spectacle of Admiral Keyes with his medal ribbons. When Attlee read Lindsay's confidential typescript, it persuaded him to reconsider Labour's previous decision.

A meeting of Labour's Parliamentary Executive was held in an upstairs committee room at 10.30 a.m. To everyone's surprise, Attlee recommended that a division be forced at the end of the debate that evening. Hugh Dalton was one of four Labour MPs not in favour, arguing that fifteen Conservatives at most would vote against the government.

Attlee overruled Dalton. At a second meeting that morning, his recommendation to vote against the adjournment motion was put to the party and accepted.

Over lunch, Attlee grilled Lindsay further about the contents of his memorandum. Attlee learned how the large British troop ships had been 'quite useless' in the small Norwegian ports; how 'not a single unit arrived properly equipped'; how 'the only aircraft we ever had were 15 Goliaths 1929 model which are slower than the German bombers'; how one squadron of Spitfires 'would have changed the campaign'; how 'the enemy was fully equipped in every respect'; how 'absolute chaos reigned at the base and in the lines of communication'; how Chamberlain's statement 'as to the limited objectives was untrue' – the operation order 'stated specifically that the object of the force was the capture of Oslo'; how it was no exaggeration to say that 'Maurice Force' was 'not an army but a rabble'; how 'the German Army showed itself an efficient and formidable force', and how its communiqués over the last few days had been 'strictly accurate'.

According to Lindsay, Attlee gave his memorandum to Herbert Morrison 'to help him open for the Opposition that afternoon'.

The Norway Debate recommenced at 4.03 p.m. in the Commons. Spears wrote: 'The House was packed and as nervous as a cat with kittens.' He soon developed cramp from being compressed into an uncomfortable sideways position.

Members had gathered in a belligerent mood. Many like Macmillan still had Amery's words 'ringing in our ears'. Violet Bonham Carter took her place in the Speaker's Gallery – with Baba Metcalfe, Mary Churchill and Anne Chamberlain – and settled down to watch 'the most dramatic debate I have almost ever heard in my whole parliamentary memory'.

Morrison spoke first. His attack was lethal. Quietly delivered, it treated Parliament as the highest court in the land. He gave no hint that he intended to divide the House. He began with Churchill and Narvik. He wished to put some hard questions to Churchill about his inexplicable obsession with Narvik. There was no apparent reason why British warships should have devoted their attention to Narvik alone. 'I should like to know what were the strategic reasons that led us first to Narvik . . . was Narvik strategically the right place to aim at first? Would it not have been wiser strategically to start at a more Southern point?'

Morrison's questions stayed in the air, unanswered. The effect was heightened by his revelation that Labour had made a request for Churchill to speak earlier, as the First Lord had 'considerable responsibility' for the Norway operations. But Churchill was going to speak last, and no one would be able to comment on his evidence. 'He is the chief witness who refuses to go into the box.'

Morrison then moved south to Namsos. His vituperation grew as he approached that section of his speech which he had based on Martin Lindsay's information. One after another he repeated Lindsay's complaints 'with all the vigour I could muster and with no holds barred'. Was it the case that A.A. guns were sent without predictors, and a week late? Was it the case that other guns were sent without ammunition? Was it the case that machine guns were sent without spare barrels? Was there any proper liaison between the port occupied by 'Maurice Force' at Namsos and the port occupied by 'Sickle Force' at Åndalsnes? Was it a fact that the military force was not supplied with snowshoes, so that 'the troops were stuck on the roads and were bombed there'?

To Henry Morris-Jones on the Liberal bench, it was a 'very formidable indictment'; to Ivan Maisky up in the Diplomatic Gallery, an 'astonishingly fierce' assault. What impressed Hugh Dalton on the Labour front bench was Morrison's impossible-to-deny complaints list. 'He has lots of detail and is very definite.' It was thanks to these details, the diplomat Oliver Harvey learned in Paris two days later, that Morrison's speech, out of all those heard in the Norway Debate, formed 'the most effective attack on the Government'.

From Namsos, Morrison turned his offensive back to the War Cabinet. Deliberately exempting the Foreign Secretary (Baba Metcalfe reported to Halifax), Morrison focused his criticism on the Prime Minister, the Chancellor and the new Secretary of State for Air – the Ministers most closely identified with appeasement. To guffaws of hilarity, Morrison read out Hoare's recent broadcast from the *Listener* and his radiant picture of operations in Norway. ' "Today our wings are spread over the Arctic. They are sheathed in ice. Tomorrow the sun of victory will touch them with its golden light" – Hon. Members understandably laugh, but I am not quoting this for the purpose of arousing amusement, because it really is serious, for it is an indication of the delusions from which the Government are suffering.' Morrison paused to stare at the stiff triumvirate whose resignation he demanded. His eyes did not release them easily. In appalled fascination, the Canadian diplomat Charles Ritchie followed Morrison's contempt-filled gaze. 'There they sat on the front bench – the three of them – Chamberlain,

Simon and Hoare, the old-fashioned solid, upper middle-class Englishmen, methodical, respectable, immovable men who cannot be hurried or bullied, shrewd in short-term bargaining or political manipulation, but with no understanding of this age – of its despair, its violence and its gropings, blinkered in solid comfort, shut off from poverty and risk.' Morrison had left his deadliest move till last. The whole 'spirit, tempo and temperament' of these three Ministers had been 'wrong, inadequate and unsuitable' – and this, he said, waiting for his pause to take effect, was why 'we feel we must divide the House at the end of our Debate today'.

Harold Nicolson in his account for the *Montreal Standard* revealed how even up to this stage a majority in the Chamber had believed that the opposition would not force a division, 'but that the Government would be allowed to reconstitute themselves with dignity and ease'. Had this been Chamberlain's understanding too?

The Prime Minister was an experienced parliamentarian, and it is unlikely that Morrison's demand took him by surprise. There was always the risk of a division – rumours had been flying into the Whips' Office since early afternoon. Most likely, he had crafted a statement in case. Certainly, the Liberal Chief Whip Percy Harris felt that Chamberlain's response took the form of 'a carefully prepared impromptu', which Clement Davies maintained was written for him by John Simon. In addition, Chamberlain looked for assistance from beyond the Cabinet, believing that 'Providence designed my speeches to be timed at the right moment to create the effect I want at that point'.*

Not on this occasion, though. Whether he had prepared it or not, whether his fury was real or assumed, Chamberlain's interruption was, in the opinion of Dingle Foot, 'perhaps the most ill-judged speech ever delivered in the House of Commons'.

Angry and worn out (Channon), showing his teeth like a rat in a corner (Dalton), with a leer of triumph (Nicolson), Chamberlain snatched Morrison's bait. Violet Bonham Carter watched the disaster unfold with horror

* During the 1935 General Election campaign, for example, after Herbert Morrison had made deprecatory remarks about Chamberlain's death's head appearance, Chamberlain replied that he would naturally not attempt to compete, in the matter of looks, with so magnificent a specimen of humanity as Mr Morrison.

and pity. 'Chamberlain jumped up & with affected surprise (for he must have known beforehand) & real indignation, said that he welcomed [the] challenge – & appealed to his friends – "for I have friends in this House" – to support him. This unfortunate phrase, which got him a Party cheer at the time, became the "leit motif" of his ruin. Anyone else might have said it with impunity – but it was so profoundly, fatally characteristic to make this tremendous issue a matter of who were, & who were not, his friends.'

'Not I,' Boothby immediately called out – and got a withering glance 'with the eyes of an arrogant blackbird'.

As the immediate context of Chamberlain's observations makes clear, he was not uttering an appeal to his personal friends. Rather, he was pointing out that Morrison had just thrown down a challenge to the government in general. Yet for Labour MP Josiah Wedgwood, Chamberlain's unwise riposte was 'the match to the explosion'. In the space of a single sentence, the Prime Minister had reminded his many critics of how he had returned politics from a national level after Munich, to a party level – and now to a personal level. Baba Metcalfe reported to Halifax that it was this inflammatory gaffe which 'turned the tide against him, as every subsequent speaker alluded to him being very unfit to lead the country as he was putting personal considerations ahead of the country'.

Seated behind Chamberlain, Chips Channon groaned inwardly. Nothing was so revolting as the House of Commons on an ugly night. 'We then knew it was to be war.'

The next hammer blow was delivered by Lloyd George, who had once said: 'The House for a Minister is a lion's den. They are always waiting. Some day you will have to fight them for your life. If you win, it's all right. If not, it is the end of you.' In John Simon's opinion, Lloyd George was 'the worst of all in his denunciation of the Prime Minister'.

It was an achievement to persuade Lloyd George to speak. He had been busy making notes during Morrison's speech 'with his usual little stump of pencil' when he disappeared in a huff, annoyed by a backbencher's remark, and so missed Chamberlain's appeal to his friends. Dingle Foot was sitting beside Megan Lloyd George when Chamberlain resumed his seat. 'There is the opening – your father must speak now.' She did not need telling. She rose and shot out of the Chamber to find him, though she was not over-confident. Her father had been playing hard to get ever since Nancy Astor inspected him for a return to government. A. J. Sylvester had subsequently learned from Frances Stevenson that Lloyd George did not plan to speak in the debate and was being 'most difficult', and anyway had several times made the journey to London intending to talk in the House, and come away without doing so.

Herbert Morrison, keen to harness the old warhorse to his battle wagon, had already sent messages through Megan asking him to speak or even to attend, and to impress on Lloyd George that this was a vital occasion. But Morrison was unable to extract a definite reply. 'Sometimes the answer was that he would think about it. Sometimes it was that he did not feel like coming to the debate.' When Morrison spotted Lloyd George on the front bench on the opening day, he had gone over and repeated that there would be great disappointment if he did not make a contribution. 'They are waiting for you and looking for you.' Lloyd George gave no sign of what he intended to do.

Morrison, Megan, Astor, Foot – these were not the only MPs pleading with Lloyd George to do something. Clement Davies and the Liberal Chief Whip Percy Harris followed Megan out to look for him. Meanwhile, Eleanor Rathbone scribbled Lloyd George a note. 'There is terrific lobbying going on to get Conservatives to vote against the Government. They say the Tories are shocked by NC making this into a personal role for or against him.' A second handwritten appeal arrived from Boothby. 'It is a direct challenge now. The P.M. has appealed to his "friends" – as against the interests of the country . . .' And that claim again: 'I think we may get as many as 40 Conservatives into our lobby.'

Davies and Harris found Lloyd George sulking in his room upstairs 'with his feet on the fender saying he had no intention of speaking and was not interested'. Davies then read him the riot act in Welsh, saying that he was behaving like a prima donna, and was no better than Chamberlain in caring more for himself than for his country. Davies told him that his speech might turn the scales, and he was throwing away this great opportunity because of a personal slight from some backbencher. 'Has the great Achilles lost his skill?' Lloyd George then raised doubts about the wisdom of his intervening, and his fear that he could not make an effective contribution without implicating his old colleague Churchill. Harris quelled these immediately. 'When

I explained the character of Neville's speech, and his personal appeal to "his friends" that seemed to decide him, and he came down to the House.'

As Father of the House, Lloyd George encountered none of Amery's problems in attracting the Speaker's attention. At 5.37 p.m. Harold Nicolson watched him rise 'with all the dignity of his white hair, with all the weight of his experience and with all the fire of his fighting days. He pawed the ground with his right foot. He whirled his arms. He pointed an accusing finger.'

Lloyd George began almost inaudibly. Members shouted: 'Speak up, please!' He brushed back his long white hair, reminding them that a Welshman generally spoke low at the beginning. His voice had been thin, without punch, when he gave his speech back in April to celebrate his fifty years in Parliament. Yet the fears soon vanished that he had lost his oratorical touch.

Within minutes, a regular visitor to Churt, Ivan Maisky, felt that Lloyd George was back to his old 'inimitable self'. He stood at the despatch box on the side of the opposition, jerking his left leg ('he was in the habit of doing so when he spoke in Parliament'), pulling his pince-nez off his bronzed nose and flashing it about 'as if it were a sword pulled from its sheath'.

Geoffrey Shakespeare, seated opposite, was familiar with Lloyd George's technique, having first seen him in action at the Albert Hall, at a Baptist rally organised by Shakespeare's father. Lloyd George had confided to him how he copied the skills of the old Welsh narrative preachers. Shakespeare wrote: 'His custom was to start slowly and cautiously, like a bather entering the sea, uncertain as to the depth of the water or the strength of the current. Then, as he gained confidence he would try a fancy stroke, he would flash out a simile or illustration; in a few minutes he had woken his audience to life and was borne along on the flood of their rising enthusiasm.'

Lloyd George spoke to the hushed, packed House as a senior politician who had been one of the nation's most successful war leaders, as well as an expert in the removal of wartime premiers from office. Charles Ritchie listened to his gathering attack. 'His speech made me think of King Lear's ranting – shot through with gleams of vision.' Violet Bonham Carter considered it 'the best & most deadly speech I have ever heard from him – voice – gesture – everything was brought into play to drive home his indictment'.

In his flexible, melodious tenor, Lloyd George talked of how the disaster in Norway, despite all the warnings, had left us in 'the worst strategic position in which this country has ever been placed'. With a scathing rebuke to the Conservative back bench, he said that Hitler did not hold himself answerable to the Whips or to David Margesson. His blue eyes gleaming with mischief, he separated Churchill from the rest of the War Cabinet in apportioning blame. When Churchill sprang up to take 'complete responsibility' for everything that had been done by the Admiralty, Lloyd George suggested to his old friend that his loyalty was misplaced, and he warned that Churchill must not allow himself 'to be converted into an air-raid shelter to keep the splinters from hitting his colleagues'. Several speakers had made the same point. None had inspired raucous laughter. Baba Metcalfe watched Churchill 'like a fat baby swinging his legs on the front bench trying not to laugh . . . stony faces on each side of him'.

Observing Lloyd George savage Chamberlain, Dingle Foot felt that in his whole career he had not seen anything to match this clash between two political enemies. 'It would be difficult to exaggerate the drama of the occasion.' Colville recorded how the opposition shouted themselves hoarse as Lloyd George became more and more vehement and less and less reasonable. 'Horace Wilson, who sat with me in the official gallery, said that the hatred written on their faces astonished him: it was the pent-up bitterness and personal animosity of years.' Not even his faithful bloodhound Chips Channon could bring consolation to Chamberlain. He sat loyally behind the Prime Minister, 'hoping to surround him with an aura of affection', but 'Little Neville seems heart-broken and shrivelled,' only stirring from time to time to glance up into the Speaker's Gallery where his wife had been sitting for two days, hardly leaving the House. 'She was in black – black hat – black coat – black gloves, with only a bunch of violets in her coat. She looked infinitely sad as she peered down into the mad arena where the lions were out for her husband's blood.'

Lloyd George's speech packed into twenty-five minutes a quarter-century of contempt. Now at last he had the Prime Minister's diminutive scalp in his sights. Only two days earlier, A. J. Sylvester had advised Lloyd George on how to trap that insultingly small head – by making Chamberlain lose his temper. Lloyd George had not been present to hear Chamberlain's unwise remark about friends, but he viciously twisted its intention to provoke the Prime Minister into making a second ill-judged intercession.

Chamberlain exploded when Lloyd George accused him of making his personality 'inseparable from the interests of the country'.

He jumped up and angrily leant over the despatch box. 'What is the meaning of that observation?' Indignantly, he denied that he was making the debate a personal issue. 'I took pains to say that personalities ought to have no place in these matters.' This time there was no mistaking his rage.

The two men glared at each other, wrote the *Daily Mirror*'s correspondent. 'Chamberlain white to the lips, his fingers twitching. Lloyd George passionate, scowling, scornful.'

'Norway'. 'Unprepared'. 'Margesson'. Another of the words that Lloyd George had earlier scribbled on a sheet of House of Commons paper and underlined with his yellow pencil was 'Sacrifice'. Lloyd George was aware that 'sacrifice' occupied a special niche in Chamberlain's lexicon. After reluctantly deciding to remove Hore-Belisha from the War Office in January, Chamberlain had written him a sympathetic note that in wartime 'no one can feel satisfied unless he has made some sacrifice'. From Hore-Belisha, Lloyd George had heard an extraordinary story that Chamberlain had told at their meeting, of a French general who saw a soldier about to be shot for cowardice, and said to him: 'You are making a great sacrifice' – explaining that 'in war everybody had to make sacrifices and contribute to the victory of the common cause'. With this potent word, Lloyd George ended his withering speech. 'I say solemnly that the Prime Minister should give an example of sacrifice because there is nothing which can contribute more to victory in this war than that he should sacrifice the seals of office.'

The strained silence of the House after Lloyd George sat down gave the impression that a taboo had been violated and all the frustrations of the past eight months released. It was the last great speech of Lloyd George's life.*

Viscount Addison was sitting in the Peers' Gallery and immediately wrote him a note. 'I have been listening to you. It did my heart good.

---

* It preyed on Chamberlain for the next forty-eight hours. He told Princess Olga of Yugoslavia over lunch at the Dorchester on his last day in office that 'Lloyd George's personal attack on him surpassed anything he had ever heard in Parliament', and it was still on his mind when Margot Oxford called at No. 10 a few hours later, shortly after he had resigned. 'The only person of whom he spoke with biting words was Lloyd George. "There are people in this world . . . who are frauds . . ."'

Nothing truer can be said than your last sentence. Get rid of the P.M. and a real coalition could become possible.'

Churchill had watched this gladiatorial display with mixed emotions. He muttered to Kingsley Wood: 'This is all making it damned difficult for me tonight.'

Churchill had come from a briefing upstairs with General Paget on the situation in Norway. The military campaign continued to be the First Lord's priority outside the Chamber. Today – Wednesday 8 May – marked the date when Admiral Cork had planned to occupy Narvik.

Since the weekend, Churchill had been holed up in the Admiralty, poring over maps of Harstad and Narvik, as he had hidden in a mineshaft after his escape from the Boers, with food and whisky smuggled in by the British mine manager, only on this occasion his manager had had to leave: Clementine had departed on the 1.45 p.m. train to Hereford to attend Bertram Romilly's funeral.

No account survives of Churchill's 5 p.m. appointment with General Paget, assuming that it took place. But Paget would have felt hardly more optimistic about the situation in central Norway than Fleming or Lindsay. The night before, Air Marshal Charles Portal, Commander-in-Chief of Bomber Command since April, had sent nine Wellingtons against Stavanger. Only one had managed to locate the airfield and bomb it. The following night, Portal would try again with nine Whitleys: they would be recalled without fulfilling their mission.

All hinged on Cork's operation 400 miles north. A victory at Narvik in time for his speech: that was what Churchill had hoped for. He had been drumming his fingers for news of this ever since 9 April.

Narvik was the one constant. 'My eye has always been fixed on Narvik,' Churchill would tell the House that evening. For the next three days, his fixation to seize Narvik shadowed his capture of the premiership.

The War Cabinet had finally given the go-ahead for the Narvik operation the day before, after Churchill pleaded that if Admiral Cork decided to attack then 'nothing should be done to stop him'.

Later that evening a signal arrived from Cork reaffirming his willingness to make the assault. 'It is as a symbol of victory before the world that I have understood occupation of Narvik was desired and why I have urged that we should take a risk to occupy the place.'

Logistical problems remained. On the same day, 7 May, Colonel Faulkner had made another reconnaissance and chosen a beach on which the battalion was to land. But the navy told him that 'they could not provide craft to land there', so the whole operation was again postponed.

'In the brown hours, when baffling news comes, and disappointing news . . .' The message that Cork was forced to put back the invasion of Narvik to 10 May left Churchill helpless and fuming. Then Cork had postponed the operation again until after General Auchinleck's arrival on 12 May. Churchill would have no triumph to break to the House.

Suddenly, the continuing stalemate in the Arctic weighed heavier than it had the previous evening. Even then, Halifax had believed that Churchill would need 'all his time' to recover from the effect of Roger Keyes's assault. The attacks by Amery and now by Lloyd George had complicated Churchill's dilemma still further, and intensified the pressure on his forthcoming speech.

In having to make the closing case for the government, Churchill was required to act as the supreme apologist for an administration that he had criticised until being invited to join it eight months earlier. John Reith wondered 'if any speaker had ever been in a more equivocal position'. In the debate in the House of Lords on that Wednesday afternoon, the opposition spokesman Lord Snell made the acerbic observation that everyone knew – 'at least until recently' – Churchill's opinion of the government, but 'today he is put up to save them from shipwreck, and we are tonight to witness the strange sight of both the horse and its rider apparently going the same way – temporarily'.

Yet Narvik was not Omdurman, when Churchill had shouted to an NCO as he drew rein: 'I hope you enjoyed that!' Over in the Commons, the American reporter Ed Murrow had earlier observed Churchill slumped in his seat, 'playing with his fingers, and watching the House and its reactions with great interest'. It had prompted Murrow to reflect that the future of the government rested in the First Lord's rather pudgy hands. 'If he should openly blame the political leadership of the country for the reverse in Norway, Mr Chamberlain's government might be forced to resign.' But how could Churchill blame anyone? As Conservative MP Quintin Hogg pointed out, this was a naval operation for which Churchill was himself 'departmentally and in fact personally largely responsible'. Churchill's dilemma was characteristic and self-defining, wrote Alan Campbell-Johnson, Political Secretary to Archie Sinclair. 'A peculiar spirit of irony, which seemed resolved always to distort and confine Churchill's splendid genius, operated once again in this the most critical moment of his career.'

As Big Ben struck off another hour, Churchill waited with fading expectations to hear some redeeming news from Norway that he could work into his speech, and so conclude the debate on the uplifting note that he had looked forward to rehearsing with Clementine.

Once before, feeling vulnerable, he had written to his wife: 'I have been sometimes a little depressed about politics and would have liked to be comforted by you.' His valet described how husband and wife shared 'the almost telepathic understanding which one finds very occasionally between brother and sister'.

Colville noticed that Clementine's judgement 'often saved her husband from unwise acts on which he had impetuously determined'. On this afternoon, Halifax had Baba Metcalfe to turn to; Chamberlain had his wife Anne, who sat in a seat in front of Baba. Without Clementine there to advise and support, Martin Gilbert wrote, 'Churchill was lonely and felt he had no ally with whom to share his deepest worries and concerns.' At this most vital time, Churchill's isolation was the deepest that it had been since the start of the war.

On the other hand, says Andrew Roberts, 'thank goodness Clementine wasn't there. She was a Liberal. She hated all his best friends, like Beaverbrook and Bracken, who were working so hard to get him a job.'

It is not known how much of his speech, if any, Clementine had vetted before she caught her train to Hereford. Churchill wrote notes for some of it on the back of an envelope. His routine would have been to have had the rest typed out on octavo sheets and then retyped in large print on smaller sheets, eight inches by four, in short separate lines, in what Halifax called 'Psalm form'. The words were short, too. Halifax once sat with Churchill to prepare the King's speech to Parliament, and noticed that he used 'monosyllables wherever possible, and always Anglo Saxon derivatives in preference to Latin'.

Unlike Lloyd George, who was able to deliver his speech impromptu, from a few key words, not having written it out, Churchill seldom spoke in public without a text, or without having rehearsed what he was going to say. He could easily spend eight hours preparing a forty-minute speech, before memorising it in front of a mirror. The fear of drying up haunted him.

What Leo Amery called the 'Winstonian diction' was not a spontaneous phenomenon. In December 1900, Churchill delivered one of his earliest speeches, about his escape from the Boers, to an audience in Canada. 'He evidently does not make any pretensions to oratory,' decided the critic of the *Ottawa Evening Journal*. 'As a lecturer he is somewhat handicapped by a lisp.' A defect in his palate gave Churchill's voice an echoing timbre which was mocked by Conservative backbenchers in Churchill's maiden speech, and caused him to admit to the Duke of Devonshire at the Free Trade Hall in Manchester, two years later, how nervous he was of talking in public. 'Quite unnecessary,' harrumphed the Duke. 'When you get to the hall, march in boldly, take your seat confidently on the platform, sit down and look around you calmly, stare people in the face and when you have had a really good look at them all, say to yourself, "I've never seen such a crowd of damn fools in all my life."'

Small, tongue-tied, with a speech impediment, Churchill was not constructed to be an orator, which was why he took no performance for granted. He told his doctor, Charles Moran, that whenever he rose in the House 'he was always fearful that he might blurt out something that would get him into trouble, and that he would wake in the morning to find that he had blighted his prospects'. Either that, or he would break down in the course of a speech like his father, who was suddenly struck with aphasia while speaking. This had happened once before to Churchill in the Commons in 1905, wrote Moran. 'He had found himself on his feet, with his mind a complete blank, while the awful silence was broken only by friendly encouraging noises; he stood his ground until he could bear it no longer; back in his seat, he could only bury his head in his hands.'

He made several more disastrous speeches. In March 1933, Brendan Bracken, Churchill's impetuous 'acolyte' as Robert Bernays called him, had 'scampered' about the House telling Bernays that he had already heard Churchill's speech 'and what a thundering indictment it was going to be'.

Bernays then witnessed the House dissolve into 'a contemptuous cascade of laughter, and from that moment Winston was done. The theatricality went out of the atmosphere, the electricity went out of his voice. He floundered bravely on. He had lost the House. Members began to chatter to one another and one by one they drifted out . . . The rest of the debate he sat in his corner seat scowling, crumpled-up by the magnitude of his failure.' The Churchill Flop was the topic for days afterwards, wrote Bernays. 'Men are really saying that Churchill is done for . . . Of course, Winston will come back. That is the essential greatness of the man, that you knock him down and everybody says he won't get up again and then he is back in the ring as fit and fierce as ever.'

Churchill suffered another flop in 1934, after Leo Amery skewered him during the India Bill; and again in 1936 during the Abdication crisis, when Churchill, loyally supporting Edward VIII, was stopped in mid-speech by savage cries of 'Drop it!' and 'Twister', and stormed out of the Chamber in tears, convinced that his 'political career was finished'.

Yet it was not, and the era of his best speech-making had hardly begun, when he would discover what Lord Woolton called 'his quite extraordinary capacity – which is probably the greatest national asset that we have in Government – for expressing in Elizabethan English the sentiments of the public'; when, as the Rector of Oslo University afterwards put it to him, his speeches 'broke like sunshine through the dark clouds of German oppression to warm and cheer our hearts'.

Later, Churchill liked to visit an eminent throat specialist called Punt who squirted his vocal cords with a mysterious spray. Churchill would sing a brief scale and depart. After his controversial broadcast on the BBC in January 1940 attacking the neutrals, he told Halifax: 'Asking me not to make a speech is like asking a centipede to get along and not put a foot on the ground.'

Even so, he preferred a live audience in the Commons to a microphone. As Maisky astutely perceived, 'Churchill sees the world in terms of the effect of a parliamentary performance. And is it any surprise? Parliament is in the blood of every Englishman, and Churchill has been warming the benches of Westminster for more than 40 years.' If Lloyd George was the House's father, Churchill was its son. He spoke from the heart when, in

1950, he addressed MPs in their new Chamber, telling them 'I am a child of the House of Commons.'

The Commons was more than its Chamber, though. All morning and afternoon, dissident and opposition groups had hurried together in upstairs committee rooms and offices, to discuss what action to take.

An orderly transfer: that was what Lord Salisbury had hoped for at the Watching Committee's first gathering at 11.00 a.m. in Arlington Street. He had 'begged' Nicolson, Amery, Macmillan, Spears and the others not to vote against the government if a division came, 'but to abstain from voting'. Their mood changed when Margesson sent Conservative MPs a telegram underlined with three thick black lines, the most urgent summons a Member could receive. Emrys-Evans made his way to the Lords after Salisbury had spoken in the debate there, and told him that the position had gone too far 'and that abstention was really impossible'.

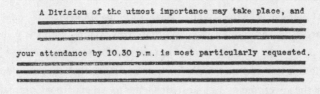

A Division of the utmost importance may take place, and

your attendance by 10.30 p.m. is most particularly requested.

DAVID MARGESSON.

At 6 p.m. Harold Nicolson joined members of the Watching Committee for a meeting with Davies's All Party Action Group. 'We agree that we must vote against the Government.' A second emergency meeting was organised for 9 p.m., shortly before Churchill's speech, to adopt this position formally.

The debate in the Commons was still going on downstairs when Amery took the chair for what, in effect, was a get-together of all three dissident groups. Boothby had persuaded Amery to assume control, flattering him that he was the obvious choice following his triumphant speech the evening before.

What fascinated Nicolson was to see who were the Conservative MPs marching into Committee Room 8. The most rebellious were dressed in military uniforms. Nicolson was heartened by the spectacle of this 'unexpected mutiny on the part of all those who had always been regarded as the firmest supporters of Mr Chamberlain'.

There were sixty-two government backbenchers on active service in the army, with a further sixteen in the RAF, and seven in the navy. Like Fleming and Lindsay, these men had first-hand experience of the inadequate state of Britain's armed forces.

Discontent had spread to all ranks. When the Conservative MP Somerset de Chair asked his colonel in the Household Cavalry for leave to travel up to London for the debate, Lord Weld-Forester questioned him, suspicious. 'Which way are you going to vote?'

'Against the Government,' de Chair replied.

'You can certainly go in that case.'

Another uniformed MP was the 'baby of the House', John Profumo, a twenty-five-year-old lieutenant with 1st Northamptonshire Yeomanry. He had never voted before in a debate, and his torment was made worse by the fact that David Margesson had been one of his sponsors.

Margesson had sent a special Whip to MPs serving with the military overseas. Already that afternoon, fourteen members of the Service Members Committee had met, with thirteen declaring that they would vote against the government. A handwritten letter to Amery from Commander Stephen King-Hall, a National Labour MP, expressed their collective anger. 'I regard the war situation as so serious that I want you to know that I am being driven to the conclusion that if this goes much further, it will be necessary in the National Interest for those who believe that a radical change in the Government is necessary, to go into open opposition to the present administration. I want you to know that is how strongly I feel.'

It was when Nancy Astor with hands on hips told Harold Nicolson of her intention to vote against the government that he realised he had no alternative but to follow suit.

Between the Watching Committee, Amery's group and Davies's All Party Group, Nicolson calculated that they might achieve Boothby's figure of forty no-votes. By now, news had leaked out of a fourth group of some thirty disaffected Conservative MPs led by Herbert Williams. In

Margesson's office the alarm bells were springing off the walls from all directions. Harold Nicolson told his Canadian readers: 'Feverishly did the Whips try to split these groups, and Private Secretaries scurried backwards and forwards making promises and offering compromises and suggesting reconstructions.'

The most active scurrier was the Prime Minister's Parliamentary Private Secretary Alec Dunglass, who accompanied Chamberlain to both days of the debate. On 8 May, Dunglass arranged for Chamberlain to meet Herbert Williams the following afternoon, and any other Members that Williams cared to bring with him. The promise of a face-to-face talk with the Prime Minister had the desired calming effect. Williams advised his associates that 'it was our duty to support him'.

Another potential rebel MP who required Dunglass's pacifying skills was Quintin Hogg, a serving officer like Profumo, and for nine months in a unit with no equipment, training or transport. Hogg spilled out his fury in a letter to Margesson. 'The fact is that there is no young officer whom I know who can wholeheartedly support the Government so long as our men are neglected and betrayed by the Administration for which the Government are responsible.' Hogg accused the Speaker of discriminating against 'men in khaki' – as FitzRoy, himself a former soldier, referred to Hogg's fellow servicemen. Hogg went on: 'Do you seriously want the P.M. to be supported by nobody but fools & rascals? Or that the voice of serving men should never be heard?'

Hogg was temporarily neutralised when, on what must have been one of the most overloaded days of his premiership, Chamberlain carved out time to see this troubled young officer to allay his fears. Half-expecting Chamberlain to haul him over the coals, Hogg 'only found a man of affectionate nature, courtesy and great humility. He asked me my particular complaints. I found them difficult to specify and blurted out some relatively trivial matters . . . I was unable to get it across that what was wrong was not detailed, but the whole spirit of Parliament and the nation and that the thing I wanted was a change. I remember now the gentleness, courtesy and generosity with which the doomed man treated his inarticulate and presumptuous young supporter who ventured to question his authority and make his task more difficult. I went out in greater agony than I had entered.'

While Hogg battled with his conscience, Dunglass fought to mollify an increasingly seditious Watching Committee. At some moment late in the afternoon, he tracked down Emrys-Evans and asked whether his senior Conservative friends would vote for the government if they could see the Prime Minister the following morning and place their demands. Dunglass gave the strongest hint yet that the Prime Minister was prepared to carry out 'a drastic reconstruction of the Government'.

But Emrys-Evans was unimpressed. 'I told him that it was too late.' The government should have been reconstructed at the beginning of the war. The Watching Committee, he went on, was 'thoroughly dissatisfied with such Ministers as Simon and Hoare, and with Sir Horace Wilson and his intolerable interference in politics and his evil influence on policy. I also explained that the attitude of the Whips' Office had been disastrous and that we did not think the Prime Minister had the right temperament for a Head of Government in wartime. I nevertheless promised to put his proposal before my friends, and a meeting was summoned for 9 o'clock that night.'

News that Herbert Williams's group had decided to support Chamberlain did not deter a single dissident MP who assembled under Amery's chairmanship. Harold Macmillan recalled how they all then unanimously agreed to vote – 'and to vote against the motion. So the die was cast.' Amery deputed Emrys-Evans to inform Dunglass of their 'fateful decision'. To Amery's satisfaction, Emrys-Evans did so by explaining that their view had been summarised in the closing sentence of Amery's speech the night before – '*In the name of God, go.*'

Amery in the meantime made his way downstairs to the Chamber to join the throng that was assembling to hear Churchill.

All through these tense and fluctuating discussions, Harold Macmillan claimed to have been consumed by two desires. 1. The government had to fall. 2. Churchill had to emerge as Prime Minister. As the moment approached for the First Lord to speak, Macmillan's chief anxiety concerned Churchill. 'We knew that he had determined to stand loyally by his colleagues and would close the debate as the spokesman of the Government . . . but how could Churchill be disentangled from the ruins?' Louis

Spears no longer felt confident that it was possible 'to save him from the wreck'. Churchill was going to have to follow his own instructions to his admirals, and steer his way with skilful care up an exposed and narrowing fjord.

Churchill shared Chamberlain's nerves in the countdown to a speech. Bernays described how Churchill wandered in and out, and stirred uneasily in his seat, in a fever of impatience to be up. 'He is like a pugilist waiting for the command "seconds out" in the ring.'

Habitually in the moments before he was due to speak, Churchill was to be found in the Smoking Room, at the centre of a group, talking in a rapid voice, breaking matchsticks into little pieces and throwing them about him on the floor.

This was how Macmillan, after leaving Amery's meeting, discovered the First Lord late on Wednesday evening.

Churchill beckoned him over, and Macmillan wished him luck, but added that he hoped his speech would not be too convincing.

'Why not?'

Macmillan regarded him over his pince-nez. 'Because we must have a new Prime Minister, and it must be you.'

According to Macmillan, Churchill answered gruffly 'that he had signed on for the voyage and would stick to the ship. But I don't think he was angry with me'.

Churchill's daughter Mary had come to support him in Clementine's absence. She watched her father make his way into the stifling Chamber. The unrest in the House 'was aggravated by Papa arriving rather late' for the opposition's winding-up speech by Labour's A. V. Alexander.

On the crowded front bench, Churchill appeared very white in the queer light of the Gothic hall which seemed to Spears 'to trail a veil of last winter's fog across the beams of its ceiling'. Members had settled down in their seats with anticipatory grins or set jaws. The question on everyone's mind: Would Winston be loyal?

At 10.11 p.m. the Speaker called his name. Mary Churchill peered over the edge of the Gallery. 'Papa rose to wind up the debate. It was the first time in 11 years that he had wound up for the Govt.'

Down in the Chamber, Nicolson watched the First Lord assemble his notes and pat his waistcoat pockets for his two pairs of reading glasses. 'The House was tense, almost awestruck. It was felt that Winston Churchill was faced by the most difficult speech of his career. He had to defend a reverse: he had to be loyal not only to the Naval Staff but to his Prime Minister. Would he diminish his own prestige? He rose, gay and determined: pugnacious and kind.'

Mary Churchill understood at once that the House 'was in a most uncertain, unpleasant & sensitive restless mood. There were frequent interruptions – also quite a lot of cheering. Papa's handling of the actual matter and of the House was nothing short of SUPERB. I listened breathless with pride [and] apprehension.'

Quintin Hogg also watched in admiration. Earlier, he had decided to vote against the government. Yet in common with several other potential dissidents, he found himself veering back in support after listening to Churchill. 'I can see him now scowling, crouching and snarling at the despatch box as the tremendous voice rolled forth its terrific sentences in defence of the Government whose imminent fall was to bring him immortal glory and a State funeral in St Paul's. As he rose to his peroration each word slammed home like a bullet in my stomach.'

Churchill was jeered and heckled, but his mind did not go blank, he did not dry up. As usual, his performance divided his audience. For Hogg, it was 'one of his greatest and most passionate speeches'; for Dingle Foot, 'the least impressive speech of his career'. A consummate actor playing an impossible part was the general verdict. Members admired Churchill's virtuosity, but they shared Chips Channon's doubt that he had thrown every ounce of his weight into it. 'How much of the fire was real, how much ersatz, we shall never know.'

No one could dispute Churchill's loyalty, though. It impressed Nicolson that Churchill accepted full responsibility – prompting shouts of 'Not you, not you!' – and then denounced Labour for forcing the division and for wilfully misrepresenting the Prime Minister's use of the accepted parliamentary term 'friends'. Nicolson wrote: 'He said not one word which could be interpreted as disassociating himself from his colleagues in the Cabinet. Not one word – yet by his manner of speech, by the prestige of his brilliance, he rose so far above them that he was no longer of them.'

Churchill devoted the first part of his speech to a 'general account' of the campaign. But after promising to tell 'the story of what happened, and why', his statement was notable for its omissions. He never alluded to his part in pressing the War Cabinet for seven months to block off Narvik with a minefield. He made no reference to his decision to disembark troops at Rosyth or to the destructive chaos that this action had caused. He revealed nothing of his reluctance to switch operations from Narvik to Trondheim, of his continuous changes of mind, of his menacing threats to Chamberlain. Instead, Churchill was as careful to defend the government – which, he insisted, was 'at every stage united . . . without the slightest difference of opinion' – as Chamberlain had been to implicate him in its disasters.

Labour MPs were not persuaded, thought Maisky. 'Defending Chamberlain is a difficult task, and it brought Churchill no laurels.' The opposition front bench interrupted him, first Morrison, then Greenwood, to insinuate that Churchill had personally 'overruled' his admirals and generals on the spot. Not only that, but he had recommended to the War Cabinet and the Prime Minister other actions than they had taken.

These serious accusations were not too wide of the truth, and provoked Churchill into an impassioned denial. They formed, he said, a 'cataract of unworthy suggestions and of actual falsehoods'. There were fierce exchanges, wrote Joseph Kennedy, and 'a couple of times when he lost his temper'.

It looked at one point as though the Deputy Serjeant at Arms might have to eject Labour MP Emanuel Shinwell, who heckled Churchill from the shadows of the furthest seat on the top back bench. Shinwell wrote: 'My interjection caused him to pause in the argument and indulge in a slashing attack on the Member "skulking" and afraid to show himself.' There was uproar as another Labour MP, 'rather the worse for drink', appealed to the Speaker to ask whether 'skulk' was a word allowed in Parliament. Violet Bonham Carter was horrified by this 'unfortunate brawl', yet Shinwell was unrepentant. 'It was enough that I had ruffled him, upsetting his discourse; it was his own method – why not use it?'

There was laughter, but the tension increased. Dalton wrote that 'a good deal of riot, some of it rather stupid, developed on our benches towards the close of Churchill's final speech', with the Opposition 'baying like hounds' and Churchill shouting angrily at the Labour benches: 'All day long we have had abuse, and now hon. Members opposite will not even listen.'

Mary Churchill sat transfixed. 'A storm of interruptions arose making Papa sit down & the speech ended amid catcalls from both sides of the House.'

To Chips Channon, it was 'like bedlam'.

17
THE DIVISION

'Something very extraordinary happened in Parliament last week ... No shots, nobody put in prison, but revolution occurred.'
ELLEN WILKINSON MP, Labour Party Conference, 13 May 1940

'The scene in the House was a disgrace.'
PATRICK DONNER MP

Churchill's speech concluded the two-day debate. At 11.00 p.m. the Speaker stood up and procedure took over. 'The Question is, That this House do now adjourn. As many as are of that opinion say, Aye.'

Some Members shouted aye.

'To the contrary, No.'

Some Members shouted no.

'Division – clear the Lobby!'

The Clerk at the table turned over the sandglass to time six minutes to the division. The Bar Doorkeeper opened the Chamber's inner doors and shouted 'Division!' to alert the Principal Doorkeeper, who activated the bell by a lever in the arm of his chair. Bells rang throughout the Commons, and the cry of 'Division!' was taken up by police officers and other staff.

The bells rang for fifty-five seconds, paused for ten seconds, and rang again for fifty-five seconds. During this time each side of the argument provided Tellers for the division. After two minutes, the Speaker again put the question, and announced the names of the Tellers: Captain Margesson and Lieutenant Colonel Kerr for the government ayes, Sir Charles Edwards and Mr Paling for the opposition noes.

Members had four more minutes to get into one division Lobby or the other. Harold Nicolson noted the 'great tensity in the air' as they began to rise from their seats.

In Andros on very hot days Chamberlain sometimes observed a waterspout forming half a mile away, rising inky black from the water and tilting inland in a tall column of dust. Inside the store, all the shutters were at once closed, plunging the storekeeper and his assistant into darkness.

It is hard to say at what point the government grasped the nature of this maelstrom. Earlier in the afternoon, Ministers had felt that the Labour decision to divide the House was a mistake, and had freely predicted that no more than a dozen Conservatives would defy their Whips. David Margesson later claimed that it dawned on him only in the winding-up speeches that the large government majority was likely to collapse. Out of the blue, a routine adjournment motion for the Whitsun holiday, which the government had expected comfortably to win, had been hijacked, using a procedural vote to expose the fragility of the Chamberlain administration. As the division bell sounded with the piercing shrill of a fire alarm, panic spread along the front bench. Euan Wallace wrote in his diary how 'at one moment the Whips were apprehensive of an actual defeat on the vote for the adjournment'.

Seated next to Mary Churchill, John Colville had gauged the mood of Chamberlain's inner circle – Alec Dunglass, Kingsley Wood, Arthur Rucker: 'All seemed to think the P.M. would have to resign unless he could get a majority of a hundred votes.' Everything depended on the dissidents, and whether Conservative waverers could be persuaded by Amery, Macmillan, Emrys-Evans, Spears, Cooper, Boothby and Nancy Astor to summon the courage to go into the opposition Lobby.

Simon, the aloof Chancellor, was one of the first Ministers to feel nervous about the government's chances. This followed an encounter in the Commons dining room with two Conservative MPs in uniform: Somerset de Chair and Stuart Russell, the latter soon to be killed in action.

Simon paused at their table. 'May I ask which way you young people are going to vote?'

'Against you,' said de Chair.

The Chancellor sat down as if punched, and pointed out the constitutional implications. 'If you succeed in bringing down the Government, as you very well may do, the King cannot send for Mr Churchill or Lord Halifax. He would have to send for Mr Attlee or Mr Greenwood. Is that what you want?' Nor would that be the only consequence. Simon prophesied that if there was a bad result in the division, 'Germany would invade Holland within 48 hours.'

Undeterred, de Chair openly expressed his feelings in the final moments of the debate as he watched Churchill shout back at the opposition. De Chair stood at the rear of the Chamber with a group of Whips and Junior Ministers, who asked him: 'How can you vote for a rabble like that against a man like that?'

'I am not voting against him. I am voting against you and you and you,' and he pointed at three of them in turn.

There was no indication of how the vote would go as Members began to move into the division Lobbies. Chips Channon found the whispering unbearable. He watched Nancy Astor rush about, 'intriguing and enjoying the fray and the smell of blood' – causing one French journalist to remark in Colville's earshot: '*Dieu! Que les femmes députées sont laides!!*'

Active until the sixth minute when the Doorkeepers turned their keys in the locks, government Whips and Ministers were still putting pressure on the dissidents. Brendan Bracken, Private Secretary to Churchill, and Jim Thomas, Private Secretary to Anthony Eden, were drawn aside and cautioned that if they voted against the government it would be taken as an indication of their Ministers' sympathies. With expressionless faces, they entered the government Lobby. But John Profumo, elected a month earlier as a pro-Chamberlain MP, had already decided against. 'It was not easy to walk into the opposition Lobby. I remember Walter Elliot, who was a Minister, spitting on my shoes as we were waiting in line. In the House.'

The tension had made everyone a punter. 'Ham' Kerr, Conservative MP for Oldham, bet that one hundred government supporters would vote against the regime, while Percy Harris reckoned that only thirteen Tories would. Up in the Diplomatic Gallery, Joseph Kennedy sat squeezed between Maisky and the Belgian Ambassador, who predicted that the Government majority would be 130, 'and everybody felt that was quite likely'. In the summer of 1939, similar votes had been won by 164 and 116.

Almost the last group to make up their minds were the Conservative dissidents in uniform. Fourteen of them sat in a group on the government back benches below the gangway. Nancy Astor overheard them discussing their dilemma, which, as Louis Spears rendered it, compelled them 'to show courage in the safety of that building when so much was being freely offered elsewhere on land, on the sea, and in the air. It was our contribution to the war, our way of fighting . . .' The lead was given by William Anstruther-Gray in the uniform of a Coldstream Guards officer. With one minute remaining, he pronounced his verdict, and led his group towards the No Lobby. They marched in, Dingle Foot recalled, 'as if they were marching four abreast', all in uniform. 'The effect was tremendous.'

This left Quintin Hogg still sitting. 'What should I do?' he agonised. 'Vote for the Government as the majority would do? Abstain as many subsequently did? Vote against and perhaps bring my country as well as the Government down? I was never more lonely in my life.'

On the Clerk's table, the grey sand in the Victorian glass trickled to a halt. The Speaker rose a second time, and called out: 'Lock the doors.' No one not already in the division Lobbies would from now on be able to vote. Next morning, Hogg wrote to Chamberlain: 'I wish I could have voted with you, or even abstained . . . but you know what I thought and I took the difficult, and less pleasant course.' Mind made up, Hogg rushed past the Doorkeeper – in one version forcing him aside – and got into the No Lobby 'as the door closed behind'.

Dingle Foot described the scene in the No Lobby as unique, a fitting culmination to what had been 'unquestionably the most important debate in Parliamentary history'. Clement Attlee saw – much to his 'pleasure and surprise' – something that he had long hoped for, but never expected to witness: Conservative MP after Conservative MP, many in khaki, navy blue and air-force blue uniforms, crowded with Labour and Liberal MPs into the same Lobby. In Ronald Blythe's phrase: 'Shifty eyes and blushes met the Labour and Liberal grins.'

At the Labour Party's meeting that morning, Dalton had forecast that the opposition would attract no more than fifteen government supporters. In fact, more than forty milled inside, including Duff Cooper who in a speech earlier had announced his intention to vote against the government, and was moved to witness 'a young officer in uniform, who had been for long a fervent admirer of Chamberlain, walking through the Opposition Lobby with the tears streaming down his face'. Dalton's eyes filled with tears as well. 'How many of these young men, I wondered, were giving the last Parliamentary vote that they would ever give – for their Country and against their Whips?' Admiral Keyes was there with them, saying in a loud voice: 'They wouldn't let me lead an expedition into Trondheim, so I'm leading an expedition into this Lobby instead.' Roy Wise, Conservative MP for Smethwick and a lieutenant colonel in the Queen's Royal Regiment, had fought in Norway with Fleming and Lindsay. He explained to Dalton: 'I came straight back from Namsos to vote against the Government.' Disgusted that his artillery had not fired a shot due to the lack of ammunition, and that his wounded had not been treated due to the lack of medical supplies, he was voting on behalf of his men, and he repeated what Lindsay had told Attlee. 'We were bombed by German aeroplanes and had nothing with which to reply, not even a machine gun.'

In contrast, the Aye Lobby seemed to Chips Channon thin for a three line whip. Two covert dissidents, Anthony Eden and Jim Thomas, 'looked triumphant'. But most Members appeared worried. 'Everyone wondered how many had dared to vote against us: so many threaten to do, and funk it at the last moment.' After casting his vote, Channon returned to his seat behind Chamberlain – who had sat with 'patience and courtesy' throughout the closing speeches – 'and we watched the insurgents file out of the Opposition Lobby'. The mood still was that the government could survive with a majority of one hundred or more.

Meanwhile, the dense pack inside the No Lobby had divided into two columns according to the first letter of the voting MP's surname, A–L in one column, M–Z in another. Spears shuffled towards the Division Clerk, who ticked off his name as he called it out. 'A quick look by the official, a line drawn with a soft pencil against that name, and you were facing the half-closed double doors through which you must pass in single file.'

Duff Cooper was a step ahead in the other line, poker-faced.

On either side of the narrow opening stood the Tellers. Spears recognised the commanding figure of David Margesson, telling for the government. 'It was very painful.' Spears had fought in the last war in the same regiment as Margesson, 'to whom I was indebted for much kindness'.

Duff Cooper stepped past, and the Chief Whip called out the new total '151' with an expression of 'implacable resentment'.

Spears was next. He bowed his head, squeezed through.

'152,' continued Margesson in a level voice.

Spears returned to the Chamber. '153, 154 . . .' Margesson's voice counted on, until Spears lost it in the general hubbub of the House as he regained his seat.

Disgusted, Chips Channon watched Cooper and Spears file back in, followed by Hubert Duggan. 'My heart snapped against him for ever.'

Some MPs emerging from the No Lobby shouted their names up to reporters to make sure that their identities would be printed. Government supporters began to hurl insults. Channon joined in. 'Quislings!' he shouted. 'Rats!'

'Yes-men!' the dissidents yelled back.

No one present ever forgot the scene in the House before the figures were announced. The Chamber, Maisky wrote, 'buzzed like a disturbed bee-hive'. The packed benches were so tense that they seemed to Spears 'to be vibrating like taut wire. Members were standing in every corner. Every seat in the Peers' and public galleries was occupied.'

The tension reached its peak when the Tellers appeared and fanned out in a line at the Bar of the House. The Chief Whip moved to the right, indicating that the government was not beaten. 'We are all right,' Channon heard one relieved voice say. But if the government had won, by what margin?

The four Tellers stepped stiffly forwards towards the Table and bowed low to the Speaker. A few feet away, Churchill's fists rested on his parted knees while he waited for the result.

In dead silence, Margesson read out the figures. 'The Ayes were 281; the Noes, 200.'

Baba Metcalfe sat with her mouth agape. 'I don't think anyone expected such a shock.'

Nicolson wrote: 'The Government's majority dropped from the 213, which it expected, to only 81. There was a gasp of astonishment from every bench.' Another few seconds passed in silence as the numbers sank in. Nicolson watched Margesson hand the division slip to the Clerk. 'Then from the Opposition rose a great howl.'

The cry came from the throat of Labour MP Josiah Wedgwood – the first, bald register of understanding that what appeared on Margesson's buff-coloured slip to be a voting victory was in every other respect a fatal moral defeat. 'It took five seconds before I recognised the significance of the figures and shouted "Resign!" Then pandemonium broke loose.'

Maisky wrote: 'Triumphant roars erupted like a storm from the Opposition benches.' Labour and Conservatives below the gangway leapt to their feet, prancing, waving order papers, yelling out the concluding words of Amery's speech: *'In the name of God, go!'*

Baba Metcalfe was appalled. 'The cries of "Go, go," "Resign," "Get out" were dreadful and shaming.'

'Then followed a scene I shall never forget,' wrote Violet Bonham Carter. 'Prim respectable Conservatives like Harold Macmillan – with his high white collar & tightly fixed pince-nez yelling "Go! Go! Go!" like inspired baboons.'

Macmillan sat beside Wedgwood below the gangway. 'We ought to sing something,' said Macmillan, who had once burnt an effigy of Chamberlain on a bonfire at his country house, Birch Grove. Wedgwood started singing 'Rule Britannia'. Macmillan joined in, but 'as neither of us could sing it was not a very successful effort'. Reith was repelled by this 'scene of disgusting jubilation' – and Euan Wallace found himself 'quite unable to go out into the Lobby afterward as I felt certain that I should have struck Harold Macmillan'.

All this while, Chamberlain sat in his place, wrote Maisky, 'white as chalk' and looking stunned at the continuing shouts of 'Go! Go! Go!' Not in an unlike manner had Gielgud made his entrance at the Old Vic – 'Howl, howl, howl' – with Cordelia in his arms. Boothby recalled how 'for a moment he blanched, but quickly recovered himself, and smiled at some of his supporters'. John Simon leant over and patted his back. Then Chamberlain stood abruptly up and picked his way, alone, without visible emotion, over the stretched-out legs of the frontbenchers, past the Speaker's Chair.

Margesson leapt to his feet and signalled with his order paper for Conservative MPs to rise. John Reith complied. 'We stood up as he left and gave him a cheer.'

Harold Nicolson watched the Prime Minister's solitary figure disappear down the blacked-out corridor. He described the final scene to his readers in Montreal. 'Neville Chamberlain with his jaw set fiercely walked slowly from the Chamber amid the applause of his immediate supporters. We knew he was beaten, but those of us who had fought him since Munich did not join in this jubilation. We were glad to see that the lone grey wolf walked out with his jaw set and his head erect.'

Chamberlain wrote to his sister that the Norway Debate 'was a very painful affair to many besides myself and in particular for its exhibition of personal and party passion'. He had asked for friendship from those who were his friends, and he had not got it. Aside from a brief appearance the following day, he would never go back into the Chamber as Prime Minister.

PART FIVE

THE AFTERMATH

18
A TERRIFIC BUZZ

*'It is not a principle of the Conservative Party to stab its leaders in the back, but I
must confess that it often appears to be a practice.'*

ARTHUR BALFOUR, 1922

The events of the next forty-eight hours have been recounted and recounted,
yet historians have not been able to establish a reliable narrative any more
definitively than the participants. This is not surprising: allegiances changed
minute by minute as Chamberlain mulled over whether to resign or stay put,
and others manoeuvred to take his place. In this atmosphere of profound
chaos, a swarm of MPs suddenly discovered that they were Men of Destiny.

David Faber can testify how all previous loyalties dissolve at such a
moment. 'At the end of the day, you're there for one purpose – to achieve
power, and that would have been more pronounced then.' Joseph Kennedy
looked down from the Diplomatic Gallery with a mighty sense that 'the
maelstrom of war' was about to cast up new parliamentary leaders – the division result acting as a starting gun, in the words of the *Daily Worker*'s lobby
correspondent, for 'every shallow cynical egotist' to press his claims and
extol his own virtues. 'Old admirals remove the moth balls from their uniforms and parade the House in an effort to explain they can kill quicker and
better than the new jacks in office. Churchill grabs his chance to swim now
that Chamberlain sinks, Hore-Belisha and Duff Cooper again dream of office
and power.' The division had transformed Barry's elegant Gothic halls into
'the green-eyed jungle', as Hugh Dalton famously called Westminster, a place
where a man's character and ambitions were laid out naked to his enemies.

Immediately after the House adjourned at 11.13 p.m. a 'terrific buzz' could
be heard in the Lobby as Members speculated on the next step and balanced
their chances. An over-excited Dalton announced that 'the Old Man' must go to

Buckingham Palace and resign. Vitriolic slanging matches took place between Conservatives. Kenneth Pickthorn snarled at Richard Law, son of the former Prime Minister Bonar Law: 'Well, I expect you'll get your reward!' Maurice Hely-Hutchinson compared Somerset de Chair and his friends to German parachutists at Stavanger, dropped behind the lines in Conservative uniforms. In the same choleric language, David Margesson carpeted John Profumo the following day. 'And I tell you this, you utterly contemptible little shit. On every morning that you wake up for the rest of your life you will be ashamed of what you did last night.' Almost at once, Quintin Hogg began to feel 'like a traitor'. In the slow train next morning back to his regiment in Lincoln, Hogg sat opposite the local MP who seized the opportunity to tell him 'at intervals of five minutes that I had made a decision which I would repent for the rest of my life.'

The sense of foreboding on the government front bench was articulated by the Air Minister, Samuel Hoare. Up until even a fortnight before, Hoare had let it be known that he 'was still planning to succeed Neville when the time came'. But speaking in the Norway Debate right after Chamberlain's damaging riposte to Morrison, 'Slippery Sam' gave an extraordinarily lame performance, and according to a member of his own department, 'muddled all his facts in his speech' – which was '_so_ bad', wrote Violet Bonham Carter, 'that he emptied the House'. When Hoare admitted that a squadron of Gladiators had been bombed on a frozen lake, one Conservative MP whispered, 'I suppose he was skating somewhere else.' Hoare told his wife Maud as they drove home, with a presentiment that proved correct: 'That is not only the last speech that I shall make as a Minister, but it is the last speech that I shall make in the House of Commons.'

The general conviction was that the division result meant a reconstruction at once, shedding unpopular Ministers like Hoare, Simon and Wood, and bringing in opposition leaders, possibly under a new Prime Minister who would be capable of inspiring more faith among all parties. A jubilant Lloyd George told the Soviet Ambassador in the Commons Strangers' Dining Room: 'Chamberlain is done for . . . he might hold on for a few weeks . . . a duck with a broken leg still flutters its wings, but its fate has been decided. The same with Neville.' The Chief Whip David Margesson braced himself for the transition of power. Colville wrote: 'I remember David said to me that very night that Chamberlain would have to resign.'

The Prime Minister had reached the same conclusion, at least in the first instance, according to Hoare. 'I was not surprised when Chamberlain told me immediately after the Debate that he would resign.'

Chamberlain wrote to his sister: 'It did not take me long to make up my mind what to do.' On leaving the Chamber, he walked down the darkened corridor to the Prime Minister's room on the left, which Halifax described as 'always hideously uncomfortable, as about six more people want to sit round the table than there is room for'. Chamberlain asked Churchill to join him, and said that 'he felt he could not go on'. He saw the time had come for a National government in the broadest sense, 'or we could not get through'.

In a strange piece of theatre, rather than concurring at once, Churchill urged Chamberlain to stay put. As Amery saw the scene, in a letter that he wrote to Halifax many years after: 'Winston cheers up Neville by telling him not to take things too seriously and that there is no reason why he should not carry on as before (possibly with his tongue in his cheek).' Chamberlain was under no obligation constitutionally to resign. A majority of eighty-one was more than ample in normal peacetime circumstances – incredibly, several government insiders had reconsidered their previous minimum figure of one hundred, and now, observed Colville, 'were fairly satisfied' by the vote. Not only that, but, as David Dilks has demonstrated, Churchill and Chamberlain had formed a partnership of growing strength. Plus, there was Churchill's special code of loyalty which held that if a Prime Minister tripped, 'he must be sustained. If he makes mistakes, they must be covered.'

Labour's riotous behaviour in the House had rekindled long-standing grudges, and aroused Churchill's combative instincts. Just as he had hours before instructed Colonel Gubbins, so he now advised Chamberlain to fight on, as though they were a small force of embattled commandos in the high mountains of Norway. 'This has been a damaging debate,' Churchill recalled himself advising Chamberlain, 'but you have a good majority. Do not take the matter grievously to heart. Strengthen your Government from every quarter, and let us go on until our majority deserts us.'

'Every quarter' was a Churchillian exaggeration. Chamberlain told John Simon in a private discussion next day that 'Winston had apparently originally taken the view that the Labour people had nothing to contribute, and that the way to broaden the government was to bring in a selection of last night's rebels instead, together of course with Archie Sinclair with whom Winston has long been in close relations.'

Looking back on their conversation from a distance of eight years, Churchill wrote that Chamberlain remained both unconvinced and uncomforted by his encouragement, 'and I left him about midnight with the feeling that he would persist in his resolve to sacrifice himself if there was no other way'.

There was a further good reason why Churchill might have wanted to shore up Chamberlain. If the Prime Minister did resign, it was unlikely that Churchill would be chosen as his replacement.

Only five hours earlier, Conservative MP George Lambert had pressed the House to answer a vital question: in the event of a change of government, as many seemed to be proposing, 'Who is to be Prime Minister? . . . After all, this is the House of Commons, democratically elected.' Had Lambert's question been put to a vote that evening, the result would not have been the First Lord by a long chalk.

It is difficult to conceive that two days before he became Prime Minister, Churchill was not viewed as the front runner in what revealed itself to be a continuously shifting pack of potential premiers, almost none of whom enjoyed the necessary cross-party support. Ida Chamberlain wrote to her brother: 'No one has yet been able to produce the names of wonderful new men who would command at once the confidence of the nation.' Euan Wallace despaired that those who had voted simply to remove Chamberlain from office 'do not appear to agree on, or even to have thought of, an efficient substitute'. Cadogan feared that the debate had weakened the government. 'But what are we going to put in its place? Winston useless. Then? Attlee? Sinclair? Sam Hoare!' Anthony Eden's Private Secretary had a hunch that Eden himself 'might step in'. The Home Secretary Sir John Anderson, an administrator of the highest ability, was another possibility – promoted by Chamberlain none other, who told Joseph Kennedy: 'Anderson might be P.M.' Again and again in these tight inner circles Churchill's name bobbed up, was contemplated briefly – and dismissed.

In one of his fireside chats with Ivan Maisky, Churchill admitted to the Soviet Ambassador that 'the Conservative party won't let anyone tell it who should be its leader'. In November, Beaverbrook had confided to Maisky that 'Churchill, apparently, has no chance at all'. Popular though he was outside Westminster, Churchill enjoyed a divisive and rickety reputation within the Commons, and not merely among opposition Labour MPs – 'who had publicly pledged themselves', according to the Communist MP William Gallacher, 'never to associate with such a villainous character as Churchill!' Emanuel Shinwell said that most Labour MPs 'had never forgotten his jibes that "Labour was unfit to govern"'. Labour leaders like Arthur Greenwood still saw in Churchill 'the grim figure' of 'the man who tried to beat us in the Great Strike', and Stafford Cripps told Lloyd George on the morning after the division that 'many of them were frightened of Winston'. The ruling Conservative Party regarded him with equal fear, distaste and mistrust. Shinwell wrote: 'Along the stone corridor he used to walk, with many Tories ostentatiously turning their backs.' A previous Conservative Prime Minister, Stanley Baldwin, acknowledged that 'our people like [Churchill]. They love listening to him in the House, look on him as a star turn . . . But for leadership they would turn him down every time.' Only ten months earlier, Samuel Hoare estimated that if there was a ballot of Conservative backbenchers, four out of five would vote against a Churchill premiership. This hostility was not limited to the back benches. The War Cabinet was stacked against Churchill – more grittily so following his erratic conduct in the Norway Campaign. The Speaker, Captain Fitz-Roy, was another obstacle, revealing in a private conversation soon after the division that he 'did not have much confidence in Winston's character and was confident he was unreliable'. To cap it all, Churchill did not have the backing of the King, whose prerogative it was to appoint any new Prime Minister. On the first day of the Norway Debate, the King's Private Secretary wrote in a memorandum to George VI that for Churchill to be Prime Minister of a coalition was 'very undesirable'. How undesirable may be guessed from a letter that Queen Mary wrote to John Colville's mother, her lady-in-waiting, to say that Colville should refuse to serve under Churchill.

In the aftermath of the division on 8 May, in the eyes of a majority whose backing he required were he to succeed Chamberlain, Churchill was not destiny's child. If anything, the Norway Campaign had served to reinforce huge reservations about his loyalty, military competence and judgement. Joseph Kennedy wrote to his wife: 'Churchill has energy and brains but <u>no</u> judgment.' Halifax had recently discussed Churchill's chances over lunch with Anthony Eden – who in April polled 28 per cent as the public's choice of next Prime Minister, against Churchill's 25 per cent. Halifax confided that 'however much people admire Winston's qualities, that admiration is constantly balanced by fear of him if he was loose!' Eden, too, doubted 'whether Churchill could ever be P.M. so bad is his judgement'. Weeks earlier, Peter Fleming's brother Ian had taken a sounding among MPs. 'In House of Commons Conservatives say: Winston is all right where he is, but could never stand strain of P.M.'s job, health wouldn't be good enough.' Even a natural ally like Harold Nicolson failed to see Churchill as the next leader, the reason being that 'Churchill is undermined by the Conservative caucus' – i.e. those MPs who could neither forgive him for his pre-war criticisms of Chamberlain, nor for having proved to be 'so abundantly right' about Hitler. Duff Cooper was a strong Churchill supporter, yet even he believed that Churchill's insuperable problem was that he had 'so many and such violent enemies'.

An archetypical enemy was Nancy Dugdale, wife of a recent Conservative Deputy Whip. Churchill did not go down well in their part of Yorkshire, she revealed in a letter to Chamberlain. 'The constant agitation in favour of Mr Churchill in the press in no way corresponds to the feeling of the people here who frankly distrust him & fundamentally dislike his boasting.' She wrote to her husband four days after the Norway Debate: 'WC is really the counterpart of Goering in England, full of the desire for blood, "Blitz Krieg" and bloated with ego and over feeling, the same treachery running through his veins, punctuated by heroics and hot air.'

This is not to say that antipathy towards Churchill flowed all in one direction. After a disquieting scene in the House, when Conservative MPs had 'howled and hooted him out', Churchill walked from the Chamber with his head lowered, and only his faithful Brendan Bracken following. As Bracken reached the door, he turned and looked round at the Conservative majority 'with hatred in his eyes and murder in his heart', recalled a witness. 'If someone at that moment had handed him a bren gun in working condition, the Tory majority would have been blasted out of the House of Commons.'

Andrew Roberts interviewed up to twenty of those Conservative MPs. He says: 'Not a single one once said or wrote that because of the fact that Winston Churchill was right about Adolf Hitler we should make him Prime Minister.' In the heated discussions in the Lobbies and Whips' rooms after the division, there was a strong inclination to downgrade Churchill's claims and to cite his reckless past rather than praise his foresight. Revisiting this period a month on, Clementine Churchill told Violet Bonham Carter 'that a great section of the Tory Party were not behind Winston', and that even his closest supporters 'were cautious in promoting his interests'.

Inevitably, there was one name that did emerge as the natural compromise leader of a government of national unity, under whom all differences might resolve themselves, acceptable to the opposition, and whom the Conservative Party would have chosen in overwhelming numbers had MPs held a snap election that night.

Lord Halifax was a politician of indisputable charm and integrity, who had capably administered an empire of 320 million people. The historian Robert Blake summed up the Foreign Secretary's attraction: 'He was widely respected across the whole party political spectrum. No breath of scandal ever touched his name.'

If, as S. J. D. Green reminds us, 'no "serious politician" during the 1930s had been "a Churchillian",' then almost the opposite was true of Halifax, who had long been touted as a premier. As far back as December 1926, at a lunch party given by Chamberlain, Viscount Mersey had asked two of those present, Victor Cazalet and Charles Cayzer, who would be the next Conservative leader after their host. 'They both said "Edward Wood [Halifax], every time."' In 1938, Beverley Baxter and several other MPs placed bets on the succession to Chamberlain, with Halifax emerging as 6-to-4 favourite and Churchill as 40-to-1 outsider. Following the invasion of Czechoslovakia, Harold Nicolson reported on a general feeling in the Commons 'that Halifax should become Prime Minister'. Even Lloyd George, when casting round for a suitable premier other than himself, looked with a grudging glance at Halifax, telling A. J. Sylvester: 'Well, there is always the pale young curate.'

The division's sensational result fixed the searchlights on the Foreign Secretary. Those who feared Churchill as leader found the opposing qualities in Halifax. Coming downstairs into the Lobby after the debate, Joseph Kennedy met Hugh Dalton and Nancy Astor conferring. 'Lady Astor immediately started for Lord Halifax for Prime Minister.'

The Foreign Secretary had been occupied all afternoon in the Lords, where he had spoken from 7.38 p.m. to 8.15 p.m. 'On the whole it went better than I expected,' Halifax wrote in his diary. 'My speech contributed nothing new but did adequately.' With viceregal detachment, he had organised for the debate in the Lords to be wrapped up in a single sitting, without a division, after persuading several speakers to drop out 'in order that I might get finished before dinner'.

His dinner date that evening was his hostess of the weekend.

Baba Metcalfe was bursting to tell Halifax about the extraordinary scenes that she had witnessed in the Commons. Over a hurried meal, at which Dorothy Halifax was also present, Baba described how she had 'popped backwards and forwards' between the Commons and the Lords, to hear Lord Salisbury and then Halifax. To go from one House to the other was 'like going from Twickenham to St Paul's'. She described the scrummage in the former: Morrison's unanticipated call for a confidence vote, Chamberlain's misplaced appeal to his friends, Lloyd George's scornful demand that the Prime Minister sacrifice himself, and the 'very sharp exchanges between Labour people and the P.M.' To Halifax, hearing this for the first time, it was clear that the position had 'suddenly become acute'.

Some years before, a bomb had exploded under his train as it approached Delhi, wrecking the restaurant carriage. Then the Viceroy's coach had leapt the gap. The challenge facing Halifax this evening was how to keep the government on the rails.

After dinner, Halifax took Baba down to the Commons since he wanted to see Chamberlain and she wanted to hear Churchill. He wrote: 'I didn't see the P.M.', but he had sat in the Peers' Gallery and caught the final moments of the debate. 'Winston was good, but got into a bit of a row at the end, and the Division was bad.' Halifax was 'amazed at the personal animosity to the P.M.', he told Baba. 'What the solution is I don't pretend to know.'

In fact, a sizeable body of MPs had decided that Halifax was the solution, and not merely Conservative Members. In the opinion of the Labour frontbencher Hugh Dalton, there was 'no other choice' but Halifax.

The swell for him had been growing all day. At the very moment that Halifax dined with Baba, Dalton called on Rab Butler, Halifax's representative in the Commons, with a radical proposal: provided that Neville Chamberlain, John Simon, Samuel Hoare and Kingsley Wood disappeared from the government, having 'such long crime sheets', then Labour would be prepared to discuss the question of entering a coalition. Dalton said: 'If I was asked who should succeed Chamberlain as Prime Minister, my own view, which I thought was shared by a number of others, was that it should be Halifax . . . Some might think of Winston as P.M., but in my view he would be better occupied in winning the war.'

This was not merely Dalton's opinion, but that of Attlee, who 'agrees with my preference for Halifax over Churchill', and of Morrison as well. Dalton asked Butler to pass their views on to the Foreign Secretary. Butler did so in a letter which he wrote to Halifax that night.

Knowledge that Halifax had the support of the Labour leadership lay behind an earlier covert approach, this time from within No. 10. The previous day, Dunglass had contacted Butler and asked him 'to talk to Halifax and persuade him to become Prime Minister'. Dunglass, too, had heard, most likely from Chamberlain, that Halifax 'was the personal choice of Mr Attlee'.

Add now to the phalanx forming behind the Foreign Secretary, Lloyd George. He recently had told Stafford Cripps, somewhat to Cripps's surprise, that 'Winston could not be P.M. and that it would have to be Halifax'. If ever there was a shoo-in for Prime Minister, then it was Edward Halifax on the evening of 8 May 1940.

Watching all this with a self-interested eye was Max Beaverbrook, who had once 'stupefied' Leo Amery 'by saying that unfit as he was for the job, he might be compelled to be Prime Minister!' Beaverbrook was suspected of supporting Lloyd George before the division, the politician he had backed in 1916 and forced to resign in 1922. Now having digested the result, he had embarked on his reluctant shift towards Churchill, even if, as Beaverbrook pointed out, the position was 'very heavily loaded' in favour of Halifax – as how could it not be? Chamberlain wished to recommend Halifax as his successor. The King wanted Halifax as his Prime Minister. And the government Chief Whip preferred Halifax – as did most Conservative MPs, three of the Labour leaders and, apparently, Lloyd George. The only person supposedly not in favour of a Halifax premiership was Halifax himself.

At some unclear point during 8 May, probably in his room behind the Speaker's Chair, Chamberlain spoke to Halifax in what was to be the first of three meetings over the next twenty-four hours in all of which he tried to talk his Foreign Secretary into becoming Prime Minister of a coalition government. With no confidence in Churchill as his successor, and no faith that Labour would endorse Churchill following the rowdy scenes in the Chamber, Chamberlain had turned over in his methodical mind the fact that Halifax had the respect and support of the Labour leaders, under whom he had successfully served when Viceroy of India. This, on top of Chamberlain's soundings that the Conservatives 'would not accept Winston' made Halifax not merely a natural choice on this seismic evening. It also made him the only one. Chamberlain now just had to convince Halifax.

Stuart Hodgson was researching Halifax's biography at this moment, and he recorded how Halifax once let slip 'that he would rather be Master of Foxhounds than Prime Minister'. Halifax's initial response to Chamberlain on 8 May was in this vein. 'I told him . . . that if the Labour people said that they would only serve under me I should tell them that I was not prepared to do it.'

Later that evening, Halifax drove Baba Metcalfe home to 16 Wilton Place. Her London house had been kept under dust sheets since the start of the war, but she continued to spend the odd night there. It was where the Duke of Windsor had stayed in September when he went to visit his brother at Buckingham Palace, and a place where Baba and Halifax could talk without being observed or overheard.

In his introduction to his father's ghost stories, which he had read to her the previous Saturday at Little Compton, Halifax remarked that 'mystery, romance, adventure, other-worldiness all played their part'. The same elements shadowed the relationship between the Foreign Secretary – with his 'mystical, Christian character', as Joseph Kennedy called it – and Lord Curzon's worldly youngest daughter, whose 'snapshot photograph' Halifax never tired of gazing at: 'It sits in a prayer book that I use every morning, and so cheers me each day!'

Baba had acted as Halifax's go-between-cum-confidante throughout the Norway Debate. She appreciated his reservations about accepting the premiership in a way that Halifax's advisers could not. As Curzon's daughter, she understood his predicament probably better even than his wife: Dorothy, Stuart Hodgson observed, was always 'jealous for her husband's fame' – something borne out by an entry in Violet Bonham Carter's diary following a talk with Clementine Churchill. 'I can't believe that Ed. Halifax wanted it. But Clemmie says she thinks Dorothy H. did.'

More pertinently: did Baba Metcalfe want it for Halifax?

For Baba, Halifax was the outstanding choice to succeed Chamberlain. She wrote in her diary: 'He would have been more dependable and better than Winston, one can't talk of them in the same breath, and England would have had a man at the helm of whom she could have been justly proud.' Baba flirted with Halifax that if he became Prime Minister it would make her more frightened of him. What further confessions she may have vouchsafed during this period are contained in letters which are missing or destroyed. But her regret at his refusal to step up to the mark is hinted at in a letter that Halifax wrote to her five days later regarding his decision. 'I can't share your feelings all together, I'm afraid – as the instinct of self defence is so strong in all the lower animals!'

Lower animals are notorious for possessing instincts other than self-defence. One among plenty of reasons why the Holy Fox might have desired Baba's company was that he could air his concerns with her. She wrote about their conversation following the division that evening: 'We discussed the chances of his having to take on that ghastly and thankless job. He thought it would never work, the difficulty of the Lords & Commons being impossible and having someone to deputise for you would always be unsuccessful. He dreaded the thought.'

The enamoured Foreign Secretary may have dreaded something else besides. A degree of caution must be exercised when looking for motives to explain his obstinate and not always utterly convincing reluctance to take on Chamberlain's mantle. The risk that the inevitable extra scrutiny and workload would expose and harm his affection for Baba Metcalfe involves an element of speculation. But if power is an aphrodisiac, then love is its antidote. It is not difficult to imagine a prudent calculation which would have dictated that Halifax remain where he was, revered, respected, untouched by any breath of scandal, yet able to go on sharing further precious hours and confidences with his 'dearest Baba'.

Back in the Commons, intense discussions continued into the early hours. Violet Bonham Carter talked in the Liberal Whips' room till nearly 1 a.m. with Percy Harris and Archie Sinclair. 'We all made our choice of P.M.'s – Winston, Halifax & Ll.G being the candidates – & all gave Winston our 1st vote tho' some thought Halifax more probable.' Lloyd George, in conversation with Attlee, thought that the King might send for the Labour leader in order to consult him. 'I told Attlee that I did not think he could be P.M. in this situation. Given the strength of Parties in the House, the P.M. must be a Conservative. He quite agreed.' An 'awestruck' Baffy Dugdale completed her diary entry for 8 May: 'I can write no more tonight but should probably put down now that I think when the King sends for Attlee he will probably advise sending for Halifax.'

By now, word of Chamberlain's preference had reached Churchill – who was sanguine about it, according to an undated account left by Beaverbrook. 'Churchill had earlier told his friends, including me, that if asked to serve under Halifax he would do so. He would lead the House of Commons and give Halifax sincere and continual support.'

If this really was the case – and as David Dilks is careful to alert us: 'It's always a mistake to believe anything said or written by Beaverbrook unless there is independent corroboration' – then it is noteworthy that one friend Churchill did not inform was a tall, burly thirty-nine-year-old Irishman with a crop of untidy flame-red hair 'who always knows everything through Winston'.

An unsatisfactory cluster of stories, all second-hand or hearsay, surround Brendan Bracken's movements during these blurry hours. They emanate from Bracken's strenuous freelance attempts to champion Churchill's claims over Halifax's. Afterwards, friends like Louis Spears were confident that Churchill was 'completely unaware' of what Bracken had been up to, but it is not impossible that Churchill was using Bracken, even before the division, to broadcast his lack of enthusiasm to play second fiddle to the Foreign Secretary.

The most arresting story was repeated by Bracken to Amery, in a conversation that took place fourteen years later. It begins on that febrile evening of 8 May when Bracken met Paul Emrys-Evans and Richard Law in Churchill's room in the Commons and declared off his own bat that 'it was unlikely that Winston would be prepared to serve under Halifax'. Bracken told Amery that he had made the same claim the night before – to the Labour leader. Even as Amery had been delivering his Cromwellian speech in the Chamber, Bracken, apparently, was dining with Attlee in an unscheduled meeting on 7 May. Bracken disclosed to Amery that Attlee had been unusually forthcoming during their dinner. 'Discussing a possible coalition, Attlee said his people would accept one under Halifax with Winston as Defence Minister. He had never forgiven W. for Tonypandy. B.B., on his own authority, said Winston was not prepared to serve under Halifax. He would get all the blame without having the real power of decision. Attlee ended by at any rate acquiescing in W. as possible.'

Yet when Amery contacted Attlee to confirm this story, Attlee denied it. 'I do not believe that I met Brendan Bracken; certainly I did not dine with him and I did not talk with him on the evening of the [7th]'* – an evening when Attlee had a lot else to do. 'I certainly never discussed whether it should be Winston or Halifax with him.'

Another anecdote that Bracken told Amery in January 1955 was how, when Bracken reported back to Churchill his conversation with Attlee, Bracken was initially 'well scourged' by Churchill who 'blew up, said he had no business to say anything of the sort & that he was quite willing to serve under H. All the same, what he now knew about Attlee no doubt confused him in hoping for himself.'

A quite separate and also unverifiable story describes Bracken's impulsive reaction upon learning that Churchill had already consented to a Halifax premiership. The source this time is Churchill's doctor, Charles Moran, in a diary entry that Moran wrote seven years later: how, early on the evening of 8 May, 'word reached Brendan that Winston had come to an agreement with Halifax that he would act as his second in command if Halifax became Prime Minister. Brendan thought this would be disastrous, that if it were carried out we should lose the war. He went about London searching for Winston. At one o'clock in the morning he found him. "You can't agree to this," Brendan spluttered, but Winston was obdurate; he said that he could not go back on his word.'

Both stories filtered out a long time after the events that they describe, and deserve to be treated with the same caution as Bracken's account of his dead brother in Narvik. His reputation as a fantasist by now preceded him, embodied in his reluctance to deny rumours – which he may have fanned – that it was he, Brendan Bracken, who was Churchill's illegitimate son, and not Giles Romilly's brother. As recently as 1 May, Beaverbrook had warned Robert Bruce Lockhart that 'Brendan was unreliable in his information'.

What is not in doubt is that on the night of the 'fatal division', as Chips

---

* Attlee writes '9th May'; Spears has it in his diary as 8 May, but Amery corrects this to 7 May.

Channon now began to call it, a consensus was gathering in Parliament and Fleet Street about what the morning was likely to bring. *The Times*, edited by Halifax's longstanding friend and reluctant advocate Geoffrey Dawson, went to press with a rousing leading letter from another Fellow of All Souls, A. L. Rowse, this time in his capacity as the Labour candidate for Penryn and Falmouth. 'I believe the Labour movement would serve under Lord Halifax as Prime Minister who has defined the moral issues of the war as no one else has done and gives the nation the right moral leadership.' Rowse's letter accorded 'with Dawson's own sentiments' and had the Labour Party's approval, and it followed Cripps's front-page letter in Monday's *Daily Mail* also calling for a Halifax administration.

The front page of the *Daily Mirror* had gone to bed as well, with the most emphatic declaration of all. 'Lord Halifax, the Foreign Secretary, is almost certain to become the new Prime Minister.'

Whatever his private reservations, to the world beyond Westminster it looked as though the Master of the Middleton Hounds was set to replace Chamberlain, and that Halifax's immediate task would be to lead the country into battle with a German 'fern-a-tic', as Chamberlain viewed Hitler, whom he had once mistaken for a footman.

Wednesday 8 May was a significant day not only in Parliament, but in the history of Europe. While Members were debating the Norway Campaign, Hitler set the final date for Operation 'Gelb'. The invasion of Western Europe was to begin at 5.35 a.m. on Friday 10 May under the code word 'Danzig'.

The absolute silence on the German border with Holland, Belgium and Luxembourg was a cause for nervous concern. Hitler had signed a non-aggression pact with each of these countries. Rumours throughout the week about a German attack on the Western Front rose to the boil at a small party which convened at Max Beaverbrook's house immediately after the division.

Bumping into a 'dog-tired' Clement Davies in the street, on his way to the Reform Club to get some sleep, Beaverbrook had persuaded the leading light of the revolt to walk on with him to Stornoway House, just off Pall Mall. There, around midnight, they found Joseph Kennedy: the American

Ambassador had come to get Beaverbrook's 'slant on the situation'. Both Beaverbrook and Davies had concluded that Chamberlain would have to resign, which Beaverbrook 'accordingly telephoned to the *Express*'. Kennedy then telephoned President Roosevelt from Beaverbrook's study, but Kennedy's report on the turbulence in Westminster was cast into shadow by Roosevelt's news, obtained from a leak in the German General Staff. 'The President told me he was very much upset as he had just heard that Germany had delivered an ultimatum to Holland.'

It was 2 a.m. when Kennedy telephoned Colville at No. 10. He next called Churchill, who responded: 'A terrible world this is getting to be.' Kennedy then rang Hoare, who was equally despondent. 'There really doesn't seem to be much hope anywhere, does there?'

Kennedy concurred. 'There is a very definite undercurrent of despair because of the hopelessness of the whole task for England.'

Clement Davies meanwhile had hurried off to report the news of Germany's ultimatum to the Dutch Ambassador, a contact of Davies's through his work for Unilever, who, barely awake and still in pyjamas, was so shocked that he collapsed in his arms.

19
THE OBVIOUS MAN

*'Do you happen to know any gentleman of your acquaintance, Mr. Taper, who
refuses Secretaryships of State so easily?'*
BENJAMIN DISRAELI, *Coningsby*

In his sixth-floor suite at the Dorchester, Halifax read the headlines on
9 May and experienced what he described to Baba Metcalfe on another occasion as a bad 'pit of the stomach feeling'. With the exception of the *Daily
Mail*, which had come out for Lloyd George, the morning papers regarded
a Halifax premiership as the likeliest outcome following the startling vote
in Parliament.

Outside, it was another beautiful spring day, the tulips almost at their
best as Halifax walked through the Buckingham Palace gardens to the Foreign Office. Awaiting him on his desk was Rab Butler's letter saying that
Labour were willing to serve under Halifax – 'Dalton said there was no
other choice than you' – plus the news that Butler had spoken after the division to Herbert Morrison, 'who said that the idea of Labour joining the
Govt. was "coming along well"'.

When at 10 a.m. Chamberlain asked the Foreign Secretary to come and
see him, Halifax could have had no doubt what he wished to discuss.

Their talk lasted forty-five minutes. The Prime Minister's agenda was
simple: to harness his skills as a chairman in order to make Halifax reconsider his unenthusiastic stance of the day before. Chamberlain later
explained to Joseph Kennedy that he and Halifax 'never had a disagreement. Except little things as between men.' His objective this morning, and
again in the afternoon, was to persuade Halifax to agree to the largest thing
in politics. Chamberlain was by now well acquainted with the habit that
had marked Halifax's political life, of raising an obstacle in the expectation

that it would be knocked down. He had interpreted Halifax's earlier reluctance as par for the course.

The only first-hand account of their 10.15 a.m. meeting in Chamberlain's office is provided by Halifax. Chamberlain began by saying that the position could not be left as it was by the division, and it was vital to restore confidence in the government. This could not be done, he thought, unless all parties were brought in. He asked Halifax for his view.

Halifax wrote: 'I told him I thought this was essential. He told me that Winston had been doubtful about it when he had spoken to him immediately after the Division last night.' But Churchill's antipathy to Labour was well known, and reciprocated in full.

The two men next discussed the chances of Labour serving under Chamberlain. Both agreed that these were negligible. Halifax braced himself for the inevitable question: who should be Chamberlain's successor? 'He thought that it was clearly Winston, or myself, and appeared to suggest that if it were myself he might continue to serve in the Government.'

For the second time in the space of a few hours, Halifax rehearsed his reservations to Chamberlain. He told Baba, with whom he had lunch shortly afterwards – and who may have been one of them herself – how he had put forward 'the many difficulties of his position'.

It is a rare politician who turns down the chance to be Prime Minister. When Rab Butler asked Halifax later in the week why he had argued against accepting the leadership, Halifax snapped: 'You know my reasons, it's no use discussing that.' His main reason was commonly understood to be his peerage, which, Halifax had persistently argued, and not just to Baba, put him out of the running by placing him, as he now explained to Chamberlain, in 'the difficult position of a Prime Minister unable to make contact with the centre of gravity in the House of Commons'. This, too, was the reason that Halifax gave six hours later to Churchill, who reported it to Anthony Eden at dinner. Eden immediately afterwards wrote in his diary: 'Edward did not wish to succeed. Parliamentary position too difficult.'

But how difficult was Halifax's position?

Seventeen years earlier, in May 1923, George V had rejected the then-favourite, Baba's father, as his Prime Minister, because, according to Baba's sister Irene, 'the Labour Opposition were unrepresented in the House of Lords, and that therefore objections to him as a Peer were insuperable'. Actually, the principal reason was not Lord Curzon's peerage so much as his temperamental unsuitability. Had Churchill himself been sitting in the Lords in May 1940, it is unlikely that he would have found 'the H of L problem' such an obstacle, as he had made clear in an essay on Curzon published in 1937. 'The principle that a Prime Minister in the Lords is an anachronism,' Churchill wrote then, 'is a question which only Parliament can settle in the presence of the personalities and circumstances of the occasion.' Lord Vansittart's observation that Curzon's peerage was a convenient rather than an insuperable obstacle was more apposite of Halifax. As Harold Macmillan put it in a note: 'No one objected to a Peer as Prime Minister on principle.'

The fact that Halifax sat in the House of Lords was indeed a genuine stumbling-block, because legislation would have been required to enable him to sit in the House of Commons, and he would then have had to find a seat and fight a by-election, all of which entailed a delay of at least a month. But these were extraordinary circumstances, and the urgency of the occasion permitted normal procedure to be suspended. At a moment when the national emergency demanded new leadership, Halifax's peerage was an irrelevance to almost everyone but himself.

Chamberlain replied to Halifax that he saw no problem about him sitting in the Lords, 'arguing that *ex-hypothesi* in the new situation there would be comparatively little opposition in the House of Commons'. Earlier in the year, 'very secret soundings' had taken place behind John Simon's back to enable a bill that would allow a peer to be made a commoner – 'dis-peered' as Chamberlain put it – so that Lord Stamp could succeed Simon as Chancellor. In the same explorative vein, as Chamberlain's leadership came under pressure in March, George VI's Private Secretary Alexander Hardinge had consulted four constitutional experts on the monarch's right to summon a person to form an administration. Hardinge's conclusion: the King need not ask the advice of the outgoing Prime Minister as to his successor, nor should the latter give such advice unless it was asked for. 'The only person who could make the formal offer of the post of Prime Minister to any individual is the King himself.' Halifax's peerage was never going to be a stumbling block for George VI – any more than it was for his daughter in 1963 when she invited Alec Dunglass (by then the Earl of Home) to become her Prime Minister. A day after Halifax's meeting with Chamberlain, the King offered to put Halifax's peerage into 'abeyance', because, he wrote in his diary, 'I thought that H was the obvious man.'

With Labour's endorsement confirmed, Halifax's peerage was even less of a barrier in the quarters where the harshest protests might have been most anticipated. Butler in his letter to Halifax delivered earlier that morning had emphasised that Attlee and Dalton 'saw no objection in the Lords difficulty'. Not only that, but Dalton had given an assurance which seemed to welcome Halifax's peerage: 'In time of war I was not concerned with the fact that he was in the Lords. Indeed, this had some advantages in relieving the strain upon him.' Significantly, on its front page that day the Labour-supporting *Daily Mirror* had no difficulty in promoting a Halifax premiership either. 'The constitutional problem of permitting a peer to sit in both Houses is likely to be overcome by means of a special emergency session of both Houses.'

Whatever the nature of Halifax's misgivings, the fact that he was a peer was, out of all his excuses, the least convincing.

So why at the height was Halifax ready to decline?

It is most unusual for a potential Minister to pass up a promotion. Chamberlain turned down the Treasury in 1924 in order to pursue his cousin Norman's social policies, which alone allowed Churchill to survive and come in as Chancellor of the Exchequer. In 1916, Bonar Law refused the premiership on Asquith's resignation, believing that Lloyd George would be the more effective war leader. In 1855, Lord Derby declined Queen Victoria's offer to form a government, hoping to return in a stronger position. Such examples are few.

To be fair to Halifax, his avowed reluctance to take power had a history. Meeting him in St James's Park in March 1938 after Halifax had been appointed Foreign Secretary, a friend asked: 'Edward, may I congratulate you?'

'No,' Halifax replied, 'you certainly may not!'

'May I condole with you?'

'Yes, you may.'

Another friend wrote to John Buchan in May 1939 after taking a long walk with Halifax. 'How wise and calm he is. He tells me that he absolutely refuses to contemplate the idea of being P.M. He is the only person at the moment who would be acceptable to the country at all.'

Halifax's refusals were less adamantine in practice, though. When Stuart Hodgson began researching his biography during these months, he noted how one of the curiosities of Halifax's career was the way in which all the great offices which he had filled one after the other seemed to have been thrust upon him against his will. Halifax's most recent biographer has well observed how Halifax used his opening refusal to reinforce the public image of an inherently modest man who was uninterested in high office, 'but dragged there by friends for his country's good'. Scrupulous never to rule out anything altogether, Halifax noted of himself that he was 'not one to burn the house down, because he would continue to hope that he might later get it back again'.

Halifax hid his ambitious side as he hid his deformed left hand. When an MP, he had appeared to be quite lacking in 'push', and had no regrets at leaving the House of Commons – 'for me it never held any great appeal'. The type of politician Halifax professed to admire was Lord Derby, with whom he had served in Bonar Law's government in 1922, and who 'took the opportunity of a change of Government to get back to his natural work in Lancashire which he always felt to have first claim on him'. A contemporary noted in 1936 that it was widely known that Halifax was only too anxious to retire from public life 'as he invariably tells everyone that his one object is to give up politics and go back and live at his home'. This was not flim-flam. Halifax admired self-abnegation. His first book was on John Keble (1792–1866), the most distinguished man of his time in Oxford, who had abandoned his university career to bury himself in a small curacy in Gloucestershire. In January 1942, Halifax envisaged to Baba Metcalfe being sacked by Churchill. 'What then? Casual political employment, interspersed with Little Compton and Garrowby.' Such a combination, 'with us all together', was 'a dream which keeps me alive & sane. When will this be?'

Halifax's aversion to political power was rooted in his genuine preference for the country life of Garrowby over the turmoil of Westminster. He was also, as Stuart Hodgson's 1941 biography diplomatically put it, 'no friend to unnecessary activity'. His immediate reaction on being offered the position of Foreign Secretary in 1938 had been to prevaricate, according to the diplomat Oliver Harvey. 'He said he was very lazy and disliked work. Could he hunt on

Saturdays?' His daughter-in-law Diana Holderness confirms: 'He was lazy. He never went to bed after 10.30 p.m. At the Embassy in Washington, he'd have dinner early, 8 p.m. at the very latest. He'd get up: "I've got to see some papers," or: "I'm going to my tower." Sometimes he stupidly would leave the door open. And you'd see him lying in bed, reading. He didn't want the nuisance.' Being Prime Minister would have entailed a lot of work. He had told Baba only a few weeks earlier that he was too tired to start that racket again.

It is important when trying to deduce his motives to recall that Halifax had already enjoyed power – he had ruled a fifth of the world's population, even if he had been answerable to a Secretary of State. Diana Holderness says: 'If you've been Viceroy, it's really grander than being P.M. You were curtseyed to.' Grand enough anyway in his own eyes, he did not need to be grander by becoming Prime Minister. Less than twelve months later, he revealed to Charles Peake what might have been his truer aspiration. 'E. said that it was his real ambition in life to become a Duke.'

Yet the general assumption that only a sense of duty had driven Halifax into politics, and that he would rather have lived the life of a country squire, was not believed in every quarter. His critics suspected that Halifax's holiness, like Gandhi's, was a convenient foil for his politics. The prominent editor of the *Daily Herald*, Francis Williams, categorically disputed Halifax's much vaunted deficiency of ambition. 'No man climbs to the top in politics without a liking for power. Such liking was concealed in Halifax's case – possibly even from himself – by an aloofness that appeared incapable of passion . . . It was as though his emotions, like his left arm, had become atrophied.' There was no man more dangerous in politics, Williams went on, 'than the man who is thought to be above them. Halifax came to be such a man.' Chips Channon agreed: 'A more ambitious man never lived.'

Moreover, as his letters to Baba bear out, Halifax *was* capable of passion.

To some observers, Chamberlain possibly among them, Halifax appeared less like Lord Derby and more like Lord Rosebery, who in March 1894 exchanged the Foreign Office for the 'dunghill' of the premiership after displaying Halifax's coquettish habit of declining positions that he had been offered, only then to take them. In this scenario, all that it required for Halifax to say yes to Chamberlain was to have someone he trusted to tell him that it was his plain duty to set aside his personal and private reasons, as his father had done in 1925 when advising him to accept the Viceroyalty ('I think you really have to go'); or else to be courted one further time, as Chamberlain did in 1938. The person who accepted the Foreign Secretaryship 'with the greatest reluctance' was the same man who revealed to Baba Metcalfe that he couldn't help himself, and it was 'the biggest thing to have a shot'; until that day arrived when Halifax was made a Duke, there was no bigger shot than the premiership.

Tellingly, Halifax said to Butler immediately after his conversation with Chamberlain on 9 May that 'he felt he could do the job'. Cadogan went further, admitting later to Lord Killearn that Halifax 'really wanted the job'. This was Eden's opinion too.

A more convincing explanation for Halifax's resistance is suggested in a letter written five days later to Stanley Baldwin by J. C. C. Davidson, former chairman of the Conservative Party. Davidson recalled that Bonar Law had refused to become Prime Minister when Lloyd George formed his first coalition in 1916, 'and I understand that Halifax refused for very much the same reason vis-à-vis Winston. Each would have been overshadowed by the Man of Destiny.' This certainly was Baffy Dugdale's immediate concern on hearing rumours of a Halifax administration with Churchill as War Minister. 'I think he will be more the captive than the master.'

Nine months before, Chamberlain had explained to General Ironside his reluctance to include Churchill in government. Ironside wrote of their conversation: 'He thinks that Winston might be so strong in a Cabinet that he would be prevented from acting.' The Norway Campaign had borne out many of Chamberlain's fears. Only Halifax had the experience and character to challenge Churchill. As Halifax told Rab Butler minutes after his interview with Chamberlain: 'Churchill needed a restraining influence.'

Halifax was one of the few people not overawed by Churchill, ever since marching into his office in March 1921 to say that he had no more wanted to be Under-Secretary to him than Churchill wanted Halifax appointed. Experience had taught Halifax that the best way of dealing with Churchill was to stand up to him. Although too often yielding to Churchill's temperament, Halifax did 'butt into' Churchill's tirades on a regular basis. 'The latter does not really mind, but grunts a bit over his cigar, and is as friendly as ever afterwards.'

They were two people as different in habits as it was possible to be, divided irreversibly by India and Munich, and by their physical, spiritual and mental attributes – Churchill, small, fat, and a massive imbiber, who twice failed to get into Sandhurst; Halifax, lean, towering and abstemious, and a Prize Fellow of All Souls. In Valentine Lawford's phrase, they spoke 'different languages'. For all Churchill's proclaimed respect for Halifax, he viewed him very suspiciously, and vice versa – Halifax protesting in his diary: 'I have seldom met anybody with stranger gaps of knowledge, or whose mind worked in greater jerks.' Diana Holderness says: 'Halifax didn't like Winston, and Winston didn't like him.' Yet as opposites, they had pedalled in tandem surprisingly well, as Baba Metcalfe observed. 'Edward and Winston are a very good combination as they act as a stimulus and brake on each other. The former is able to check the times when Winston desires to stampede into action.'

Rab Butler had waited in Halifax's room at the Foreign Office to hear about the meeting with Chamberlain. After Halifax came back up in the lift, he told

Butler that the issue boiled down to this: 'Could that restraint be better exercised as Prime Minister, or as a Minister in Churchill's Government?' Even if Halifax chose the first role, Churchill's qualities and experience 'would surely mean that he would be "running the war anyway" and Halifax's own position would speedily turn into a sort of honorary Prime Minister'.

Halifax's opinion remained remarkably constant. He may have wanted to be Prime Minister, but not this sort of Prime Minister, and not at this moment, with Churchill breathing down his neck. Halifax had admitted on 2 May that he was no military strategist, and not competent to say whether Trondheim should have been attacked; he was a 'layman' in all things military, he later told Peake. He very probably realised that he himself did not have the qualities of a Prime Minister conducting a war in such grim circumstances; and if he did so reason, he was correct, says David Dilks, 'for, while quick in the uptake, he was slow to make up his mind about big issues, and frequently referred to the fact'. Alexander Cadogan saw Halifax every day and was never convinced of his boss's suitability. 'I think he is not the stuff of which a P.M. is made in such a crisis.'

On the other hand, Halifax recognised the value, militarily, of Churchill's energy and belligerence. Back in February, Halifax had predicted that a Churchill premiership would arise only if the war was going badly, 'and he would in those circumstances be exactly what the nation needed'. It was Halifax's 'cool altruism', wrote another of his biographers, which made him decide that he was not the man for this hour, and why he felt, as he told Butler, 'W. had better run it all'. In this respect, too, he was like Lord Curzon, of whom Curzon's daughter Irene wrote: 'My father put his duty to his country and his Party before all petty personal disappointment.'

Briskly, Halifax explained his decision in the letter that he wrote to Baba Metcalfe four days later. 'I simply don't think it would have been at all a tolerable position for me to get into.' As for why not, there were, he insisted, 'many reasons' which enticingly he promised to 'go into' when they next met. 'When will that be? I hope soon. Let me know.'

Probably the greatest power that Halifax ever exercised was to rule himself out. Umpteen arguments can be advanced to explain his refusal. His peerage; his emotional entanglement with Curzon's youngest daughter; his innate aversion to 'unnecessary activity'; his genuine conviction that

Churchill would be a better leader at this dangerous time; his pragmatic calculation that if Churchill failed quickly, as the Norway Campaign suggested was likely, and as Halifax may ultimately have believed, then Churchill could be swept clean away, leaving Halifax sole heir. ('I don't think WSC will be a very good P.M.,' he wrote to Baba in the same letter, 'though I think the country will think he gives them a fillip.') All of these considerations in varying degrees played their part in Halifax's reckoning. But perhaps the most convincing proof of his reluctance was his stomach ache.

In April 1916 in Ypres, Chamberlain's cousin Norman had felt a sinking in the stomach which caused him to understand the expressions 'having cold feet' and 'having no stomach for a fight'. He wrote: 'My poor tummy did feel as if it had retired and got the most awful indigestion for a time! I never realised the real literal connection of such slang before!'

The same sort of physical manifestation appears to have afflicted Halifax towards the end of his Thursday-morning meeting with Chamberlain. 'The conversation and the evident drift of his mind left me with a bad stomach ache.'

Halifax wound up their talk by repeating that if Labour said they would only serve under him, as he knew now from Butler was their position, then he would tell them that he was still not prepared to do it, 'and see whether a definite attitude would make them budge. If it failed we should all, no doubt, have to boil our broth again.'

With the obduracy of the planter who is damned if his crop won't grow, Chamberlain left it open for Halifax to change his mind, to re-boil the broth as it were. He told Halifax that 'he would like to go over the ground again' in the afternoon with 'Winston and me together'. Obedient to his stubborn nature and to his occult faith in 'the Chamberlain touch', the Prime Minister had not accepted Halifax's position. When the meeting ended at 11 a.m., there was still lodged in a corner of Chamberlain's head the possibility that all it needed was one more push, one more appeal to Halifax's sense of civic duty. Chamberlain held fast to this belief for the rest of that day, though only to close advisers like Kingsley Wood and John Simon did he confide these thoughts. When Chamberlain saw Simon at 4 p.m., he maintained that his inclinations 'were to resign and advise the King to send for Halifax'.

20
THE LIMPET

'Politics are an uncertain career. A man who one year is hailed as the epitome of all that is best in England or even as the saviour of the country, may be execrated the next as an example of lethargy or surrender. But that is our system.'

VISCOUNT MERSEY, 9 May 1940

'The sooner some of these damned Labour people are made to join the Cabinet the better it will be.'

CUTHBERT HEADLAM MP, 5 May 1940

Even as he coaxed Halifax into his shoes, Chamberlain was laying separate plans for a coalition with Labour. Since 3 September he had made two unsuccessful overtures to the opposition, whose official view until 8 May had been 'complete non-cooperation'. He now reached out a third time, and requested that Clement Attlee and his tall, bibulous deputy Arthur Greenwood 'come into the administration and take their share of responsibility for the war'.

Chamberlain was on the telephone to the Labour leaders when, early on 9 May, the King's Private Secretary rang No. 10 anxious to know the Prime Minister's position following the division, and spoke to David Margesson. The Chief Whip had been analysing the votes: 481 MPs had voted out of 615, with 41 of its supporters voting against the government, including 33 Conservatives, of whom nearly half were in uniform. 88 Conservatives had not voted; of these, up to 60 were deliberate abstentions.*

Parliament's protest would not be ignored, Margesson assured Hardinge.

---

* Margesson kept no diary, and records were destroyed in the incendiary bomb of 10 May 1941, so that the extent of the vote against Chamberlain is still unclear and often exaggerated. The figures vary widely, from 60 Conservative abstentions, to 36 (Rasmussen), to as low as 20 (Smart).

All were agreed that 'the Government would have to be constructed on a broader basis'. To this end, Chamberlain was even now contacting the opposition parties, and proposing a fundamental reshuffle to include the dismissal of his most unpopular Ministers. According to Labour's foreign affairs spokesman Hugh Dalton, Chamberlain 'was telephoning personally from 8 a.m. that morning, trying to conciliate opponents of yesterday. He seemed determined himself to stick on – "like a dirty old piece of chewing gum on the leg of a chair" one Tory rebel said to me. He was offering to sacrifice Simon or Hoare, or even Kingsley Wood, if that would propitiate the critics.'

Chewing gum was not the most insulting epithet used to describe Chamberlain's adhesive behaviour over the next thirty-six hours. Dalton likened the Prime Minister to an old limpet, 'always trying new tricks to keep himself firm upon the rock'.* To Ellen Wilkinson, he clung to office like 'an old widow in a boarding-house, jabbing at critics with knitting needles'. Brendan Bracken had long recognised his tenacious grip. 'To me Chamberlain appears a tough old gentleman who will fight with all his might against any "real national government" in which he will not hold the first place.'

Chamberlain's manoeuvres can be seen in the context of his overnight change of heart. He had gone to bed having made up his mind to resign. Yet to resign was to ignore one of the most vital lessons of his upbringing: 'Remember,' his dominating father would say, 'never withdraw.' On Andros more than forty years before, a sense of despair had assailed Chamberlain after the failure of his first crop – before the strict reminder came from Birmingham that his family motto was *Je Tiens Ferme*. Early on 9 May, a transformation like the one in his thatched hut on Mastic Point seems to have taken place in the Prime Minister's bedroom at the top of No. 10. Almost from the moment that Chamberlain woke, Dunglass recalled, he 'fought like a tiger to keep power'.

---

* The limpet comparison was applied as well to Labour's deputy leader Arthur Greenwood, who reminded Kingsley Wood of the Slipper Limpet. 'It has a great capacity for repeated functional changes. When it becomes attached to a shell of a more mature and stabler species, it passes through the most robust and vigorous state of its existence. When it leaves the shell . . . it reverts and becomes one of the weaker and less dependable animals.'

Chamberlain had slept on Churchill's reassurance of the night before that the division was not fatal. Chips Channon was another who believed this. 'I think, with a majority of 81, Neville could still make minor changes and remain.' Chamberlain's sister Ida added her uncritical support. 'The only comment I have heard on the debate so far was a Mr Beckett recently come to Odiham who meeting Hilda in the Post Office hurried up to congratulate her on the result of the debate! So he at any rate considers the Govt. had a triumph.' In short, there is evidence that Chamberlain was tempted by the siren chorus of Churchill, Channon, Colville, the example of 'the good British public' like Mr Beckett, and the voices of the party faithful. And what he concluded after listening to their seductive message was that the prospects of restoring confidence in his administration were not so negligible as Halifax believed.

Another motive for fighting on was to keep the government's reins away from Churchill, whose conduct in the Norway Campaign had stirred up fresh worries about how he might behave were he 'loose'. From first light on that Thursday morning, Chamberlain was bombarded with letters urging him to stay put for this very reason. Lord Hankey wrote a handwritten plea from the Treasury Chambers. 'You are the only man who can hold Winston, who is amazingly valuable, but whose judgement is not 100% reliable. You are also the most resourceful member of the Cabinet, bar none.' The chairman of the 1922 Committee, Sir Patrick Spens, wrote to say that Chamberlain alone had the confidence of the great mass of moderate Conservative opinion, and his removal from office would lead within weeks to 'a grand National disaster' – i.e. Churchill – a sentiment with which Sir Auckland Geddes, Commissioner of Civil Defence for the South-West Region, was in total concurrence. 'So far I have met no one in the Region who would like to see Winston Prime Minister.' A letter even more flattering came from Sir Robert Gower, MP for Cheltenham. 'There is no member here who is more in touch with his fellow backbenchers than I am, and I can assure you that you have personally the fullest confidence and the great affection of almost without exception the whole of your Party colleagues in the House, including the large majority of those who voted in the Opposition Lobby last night.'

If the feeling at the Beefsteak, where Harold Nicolson had lunch, was unanimous 'that Chamberlain must go', then opinion within Downing Street tugged in the opposite direction. Back in the saddle, Chamberlain told his sisters that he was inclined to take his guidance from those letters he had received from MPs who 'had nothing against me except that I had the wrong people in my team'. A telegram from his chief agent in Sheffield spurred him in his new resolve: 'SHEFFIELD STRONG FOR CHAMBERLAIN NO RESIGNATION OR PANDERING TO SOCIALIST FAILURES AND CONSERVATIVE NITWITS'.

The most poignant request for Chamberlain to stay on and fight was a letter from a Sidmouth auctioneer whose nineteen-year-old pilot son had died over the North Sea during the early stages of the Norway Campaign. The auctioneer had observed 'with utmost detestation' the attacks made on Chamberlain. 'Our boy went out to meet his end, I believe, with unflinching courage. You, I know, will meet and destroy all attacks made upon you with the same high spirit and the like noble object in mind.' No appeal seemed more calculated to arouse Chamberlain's renewed sense of patriotic duty, vanity, and determination not to roll over and die.

Chewing gum, limpet, old lady, tiger. Chamberlain's manipulations on 9 May more resembled one of the writhing native octopuses which as a young plantation owner he had landed on the deck of the *Pride*. By mid-morning, his tentacles had uncoiled in every direction, to independent and contradictory ends. With one tentacle, Chamberlain wrapped his suckers around Halifax to take over should he resign. Still hoping that he might not have to resign, Chamberlain put out feelers to bring in Attlee and Greenwood. He would extend another tentacle to loyalist MPs like Herbert Williams and Victor Cazalet, reassuring them of his radical plans to reconstruct the Cabinet along purely Conservative lines.

There were also reports that Chamberlain had thrashed out, humiliatingly, to reel in Leo Amery and his dissidents.

Many of the records of these days of tumult are deeply unreliable. A prime example is Ivan Maisky's account of the Prime Minister's overture to Amery. 'At nine in the morning, Chamberlain summoned Amery and told him that he thought a serious government reshuffle was in order. Measures should be taken, however, to prevent Labour from coming to power. The government must remain in Tory hands. The Prime Minister went on to offer Amery any portfolio he wanted (except the P.M.'s), including those of Chancellor of the Exchequer or Foreign Secretary.'

The notion that Chamberlain was peddling Halifax's job one hour before he summoned Halifax to vet him for the premiership strains the imagination, even if Maisky's account was corroborated by Dalton who had heard it from Macmillan. In a slightly different version, the not always trustworthy A. L. Rowse claimed that Amery did not meet Chamberlain face to face, but received a personal telephone call. 'A fact that Amery himself told me . . . is that the morning after the debate Chamberlain rang him up, expressing regret that no place had been found for him hitherto, would he now join the government.' It would have been their first communication since the debate. Yet it is quite incredible that the graphomanic Amery would not record such an approach. The sole mention in his diaries is a second-hand rumour emanating from the Cabinet Office that Horace Wilson 'was proposing . . . that Neville should offer me some office'. Amery dismissed this as 'truly typical of the Horace Wilson methods,' and there is no further evidence that Amery and Wilson met, or even spoke. At any rate, Amery 'categorically refused the offer' according to Maisky.

Rumours that Amery might have gone to see Chamberlain fed into a much wilder scenario that echoed Greenwood's description of the House on the outbreak of war. 'If someone had come along and told me "Jo Stalin has gone to Rome and is kissing the Pope's toe", I should have believed him!' On 9 May, the tension and suspense reached the same pitch of frenzy. When the Cabinet met at 11.45 a.m. in the Commons, a peevish Alexander Cadogan wrote that 'the air was full of rumours of impending resignations' and 'we had to wait about, as that blasted H of C was sitting and wrangling and intriguing'.

In this hectic atmosphere, charged with plots and counter-plots, there was talk that a third candidate would be the solution.

His speech telling the Prime Minister to go had suddenly made Leo Amery a credible successor in one or two people's minds. He was not tarred with the Munich brush. His record was even cleaner than Churchill's, having been out of office since 1929. He was one of few contemporaries whom

Churchill could not browbeat; and he had a reputation for honesty. Amery had long regarded himself as a potential leader. As S. J. D. Green has summarised it, for a few hours on 9 May 'anything – even this strange outcome – seemed plausible'.

Amery's ambition for the top job reached back to his first day in the House in 1911. His hopes had recently mounted as the editor of *The Times* grew more critical of the government. When in January Dawson alluded to the untapped skills of 'ex-ministers', Amery had no doubt that his All Souls comrade 'was referring to me'. (He was not.) Then, on the morning after his speech on 7 May, Amery's name appeared in the *Daily Herald* as someone who 'according to some prophets may be in the next reconstituted Government'. Twenty-four hours later, when Leslie Hore-Belisha took a self-interested look at the ferment in the Commons, he concluded that 'the turn of the wheel' might bring none other than Leo Amery 'into Downing Street'.

Amery was a man of extraordinary abilities and courage, but frequently a nightmare to deal with. It is scarcely conceivable that Churchill, Halifax and Eden would have wished to serve under him. On that particular Thursday, however, Hore-Belisha divined that all certain bets were off.

At 9.30 a.m. Amery attended a meeting of the Watching Committee in Arlington Street. There was general agreement even among those who at the last minute had voted with the government that Chamberlain must resign, along with Simon, Hoare and Wood, and that either Halifax or Churchill should form a National coalition. A 'distressed' Lord Salisbury was deputed to convey the Committee's resolution to the Foreign Secretary, who remained their favoured candidate.

Amery then went down to the House to attend the formal adjournment motion for the Whitsun recess. He had hardly arrived when a short man approached in grey felt-topped boots and smoking a cigarette. Hore-Belisha had come that morning from his farm in Wimbledon, leaving his two dogs behind. He needed, he said, to talk with Amery.

A publicity-conscious politician remembered for his orange traffic beacons when Minister of Transport, Hore-Belisha was as ambitious politically as he was socially. Halifax's Private Secretary Valentine Lawford had watched him at a party in the Paris Embassy after Hore-Belisha had been promoted to the War Office. 'What a grotesque person ... the laughing stock of all the young women of Paris, as he goes around paying them flowery compliments and giving them expensive presents. I think his aim is to marry someone very <u>chic</u> but so far none of the girls will have him.' Baba Metcalfe had had to warn her sister Irene, one of those courted by him, that Hore-Belisha wanted to marry a baroness (which Irene was), and had asked whether 'if he married a baroness he would become a baron!' Hore-Belisha – who modelled himself on Disraeli and kept a bust of Napoleon in his room – carried the same unrealistic notions into his politics. Up until 4 January, he had considered himself to be a 'national hero' who was 'in a wonderful position heading straight for the Premiership'. His self-belief was expressed in language similar to Amery's. 'My position is good, I have my public, and if trouble comes and there is use for me, I shall be there.' After being dismissed from his Ministry, following pressure from the War Office and the King, and having refused the offer of the Presidency of the Board of Trade, Hore-Belisha groused to Chamberlain: 'Is there any MP who doesn't want to be Prime Minister? Is there any waiter who doesn't want to be a head waiter?' Four months later and still aggrieved, Hore-Belisha prepared to marshal his forces behind Amery.

The former War Minister told Amery that he was the leader they needed. What was more, Max Beaverbrook agreed – the two men had been discussing it at breakfast. They had decided that what was wanted was 'a clean sweep eliminating the old Conservative gang as far as possible', and that the best way of emphasising this was that Amery should be Prime Minister 'as the man who had turned out the Government and also as best qualified all round'.

Hore-Belisha proposed to lobby discreetly on Amery's behalf.

Amery suspected Hore-Belisha's motive for fomenting a pro-Amery movement. 'He no doubt started it in the hope that it might bring him back again as a reward for helping.' But Amery was flattered too. His congested reaction mimicked Halifax's. 'This was rather sudden and I discouraged the idea, at any rate as long as there was a chance of Winston or Edward accepting.'

Still, it was impossible not to be tantalised by the thought that his name was being canvassed – and by Lord Beaverbrook, 'that mercurial, irresponsible and not infrequently evil man', as David Dilks says of him. Amery had sought out Beaverbrook on 1 May, going to see him in his capacity as a kingmaker. The possibility that the press baron might now throw his weight behind Amery could not be set aside so casually.

When Amery looked very steadily at himself, he saw a sixty-seven-year-old mountaineer who felt unnecessarily fat, with a touch of rheumatism in the left shoulder, a little grey about the temples, and too weak to pull himself up by the fingertips. Was this the face of a man fit for leadership? Did Amery see flashing across his mind the swimming pond at Harrow, the empty tent in Natal? Had the moment arrived, finally, for him to reassert his primacy over Churchill?

The first thing Amery had to consider was the attitude of the Labour leaders. He was shrewd enough to recognise that any Prime Minister's future lay in the hands of Attlee and Greenwood. What was their position? It took no time at all to discover that they, too, as it happened, were in favour of an Amery premiership.

'Curiously enough Clem Davies just a few minutes later told me that he had been talking with some of the Labour Front Bench, who had suggested to him that the Tory whom they would soonest serve under would be myself.' One of the two Labour leaders that Davies had spoken to was the exuberant Arthur Greenwood.

'Of course, the idea was not serious enough to be worth considering,' repeated Amery. Yet he could not stop considering it. 'At the same time it is interesting to find oneself after ten years of backwater suddenly regarded as at any rate worth talking about as a possible.'

After a further encouraging conversation – with the Liberal leader Archie Sinclair – Amery mulled over why, actually, the idea of an Amery premiership ought to be discouraged. It was not because he lacked confidence in himself, 'for, like Churchill, "I thought I knew a good deal about it all"'. He was well qualified, 'both by experience and study of war'. On the minus side, Amery was not so well known as Churchill, and he worried that he would not be acceptable to the bulk of the party after his attack on Chamberlain.

All these considerations were swirling through Amery's mind when at 3 p.m. he chaired a meeting of what *The Times* called his 'malcontents'. Once again he resisted the calls of Boothby, Macmillan and Davies to come out for Churchill. 'I got them to agree we would support any P.M. who would form a truly National Government appointing its men by merit and not on Whips' lines ... The personal issue I carefully kept out of the picture in order to avoid waste of time discussing alternatives.'

In his speech in the Norway Debate and in each of the dissident meetings he had chaired, Amery had taken care not to make any recommendation as to who should replace Chamberlain. His continuing refusal to discuss personalities left the door open for a third contender: the Conservative Member for Birmingham Sparkbrook, Leo Maurice Amery. Had Amery decided at that moment to become a candidate, Hore-Belisha wrote to him afterwards, 'you would have stood out and had my support'.

Hore-Belisha attended Amery's crowded meeting in Committee Room 8, and he came up afterwards to say that in spite of Amery discouraging him he had sounded out Duff Cooper and one or two others 'who were quite prepared to back his idea'. In contrast to Amery, Churchill was generally regarded as a 'washout' who was lacking in energy, and in Cabinet 'not the man he was or is supposed to be'.

The time had come for the President of the Alpine Club to decide if he was the Man of Destiny that for thirty years he had chafed to be.

When in 1929 Leo Amery made the first ascent of Mount Amery, the peak that the Geographical Board of Canada had named after him, atrocious weather prevented him from seeing where he was, 'and I was worried we weren't quite on top'. Eleven years later, at what turned out to be the summit of his political achievement, Amery once again saw no clear route ahead. When the chance came to stake his claim, he was rigid in maintaining his previous self-denying position. He told Hore-Belisha that he had no doubt 'that the matter would be dealt with in the Inner Circle and that it lay between Halifax and Winston'.

21

A GREAT TIDE FLOWING

'Who would have believed seven years ago that Winston Churchill had any kind of
political future before him?'

GEORGE ORWELL, 8 June 1940

Colonel Bertram Romilly was buried on the afternoon of 9 May in the churchyard of St Thomas à Becket outside the village of Huntington. With Clementine away at the funeral, there was no one to screen visitors to Churchill's top-floor quarters at Admiralty House. Throughout that Thursday, the First Lord received a stream of callers, including one or two that his wife might have chosen to shield him against had she remained in London.

The first person to knock on his door was Anthony Eden, whom Churchill telephoned at 9.30 a.m. and asked to come at once to the Admiralty. Valentine Lawford later worked for Eden, and left a description of the then Dominions Secretary who turned up to see Churchill that morning in a light grey suit, vivid tie, and a black felt homburg that was as inseparable a part of Eden's persona as Chamberlain's umbrella and Churchill's 'seldom-lit' cigar. Known as 'Draughty Mouth' by Halifax and Baba Metcalfe, and by Lord Haw-Haw as 'handsome Anthony', few Ministers, wrote Lawford, matched Eden's physical presence. 'Eden moved always with the fluent ease of a river between its banks, almost with a suggestion of bravura.' His appearance went far to realise his ambition. 'Eden's fine eyes, with their fringes of dark lashes, his regular head, handsome hair and well-knit body, caused many to admire and some to envy him for such unashamed good looks.' Maisky was less swayed, and suggested that a jelly-fish might be in possession of a greater backbone. 'Eden is not made of iron, but rather of soft clay, which yields easily to the fingers of a skilful artisan.' Even so, Chips Channon strongly suspected his designs. 'Eden is on the fringe and is watching and waiting his chance.'

While shaving, Churchill told Eden about his midnight conversation with Chamberlain: how he had advised the Prime Minister to fight on and not seek help from Attlee and Greenwood. Churchill predicted 'that Neville would not be able to bring in Labour & that a national Government must be formed.' In the event that Halifax ruled himself out, Churchill, peering one precautious step ahead, had begun to build a Cabinet in his mind. That was why he had sent for Eden. On that Thursday, Churchill breakfasted, lunched and dined with Eden, and at the end of the day he told Eden that he wished him 'to take War'.

Churchill's next visitor was Beaverbrook, nicknamed 'the Toad' by Baba Metcalfe and Halifax, a man Clementine despised, once writing to her husband: 'My darling – Try ridding yourself of this microbe which some people fear is in your blood – Exorcise this bottle Imp & see if the air is not clearer & purer.' In an undated note which described a meeting unrecorded in his appointments book, Beaverbrook wrote: 'I saw Churchill in the morning of May 9th 1940. I asked – do you intend to serve under Halifax. He answered – I will serve under any Minister capable of prosecuting the War.' His answer allegedly disappointed Beaverbrook, but Churchill appeared immoveable in his loyalty. 'He would not stake his own claim.'

Moments after Beaverbrook left the Admiralty – he would be back twice the following day – another of Clementine's bêtes noires arrived, Brendan Bracken, whom she regarded as an 'outlandish and potentially malign influence' on her husband. Possibly at this meeting, if not in a previous conversation in the early hours, Bracken made his celebrated recommendation to Churchill not to answer should Chamberlain summon him to No. 10 to ask if he would consent to serve under Halifax. After 'much argument', apparently, Churchill promised to remain silent. They then discussed a theoretical Churchill Cabinet. On an envelope under the heading 'Humble suggestions', Bracken wrote out the names of Chamberlain, Attlee, Wood, Halifax and Lloyd George, but not, interestingly, Eden.

Churchill's recall of these hours was conveniently porous. 'I do not remember exactly how things happened during the morning of May 9.' Yet rather than helplessly letting 'events unfold', as he maintained in *The Gathering Storm*, Churchill played a more active role in exploiting Chamberlain's vulnerability than he was prepared to admit in his memoirs. At the 'very summit' of the crisis, he could be observed in the Commons smoking room, 'waving a gigantic cigar, sipping his ginger ale, and reducing two Labour back-benchers to delighted paroxysms of laughter'. He had cause to be cheerful. By midday, Churchill had detected the same reversal in the currents bearing Halifax to power as had Violet Bonham Carter, who wrote him a note of support. 'There is a great tide flowing which you can direct.' That Churchill was doing so already is suggested by a remark that he is reported to have made to Clement Davies before attending the 11.45 a.m. War Cabinet in Chamberlain's room at the Commons. Churchill spotted Davies, who was preparing to move an amendment against the adjournment motion, and he crossed the floor of the House and said to him: 'It can only be a question of hours and I have taken the necessary dispositions.'

Meanwhile, events were unfolding across the Channel. The Chiefs of Staff were now apprehensive of 'a general attack in the near future', though the head of Intelligence downplayed the overnight rumours, which had since proved false, about German paratroopers having seized Rotterdam: he advanced Hungary as Hitler's likeliest next target. Churchill reassured the War Cabinet that should Germany invade Holland, then the Royal Navy was ready, and he described the naval movements which he had ordered.

Still the Cabinet's 'heavy business' on 9 May concerned Norway. Churchill confirmed that Colonel Gubbins had landed at midnight at Mosjöen with two Commando groups armed with explosives, and with orders to blow up bridges and defiles north of Namsos. And he obtained Cabinet consent to warn local authorities in Britain about 'the type of danger to be expected' following the failure of the military expedition.

The flattened towns of Åndalsnes, Namsos and Steinkjer were graphic reminders of the fate that awaited English villages and homes if Hitler – 'that drivelling Corporal' – was not stopped there and then. For Churchill, the key to Hitler's defeat lay, as it had since September, in Narvik.

Stiff bombing had again postponed Allied plans to seize the ore-town. Ironside wrote in his diary: 'Narvik goes none too well. Cork has wired that all the military officers have advised against a direct landing.' Despite the Norwegian Defence Minister's promise of a functioning runway, Admiral Cork had visited the local air strip and reported that it could not be used for nine days, being under a foot of ice 'of iron consistency' that 'would need a lot of men to shift'. Four of the eight A.A. guns which had reached Cork on 6 May would not be ready for three more days 'on account of bad roads'. Cork was desperate for Hurricanes, 'as these were the only aircraft capable of dealing with Heinkels'. There was no disguising the shambles, which Cork would not be allowed to write about in his memoirs, and so condensed into a single line. 'I formed the opinion that the position in Norway had never been really understood.'

The War Cabinet over, Churchill returned to the Admiralty. In contrast to the frozen gridlock in Narvik, Westminster was in full spate. That the tide might be flowing at last in Churchill's direction was confirmed by a member of Chamberlain's innermost court who arrived early for lunch bearing news of the strictest confidentiality from inside No. 10.

Kingsley Wood was the spruce, plump solicitor son of a Wesleyan minister from Hull. He was short, bespectacled, with a squeaky voice, and a bland, cherubic smile that misled others into underestimating his ambitions. An owl. An elderly choirboy. 'A chicken-hearted little mutton-head.' Not one other Minister saw in Wood the potential to be a national leader – save for Neville Chamberlain.

Lord Privy Seal since 2 April, the former Air Minister was known to be 'Chamberlain's man', with his colours pinned visibly to the Prime Minister's mast. For sixteen years, Wood had endlessly jumped up and down whenever he saw his master, whose Parliamentary Private Secretary he had been, performing the same service of obsequious adulation and unquestioning loyalty as Bracken performed for Churchill – it was Wood who had visited Chamberlain on 26 April to warn him of the threat posed by his disaffected First Lord. Wood walked in St James's Park with Chamberlain most mornings, and there was little on which the Prime Minister did not feel able to consult him. As Churchill saw it: 'They had long worked together in complete confidence.' When judging Wood's value to the Prime Minister, Chamberlain's biographer Derek Walker-Smith wrote that Kingsley

Wood had 'the qualities of accessibility and bonhomie to a degree which Mr Chamberlain never possesses'. Chamberlain rewarded him with the Air Ministry and, as previously mentioned, told Chips Channon shortly after the outbreak of war that he intended to make Wood the next Prime Minister; Halifax would only be 'a stop-gap'.

Then, in January, Wood's unswerving loyalty to Chamberlain suffered a jolt when Hore-Belisha was fired. A shocked Wood had dashed after him, saying in his high-pitched voice: 'What strikes me is if this can happen to you it can happen to me.' Hore-Belisha's reply: 'Precisely, Kingsley, that is the right philosophy.'

Although a wizard at memos, 'colourful Kingsley Wood', as Evelyn Waugh crushingly called him in *Scoop*, was soon out of his depth as Air Minister – just as Churchill predicted he would be: he 'does not know a Lieutenant General from a Whitehead torpedo'. A politician whose favourite subjects were insurance and housing, it had been Wood's idea to bombard Germany with up to twelve million leaflets – which were full of spelling mistakes and printed in an obsolete Gothic type.* The failure of these 'truth raids', as Wood called them, was piled at his door. So, too, was the 'awful' rate of air production. At the end of April an overworked Wood confessed to John Reith that there was a demand for his dismissal on the grounds of 'general incompetence'.

Cadogan met Wood on 2 May, the day that Chamberlain announced the evacuation from Namsos, and observed that 'he has the air, now, of a dog that has stolen the ham off the sideboard'. On the same day, unknown to Cadogan, Wood had a lunch meeting alone with Churchill, having also lunched with him (as Clementine wrote in her appointments book) on 24 and 26 April. According to Violet Bonham Carter, Wood was 'one of those who before the change of Govt. used to come to W. to say he thought things "cldn't go on like this"'. This may explain Wood's inclusion on Bracken's list of Churchill's future Ministers.

In the hours after the Norway Debate, *Times* journalist Colin Coote formed the clear impression that Kingsley Wood was moving away from

---

* When one bundle failed to open, containing extracts from Chamberlain's speeches, a German civilian whom it hit was reported killed, the first victim of British aerial bombardment.

adulation of his former idol. 'He was an extremely barometrical politician.' In 1925, Coote had written of him: *'Kingsley could/If he would/But if he shouldn't/Kingsley wouldn't.'* Before the division, Wood was one of those who were convinced that Chamberlain would have to resign unless he had a majority of 100. The government's slenderer figure of 81 prepared the way for Wood's next move. On the morning of 9 May, Wood learned, probably from a distraught Sam Hoare, that Chamberlain was busily offering Wood's head on a crowded platter to Attlee and Greenwood. Recalling Hore-Belisha's peremptory dismissal, and recognising that power was fast draining away from Chamberlain, Wood decided to jump ship, or, in Leo Amery's image from the Boer War, change donkeys mid-stream.

When Wood arrived at the Admiralty on 9 May he carried with him a speech that he was due to deliver that afternoon on the latest methods of preserving food. Wood's keenness to safeguard his own position was evident from his self-invitation to lunch. Violet Bonham Carter wrote: 'I can't help suspecting that the old boy was feathering his future nest.'

Wood had seen the Prime Minister early that morning. He was in the act of passing on to Churchill everything that Chamberlain had told him in confidence when Anthony Eden arrived to join them for lunch.

Eden was a little 'surprised' to see Wood there, knowing him to be in the Prime Minister's camp, and when Eden was surprised, noted Maisky, he would make a startled comic gesture 'as if he were fending off a ghost that had suddenly appeared before him'. It further amazed Eden when Wood repeated what he had moments before told Churchill – 'that Neville had decided to go'. The future was then discussed. Wood made it clear where his loyalties now lay: he thought that Churchill should take over rather than Halifax. However, Wood warned that this was not the Prime Minister's intention. 'Chamberlain would want Halifax to succeed him and would want Churchill to agree.' His next remark betrayed that he might have conferred with Bracken. He advised Churchill in a conspiratorial falsetto: 'Don't agree, and don't say anything.' And something else. Churchill needed to 'make plain his willingness' to become Prime Minister.

Up until this point, Eden had thought of Kingsley Wood as a genial Pickwickian loyalist, a nonentity who with modest success had run the Post Office and telephone exchange. He did not know if he was flabbergasted more by Wood's betrayal, or by his pragmatism. 'I was shocked that Wood should talk in this way, for he had been so much Chamberlain's man, but it was good counsel and I seconded it.'

No story is more revealing of the machinations and rumours which punctuated Thursday 9 May than Wood's later counter-claim that Chamberlain did not want Halifax to succeed him; rather, that Chamberlain had long preferred Churchill to be his heir, yet did not wish this to be broadcast. Wood made his fantastic assertion in an interview with Beaverbrook, the only authority for the story. Wood apparently said to Beaverbrook: 'Quite soon after the start of the war, Chamberlain himself told me he would have to give way to Churchill. He never intended that Halifax should be Prime Minister, he always intended Churchill to be his successor ... I started negotiations with Churchill which resulted in the change.' Exactly what motivated Wood to say this is unclear, unless to recast himself in a less Iago-ish light following Chamberlain's death. Historians have taken Wood's words to suggest that Chamberlain contemplated the 'possibility of another Premiership after the war', as Chamberlain wrote in his diary on 9 September 1940. In this scenario, Churchill and not Halifax would have made the better stopgap in May, being older than Halifax and not popular with Conservative MPs. Such an interpretation defies the evidence of Chamberlain's known preference for Halifax which he expressed to his sisters. It also contradicts Wood's statement at lunch that Chamberlain wanted Halifax.

Wood died in 1943. Interviewed in 1967, Horace Wilson pooh-poohed the idea that Wood had negotiated with Churchill on Chamberlain's behalf. What Wilson did clearly recall, however, was that Chamberlain was 'misled' by Wood in the last months of his premiership. 'I didn't realise how far Kingsley Wood had gone in his association with the Opposition. He didn't warn Chamberlain.'

The division the night before had not marked the official end of the Norway Debate, which resumed at 12.17 p.m. on Thursday, but this time the vehicle was the motion that the House should adjourn that day until 21 May.

Clement Davies, one of the architects of Wednesday's rebellion, spoke first. He challenged the motion for the Whitsuntide adjournment, arguing that Parliament must reconvene the following Tuesday, 14 May. His amendment was supported by Bob Boothby, who said that the events of 8 May proved that the government as it was presently constituted did not possess the confidence of the House and country. But the amendment was not pressed after Margesson gave an undertaking that the House would be summoned earlier should the situation demand it.

The last words that Neville Chamberlain spoke in the Commons as Prime Minister were in response to Attlee's hope that when the House next met on 21 May there would be a debate on the economic war which Chamberlain had made his priority, and which the Norway Campaign had rendered vastly more difficult. Chamberlain's equivocating answer reflected the uncertainty of his position. 'We have no desire unduly to restrict the scope of the Debate, and I will consider the suggestion of my Hon Friend.' With that, he left the Chamber.

The speech of the afternoon was made by Richard Law who said that the lesson to be learned from the past three days was that if you sat on the safety valve long enough the boiler would blow up.

At 3.49 p.m. the House adjourned till 21 May. Afterwards, the Liberal MP Henry Morris-Jones, who had spoken in support of Davies, had tea with Lloyd George and his daughter Megan. 'General opinion that Neville will either have to go or drastically reorganise.'

The success of Chamberlain's attempts to reorganise his government can be measured by the alterations in his mood through the day.

The Prime Minister had entered the Chamber 'calmly', wrote Chips Channon, who had a talk with him behind the Speaker's Chair. 'He was geniality itself and did not even look tired.' Encouraging news had come from one of his feelers to the opposition, Sir Patrick Hannon, about the proposal to drop Simon and Hoare. 'So far as I can gather from Attlee, Greenwood and Sinclair they are prepared to serve under you if the two statesmen . . . will be eliminated.'

By mid-morning, though, the opposition leaders were changing tack.

Despatched by Dunglass to sound out Labour's attitude, Chips Channon approached Colonel Nathan, Labour MP for Wandsworth. 'At first he thought something might be arranged, but after several conferences he reported the position was hopeless . . . Sadly I passed this information on.'

Shortly after noon, Chamberlain walked down the corridor to his room in the Commons, late, to join the War Cabinet. This time, noticed Cadogan, he looked 'v tired and "effarouché"'. By 3 p.m., when Herbert Williams and three prominent Chamberlain loyalists were ushered into his presence, they had 'a pathetic interview' with a 'terribly shaken' Prime Minister. 'It was as if he had been struck a severe blow, because as we were walking into his room he seemed unable to get out of his chair.' Williams never forgot Chamberlain's harrowed expression. 'Some day I suppose somebody will write the history of the intrigue which pushed out of the premiership one of the ablest administrators who has ever held that office.'

Williams agreed to continue his support if Simon, Hoare and Wood were discarded. Immediately after Williams left, Chamberlain summoned his Chancellor.

Sir John Simon was a shy and awkward man who has been damned time and again, like Hoare, for reasons which do not always stand scrutiny. A lawyer with the face of a worldly prelate, he was known for possessing 'a Rolls Royce mind, without a driver'. Among his weaknesses were: an over-fondness for quoting the Classics; a reluctance to declare his mind (he had sat on the fence so long, said Lloyd George in one of several memorable put-downs which Simon inspired, that the iron had entered his soul); and his longing to be liked. David Dilks says: 'He did not wish to be called "Johnnie", but did enourage friends to address him as "Jack"' – which some of them did, like Uncle Geoffrey. His friendliness alienated because it seemed awkwardly married to his ambition; for example, in his habit of slapping colleagues on the back and calling them by the wrong Christian name, and in possibly suggesting to Chamberlain the line: 'I have friends in this House.' In the lethal phrase of A. L. Rowse, a colleague of Simon's at All Souls along with Amery, Halifax and Dawson: 'Nobody loved him. The more he tried, the less they loved him.' He had recently ranked bottom in a poll as the people's choice for the next leader. Yet not very long before, Maisky had observed how Simon, who was much better liked than this suggests, 'is obsessed with the quite fantastic idea of becoming prime minister'.

Simon arrived eleven minutes after the House adjourned, at 4 p.m. As he wrote in his diary, he was another MP who believed that 'the one indispensable thing was the Prime Minister should remain Prime Minister'.

Intuiting that Chamberlain intended to carry out the promise that he had been making all day – i.e. to sack him – Simon got there first. With a smile on his long narrow face that his enemies likened to a brass plate on a coffin, he proposed that Chamberlain should at once get rid of him and Hoare. 'If that would stop the rot nobody would cheer more loudly than I should. The P.M. said: "That is just like you, John," and I was glad to feel that he was really moved.'

In a grateful outpouring of relief, Chamberlain let go the emotions that had accumulated since the division. He admitted that 'this sort of change' was probably too late anyway and 'that someone else should be Prime Minister', and that he was going to resign and recommend Halifax to the King.

Simon left at 4.15 p.m. Fifteen minutes later, Chamberlain was back in Downing Street to receive Halifax and Churchill.

Clementine Churchill sat beside her sister in the uncomfortable black oak pew. At 4.30 p.m. the funeral of Nellie's husband was drawing to its close. Bertram Romilly had died in his bed at Huntington Park following 'a serious illness borne with great fortitude'. He had been hastened to his grave by the capture of his favourite son in Norway on the opening day of the campaign that Churchill had made his own.

Neither of Romilly's sons attended the service, which had begun at 3 p.m. Esmond was in America. No one knew where Giles was. His absence was noted by a journalist from the *Hereford Times*. 'Mr Giles Romilly, a member of the staff of a London newspaper, is reported as having been taken prisoner by the Germans at Narvik.' Lady Lettice Cotterell, chairman of the local Red Cross, had sent Giles a food parcel, following a piano concert that raised £42 for prisoners of war.

Romilly's coffin, covered with a Union flag and surmounted by his colonel's sword, medals and military cap, had been borne into St Thomas à Becket church by his tenant farmers. His regiment, the Scots Guards, had sent a wreath as well as two pipers who 'played the coffin' from the churchyard gate to the church. A choral service followed. Clementine listened to the former vicar of Kington extol Bertram's skills with a shotgun and rod, and pay tribute to his gallantry.

In a strange mirror, Colonel Romilly had fought in the same arenas as Churchill – the Boer War; Sudan, where he had commanded the Camel Corps against the Nuba tribes; and in France, where he was 'grievously wounded', when a shrapnel shell burst above his head and he received the full force, requiring a metal plate to be inserted into his skull.

His grandson says: 'Thereafter, soldiers and other people, if passing by, would tap the thing for luck!'

Churchill might have borrowed his tight-fitting uniform to go and fight the Germans, but Bertram Romilly had not been so lucky as his brother-in-law, who was another conspicuous absentee from the funeral. Unlike the case for Giles, everyone seated in the small thirteenth-century church knew where Winston Churchill was at that moment.

Even as Prebendary Greene motioned for the bearers to lift up Bertram's coffin and carry it outside to his grave, the First Lord was walking from the Admiralty to the back garden gate at No. 10 to attend a meeting that would alter the war.

22
THE SILENCE

It required the votes of 199 Conservative MPs for Theresa May to become Prime Minister in July 2016. Only three MPs and a peer decided who was to be this country's next leader during a discussion on 9 May 1940 at which no minutes were taken. Few meetings in British political history can have had consequences more far-reaching.

Halifax, the favourite of both Houses of Parliament, Whitehall, Downing Street, Fleet Street and Buckingham Palace, had come from lunch with Baba Metcalfe, at which he told her about his morning's interview with Chamberlain, and how he had put 'all the arguments I could think of against myself'. Afterwards, Baba dropped him off at the Foreign Office for an appointment with Charles Corbin, to reassure the French Ambassador of Admiral Cork's undimmed determination to seize Narvik. Halifax then walked the short distance from his office to No. 10.

Rab Butler was in the Cabinet Room when Halifax entered with Chamberlain, Churchill and the Chief Whip. Churchill banished Butler with a good-humoured and, as it turned out, prescient remark. 'There is no place for you here. Your turn will come later.* You had better go.'

The two outer doors, padded with green baize to exclude noise, had

---

* Butler nearly became leader in 1957 and 1963, the only serious alternative to the man chosen, in the first instance Macmillan, in the second Home.

closed behind them when Hardinge arrived on the King's behalf soon after 4.30 p.m., keen to learn what was going on. He was told by Chamberlain's Principal Private Secretary, the 'sound and sensible' Arthur Rucker, that the four men on the other side were working out what approach should be made to Labour. 'The idea then was that in the event of the Labour Party refusing to serve under Mr Chamberlain, the latter would resign, and, on the King asking his advice, he would recommend Lord Halifax.' The strong expectation of Rucker and the Downing Street staff waiting in the adjacent rooms was that when the double doors opened the Foreign Secretary would emerge as the Prime Minister designate.

What went on inside the Cabinet Room during the afternoon of Thursday 9 May has been debated from the moment that the meeting broke up. When Amery (in 1954/55) and Beaverbrook (in 1960) tried to reassemble the narrative, they discovered that not one of the subsequent accounts of what had happened aligned with another. It drove Amery to conclude 'that diaries are by no means accurate evidence of fact'.

Many questions are still unanswered. Did the Prime Minister urge Halifax to take his place (Peake, Cadogan), and suggest that Churchill would not have Labour's support (Churchill); or did Chamberlain make no distinction as to which of the two men he was prepared to serve under (Halifax)? Did Margesson say that the House of Commons was in favour of Halifax (Beaverbrook, Cadogan) or of Churchill (Peake); or did Margesson make no pronouncement (Halifax)? Was Churchill's historic silence long (Churchill, Peake), short (Killearn), or was there no silence at all (Halifax, Cadogan)? Did the four men sit for the meeting (Halifax, Churchill)? Did they stand (Colville)? Or were there three and not four people present (Churchill)? Was their discussion polite (Halifax, Channon, Cadogan) or was it heated (R. Churchill, Macdonald, Killearn)? Did the crucial part of the conversation occur before the Labour leaders Attlee and Greenwood arrived at 6.15 p.m. (Halifax, Churchill, Peake), or after they had left (Cadogan, Gilbert, Manchester)? When in actual fact did the meeting take place? Churchill puts it a whole day later, at 11 a.m. on Friday 10 May, but no one else agrees with his time (Andrew Roberts opts embracingly for Friday 9 May). Halifax told Amery tersely: 'Winston's chronology is inaccurate.' Churchill's timing was not the only detail awry. Dictated eight years later, his self-dramatising account of the interview is, wrote David Reynolds, 'one of the most misleading passages in *The Gathering Storm* . . . about an event so personal that his Syndicate [of researchers] could not check'.

So familiar is Churchill's version that it pays to begin with an unpublished account. In a private conversation in Washington on 5 June 1941, Halifax gave the following resumé to his Boswell, Charles Peake, who instantly wrote it down. This entry in Peake's diary has never been quoted in full before:

'Neville began by saying that it was clear that the House of Commons & the country wanted a change. He had therefore decided to resign and the question arose, whom should he advise the King to send for. He had thought it out very carefully, had searched his mind, and he had come to the conclusion that the man to succeed him was Edward. Edward had remarkable qualities. The <u>whole</u> country (emphasis on the whole) trusted him, and he hoped that Edward would respond and take over these duties etc etc.

'Edward said a silence then fell wh: he did nothing to break. Then finally David Margesson spoke up and said he was a great admirer of Edward, yes, he thought he could say that no-one admired Edward more than he. Edward had wonderful qualities. Wonderful qualities, & he had so much respect and admiration from so many people. But he felt bound to say that much as he admired Edward he rather thought that at the moment Winston was more the kind of man they were looking for. This meant no disrespect for Edward, but was just an honest opinion etc etc etc.

'Edward then said he joined in at this point to say he could not see why they were having a discussion at all. There could, he thought, be no two opinions, there were certainly not two in the country, that Winston was the only possible successor to Neville. No other choice was possible. From every point of view Winston had fitted himself by his talents, his character, his long experience and his genius to be the chosen leader of a united country. He greatly hoped therefore that the discussion might quickly terminate in order that Winston might receive the seals of office as speedily as possible.

'Winston, he then added, looked up & said, "Edward, Edward, allow me to congratulate you. You have spoken better than I have ever heard you, and you have put the thing in a nutshell. I really think there is nothing more that anyone can add." The matter was resolved accordingly and the meeting terminated.'

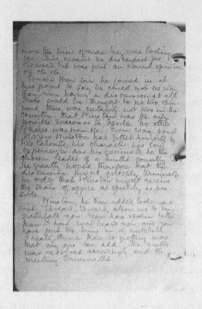

Recorded thirteen months after the event, Peake's version is interesting for several reasons. It is the first to mention any silence – which is broken by Margesson. Chamberlain unambiguously declares his hand for Halifax. Margesson comes down emphatically on the side of Churchill. The matter was resolved to everyone's satisfaction by teatime.

Is this what happened?

Churchill claimed to have been 'neither excited nor alarmed' when he entered the Cabinet Room. Yet the meeting took place only three days after he had suffered a spasm of fear in the same room, and accused Halifax of high treason. To Chips Channon, briefed by Chamberlain after the meeting, the discussion seemed to have been conducted in a spirit of strange and intense politeness, with Churchill, Halifax and Chamberlain saying to one another: 'You must be Prime Minister' – and each one, Channon observed drily, no doubt wanting it for himself.

Questioned by Amery well after the war, Halifax insisted that his recollection was 'perfectly clear as far as it goes'. In Halifax's version, written up or dictated the following morning, the four men had entered the room and 'sat down to it' at the long table.

The twenty-five-foot dark table was covered with a green cloth. From contemporary accounts, there were black leather blotters on it, Georgian candlesticks, water carafes and tumblers, and a green telephone with a scrambling device. Chamberlain sat in the only chair with arms, with his back to the marble fireplace, the coals unlit on that hot afternoon, and facing the tall shuttered windows that looked out over an L-shaped garden with an oak tree and the low wall onto Horse Guards Parade. Halifax, Churchill and Margesson sat in three of the eighteen red leather padded chairs. In a table plan of the daily War Cabinet sketched by Cadogan, Halifax is seated with his back to the window, directly opposite Chamberlain, and with Churchill on his left. This was Churchill's recollection, though he makes no mention of the Chief Whip. If the traditional placements were observed, Margesson would have sat across the table beside Chamberlain, in a chair normally occupied by the Chancellor.

In Halifax's account, Chamberlain recapitulated the situation. He had made up his mind to go. Either Halifax or Churchill must take over – though Chamberlain had no plans to vanish from the scene. 'He would serve under either.' But first he needed formally to ask the Labour leaders before they went to Bournemouth if in principle they would join the government under Chamberlain, or under another Conservative leader.

Consulted for his opinion, Margesson said that unity was essential and probably impossible under Chamberlain. Following the Prime Minister's lead, he 'did not at that moment pronounce very definitely' between Churchill and Halifax.

Yet interviewed by Beaverbrook in May 1960, five months after Halifax's death, Margesson disputed Halifax's account that he had remained neutral, and also the Halifax–Peake version in which, by contrast, Margesson had favoured Churchill. Instead, what the Chief Whip had answered when Chamberlain asked him who the House of Commons would prefer to succeed to the premiership was 'that the House of Commons would prefer Halifax'. This appears to chime with Chamberlain's declared preference – for some reason glossed over by Halifax in his diary, but not in Halifax's summary to Peake the following June; nor, intriguingly, in the account that Halifax shared hot off the boil with his Permanent Under-Secretary on getting back to his office, and which Cadogan wrote down that night. In the

Halifax–Cadogan rendition, the earliest to be recorded and for all the obvious reasons the most reliable, Chamberlain is reported as saying that Halifax 'was the man mentioned as the most acceptable'.

Churchill's much later account of what Chamberlain said is not helpful. 'I do not recall the actual words he used,' Churchill writes in *The Gathering Storm*. But he did remember Chamberlain's implication that Churchill's 'heated controversy' with Labour at the end of the Norway Debate was 'an obstacle to my obtaining their adherence'.

Whatever Chamberlain and Margesson said to Halifax – and the evidence points to one or both of them preferring Halifax – it caused the return of his morning's pain, 'and my stomach ache continued'.

Most likely it was at this juncture that Chamberlain turned to Churchill, looking at him sharply in the version that Churchill 'several times' afterwards rehearsed to Colville, and said: 'Can you see any reason, Winston, why in these days a Peer should not be Prime Minister?'

This was the trap that Kingsley Wood had warned Churchill about at lunch.

In the Churchill–Colville version, Churchill felt 'that it would be difficult to say yes without saying frankly that he thought he himself should be the choice. If he said no, or hedged, he felt sure Mr Chamberlain would turn to Lord Halifax and say, "Well, since Winston agrees I am sure that if the King asks me I should suggest his sending for you." '

This was also the trap that Bracken had supposedly warned Churchill about, not once but three times – late the night before (Moran), yet again that morning (Beaverbrook), and a third time only a few moments earlier as Bracken walked with Churchill across Horse Guards Parade '& told him he must on no account open his mouth, but let the decision come his way' (Bracken in his 1955 conversation with Amery).

Before the myth of the great silence took hold, a number of contradictory reports sprang up about how quickly, or how slowly, Churchill had answered, and in what tone of voice. In 1942, Cadogan told Lord Killearn that Churchill 'at once and much to Halifax's bewilderment replied that he certainly thought he had better qualifications and should be offered the job!' In 1946, Malcolm Macdonald insisted that Churchill's reply was very brief: 'In this crisis there is only one possible Prime Minister – and that is me.' Violet Bonham Carter learned soon after the meeting that it was not Churchill who replied, nor Margesson, but Halifax – 'I think I should be rather a fish out of water.' A variation on Halifax's intercession was heard by Joseph Kennedy in October 1940, with Halifax saying: 'Perhaps I can't handle it being in the House of Lords,' to which Churchill expressed blunt agreement. 'I don't think you could.' In 1946, Randolph Churchill revealed that Halifax had said that he would not be captain of his own ship with Churchill on board. Churchill's response: 'I am sure you wouldn't.'

In Churchill's version, published in 1948, he did not open his mouth. He remained silent, and 'a very long pause ensued'.

If a notable silence did follow the Prime Minister's question to Churchill, then this was not the first provoked by Chamberlain. Hitler's interpreter Paul Schmidt witnessed how Hitler had sat 'completely silent and unmoving' when Chamberlain's ultimatum was translated to him on 3 September. After an interval 'which seemed an age', Hitler turned to von Ribbentrop, Chamberlain's former tenant in Eaton Square, who had remained standing by the window, and asked with a savage look: 'What now?'

'The Great Silence that saved Britain' was how Beaverbrook baptised the moment in the Cabinet Room. 'Here was the most eloquent man of his age never at a loss for the striking phrase and the resounding peroration. Yet he turned the tide of history on that critical occasion by refusing to speak.' Beaverbrook remained convinced that if Churchill had spoken, he would have kept to his original decision that he was ready to serve loyally in any capacity. 'Patriotism would have compelled him to accept a position which was certain to be difficult and might have become intolerable.'

Churchill admitted to being verbose. 'Usually I talk a great deal.' Only when standing or sitting at the easel was he known to remain silent. Brush in hand, he became all-absorbed. 'One sees everything with a different eye; the shadow cast by a lampshade; by the telegraph posts on the road; all the things I never noticed before I took up painting.' This did not mean that he always recorded faithfully what he saw. In a different context, Chamberlain once wrote to his wife: 'Accuracy of drawing is beyond his ken.'

The scene that Churchill painted in *The Gathering Storm* is, as Amery pointed out to Halifax, 'very circumstantial and dramatic'. He might have been composing it for posterity, 'hamming up' in the words of one of his researchers. Further details can be added from the myriad accounts. He sucks slowly at his cigar. Then swivels round in his chair, turning his back on the others; or, if he is standing, goes over to the window and gazes out at Horse Guards Parade. The only sound is the quarterly chime of the Horse Guards clock. The cracked and tinkling note prolongs the silence, for which Churchill made this claim: 'It certainly seemed longer than the two minutes which one observes in the commemorations of Armistice Day.'

It is accepted as inconceivable that the silence lasts so long.

By exquisite coincidence at about this time a minute's silence is being observed in a small churchyard in Herefordshire where Churchill's brother-in-law has been buried with military honours. The two pipers have played his coffin through the churchyard to the graveside. A young bugler from the Royal Engineers has just sounded the 'Last Post'. The bugler – named D. Coles, according to the *Hereford Times* – is about to raise the brass shank mouthpiece to his lips to break the silence with the 'Reveille'.

A voice returns him to the room. Halifax is speaking, a tenor voice pleasant to listen to, according to Halifax's Private Secretary, even if 'one was inclined to look far above him as he spoke, as though it had been less from his mouth that one would catch his words than from an echo up in the rafters'.

The Foreign Secretary is making his own renunciation. It is everything that he has told Baba Metcalfe at lunch – everything he has told her at dinner the previous evening, at the weekend in Little Compton, at their tête-à-tête dinners in the Dorchester – but without mentioning Baba.

'I then said that I thought for the reasons given the P.M. must probably go, but that I had no doubt at all in my own mind that for me to take it would create a quite impossible position.

'Quite apart from Winston's qualities as compared with my own at this particular juncture, what would in fact be my position? Winston would be running Defence, and in this connection one could not but remember how rapidly the position had become impossible between Asquith and Lloyd George, and I should have no access to the House of Commons. The inevitable result would be that being outside both these vital points of contact I should speedily become a more or less honorary Prime Minister, living in a kind of twilight just outside the things that really mattered.

'Winston, with suitable expressions of regard and humility, said he could not but feel the force of what I had said, and the P.M. reluctantly, and Winston evidently with much less reluctance, finished by accepting my view.'

Chamberlain had tried to drag Halifax by the hair to take his place, rather as Mussolini two weeks earlier had accused Germany of attempting to pull Italy into the war. But as Mussolini explained: 'Luckily, I am bald.' In short, Halifax said that 'he would prefer not to be sent for as he felt the position would be too difficult and troublesome for him'.

The meeting was over by 6 p.m. Halifax was relieved, if not yet free of the woods. He told Amery in 1954: 'The question of the future Prime Minister was practically settled, subject to two points that were still uncertain, i.e. when the change should be made and what would be the attitude of Labour, both as regards Neville and as regards anyone else.' Until this uncertainty was cleared up, it obliged Halifax to remain on standby, since it was still entirely possible that Labour would refuse to serve under Churchill – 'there were a good many forces both inside and outside the Labour Party who were not at all anxious to have Winston'. There was, too, the wisp of a chance that Labour would agree to serve under Chamberlain. A Junior Minister, Euan Wallace, was even now hearing reports that Labour's negative attitude towards Chamberlain might be changing, 'opposed by a growing body of opinion inside the Party'.

Chamberlain had wanted to summon the Labour leaders to ask them 'the definite question whether the Labour Party would join a Government under me or if not under someone else'. Their official confirmation was necessary, 'if only to justify my resignation to my own party'. He requested that Halifax and Churchill wait for their arrival.

The two men went out into the garden and sat in the bright sun, having a cup of tea while Chamberlain kept an appointment with Lord Camrose.

Churchill's bodyguard had noticed that 'sitting in the sun did not suit Winston'. Nor was tea a Churchillian meal. He had refused it three months before, at Admiralty House in Portsmouth, on medical grounds. 'My doctor has ordered me to take nothing non-alcoholic between breakfast and dinner.' Offered a cup of tea on another occasion, he spluttered: 'Good God, I think my wife drinks that. Get me a brandy.'

Chamberlain's wife Anne had not left her seat during the Norway Debate. She returned to Downing Street soon after the House adjourned at 3.49 p.m. The diplomat Lord Killearn described Anne as 'a curious detached sort of woman ... One feels that her mind is miles away all the time.' Had she looked down from her top-floor window on that blistering afternoon, what might she have observed? Two old men seated side by side on a painted iron garden seat. Even as her husband's fate was being decided would Anne have recalled gazing as a child into a crystal ball with W. B. Yeats, and seeing two strange figures under an archway? Or would the ilex have drawn her attention? She associated the oak with a walk that she took with Neville on the morning that he flew to Munich. As they passed the tree, her husband had stopped and said: 'I would gladly stand up against that wall and be shot if only I could prevent war.' It is impossible to know what was going through her mind because, like her husband, she published no memoirs.

Nor did the two men on the bench leave behind a record of their conversation. Discreet, polite, with the prospect of a German attack at any hour, it was a very English scene. A momentous interval in both their lives, in the history of the nation – yet neither man saw fit to record a single pleasantry that they exchanged while they sipped or ignored their tea, and talked, in Churchill's recollection, 'about nothing in particular'. The other absent voice is David Margesson's. The Chief Whip died in the house of his mistress, in Nassau, and not even his daughter knows where he is buried.

Behind another window, Lord Camrose finished his meeting with Chamberlain. 'Just as I left he told me that I would have the satisfaction of knowing that I was the first person outside the three people immediately concerned who knew what his determination was.' On his way out, Camrose passed Clement Attlee and the tall, lithe figure of Arthur Greenwood coming down the corridor, 'both of them rather pale and evidently in a state of tension'.

Attlee and Greenwood had come from a charged two-hour meeting with Clement Davies to agree on Labour's position.

If Samuel Hoare and John Simon were regarded as the Tweedledum and Tweedledee of the government, then the Labour leader and his deputy were the opposition's Laurel and Hardy. Meeting them together, Maisky observed that Greenwood did most of the talking, constantly addressing Attlee with the words, 'Isn't that so, Clem?' while Attlee replied, 'Oh yes, absolutely.' If Attlee's habit of not saying much had earned him his nickname 'the Clam', then the jaunty Greenwood, by contrast, had a booming Yorkshire voice, dropped cigarettes wherever he went, and 'drank a lot, as is his wont, while Attlee merely sipped his cherry brandy'.

The forceful Davies had summoned the pair to the Reform Club as a matter of urgency having heard that Attlee was wavering. Attlee's hesitancy arose from a talk with the Liberal leader, Archie Sinclair, whose memories had gone back to the last war, and caused him to stammer out his doubts – which Attlee admitted to sharing. Attlee had served at Gallipoli, leaving with the last party from Anzac in December 1915, and he had witnessed the chaos that ensued when the 'donkeys' in command were changed mid-river. Reports of an imminent German invasion moved Attlee and Sinclair to consider letting the Prime Minister stay temporarily in office. On this subject, Labour's leader had become 'platitudinous and indecisive', according to Davies, who was very upset.

Davies not only wanted Chamberlain to resign immediately. He also no longer believed that the Labour Party should champion Halifax, whose credentials to place the government 'on a virile, thrusting war footing' the Norway Debate had thrown into question. Davies warned: 'The tension is increasing: the overwhelming blow may fall at any moment through Holland and Belgium on us and the French . . . and we are still a disorganised country, meandering along as if time were on our side with all the complacency that self-satisfaction can give.'

Mercilessly calling in a favour, Davies turned to Greenwood for help in talking Attlee out of his support for the Foreign Secretary. Davies knew that Greenwood was 'in a bad way with drink'. He was also conscious that the Labour deputy leader would not be able to ignore his appeal.

A reformed drinker, Davies was sympathetic to Greenwood's alcoholism. He told Amery how, on the eve of the war, he had found Greenwood 'hopelessly drunk, took him home to his flat in Dolphin Square, dumped him in his bed and then came back in the morning. Looking round for breakfast he found nothing but a bottle and a half of whisky which he poured into the sink and then took Greenwood back to the Reform for a good breakfast and put his Unilever car at his disposal and so helped him to be in a condition to "speak for England" a day or two later.'

Now it was Greenwood's turn to bail out Davies.

In the same club in Pall Mall where Clement Davies had dried him out in September, Greenwood sat and argued alongside the former barrister. For two hours, they piled pressure on Attlee. Davies used his energetic power to charm, and his formidable legal skills – which had made him the highest paid young lawyer in Britain, and after that a KC – to put the case against Chamberlain, arguing that he had lost all credibility, and pleading with the Labour leader to resist any offer that Chamberlain was bound to propose. It took until 6 p.m. to convince 'the Clam' that the urgency of the situation made it vital to appoint another Prime Minister. Further, this should not be the Foreign Secretary, who was too closely identified with Chamberlain's failed policies.

At the end of this long and often tense conversation, Davies sent a relieved note to Bob Boothby. 'Attlee & Greenwood are unable to distinguish between the P.M. & Halifax and are not prepared to serve under the latter.'

Later in the evening, Boothby conveyed a message to Churchill. 'Opinion is hardening against Halifax as Prime Minister. I am doing my best to foster this, because I cannot feel he is, in any circumstances, the right man.' A mightily lubricated Greenwood by and by gave Chamberlain his forthright reason why not. 'Lord Halifax is a God-fearing Christian gentleman, but he's no bloody good for a war.'

With their minds freshly made up, Attlee and Greenwood entered the Cabinet Room. They had no idea of the discussion that had taken place here less than an hour before. They sat where Halifax and Churchill had sat, with the latter two now seated on either side of Chamberlain.

Chamberlain began. He said that there was a paramount need for a National government, and he asked if they would join it and serve under him.

Attlee afterwards confessed surprise that the Prime Minister showed no sign that he was finished. 'He appeared calm. He was hardly worried and still seemed to think he could carry on.'

Churchill, to Attlee's further surprise, 'vigorously supported' everything the Prime Minister had just said. He urged Attlee and Greenwood to come in under Chamberlain, telling them 'what a splendid fellow Neville is to work under', and delivering an eloquent eulogy on the Prime Minister's efficiency and personal charm.

Attlee was so 'completely flabbergasted' that he did not know how to respond.

Unable to stomach more of this, Greenwood broke in. He glared through his spectacles at Churchill, his dank fair hair falling on either side of his forehead, swaying a little in his chair. In his cigarette-furred, north-country voice, he said: 'We haven't come here to listen to you orating, Winston. Whatever we ourselves wish to do in these circumstances, we've no choice but to refuse because Members of our Party have got absolutely no confidence in the Prime Minister.' They not only disliked Chamberlain, but regarded him as something evil.

It was now that Attlee opened his mouth. He could understand Churchill's loyalty – 'Winston had Norway on his back' – but he thought it best to be frank. 'It is not pleasant to have to tell a Prime Minister face to face that he must go, but I thought it the only thing to do. I said: "Mr Prime Minister, the fact is our Party won't come in under you. Our Party won't have you and I think I am right in saying that the country won't have you either."'

Chamberlain remained silent, 'apparently startled and hurt'. It was the second significant silence to fall in the Cabinet Room that afternoon. Attlee wrote: 'Until that moment I think Chamberlain believed it would be possible for him to remain as Prime Minister.'

Then Chamberlain asked if Attlee would serve under someone other than himself. Chamberlain later explained to his sister: 'I did not name the someone else to them, but I understood that they favoured Halifax, and I had him in mind.' Even though Halifax had now declined three times, Chamberlain was doggedly keeping the door ajar for him. He had not yet learned that the Labour leaders had a short time ago changed their minds.*

* Chamberlain's account to Ida diverges from what he purportedly told Lord Camrose in their 6 p.m. conversation moments earlier. According to Camrose's typed-up notes, but impossible to corroborate, Chamberlain confided that the Labour party had 'swung against Halifax' – and therefore he had decided to 'advise the King to send for Winston' if Labour refused to serve under him. To his sister, however, Chamberlain implied that only 'later' did he discover Attlee's volte-face.

Attlee responded positively. 'I said I thought yes, but of course I could not answer for my Party without consultation.' He would have to put the matter to his National Executive, and it was possible to do so quickly as they were meeting at Bournemouth the next day for the usual Whitsuntide conference. Attlee was travelling there with Greenwood in the morning.

Chamberlain pointed out with a streak of impatience 'that it was perfectly impossible in the middle of a great war, and with the prospect of an immediate German attack, to debate this subject publicly at Bournemouth'.

Attlee said that the matter would be discussed in private session with the Executive. 'In order that there should be no doubt I said I would put to them two questions 1) Are you prepared to serve under Chamberlain? 2) Are you prepared to serve under someone else? and would wire or telephone back.* On that we parted politely.'

The meeting had lasted forty-five minutes.

The rest of the day passed in a tense limbo, everything up in the air until Attlee telephoned from Bournemouth. Cadogan wrote in his diary: 'There it is – waiting on Labour decision.' When Chips Channon left at 8 p.m. after picking up what gossip he could from Chamberlain's typist, he was not optimistic. 'Neville still reigns, but only just.'

Chamberlain's Principal Private Secretary, Arthur Rucker, was meanwhile fulfilling his promise to keep the Palace informed. Rucker arrived at Hardinge's flat in St James's Palace just as the King's Private Secretary was settling down for dinner, and he told him that Churchill was coming to be viewed as the most favoured candidate. Hardinge, conscious of George VI's historic lack of appetite for Churchill, said that the King 'might want to try, once Chamberlain had resigned, to persuade Lord Halifax to reconsider his position, and I suggested that Rucker should mention this to the Prime Minister'.

Halifax's stomach ache had cleared up. Even as Rucker acted behind the scenes to salvage a Halifax premiership, the Foreign Secretary was writing to Baba Metcalfe from his hotel suite. He wrote on Foreign Office paper, but 'Foreign Office' was crossed out and 'Dorchester 9 May Secret & Burn'

---

* Chamberlain appears to have scribbled these down. Later that evening, Greenwood showed Clem Davies a sheet of paper – and 'written in Neville's hand the double-barrelled question'.

was written in its place. 'My dear Baba, a line to tell you that I have hopes of things working out so that you will not be more frightened of me than you have hitherto! And at the same time procuring good broad results.' He went on: 'Your [illegible word: perhaps 'understanding'] and encouragement have been of great support these days. Bless you. E.'

Churchill had returned to the Admiralty. He telephoned Clementine at Huntington Park and asked her to come back to London as soon as possible, 'sensing that events were moving towards a climax'. She said that she would be on the 4 p.m. train from Hereford the following afternoon, and conveyed how anguished she had felt not to be with him 'during these days'. He dined that night with Anthony Eden, their third meeting since breakfast. 'W. quiet and calm,' Eden wrote in his diary. 'He told me he thought it plain N.C. would advise King to send for him.' After dinner, Churchill's son Randolph telephoned from Kettering, where his Territorial unit was still based, wanting to know if there was any news. Churchill told him: 'I think I shall be Prime Minister tomorrow.'

In Berlin, the Dutch military attaché Colonel Gijsbertus 'Bert' Sas had finished eating a 'funereal' dinner in Zehlendorf with 'his intimate friend for many years', Colonel Hans Oster, a close associate of Admiral Canaris in the Abwehr and an important anti-Nazi who already on several occasions had leaked German military secrets to the Allies. Oster had learned that A-Day ('Angriffstag') was 10 May, though he took care to remind Sas that so often in the past eight months there had been a last-minute deferral, as in April when Hitler had put everything on hold to invade Norway. Sas waited round the corner in the shadows while Oster called in at the OKW headquarters. Oster returned to confirm that Hitler had departed in his train, 'the Führer Special', to the Western Front, and there had been no cancellation of Operation 'Gelb'. Sas hurried back to his Legation to make an urgent call to the Hague. There was no time to send a coded message. He took the risk of talking on an open telephone line, telling the young Dutch officer who answered, 'Tomorrow morning at dawn . . .'

In Buckingham Palace, George VI was writing up his diary for 9 May. 'An unprofitable day.'

23
HINGE OF FATE

*'Well, I suppose they had to make someone carry the can after the balls-up in
Norway.'* EVELYN WAUGH, *Men at Arms*

'Norway was Winston's adventure and poor Neville was blamed for it.'
CHIPS CHANNON MP, 11 May 1940

Mary Churchill was dancing at the Savoy – 'gaily & so unheedingly' – when
in the cold grey dawn General Guderian and 1st Panzer Division rolled over
the Luxembourg border near Viandin. Further north, General Rommel's
7th Panzer Division crossed the Belgian frontier and sped towards Dinant.
Overhead, Ju-52s of 22nd Airborne Division carried 4,000 paratroopers.

General Ismay was woken by a telephone call from the Cabinet Office. The
same officer was on duty who had rung him following the invasion of Norway.
'But this time there was no doubt about his meaning; nor did his message
come as a surprise. The German attack on the Low Countries had started.'

Ticker-tacker, ticker-tacker. A tape machine jerked into life in the office
that Peter Fleming had occupied until he was ordered to Namsos. Major
Denzil Batchelor had come in early to finish his report on the Norway
Debate. The Intelligence officer thrust himself from his chair to pick up a
page that had fallen to the floor, and read: 'Hotler's troops have overrun
Luxembourg; Dutch and Belgian cabinets appeal to France; Hotler pro-
claims fall of Belgium and Holland; Hotler says he will crush Britain; Hotler
says . . .' The machine paused. Then out rolled another sheet. 'Correction for
Hotler; read Hitler and the meaning will immediately become apparent.'

On receiving a call to say that German parachutists were falling from the
Dutch sky 'like flocks of starlings', Frances Partridge stood immobilised in
her Wiltshire farmhouse. 'I felt a grip of fear and excitement mixed, as if a
giant's hand had seized me round the waist where I stood by the telephone,

picked me up and dropped me again.' In Wales, Henry Morris-Jones did not budge from his wireless as the announcer talked of a 'possible invasion of England by air'. German bombs were said to have fallen on Chilham in Kent. In the capital, the Labour peer John Sankey wrote in his diary: 'Intense excitement. London threatened.' Peter Fleming caught sight of a confidential message, sent from the Air Ministry to the Admiralty and the War Office, describing how enemy parachutists had behaved a month before in Stavanger, and were expected to act in Britain. 'Information from Norway shows that German parachute troops when descending hold their arms above their heads as if surrendering. The parachutist, however, holds a grenade in each hand. These are thrown at anyone attempting to obstruct the landing.' Charles Peake received an internal memo from the Ministry of Information concerning reports received from Norway of a new secret weapon used by the Germans called 'Nerve Gas'. 'The effect of this is to paralyse nerves and muscles, so that the victim cannot control his movements.'

Hitler had signed off his orders for 10 May: 'The battle beginning today will decide the future of the German nation for the next thousand years.' He had thrown everything into Operation 'Gelb'. This time there was no disguising the danger that the Allies were in. In his office at Buckingham Palace, Hardinge felt 'that the greatest battle in history had broken out, on which the future of civilization depended'.

Alerted at 6 a.m. by the US State Department, Joseph Kennedy called the Admiralty and was put through to the Map Room. 'It struck me that they didn't have the slightest idea of what was going on.' Moments later, the Dutch Ambassador knocked on Halifax's door at the Dorchester. The two men had a cup of tea while the Ambassador made a formal appeal for help. Soon afterwards, the Belgian Ambassador arrived on a similar mission. Halifax telephoned Cadogan, who reassured him that the Allied armies in France were responding smoothly and were, this time, 'prepared to the last gaiter button'.

Political in-fighting ceased. The Air Minister, Samuel Hoare, until December one of the favourites to succeed Chamberlain, and someone the First Lord only days before had regarded as a snake, arrived at the Admiralty at 6.30 a.m. with the War Minister, Oliver Stanley, to discuss the situation with Churchill. 'We had had little or no sleep and the news could not have been worse,' wrote Hoare. 'Yet there he was, smoking his large cigar, and eating fried eggs and bacon, as if he had just returned from an early morning ride.'

John Colville had been dancing at the Savoy in the same party as Mary Churchill, and had gone riding in Richmond Park. 'As I dismounted the groom told me that Holland and Belgium had been invaded.'

A meeting of the Military Coordination Committee was held at 7 a.m. in the Admiralty's Upper War Room, and ordered the immediate execution of Operation 'Royal Marine'. It was too late to divert the two Hurricane squadrons already en route to Narvik, but a decision was taken to send two fighter squadrons to France without delay. General Ironside 'sat for half an hour listening to rumours that were coming in'. There was little detailed news.

At 7.30 a.m. Randolph Churchill rang his father, having heard on the BBC that forty-one had been killed and eighty-two injured in a bombing raid on Brussels. 'What's happening?'

Churchill passed on the latest information which the French Ambassador had rung through minutes earlier. 'Well, the German hordes are pouring into the Low Countries, but the British and French armies are advancing to meet them and in a day or two there will be a head-on collision.'

'What about what you told me last night about you becoming Prime Minister?'

'Oh, I don't know about that. Nothing matters now except beating the enemy.' When recalling this conversation with his father, Randolph swore that 'about the big job . . . he was not even interested'. Churchill was 'only thinking of armies and military matters'.

Blundering about downstairs, General Ironside and the other Chiefs of Staff were trying to leave the Admiralty after the MCC meeting. The doors were treble-locked, and they could find no nightwatchmen with keys. 'I walked up to one of the windows and opened it and climbed out. So much for security.'

Outside, it was the beginning of another beautiful spring day with bluebells and primroses in flower everywhere.

Ironside tramped across Horse Guards Parade to Downing Street where the War Cabinet was assembling for the first of its three meetings that day. His irritation soon yielded to exasperation. 'The P.M. at once began asking where the Germans had landed and seemed quite surprised to know that everything was uncertain.'

Chamberlain's ignorance confirmed to Ironside the 'measly' nature of a Cabinet 'which doesn't know if it is on its head or its heels'. The situation was not much clearer by the time the Cabinet broke up thirty-five minutes later, with Churchill airily telling photographers as he left: 'Plenty happened last night, and something is happening today.' When Halifax attempted with Amery to build a chronology for 10 May, he failed to recall at the 8 a.m. meeting 'any discussion at all of Neville's intimation that he thought the domestic situation must stand still for the moment'. No one knew whether the Prime Minister planned to stay in office; or, were he to resign, who would take over. The same confusion paralysed the Foreign Office where Chips Channon found many 'downhearted' Mandarins. 'It was the popular view this morning that Neville was saved.'

Chamberlain seems to have taken his cue from the French Prime Minister. In Paris, news of Hitler's attack on the Low Countries had persuaded Reynaud to withdraw the resignation that he had submitted the afternoon before. For eight electrifying hours on 10 May, Operation 'Gelb' convinced Chamberlain that the crisis in Europe made it his duty to remain in power too.

The earliest intimation that Chamberlain had decided to stay firm came moments after the War Cabinet ended, when he told Hoare, who supported him warmly, that his 'first inclination was to withhold his resignation until the French battle was finished'. Chamberlain then wrote to the Archbishop of Canterbury: 'Hitler has, I think, now put domestic quarrels out of our minds.' And, famously, to Beaverbrook: 'Hitler has seized the occasion of our divisions to strike the great blow and we cannot consider changes in the Government while we are in the throes of battle.'

The occasion of our divisions. Chips Channon and John Simon were not the only Conservative MPs to suspect that Hitler had acted in response to the Norway Debate. Sir George Broadbridge spoke for many backbenchers when he wrote to Chamberlain evincing 'not the slightest doubt that the disgraceful episode in the House of Commons on Wednesday and continued again yesterday' had been the signal for the Germans 'to start their *blitzkrieg* immediately'.

All morning, the Transport Minister Euan Wallace watched Conservative MPs who had voted against Chamberlain going to see him to apologise, as if they had suddenly recognised 'the dangers of having an entirely new set of people in the middle of a crisis'. And not merely rebel Conservatives like Roy Wise. The already conflicted Liberal leader Archie Sinclair met in hurried conclave with his Chief Whip Percy Harris, who recorded the outcome in his diary. 'Decided in light of this new threat Neville better carry on & after discussion sent communication to Press that though radical change of the Government wanted NOW is not the time for it.'

In a dramatic gesture, Sinclair called on Chamberlain in person to apologise for 'any insolence or rudeness' that he had shown him, and said that he would be ready to work under Chamberlain 'should the composition of the Government be sufficiently altered'. Long black hair, deepset greenish-brown eyes, a ghostly pallor – Sinclair's matinée-idol looks compelled one contemporary to describe him as 'the complete tragic actor'. His performance won over Chamberlain, who up till that morning had dismissed Sinclair as a stuttering conspirator without 'consequence or value'. Sinclair's offer of reconciliation was proof that Churchill, too, was on board.

It rallied the Prime Minister to know that he had behind him one of Churchill's best and oldest friends, plus 'a million Liberals up and down the country'. Sinclair's backing set the seal on Chamberlain's decision to carry on: it returned him into thinking that he was still 'the best P.M. in sight', which was what Cadogan and many in Whitehall and Westminster continued to believe. As Colville saw it, and doubtless communicated to Chamberlain: 'The fundamental difficulty is that no alternative Prime Minister seems to be available.' Wallace was another loyalist who regarded Neville Chamberlain as Chamberlain at that moment perceived himself. 'The people who know anything of the inside working of the Government machine are unanimous in thinking that he is the best man for the job of Prime Minister.' The Information Minister had pedalled the same tune. Chamberlain wrote to Hilda: 'Reith tells me that my prestige with the chfs of staff is "tremendous" & and that they say I am "the one man whose judgement they trust."' Even at this late hour, Chamberlain remained 'hard to dead' and powerfully vulnerable to the myth of his indispensability which Sinclair's message of solidarity had served to reaffirm.

Eager to bring in Labour as well, Sinclair visited Clement Attlee at his room in the Commons to suggest to him 'that in view of the morning's events it might, after all, be desirable for Chamberlain to remain Prime Minister for a time'. At more or less the same moment, a resurgent

Chamberlain appealed to Attlee to ask whether, pending an answer to his two questions, Attlee would 'send a message saying that the Labour Party supported the Government at this grave crisis of the war'.

How Attlee responded to Chamberlain's approach is uncertain. How Chamberlain understood him to have responded dictated the Prime Minister's actions over the next hours.

Years later, Attlee insisted that he had had no personal communication with Chamberlain before he left for Bournemouth on the 11.34 a.m. train. But this flies in the face of what Chamberlain told Anthony Eden that morning, and which Eden jotted down in his diary: the Prime Minister said 'that new attack must cause hold-up, only temporary. He had communicated with Attlee in this sense, who had accepted. He had asked Attlee to put out notice which would include support of Government pro tem.'

Attlee's denial that he had been in touch with Chamberlain also contradicts what Chamberlain told John Reith at 11.15 a.m. Chamberlain had asked to see Reith, who was about to attend his first War Cabinet as Information Minister. Reith found the Prime Minister 'in quite good form', as though rejuvenated by the backing that he had gained, or imagined that he had gained, first from the Liberal and now from the Labour leaders. According to Reith's diary, Chamberlain had already met with Attlee and Greenwood: 'he had seen them this morning again after the Low Countries news', and Reith 'understood quite clearly that they had agreed to defer the political crisis and support the government in view of the other crisis'.

Did Chamberlain make up this conversation with Attlee? It seems unlikely. Or did Attlee forget when he told Leo Amery in November 1954 that 'he had no direct communication one way or another with Neville that morning'? Possibly. In the mayhem of that day, Horace Wilson recalled how 'many messages came into No. 10 and many things were happening'. Cadogan's diary alludes to the floundering chaos in which everyone had to operate. 'Confused news,' Cadogan wrote. 'It is difficult to know what to believe.'

Possible, too, is that Reith may have misunderstood the nature of Chamberlain's contact with Attlee, less likely a face-to-face interview at this moment than a telephone call – which is how Leo Amery remembered it. Amery was told at the time by Clement Davies that 'before the Labour leaders went down to Bournemouth, Neville rang up Attlee and suggested that the German attack had changed the whole situation, presuming that he would continue in office at any rate for the time being. Attlee replied "Not at all" and that he had better make way as quickly as possible.' Again, this response of a bold, decisive Attlee echoes rather too comfortably what Davies may have been craving to hear. An unpublished manuscript written by someone in touch with Davies at this pivotal moment hints at a more plausible, less clear-cut reaction from Attlee, as if he had reverted to his hesitant position of the previous afternoon. 'After the invasion of Holland and Belgium, Attlee had wavered considerably and had expressed the view that now bullets were flying they should not change horses in midstream.' Were Attlee to have shared this view with a more bullish Labour front-bencher like, say, Hugh Dalton, after Chamberlain and Sinclair had got hold of Attlee that morning, then the chances are that Dalton would have talked the Labour leader out of it. This is what may have happened.

The most likely scenario is that Chamberlain – or Horace Wilson – did speak to a vacillating Attlee by telephone, and believed that he had extracted a promise of sorts from him, exactly as Chamberlain reported to Reith. When challenged by Amery in 1954, Reith admitted that his diary was 'possibly dictated two or three days later', but he reiterated that 'Chamberlain told me he had understood "quite clearly" that Attlee and Greenwood had "agreed" to defer the political crisis.'

In the quiet of the Cabinet Room, fortified by this knowledge, Chamberlain went on to summarise to Reith his position, as he saw it, since the Norway Debate. 'He could put out of his mind what had happened in the last two or three days. Sinclair, he said, had apologised; he had no feelings against Attlee; Lloyd George and he would never be friendly. He did not refer to Amery or any of the other Conservatives who had attacked him . . . he was ready for action if encouraged and authorised to act.' A measure of Chamberlain's renewed confidence was his instruction to Reith that he had made up his mind for Reith to attend all Cabinet meetings 'beginning with the one about to assemble'. This was not the action of a leader who had decided to surrender his seals.

Chamberlain had already begun spreading the news through the Whips' Office that he considered it his duty to remain in office, and there would be no change for the moment. Horace Wilson felt secure enough to make the unambiguous claim that Labour was prepared now to serve under Chamberlain, giving the following alert to Euan Wallace and other Junior Ministers: 'An announcement would shortly be made both by Labour and Opposition Liberals that in view of the very critical situation they intended to support whatever measure the Government thought necessary to deal with it.'

Yet Labour's support when eventually it came was the thinnest of gruels.

The boundlessly energetic Hugh Dalton, one of the party's 'tough guys' as Attlee called him, was charged with framing a reply to Chamberlain's request for Labour's backing. Dalton accordingly drafted and issued a message to which Attlee and Greenwood put their names. The statement arrived on a piece of ticker-tape in the middle of the second War Cabinet, which had begun at 11.30 a.m.

The tape was handed to Horace Wilson – who, Eden observed, 'was specially indignant' – and then passed over the table to Reith, who recalled that 'both Chamberlain and Wilson were surprised by what the tape message said'. It was not the strong reinforcement that they had hoped for. The Prime Minister and his closest adviser read: *The Labour Party, in view of the latest series of abominable aggressions by Hitler while firmly convinced that a drastic reconstruction of the Government is vital and urgent in order to win the war, reaffirms its determination to do its utmost to achieve victory. It calls on all its members to devote all their energies to this end.* This vague bromide, wrote Reith, seemed 'to leave things just as they were before the war blew up'.

Outside, the sun was nearing its zenith. The second meeting of the War Cabinet lasted barely thirty minutes. It exposed the switching fortunes of Chamberlain and his First Lord, who, whatever he may have said to Randolph Churchill earlier, was already sizing up the Prime Minister's armchair.

An hour before, Churchill had summoned Admiral Keyes to his office. Keyes wore his uniform and carried a small suitcase. Churchill had, at last, an important task for the Hero of Zeebrugge. Aware that Keyes was a personal friend of the Belgian Royal Family, he was sending him to Brussels to act as a liaison officer between King Leopold and London.

The Keyes mission was not the only indication that Churchill was flexing muscles in areas where he was not yet strictly entitled to wander. A huffy John Simon had learned in the course of the morning that 'despite the attacks in Flanders, Churchill was pressing for early changes in the Government'. When Simon complained of this to Maurice Hankey shortly before the 11.30 a.m. War Cabinet, Hankey revealed the extent to which Chamberlain's grip on his government, tight for so long, was loosening. He remarked in a quiet, firm voice: 'Personally, I think that if there are to be changes, the sooner they are made the better.'

Even before the War Cabinet got under way, a noticeably exuberant Churchill was observed setting the agenda. He had asked his pet scientist Frederick Lindemann to set up a rocket-shaped contrivance on a table in the window of the Cabinet Room nearest to the secretaries' office. Churchill was eager for 'the Prof' to demonstrate his latest invention, an anti-aircraft homing fuse. Ironside stood in silent fury as Churchill promised that 'it wouldn't take a minute. And then we had a description of what it was.' Ironside turned to Reith, bristling. 'Do they think this is the time for showing off toys?'

Halifax appeared, after taking a walk around St James's Park with his wife and dachshund. Then the Prime Minister walked in, and the War Cabinet began. Halifax recalled that 'the information was rather confused, but the Dutch seemed to be acting with vigour and dealing with German parachutists'.

Chamberlain was telling Ministers what had happened on the Home Front when Attlee's ticker-tape message arrived.

Labour's tepid expression of support was the cue for Chamberlain to make a statement about his intention not to resign. Halifax wrote in his diary: 'The P.M. told the Cabinet . . . that he thought it would all have to wait over till the war situation was calmer.' For a moment no one reacted.

A surprised Eden glanced at the faces of the other Ministers. They were equally nonplussed, he could tell, by Chamberlain's announcement. 'This impressed many present with difficulty of prolonged delay, specially as conditions for change might become more rather than less difficult. For P.M. personally there was also risk to personal position if appearance of clinging on were given.' Yet if this was the critical opinion of a majority around the table, 'no one expressed it'. The only person to speak up, and in favour of Chamberlain, was Samuel Hoare, who confided to his diary that Halifax was 'quite heartless' by not publicly siding with the Prime Minister.

But not so heartless as Kingsley Wood.

Few in the room were aware that Chamberlain's former protégé had gone over to Churchill's side the day before. Nor that Wood had been to see Chamberlain earlier that morning, and begged him to stand down. The Lord Privy Seal was reacting to a rumour that Chamberlain had decided to stay on. When Chamberlain confirmed this to be true, Wood said to him, in a remark which Horace Wilson considered treacherous, that 'on the contrary, the new crisis made it all the more necessary to have a National Government which alone could confront it'. To have a Minister tell him this who had slavishly danced to his tunes for sixteen years would have been a disappointment – one commentator quipped that it 'must have felt like being bitten by a gramophone!' Chamberlain was constructed of tough fibre, however. He told Wood that he accepted his view, but appears not to have listened to him.

Frustrated and resentful, Wood made a bee-line for the Admiralty to blurt out – for the second time in twenty-four hours – the gist of their private conversation to Churchill, revealing how the Prime Minister 'was inclined to feel that the great battle which had broken upon us made it necessary for him to remain at his post', and how Wood had told Chamberlain that he could not go on.

How long did Chamberlain intend to continue *in situ*? Halifax confessed to having no idea. Chamberlain had assured Eden that the hold-up was only temporary. Then Eden heard a report 'that all changes postponed; it seemed for some time'. History was galloping by at a pace so frenetic that no one could be certain.

After wiring Labour's non-committal message to Downing Street, Attlee decided to press on to the Labour conference in Bournemouth. If he remained in London, he risked being snatched like Sinclair into Chamberlain's agenda. Attlee shared a taxi with Dalton to Waterloo station. During the short journey, Attlee 'with rather an engaging smile' commended Dalton for the toughness with which he had deflected Chamberlain's appeal.

Herbert Morrison saw them off. Morrison's responsibilities as head both of the London County Council and Anti-Aircraft Defence obliged him to stay in London in the event of a German air raid. It would look bad if he was down at Bournemouth when the first bombs fell, he said.

The Labour frontbencher A. V. Alexander had earlier telephoned from Manchester to suggest that Parliament ought to cancel the Whitsun recess and meet. Dalton opposed the idea. It would present Chamberlain's cheer-leaders with the opportunity to keep the Old Man in power.

Even as Attlee, Dalton and Greenwood travelled by rail to Bournemouth, the news was ebbing out that there was to be no reconstruction of the government. Paul Emrys-Evans was walking down St James's Street after a noon meeting of the Watching Committee when he saw Brendan Bracken stepping into a taxi, and jumped in after him. 'He said things were not going well and it all depended on Labour as Neville was making a great effort to stay.' A seething Bracken had already telephoned Harold Macmillan at his publishing firm, telling him: 'It's like trying to get a limpet off a corpse.'

The taxi dropped off Emrys-Evans at the Travellers Club where he had arranged to meet Harold Nicolson and Richard Law for a pre-prandial drink. 'Saw Alec Dunglass there. He said that Winston, Halifax and Neville were working closely together, and that the formation of a new Government might be postponed.' Nicolson recorded the loyal Dunglass's conviction that this triumvirate was needed 'to carry us over these first anxious hours' and that 'the actual danger of the moment really makes it impossible for the Government to fall'.

In a depressed mood, Nicolson and his friends dispersed for lunch.

Contemplating the situation from his office at *The Times*, Geoffrey Dawson believed on 10 May that Great Britain faced probably the greatest danger which had confronted it since 1066. Yet incredibly on that day no one felt it necessary to work through the lunch hour. Emrys-Evans and Law lunched at Jules, Nicolson at the Beefsteak, Dunglass at the Travellers, Cadogan at home, Churchill at the Admiralty with Beaverbrook (who had replaced Eden as his confidant), and Halifax and Chamberlain at the Dorchester – at a luncheon hosted by Halifax for the Prime Minister to meet Princess Olga of Yugoslavia. Chamberlain, according to Olga, was 'calm and charming and showed little effects of the battle that has been raging about him'.

At some point during the meal the Prime Minister drew his Foreign Secretary aside to comment briefly about his earlier statement to the War Cabinet. Halifax had a lucid memory of Chamberlain saying 'that he had a feeling that Winston did not approve of the delay, and left me guessing as to what he meant to do'.

All seemed to hang on a telephone call from Bournemouth. Halifax understood that Chamberlain would not take 'the final decision before he heard the Labour answer'.

Adverts for the ten-day Whitsun break promised an ample ration of sunshine at Bournemouth 'and just about everything else for the enjoyment of a well-earned holiday. Make Bournemouth your permanent residence!'

On the terrace in front of the crowded Highcliffe Hotel, Labour delegates sat in the sun, 'fat gents in black coats all talking very loud'. A lot of beer was being drunk. Along the seafront towards the Pavilion gardens a surprising amount of German could be heard, spoken by prosperous-looking refugee families. Outside the Pavilion, where the orchestra played Sibelius's 'Valse Triste', a boy sold the *Daily Worker*, as Giles Romilly had done in the East End before he went to Spain. The paper had gone to bed too early to carry the news that the Whitsun holiday had been cancelled for civil servants, and that it was the duty of everyone to stay at work 'where practicable'.

In the lounge of the Highcliffe Hotel, groups of men and women wearing hats and suits gathered around trays of tea, talking, or listening to the wireless which was switched on at all the news times. People leant forward in their chairs in a tense attitude. Even though the wireless was very loud, some delegates huddled up close to it. One young woman absorbing the scene was the reporter Zita Crossman. 'People smoke a lot and the great thing seems to be to avoid anybody's eye . . . The word "parachutist" was frequently heard.' German planes were said to be bombing Canterbury.

Crossman observed the bald, imposing figure of Hugh Dalton walk past, looking strung-up. 'There was a general feeling of Big Things are being decided as we saw members of the National Executive rushing to the telephones and having tremendous urgent confabs with each other.' At one point, Crossman peered through a basement window and saw Labour's National Executive sitting – 'about 40 of them it seemed. All very solemn. Someone scowled at us for looking.'

In this stuffy underground hotel room, shortly after 3.30 p.m. – at a moment, Arthur Greenwood wrote in an unpublished memoir, 'when the grim thunder of guns had come near enough to England to be heard sounding inland across Essex and Kent' – the fate of Chamberlain, Halifax, Churchill, of England too, was determined.

Ever since the departure of the 11.34 a.m. train for Bournemouth, Clement Davies had been on the telephone in Boothby's flat in Pall Mall, trying to reach Attlee. Davies was frantic to know what substance there was to Horace Wilson's story, now being excitedly repeated in the Reform Club opposite, that the Labour leaders had agreed to serve under Chamberlain. After dialling fruitlessly for two hours, Davies, who had not slept for three nights, managed to catch Greenwood at the Highcliffe Hotel soon after his arrival there with Attlee and Dalton. Livid, Greenwood assured Davies that the report contained not a word of truth. Davies at once telephoned the press agencies and Reuters, telling them this.

Meanwhile in Bournemouth, the Labour leaders went downstairs to put Chamberlain's questions to their party's National Executive.

The discussion did not take long, even though many delegates were more talkative than usual. As anticipated, the Executive Committee refused categorically to serve under Chamberlain, but agreed to be a part of a government under another Prime Minister, on condition that Labour was 'sufficiently represented' in the key positions. The meeting ended at about 4.30 p.m. In Downing Street, the third and last War Cabinet of 10 May was getting under way.

Still not having heard from Attlee, who had promised to try and telephone the result by 2 p.m., Chamberlain had told a secretary to ring the Highcliffe Hotel and ask whether the Labour leader was in a position yet to answer the two questions that Chamberlain had written down for him the previous evening. Attlee was preparing to leave with Greenwood to catch the 5.15 p.m. train to Waterloo. He dictated his reply from one of the public telephone boxes in the hotel lobby. 'The answer to the first question is, no. To the second, yes.' He then read out the resolution which the National Executive had approved, he stressed, unanimously. Labour, Attlee slowly dictated in his quiet, clipped voice, were prepared 'to take our share of responsibility in a new Government which, under a new Prime Minister, would command the confidence of the nation'. Dalton had inserted the phrase 'under a new Prime Minister'. Attlee, dithering to the last, had doubted whether the words were necessary, but Dalton in his booming baritone had insisted. 'If you don't make it absolutely plain, the Old Man will still hang on.' It was 4.45 p.m. when Attlee put down the receiver.

Neville Chamberlain had had a hunch that the war would end in the spring of 1940. It ended for him shortly before 5 p.m. when a secretary entered the Cabinet Room and handed Attlee's typed-out answer to Horace Wilson, who read it and without comment slid it along the green cloth to the Prime Minister.

Every one of the eighteen people around the table knew the significance of that sheet of paper, what it portended. Intently, they watched Chamberlain's lean face as he took in its contents, his hair white over the ears, in one description, as if he had laid a palm covered with powder on his temples.

Was Labour prepared to serve under Chamberlain, as recent feverish reports were suggesting? Or was Labour still refusing to serve under him, but declining to accept Churchill as Prime Minister? And that being the case, would Halifax be pleaded with at this eleventh hour, which history had taught was his favourite moment, to fulfil his duty and step in?

The scrutiny of the Prime Minister's face by the First Lord was unusually keen. Seated opposite Chamberlain, between Halifax and Pound, Churchill had by now sketched out the nucleus of his War Cabinet, 'in anticipation of the decision', as Halifax later wrote to Amery, 'but feeling quite sure in his own mind that the decision was inevitable within an hour or two'. Amery had been to see Churchill after lunch 'when he told me something of his plans for the Cabinet and indeed suggested to me that I might take on Supply'. Churchill then told Amery 'under the pledge of strictest secrecy that he meant to keep Neville in the Government as leader of the largest party'. These plans were dust if Labour decided not to back Churchill.

Not Winston, Attlee had told Harold Wilson. He was too old. Now he had Norway on his back. Then there was his long and hostile history with Labour, an antagonism unchanged since 1922, when as Secretary of State for War, Churchill had accepted an invitation from the President of the Cambridge Union, Geoffrey Shakespeare, to oppose the motion *That this House considers the time is now ripe for a Labour Government.* 'Labour was a class party,' Churchill had informed the undergraduates. 'Labour made and kept men equal.' To cries of 'No', he retorted: 'It is no good saying "no", it is so; dead equality except for the political bosses.' Churchill had won that debate by 651 votes to 265, going on to stand as an 'anti-Socialist' candidate in the 1924 election. Since then, Colin Coote had observed, there had been 'not one injurious epithet in the English language which the Socialists had not applied to Winston' – and Churchill had retaliated in kind, right up to his recommendation to Chamberlain, immediately following the Division, that the government required no help from the Socialists. Less than forty-eight hours later, could Churchill succeed in winning over Labour's political bosses by bringing them into government? Out of all the men around that Cabinet table trying to read Chamberlain's face, Churchill had shown perhaps the least interest in forging a coalition with Attlee and Greenwood.

Professional chairman to the end, Chamberlain impassively put aside the piece of paper and carried on with the War Cabinet. Operation 'Royal Marine' was fixed for 9.00 that night. The Allied bombing of the Ruhr was postponed until the following evening. It was agreed to warn British troops stationed in Britain about parachutists attempting to land.

The final item concerned the political situation at home. Chamberlain said that he had thought matters over, and since Labour had said yes to service under another Prime Minister, he had decided 'in the light of this answer' not to wait, and he proposed to see the King that evening and tender his resignation. All members of the War Cabinet were expected to offer their resignations to the new Prime Minister. Immediately afterwards, at 5 p.m., Chamberlain told a gathering of Ministers not in the War Cabinet 'that he would be willing to serve in the new Government, but could not indicate the name of his successor since it would be for the King to decide who to send for'.

Colville voiced the squeals of the Downing Street staff. 'We at No. 10 had hoped so much that the King would send for Halifax.' Their hopes were kept flickering by the highly unlikely possibility of George VI, who 'is understood not to wish to send for Winston, being able to persuade Halifax to recant his determination not to be P.M.'

But it required prompt action if the Foreign Secretary was to pip Churchill to the post. For a small inner gang of hangers-on led by Dunglass, and including Colville, Butler and Channon, the fact that Chamberlain lingered in Downing Street – having at first promised to go 'at once' to the Palace – was the spur for them to act. Channon wrote: 'Neville hesitated for half an hour, and meanwhile Dunglass rang me – could not Rab persuade Halifax to take it on?' Dunglass then suggested to Colville that they walk over to the Foreign Office and talk to Butler.

Rab Butler at once expressed doubts when approached by this posse from No. 10. 'Easier said than done,' he remarked thirty years later. Urged on by Rucker at Hardinge's request, Butler twice already – that morning and the day before – had had earnest conversations with 'the Pope', as he called Halifax. But the Foreign Secretary was steadfast in his decision not to enter the lists: 'He would not be Prime Minister.' Even so, when egged on by Dunglass, Colville and Channon, Butler consented to go and speak personally to Halifax 'for one last final try'. Butler rang through to Valentine Lawford to let Halifax know that he was on his way.

Butler's father, a member of the Indian Civil Service, had passed on this advice to his son: 'You can do a great deal by getting to a meeting ten minutes early.' Butler's weakness was his unpunctuality. When he arrived at Halifax's room, he was told by Lawford, 'the rather "Second Empire" secretary' as Channon called him, that the Foreign Secretary had slipped out to the dentist. By neglecting to warn Halifax in time that Butler was coming to see him, Channon suggested that Lawford 'may well have played a decisively negative role in history . . .' Yet a handwritten note by Lawford in the printed edition of Channon's diary states the following. 'I am not sure of this! E[dward] didn't want to see Rab again, obviously.'

Along with his stomach ache, Halifax's dental appointment has since become a motif of his determination not to be Prime Minister. Lawford wrote in another note: 'It was H who insisted on going to the dentist – and didn't want to be P.M. anyhow, at all.' To a disappointed Colville, Halifax's behaviour was 'true to form'.

A peculiar feature of Friday 10 May is the number of politicians affected on that day by dental issues. After lunching at the Beefsteak, Harold Nicolson had travelled down to Sissinghurst. 'It is all looking too beautiful to be believed, but a sort of film has obtruded itself between my appreciation of nature and my terror of real life. It is like a tooth-ache.'

Even as news came in of Germany's invasion of Holland and Belgium, Lord Sankey was having 'two teeth stopped' by his dentist, Mr Brown. 'He says they ought to be all right for a time now, thank God.'

It is not known whether Halifax shared the same dentist as Sankey – or as Chamberlain, who in February 'had to bolt off to my dentist! A tooth had been worrying me for several days & was showing signs of flaring up.' But

Halifax was regarded in the Foreign Office as something of a dental expert. A month before, Britain's Ambassador to Brussels told Cadogan that he wanted 'to stay 2 or 3 days for his Dentist! Referred him to H!' Plus, it is perfectly possible that Halifax did need dental treatment, and this was not a variation of his psychosomatic stomach ache earlier. He wrote in his diary on the eve of the Blitz, three months later: 'Having been tormented with toothache for about a week I was persuaded to have it out last Friday with a local anaesthetic. The sequel has been that it ached worse than ever, and has just begun to abate. Very bad for the temper.'

With Halifax in the dentist's chair, the road was clear. Hardinge arrived at Downing Street shortly after the reply from Bournemouth had been received. Chamberlain had resigned and was preparing to go to the Palace. An audience had been arranged for 6 p.m. 'I was informed that in the event of the King asking his advice as to his successor, he would <u>without hesitation</u> recommend Mr Churchill.'

A single word is scrawled in pencil in Chamberlain's pocket diary for 10 May: 'Resigned.'

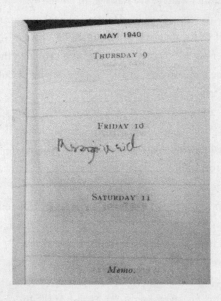

Forty-four years earlier, Chamberlain had written an anguished letter to his father. 'The plants don't grow . . . All the order & discipline that I have worked up will be lost . . . this is *my* failure.' And two months later: 'No doubt a sharper man would have seen long ago what the ultimate result was likely to be.'

He was now seventy-one. Once again a venture had failed into which he had ploughed so much, and the outcome of which many had predicted. 'All my world has tumbled to bits in a moment,' he wrote to Hilda. For one of the last times in his life, he credited a force greater than himself. 'Perhaps it was providential that the revolution which overturned me coincided with the entry of the real thing.'

Accompanied by Dunglass, Chamberlain drove to Buckingham Palace. His audience with George VI lasted half an hour. They had not spoken since the first night of the Norway Debate, when Chamberlain had declined the King's offer to tell Labour's leaders that they must pull their weight and join a National government.

George VI wrote this famous diary entry about his conversation that evening with Chamberlain: 'He told me that Attlee had been to see him & had told him that the Labour Party would serve in the new administration of a new Prime Minister but not one with himself as P.M. He then told me he wished to resign . . . I accepted his resignation, & told him how grossly unfair I thought he had been treated & that I was terribly sorry that all this controversy had happened. We then had an informal talk over his successor. I, of course, suggested Halifax . . . as I thought H. was the obvious man, & that his peerage could be placed in abeyance for the time being.'

Significantly, the King had not waited to ask for Chamberlain's recommendation. Aside from revealing his definite preference, the immediacy of George VI's reaction hints at his continuing hope that the new Prime Minister could somehow, even now, be Halifax.

The monarch still had political power, thanks to the unwritten British constitution. It was George V who decided that Bonar Law was the best person to form a government in 1922. A year later, Baba's father had been rejected in place of Baldwin – a straight result, Curzon wrote to his wife, 'of the step taken by the King'.

If the King had exercised his prerogative to ask Halifax directly, and if

Chamberlain had recommended the King to send for the Foreign Secretary, as Churchill was aware lay within his power – 'I owe something to Chamberlain, you know,' Churchill later told the *Manchester Guardian*. 'When he resigned he could have advised the King to send for Halifax and he didn't' – then it is possible that George VI might have been able to persuade one of his most dedicated public servants 'whose wisdom and urbanity had often dispelled the depression of the last few months'.

At the final moment, after learning that Labour had 'changed their minds and were veering towards Winston', Chamberlain did not make this recommendation. The King wrote in his diary: ' . . . he told me that H was not enthusiastic, as being in the Lords he would only act as a shadow or a ghost in the Commons where all the real work took place. I was disappointed over this statement.' Fascinated though Halifax was by ghosts, he was not interested in becoming one. The King could do little more than stutter his regret next day when he came across Halifax in the Buckingham Palace gardens, saying: 'I was sorry not to have him as P.M.' – to which Halifax replied, as he wrote in his diary: 'with suitable expressions of gratitude, but also of hope that he had thought my reasons for judging differently were sound. On the whole he did not contest this.'

With Halifax ruling himself out, and the outgoing Prime Minister not expected to volunteer an alternative, it was for the Sovereign to decide whether to ask Chamberlain for advice about his successor. Because of the party's large majority, the Prime Minister had to be a Conservative, which precluded Attlee and Lloyd George.

Eden? Wood? Amery? Hoare?

'Then I knew that there was only one person I could send for to form a Government who had the confidence of the country, & that was Winston. I asked Chamberlain his advice & he told me Winston was the man to send for.'

The King thanked Chamberlain for all his help to him, and repeated that he would greatly regret losing Chamberlain as his Prime Minister, but he would make it 'a condition that he should remain in the Cabinet and be the Leader of the House'. Then, according to Hardinge, 'after further thought, Mr Churchill was asked to come to the Palace'.

Hardinge's choice of the words 'further thought' deserves lingering over for the lack of enthusiasm it reveals. There is no record of what the King said to his Private Secretary, yet it is extremely hard to believe that their conversation did not touch on the hazards of a Churchill administration. The opinion which Hardinge had held until recently – that a Churchill premiership was 'very undesirable' – coincided with the King's own. On 6 April 1955, George VI's biographer Jack Wheeler-Bennett let slip to Harold Nicolson, in a diary entry not published, how 'according to his research, the King "was bitterly opposed to Winston succeeding Chamberlain" . . . the adverb employed is instructive'. There was no personal spark between the two men, as between Churchill and the King's elder brother. Halifax recorded in his diary how George VI 'was funny about Winston and told me he did not find him very easy to talk to', and 'was clearly apprehensive of Winston's administrative methods'. In a private conversation with another Minister, George VI said that Churchill had no understanding 'of the mind of the people'. The King was on record as telling President Roosevelt that only in exceptional circumstances would he consent to Churchill being made Prime Minister. The Queen, too, thought Churchill brash, and according to a Palace official was 'very anti-Winston', not having forgiven him for his support of Edward VIII at the time of the Abdication. It would have been extraordinary if these reservations had not jittered through George VI's mind while he sat waiting in his room on the first floor, in his striped morning dress trousers, black waistcoat and jacket, to receive the First Lord of the Admiralty.

Chamberlain's sister Hilda believed that Winston Churchill was not an empathetic character. 'I doubt if any Churchill has been made to realise what is meant by consideration for others.' Yet oddly no one would have respected the King's qualms at this moment more than Churchill, whose prominent role in the Norway Campaign had inspired that morning's editorial in the *Daily Worker*. 'Now the veil has been torn aside, revealing the crime of the Norway adventure in all its horror; reckless adventurism, ill-equipped troops sent to their death, colossal military and naval blunders . . . He now has two Gallipolis to his credit.' Lord Woolton succinctly observed of him: 'Few people have succeeded in obtaining such a public demand for their promotion as the result of the failure of an enterprise.'

Afterwards, Churchill called his elevation 'a marvel' – and really did not know how he had survived in the public's esteem 'while all the blame was thrown on poor Mr Chamberlain'. On his last visit to Chamberlain, when he was dying of stomach cancer, Joseph Kennedy remarked that the Norway failure had made Churchill Prime Minister. 'True,' said Chamberlain, smiling sadly. Churchill, who only four days before the debate had 'come round to the view that it was providential we didn't succeed' in Norway, was still ruminating on the events which had brought him to power when he visited Oslo eight years later. He told his Norwegian audience at the banquet in his honour: 'In my long life, very long life . . . I have noticed the way in which human judgement is falsified. You may do a very wise thing and it may turn out most badly. You may do a foolish thing and it may save your life.'

Clementine had taken the afternoon train from Hereford. One reason given for cancelling the Whitsun holiday was not to place any unnecessary demand on public transport. In the event, her train was on time. She arrived back at Admiralty House shortly before Churchill climbed into the Humber with his bodyguard for the short drive to Buckingham Palace. Minutes later, another impatient telephone call was put through to Churchill's secretary who, on being asked if there was any news, was able to reply to Randolph: 'Only just to say that your father has gone to the Palace and when he comes back he will be Prime Minister.'

The streets and parks were unnaturally empty, and no one crowded the railings. Posters advertised news that was already history. 'Brussels bombed, Paris bombed, Lyons bombed, Swiss railways bombed.' The population had remained indoors, listening to the wireless. Figures showed that cinema and theatre attendance dropped on this evening by 50 per cent. The drama was going on elsewhere.

Whatever his private misgivings, the King received Churchill 'most graciously'. In *The Gathering Storm*, Churchill wrote that George VI looked at him searchingly and quizzically for some moments, and then said: 'I suppose you don't know why I have sent for you?'

Churchill replied: 'Sir, I simply couldn't imagine why.'

The King laughed and said: 'I want to ask you to form a Government.'

Frank Longford had raised a laugh in 1923 at the Eton Political Society when he asked the question: 'Do you think that Mr Winston Churchill has any future?' Less than a year later, when Baldwin invited Churchill back into the Conservative fold as Chancellor, after Chamberlain had turned down the position, Churchill wanted nothing more than to answer: 'Will the bloody duck swim?'

On this more sombre occasion, he told the King: 'I will certainly do so.'

The ride back from the Palace was made 'in complete silence', according to his bodyguard. Only when he stepped out of the Humber did Churchill speak.

'You know why I have been to Buckingham Palace, Thompson?'

'Yes, sir,' Walter Thompson answered, and congratulated him.

Churchill looked tense and strained. 'All I hope is that it is not too late. I am afraid it is, but we can only do our best.'

Thompson recalled that tears came into Churchill's eyes. As he turned away, he muttered something to himself. 'Then he set his jaw, and with a look of determination, mastering all emotions, he entered the side door of the Admiralty and began to climb the stairs.'

Those waiting to listen to the news at 9 p.m. were puzzled when the pips sounded and the announcer began: 'This is the Home Service. Here is the Right Honourable Neville Chamberlain MP who will make a statement.' Why had the speaker not announced him as 'the Prime Minister'?

Chamberlain had scribbled it off on his return to Downing Street. It was short, simple, dignified, and 'came quite spontaneously from what was in my mind'. The Queen told Halifax that Princess Elizabeth burst into tears when she heard it. Harold Nicolson thought it 'magnificent', and felt all his hatred for Chamberlain at once subside 'as if a piece of bread were dropped into a glass of champagne'. Ida wrote to her brother after hearing his broadcast: 'You have acted nobly, like yourself & like a Chamberlain.'

'I am not now going to make any comments on the debate in the House of Commons which took place on Tuesday and Wednesday, but when it was over I had no doubt in my mind that some new and drastic action must be taken if confidence was to be restored to the House of Commons and the war carried on with the energy and vigour essential to victory . . .'

Chamberlain stated that he believed unanimity of all parties was essential at this stage to present a united front to the enemy, and that it could not be obtained under him. *'His Majesty has now entrusted to my right honourable colleague . . .'* The journalist Virginia Cowles was certain that he was about to say 'Lord Halifax'. Nicolson would not have been surprised to hear the name 'Lloyd George'. Even ardent Churchill supporters like General Ismay had not anticipated the next half of the sentence. Ismay had been appointed Churchill's Chief of Staff on 1 May. 'The idea is prevalent that backroom boys know everything that is going on behind the scenes. I can only say that, although I was in almost constant attendance on Mr Churchill during these days, my first intimation that he was to be Prime Minister was his summons to Buckingham Palace.'

'. . . Mr Winston Churchill the task of forming a new Administration.'

Another person listening was Baba Metcalfe. 'My relief when at last he said Winston was going to be P.M. evoked a "Thank God" from me. I was so intensely glad that Edward was not going to have to carry out that ghastly responsibility. Those are purely personal grounds.'

In the early hours of the next morning, Sir Edward Bridges, the self-effacing Cabinet Secretary, went into the Admiralty to see Churchill who was still at his desk composing his War Cabinet, and said in a cautious voice: 'May I wish you every possible good fortune?'

Churchill grunted. 'Hum. "Every good fortune!" I like that! These other people have all been congratulating me. Every good fortune!'

Britain's new Prime Minister was quite right to be sceptical. There had been no Providential intervention. Events and individuals had decided the outcome.

For John Colville, it had been an exceptionally long day at No. 10. 'I went home to a solitary dinner and read *War and Peace.*' Colville's last boss had been, as he said of himself, 'a man of peace to the depths of my soul'. Chamberlain had had a lust for peace, said Churchill. Now was needed a man of war.

Even so, the imminent arrival of Churchill – whom Butler only hours earlier had described as 'the greatest adventurer of modern political history' – seemed to pose 'a terrible risk', Colville thought. 'It involves the danger of rash and spectacular exploits, and I cannot help fearing that this country may be manoeuvred into the most dangerous position it has ever been in . . . everybody is in despair here at the prospect.' Colville wrote this under the influence of Chips Channon's lukewarm champagne, a bottle produced from a filing cabinet and shared between Colville, Channon, Butler and Dunglass after the four of them lugubriously clinked glasses in a Jacobite toast to their 'King over the Water', Neville Chamberlain. 'Well, we had better drink together,' Butler is reported to have said, 'because this is the end.'

The drama of 10 May touched few people more personally than Margot Oxford. Her late husband, Herbert Asquith, had been ousted by Lloyd George in the First World War in similar circumstances. 'I remember what I felt when Ll G turned us out after 10 years of Downing Street.'

On Friday night, she was at her house in 44 Bedford Square. 'I felt very sad & lonely & was alone here, so after dinner, I thought I would take a taxi & say Goodbye to the Chamberlains.' Dressed from head to toe in black satin, she approached the door of her former home, rapped the lion-headed knocker, and 'sent my card up'.

A familiar manservant came down the ill-lit, red-carpeted corridor 'which I know so well!' and to her surprise said that the Chamberlains would be 'delighted to see me'. With some emotion Margot kissed Anne, and shook hands with Neville. 'They were both rather moved. He said that no one could have been nicer than Winston . . . that nothing just now mattered in any way about him or about any individual; all that mattered was that they should be United.'

In that instant, she felt that Chamberlain had less self-pity and self-love than any man she knew. 'I looked at his spare figure and keen eye and could not help comparing it with Winston's self-indulgent rotundity.'

But she knew how much Churchill loved making war and how he relished being on the bridge of a fighting frigate in the middle of a gale.

Margot's impromptu return to No. 10 carried her back twenty-six years to another fateful evening. The night of 4 August 1914, moments after her husband had declared war on Germany. She was passing the foot of the same staircase on her way to bed when she glanced down the corridor and saw Winston Churchill 'with a happy face' striding towards the double doors of the Cabinet Room.

EPILOGUES

'So it is to be Winston! The one thing I thought he could never be is P.M.'

BAFFY DUGDALE, 10 May 1940

*'The substitution of Churchill for Chamberlain is received
here with absolute indifference; by the Duce with irony.'*

COUNT GALEAZZO CIANO, 10 May 1940

CHURCHILL'S WAR CABINET was announced on 11 May and, to start with, satisfied nobody – full of 'symbolic sexagenarians' who failed, wrote Violet Bonham Carter, to present a surface 'on which a mind could strike'. Chamberlain loyalists referred to it as the 'Treachery Bench'. Even a natural supporter like Geoffrey Shakespeare felt it a pity that Churchill's new team 'should have been launched on a wave of pettiness and spite'. In fact, Churchill's Administration included twenty-one out of thirty-four Ministers who had served under Chamberlain. Clement Attlee became Lord Privy Seal. Arthur Greenwood replaced Hankey as Minister without Portfolio. No appointment raised eyebrows higher than the promotion of that 'indispensable Judas' Kingsley Wood, who, *'incredibile dicta'*, marvelled Reith, took over from John Simon at the Exchequer. Like most others, Violet Bonham Carter perceived Wood's new job as a reward for his sudden shift of allegiance: 'According to Clemmie it was largely Kingsley Wood who persuaded Chamberlain to recommend the King to send for W.' John Simon was elevated out of the way and made Lord Chancellor, 'and so,' observed Cuthbert Headlam, 'he has definitely given up the hope of becoming P.M.' Another Minister who had harboured leadership ambitions was Samuel Hoare, replaced by Archie Sinclair as Secretary of State for Air. Hoare had set his heart on a viceroyalty ('will take nothing short of India!' Cadogan reported), but, blamed by Churchill even now for the 1935 Government of

India Act, on top of other well-nursed grievances, he was sent as Ambassador to Madrid. *Times* journalist Leo Kennedy was walking past Buckingham Palace when he saw 'poor old Sam Hoare being driven away in his car, looking like nothing on earth'. Upset, Hoare wrote to Chamberlain on 14 May: 'No one has said a word in my defence . . . I, alone of the four of us who went through Munich, am left isolated to stand this unjust criticism.' Anthony Eden replaced Oliver Stanley as Secretary of State for War, the first news Stanley receiving of this being a call from Buckingham Palace 'asking if 10.30 tomorrow would suit him to deliver up his Seals!' Churchill's small team of supporters – those whom Nancy Dugdale dubbed his 'reptile satellites', J. C. C. Davidson 'the jackals', and Geoffrey Dawson the 'Thugs' – were recompensed with junior Ministries. At the Ministry of Information, Duff Cooper replaced John Reith (who 'within ten minutes' had collected all his gear and left the building). Lord Beaverbrook was made Minister of Aircraft Production; Bob Boothby, Parliamentary Secretary (Food); Harold Macmillan, Parliamentary Secretary (Supply); Harold Nicolson, Parliamentary Secretary (Information). The only Churchill recommendation which placed the King 'in a difficulty' was for Brendan Bracken to be created a Privy Counsellor. George VI felt that it was 'most important to maintain the high standard of qualification for membership' – and in this respect, it was implied, Bracken fell short. (A journalist later told Bracken when he became Minister of Information: 'Everything about you, Minister, is phoney; even your hair which looks like a wig, is really your own!') The King hoped that the appointment could be postponed for the time being, but Churchill dug in his heels, insisting: 'He has sometimes been almost my sole supporter in the years when I have been striving to get this country properly defended . . .'

CLEMENT DAVIES was lauded on 12 May in Beaverbrook's *Sunday Express* as 'the man who pulled down Chamberlain to set up Churchill'. He entered the Chamber next day to cries of 'Warwick!' Amery had pressed Churchill to give him a Ministry. 'I do hope you will not forget Clem Davies, whose indefatigable and well-directed energy contributed so much to the bringing about of a National Government . . .' Instead, Churchill offered Davies a viscountcy, which he turned down. He became leader of the Liberal Party in 1945 after Sinclair lost his seat. He died in 1962.

LEO AMERY was not offered the Supply Ministry, nor a place in the War Cabinet, but he was made Secretary of State for India, the country of his birth. He continued to spar with Churchill. On 28 July, Halifax reported that Churchill came to see him at the Dorchester and 'poured out his soul on India and Leo Amery. I think I persuaded him that Leo was more fool than knave.' He died in 1955.

PAUL EMRYS-EVANS, Honorary Secretary of the Watching Committee and, with Amery and Davies, a principal player in Chamberlain's overthrow, was likewise overlooked. 'As I was leaving the House [on 13 May], Brendan Bracken told me that although my name had been considered for an appointment, it was decided not to give me one.'

HORACE WILSON – according to Maisky, 'now referred to by all and sundry as Sir Horace Quisling' – was shifted from No. 10 back to the Civil Service, of which he had been head since 1939, with a warning that if he ever again visited Downing Street he would be made 'Governor of Greenland'. Right up to the end, Chamberlain maintained that Wilson had been unjustly criticised, and that he, Wilson, had a strong political sense, telling Halifax in their last conversation that 'nobody had served him more loyally'. When the vergers came to close Westminster Abbey on the day of Chamberlain's funeral, at nightfall, 'they found Horace Wilson there, still praying'. Churchill continued to demonise him, and refused to sign a formal letter of thanks for Wilson's services when the latter retired at the normal age of sixty, in the summer of 1942. He died in 1972.

LLOYD GEORGE went on flirting with a return to government. 'Many people want to see Lloyd George in office,' the New Yorker reported on 12 May. He told Maisky that he saw himself as 'general commissioner for food production with special powers'. Yet he refused to accept a position while Chamberlain remained in the War Cabinet, writing to Churchill: 'After deep and very anxious reflection I have come to the conclusion that I will be more useful to you outside rather than inside the WC as it is at present constructed.' On 3 October, Lloyd George confided to Sylvester: 'I shall wait until Winston is bust.' Churchill and Chamberlain discussed whether he wished to be the British Pétain, and

Chamberlain offered his resignation if Churchill believed it essential to get Lloyd George into the government; Churchill brushed this suggestion aside on the grounds that Chamberlain was giving him far more help than Lloyd George ever could. Meanwhile, Sylvester noted, Lloyd George put his energies into digging an air-raid shelter at Churt, 'sixty feet below the earth's crust ... like Piccadilly underground station. It has certainly not cost less than £6,000 [£350,000 in today's prices] and it is the talk of the place.' Before approaching Halifax, Churchill offered Lloyd George the Embassy in Washington, but he refused. By Christmas 1940, even Sylvester was 'completely tired of Lloyd George's mucking about. The man is doing nothing for his country, and is just living amongst the clouds, quarrelling with everybody.' He died in 1945.

LORD HALIFAX gave no indication that he regretted turning down the premiership, though he looked with distaste at Churchill's appointments. 'The gangsters will shortly be in complete control.' He had used a similar phrase when describing Hitler's invasion of Norway ('a well-executed piece of brigandage'). Much against his will, in January 1941 he was sent as Ambassador to Washington, following the death of Lord Lothian, who had been responsible for calling Halifax a 'saint'. He had seen Baba Metcalfe more or less every day until his departure on 14 January, when he hurriedly wrote to her: 'In the train. I have just opened your note, Baba darling. It has made it seem a little less beastly in one way wishing you goodbye this morning and in another infinitely worse. You need not be afraid that I will forget you or stop loving you – for I don't think that would be possible – and the memory of you, & knowing that you are remembering me in your thoughts and your prayers, will be of quite untold help.' When in 1943 Churchill offered him the India Office, Halifax declined, explaining that he had 'no political ambitions, and that when he, or anybody else, thought that I had ceased to be useful in Washington I had plenty of my own things to do'. After retiring in 1946, he was made Chancellor of the Order of the Garter, 'which I have always thought an intensely agreeable order'. He never achieved his ambition to become a Duke. He died in 1959.

BABA METCALFE left instructions for her diaries to be destroyed ('They are of great interest'), but an edited typescript survived, as did Lord Halifax's letters to her – now lodged in the Borthwick Institute. So far, only one letter from Baba to Halifax has been traced. Halifax's son Richard wrote to her: 'There are none at Garrowby. It is a mystery.' After the war, she shifted her emotional interest to Halifax's son-in-law, Lord Feversham. She divorced Fruity in 1955. In 1962, she returned to Simla to open a refuge for Tibetan children. She died in 1995, never having disclosed the nature of her relationship to 'Edouard'. 'But she enjoyed hinting at it,' says Philip Ziegler. 'She knew it was the gossip of the day, and rather relished the fact.'

PETER FLEMING died in 1971 with a Norwegian flag brought back from Namsos beside his bed. He had revisited the town only the year before, when he was reunited with Fanny Fahsing and the harbourmaster. In *The Sett*, an unfinished novel that he wrote on his return from Norway in 1940, he imagined what would have happened if Hitler had invaded Britain with Chamberlain still in power. Ju-52s at RAF Benson; the BBC transformed into the New Nordic Broadcasting Station; Buckingham Palace now the Brown House, residence of the Nazi Governor-General, Rudolf Hess; and the British government and the King evacuated to Ottawa.

MARTIN LINDSAY was mentioned in despatches for his service in Norway. In June 1945, he became Conservative MP for Solihull, defeating his Labour opponent, Roy Jenkins, by 5,049 votes. In 1947 he published his history of the House of Commons. His Norway Memorandum was not the only instance when he contacted Attlee over an issue of national importance. In October 1946, after Attlee had succeeded Churchill as Prime Minister, Lindsay ventured to send him 'some confidential information which I think you may not be in possession of'. Five years later, in an envelope marked 'secret', Lindsay communicated with Attlee again: 'Dear Prime Minister, I have hesitated a good deal before sending you the following information . . . the fact that British prestige abroad is involved has caused me to write'. He died in 1981.

TOM FOWLER went back to Krogs Farm in 2010 and was reunited with the farmer's daughter, Torlaug Werstad, who still lives there. On 26 April 2016, the Norwegian Honorary Consul in Grimsby presented him with the Norwegian Memorial Medal in recognition of his part in helping to restore Norway's freedom during the Second World War.

FRANK LODGE continued to fight for recognition. In 2008, he wrote a letter to the Defence Secretary: 'The family of a soldier who lost his life in Burma would receive the Burma star, in Italy the Italy Star, in North Africa the Africa Star, in France or Germany the French Germany star, but for the families of those who gave their lives in Norway, 1940 – nothing.' He died in 2012. There is still no specific Norway Campaign medal.

THE STEINKJER MEMORIAL, commemorating eleven British soldiers who lost their lives in the battle for Steinkjer, was unveiled on 21 April 2010, exactly seventy years to the day after Steinkjer town centre was destroyed by German bombs.

GILES ROMILLY was flown from Narvik to Germany where he spent five months in solitary confinement at Stalag XIIIA, then taken to Stalag VIIIB at Tost, and then in November 1941 to Colditz, where he became the first POW to be held hostage as a 'Prominente' in case things went badly for Hitler. A letter written to his parents on 27 April 1940 failed to reach Huntington Park in time for Colonel Romilly to know that his son was alive. 'Dearest Mummy and Daddy, Well, my caravan has halted at last, and I am in Germany ... Some day I will be able to tell you the whole story, there are good bits in it. But of course you, Mummy, were once a prisoner of war yourself – so naturally you will be a bit blasé about the whole business. Wasn't a potato pushed at you through iron bars? I seem to remember that detail. I must think up some rather more modern embellishments to tell you ... Narvik was dreadful. When I left, early one preposterously cold morning, snow was still whirling down from a leaden sky so low it almost touched the ground. I was glad to be moving swiftly southward towards the spring. A pity Uncle Winston didn't know when I was leaving – though I daresay he wouldn't have bothered ... I got captured through being too interested in the "story"! I send all my love, hoping you are both well and happy.' Only weeks later did Giles learn that his father had died on 6 May. Reunited after the war with his Narvik diary, he typed it out and gave a copy to his 'dear uncle Winston', as background for the Norwegian section of *The Gathering Storm*. 'Please raid for facts and impressions, if you find anything useful, and accept this typescript as a Birthday Present.' He died in California in 1967. His ashes are buried with his mother's in the churchyard at Huntington, next to his father's grave.

NARVIK was finally captured on 28 May 1940 according to General Mackesy's original plan, with only 150 casualties, and with French, Polish and Norwegian troops, and no British soldiers involved at all, merely a British artillery unit positioned on a hill west of the town. Any earlier, and the chances were strong that Churchill might have seen repeated the massacre of Suvla Bay in the Turkish campaign – a campaign that had earned him the nickname 'the butcher of Gallipoli'. After Narvik's seizure by an Allied force which had changed its name once again (to the North West Expeditionary Force), Admiral Cork's Chief of Staff, Captain Loben Maund, walked along the beach, and confirmed that British troops would have had to wade a considerable distance ashore, 'well-covered by machine-gun posts that could not have been neutralised by fire from the sea'. Colonel Kurt Herrmann, last survivor of General Dietl's staff, told General Mackesy's son Piers that he believed that the British attack as originally conceived and promoted by Churchill would have failed. This is also the opinion of a former machine-gunner from the Norwegian 6th Division. At ninety-seven, Ivan Vanya is the oldest living soldier to have fought the Germans before Narvik's capture in May. On 23 April, his team were pinned down for a day and a half by a German machine-gun unit on Mount Leigas. For a whole night, Vanya, an expert skier, had to play dead, digging his face into the snow while tracer bullets ripped overhead. He says: 'The British did the right thing not to land. It would have been very stupid to go with Churchill's idea. They were not well equipped. They would have lost many lives.' Peter Fleming, allegedly the first British soldier to land on the Norwegian mainland, had taken part in the earlier military withdrawal from central Norway, and recorded how 'the end of the difficult affair at Narvik attracted little attention at the time and is today scarcely remembered as a victory'. After the efforts made to occupy the town, it was held by the Allies for ten days, then evacuated on 8 June 1940 in order to throw every man who could be spared, every gun and every plane, into the battlefield in France. Captain Maund was among the evacuees. 'The withdrawal though successful in that not one of the 31,000 men was left behind was perhaps one of the saddest journeys most of us had ever made. Across the waters ahead of us France had collapsed; Italy declared war and few anywhere outside Great Britain ever imagined England could survive.'

NEVILLE CHAMBERLAIN remained leader of his party, as Asquith had in December 1916, and became Lord President of the Council. Offered the Order of the Garter, which would have made him a knight, he turned it down, preferring, he told Churchill, to die plain Mr Chamberlain, 'like my father before, unadorned by any title'. Joseph Kennedy saw him on 16 May. 'He is definitely a heartbroken and physically broken man. He looks ghastly.' Chamberlain had the example of his cousin Norman, who lost his captaincy in 1917, days before attempting to lead his men 'unswervingly under extremely heavy fire' to their objective. 'At bottom it was the humiliation of being degraded in rank that poisoned everything.' A similar bane afflicted Chamberlain, even if he half-welcomed Churchill's accession, now that the battle had intensified. He confessed to Anthony Eden that he had agreed to stay on in the War Cabinet only 'with a heavy heart'. The loss of Chequers was a further blow. He drove down with Anne one evening in June to collect his wood-saw and say goodbye. Jones, the gardener, was in tears. Chamberlain gave him a copy of William Robinson's *English Flower Garden*. Then, before he stepped into the Armstrong Siddeley, his eyes took in the shrubs that he had planted: the magnolias on the north lawn, the flowering cherries, and the tulip tree in the east forecourt which was later chosen as his memorial tree (and continues to thrive). After they had to relinquish the house, the Chamberlains could not bear to speak of the place by its name – as in childhood his father had not talked of his mother. Anne wrote: 'It was like someone we loved had gone.' He wrote to his sister Ida: 'There is no pleasure in life for us just now. Week ends cannot be distinguished from week days.' Yet within a short time Chamberlain discovered that he had become indispensable to the new tenant. Churchill had written to him on the evening of 10 May: 'To a very large extent I am in your hands – and I feel no fear of that.' Neither did Churchill lack the courage to inform Lloyd George that 'I have received a very great deal of help from Chamberlain. His kindness and courtesy to me in our new relations have touched me. I have joined hands with him and must act with perfect loy-alty.' Chamberlain was quick to reciprocate. 'Winston has behaved with the most unimpeachable loyalty. Our relations are excellent and I know that he finds my help of great value to him.' When Churchill was away in France on 22 May, Chamberlain once again presided over the government, causing Churchill later to admit to Halifax and others: 'I shall never find such a col-league again.' Yet Churchill's dependence on Chamberlain – and on Chamberlain henchmen like David Margesson, who remained Chief Whip – was not popular. On 21 June, Cecil King wrote in his diary: 'He is now so much in the grip of the old bunch that people are calling him Nev-ille Churchill.' Even as British pilots defended the skies that summer, Maisky noted how 'the officers and soldiers returning from Flanders take every opportunity to curse the former government which *let them down* with arms and equipment. Many demand that Chamberlain should be brought to court for high treason!' Against rising criticism, Chamberlain wryly reflected that it was he and Lord Swinton who had pushed ahead with the production of the Hurricanes and Spitfires that were winning the Battle of Britain, against the advice of both Churchill, who six months before Munich had written to Chamberlain criticising these selfsame fighter planes, and that of the Air Staff, who had championed bombers. 'If I am personally responsible for deficiencies of tanks and A.A. guns, I must equally be responsible for the efficiency of the Air Force & Navy.' One of those RAF pilots was Conservative MP Patrick Donner, who, though he had voted against the government in the Norway Debate, refused to join in the clamour to traduce Chamberlain. Donner directed his most burning criticism towards those who 'having held an erroneous view of Neville Chamberlain for many years . . . do not possess the resilience of mind to change that view in the light of facts previously unknown to them'. Donner concluded: 'Must not the final verdict be . . . that Neville Chamberlain and Winston Churchill between them saved this country. Neither statesman would have achieved our salvation without the other' – a sentiment echoed by one of Chamberlain's constituents, a Mrs Hodges who wrote to him on the day he died, saying that 'you saved the life of our Country and we always think of you with deep and everlasting gratitude', and adding this PS: 'I have a portrait of you and Mr. Churchill side by side on my mantelpiece.' That the relationship between the two men remained unresolved is hinted at in a story told by Chamberlain's doctor, Thomas Horder, when on 22 September 1940 Chamberlain took the reluctant decision to retire from active public life after confessing to 'having trouble with my inside'. In the last stages of stomach cancer, Chamberlain wrote a letter to Churchill, entrusting it to Horder to deliver. Churchill took the letter, but before open-ing it asked: 'Did he say anything about the Leadership?' As A. J. Sylvester wrote in his diary: 'The fact is Winston is afraid of NC.' Six months after the Norway Debate, on 7 November 1940, Halifax visited Chamberlain, who pointed to a chair by his bed and said: 'Sit there.' They talked for ten minutes, Halifax finding Chamberlain 'very steady and brave' and even able to make a parliamentary joke. Chamberlain told him with a half-laugh: 'Approaching dissolution, I suppose, brings relief.' Halifax's diary contin-ued: 'Then he spoke of our work together, and what it had meant to him, in a way that moved me much. He took my hand in both his, and held it, and so with no more said but with the full understanding of friends who go to different duties, we parted.' On 9 November, a wet Saturday evening, Halifax was staying with Baba Metcalfe at Little Compton when Horace Wilson telephoned to say that Chamberlain had died. The time and place were kept secret for his cremation the following week. The *Daily Telegraph* lamented: 'Never before in England's history has so much secrecy surrounded a former Prime Minister's funeral. The public was left completely in the dark about the burial arrangements because London is in the front line of battle.' On 13 November, Chamberlain was cremated in Golders Green without a ceremony, with only Anne and 'two household servants alone' being present, and no one from the Clique, not his sisters Ida and Hilda, not his son Frank, with the Royal Artillery in Malta, or daughter Dorothy, nor his niece Valerie, who was training as a nurse in Glasgow. The next day a service to pay homage to his ashes was held in a chilly Westminster Abbey to the wail of air-raid sirens and with the draught from the blown-out stained-glass windows whirling about his empty coffin. As the service reached its climax, one mourner noticed with concern that the congregation was singing 'the chief hymn to a wrong tune'. Chamberlain's public image has been out of key with his private persona ever since.

WINSTON CHURCHILL returned from Buckingham Palace on the evening of 10 May having 'acquired the chief power in the State, which henceforth I wielded in ever-growing measure for five years and three months of world war, at the end of which time all our enemies having surrendered unconditionally or being about to do so I was immediately dismissed by the British electorate from all further conduct of their affairs'. He became Prime Minister again from 1951 to 1955. He died in 1965.

MARTIN LINDSAY'S MEMORANDUM TO CLEMENT ATTLEE

Private & Confidential

May I use a private friendship to bring a public matter to your notice in the hope that it may be of some service to the country?

I have just returned from the Southern front in Norway after serving in a very humble position on the Staff. Now that all those who will ever get back have got over, I think that the facts as observed by myself and my comrades should be brought to the notice of responsible persons so that those responsible are not able to cover up their misdeeds next week in Parliament. The facts as regards the front itself come from eye witnesses, some of whom have seen this letter and state that, in their opinion, it does not fully disclose the extent of the disorganisation and incompetence exhibited.

Within a week of the German invasion of Norway a convoy containing about 40,000 men was assembled on the Clyde in ships all over 10,000 tons and some over 30,000 tons. The ports in Norway available to us were very small, and these ships were quite useless. Even at this stage there were numerous cases of persons and units being sent on the wrong boats. In many cases it was necessary to telephone the War Office to find out where to go as the local staff were entirely ignorant.

The troops at the front consisted of three battalions of regulars and two of semi-trained territorials. The only artillery were one or two guns run by the Royal Marines. A ship containing artillery and A.A. guns was torpedoed in the second convoy. The enemy was fully equipped in every respect. The front lines of communication and base undefended by any anti-aircraft guns except pom-poms were *subjected* [handwritten] to *continuous* [handwritten] bombing from dawn to dusk. Only a very few wounded were got back as the enemy regularly machine-gunned the stretcher bearers, the one road, and of course the civilians. No building except the station was standing within four miles of the base The only aircraft we ever had were 15 Goliaths 1929 model which are slower than the German bombers; of these only three were in action the last five days. It has been stated that Hurricanes and Spitfires could not be used owing to their landing speed. The Wing-Commander in charge states that this is not the case. One squadron would have changed the campaign.

So far as I have been able to ascertain, not a single unit arrived properly equipped. Vital parts left behind or on wrong boats, *no* [handwritten] transport, no medical equipment and very little food. Senior Staff Officers asking junior Officers what they should do next. Absolute chaos reigned at the base and in the lines of communication. Considering these impossible conditions the behaviour of the troops was admirable; but a very high percentage of shock cases exist, due to unremitting bombing with nobody replying.

The operation order stated specifically that the object of the force was the capture of Oslo; this order I have seen and copies exist. The P.M. statement as to the limited objectives was untrue, as also was his statement that the evacuation was effected without loss. The first night of the evacuation I myself saw two men killed. The embarkation was done under continuous bombing raids. There was one A.A. gun firing only.

It is no exaggeration to say that the force was not an army but a rabble, and given the facts as set out above very few troops would not have bolted. It speaks volumes for the rank and file and their immediate leaders that this was not the case.

In the whole story of muddle and incompetence which has resulted in one of the most complete disasters in our military history, the efficiency of the Navy stands out. To them, those of us who got back owe our lives. With them only was one immediately conscious that every officer and man knew his job and did it in keeping with the highest traditions of that great service.

If the lessons of this disaster are not learned, and the people responsible weeded out the prospects of our winning this war are slender. I may add that the German Army showed itself an efficient and formidable force. I am aware that for an officer to write as I have written is against the regulations, but I consider that the truth should be made *known* [handwritten] in the public interest and not buried. I may add that the German High Command Communique[s] of the last few days have been strictly accurate.

NOTES AND SOURCES

AM – Alexandra ('Baba') Metcalfe diary
BCA – Balliol College Archives, Oxford
BI – Borthwick Institute, York
BL – British Library
BOD – Bodleian Library, Oxford
CA – Churchill Archives Centre, Cambridge
CP – Charles Peake diary
CRL – Cadbury Research Library, Birmingham University
FRO – Flintshire Records Office
PA – Parliamentary Archives
RU – Special Collections, Reading University
SP – Salisbury Papers

PROLOGUE
foul and treacherous, W. S. Churchill, *Churchill's visit to Norway*, 15
one of the black . . . world, ibid., 31
known all over, ibid., 8
Oh no . . . Britain, ibid., 42

1 PERFECT BLACKOUT
Is there any, Cecil King, *With Malice Toward None*, 15
blown to pieces, Churchill, *Churchill's Visit to Norway*, 36

his face covered, Vernon Bartlett, *And Now, Tomorrow*, 90
we pride ourselves, Churchill, *Churchill's Visit to Norway*, 35
only known record, Sir Benjamin Stone took a formal photograph in 1903, but Members posed for this.
splendid upheaval, A. J. P. Taylor, *A Personal History*, 153
almost inevitable, Vernon Bartlett, *I Know What I Liked*, 139
We are meeting to-day, Pierse Loftus MP, Hansard, 9/5/1940
the most momentous, Beaverbrook papers, PA HC/BBK/G/11/11; Stafford Cripps, too, called the debate 'the most momentous that has ever taken place in the history of Parliament', Hansard, 9/5/1940
altered the history, Harold Macmillan, *The Blast of War*, 54
a little suspicious, Austen Mitchell, 'A Forbidden Glimpse of History', *The House* magazine, 20/8/1992; *Sunday Times*, 1/5/1966
sitting on a jelly, John Moore-Brabazon, *The Brabazon Story*, 55
In vain we look, BOD MSS Macmillan dep c.874

rather like a biologist, Ivan Maisky, *The Maisky Diaries*, xvi

It was then, W. S. Churchill, *Great Contemporaries*, 38

Curious what, Borthwick Institute Edward Halifax diary, 21/3/1940

Whenever the English, Elias Canetti, *The Human Province*, 13

pinnacle of deathless, W. S. Churchill, *A History of the English-Speaking Peoples*, vol. I, 26

If ever there was, Philip Ziegler interview with author, 24/11/2015

Six more weeks, Alan Campbell-Johnson, *Viscount Halifax*, 557

the number of people, BOD MSS Woolton 76

I think that Kingsley, Henry Channon, *Chips: The Diaries of Sir Henry Channon*, 221

People are saying, Harold Nicolson, *Diaries and Letters; 1939–1945*, vol.2, 75

in the light of, BI EH diary, 16/4/1940

History goes past, Hugh Dalton, *The Second World War Diary of Hugh Dalton*, 347

What you tell me, CA Amel 8/76, Hore-Belisha to LA, 5/10/1954

upon what small, D. R. Thorpe, *The Uncrowned Prime Ministers*, 138

the one time, Lord Hailsham, *Desert Island Discs*, BBC, 27/3/1988

got slightly confused, Andrew Roberts, *The Holy Fox*, 289

It's all destiny, Frances Campbell-Preston interview with author, 4/5/2015

the P.M. considers, Maisky, 161

things were "written", Edmund Ironside, *The Ironside Diaries*, 40

I heard Churchill, James Stuart, *Within the Fringe: An autobiography*, 96

Churchill wrote of, David Dilks interview with author, 29/4/2015

extended essay . . . distortion, David Reynolds, *In Command of History*, 128, 119

It is a pity, Leo Amery, *The Leo Amery Diaries*, vol. 1, 1896–1929, 592

the public of our, Patrick Beesly, *Very Special Admiral*, 297

raising his hand . . . clouded, Somerset de Chair, *Buried Pleasure*, 225

ought to be a model, WSC, Hansard, 12/11/1940

Of course, I could, Randolph Churchill and Martin Gilbert, *Finest Hour: Winston S. Churchill, 1939–41*, 902

this narrow, obstinate, Dingle Foot, *British Political Crises*, 162

I myself can, Neville Chamberlain, *Norman Chamberlain: A memoir*, vi

consistently misjudged, Edward Halifax, *Fulness of Days*, 227

less than justice, ibid., 198

For a long time, Dilks interview with author

Halifax felt it, Zeigler interview with author

unwittingly inaccurate, Halifax, 185

the real thing, Edward Spears, *Prelude to Dunkirk*, 133

trying to construct, Churchill, Hansard, 12/11/1940

Churchill's writing of history, Ziegler interview with author

He sees himself, Cecil King, 60

to defend . . . proceeding, CA WCHL 1/14

it would reveal, Dilks interview with author

They often get, CA Amel 7/86, LA to EH, 22/11/1954

He is a very emotional, Maisky, 337

good anti-Nazi, CA Amel 7/86, LA to Lord Lytton, 4/8/1940

who wrote history, Otto Mohr, *Churchill's Visit to Norway*, 13

keen sense of justice, *Manchester Guardian*, 11/5/1950

the irrational . . . crucial, David Dilks, 'Appeasement Revisited': *University of Leeds Review*, vol. 15, no. 1, May 1972

When the clamour, C. L. Lundin, *Finland in the Second World War*, ii

on the precise, Nick Smart, 'Four Days in May: The Norway Debate and the Downfall of Neville Chamberlain', *Parliamentary History*, vol. 17, no. 2, 1998, 231

barbed-wire, holes, Moore-Brabazon, 97

so as to introduce, Geoffrey Shakespeare, *Let Candles Be Brought In*, 227

indefatigable second, Beverley Baxter, *Men, Martyrs and Mountebanks*, 255

saved from, Geoffrey Shakespeare, 40

the Victorian sandglass: A sandglass measured the time until May 1941, when it was replaced by a clockwork instrument called 'the clock'. This was started by pressing a button. Four more minutes were allowed for Members to get into the voting lobbies between the 'second call' and the order to lock the doors. 'At the end of the four minutes a very small bell strikes and the dial hand stops.' Dennis Herbert, *Backbencher and Chairman*, 131

2 'NAR-VIK'

My eye has, Churchill, Hansard, 8/5/1940

Who will want, in Stephen Spender, *New Selected Journals*

the focal point . . . disaster, John Shakespeare interview with author, 4/1/2016

NAR-vik, Frances Partridge, *A Pacifist's War, Diaries 1939–45*, 36

no time . . . hope, ibid., 37

an outlandish place, Ronald Blythe, *The Age of Illusion*, 153

a battleship could, Giles Romilly, *The Privileged Nightmare*, 8

That day lightning, Theodore Broch, *The Mountains Wait*, 74

abominable, insulting bangs, Romilly, 9

I was going to, *Armidale Express*, 28/6/1940

What he did, Edmund Romilly interview with author, 8/9/2016

Yes. Yes . . . rails, Romilly, 9–10

I dashed . . . gone, CA CH 4/142, Romilly diary, 9/4/40

I want to make, Broch, 79

I got captured, GR to parents 27/4/1940, private collection

fluttered around crazily, CA CH 4/142

He was upset, Mary Marshall interview with author, 10/9/2016

Das ist Pech für Sie, Romilly, 11

What ship are . . . journy!, ibid., 12–13

a forest of mast tops, CA CH 4/142

dominating and brutal, Broch, 109

without a stitch . . . available, CA CH 4/142

on the general, GR's affidavit at General Keitel's trial, 14/3/1946

Monday April 8 . . . miles out, CA CH 4/142

In war, speed, Romilly, 21

We did not . . . Sun, Broch, 102

Six mounted . . . uniform anywhere, Leland Stowe, *No Other Road to Freedom*, 72

the most important, ibid., 118

an unbelievable . . . hours, ibid., 83–4

practically on starvation, CA CH 4/142

the snow, snow, *Armidale Express*, 28/6/1940

You can't imagine, GR to parents, 27/4/1940

Well, Mr Romilly . . . Churchill, Romilly, 23

Winston Churchill, the greatest, Narvik War Museum

The Nazis are taking, CA CH 4/142

caused him no, BI EH diary, 12/4/1940

The British have, Geirr Haarr interview with author, 12/5/2016

Everyone knows . . . imagination, Kevin Ingram, *Rebel: The Short Life of Esmond Romilly*, 17

reading telegrams, John Colville, *The Fringes of Power*, 538

a stern-looking, Anna Gerstein, *Misdeal*, 3

No, no, ibid., 35

I don't believe, Mary Soames, *Speaking for Themselves: The personal letters of Winston and Clementine Churchill*, 118

a perambulating, Meredith Whitford, *Churchill's Rebels: Jessica Mitford and Esmond Romilly*, 47

a big-shouldered structure, Giles Romilly, unpublished MS

For the latter part, Giles and Esmond Romilly, *Out of Bounds*, 209

a very tough . . . attacks him, T. C. Worsley, *Fellow Travellers*, 86

it would kill, Ingram, 184

who was inclined, John Sutherland, *Stephen Spender*, 223

hideous blow . . . captors, Whitford, 257

You shall . . . heads, Nellie Hozier, 'Prisoners in Germany', *English Review*, Feb 1915

I needn't tell . . . sorrow and pain, Whitford, 258

sympathy for . . . young people, Colville, *Action this Day: Working with Churchill*, 55, 65

sentimental about people, David Carlton, *Anthony Eden*, 159; Nicolson diary, 6/1/1940

supreme question, *The Argus* (Melbourne), 20/11/1937

3 OPERATION 'WILFRED'

A lot of nonsense, quoted in Beesly, 153

I can't help . . . publicly, Soames, 143, 150

This so called, Alexander Cadogan, *The Diaries of Sir Alexander Cadogan*, 244

the importance of stopping, W. S. Churchill, *The Gathering Storm*, 421

doing Narvik, Cadogan, 242

It is like, Ironside, 192

the power of, Martin Gilbert, *The*

Churchill War Papers: At the Admiralty, vol. I, 101

900 bombers . . . communication, SP Lord Londonderry to Lord Salisbury, 22/9/1939

abject depression, Robert Self ed., *The Neville Chamberlain Diary Letters*, vol. 4, 466

However much, ibid., 456

Winston, of course, Colville, *Fringes of Power*, 60

needed a diet, J. H. Godfrey, *The Naval Memoirs of Admiral J. H. Godfrey*, vol. 5, 326

it would give, Christopher M. Bell, *Churchill and Sea Power*, 174

into an imprudent, Churchill and Gilbert, *Finest Hour*, 178

I can manage, Soames, 92

A modern fleet . . . come, Ironside, 41

obsessed with the idea, Godfrey, vol. 8, 18

The search for, *At the Admiralty*, 127

And when he digs, Maisky, 473

If Germany can . . . decisive, *At the Admiralty*, 523

Our defeat . . . guide, ibid., 524

My wife doesn't . . . party, Ralph F. De Bedts, *Ambassador Joseph Kennedy 1938–40: An anatomy of appeasement*, 197

much to the disgust, Ironside, 196

to turn down . . . split, Cadogan, 245

I have felt very, *At the Admiralty*, 638

technical infringement, Geirr Haarr, *The German Invasion of Norway: April 1940*

he wanted to do, Godfrey, vol. 5, 327

brought the whole, ibid., 328

by a full three, Roberts, *Holy Fox*, 189

very seldom, Hastings Ismay, *The Memoirs of General the Lord Ismay*, 103

the endless procession, *At the Admiralty*, 760

Halvorsen was unaware, Haarr interview with author

We are sitting opposite, *At the Admiralty*, 773

one or two . . . went ahead, BI EH diary, 16/2/1940

You should board, *At the Admiralty*, 772

Winston rang me, BI EH diary, 17/2/1940

At 7.45 before, *NC Diary Letters*, vol. 4, 499

Come on up, Geirr Haarr, *The Battle for Norway: April–June 1940*, 429

You must have, CHAR 1/355/17

under the noses . . . Navy is here", *At the Admiralty*, 794–95

Altmark – drawn cutlasses . . . our way, Ronald Tree, *When the Moon Was High*, 112

the most flagrant, *At the Admiralty*, 760

Most of them, CHAR 1/355/17

complete subservience, François Kersaudy, *Norway 1940*, 28

pleaded earnestly, *At the Admiralty*, 796

Strike while the iron, ibid., 761

The operation being, ibid., 780

medieval story, Florence Harriman, *Mission to the North*, 246

certain indications . . . territory, Erich Raeder, *Struggle for the Sea*, 158–9 the war could not be, Klaus A. Maier, 'German Strategy', *Germany and the Second World War*: vol. 2, 185

all-destroying blow, Rauschning, *Hitler Speaks*, 20

if Germany were, Geirr Haarr, *The German Invasion of Norway: April 1940*, 127–30

a trustworthy impression, ibid., 140

upon mentioning . . . time, Kersaudy, 42

Führer orders investigation, ibid., 42

issue of Norway, Haarr, *German Invasion of Norway*, 6

the awful difficulties, Churchill, *Gathering Storm*, 554

a decisive blow, Paul Reynaud, *In the Thick of the Fight*, 266

in complete ignorance, Kersaudy, 44

on a theoretical, ibid., 43

This incident put, Raeder, 163

No opposition, Haarr, 6

Really stupid initiative, Kersaudy, 44

siege of Great Britain, ibid., 38

a north-Germanic, Peter Longerich, *Goebbels*, 449

human material . . . upbreeding of men, H. D. Loock, 'Weserübung – A Step towards the Greater Germanic Reich', *Scandinavian Journal of History* 2, 1977, 67–88

the boarding of, Kersaudy, 45

to launch a, ibid., 45

Once outside, ibid., 46

I cannot and I, Loock, op. cit.

It was remarkable, Raeder, 167

We have no, Ironside, 190

To help form, Information from Geirr Haarr

utmost importance . . . operation, Kersaudy, 48

into a rage, Maier, 'German Strategy', 192

expressed his . . . losses, Kersaudy, 49

breakfast, Haarr, *German Invasion of Norway*, 44

cross-examined . . . war, Kersaudy, 49

Wesertag ist der, Haarr, *German Invasion of Norway*, 44

Everything has, Peter Longerich, *Goebbels*, 446

First we will keep, Ian Kershaw, *Hitler 1936–45: Nemesis*, 288

A hundred . . . available, Harriman, 246

Have you read, *NC Diary Letters*, vol. 4, 498

a very pleasant, Amery, *Diaries*, vol. 2, 553

When I wage . . . Norway, Hermann Rauschning, *Hitler Speaks*, 128

1. that Denmark . . . ships, CA HNKY 10/7-8

the danger came, ibid.

a fantastic story . . . nerve war, William L. Shirer, *Berlin Diary*, 229

would be taken, Haarr, *German Invasion of Norway*, 48

Recent information, Reynaud, 270

the Germans were, Amery, *Diaries*, vol. 2, 592

did not support, Haarr, 48

a mad expedition, Beesly, 151

Information reached us, CA HNKY 10/7–8

vain boggling, Churchill, *Gathering Storm*, 458

one of the most, Kersaudy, 49

you should never, *NC Diary Letters*, vol. 4, 21

Apparently Cabinet, Cadogan, 255

I am concerned, Geoffrey Shakespeare, 232

that Mr Churchill, ibid., 231

so I might be, ibid., 234

on which Winston, NC Diary Letters, vol. 4, 504

rash suggestions, ibid., 407

conscious that Winston, ibid., 508

I said that for once, ibid., 505

a bull with snails, NC Diary Letters, vol. 4, 512

kill two birds, Graham Rhys-Jones, Churchill and the Norway Campaign, 5

We had everything, At the Admiralty, 532

I think the whole, John Kennedy, The Business of War, 51

amateurish and half-hatched, Cadogan, 263

We had a dreadful . . . consider, Ironside, 227

tired and lugubrious . . . go, John Kennedy, 50

My dear Edward . . . not, At the Admiralty, 883–84

The first step, ibid., 854

to do something, Colville, Fringes of Power, 92

It is time we stopped, Hansard, 19/3/1940

the delay, the vacillation, Macmillan, 59

Great Britain and France, The Times, 20/3/1940

a foxy expression, NC Diary Letters, vol. 4, 512

I rejoice that you, At the Admiralty, 909

the battle of iron, Reynaud, 267

because of his loyalty, Colville, Fringes of Power, 96

as I believe, BI EH diary, 6/4/1940

the necessity of throwing, Colville, Fringes of Power, 97

by the spring, NC Diary Letters, vol. 4, 456

Attlee actually looks, ibid., 410

of the gathering, Maisky diary, 4/4/1940

This I heard later, BI EH diary, 4/4/1940

very warmly received, NC Diary Letters, vol. 4, 38, 6/4/1940

we showed a lamentable, Spears, 99

I doubt if, Normanbrook, Action This Day, 29

We are ready, Express, 4/4/1940

to speak more, SP Lord Salisbury to Lord Wilmer, 2/4/1940

There is a curious, NC Diary Letters, vol. 4, 515

When an operation, At the Admiralty, 893

deplorably insecure, Cadogan, 262

an alarming communiqué, Colville, Fringes of Power, 92

indicated a decision, Dilks, 'Great Britain and Scandinavia in the Phoney War'

You cannot keep, Ironside, 221

Gamelin on his visit, Kersaudy to author

and stated it, CA CHU 4/142

were talked about, Raymond E. Lee, Journals, December 1940

If anyone starts, Geoffrey Shakespeare, 234

See the midnight . . . Norway, D. J. L. Fitzgerald, History of the Irish Guards in the Second World War, 10

tragic impasse, Paul Baudouin, *Private Diaries*, 11

Thanks to our, Reynaud, 266

a game of musical chairs (footnote), CRL AP20/1/20-20A, Eden diary, 1/4/1940

Why take the trouble (footnote), Amery, *Diaries*, vol. 2, 586

Winston has hankered, Amery, *Diaries*, vol. 1, 590

1st L now becomes, CA GBR/0014/INKP, Inskip diary 9/4/1940

putting Churchill in charge, Maisky diary, 4/4/1940

Winston is in seventh, *NC Diary Letters*, vol. 4, 496

personally doubted whether, *At the Admiralty*, 951

always rather pooh-poohed, Patrick Donner, *Crusade*, 272

commit some overt, *At the Admiralty*, 762

the moment the Germans, T. K. Derry, *The Campaign in Norway*, 15

new officers, Haarr, *German Invasion of Norway*, 51

and found forts, BOD MSS Dawson 81/39–41/13

German warships, Haarr, *German Invasion of Norway*, 50

well dined, ibid., 86

I don't think so, Henry Denham, *Inside the Nazi Ring*, 4

100 Ships, *At the Admiralty*, 977

some operation against, Haarr, *German Invasion of Norway*, 49

in principle fantastic, Derry, 28

evidently doing [an] exercise, Admiralty War Diary 223/126; Haarr, *German Invasion of Norway*, 50

All these reports, *At the Admiralty*, 977

The war is going, Haarr, *German Invasion of Norway*, 41

the silliest thing, Cadogan, 268

he was like, Ironside, 248

all gone without, BI EH diary, 8/4/1940

Winston very optimistic . . . 10.30, J. A. Cross, *Samuel Hoare*, 313

The man who, Simon Garfield, *We are at War*, 194

4 THE FIRST CRUNCH

Faultless timing, Evelyn Waugh, *Put Out More Flags*, 31

It was the Duty, Ismay, 118

No news from, Cadogan, 268

Our information was, *At the Admiralty*, 989

We listened to the news, Colville, *Fringes of Power*, 100

The German Government, Shirer, 245

In the same way, Loock, 67–88

What a sharp . . . of the day, Maisky, 270

Little girls could, Spears, 102

no chance of Narvik, Nicolson, 69

crackling in the forests . . . flowers growing (footnote), CRL NC 11/2/1a, Anne Chamberlain journal, 29/1/1940

beyond all challenge (footnote) Churchill, *A History of the English-Speaking Peoples*, vol. 1, 21

totally failed to blow up (footnote), BI EH diary, 25/4/1940

despatches in hand . . . unexpected, Paul Baudouin, 9

Norway was against, *The Diaries of William Lyon Mackenzie King*, http://www.bac-lac.gc.ca, 9/4/1940

Judging by the way, Spears, 105

clock-like precision, BOD MSS Simon diary 11, 12/4/1940

and we were ninnies, Colville, *Fringes of Power*, 100

all had one, Maisky, 270

We have bungled, Ironside, 250

It is sometimes, *At the Admiralty*, 996

I consider Germans, ibid., 996

The First Lord, Colville, *Fringes of Power*, 99

even more ... hours, Basil Liddell Hart, *Memoirs*, vol. 2, 278

that something very, A. J. Sylvester papers, PA LG/g/241/1

only one enemy, *At the Admiralty*, 993

an entirely different, ibid., 998

gloomy news . . . bad day, John Wheeler-Bennett, *King George VI*, 438

with monkeyish, Ironside, 250

nagging at everybody, Cross, 314

excellent, Donner, 272

paramount necessity ... expedition, *At the Admiralty*, 999

lack of information, ibid., 993

like cut flowers, BI EH diary, 9/4/1940

and said "Look at it! W. P. Crozier, *Off the Record*, 169

a sideshow in, Peter Fleming, *Invasion 1940*, 156

first love, Churchill, *Gathering Storm*, 493

the trophy at, *At the Admiralty*, 1100

As enemy is, Haarr, *German Invasion of Norway*, 353

It is at your, ibid., 336

that I did not, ibid., 338

the Admiralty's intolerable, Stephen Roskill, *Churchill and the Admirals*, 101

A miraculous change, *New Statesman*, 13/4/1940

8 a.m. news, Partridge, 35

something considerable, Margery Allingham, *The Oaken Heart*, 133

There's something about, Collin Brooks, *Fleet Street, Press Barons and Politics*, 265

the British had effected, Mackenzie King, 10/4/1940

Everywhere, in the, Brooks, 265

You can take it, Allingham, 171

"We have the Germans, Garfield, 194

the shores of Norway, Fitzgerald, 13

The papers were, BOD MS Eng hist 496, Euan Wallace diary

The world was, BOD MSS Dawson 44 diary

In that speech, Hansard, 7/5/1940

such a damaging effect, Hansard, 8/5/1940

We have been completely, *At the Admiralty*, 1001

terribly despondent . . . out, ibid., 999

entirely fictitious, Tree, 112

I had to manoeuvre, *At the Admiralty*, 999

It is said of Sam, A. J. Sylvester papers, PA LG/g/241/1

Aunt Tabitha, Nicolson, 56

He is indignant, *At the Admiralty*, 1006

I must apologise, ibid., 1013

obvious signs, SP Clement Davies to Lord Salisbury, 15/4/1940

His speech in the House, BI EH diary, 11/4/1940

He hesitates, Nicolson, 70

I had never seen, Maisky, 270

As I listened, BOD MSS Dawson 44 diary

The prevailing mood, Maisky 271

looking bent, Brooks, 265

his physique must, Ironside, 248

5 IN GREAT STRENGTH

Everyone said, Waugh, *Put Out More Flags*, 183

Norway was a disaster, Robert Blake and Wm. Roger Louis ed., *Churchill*, 261

You provoked action, *The Keyes Papers*, *Vol. III: 1939–45*, 26

running riot, Godfrey, vol. 5, 308

zest for taking charge, ibid., vol. 8, 19

stimulating martyrdom . . . technical, Arthur Bryant, *The Turn of the Tide*, 301

The tragedy of Churchill, Beesly, 297

tormenting telegraphic . . . Admiralty, Godfrey, vol. v, 302

All the careful, Beesly, 153

an exceptional measure, Churchill, *Gathering Storm*, 528

almost malicious, Roskill, 285

how firmly Churchill, Geoffrey Shakespeare, private archive

Winston entered, Roskill, 106

The exact opposite, Robert Boothby, *Recollections of a Rebel*, 55

every misstep, Bell, 6

all the daily, Roskill, 290

no power to take, *At the Admiralty*, 981

no decision over Norway, *NC Diary Letters*, vol. 4, 522

hard to believe, *At the Admiralty*, 978

undoubtedly making . . . engaged, *At the Admiralty*, 979

He sounded optimistic, BI EH diary, 8/4/1940

the clearest . . . silence, Roskill, 98–99

much to my . . . Commander-in-chief, Roskill, 99

Admiral Pound telephoned, Admiralty War Diary 199/388, Diary of 1st Cruiser Squadron

You seem to have, Waugh, *Put out More Flags*, 180

Though I generally, Haarr interview with author, 15/2/2016

everything went wrong, Macmillan, 50

violated all the rules, Klaus Maier, 'Germany Strategy', *Germany and the Second World War: vol. 2*, 195

Rarely in history, Hansard, 7/5/1940

We hadn't been, Tom Fowler interview with author, 4/11/2015

so that it stands, Amery, *Diaries*, vol. 2, 582

I was in, Frank Lodge memoir, private collection

Gentlemen, I have just, Fitzgerald, 13

Military assistance, Kersaudy, 92

the only base, Haarr, *Battle for Norway*, 30

It really is the devil, BI EH diary, 6/5/1940

threatened to resign, Hugh Dalton, *The Fateful Years: 1931–1945*, 304

for all practical, Haarr, *Battle for Norway*, 30

the only thing, Cadogan, 270

imperative from, Bell, 188

no serious operations, *At the Admiralty*, 1007

lead to a bloody, ibid., 1041

mar its integrity, ibid., 1043

Once Narvik is cleared, ibid., 1031

very important political, Kersaudy, 95

Most urgent that, Haarr, *Battle for Norway*, 30

Trondheim is now, ibid., 31

immediate military and aerial, Haarr, *German Invasion of Norway*, 183

we began this war, Haarr, *Battle for Norway*, 22

a very level . . . recover, ibid., 22

One plane in . . . breath, CA CH 4/142, Romilly diary

without a single, ibid.

thoroughly frightened . . . delay, *At the Admiralty*, 1054

for which long, ibid., 1000

deed of fame, ibid., 1084

staking out, Ironside, 253

half-cocked . . . show, *At the Admiralty*, 1030

Maddening . . . another, Ironside, 258

brilliant operation, *At the Admiralty*, 1057

a direct attack, *NC Diary Letters*, vol. 4, 525

Tiny, we are . . . some heat, Ironside, 257

on his own . . . in 1915, Godfrey, vol. 8, 14

bright ideas . . . the whole, John Kennedy, 168

Left to myself, Churchill, *Gathering Storm*, 562

WE ARE COMING, Haarr, *Battle for Norway*, 22

6 FLEA AND LOUSE

We disembarked, Martin Lindsay, 'Reconnaissance', *Spectator*, 17/5/1940

No single action of mine, Peter Fleming, 'Return to Namsos', *Spectator*, 16/5/1970

While the Germans, Reynaud, 277

wounding the still, Duff Hart-Davis, *Peter Fleming*, 224

A better pair . . . paper, Adrian Carton de Wiart, *Happy Odyssey*, 166–7

He was taciturn, Duff Hart-Davis interview with author

a preoccupation . . . imperturbably, Anthony Powell, *To Keep the Ball Rolling*, 76

He was a four-square, Joan Bright Astley, *The Inner Circle*, 76

Should have been, Hart-Davis, 215

my dear Peter, CA CHUR/2/149A-B

terribly slowly . . . picture, Robert Bernays, *Diaries*, 88

for whom I had, CA CHUR/2/149A-B

As the war, *Times*, 25/5/1917

a blend of . . . Front, W. H. Auden and Christopher Isherwood, *Journey to a War*, 214

to proceed by air, Peter Fleming, *Report on measures taken at Namsos in connection with the landing of an Allied Expeditionary Force*, private collection

Come to Norway . . . doing, Hart-Davis, 222

to communicate with, Lindsay 'Reconnaissance'

Nobody, even in, Hart-Davis, 222

ascertain whether . . . SECRECY, PF Report

Suddenly, swinging round, PF diary, 13/4/1940, private collection

We had no more idea, PF 'Return to Namsos'

like an old woman, Waugh, *Put out More Flags*, 206

a susurrus which, PF *Report*

I was there, Storm Evensen interview with author, 17/10/2015

It is perhaps, PF *Report*

and once more, Lindsay 'Reconaissance'

buying up all, ibid.

In the middle, Carton de Wiart, 165

cocoon of self-sufficiency . . . motives, RU MS 1391 B/13–17; MS1391B44

with the dripping head, Waugh, *Men at Arms*, 74

a damn nice, PF diary, 19/4/1940

swatting the muzzles, RU MS 1391 B/13

My godfather, draft for BBC broadcast January 1964, RU MS 1391 B/44

between 20 and 30 . . . children, RU MS 1391 B/14

a rather cool, RU MS 1391 B/27

a campaign for, Haarr, *Battle for Norway*, 115

that no operation, *At the Admiralty*, 1118

We did not seem, Carton de Wiart, 166

which would be, PF *Report*

the difficulties presented, David Brown, *Naval Operations of the Campaign in Norway*, 73

The cards were, *Action this Day*, 40

a special attachment, Fleming, *Invasion 1940*, 232

naval lads tossing, Frank Lodge memoir

Our skipper guided, Fowler interview with author

The names on, Lodge memoir

in a flurry of frothing, Donald Macintyre, *Narvik*

Have brought, Haarr, *Battle for Norway*, 112

not dissimilar . . . firing, ML 'Reconnaissance'

cumbered with . . . yesterday, PF 'Return to Namsos'

German Intelligence did, PF *Report*

probably the best troops, *At the Admiralty*, 1066

Chattering, overloaded, PF diary, 19/4/1940

Took Carton de W, ibid.

elfin-like, PF 'Return to Namsos'

She thought it, Wenche Fahsing interview with author, 17/10/2015

My orders were, Carton de Wiart, 168

pincer movement, Ironside, *Diaries*, 257

a new conception, *At the Admiralty*, 1055

to confuse and distract, ibid., 1084

this important project, ibid., 1064

to destroy places, Haarr, *Battle for Norway*, 106

There was a roaring, Evensen interview with author

"Dispersons!" cried . . . dead, PF diary

making even thinking, Haarr, *Battle for Norway*, 119

Huge fires . . . of death, ML 'Death of a Town'

it is a most unnerving, Carton de Wiart, 172

They went for, PF diary, 20/4/1940

blew the town . . . fire, ibid.

and the glare, Haarr, *Battle for Norway*, 120

Enemy aircraft, ibid., 120

7 THE FIRST LAND BATTLE

so I had to, Information from Elaine Lodge

That's where, Fowler interview with author

Fix bayonets!, John Benson, *Saturday Night Soldiers*, 28

Torlaug Werstad interview with author, 17/10/2016

We were in, Fowler interview

Beside those German, Stowe, 110

ancient and modern, Churchill, *My Early Life*, 186

The British have planned, Colville, *Fringes of Power*, 116

so ill-informed . . . darkness, George Orwell, *Collected Essays, Journalism and Letters*, vol. 2, 341

of any force . . . one, Hansard, 7/5/1940

The Jerries could, Stowe, 111

there was no, Joe Kynoch, *Norway 1940*, 57

Even more important, Martin Lindsay, *World at War*, Thames TV 1973

There seemed to be, Broch, 162

We could hear, Stowe, 111

. . . men shouting, Kynoch, 100

I felt in my bones, Carton de Wiart, 167

catastrophic British defeat, Stowe, 92

It's the planes . . . awful, ibid., 111

What we need, ibid., 112

I'm glad you're, ibid., 144

For God's sake, ibid., 145

Damned unfair!, RU MS 1391 B/13

Still I waited, Carton de Wiart, 171

paramount need for speed, Rhys-Jones, 86

A peculiar fatality, Ironside, 269

The only clue . . . Norway, Julian Paget, *The Crusading General*, 29

My instructions, H.R.S. Massy, Despatch on 'Operation in Central Norway, 1940', *London Gazette No. 37584*, 29/5/1946

We had to tear, Paget, 29

The scene below, Dudley Clarke, *Seven Assignments*, 92

a vast pyramid, J. L. Moulton, *The Norwegian Campaign of 1940*, 174

several fishing rods, Kersaudy, 141

great strength, Haarr, *Battle for Norway*, 22

in full association, Haarr, *German Invasion of Norway*, 184

little more than children, Haarr, *Battle for Norway*, 67

the Luftwaffe's almost, Fleming, *Invasion 1940*, 20

with no aerodromes, BI EH diary, 2/5/1940

information necessarily, Portal to Newall, 8/5/1940; Denis Richards, *Portal of Hungerford*, 147

just as they liked, Clarke, 152

constantly flew without, Evelyn Waugh, *Diaries*, 470

adequate air support, Massy, *London Gazette*

We saw ourselves . . . along, Victor Macclure, 'Gladiators in Norway', *Blackwood's Magazine*, February/March 1941, vol. 249

a scenario that, Paget, 35

the various & changing, At the Admiralty, 1076

Winston changed his, *NC Diary Letters*, vol. 4, 527

gave no idea Godfrey, vol. 7 pt 2, 228

We are aiming at, *At the Admiralty*, 1070

prejudice the effectiveness, ibid., 1074

the opportunity for, ibid., 1084

not . . . very keen on, Churchill, *Gathering Storm*, 492

unless you are, Haarr, *Battle for Norway*, 35

The Crazy Gang . . . volatile, Henry Pownall, *Chief of Staff*, 297

unpredictable and, Jacob, *Action this Day*, 162

They may not be, PA LG/g/241/1

talking a lot, *At the Admiralty*, 1086

Everyone is very, ibid., 1032

a company commander, Ironside, 260

great as are, Pownall, 304

his judgement is, BOD MSS Simon 11, 8/5/1940

A farce . . . bottom, *At the Admiralty*, 1063

meddling . . . wobbles, Cross, 314

conservative, Clive Ponting, *Churchill*, 426

disagreed entirely . . . hole, *At the Admiralty*, 1071-2

The result was magical, *NC Diary Letters*, vol. 4, 520

Oh dear! . . . your Winston, CRL NC 18/2/1161–1198, 2/5/1940

You do manage, CRL NC 18/2/1161–1198, 23/2/1940

Had I been, Churchill, *Gathering Storm*, 580

You can't buy meat, Claire Simpson, *Neville's Island*

just the price, *NC Diary Letters*, vol. 4, 517

getting into a sad, ibid., 519

with the least possible delay, *At the Admiralty*, 1073

in the best, *NC Diary Letters*, vol. 4, 520

a vehement and decisive, Churchill, *Gathering Storm*, 625

complete alteration, *At the Admiralty*, 1093

a blithe disregard, Fleming, *Invasion 1940*, 20

considerable advance, *At the Admiralty*, 1092

unexpected success, Churchill, *Gathering Storm*, 625

That he used to doze (footnote), Godfrey, vol. 5, 39

But at the mention, Arthur Bryant, *The Turn of the Tide*, 209

there was no . . . yellow, Bruce Lockhart, 52

Churchill never for, BOD MSS Simon 11

Great efforts are, BI EH diary, 3/5/1940

which he . . . at once, *NC Diary Letters*, vol. 4, 527

There are few, Percy Groves, *Behind the Smoke Screen*, 262

All Trondheim plans, Cadogan, 272

a dud plan, Pownall, 305

Enemy aircraft again, Brown, 77

He is so like, Ironside, 278

8 WORST OF ALL EXPERIENCES

Ah, it is all, L. E. H. Maund, *Assault from the Sea*, 40

Chamberlain was destroyed, Simon Ball, *The Guardsmen*, 212

I am convinced, Churchill, *Gathering Storm*, 483

primary strategic, Rhys-Jones, 122

Once this is, *At the Admiralty*, 1100

Gilbertian, Derry, 244

a mystery which, Haarr, *Battle for Norway*, 200

plans by . . . effort, ibid., 271

Narvik was really, ibid., 221

a typical advance, ibid., 220

we take every, ibid., 200

disliked the suggestion, ibid., 201

very strongly held, Brown, 22

ridiculous appointment . . . Fleet, Godfrey, vol. 5, 308

and he did . . . commanders, Piers Mackesy, 'Churchill on Narvik', *Journal of the Royal United Services Institution*, December 1970, 28–33

to turn the enemy, Haarr, *Battle for Norway*, 199

The crowd lining . . . interested, William Boyle, *My Naval Life*, 192

with diametrically . . . landing, 'The Norway Campaign of 1940', *London Gazette*, Supplement, 8/7/1947

fire in retaliation, Haarr, *German Invasion of Norway*, 40

If there was one thing, Macclure, 'Gladiators in Norway'

missing a low-flying, Fitzgerald, 32

Narvik in Allied . . . we are?, ibid., 37

all the battles . . . experiences, ibid., 16

For submarines, please, ibid., 25

quite inadequate, *London Gazette*, Supplement, 3/7/1947, 297

I must point . . . ruled out, *At the Admiralty*, 1096

seldom greater than, *London Gazette*, 8/7/1947

Until snow melts, Haarr, *Battle for Norway*, 223

most urgent, *At the Admiralty*, 1083

an assault . . . success, ibid.

to sit down, ibid., 1084

failure to take Narvik . . . reasons, ibid., 1105

why we are . . . wrong, Amery, *Diaries*, vol. 2, 587

There was no apparent, *Spectator*, 9/5/1940

He always imagined, Maisky, 353

The question of who, Godfrey, vol. 7, 127

pondered a good, Churchill, *Gathering Storm*, 490

iron of the Dardanelles, ibid., 496

Of all the harebrained, Pownall, 282

might . . . prove a Gallipoli, Oliver Harvey, *Diplomatic Diaries*, 339

a little worried, Colville, *Fringes of Power*, 104

bruised . . . offensive operations, Maisky, 455

I thought he, Soames, *Winston and Clementine*, 107

there were political, Mackesy, 'Churchill on Narvik'

that Winston is worried, PA LG/g/241/1

determined that he, Beesly, 124

the damaging deadlock, Haarr, *Battle for Norway*, 225

to start monkeying, Ironside, 262

at once unexpected, *At the Admiralty*, 1078

How can one, Mackesy, 'Churchill on Narvik'

sheer bloody murder, Haarr, *Battle for Norway*, 224

So far as I am, ibid., 224

in a thoroughly disgruntled, Ironside, 269

non-existent . . . neutralisation, Derry, 153

so evidently contemplated, Churchill, *Gathering Storm*, 487

taken aback, *At the Admiralty*, 1084

Where is the oil? Geoffrey Shakespeare, 229

Should you consider, *At the Admiralty*, 1086

If this Officer, ibid., 1118

the apparent lack . . . operation, ibid., 1113

test the snow . . . exhausting, Kersaudy, 127

What is really, *At the Admiralty*, 1110

It is a curious . . . available, Fitzgerald, 26

There is not . . . proposed, Haarr, *Battle for Norway*, 226

3.30 Romilly taken, CA CHU 4/142, Romilly diary

Negative embarkation . . . the shore, Fitzgerald, 28

We want a bit, Haarr, *Battle for Norway*, 29

he is *unlucky*, Pownall, 304

an unlucky star . . . mistake, Harvey, 339

Attack at dawn, Anthony Dix, *The Norway Campaign and the Rise of Churchill*, 60

It was suicidal, Trond Kristiansen interview with author, 15/10/2015

a wall of ships . . . rifles, Haarr, *Battle for Norway*, 206

Nicholas Rodger interview with author, 15/5/2016

Gunnar Hojem interview with author, 17/10/2015

9 THE WINSTON IMPASSE

He was all, Philip Willamson and Edward Baldwin, *Baldwin Papers*, 475

An ill fate . . ., Philip Joubert de la Ferté, *The Fated Sky*, 173

overburdened with, CA WDVS 1/3, William Welclose Davies unpublished autobiography

immediate offensive action, Cecil Aspinall-Oglander, *Roger Keyes*, 345

What better way, CA WDVS 1/3

genius for making, CA CHAR 19/2B/194–5

with his Union Jack, Aspinall-Oglander, 63

as the finest, ibid., 221

to revive in, ibid., xiii

that as soon . . . Star, ibid., 339

oddments, CA CHAR 19/2C/233–37

smash up the Norwegian, *Keyes Papers*, 27

Some of the great, Aspinall-Oglander, 346

He rang the bell, *Keyes Papers*, 23, 37

Let me organise . . . linked, Aspinall-Oglander, 346

I know I represent . . . attack, CA CHAR 19/2C/233–37

a combination . . . to me, *Keyes Papers*, 33

to hammer a way, ibid., 37

very devoted, *Keyes Papers*, 26

I have to be guided, *At the Admiralty*, 1131

the universally recognised, CA CHAR 19/2B/194–5

the letter of, Soames, *Clementine Churchill*, 142

but he has . . . Germany, ibid., 142

It was a nasty . . . after all?, CA CHAR 19/2B/194–5

Do-Nothing Dudley, King, 85

so excited as, D. R. Thorpe, *Alec Douglas-Home*, 100

damnably . . . short-sighted, *Keyes Papers*, 41

Steinkjer will stink, ibid., 42

The Military situation, ibid., 34

If the scuttle, ibid., 36

the chief author, Amery, *Diaries*, vol. 2, 589

I don't think, *Keyes Papers*, 25

He was very, Ironside, 268

a curious creature, ibid., 263

I still see the map, *At the Admiralty*, 1152

and had reported, ibid., 1082

The Norwegian Minister, Colville, *Fringes of Power*, 111

by the atmosphere, Alan Moorehead, *Gallipoli*, 40

Winston was a, Ironside, 282

being maddening, declaring, Colville, *Fringes of Power*, 107

his verbosity and recklessness, ibid., 108

The P.M. is depressed, ibid., 107

in fact he seems, Channon, 242

one of the worst, *NC Diary Letters*, vol. 4, 521

most difficult . . . powers, ibid., 522

the public must not, King, 16

I have been, *At the Admiralty*, 1128

He is proving, Colville, *Fringes of Power*, 107

My dear Neville . . . action, CA CHAR 19/2C/308

there would then, *At the Admiralty*, 1137

at a loss how, ibid., 1137

a revival in some form, Gilbert, *Finest Hour*, 264

10 EVACUATION

The evacuation of, Hansard, 8/5/1940

Norway was the dullest, Carton de Wiart, 174

Steinkjer has . . . this, Haarr, *Battle for Norway*, 128

sitting out like, Carton de Wiart, 171

Never reinforce . . . with em, Waugh, *Men at Arms*, 144

For political reasons, Carton de Wiart, 171

Many congratulations, PF diary, 27/4/1940

had a ghastly time, Hart-Davis, 229

in silk combinations . . . well do!, ibid., 229

dear Peter, CA CHUR 2/149A-B

Communications with "Sickle Force", Ironside, 308

Pretty awful!, Cadogan, 273

in the greatest secrecy, *At the Admiralty*, 1141

Today our wings, *Listener*, 6/5/1940

We should then, *At the Admiralty*, 1140

a secret, complicated, RU MS1391 B/6

You can really, Carton de Wiart, 171

Evacuation decided, WO 106/1895

First to evacuate, Carton de Wiart, 173

unsound in . . . at Namsos, Haarr, *Battle for Norway*, 156

Orders have been, Lodge memoir

The Germans had bombed, Fowler interview with author

British expeditionary . . . crazy, Stowe, 113–14

wore all these things, Carton de Wiart, 169

like blackened totem, Lindsay, *Spectator*, 'Death of a Town'

whether British ... little, Walter Hingston, *Never Give Up*, 78

the only unenvied, Carton de Wiart, 173

that last, endless day, ibid., 174

absolute destruction such, *The Times*, 9/5/1940

It sounded as if, ML 'Death of a Town'

Our house was pulverised, Hjørdis Mikalsen interview with author, 17/10/2015

The expression which ... the air, Reynolds, 124–5

this brief campaign, Feiling, 438

for the first time, Fleming, *Invasion 1940*, 21

It was the fog, Ironside, 291

had made ... coal, PF 'Return to Namsos'

a very important, Evensen interview with author

It is with the deepest, Haarr, *Battle for Norway*, 172

physically sick ... Germany, Partridge, 37–8

In unresting pursuit, *Daily Herald*, 3/5/1940

It would be hard, Shirer, *This is Berlin*, 3/5/1940

Hitler claims complete, Mackenzie King, 30/4/1940

There was a whole, Elaine Lodge interview with author, 12/11/2015

I said "I lost . . . Norway, Fowler interview with author

The whole thing, Waugh, *Put out More Flags*, 211

From the military, Laurence Thompson, *1940*, 64

lamentable, footling, Spears, 117

We are on, Ironside, 295

Today there is no, Rauschning, 124

It must be a dark, Mackenzie King, 3/5/1940

we were heading, Spears, 112

The general impression ... gloom, Nicolson, 74

would be beaten, John Reith, *Diaries*, 246

You don't think ... possible, Partridge, 37

For hundreds, perhaps, RU MS1391 B/6

When men escape, Fleming, *Invasion 1940*, 23

however daringly, ibid., 156

untiring, resourceful, PF *Report*

My father was direct, Jacynth Fitzalan Howard interview with author, 18/12/2014

the skilful ... hunger, Simon Courtauld, *The Watkins Boys*, 48

a very high ... little food, SP S (4) WC1/64 'Lindsay Memorandum'

gallant picnic, Brooks, *Fleet Street*, 28/4/1940

This was a, Alexander Mackintosh, *Echoes of Big Ben*, 69

never seen the House, SP Tree to Cranborne, 2/5/1940

very shaken ... extremis, SP E-E to Cranborne, 5/5/1940

under the very ... advantage, Hansard, 2/5/1940

He might have, Sylvester, 258

Chamberlain is clearly, Maisky, 272

there was a flat, Ed Murrow, *This is London*, 98

What a Govt, BOD MS Eng hist d.360, Crookshank diary

The campaign ... excitement, Partridge, 35

on the pretext ... opinion, PA LG/g/241/1, 27/4/1940

the tremendous ... news, Allingham, 132

the false news, Amery, *Diaries*, vol. 2, 591

we have been given, Mackenzie King, 3/5/1940

partially misled, Colville, *Fringes of Power*, 110

no more about, Reith, *Into the Wind*, 377

the smell of failure, Waugh, *Men at Arms*, 220

completely "winded", Violet Bonham Carter, *Champion Redoubtable*, 208

almost indescribable ... danger, Allingham, 166

scarcely capable ... history, Fleming, *Invasion 1940*, 25

if the Germans, Maisky, 290

Each day and night, Irene Ravensdale diary, 24/5/1940

immediately on a pass-word ... this idea (footnote), BCA Dep. Monckton Trustees file 2, 13/5/1940

Everything was very, Stowe, 112

one of America's, PA LG/g/241/1

He told me, Kingsley Martin, *Editor*, 279

We talked about, Campbell-Preston interview with author

who had muffed, Allingham, 168

was like following, ibid., 67

something far more, ibid., 168

the debate is, BI EH diary, 3/5/1940

no doubt ... mischief, ibid., 2/5/1940

the fiasco in Norway, Dalton speaking in Cambridge, 5/5/1940

What disgusts me, Colville, *Fringes of Power*, 118

A Westminster war, Channon, 244

were thinking more, Ironside, 288

there is a first-class, ibid., 293

Well, Steinkjer was, Stowe, 118

It is all terrible, Leo Amery, *My Political Life*, vol. 3, 357

Most of the Ministers, Ironside, 295

11 MONSIEUR J'AIMEBERLIN

Chamberlain. What a man, Martha Gellhorn, *Letters*, 64

He seemed the reincarnation, Channon, 172

When the perspective, Hansard, 12/11/1940

much needed rest, *NC Diary Letters*, vol. 4, 524

One may as well, Information from David Dilks

light-hearted, Reith, *Diaries*, 248

the good British, ibid., 527

When they went, Valerie Cole, taped interview with Martyn Downer, 2009

She was very, ibid.

an almost complete, Derek Walker-Smith, *Neville Chamberlain*, 189

the biggest practical, Dilks interview with author

incurably modest, Martyn Downer, *The Sultan of Zanzibar*, 238

I often think, *NC Diary Letters*, vol. 4, 418

the sort of man, Bernays, 53

this extraordinary man ... father, Churchill, *Great Contemporaries*, 63

There is too deep, Self, *Chamberlain*, 121

was sent as Ambassador, *Birmingham Post*, 18/1/1907

the wild man, Thomas Dugdale to Nancy Dugdale, 12/5/1940, private collection

Hectic preparations, CA GBR/0014/MCHL, Mary Soames diary

I said no oysters ... dingy." CRL NC 11/2/1a, Anne Chamberlain journal 1940

my father was gripped, Soames, *A Daughter's Tale*, 129

What a pity Hitler, Churchill, *Gathering Storm*, 495

really the only, ibid., 495

the finest cigars, CRL NC 3/2/1

Then he ain't look ... lumbah!, Simpson

spontaneously attached, Keith Feiling, *The Life of Neville Chamberlain*, 31

the best site, David Dilks, *Neville Chamberlain: vol. 1*, 47

seven thousand acres, Feiling, 31

I'm goin' 'ome!, Simpson

in spite of all, ibid., 30

very tough fibre, WSC BBC broadcast, 12/11/1939

All the time, Feiling, 16

in a position, ibid., 71

which had but a poor, note re NC's donation of forty-nine birds (1896/7), Natural History Museum, Tring

I'd never heard ... sisal, Hein van Grouw interview with author, 18/12/2015

the world's life-buoy, Halifax, *Fulness of Days*, 202

The house was full, Valerie Cole interview

the greatest miracle, Geoffrey Lewis, *Lord Hailsham*, 56

Did you ever, Halifax, *Fulness of Days*, 195

since he loves to fish, *Sydney Sun*, 3/10/1938

divinely led, *The Times*, 16/9/1938

The day may come, John Evelyn Wrench, *Geoffrey Dawson and Our Times*, 416

the precious ... ears, Geoffrey Shakespeare, 193

species of insanity, Dutton, *Chamberlain*, 130

and his friends ... politically impossible, Hansard, 31/3/1947

The task of rehabilitating, Richard Gott, *Guardian*, 22/11/1984

It can ingest, Canetti, *Notes from Hampstead*, 38

No, just the same, Arthur Chamberlain interview with author, 3/12/2015

Neville's my name ... Randolph, Francis Chamberlain interview with author, 3/10/2015

the most disastrous, Attlee, in Francis Williams, *A Pattern of Rulers*, 193

a man ill-timed, CA Amel 8/76/5, Feiling to LA, 15/11/1954

Poor Chamberlain, Brooks, 268

He was . . . world, Alec Douglas-Home, *The Way the Wind Blows*, 60

His intimates, Nicolson, *Spectator*, 16/5/1940

What do you want?, Douglas-Home, 60

accursed shyness, *NC Diary Letters*, vol. 2, 6

I never knew . . . eye, G. S. Harvie-Watt, *Most of My Life*, 42

I can't really, Self, *Chamberlain*, 206

the mind and manner, Nicolson, 345

if the b——, Walter Citrine, *Men and Work*, 367

Boiled down, Robert Self ed., *The Austen Chamberlain Diary Letters*, 259

What a good, CA GBR/0014/LWFD 2/2, Valentine Lawford diary, 1/11/1940

Many people who, Cadogan, 132

She had got him . . . governments, Halifax, *Fulness of Days*, 227–33

I have increasing, *NC Diary Letters*, vol. 4, 548

his reputation is, Valerie Cole interview

You have a wonderful, CRL NC 18/2/1161–1198

Why look at our boss, Simpson

The Chamberlains, Francis Chamberlain interview with author

Papa could not, CRL NC 9/2/10, Ida Chamberlain memoir

Naturally reserved, shut, Chamberlain, *Norman Chamberlain*, 160

I was counting, ibid., 1

how greatly Norman, ibid., v

the statesman in, ibid., 80

The terror I suffered, ibid., 106

Everything is mud, ibid., 123

I do want to say, Francis Chamberlain to NC, 21/10/1940, private collection

stale digestive biscuits, Hart-Davis, 213

Look at his head . . . him, Sylvester, 235

advanced towards, Colin Coote, *Editorial*, 290

He looks well, Hart-Davis, 218

He is slow, ibid., 218

whole appearance, *The Times*, 20/3/1940

Not unsatisfactory, *NC Diary Letters*, vol. 4, 487

Every night I have, ibid., 473

surprisingly well, ibid., 518

pure ecstasy, CRL 11/2/5

He told us, Hart-Davis, 218

He gave a most humorous, CRL NC 9/2/9

good cooked breakfast, Anthony Seldon, *10 Downing Street*, 135

strong burnt chicory . . . excellence, Colville, *Fringes of Power*, 45

his years in the Bahamas, King, 25

I have occasionally times, *NC Diary Letters*, vol. 4, 444

green and shapeless . . . mine, CRL NC 11/2/1a

Even walking near, *NC Diary Letters*, vol. 4, 466

I must remain P.M., ibid., 415

no young trees, CRL NC 2/26

dark halls, old paintings, Maisky, 372

always there . . . country, CRL NC 18/2/1161–1198

where one can be, Norma Major, *Chequers*, 186

It was his saw, CRL NC 11/2/5

It was given me, Kenneth Clark, *Another Part of the Wood*, 271

If ever that silly, Ivone Kirkpatrick, *The Inner Circle*, 135

One must have something, NC *Diary Letters*, vol. 4, 459

full, as was to, ibid., 490

I find it is, ibid., 491–2

one of the loveliest, CRL NC 13/17, NC to Morrison Bell 5/5/1940

It gives him, Maisky, 364

feeble, fatuous, BOD MS Eng hist 496, Wallace diary

a bad British, *The Times*, 6/5/1940

Then an encouraging, Dalton, 303

storm of abuse . . . hand, Channon, 244

Your endurance and courage, Reith, *Into the Wind*, 381

Chamberlain hates criticism, Crozier, 123

very down and depressed, Self, *Chamberlain*, 422

Our failure in Norway, *At the Admiralty*, Channon papers, 1136

covered in blood, Douglas-Home, 71

It was a massive, Francis Chamberlain interview with author

square with the picture, NC *Diary Letters*, vol. 4, 527

too apt to look, ibid., 527

more trouble than, ibid., 517

It was a shattering, BOD MSS Dawson 44 diary, 19/4/1940

strong inclination, NC *Diary Letters*, vol. 4, 523

he didn't think, Joseph Kennedy, *Letters*, 399

half a dozen people, NC *Diary Letters*, vol. 4, 445

I don't see that other, ibid., 493

ubiquitous . . . cadaverous-looking, Spears, 15, 106

like a teak-faced, Chair, *Die? I thought I'd Laugh*, 132

Our Secret Service, Feiling, 347

he had a devious, CA Amel 8/76, Vansittart to LA 12/7/1954

had been fixed up, Guy Liddell, *Diaries*, 55

The telephone check, ibid., 71

the seamy side . . . organisation", J. C. C. Davidson, *Memoirs of a Conservative*, 272

had the gall, Tree, 76

Ring me there, SP Tree to Cranborne, 2/5/1940

Hoare's star is, AM diary, 16/2/1940

Winston himself is very, NC *Diary Letters*, vol. 4, 432

It is very difficult, BCA Dep. Monckton Trustees file 17, 13/11/1939

To WHOMSOEVER, ibid.

What we really want, BCA Dep. Monckton Trustees file 24, 23/6/1940

carrying on a regular, NC *Diary Letters*, vol. 4, 351

whether there is, Hansard, 13/4/1939

and that his job, Andrew Roberts interview with author, 11/12/2014

You have been, Gerald de Groot, *Life of Sir Archibald Sinclair*, 22

Archie knows or guesses, ibid., 23

used to play football, Bernays, 134

blinded by prejudiced hatred, Colville, *Fringes of Power*, 91

scuttle away, Groot, 152

We had the impression, PA Harris papers HRS/1

close relations, BOD MSS Simon 12, 9/5/1940

this brilliant, puffing, *At the Admiralty*, Channon papers, 1136

Chagrined by his failure, Channon, 242

Tonight Churchill sat, ibid., 244

playing politics ... everybody, PA LG/g/241/1

Winston still seems, Rhodes James, *George VI*, 192

that Winston's attitude, ibid., 187

You cannot expect, Martin Gilbert, *Winston S. Churchill, companion vol. v, Part Three, The Coming of war, 1936–1939*, 1205

full of fight still, Channon, 244

pumped ... Neville's head, *At the Admiralty*, Channon papers, 1136

inflated ... no doubt, Reith, 249

there is a movement, King, 31

The Government was obviously, CA Amel 8/76, EE-E to LA, 21/6/1954

that the whole, Nicolson, 74–5

exceptionally slanderous ... trusted, Emanuel Shinwell, *I've Lived Through It All*, 157

I am no good, Dilks, *Churchill & Company*, 30

captain ... heart's desire, *At the Admiralty*, 83

I'm proud to follow, Cadogan, 253

Winston had made, PA LG/g/241/1

Churchill was on, *At the Admiralty*, 1190

What a brilliant creature, Dilks, *Churchill & Company*, 24

like arguing with, Dugdale, *Baffy*, 3

Winston is very, Dilks, *Churchill & Company*, 25

see W. Chu Prime Minister, Graham Stewart, *Burying Caesar*, 73

never founded on, Dilks, *Churchill & Company*, 25

He won't give, Stewart, 272

had behaved ... terms, BI EH diary, 1/4/1942

He has throughout, BOD MSS Simon 12, 9/5/1940

With enormous solemnity, Manchester, 603

To me personally, *NC Diary Letters*, vol. 4, 513

was profuse in, ibid., 522

I do believe that, CRL NC 18/2/1161–1198

I am extremely anxious, *NC Diary Letters*, vol. 4, 527

Now I've got, Crozier, 169

playing a deep game, Channon, 244

set out & defined ... meet him, *NC Diary Letters*, vol. 4, 527

I shall have, ibid., 526

quite convinced that, Ball, 209; SP Cranborne to EE-E, 15/4/1940

My reasoning power, CRL NC 11/2/2

it no use to wex, Simpson

strong as de debble, ibid.

I keep tightening, Self, *Chamberlain*, 23

a much stronger, CA Amel 8/79, LA to Feiling, 19/11/1954

where he is interested, Dugdale, *Baffy*, 89

a Führer now, Dalton, *Fateful Years*, 162

If Chamberlain says, Nicolson, *Diaries and letters: 1930–1939*, 397

not malevolent at all, *NC Diary Letters*, vol. 4, 526

to try and get, BI EH, 19/4/1940

and forget the war, BI EH diary, 21/3/1940

More & more, NC Diary Letters, vol. 4, 411

the Chamberlain touch, ibid., 264

Yes, it must, Walker-Smith, 194

It is a vile, NC Diary Letters, vol. 4, 528

12 THE MASTER OF GARROWBY

We human beings, BOD MSS Woolton 76

What a different, Stuart Hodgson, Lord Halifax, 19

I have a stomach, Charles Peake diary, private collection

motored off ... garden etc., BI EH diary, 5/5/1940

It was no good ... possibility, Anne de Courcy, 351; Georgia Sitwell diary, 3/5/1940

He should have, Davina Eastwood interview with author, 17/12/2014

There still seems, Bernays, 394

Halifax might sometimes, CA GBR/0014/LWFD 2/2

There is nothing, BOD MSS Dawson 82/78

even in times, Cadogan, 168

the well-assorted, Halifax, Fulness of Days, 153

inconceivably incompetent, IR diary, 20/8/1939

the material of, Halifax, Fulness of Days, x

a disastrous ... Castle!, Robert Vansittart, The Mist Procession, 273

to order my life, Halifax, Fulness of Days, 83

to direct affairs, A. L. Kennedy, The Times and Appeasement, 240

he was wasting time, CA GBR/0014/ LWFD 2/2

Halifax was now ... Winston, NC Diary Letters, vol. 4, 504

if Halifax would, Amery, Diaries, vol. 2, 584

a roaring farce, BOD MSS Dawson 44 diary, 1/4/1940

a leading member, Daily Mail, 6/5/1940

a small Committee, BL Add 58245, Salisbury to EE-E 31/3/1940

an appearance of, SP Salisbury to EH, 22/9/1939

The question which, SP Memorandum by Salisbury, 27/3/1940

The economic war, SP Cranborne to Salisbury, 18/4/1940

of the necessity, SP EE-E to Cranborne, 18/4/1940

very respectable Conservatives, Nicolson, 58

inefficient and talkative people, Colville, Fringes of Power, 96

keep the Government, SP Salisbury to Lord Cecil, 26/9/1939

Birmingham politics, SP Salisbury to Cranborne, 13/4/1940

Personally I was, SP Salisbury to Margot Oxford 13/5/1940

as my house, BL Add 58245, Emrys-Evans 9/4/1940

Your last letter, BL Add 58245, Trenchard 13/4/1940

at 9.30 any morning, BL Add 58245, Salisbury to EE-E, 1/5/1940

An interim Government, SP EE-E to Cranborne, 5/5/1940

a sign of softness, SP Salisbury to Halifax, 25/4/1940

told him ... cross-examined, BI EH diary, 24/4/1940

diffuse and unimpressive, Amery, *Diaries*, vol. 2, 589

a dinner at All Souls, SP E-E to Cranborne, 5/5/1940

In effect they, S. J. D. Green, 257

It is not encouraging ... apathy, SP Salisbury to Cranborne, 30/4/1940

Upon the general, SP Salisbury to Cranborne, 25/4/1940

Lord Halifax, we are, BL Add Ms 89013/2/1//9

Halifax had a most, SP E-E to Cranborne, 5/5/1940

in thoroughly critical ... murdered!, BI EH diary, 29/4/1940

Architecturally, CA GBR/0014/LWFD 2/2, 'Three Ministers'

almost three foot ... underneath, ibid.

One couldn't say, Diana Holderness interview with author, 17/11/2014

He had landed, CP diary, 26/7/41

tried to get ... nerve, ibid., 27/1/41

Anything, though ever, Halifax, *Fulness of Days*, 12

It is so terribly, CP diary, 16/1/1941

not so much, Hodgson, 89

Queer bird, Halifax, Francis Beckett, *Clem Attlee*, 157

singularly inscrutable ... do, Dilks interview with author

who possessed both, HN to AM, 10/1/1960, private collection

His strong point, AM diary, 5/9/41

a life of unselfish ... Majesty.", CA GBR/0014/LWFD 2/2

liked Halifax's telegrams, Roberts, *Holy Fox*, 202

The Queen has repeatedly, BI EH diary, 6/5/1940

statesman that only this, Geoffrey Shakespeare, 101

into broad Yorkshire, Hodgson, 246

pious old fool ... principle today!, Maisky, 282, 145, 250

a landlord's heart, ibid., 228

always mindful, ibid., 102

fascinates and bamboozles, Channon, 184

extraordinary ... ends, ibid., 313

How mistaken ... friends, CP diary, 29/1/1941

which has constantly, ibid., 1/4/1941

if greatness means, ibid., 27/1/1941

With all his, ibid., 30/1/1941

the most appalling ... inhuman, ibid., 1/4/1941

I always make, ibid., 8/3/1941

while under their, Alfred Duff Cooper, *Diaries*, 40

Very chic, but exquisite, Nicholas Mosley interview with author, 7/10/2015

I never hear, NA to AM, 15/5/1943

Gosh! She is selfish, IR diary, 23/3/1938

She was cold, Information from Anne de Courcy

you keep me, BCA Dep. Monckton Trustees file 24, WM to AM April 1941

I like her, although, James Lees-Milne, *Through Wood and Dale*, 213–14

deliberate action ... quietly bulldozing, ibid., 268

She ran the show ... thing, David Metcalfe interview with Anne de Courcy, 19/11/1996 my hated rival, Anne de Courcy, *The Viceroy's Daughters*, 366

We wanted a boy, Irene Ravensdale, *In Many Rhythms*, 20

We left Simla, AM diary, private collection

I have no money, Anne de Courcy, 112

Which tie shall, ibid., 252

Baba rang up, IR diary, 27/11/1937

except how wonderful, David Faber, *Munich, 1938*, 32

when I heard, Halifax, *Fulness of Days*, 185

that indefatigable, BI EH diary, 16/9/1940

My dear Baba, BI EH to AM, 14/2/1938

in the big . . . those days, BI EH to AM, 13/5/1942

The Eden, Churchill type, AM diary, 22/8/1939

Edward said he would, ibid., 6/10/1939

He thought Kingsley, ibid., 15/2/1940

Lady Astor, BI EH diary, 29/4/1940

in a flat, Halifax, *Fulness of Days*, 218

to come & cheer, BI EH to AM 4/10/1939

Really, it is intolerable, AM diary 30/1/1940

incredible that a man, ibid., 30/1/1940

terrified, ibid., 10/5/1940

What better monument, ibid., 3/11/1940

Winston is causing, ibid., 19/3/1940

Baba dearest, BI EH to AM, 17/4/41

for heaven's sake . . . the man, BI EH to AM, 27/5/1943

He showed me, AM diary, 30/1/1940

an evening of, ibid., 31/8/1940

by far the best, Hodgson, 225

It lacks strength, AM diary, 16/2/1940

early church . . . much, ibid., 4/10/1940

It is perfect, BI EH to AM, 21/7/1944

I have to go . . . moment, Bruce Lockhart, *Diaries vol. 2, 1939-1965*, 50

"Not tight, CP diary, 11/2/1941

a large buxom, Nicholas Mosley interview with author

Lord Halifax can, IR diary, 14/11/1940

unfortunate . . . might talk, ibid., 13/12/1940

it was not fair . . . plane, ibid., 14/12/1940

We could not, ibid., 19/8/1941

Discussed with Victor, ibid., 27/9/1940; Anne de Courcy, 365

The sweet test, Ravensdale, 11

I can't tell you, BI EH to AM, 10/10/1942

All I have, BI EH to AM, 10/2/1940

lace brassiere, IR diary, 10/9/1940

I said she loved, ibid., 30/9/1943

Irene said to Baba, Mosley interview with author

My dear, was it *thorough-going?* Leslie Bonham Carter interview with author, 10/11/2015

Asked me . . . somehow, James Lees-Milne, *Ceaseless Turmoil*, 277

intercourse in shop doorways, William Manchester, *The Caged Lion*, 609

a girl curfew, Adrian Fort, *Nancy: The Story of Lady Astor*, 274

Edward was purely, Earl of Birkenhead, *Halifax*, 461

psychical rather than, Michael Bloch, *Duchess of Windsor*, epilogue

a herd of unicorns, Anne de Courcy, 234

They seem to, Davina Eastwood interview with author

some large wounded, IR diary, 4/10/1937

a v ugly diatribe ... Ld H, ibid., 3/9/1940

Was the relationship, Diana Holderness interview with author

almost as if, King, 62

was perhaps the, CA GBR/0014/LWFD 2/2

a bit of a, Roy Jenkins to author, 1991

Naldera, darling, DG to AM, 12/5/1939, private collection

My father told me, Nicholas Mosley interview with author

then it was ... public image, Andrew Roberts interview with author

Everyone tells me, WS to AM, 30/11/1939, private collection

I can't conceive, BI EH to AM, 6/5/1940

Baba doing the, IR diary, 30/12/1941

still living in, EH to AM, 9/10/1940

We could ... soul, Halifax, Fulness of Days, 223

it was lovely, BI CP to AM, 16/8/1940

so light-hearted, BI DH to AM, 11/11/1940

There was no, Halifax, Fulness of Days, 220

I shall take, ibid., 226

to ring only, ibid., 220

Is it possible ... raped, ibid., 291

Edward is ... delay, AM diary, 5/5/1940

If I were dictator, Anne de Courcy, 405

the delay in sending, Channon, 243

It is very difficult, BI EH diary, 6/5/1940

tried to make ... away, ibid., 5/6/1940

The world is foul, BI EH to AM, 6/5/1940

There is considerable, BI EH diary, 6/5/1940

will remain in, AM diary, 5/5/1940

13 THE WILD MAN

I don't know, Hickman, Churchill's Bodyguard, 76

I wonder whether, Field Marshal Lord Alanbrooke, War Diaries, 450

He was still playing, Emanuel Shinwell, Conflict without Malice, 148

the Norwegian fiasco, Spears, 112

would only reflect, Josiah Wedgwood, Memoirs of a Fighting Life, 243

This war was, Thompson, 63

her heart's delight, Gerstein, Misdeal, 4

American sources ... news, Whitford, 258

in a terrible state, Jessica Mitford, Decca, 41

He had reached, CA CHAR 1/355/27

I am only, ibid.

Norway might have, Reynolds, 126

unassailable, Colville, Fringes of Power, 111

If I were the first ... case, ibid., 90

is more directly, BOD MSS Simon 11

is probably more, Pownall, 306

The prime responsibility, Liddell Hart, 278

figured enormous, Whitford, 258

Churchill? He's the man, A. J. P. Taylor, Beaverbrook, 408

The mere thought, Colville, Action this Day, 48

We all felt very uneasy, Godfrey, vol. 7 pt 2, 229

he could not, BI EH diary, 13/5/1940

your being generally, CA CSCT 1

he was not quite, At the Admiralty, 1191

was tight most, Mackenzie King diary, 29/4/1940

superannuated drunkard, Paul Fussell, *Wartime*, 122

It is at times, Ponting, 428

white wine on occasion, Ian Jacob in *Action this Day*, 182

To Mr Churchill ... evening, Phyllis Moir, *Life Magazine*, 21/4/1941, 79

a real risk, SP Cranborne to Salisbury, 18/4/1940

Frankly, I was ..., SP Salisbury to Cranborne, 20/4/1940

very deadly, *At the Admiralty*, 1206

rumpled slump, Tom Hickman, *Churchill's Bodyguard*, 22

jumpy, *Keyes Papers*, 24

He was very tired, ibid., 23

pale features, reddish, Churchill War Rooms

the chief difficulty, CA GBR/0014/MART

Churchill's dentures, Dan Rootham interview with author, 4/11/2015

never bothered about, BOD MSS Woolton 76 diary 2

made the telephone, Reynaud, 239

I must confess, CA CSCT 1

slightly bloodshot, BI EH to AM, 22/6/1941

as always happens, Maisky, 442

may be silly, *At the Admiralty*, 1205

I had a spasm ... frustration, ibid., 1206

He is overdoing, CA LKEN 1/23 diary May 1940

We had yesterday, Ironside, 294

amazed at the speed, CA EADE 2/1

the sombre countenance, Charles Moran, *Churchill: the Struggle for survival*, 9

fairy-tale fortress, Maisky, 230

leaves its mark, BOD MS Eng hist 496, Wallace diary

Sir, we have gained, Noel Mostert, *The Line Upon a Wind*, 508

from a shoal ... charts, Diana Cooper, *Autobiography*, 523

where all ... light, CRL NC/11/2/1a

The lamp was ... again, Maisky, 230

and a very tidy, CRL NC/11/2/1a

I have a very delicate, Violet Bonham Carter, *Winston Churchill*, 173

bit of pelt, Gilbert, *Churchill*, 100

he had just dressed, CA BRGS 1/1

That is why, Geoffrey Shakespeare, 229

I had to test ... Commons, Norman McGowan, *My Years with Churchill*, 24

He wanted me ... 11 p.m., Geoffrey Shakespeare, 'Winston Churchill at War', private papers

But after 11 p.m ... On he went, ibid.

His speeches must, McGowan, 36

I tell her everything, Maisky, 125

He always needed, David Cannadine lecture, 'Churchill and Leadership', Exeter College, Oxford, May 2016

England – old statesmen!, Romilly, 22

It makes no difference, Manchester, 263

Mr Pug is very sweet, Soames, *Clementine Churchill*, 301

Churchill needed a victory, Godfrey, vol. 8, 20

What about a visit, Geoffrey Shakespeare, 229

We have nothing ... face, Dalton, *Fateful Years*, 302

until it was clear, BCA Dep. Monckton Trustees file 2, 4/5/1940

There is nothing, *The Times*, 6/5/1940

It would show, *At the Admiralty*, 1205

I must regard, ibid., 1187

I shall be glad, ibid., 1192

exactly NIL ... lunacy, Rhys-Jones, 143

like a caged lion, Geoffrey Shakespeare, 229

one of the worst, *The Times*, 6/5/1940

skedaddling habits, Macclure, 'Gladiators in Norway'

A measure of their anger, Information from Geirr Haarr

Winston seems to, Ironside, 295

clamber let alone, *At the Admiralty*, 1201

absolutely unjustified, ibid., 1201

great reluctance ibid., 1200

Her bulk at, ibid., 1222

to provoke a, Rhys-Jones, 149

Bertram, CA Clementine's engagements book 1940

14 THE REBELS

Oh! the excitement, Channon, 243

In vain we look ... 1916, BOD MSS Macmillan dep c.874

People are so, Nicolson, 75

on all sides ... storm, Liddell Hart, 279

What would quicken, *The Times*, 7/5/1940

as artful as, Sylvester, *Life with Lloyd George*, 244

never forget the fearful days, PA WSC to LG, 8/11/1924

To think that I, Amery, *Diaries*, vol. 2, 601

he was quite, BOD MS Eng hist 497, Wallace diary

I am always, Sylvester, 249

I have a great, ibid., 251

Well, there was, Geoffrey Shakespeare, 62

Every day he is crazy, Sylvester, 239

I heard men ... interested, PA LG/g/241/1

sound ... play, Thomas Jones, *Diary with Letters*, 457

Nancy welcomed ... longer, ibid., 457

very soul ... Asquith, Roskill, *Hankey*, 270

more presence than, Information from Christopher Clement-Davies

I gather I owe, Amery, *Diaries*, vol. 1, 78

knowing my Neville, Amery, *Diaries*, vol. 2, 578

Give this to, Geoffrey Shakespeare, 60

standing in ... urchin, Faber, *Speaking for England*, 18

How could ... grip, Churchill, *My Early Life*, 18

fully-clothed (footnote), Wm. Louis, *In the Name of God, Go!*, 30

the best ducking, Amery, *Diaries*, vol. 2, 104

for lectures and, Faber, 38

to desert his Liberal, ibid., 176

at sixes and sevens, Amery, *Diaries*, vol. 2, 590

What I shall achieve, Amery, *Diaries*, vol. 1, 78

an immense advantage ... in the right, ibid., 78

being right, Amery, *Diaries*, vol. 2, 257

the greatest law-giver, Blake & Louis, *Churchill*, 258

a bigger man, Amery, *Diaries*, vol. 2, 397

alpinising energy, Vansittart, 354

a steep snow-crowned, *Canadian Alpine Journal*, 1929, 3

Oh, Leo's on the executive, Information from Frances Campbell-Preston, 4/5/2015

I . . . made him, Faber, 267

a reward of successful, Amery, *Diaries*, vol. 1, 244

if only he, *NC Diary Letters*, vol. 2, 104

listened to with, *NC Diary Letters*, vol. 3, 170

pull his coat, Faber, 239

moral collapse . . . leader, Amery, *Diaries*, vol. 2, 226

with such gifts, ibid., 538

I shall be justified, ibid., 396

there are always, Faber, 275

What a difference, Amery, *Diaries*, vol. 2, 443

spoke of my, ibid., 55

the cleverest . . . politics, Faber, 240

He had, David Faber interview with author, 28/1/2015

a scheming little, Faber, 102

combative and persistent, Macmillan, *Blast of War*, 69

a wise and benevolent, Spears, 39

I had the best, Amery, *Diaries*, vol. 2, 1069

irritated snort, Faber, 356

as if stung, Dugdale, *Baffy*, 2/9/1939

most insulting, *NC Diary Letters*, vol. 4, 443

killed off all, Amery, *Diaries*, vol. 2, 570

the smaller . . . Quisling, *NC Diary Letters*, vol. 4, 526

very hard not, Amery, *Diaries*, vol. 2, 453

he has not been, CA Amel 2/1/31, LA to Jacques Bardou

just senior to Winston, BOD MSS Dawson 81 39-41/13

would make a real . . . today, BOD MSS Dawson 81

always seeing further, Amery, *Diaries*, vol. 2, 257

distorted or damaged, C. F. Amery, *Notes on Forestry*, 35

Every tree threatening, ibid., 38

to harass the, Amery, *Diaries*, vol. 2, 558

Are you aware, ibid., 559

insane ban . . . Norway, BOD MSS Dawson 81 39-41/1

helplessness and vacillation, Amery, *Times History of the War in South Africa*, vol. 2, 305

not merely to upset, CA Amel 2/1/31 1940

Neville giving place, Amery, *Diaries*, vol. 2, 580

a pale-faced, *Sunday Express*, 12/5/1940

I have no doubt, Boothby letter to *Observer*, 4/9/1966

Thank God, Alun Wyburn-Powell, *Clement Davies*, 110

I do deplore, CA Amel 8/76/5, CD to LA, 21/10/1954

a very live wire, Amery, *Diaries*, vol. 2, 576

an able and successful, SP Wolmer to Salisbury, 15/4/1940

treacherous Welshman, *NC Diary Letters*, vol. 4, 535

to take the measures, *Liberal Magazine*, 1949, vol. 48, 65

an orchestra without, *Montgomeryshire Express*, 17/2/1940

brought things to, CA Amel 2/1/31 1940

The Government must, Cross, *Hoare*, 255

almost criminal, *The Times*, 4/5/1940

big words ... Cabinets, Bruce Lockhart, 52

at the complacent, CA Amel 2/1/31 1940

to scotch the Opposition, PA LG/g/241/1

without bothering ... founder", Amery, *Diaries*, vol. 2, 590

Clam Attlee ... reputation, Citrine, 367

If I pass you, William Douglas-Home, *The Prime Ministers*, 237

unseating Chamberlain ... at all, Orwell, *Collected Essays*, vol. 2, 359

sordid gatherings, Self, *Chamberlain*, 440

He has told us, Bonham Carter, *Champion Redoubtable*, 208

Again and again, Hansard, 1/2/1940

To my mind, SP CD to Salisbury, 15/4/1940

Not Winston ... Churchill, Harold Wilson, in *Attlee as I Knew Him*, 42

gollywog itching, Jeremy Lewis, *David Astor*, 183

plump for Winston ... crowd, *At the Admiralty*, 1186; Taylor, *Beaverbook*, 407

very changeable ... prostitute, Maisky, 239

a mixture of scorn, Colville, *Inner Circle*, 91

In every case, Taylor, *Beaverbrook*, 407

We have this ... combat, *The Times*, 4/5/1940

We'll all swing, Bruce Lockhart, 54

good politically ... through tomorrow, Colville, *Fringes of Power*, 91–92

assured by the intelligence, *Daily Herald*, 7/5/1940

no one expected, AM diary, 7/5/1940

thought they would, *At the Admiralty*, 1191

P.M. is expected, Jones, 457

I think there ... storm, PA LG/g/241/1

Should one expect ... We'll see, Maisky, 273

Remember the good ... out, *The Times*, 7/5/1940

as heroes, *At the Admiralty*, 1196

to prevent all sorts, Reith, *Into the Wind*, 381

shattering rumour ... look over, BOD MSS Dawson diary 1940

just returned ... military history, SP S (4) WC1/64

Yes, I'm 99.9 per cent, Jacynth Fitzalan Howard to author, 27/9/2016

have seen ... slender, SP S (4) WC1/64

the whole ... information, SP Salisbury to Cranborne, 2/5/1940

15 TUESDAY 7 MAY

The dead columns, Duff Cooper, *Old Men Forget*, 277

might still lie, Moorehead, 128

The general ... historic, Nicolson, *Montreal Standard*, 11/5/1940

Listening to the bores, Henry Morris-Jones, *Doctor in the Whips' Room*, 158; Dennis Herbert, *Backbencher and Chairman*, 90

I never saw, Dugdale, *Baffy*, 168

Well staged, David, *Daily Herald*, 8/5/1940

I confess that, *NC Diary Letters*, vol. 4, 491, 20/1/1940

sick to see such, ibid., 491

Silly bladders!, Cadogan, 18

I feel just, Geoffrey Shakespeare, 41

He has no charm, Cooper, 'A Candid Portrait', *American Mercury*, January 1940

When he said, Christopher Sylvester ed., *Literary Companion to Parliament*, 414

there is little or no, Walker-Smith, 15

No one anticipated, Herbert, 226

if he rallies, PA LG/g/241/1

terrible place, Martin Lindsay, *The House of Commons*, 11

everything mahn want, Simpson

by allowing the, Nicolson, *Montreal Standard*

rather feminine, Nicolson, 76

looked a shattered man, FRO D/MJ/21 Diary 1940

No one listening, Foot, 178

Germany has invaded, *New Statesman* 9/5/1940

That Churchill had, Amery, *My Political Life*, 359

thin and burning-eyed, Blythe, 266

his obvious satisfaction, Amery, *My Political Life*, vol. 3, 359

was simply rot, Maisky, 274

that the Government, Colville, *Fringes of Power*, 92

a little mouse, Dalton, *War Diary*, 196

When a Premier, *Daily Worker*, 8/5/1940

made it much easier, Amery, *My Political Life*, vol. 3, 358

a bad speaker, AM diary, 7/8/1940

eloquent and venomous . . . inside information, Colville, *Fringes of Power*, 117

Violent attacks . . . out, Groot, 153

but not devastatingly, Dugdale, *Baffy*, 168

Up to that moment, Nicolson, *Montreal Standard*

determined not to, Dugdale, *Baffy*, 168

This active and high-minded, Nicolson, *Montreal Standard*

agonised discomfort, Amery, *My Political Life*, vol. 3, 359

very distinguished, Herbert, 58

a certain customary . . . trouble, ibid., 360

to kill the debate, Amery, *Diaries*, vol. 2, 592

a dreary and not, AM diary, 7/8/1940

a veteran Socialist . . . wills, Nicolson, *Montreal Standard*

Questionable taste, Channon, 245

I am not very quick, *Keyes Papers*, 36

very disappointed . . . all idea, Carton de Wiart, 176

Now the Admiral . . . 101, Nicolson, *Montreal Standard*

He stumbled, got confused, Maisky, 274

The sincerity that, Cooper, *Old Men Forget*, 278

Keyes's words, Maisky, 274

It knocked the House, Dugdale, *Baffy*, 168

on the lines, AM diary, 7/5/1940

The House notices, Nicolson, *Montreal Standard*

There is a . . . effort, ibid.

divided between, Amery, *My Political Life*, vol. 3, 359

The whole effect, ibid., 360

barely a dozen . . . day, ibid., 360

cherubically asleep . . . African history, Amery, *Diaries*, vol. 2, 242–3

Austen told me, ibid., 229

Very rowdy meeting, Herbert Williams, *Politics – Grave and Gay*, 220

a curious sing-song, Macmillan, 58

Spoke with considerable, Amery, *Diaries*, vol. 1, 79

my favourite old quotation, Amery, *Diaries*, vol. 2, 592

Your troops are, Oliver Cromwell, *Letters and Speeches*, 300

too strong meat . . . finish, Amery, *Diaries*, vol. 2, 592

doubtful whether I, CA Amel 8/76

The temperature . . . point, Nicolson, *Montreal Standard*

a case of parliamentary, Roberts, *Holy Fox*, 195

and naturally I, CA Amel 8/76, CD to LA 21/10/1954

murmured in my, Amery, *My Political Life*, vol. 3, 360

In the meantime, CA Amel 8/76, CD to LA 21/10/1954

I've seen it, David Faber interview with author

far beyond his, Macmillan, 58

a tribute less, Amery, *Diaries*, vol. 2, 592

a squashed little, Blythe, 270

There are few sights, ibid., 269

ear of the . . . action, Amery, *My Political Life*, vol. 1, 370

I found myself, Amery, *Diaries*, vol. 2, 592

The crash of glass, Spears, 120

the impression of volleys, ibid., 119

I could only . . . round me, Amery, *My Political Life*, vol. 3, 364–5

that I cast prudence, Amery, *Diaries*, vol. 2, 592

The debate in, Allingham, 168

My dear Leo, CA Amel 2/1/31 1940

so consistently helpful, Amery, *Diaries*, vol. 2, 21/10/1938

not without real, CA Amel 2/1/31, LA to NC, 6/10/1940

the pained faces . . . there, ibid.

both Chamberlain and Churchill, King, 35

His last words, Nicolson, *Montreal Standard*

There is little doubt, Rhodes James, *George VI*, 187

for some time past, ibid. 187

and had asked . . . National Government, ibid., 189

Neville Chamberlain, Frances Campbell Preston interview with author

he felt he had, BI EH diary, 7/11/1940

was always subject, Rhodes James, *George VI*, 187

Harold Macmillan and, BOD MS Eng hist 497, Wallace diary

Members began seriously, Foot, *Guardian*, 8/5/1965

effectively destroyed, Macmillan, 55

It settled the fate, Amery, *Diaries*, vol. 2, 592

Your great speech, CA Amel 8/76

which tipped the scale, Amery, *Diaries*, vol. 2, 670

the Government had undergone, J. E. Sewell, *Mirror of Britain*, 164

not want a change, Dugdale, *Baffy*, 168

There is no doubt, Nicolson, 77

the Labour leaders, Amery, *Diaries*, vol. 2, 593

was still unclear, Maisky, 274

Even the usually, Macmillan, 58

the Old Man would, Dalton, *War Diary*, 341

Labour is not to press, Brooks, 268

more death and destruction, *Mirror*, 9/5/1940

on account of his report, Shirer, *Berlin Diary*, 260

16 WEDNESDAY 8 MAY

If it's piracy, quoted in Julian Amery, *Approach March*, 46

If Lady Alexandra, BI EH note

I was the first, *World at War*, Thames Television, 1973

battle-stained service, Martin Lindsay, *So Few Got Through*, v

private friendship, SP S (4) WC1/64 'Lindsay Memorandum'

and I gave him, *World at War*

His first-hand information, Oliver Lindsay in *So Few Got Through*, introduction, v

that discontent had, CA Atle 1/7-1/17

quite useless . . . accurate, SP 'Lindsay Memorandum'

to help him, *World at War*

The House was packed, Spears, 123

ringing in our ears, Macmillan, *Blast of War*, 59

the most dramatic, Bonham Carter, *Champion Redoubtable*, 209

with all the vigour, Morrison, *Autobiography*, 173

very formidable indictment, FRO D/MJ/21 Diary 1940

astonishingly fierce, Maisky, 274

He has lots, Dalton, *War Diary*, 340

the most effective, Harvey, 355

There they sat, Charles Ritchie, *The Siren Years*, 51

a carefully prepared, PA HRS/1

Providence designed, *NC Diary Letters*, vol. 4, 402

perhaps the most, Foot, 178

Chamberlain jumped, Bonham Carter, *Champion Redoubtable*, 209–10

Not I . . . blackbird, Boothby, *Recollections of a Rebel*, 143

the match to, Wedgwood, 244

turned the tide, AM diary, 8/5/1940

We then knew, Channon, 245

The House for a Minister, Walter Elliot, *Long Distance*, 3

the worst of all, BOD MSS Simon 11

with his usual little, CA Amel 8/76, LA to CD 26/7/1954

There is the opening, Foot, 178

Sometimes the answer . . . you, Morrison, 174

There is terrific lobbying, PA LG/G/3/13

It is a direct . . . lobby, PA LG/G/3/13

with his feet, CA Amel 8/76, LA to CD 26/7/1954

Has the great Achilles, National Library of Wales, Clement Davies I/2/8

When I explained, Percy Harris, *Forty Years in and out of Parliament*, 150

with all the dignity, Nicolson, *Montreal Standard*

inimitable self, Maisky, 274

he was in ... sheath, Maisky diary, 4/4/1940

His custom was, Geoffrey Shakespeare, 54

His speech made, Ritchie, 51

the best & most, Bonham Carter, *Champion Redoubtable*, 210

like a fat baby, AM diary, 8/5/1940

It would be, Foot, *Guardian*, 8/5/65

Horace Wilson, who sat, Colville, *Fringes of Power*, 119

hoping to surround ... husband's blood, Channon, 245

Chamberlain white, *Daily Mirror*, 9/5/1940

Norway ... Sacrifice, PA LG/G/190

no one can feel, Minney, 271

You are making, King, 16

in war everybody, BOD MSS Simon diary 11, 15/1/1940

Lloyd George's personal (footnote), Channon, 249,

The only person ... frauds (footnote), Wrench, 415

I have been listening, PA LG/G/3/13

This is all making, Dalton, *Fateful Years*, 306

My eye has always, *At the Admiralty*, 1244

nothing should be, ibid., 1209

It is as a symbol, ibid., 1221

they could not, Fitzgerald, 38

In the brown hours, Hansard, 8/5/1940

all his time, BI EH diary, 7/5/1940

if any speaker, Reith, *Into the Wind*, 382

I hope you enjoyed that!, Somerset de Chair, *Buried Pleasure*, 50

playing with his fingers, Ed Murrow, *This is London*, 98

If he should openly, ibid., 99

departmentally and in fact, CA HLSM 4/1/4

A peculiar spirit, Campbell-Johnson, *Halifax*, 556

I have been sometimes, Martin Gilbert, *Winston Churchill: The Wilderness Years*, 129

the almost telepathic, Mcgowan, 36

often saved her, Colville, *Inner Circle*, 33

Churchill was lonely, Gilbert, *Wilderness Years*, 212

thank goodness, Andrew Roberts interview with author

monosyllables wherever, Halifax, *Fulness of Days*, 229

Winstonian diction, Amery, *Diaries*, vol. 1, 546

Quite unnecessary, Dilks, 'Appeasement Revisited', University of Leeds Reviews, vol. 15, no. 1, May 1972

he was always fearful, Moran, 132

He had found, ibid., 132

scampered ... as ever, Bernays, 62–63

political career was finished, Gilbert, *Wilderness Years*, 171

his quite extraordinary, BOD MSS Woolton 11

broke like sunshine, Mohr, *Churchill's Visit to Norway*, 13

Asking me not, Roberts, *Holy Fox*, 189

Churchill sees the world, Maisky, 440

I am a child, Hansard, 24/10/1950

We agree that, Nicolson, 79

begged . . . voting, ibid., 78

and that abstention, BL Add Ms 89013/2/1/9

unexpected mutiny, Nicolson, *Montreal Standard*

Which way . . . case, Chair, *Die? I Thought I'd Laugh*, 150

I regard the war, CA Amel 2/1/31 1940

Feverishly did the Whips, Nicolson, *Montreal Standard*

it was our duty, Williams, 112

The fact is . . . heard? CA HLSM, 1/1/6

only found a man, CA HLSM, 4/1/4

a drastic reconstruction, BL Add Ms 89013/2/1/9

I told him . . . night, ibid.

and to vote, Macmillan, 61

We knew that, ibid., 59

to save him, Spears, 122

He is like, Bernays, 122

Why not? . . . angry with me, Macmillan, 61

was aggravated by, CA GBR/0014/ MCHL

to trail a veil, Spears, 138

Papa rose to, Soames, *A Daughter's Tale*, 139

The House was tense, Nicolson, *Montreal Standard*

was in a most uncertain, Soames, *A Daughter's Tale*, 202

I can see him, CA HLSM 4/1/4

one of his greatest, ibid.

the least impressive, Foot, *Guardian*, 8/5/1965

How much of, Channon, 246

He said not, Nicolson, *Montreal Standard*

Defending Chamberlain, Maisky diary, 8/5/1940

a couple of, Joseph Kennedy, *Letters*, 422

My interjection caused, Shinwell in Charles Eade, *Churchill by his Contemporaries*, 125

rather the worse, Channon, 246

unfortunate brawl, Bonham Carter, *Champion Redoubtable*, 210

It was enough, Eade, 125

a good deal, Dalton, *Fateful Years*, 306

baying like hounds, Chair, *Die? I Thought I'd Laugh*, 151

A storm of interruptions, CA GBR/0014/MCHL

like bedlam, Channon, 246

17 THE DIVISION

The scene in the House, Patrick Donner, *Crusade*, 273

great tensity in, Nicolson, 79

at one moment, BOD MS Eng hist 497, Wallace diary

All seemed to think, Colville, *Fringes of Power*, 119

May I ask . . . and you, Chair, *Die? I Thought I'd Laugh*, 151

intriguing and enjoying, Channon, 246

Dieu! Que les femmes, CA GBR/0014/ MCHL

It was not easy, David Profumo, *Bringing the House down*, 77

and everybody felt, Joseph Kennedy, *Letters*, 422

to show courage, Spears, 129

as if they were, Foot, *Guardian*, 8/5/1965

What should . . . life, CA HLSM 4/1/4

I wish I could . . ., CA HLSM 1/1/6

unquestionably the most, Foot, 178

pleasure and surprise, Francis Williams, *A Prime Minister Remembers*, 32

Shifty eyes and blushes, Blythe, 276

a young officer, Cooper, 279

How many of . . . instead, Dalton, *Fateful Years*, 306

I came . . . machine gun, ibid., 308

looked triumphant . . . Opposition Lobby, Channon, 247

A quick look, Spears, 128

It was very . . . kindness, ibid., 129

My heart snapped, Channon, 247

buzzed like a disturbed, Maisky, 275

to be vibrating, Spears, 129

We are all right, Channon, 247

I don't think anyone, AM diary, 8/5/1940

The Government's majority . . . howl, Nicolson, *Montreal Standard*

It took five, Wedgwood, 244

Triumphant roars, Maisky, 275

The cries of "Go, go", AM diary, 8/5/1940

Then followed a scene, Bonham Carter, *Champion Redoubtable*, 211

We ought to sing, Wedgwood, 244

as neither of us, Macmillan, 62

scene of disgusting, Reith, 249

quite unable to, BOD MS Eng hist 497, Wallace diary

white as chalk, Maisky, 275

for a moment, Boothby, *I Fight to Live*, 218

We stood up, Reith, 249

Neville Chamberlain . . . erect, Nicolson, *Montreal Standard*

was a very, *NC Diary Letters*, vol. 4, 528

18 A TERRIFIC BUZZ

It is not a principle, Thorpe, *Uncrowned Prime Ministers*, 237

the maelstrom of war, Joseph Kennedy, *Letters*, 385

every shallow . . . power, *Daily Worker*, 10/5/1940

the green-eyed jungle, Thorpe, 237

terrific buzz, Dalton, *War Diary*, 342

Well, I expect, Roberts, *Churchill: Embattled Hero*, 8

And I tell you, Tim Renton, *Chief Whip*, 267

like a traitor . . . life, CA HLSM 4/1/4

was still planning, Cuthbert Headlam, *Diaries*, 190

muddled all his, King, 37

so bad, Bonham Carter, *Champion Redoubtable*, 210

I suppose he, *Daily Herald*, 10/5/1940

That is not only, Samuel Hoare, *Nine Troubled Years*, 431

Chamberlain is done for, Maisky, 275

I remember David, CA MRSN 2/1, Colville to J. E. B. Hill 7/11/1978

I was not surprised, Hoare, *Nine Troubled Years*, 431

It did not take me, *NC Diary Letters*, vol. 4, 529

always hideously, BI EH diary, 8/3/1940

he felt he could . . . through, Churchill, *Gathering Storm*, 661

Winston cheers up Neville, CA Amel 8/76, LA to EH, 28/12/1954

were fairly satisfied, Colville, *Fringes of Power*, 119

he must be sustained, Churchill, *Their Finest Hour*, 15

This has been . . . deserts us, Churchill, *Gathering Storm*, 661

Winston had apparently, BOD MSS Simon diary 11

and I left him, Churchill, *Gathering Storm*, 661

No one has yet, CRL NC 18/2/1161–68

do not appear to, BOD MS Eng hist 497, Wallace diary

But what are, Cadogan, 277

might step in, Roberts, *Churchill: Embattled Hero*, 5

Anderson might be PM, Joseph Kennedy, *Letters*, 476

the Conservative party, Maisky, 108

Churchill, apparently, ibid., 239

who had . . . Chuchill, William Gallacher, *Last Memoirs*, 273

had never forgotten, Shinwell, *Conflict Without Malice*, 149

the grim . . . Strike, Addison, 76

many of them, P. F. Clarke, *The Cripps Version*, 172

Along the stone, Shinwell, 148

our people like, Gilbert, *Wilderness Years*, 11

did not have much, PA HRS/1

very undesirable, Rhodes James, *George VI*, 188

Churchill has energy, Joseph Kennedy, *Letters*, 391

however much people, BI EH diary, 18/3/1940

whether Churchill could, Harvey, 326

In House of Commons, Bruce Lockhart, 48

Churchill is undermined, Nicolson, 75

so abundantly right, Wheeler-Bennett, *George VI*, 441

so many and such, Cooper, 256

The constant agitation, CRL NC 13/17, ND to NC 11/5/1940

WC is really, Crathorne papers, ND to TD 12/5/1940

howled and hooted . . . Commons, Gallacher, *Rolling of the Thunder*, 214

Not a single one, Andrew Roberts interview with author

that a great section, Bonham Carter, *Champion Redoubtable*, 224

He was widely, Blake & Louis, 264

no "serious politician", S. J. D. Green, 259

They both said, Charles Mersey, *A Picture of Life*, 334

that Halifax should, Nicolson, *Diaries and Letters 1930–1939*, 393

Well, there is always, Sylvester, 235

Lady Astor immediately, Joseph Kennedy, *Letters*, 422

On the whole . . . dinner, BI EH diary, 8/5/1940

popped backwards . . . St Paul's, AM diary, 8/5/1940

very sharp . . . was bad, BI EH diary, 8/5/1940

amazed at the, AM diary, 8/5/1940

What the solution, BI EH diary, 8/5/1940

no other choice, Birkenhead, *Halifax*, 453

such long crime, Dalton, *Fateful Years*, 307

If I was asked . . . Churchill, ibid., 307

agrees with my, ibid., 308

to talk to Halifax, Butler, *Art of the Possible*, 83

was the personal, Douglas-Home, *The Way the Wind Blows*, 75

Winston could not, Eric Estorick, *Stafford Cripps*, 234

stupefied . . . Prime Minister!, Amery, *Diaries*, vol. 2, 73

very heavily loaded, PA BBK/G/11/11

would not accept, CA Amel 8/76 EE-E to LA, 14/1/1955

that he would, Hodgson, 11

I told him, BI EH diary, 9/5/1940

mystery, romance, adventure, *Lord Halifax's Ghost Book*, 4

mystical, Christian, Joseph Kennedy, *Letters*, 384

snapshot photograph . . . each day!, BI EH to AM, 30/5/1941

jealous for her, Hodgson, 149

I can't believe, Bonham Carter, *Champion Redoubtable*, 224

He would have been, AM diary, 10/5/1940

I can't share, BI EH to BM, 13/5/1940

We discussed the chances, AM diary, 8/5/1940

We all made our, Bonham Carter, *Champion Redoubtable*, 211

I told Attlee, Dalton, *Fateful Years*, 309

awestruck . . . for Halifax, Dugdale, *Baffy*, 169

Churchill had earlier, PA BBK/G/11/11

It's always a mistake, Dilks interview with author

who always knows, BOD MSS Eng hist d.360, Crookshank diary, 4/1/1940

completely unaware, Spears, 130

it was unlikely, BL Add Ms 89013/2/1/9

Discussing a possible, CA Amel 8/76, LA talk with BB 22/1/1955

I do not believe . . . with him, CA Amel 8/76, Attlee to LA, 15/11/1954

well scourged, Amery, *Diaries*, vol. 2, 595

blew up, CA Amel 8/76, 22/1/1955

word reached Brendan, Moran, 347

Brendan was unreliable, Bruce Lockhart, 52

fatal division, Channon, 249

with Dawson's own, Rowse, *All Souls and Appeasment*, 107

fern-a-tic, Joseph Kennedy, *Letters*, 477

slant on the situation, ibid., 422

The President told, ibid., 423

A terrible world . . . for England, ibid., 423

19 THE OBVIOUS MAN

pit of the stomach, BI EH to AM, 25/5/1941

Dalton said there, Birkenhead, 453

who said that, Butler, *Art of the Possible*, 83

never had a disagreement, Joseph Kennedy, *Letters*, 476

I told him . . . Government, BI EH diary, 9/5/1940

the many difficulties, AM diary, 9/5/1940

You know my reasons, Blake & Louis, 273

the difficult position, BI EH diary, 9/5/1940

Edward did not, CRL Avon papers, AP20/1/20–20A

the Labour Opposition, Ravensdale, 38

the H of L problem, Thorpe, *Uncrowned Prime Ministers*, 153

The principle that, Churchill, *Great Contemporaries*, 225

No one objected, BOD MSS Macmillan c.874

arguing that *ex-hypothesi*, BI EH diary, 9/5/1940

very secret soundings, Self, *Chamberlain*, 408

dis-peered, ibid., 408

The only person, Rhodes James, *George VI*, 187

abeyance ... obvious man, Wheeler-Bennett, *George VI*, 444

saw no objection, Birkenhead, 453

In time of war, Dalton, *War Diary*, 342

Edward, may I, Headlam, 125

How wise and calm he is, Rhodes James, *Victor Cazalet*, 211

but dragged there, Roberts, *Holy Fox*, 198

not one to burn, Thompson, 150

for me it never, Halifax, *Fulness of Days*, 101

took the opportunity, ibid., 178

as he invariably, CRL NC7/11/29/37

What then ... this be? BI EH to AM 26/1/1942

no friend to unnecessary, Hodgson, 39

He said he, Harvey, 100

He was lazy ... curtseyed to, Diana Holderness interview with author

E. said that, CP diary, 8/3/1941

No man climbs, Francis Williams, *A Pattern of Rulers*, 228

A more ambitious man, Channon, 249

dunghill, Michael Bloch, *Closet Queens*, 25

I think you really, Hodgson, 69

with the greatest ... shot, Halifax, *Fulness of Days*, 195

he felt he, Butler, 84

really wanted the job, Miles Lampson, *The Killearn diaries*, 234

and I understand, Davidson to Baldwin, 14/5/1940; in Sheila Lawlor, *Churchill and the Politics of War*, 31

I think he will, Dugdale, *Baffy*, 169

He thinks that, Ironside, 83

Churchill needed, Butler, 84

butt into ... ever afterwards, BI EH diary, 30/4/1940

different languages, CA GBR/0014/ LWFD 2/2

I have seldom met, BI EH diary, 11/5/1940

Edward and Winston, AM diary, 11/12/1940

Could that restraint ... Minister, Butler, 84

layman, Roberts, *Holy Fox*, 203

I think he is not, Cadogan, 280

and he would, BI EH diary, 25/2/1940

cool altruism, Campbell-Johnson, 557

W had better, Thorpe, 178

My father put, Ravensdale, 38

I simply ... know, BI EH to AM 13/5/1940

having cold feet ... before!, Chamberlain, *Norman Chamberlain*, 107

The conversation ... broth again, BI EH diary, 9/5/1940

he would like, ibid.

were to resign, BOD MSS Simon 12

20 THE LIMPET

Politics are an uncertain, Mersey, 432

The sooner some, Headlam, 195

complete non-cooperation, BOD MS Eng hist 497, Wallace diary

come into the, BOD MSS Simon 12

the Government would, Rhodes James, *George VI*, 190

was telephoning personally, Dalton, *Fateful Years*, 308

always trying, ibid., 309

It has a great (footnote), BOD Greenwood MS Eng c 6262

an old widow, John Bew, *Citizen Clem*, 241

To me Chamberlain, Charles Lysaght, *Brendan Bracken*, 160

Remember . . . never withdraw, Thorpe, *Uncrowned Prime Ministers*, 50

fought like a tiger, D. R. Thorpe interview with author, 12/1/2015

I think, with a majority, Channon, 247

The only comment, CRL NC/18/2/1161–1198

You are the only, CRL NC 13/17

a grand National, CRL NC 13/17

So far I have, CRL NC 13/17

There is no member, CRL NC 13/17/106

that Chamberlain must go, Nicolson, 81

had nothing against, *NC Diary Letters*, vol. 4, 529

SHEFFIELD STRONG, CRL NC 13/17

with utmost . . . in mind, CRL NC 13/17

At nine in the morning, Maisky, 275

A fact that Amery, Rowse, 107

was proposing . . . methods, Amery, *Diaries*, vol. 2, 612

categorically refused, Maisky, 275

If someone had come, Campbell-Johnson, 545

the air was full of rumours, Colville, *Fringes of Power*, 120

we had to wait, Cadogan, 280

anything – even this, S. J. D. Green, 258

was referring to me, Amery, *Diaries*, vol. 2, 580

the turn of the wheel, CA Amel 8/76, HB to LA 5/10/1954

What a grotesque person, CA GBR/0014/LWFD 2/2

if he married a baroness, IR diary, 13/10/1939

in a wonderful, King, 17

My position is good, Crozier, 137

Is there any MP, King, 15

a clean sweep . . . all round, Amery, *Diaries*, vol. 2, 611

He no doubt . . . possible, ibid., 611–612

Curiously enough, ibid.

for, like Churchill, Amery, *My Political Life*, vol. 3, 370

both by experience, CA Amel 8/76, LA to HB 28/9/1954

I got them to agree, Amery, *Diaries*, vol. 2, 612

you would have stood, CA Amel 8/76

who were quite prepared, Amery, *Diaries*, vol. 2, 612

washout . . . to be, Crozier, 152

and I was worried, Brian Patton, *Tales from the Canadian Rockies*, 228

that the matter, CA Amel 8/76

21 A GREAT TIDE FLOWING

Who would have, Orwell, 346

seldom-lit . . . good looks, CA GBR/0014/LWFD 'Three Ministers'

Eden is not made, Maisky, 92

Eden is on the fringe, Channon, 242

that Neville . . . take War, Eden diary, CRL AP20/1/20-20A

My darling – try, Richard Hough, Winston and Clementine, 459

I saw Churchill, Taylor, Beaverbrook, 409

He would not stake, Anne Chisholm and Michael Davie, Beaverbrook, 374

outlandish and potentially malign, Colville, The Churchillians, 42

much argument, Taylor, 409

Humble suggestions, CA Char 20/11/40-41

I do not remember, Churchill, Gathering Storm, 522

very summit . . . laughter, Spectator, 16/5/1940

There is a great, At the Admiralty, 1265

It can only be, CA Amel 8/76

a general attack, BOD MS Eng hist 497, Wallace diary

heavy business, At the Admiralty, 1262

the type of danger, ibid., 1256

that drivelling Corporal, Chair, Buried Pleasure, 254

Narvik goes none, Ironside, 297

of iron . . . to shift, Macclure, 'Gladiators in Norway'

as these were, At the Admiralty, 1257

I formed the opinion, William Boyle, My Naval Life, 192

A chicken-hearted, Cadogan, 272

They had long, Churchill, Gathering Storm, 522

the qualities of accessibility, Walker-Smith, 202

What strikes me, R. J. Minney, Private papers of Hore-Belisha, 277

colourful Kingsley Wood, Evelyn Waugh, Scoop; see also BOD MSS Dawson diary, 13/5/1940

does not know, Gilbert, Wilderness Years, 146

When one bundle failed (footnote), H. Wilson, A Prime Minister Remembers, 235

general incompetence, Reith, Into the Wind, 379

he has the air, Cadogan, 276

one of those, Bonham Carter, Champion Redoubtable, 224

He was an extremely barometrical, Colin Coote, Editorial, 203

Kingsley could, ibid., 203

I can't help, Bonham Carter, Champion Redoubtable, 224

surprised, CRL AP20/1/20-20A

as if he were fending, Maisky, 101

that Neville . . . seconded it, CRL AP20/1/20-20A

Quite soon after, PA BBK/G/11/11

misled . . . warn Chamberlain, Paul Addison, The Road to 1945, 102

General opinion that Neville, FRO D/MJ/21 Diary 1940

calmly . . . look tired, Channon, 247–8

So far as I can, Addison, 99

At first he thought, Channon, 248

v tired and "effarouché", Cadogan, 280

a pathetic interview . . . office, Williams, 113

Nobody loved him, Rowse, 16

is obsessed with, Maisky, 43

the one indispensable . . . Prime Minister, BOD MSS Simon 12 a serious ... grievously wounded, *Hereford Times*, 11/5/1940

Thereafter soldiers, Edmund Romilly to author, 8/5/2017

22 THE SILENCE

Winston's account, CA Amel 8/76, Halifax to LA, 20/11/1954

I won't ask whether, CA Amel 8/76, LA to Halifax, 18/11/1954

all the arguments, BI EH diary, 9/5/1940

There is no place, Butler, 84

sound and sensible, Colville, *The Churchillians*, 53

The idea then was, Rhodes James, *George VI*, 190

that diaries are, CA Amel 8/76, LA to EH, 22/11/1954

Friday 9 May, Roberts, *Churchill and Hitler*, 96

Winston's chronology, CA Amel 8/76, EH to LA, 24/11/1954

one of the most, Reynolds, 127

Neville began ... terminated, CP diary, 5/6/1941

neither excited nor, Churchill, *Gathering Storm*, 522

You must be Prime Minister, Channon, 248

perfectly clear, CA Amel 8/76, EH to LA, 24/11/1954

sat down to it, BI EH diary, 9/5/1940

He would serve ... definitely, ibid.

that the House of Commons, PA BBK/G/11/11

was the man, Cadogan, 280

I do not recall ... adherence, Churchill, *Gathering Storm*, 663

and my stomach, BI EH diary, 9/5/1940

several times ... sending for you, Colville, *Fringes of Power*, 123

& told him, CA Amel 8/76, LA talk with BB, 22/1/1955

at once and much, *Killearn diaries*, 234

In this crisis, Bruce Lockhart, 543

I think I should be, Bonham Carter, *Champion Redoubtable*, 224

Perhaps I can't handle, Joseph Kennedy, *Letters*, 476

I am sure you, Bruce Lockhart, 563

a very long, Churchill, *Gathering Storm*, 663

completely silent ... What now?, Moorhouse, *Berlin at War*, 26

Here was the ... intolerable PA BBK/G/11/11

Usually I talk, Churchill, *Gathering Storm*, 663

One sees everything, Dilks, *Churchill & Company*, 3

Accuracy of drawing, Stewart, 41

very circumstantial, CA Amel 8/76, LA to EH 22/10/1954

hamming up, Reynolds, 127

It certainly seemed, Churchill, *Gathering Storm*, 663

one was inclined, CA GBR/0014/ LWFD 2/2, 'Three Ministers'

I then said ... view, BI EH diary, 9/5/1940

Luckily, I am bald, Colville, *Fringes of Power*, 108

he would prefer, *At the Admiralty*, 1261

The question of, CA Amel 8/76, EH to LA 24/11/1954

there were a good, CA Amel 8/76, EH to LA 29/12/1954

opposed by a growing, BOD MS Eng hist 497, Wallace diary

the definite question ... party, *NC Diary Letters*, vol. 4, 529

sitting in the sun, Tom Hickman, *Churchill's Bodyguard*, 35

My doctor has, *At the Admiralty*, 764

Good God, I think, notice in Churchill War Rooms

a curious detached, *Killearn diaries*, 86

I would gladly, Self, *Chamberlain*, 322

about nothing in particular, Churchill, *Gathering Storm*, 596

not even his daughter, Gay Charteris interview with author, 8/1/2015

Just as I ... tension, *At the Admiralty*, 1261

Isn't that ... brandy, Maisky, 271

platitudinous and indecisive, Wyburn-Powell, 108

on a virile ... give, S (4) WCI/96

in a bad way ... two later, CA Amel 87/6, LA to Davies 27/7/1954

Attlee & Greenwood, *At the Admiralty*, 1265

Opinion is hardening, ibid., 1263

Lord Halifax is, Bruce Lockhart, 59

He appeared calm ... remember, Williams, *A Prime Minister Remembers*, 32

a bit evasive, BI EH diary 9/5/1940

vigorously supported, Roy Jenkins, *Mr Attlee*, 218

what a splendid fellow, CA Amel 87/6

completely flabbergasted, CA Amel 87/6

We haven't come, Thompson, *1940*, 87

Winston had Norway, Kenneth Harris, *Attlee*, 174

It is not pleasant, Williams, 32

apparently startled and hurt, King, 38

Until that moment ... parted politely, Williams, 32

I did not name, *NC Diary Letters*, vol. 4, 529

swung against Halifax ... Winston (footnote), *At the Admiralty*, 1261

I said I thought, Williams, 32

that it was perfectly, BOD MSS Simon 12

In order that, Williams, 32

written in Neville's (footnote), CA Amel 8/76 file 5, Leo Amery talk with Clem Davies 26/7/1954

There it is, Cadogan, 280

Neville still reigns, Channon, 248

might want to try, Rhodes James, *George VI*, 190

My dear Baba, Roberts, *Holy Fox*, 206; and Andrew Roberts papers

sensing that ... these days, *At the Admiralty*, 1282

W quiet ... for him, CRL AP20/1/20-20A

I think I shall, *At the Admiralty*, 1266

his intimate friend, Guy Liddell, *Diaries*, 75

An unprofitable day, Rhodes James, *George VI*, 191

23 HINGE OF FATE

Well, I suppose, Waugh, *Men at Arms*, 176

gaily & so unheedingly, Soames, *A Daughter's Tale*, 140

But this time, Ismay, 124

Hotler's troops, Bright Astley, 76

like flocks ... me again, Partridge, 38

possible invasion, FRO D/MJ/21 Diary 1940

Intense excitement, BOD MSS Sankey diary, 10/5/1940

Information from Norway, Fleming, *Invasion 1940*, 54

The effect of this, BCA Dep. Monckton Trustees 2

The battle beginning, Shirer, *Berlin Diary*, 261

that the greatest battle, Rhodes James, *George VI*, 191

It struck me, Joseph Kennedy, *Letters*, 423

prepared to the last, BI EH diary, 10/5/1940

We had had little, *At the Admiralty*, 1268

As I dismounted, Colville, *Fringes of Power*, 121

sat for half an hour, Ironside, 301

Well, the German . . . enemy, Gilbert, *Finest Hour*, 306

about the big . . . matters, Bruce Lockhart, 564

I walked up . . . heels, Ironside, 301

Plenty happened, *Hereford Times*, 11/5/1940

any discussion at all, CA Amel 8/76, EH to LA 29/12/1954

downhearted . . . was saved, Channon, 249

first inclination was, Hoare, *Nine Troubled Years*, 432

Hitler has, I think, Nick Smart, 'Four days in May: downfall of Neville Chamberlain', *Parliamentary History*, vol. 17. no 2. 1998

Hitler has seized, Taylor, *Beaverbrook*, 410

not the slightest doubt, CRL NC 13/17

the dangers of, BOD MS Eng hist 496, Wallace diary

Decided in light, PA HRS/1

any insolence or rudeness, Colville, *Fringes of Power*, 121

should the composition, Maisky diary, 13/5/1940

the complete tragic, King, 49

consequence or value, *At the Admiralty*, 1191

a million Liberals, ibid.

the best P.M., Cadogan, 277

The fundamental difficulty, Colville, *Fringes of Power*, 120

The people who, BOD MS Eng hist 496, Wallace diary

Reith tells me, *NC Diary Letters*, vol. 4, 528

that in view of, Williams, 33

send a message, Dalton, *Fateful Years*, 310

that new attack, CRL AP20/1/20-20A

in quite good . . . other crisis, Reith, *Diaries*, 250

he had no direct, CA Amel 8/76, CA to LA 19/11/1954

many messages, CA Amel 8/76, HW to LA 26/11/1954

Confused news, Cadogan, 281

before the Labour, Amery, *Diaries*, vol. 2, 613

After the invasion, National Library of Wales, I/2/8

possibly dictated . . . crisis, CA Amel 8/76, Reith to LA 15/11/1954

He could put out . . . assemble, Reith, *Into the Wind*, 382

An announcement, BOD MS Eng hist 496, Wallace diary

tough guys, Dalton, *Fateful Years*, 311

was specially indignant, CRL AP20/1/20-20A

both Chamberlain and, CA Amel 8/76, Reith to LA 24/11/1954

Chamberlain would have, Faber interview with author

to leave things, Reith, *Diaries*, 250

despite the attacks, CRL AP20/1/20-20A

Personally, I think, ibid.

it wouldn't take, *At the Admiralty*, 1275

Do they think, CA Amel 8/76, Reith to LA 24/11/1954

the information was . . . calmer, BI EH diary, 10/5/1940

This impressed many . . . expressed it, CRL AP20/1/20-20A

quite heartless, Cross, 318

on the contrary, Churchill, *Gathering Storm*, 662

must have felt, Coote, *Editorial*, 203

was inclined to, Churchill, *Gathering Storm*, 662

that all changes, CRL AP20/1/20-20A

with rather an engaging smile, Dalton, *War Diary*, 345

He said things, BL Add Ms 89013/2/1/9

It's like trying, Macmillan, 64

Saw Alec Dunglass, BL Add Ms 89013/2/1/9

to carry us . . . to fall, Nicolson, 82

calm and charming, Channon, 249

that he had, BI EH diary, 10/5/1940

the final decision, CA Amel 8/76, EH to LA 3/12/1954

fat gents in black, Zita Crossman, 'The 1940 Labour Party Conference', in *Speak for Yourself: A Mass Observation anthology, 1937–1949*, 188–99

People smoke . . . frequently heard, ibid.

There was a . . . looking, ibid.

when the grim thunder, BOD MS Eng d 2989, Greenwood memoirs

The answer to . . . nation, Williams, 34

If you don't, Dalton, *Fateful Years*, 311

a palm covered, Spears, 130

in anticipation . . . or two, CA Amel 8/76, EH to LA 3/12/1954

when he told me, CA Amel 8/76, LA to EH 22/11/1954

under the pledge, Amery, *Diaries*, vol. 2, 613

Labour was a class . . . bosses, 'Winston Churchill at the Cambridge Union', Geoffrey Shakespeare private papers

not one injurious epithet, Coote, 210

in the light of, Manchester, 674

that he would be, BOD Wallace diary MS Eng hist, 496

We at No. 10, Colville, *Action this Day*, 49

is understood not, Colville, *Fringes of Power*, 121

Neville hesitated, Channon, 249

Easier said than done, Patrick Higgins, unpublished biography of Rab Butler

He would not . . . final try, Channon, 249

You can do a great deal, Thorpe, *Uncrowned Prime Ministers*, 181

the rather "Second Empire", Channon, 249

may well have played, ibid., 249

I am not sure of this!, Information from Herry Lawford

It was H who, ibid.

true to form, Colville, *Fringes of Power*, 122

It is all looking, Nicolson, 83

two teeth ... thank God, BOD MSS Sankey diary, 10/5/1940

had to bolt off, *NC Diary Letters*, vol. 4, 501

to stay 2 or 3 days, CA ACAD 1/9 1940, unpublished entry Cadogan diary 9/4/1940

Having been tormented, BI EH diary, 30/7/1940

I was informed, Rhodes James, *George VI*, 191

Resigned, CRL NC 2/29/37

The plants ... my failure, Feiling, 28

No doubt a sharper, CRL NCP, 1/6/10/114, NC to Joseph Chamberlain, 28/4/1896

All my world, *NC Diary Letters*, vol. 4, 531

Perhaps it was providential, ibid.

He told me, Wheeler-Bennett, *George VI*, 443

of the step, Kenneth Rose, *The Later Cecils*, 192

I owe something, Crozier, 175

whose wisdom, Wheeler-Bennett, *George VI*, 443

changed their minds, *NC Diary Letters*, vol. 4, 529

... he told me, Wheeler-Bennett, *George VI*, 444

I was sorry not, ibid.

with suitable expressions, BI EH diary, 11/5/1940

Then I knew, Wheeler-Bennett, *George VI*, 444

a condition that, *At the Admiralty*, 1261

after further thought, Rhodes James, *George VI*, 191

very undesirable, ibid., 191

according to his research, ibid., 193

was funny about Winston, BI EH diary, 5/6/1940

was clearly apprehensive, BI EH diary, 11/5/1940

of the mind of, BOD MSS Woolton 76, 19/3/1942

very anti-Winston, Rhodes James, *George VI*, 192

I doubt if any, CRL NC 18/2/1161–1198

Few people have, Frederick Woolton, *Memoirs*, 174

a marvel ... poor Mr Chamberlain, CA CHUR 4/109/42-3

"True," said Chamberlain, Joseph Kennedy, *Letters*, 477

come round to, *NC Diary Letters*, vol. 4, 527; Reith, *Into the Wind*, 381

In my long life ..., Churchill, *Churchill's Visit to Norway*, 33

Only just to say, *At the Admiralty*, 1283

most graciously ... Government, ibid., 1283

Do you think, Frank Longford, *Eleven at No. 10*, 54

Will the bloody, Blake & Louis, 79

I will certainly, *At the Admiralty*, 1283

in complete silence ... stairs, Hickman, 90–91

came quite spontaneously, *NC Diary Letters*, vol. 4, 530

magnificent ... champagne, Nicolson, 84

You have acted nobly, CRL NC 18/2/ 1161-1198

The idea is prevalent, Ismay, 115

My relief when, AM diary, 10/5/1940

May I wish ... fortune!, Bridges, *Action this Day*, 219

I went home, Colville, *Fringes of Power*, 122

a man of peace, Walker-Smith, 334

the greatest adventurer, Self, *Chamberlain*, 431

a terrible risk . . . at the prospect, Colville, *Fringes of Power*, 122

Well, we had better, BOD MSS Woolton 76 diary 2

I remember what, SP MO to Salisbury, 16/5/1940

I felt very sad . . . card up, ibid.

which I know so well!, Wrench, 415

delighted to see me, ibid.

They were both rather . . . rotundity, ibid.

with a happy face Foot, *British Political Crises*, 183

EPILOGUES

So it is to be Winston!, Dugdale, *Baffy*, 169

The substitution of Churchill, Galeazzo Ciano, *Ciano's Diary*, 248

symbolic sexagenarians, Bonham Carter, *Champion Redoubtable*, 213

should have been, BOD MSS Simon 86, GS to JS, 14/5/1940

indispensable Judas, Maurice Cowling, *The Impact of Hitler*, 385

incredibile dicta, Reith, *Into the Wind*, 384

According to Clemmie, Bonham Carter, *Champion Redoubtable*, 224

and so he has, Headlam, 198

will take nothing, Cadogan, 282

poor old Sam Hoare, CA LKEN 1/23

No one has said, CRL NC7/11/33/98, SH to NC 14/5 1940

asking if 10.30, BOD MS Eng hist 497, Wallace diary

within ten minutes, Reith, *Into the Wind*, 383

in a difficulty . . . membership, CA CHAR 20/7/96–105

Everything about you, Kingsley Martin, *Editor*, 266

He has sometimes, CA CHAR 20/7/96-105

I do hope you, CA Amel 2/1/31 1940, LA to WC 14/5/1940

poured out his soul, BI EH diary, 28/7/1940

As I was leaving, BL Add Ms 89013/2/1/9

now referred to, Maisky, 280

nobody had served, BI EH diary, 7/11/1940

they found Horace, CA GBR/0014/LWFD 2/2, Lawford diary, 7/12/1940

general commissioner, Maisky diary, 18/5/1940

After deep and very, PA LG/G/4/4

I shall wait, Sylvester, 281

sixty feet below, ibid., 281

completely tired, ibid., 282

The gangsters will, Roberts, *Holy Fox*, 209

a well-executed, BI EH diary, 9/4/1940

In the train, BI EH to AM, 14/1/1941

no political ambitions, BI EH diary, 18/10/1943

which I have always, CP diary, 16/2/1941

They are of great interest, BI AM to Richard Halifax

There are none, BI RH to AM, 30/10/1985

some confidential, BOD MSS Attlee dep 42, fols. 105, 129, 10/10/1946

Dear Prime Minister, BOD MSS Attlee dep 42, 117, fols. 204–5

The family of, FL to Defence Minister, June 2008, private collection

Dearest Mummy and Daddy, GR to parents, 27/4/1940

dear uncle ... Birthday Present, CA CHU 4/142

well-covered, Maund, 52

The British did, Ivan Vanya interview with author, 18/10/2015

the end of, Fleming, Invasion 1940, 146

The withdrawal, Maund, 58

like my father before, Self, Chamberlain, 445

He is definitely, Joseph Kennedy, Letters, 427

unswervingly under extremely, NC Diary Letters, vol. 1, 239

At bottom it was, ibid., 242

with a heavy heart, CRL AP20/1/20-20A, Eden diary 12/5/1940

It was like, CRL NC 11/2/5

There is no pleasure, NC Diary Letters, vol. 4, 533

To a very large, Feiling, 442

I have received, Dilks, 'The Twilight War and the Fall of France: Chamberlain and Churchill in 1940', Royal Historical Society, Vol. 28, 1978, 61–86

Winston has behaved, NC Diary Letters, vol. 4, 543

I shall never, Rhodes James, Cazalet, 278

He is now, King, 56

the officers and soldiers, Maisky diary, 4/6/1940

If I am personally, NC Diary Letters, vol. 4, 547

having held an, Donner, 245

Must not the final, ibid., 246

you saved the life, Dutton, 121

having trouble with, NC Diary Letters, vol. 4, 554

Did he say, Thompson, 94

The fact is Winston, PA LG/g/241/1, 19/6/40

Sit there, CRL NC 11/2/1a, Anne Chamberlain diary, 7/11/1940

very steady and brave, EH to WSC, 7/11/1940

Approaching dissolution ... we parted, BI EH diary 7/11/1940

Never before ... servants, Telegraph, 15/11/1940

the chief hymn, BOD MSS Eng hist d.360, Crookshank diary

acquired the chief, Churchill, Gathering Storm, 528

BIBLIOGRAPHY

The most satisfying overviews of this period are Paul Addison's *The Road to 1945*, Lynne Olson's *Troublesome Young Men*, Graham Stewart's *Burying Caesar*, and Laurence Thompson's *1940*.

Of contemporary diarists, Ivan Maisky – thanks to Gabriel Gorodetsky's rehabilitative editing – deserves to take his place alongside Chips Channon, John Colville and Harold Nicolson.

The Norway Campaign: Geirr Haarr is the indisputable Norwegian authority. No one has covered the French involvement with more elegance than François Kersaudy. For the British perspective, there are good recent accounts by Christopher Bell, John Benson, Anthony Dix and Graham Rhys-Jones.

Neville Chamberlain: Robert Self's four volumes of diaries and letters are a monument of scholarship. Alongside Self's one-volume life of Chamberlain, the first part of David Dilks's as yet unfinished biography stands out. David Dutton and Nick Smart have also written invaluable studies. A rewarding account of Chamberlain's time on Andros is Claire Simpson's *Neville's Island*.

Lord Halifax: Andrew Roberts's life remains the most complete and insightful. Also recommended is Anne de Courcy's portrait of Baba Metcalfe in *The Viceroy's Daughters*.

Churchill: A recent review in the *TLS* began: 'There are more than fifty books whose main title begins "Churchill and . . ."' Of the legion of experts on the life and times of WSC, I would like to pay tribute to David Dilks, William Manchester and David Reynolds. No scholar, though, is likely to eclipse the achievement of Martin Gilbert. *The Churchill War Papers: At the Admiralty* is indispensable.

BOOKS

Jack Adams, *The Doomed Expedition: The Norwegian Campaign of 1940*, Leo Cooper, 1989

Paul Addison, *The Road to 1945*, Cape, 1975

Field Marshal Lord Alanbrooke, *War Diaries 1939–1945*, ed. Alex Danchev and Daniel Todman, Weidenfeld & Nicolson, 2001

Margery Allingham, *The Oaken Heart*, Michael Joseph, 1941

C. F. Amery, *Notes on Forestry*, Trübner & Co., 1875

Julian Amery, *Approach March: A Venture in Autobiography*, Hutchinson, 1973

Leo Amery, *The Times History of the War in South Africa*, 1899–1902, vol. 2, Samson Low, 1901

—*My Political Life*, 3 vols, Hutchinson, 1953–55

—*The Leo Amery Diaries, vol. 1, 1896–1929*, ed. John Barnes and David Nicholson, Hutchinson, 1980

—*The Empire at Bay: The Leo Amery diaries vol. 2, 1929–1945*, ed. John Barnes and David Nicholson, Hutchinson, 1988

Cecil Aspinall-Oglander, *Roger Keyes: Being the biography of Admiral of the Fleet Lord Keyes of Zeebrugge and Dover*, Hogarth, 1951

Joan Bright Astley, *The Inner Circle: A view of war at the top*, Hutchinson, 1971

W. H. Auden and Christopher Isherwood, *Journey to a War*, Octagon, 1972

Edward Baldwin and Philip Williamson, *Baldwin Papers: A conservative statesman, 1908–1947*, CUP, 2004

Simon Ball, *The Guardsmen: Harold Macmillan, three friends, and the world they made*, HarperCollins, 2004

Vernon Bartlett, *And Now, Tomorrow*, Chatto & Windus, 1960

—*I Know What I Liked*, Chatto & Windus, 1974

Paul Baudouin, *The Private Diaries of Paul Baudouin*, Eyre & Spottiswoode, 1948

Beverley Baxter, *Men, Martyrs and Mountebanks*, Hutchinson, 1940

Francis Beckett, *Clem Attlee*, Richard Cohen, 1997

Ralph F. De Bedts, *Ambassador Joseph Kennedy 1938–40: An anatomy of appeasement*, Peter Lang, 1985

Patrick Beesly, *Very Special Admiral: The life of Admiral J.H. Godfrey*, Hamish Hamilton, 1980

Christopher M. Bell, Churchill and Sea Power, OUP, 2012

John Benson, *Saturday Night Soldiers: The 4th Battalion of the Lincolnshire Regiment in World War II*, Boston, 2002

Isaiah Berlin, *Mr Churchill in 1940*, John Murray, 1964

Robert Bernays, *Diaries and Letters of Robert Bernays 1932–39*, ed. Nick Smart, E. Mellen Press, 1996

John Bew, *Citizen Clem*, Riverrun, 2016

Earl of Birkenhead, *Halifax*, Hamish Hamilton, 1965

Robert Blake and Wm. Roger Louis ed., *Churchill: A major new assessment of his life in peace and war*, Norton, 1993

Michael Bloch, *Duchess of Windsor*, Weidenfeld & Nicolson, 1996

—*Closet Queens*, Little Brown, 2015

Ronald Blythe, *The Age of Illusion: England in the twenties and thirties*, Hamish Hamilton, 1963

Violet Bonham Carter, *Champion Redoutable: The diaries and letters of Violet Bonham Carter, 1914–1945*, ed. Mark Pottle, Weidenfeld & Nicholson, 1999

—*Winston Churchill: An intimate portrait*, Harcourt Brace, 1965

Robert Boothby, *I Fight to Live*, Gollancz, 1947

—*Recollections of a Rebel*, Hutchinson, 1978

Andrew Boyle, *Poor, Dear Brendan: The quest for Brendan Bracken*, Hutchinson, 1974

William Boyle, *My Naval Life, 1886–1941*, Hutchinson, 1942

Theodore Broch, *The Mountains Wait*, Michael Joseph, 1943

Leslie Brody, *Irrepressible: The life and times of Jessica Mitford*, Counterpoint, 2010

Collin Brooks, *Fleet Street, Press Barons and Politics: The journals of Collin Brooks, 1932-1940*, CUP, 1998

Anthony Montague Brown, *Long Sunset: Memoirs of Winston Churchill's last private secretary*, Cassell, 1995

David Brown, *Naval Operations of the Campaign in Norway*, Routledge, 1970

Arthur Bryant, *The Turn of the Tide: Based on the War Diaries of Field Marshal Viscount Alanbrooke*, Collins, 1957

Richard Austen Butler, *The Art of the Possible: The memoirs of Lord Butler*, Hamish Hamilton, 1971

Alexander Cadogan, *The Diaries of Sir Alexander Cadogan*, ed. David Dilks, Cassell, 1971

Angus Calder and Dorothy Sheridan ed., *Speak for Yourself: A Mass Observation anthology, 1937–1949*, Cape, 1984

Alan Campbell-Johnson, *Viscount Halifax: A biography*, Hale, 1941

Elias Canetti, *The Human Province*, Deutsch, 1985

—*Notes from Hampstead: The Writer's Notes: 1954–71*, Farrar Straus & Giroux, 2005

David Carlton, *Anthony Eden*, Allen Lane, 1981

Adrian Carton de Wiart, *Happy Odyssey*, Cape, 1950

Somerset de Chair, *Buried Pleasure*, Merlin, 1985

—*Die? I Thought I'd Laugh*, Merlin, 1993

Austen Chamberlain, *The Austen Chamberlain Diary Letters*, ed. Robert Self, CUP, 1996

Neville Chamberlain, *Norman Chamberlain: A memoir*, John Murray, 1923

The Neville Chamberlain Diary Letters, vols. 1–4, ed. Robert Self, Ashgate, 2000–05

Henry Channon, *Chips: The Diaries of Sir Henry Channon*, ed. Robert Rhodes James, Weidenfeld & Nicolson, 1967

John Charmley, *Winston Churchill: The end of glory*, Hodder & Stoughton, 1993

—*Duff Cooper: The authorized biography*, Weidenfeld & Nicolson, 1986

Alfred Chatfield, *The Navy and Defence: The autobiography of Admiral of the Fleet Lord Chatfield*, Heinemann, 1947

Anne Chisholm and Michael Davie, *Beaverbrook: A life*, Hutchinson, 1992

Randolph Churchill and Martin Gilbert, *W. S. Churchill, Finest Hour, 1939–41*, Houghton Mifflin, 1983

Winston Churchill, *My Early Life*, Butterworth, 1930

—*Great Contemporaries*, Butterworth, 1937

—*Churchill's Visit to Norway: Speeches delivered by Winston S. Churchill in Oslo, May 1948, together with addresses by Otto Lous Mohr, Jacob S. Worm-Müller, Gunnar Jahn*, Oslo, 1949

—*A History of the English-Speaking Peoples*, vol. 1, Cassell, 1951

—*The Second World War, The Gathering Storm*, vol. 1, Cassell, 1948

Galeazzo Ciano, *Ciano's Diary, 1939–1943*, ed. Malcom Muggeridge, Heinemann, 1947

James Cilcennin, *Admiralty House, Whitehall*, Country Life, 1960

Walter Citrine, *Men and Work*, Hutchinson, 1964

—*Two Careers*, Hutchinson, 1967

Alan Clark, *The Tories: Conservatives and the nation state, 1922–1997*, Phoenix, 1999

Kenneth Clark, *Another Part of the Wood*, Harper & Row, 1975

Dudley Clarke, *Seven Assignments*, Cape, 1948

Peter Clarke, *The Cripps Version: The life of Sir Stafford Cripps, 1889–1952*, Allen Lane, 2002

John Colville, *The Fringes of Power, Downing Street Diaries 1939–1955*, Hodder & Stoughton, 1985

—*Winston Churchill and his Inner Circle*, Wyndham, 1981

—*Footprints in Time*, Collins, 1976

—*The Churchillians*, Weidenfeld & Nicolson, 1981

Ian Colvin, *Vansittart in Office*, Gollancz, 1965

Diana Cooper, *Autobiography*, Michael Russell, 1979

Alfred Duff Cooper, *The Duff Cooper Diaries*, ed. John Julius Norwich, Weidenfeld & Nicolson, 2005

—*Old Men Forget*, Hart-Davis, 1953

Colin Coote, *Editorial*, Eyre & Spottiswoode, 1965

—*A Companion of Honour: the story of Walter Elliot*, Collins, 1965

Patrick Cosgrave, *Churchill at War*, Collins, 1974

Anne de Courcy, *The Viceroy's Daughters: The lives of the Curzon sisters*, Weidenfeld & Nicolson, 2000

—*Margot at War: Love and Betrayal in Downing Street 1912–1916*, Weidenfeld & Nicolson, 2015

Simon Courtauld, *The Watkins Boys*, Michael Russell, 2010

Virginia Cowley, *Looking for Trouble*, Hamish Hamilton, 1941

Maurice Cowling, *The Impact of Hitler: British politics and British policy, 1933–1940*, CUP, 1975

Henry Page Croft, *My Life of Strife*, Hutchinson, 1948

Oliver Cromwell, *Letters and Speeches*, ed. Thomas Carlyle, 1860

J. A. Cross, *Samuel Hoare: A political biography*, Cape, 1977

Robert Crowcroft, *Attlee's War: World War II and the making of a Labour leader*, I. B. Tauris, 2011

Nick Crowson, *Facing Fascism: The Conservative Party and the European dictators, 1935–1940*, Routledge, 2002

W. P. Crozier, *Off the Record: Political interviews 1933–1943*, ed. A. J. P. Taylor, Hutchinson, 1973

Hugh Cudlipp, *Walking on the Water*, Bodley Head, 1976

Hugh Dalton, *The Second World War Diary of Hugh Dalton*, ed. Ben Pimlott, Cape, 1986

—*The Fateful Years: 1931–1945*, Muller, 1957

J. C. C. Davidson, *Memoirs of a Conservative*, Weidenfeld & Nicolson, 1969

Wilhelm Deist, *Germany and the Second World War*, vol. 2, Oxford, 1990

Henry Denham, *Inside the Nazi Ring*, John Murray, 1984

T. K. Derry, *The Campaign in Norway*, HMSO, 1952

David Dilks, *Retreat from Power: Studies in Britain's foreign policy of the twentieth century*, Macmillan, 1981

—*Neville Chamberlain, vol. 1, 1869–1929*, CUP, 1984

—*Churchill & Company: Allies and Rivals in War and Peace*, I. B. Tauris, 2012

Anthony Dix, *The Norway Campaign and the Rise of Churchill 1940*, Pen & Sword, 2014

Patrick Donner, *Crusade: A life against the calamitous twentieth century*, Sherwood Press, 1984

Bernard Donoughue and George Jones, *Herbert Morrison: Portrait of a politician*, Weidenfeld & Nicolson, 1973

Alec Douglas-Home, *The way the wind blows: An autobiography*, Collins, 1976

—*Letters to a Grandson*, Collins, 1983

William Douglas-Home, *The Prime Ministers: Stories and anecdotes from Number 10*, W. H. Allen, 1987

Martyn Downer, *The Sultan of Zanzibar: The bizarre world and spectacular hoaxes of Horace de Vere Cole*, Black Spring Press, 2010

Tom Driberg, *Beaverbrook: A study in power and frustration*, Weidenfeld & Nicolson, 1956

Blanche Dugdale, *Baffy: The diaries of Blanche Dugdale, 1936–1947*, ed. N. A. Rose, Mitchell Valentine, 1973

David Dutton, *Neville Chamberlain*, Arnold, 2001

—*Simon: A political biography of Sir John Simon*, Aurum, 1992

Charles Eade, *Churchill by his Contemporaries*, Hutchinson, 1953

Anthony Eden, *The Eden Memoirs, 3: The reckoning*, Cassell, 1965

Paul Einzig, *In the Centre of Things*, Hutchinson, 1960

Walter Elliot, *Long Distance*, Constable, 1943

Erick Estorick, *Stafford Cripps*, Heinemann, 1949

David Faber, *Speaking for England: Leo, Julian and John Amery, the tragedy of a political family*, Free Press, 2005

—*Munich, 1938: Appeasement and World War II*, Simon & Schuster, 2008

Keith Feiling, *The Life of Neville Chamberlain*, Macmillan, 1946

Philip Joubert de la Ferté, *The Fated Sky*, London, 1977

D. J. L. Fitzgerald, *History of the Irish Guards in the Second World War*, Gale & Polden, 1949

Peter Fleming, *Invasion 1940*, Rupert Hart-Davies, 1957

Dingle Foot, *British Political Crises*, W. Kimber, 1976

Adrian Fort, *Nancy: The Story of Lady Astor*, Cape, 2012

Willi Frischauer, *"The Navy's Here!": The Altmark affair*, Gollancz, 1955

Paul Fussell, *Wartime: Understanding and behaviour in the Second World War*, OUP, 1989

William Gallacher, *The Rolling of the Thunder*, Lawrence & Wishart, 1947

—*Last Memoirs*, Lawrence & Wishart, 1966

Simon Garfield, *We are at War*, Ebury, 2005

Martha Gellhorn, *The Letters of Martha Gellhorn*, ed. Caroline Moorehead, Chatto & Window, 2006

Anna Gerstein, *Misdeal*, Lond. & Co, 1932

Martin Gilbert, *Winston S. Churchill, companion vol. 5, Part Three, The Coming of War, 1936–1939*, Houghton Mifflin, 1983

— *The Churchill War Papers: At the Admiralty*, vol. 1, Norton, 1993

Hubert Gladwyn Jebb, *The Memoirs of Lord Gladwyn*, Weidenfeld & Nicolson, 1972

J. H. Godfrey, *The Naval Memoirs of Admiral J. H. Godfrey*, 8 vols, Hailsham, 1964

S. J. D. Green and Peregrine Horden, *All Souls and the Wider World: Statesmen, scholars, and adventurers*, OUP, 2011

Ian Grimwood, *A Little Chit of a Fellow: A biography of the Right Hon. Leslie Hore-Belisha*, Lewes, 2006

Gerard de Groot, *Liberal Crusader: The life of Sir Archibald Sinclair*, Hurst, 1993

Percy Groves, *Behind the Smoke Screen*, Faber, 1934

Francis de Guingand, *Operation Victory*, Hodder and Stoughton, 1947

Geirr Haarr, *The Battle for Norway, April–June 1940*, Seaforth, 2010

—*The German Invasion of Norway: April 1940*, Seaforth, 2011

Charles Wood, Viscount Halifax, *Lord Halifax's Ghost Book: A collection of stories of haunted houses, apparitions and supernatural occurrences*, Geoffrey Bles, 1939

Edward Wood, Earl of Halifax, *Fulness of Days*, Collins, 1957

—*John Keble*, Mowbray, 1909

—with Sir G. Lloyd, *The Great Opportunity*, London, 1918

Florence Harriman, *Mission to the North*, Harrap, 1941

Kenneth Harris, *Attlee*, Weidenfeld & Nicolson, 1995

Percy Harris, *Forty Years In and Out of Parliament*, A. Melrose, 1947

Duff Hart-Davis, *Peter Fleming*, Cape, 1974

Oliver Harvey, *The Diplomatic Diaries of Oliver Harvey, 1937–1940*, Collins, 1970

George Harvie-Watt, *Most of My Life*, London, 1983

Max Hastings, *Finest Years: Churchill as warlord*, HarperPress, 2009

Cuthbert Headlam, *Parliament and Politics in the Age of Churchill and Attlee: The Headlam diaries*, ed. Stuart Ball, CUP, 1999

Dennis Herbert, *Backbencher and Chairman: Some parliamentary reminiscences of Lord Hemingford*, John Murray, 1946

Tom Hickman, *Churchill's Bodyguard: The authorized biography of Walter H. Thompson*, Headline, 2005

Walter Hingston, *Never Give Up: The history of the King's Own Yorkshire Light Infantry, 1919–1942*, Lund Humphries, 1950

Samuel Hoare, *Nine Troubled Years*, Collins, 1954

—*The Unbroken Thread*, Collins, 1949

Stuart Hodgson, *Lord Halifax: An Appreciation*, Christophers, 1941

Leslie Hore-Belisha, *The Private Papers of Hore-Belisha*, ed. R. J. Minney, Aldershot, 1960

Richard Hough, *Winston and Clementine*, Bantam, 1991

Kevin Ingram, *Rebel: The Short Life of Esmond Romilly*, Weidenfeld & Nicolson, 1985

Edmund Ironside, *The Ironside Diaries: Edmund Ironside*, ed. R. Macleod and D. Kelly, Constable, 1962

Hastings Ismay, *The Memoirs of General the Lord Ismay*, Viking, 1960

Roy Jenkins, *Attlee: An interim biography*, Heinemann, 1948

—*Churchill*, Macmillan, 2001

Thomas Jones, *A Diary with Letters, 1931–1950*, OUP, 1954

A. L. Kennedy, *The Times and Appeasement: The journals of A. L. Kennedy*, ed. Gordon Martel, CUP, 2000

John Kennedy, *The Business of War*, Hutchinson, 1957

Joseph Kennedy, *Hostage to Fortune: The letters of Joseph P. Kennedy*, ed. Amanda Smith, Viking, 2001

François Kersaudy, *Norway 1940*, William Collins, 1990

—*Churchill contre Hitler: Norvège 1940, la victoire fatale*, Tallandier, 2002

Ian Kershaw, *Hitler 1936–45: Nemesis*, Penguin, 2001

Roger Keyes, *The Keyes Papers, Vol. III: 1939–45*, ed. Paul Halpern, Allen & Unwin, 1981

Lord Killearn, *The Killearn Diaries, 1934–1946: The diplomatic and personal record of Lord Killearn* [Sir Miles Lampson], Sidgwick & Jackson, 1972

Cecil King, *With Malice Toward None: A war diary*, Sidgwick & Jackson, 1970

William Mackenzie King, *The Diaries of William Lyon Mackenzie King*, http://www.bac-lac.gc.ca

Ivone Kirkpatrick, *The Inner Circle*, Macmillan, 1959

Halvdan Koht, *Norway, Neutral and Invaded*, Hutchinson, 1941

Joe Kynoch, *Norway 1940: The Forgotten Fiasco*, Airlife, 2002

Sheila Lawlor, *Churchill and the Politics of War 1940–1941*, CUP, 1994

Raymond Lee, *The London Journal of General Raymond E. Lee, 1940–1941*, Little Brown, 1971

James Lees-Milne, *Through Wood and Dale: Diaries, 1975–1978*, John Murray, 2001

—*Ceaseless Turmoil: Diaries, 1988–1992*, John Murray, 2004

Geoffrey Lewis, *Lord Hailsham: A life*, Cape, 1997

Jeremy Lewis, *David Astor*, Cape, 2016

Guy Liddell, *The Guy Liddell Diaries: MI5's director of counter-espionage in World War II*, ed. Nigel West, Routledge, 2005

Basil Liddell Hart, *The Liddell Hart Memoirs: The later years*, vol. 2, Putnam, 1965

David Lindsay, *The Crawford Papers, The Journals of David Lindsay, 1892–1940*, ed. John Vincent, MUP, 1984

Martin Lindsay, *The House of Commons*, Collins, 1947

—*So Few Got Through*, Pen & Sword, 2012

Robert Bruce Lockhart, *The Diaries of Sir Robert Bruce Lockhart: 1939–65*, Macmillan, 1973

Peter Longerich, *Goebbels*, Bodley Head, 2015

Frank Longford, *Eleven at No. 10: A personal view of Prime Ministers, 1931–1984*, Harrap, 1984

David Lough, *No More Champagne: Churchill and his money*, Head of Zeus, 2015

Wm. Roger Louis, *In the Name of God, Go!: Leo Amery and the British empire in the Age of Churchill*, Norton, 1992

John Lukacs, *Five Days in London, May 1940*, Yale, 1999

C. L. Lundin, *Finland in the Second World War*, Bloomington, 1957

Charles Lysaght, *Brendan Bracken*, Allen Lane, 1979

Norman McGowan, *My Years with Churchill*, Souvenir Press, 1958

Donald Macintyre, *Narvik*, Evans, 1959

Alexander Mackintosh, *Echoes of Big Ben: A journalist's parliamentary diary*, Jarrold, 1945

Harold Macmillan, *The Blast of War, 1939–1945*, Macmillan, 1967

Ivan Maisky, *The Maisky Diaries: The wartime revelations of Stalin's ambassador in London*, ed. Gabriel Gorodetsky, Yale, 2016

Norma Major, *Chequers*, Cross River Press, 1997

William Manchester, *The Caged Lion: Winston Spencer Churchill, 1932–1940*, Michael Joseph, 1988

L. E. H. Maund, *Assault from the Sea*, Methuen, 1949

Charles Mersey, *A Picture of Life*, John Murray, 1941

Jessica Mitford, *Decca: The Letters of Jessica Mitford*, ed. Peter Sussman, Weidenfeld & Nicolson, 2006

John Moore-Brabazon, *The Brabazon Story*, Heinemann, 1956

Alan Moorehead, *Gallipoli*, Hamish Hamilton, 1956

Roger Moorhouse, *Berlin at War: Life and death in Hitler's capital, 1939– 45*, Bodley Head, 2010

Charles Moran, *Churchill at War, 1940–1965*, Constable, 2002

Henry Morris-Jones, *Doctor in the Whips' Room*, Hale, 1955

Herbert Morrison, *An Autobiography*, Odhams, 1960

Morris Moses, *Spy Camera – The Minox Story*, Hove Foto Books, 1990

Nicholas Mosley, *Paradoxes of Peace*, Dalkey Archive Press, 2009

Noel Mostert, *The Line Upon a Wind*, Norton, 2008

J. L. Moulton, *The Norwegian Campaign of 1940*, Eyre & Spottiswoode, 1966

Ed Murrow, *This is London*, Cassell, 1941

John Naylor, *A Man and an Institution: Sir Maurice Hankey*, CUP, 1984

Elizabeth Nel, *Mr Churchill's Secretary*, Hodder & Stoughton, 1958

Harold Nicolson, *Diaries and Letters: 1930–1939, vol.1*, Collins, 1968

—*Diaries and Letters; 1939–1945, vol.2*, Athenaeum, 1966

John Julius Norwich, *Trying to Please*, Dovecote Press, 2008

Chris Ogden, *Life of the Party: The biography of Pamela Digby Churchill Hayward Harriman*, Little Brown, 1994

Lynne Olson, *Troublesome Young Men: The rebels who brought Churchill to power in 1940 and helped to save Britain*, Bloomsbury, 2007

George Orwell, *The Collected Essays, Journalism and Letters of George Orwell*, vol. 2, Secker & Warburg, 1968

Julian Paget, *The Crusading General: The life of General Sir Bernard Paget*, Pen & Sword, 2008

Frances Partridge, *A Pacifist's War, Diaries 1939–45*, Hogarth Press, 1978

Brian Patton, *Tales from the Canadian Rockies*, McClelland & Stewart, 1993

Clive Ponting, *Churchill*, Sinclair-Stevenson, 1994

Anthony Powell, *To Keep the Ball Rolling*, Heinemann, 1980

Henry Pownall, *Chief of Staff*, Archon, 1973

David Profumo, *Bringing the House Down: A family memoir*, John Murray, 2006

Erich Raeder, *Struggle for the Sea*, Kimber, 1959

Hermann Rauschning, *Hitler Speaks*, Butterworth, 1939

Irene Ravensdale, *In Many Rhythms: An autobiography*, Weidenfeld & Nicolson, 1953

John Reith, *Into the Wind*, Hodder and Stoughton, 1949

—*The Reith Diaries*, ed. Charles Stuart, Collins, 1975

Tim Renton, *Chief Whip: People, power and patronage in Westminster*, Politico, 2004

Paul Reynaud, *In the Thick of the Fight, 1930–1945*, Cassell, 1955

David Reynolds, *In Command of History*, Allen Lane, 2004

Robert Rhodes-James, *Victor Cazalet: A portrait*, Hamish Hamilton, 1976

—*A Spirit Undaunted: The political role of George VI*, Little Brown, 1998

Graham Rhys-Jones, *Churchill and the Norway Campaign*, Pen & Sword, 2008

Denis Richards, *Portal of Hungerford*, Heinemann, 1978

Charles Richardson, *From Churchill's Secret Circle to the BBC: The biography of Lieutenant General Sir Ian Jacob*, Brassey's, 1991

Charles Ritchie, *The Siren Years: Undiplomatic diaries, 1937–1945*, Macmillan, 1974

Andrew Roberts, *The Holy Fox: A biography of Lord Halifax*, Weidenfeld & Nicolson, 1991

—*Eminent Churchillians*, Weidenfeld & Nicolson, 1994

— *Churchill: Embattled Hero*, Phoenix, 1996

—*Hitler and Churchill: Secrets of leadership*, Weidenfeld & Nicolson, 2003

Giles Romilly, *The Privileged Nightmare*, Weidenfeld & Nicolson, 1954

Giles and Esmond Romilly, *Out of Bounds*, Hamish Hamilton, 1935

Kenneth Rose, *The Later Cecils*, Weidenfeld & Nicolson, 1975

Stephen Roskill, *Hankey: man of secrets*, Collins, 1974

—*Churchill and the Admirals*, Morrow, 1977

A. L. Rowse, *All Souls and Appeasement*, Macmillan, 1961

Anthony Seldon, *10 Downing Street: The illustrated history*, HarperCollins, 1999

Robert Self, *Neville Chamberlain: A biography*, Ashgate, 2006

J. E. Sewell, *Mirror of Britain*, Hodder & Stoughton, 1941

Geoffrey Shakespeare, *Let Candles Be Brought In*, Macdonald, 1949

Emanuel Shinwell, *Conflict without Malice*, Odhams, 1955

—*I've Lived Through It All*, Gollancz, 1973

—*Lead with the Left: My first ninety-six years*, Cassell, 1981

William Shirer, *Berlin Diary: The journal of a foreign correspondent, 1934–1941*, Hamish Hamilton, 1941

—*This is Berlin: Reporting from Nazi Germany, 1938–40*, Hutchinson, 1999

Claire Simpson, *Neville's Island*, Amazon, 2012

Nick Smart, *Neville Chamberlain*, Routledge, 2010

Mary Soames, *A Daughter's Tale: The memoirs of Winston Churchill's Youngest Daughter*, Random House, 2011

—*Clementine Churchill*, Cassell, 1979

Mary Soames, ed., *Speaking for Themselves: The Personal Letters of Winston and Clementine Churchill*, Doubleday, 1998

Edward L. Spears, *Prelude to Dunkirk*, William Heinemann, 1954

Stephen Spender, *New Selected Journals, 1939–45*, ed. Lara Feigel and John Sutherland, Faber, 2012

David Stafford, *Churchill and Secret Service*, John Murray, 1997

Graham Stewart, *Burying Caesar: Churchill, Chamberlain and the battle for the Tory Party*, Weidenfeld & Nicolson, 1999

Leland Stowe, *No Other Road to Freedom*, Faber, 1942

James Stuart, *Within the Fringe: An autobiography*, Bodley Head, 1967

John Sutherland, *Stephen Spender: The authorized biography*, Viking, 2004

Philip Cunliffe Lister, Earl of Swinton, *Sixty Years of Power: Some memories of the men who wielded it*, Heinemann, 1966

A. J. Sylvester, *Life with Lloyd George: The diary of A. J. Sylvester, 1931–45*, ed. Colin Cross, Macmillan, 1975

A. J. P. Taylor, *Beaverbrook*, Hamish Hamilton, 1972

—*A Personal History*, Hamish Hamilton, 1982

Laurence Thompson, *1940*, Collins, 1966

D. R. Thorpe, *The Uncrowned Prime Ministers*, Darkhorse, 1980

—*Alec Douglas-Home*, Sinclair-Stevenson, 1996

John Tilley, *Churchill's Favourite Socialist: A life of A. V. Alexander*, Manchester, 1995

Daniel Todman, *Britain's War*, Allen Lane, 2016

Philip Toynbee, *Friends Apart: A memoir of Esmond Romilly and Jasper Ridley in the thirties*, Sidgwick & Jackson, 1954

Ronald Tree, *When the Moon Was High*, Macmillan, 1975

Robert Vansittart, *The Mist Procession*, Hutchinson, 1958

Tristan de Vere Cole, *The Last Bastard?*, Wilton65, 2015

Philip Vian, *Action this Day: A war memoir*, Muller, 1960

Derek Walker-Smith, *Neville Chamberlain: Man of Peace*, Hale, 1940

Evelyn Waugh, *Put Out More Flags*, Penguin, 1943

—*Men at Arms*, Chapman & Hall, 1961

—*The Diaries of Evelyn Waugh*, ed. Michael Davie, Weidenfeld & Nicolson, 1976

Josiah Wedgwood, *Memoirs of a Fighting Life*, Hutchinson, 1940

John Wheeler-Bennett, *King George VI: His life and reign*, Macmillan, 1958

—ed., *Action this Day: Working with Churchill*, Macmillan, 1968

Meredith Whitford, *Churchill's Rebels, Jessica Mitford and Esmond Romilly*, Umbria Press, 2014

Francis Williams, *A Prime Minister Remembers*, Heinemann, 1961

—*Nothing so strange: an autobiography*, Cassell, 1970

—*A Pattern of Rulers*, London, 1965

Herbert Williams, *Politics – Grave and Gay*, Hutchinson, 1949

Harold Wilson, *A Prime Minister on Prime Ministers*, Weidenfeld & Nicolson, 1977

—*Attlee as I Knew Him*, ed. Geoffrey Dellar, London, 1983

Edward Winterton, *Orders of the Day*, Cassell, 1953

Frederick Woolton, *Memoirs*, Cassell, 1959

T. C. Worsley, *Fellow Travellers: A memoir of the thirties*, London, 1971

John Evelyn Wrench, *Geoffrey Dawson and Our Times*, Hutchinson, 1955

Alun Wyburn-Powell, *Clement Davies: Liberal leader*, Politico, 2003

JOURNALS, PERIODICALS AND LECTURES

Canadian Alpine Journal, 1929

David Cannadine, 'Churchill and Leadership: What lessons for today?', lecture delivered at Exeter College, Oxford, 23/5/2016

N. J. Crowson, 'Conservative Parliamentary Dissent Over Foreign Policy During the Premiership of Neville Chamberlain: Myth or Reality?' *Parliamentary History*, Vol. 14, 1995, 315–36

David Dilks, 'Appeasement Revisited', *University of Leeds Review*, vol. 15, no. 1, May 1972

—'Great Britain and Scandinavia in the Phoney War', *Scandinavian Journal of History*, 2, 1977, 29–51

—'Britain and Canada in the Age of Mackenzie King', Canada House lecture series 4, 1978

—'The Twilight War and the Fall of France: Chamberlain and Churchill in 1940', *Royal Historical Society*, Vol. 28 (1978), 61–86

—'Three Visitors to Canada: Baldwin, Chamberlain and Churchill', Canada House lecture series 28, March 1985

—'Britain and Germany before the War', lecture delivered at the Ludwig-Maximilians-University, Munich, 13 July 1998

Alfred Duff Cooper, 'A Candid Portrait', *American Mercury*, January 1940

John D. Fair, 'The Norway Campaign and Winston Churchill's rise to power in 1940: A study of perception and attribution', *English Historical Journal*, vol. 9, no. 3, Aug 1987

Peter Fleming, 'Return to Namsos', *Spectator*, 16/5/1970

Dingle Foot, 'Chamberlain's Downfall', *Guardian*, 8/5/1965

Patrick Higgins, unpublished biography of Rab Butler

Nellie Hozier, 'Prisoners in Germany', *English Review*, Feb 1915, 305–323

Kevin Jefferys, 'May 1940: The downfall of Neville Chamberlain', *Parliamentary History*, vol. 10, 1991, 363–78

Martin Lindsay, 'Reconnaissance', *Spectator*, 17/5/1940

—'Death of a Town', *Spectator*, 23/5/1940

London Gazette, Supplement, 8/7/1947

H. D. Loock, *'Weserübung* – A Step towards the Greater Germanic Reich', *Scandinavian Journal of History* 2, 1977, 67–88

Victor Macclure, 'Gladiators in Norway', *Blackwood's Magazine*, February/March 1941, vol. 249

Piers Mackesy, 'Churchill on Narvik', *Journal of the Royal United Services Institution*, 115, December 1970, 28

H. R. S. Massy, 'Operation in Central Norway, 1940', *London Gazette no. 37584*, 29/5/1946

Austen Mitchell, 'A Forbidden Glimpse of History', *The House* magazine, 20/8/1992

Phyllis Moir, 'I was Winston Churchill's Private Secretary', *Life Magazine*, 21/4/1941, 79

Harold Nicolson, 'Drama in Parliment', *Montreal Standard*, 11/5/1940

J. S. Rasmussen, 'Party Discipline in Wartime: The Downfall of the Chamberlain Government', *Journal of Politics*, xxxii, 1970, 379–406

David M. Roberts, 'Clement Davies and the Fall of Neville Chamberlain, 1939–40', *Welsh History Review*, viii, 1976

Nick Smart, 'Four Days in May: The Norway Debate and the Downfall of Neville Chamberlain', *Parliamentary History*, vol. 17, no. 2, 1998, 231

ACKNOWLEDGEMENTS

A private historian who is a novelist is also a fool if he does not step with special care into a territory which professional historians have mulled over now for more than seventy-five years. I am grateful to Noel Malcolm for strengthening a conviction that the writing of history need not be the domain solely of academics and specialists. We might not in each and every instance use the same methods, and we may ask different questions, yet all of us, novelists included, aim towards the same end: a faithful and plausible narrative reassembled from the material available.

To Andy Harries, I owe my initial research into the Norway Debate. I am indebted to him and to Kerry Gill-Pryde for sowing the idea that Churchill's sudden arrival in No. 10 merited closer analysis.

I am grateful to the Warden and Fellows of All Souls College, Oxford, for giving me a Visiting Fellowship in 2016, which, aside from a sizeable metal key to the matchless Codrington Library, provided a daily reminder of several of the players in this dramatic story – not least through the intense gaze of their portraits: Leo Amery, John Simon, Geoffrey Dawson, Quintin Hogg, and Edward Halifax, who regarded All Souls as 'a second home', and, being six foot five, installed in the Warden's Lodgings (according to Keith Thomas, who overlapped with him), an extra-long bath so that he might turn off the taps with his toes.

In the House of Commons, I am grateful to Robin Fell, former Door-keeper and acting Deputy Serjeant at Arms for making real the division procedure; and to Lord Lisvane, former Chief Clerk, for the benefit of his constitutional expertise, and for showing me the Chamber and the voting Lobbies, and to Louise Clarke for letting me hold the sandglass used for measuring the six minutes before the vote of 8 May 1940.

For access to collections at the Bodleian, I am grateful (as I have been for twenty-five years) to Colin Harris of the Special Collections Department, and to Michael Hughes.

For permission to quote from the Neville Chamberlain papers, I would like to thank the Cadbury Research Library, University of Birmingham, and Martin Killeen.

For permission to quote from the Churchill papers at the Churchill Archives Centre in Cambridge, I am grateful to Churchill College and Emma Soames, and to Allen Packwood for his advice and guidance.

For permission to quote from Lord Halifax's papers at the Borthwick Institute in York, I would like to thank the Earl of Halifax and Colin Webb.

For permission to quote from Baba Metcalfe's diaries and letters, I would like to thank Julian Metcalfe.

For access to and permission to quote from Charles Peake's diary, I would like to thank Michael Peake.

For access to and permission to quote from the Salisbury Papers, I would like to thank Robert Salisbury and Robin Harcourt Williams; also Shana Fleming, and Sarah Whale at the Archives and Historic Collections Department at Hatfield House.

For access to and permission to quote from Peter Fleming's diaries, letters and papers, I would like to thank Kate Grimond, and Kate Arnold-Foster at the University of Reading's Special Collections.

For permission to quote from the Parliamentary Archives, I would like to thank Mari Takayanagi and Annie Pinder.

For access to and permission to quote from the Clement Davies Papers in the National Library of Wales Archives, I would like to thank Martin Robson Riley and Christopher Clement-Davies.

For permission to quote from his taped interview with Valerie Cole, I would like to thank Martyn Downer.

For securing a copy of Harold Nicolson's article in the *Montreal Standard,* I would like to thank Janis Johnson and Andrew Miller at the Canadian Senate in Ottawa.

For access to Neville Chamberlain's bird collection, I would like to thank Hein van Grouw and Robert Prys-Jones at the Natural History Museum, Tring.

For assistance in tracking down survivors of 'Maurice Force' and for taking me to Krogs Farm, and for permission to use his photographs, I would like to thank Paul Kiddell.

I am indebted to Anne de Courcy for putting at my disposal her archives, including her transcriptions of Irene Ravensdale's diaries and related material.

For permission to quote from the Harry Crookshank papers at the Bodleian, I would like to thank Elizabeth Crookshank.

For permission to quote from the John Simon papers at the Bodleian, I would like to thank John Simon.

For permission to quote from the Arthur Greenwood papers at the Bodleian, I would like to thank Susie Greenwood.

For permission to quote from Lord Woolton's papers at the Bodleian, I would like to thank the Earl of Woolton.

For permission to quote from the Walter Monckton papers at Balliol College, I would like to thank Walter Monckton's Trustees and Balliol College, Oxford.

For permission to quote from the Mary Soames papers at the Churchill Archives Centre, I would like to thank Emma Soames and Curtis Brown Group Ltd.

For permission to quote from the Leo Amery papers at the Churchill Archives Centre I would like to thank Churchill College, Cambridge.

For permission to quote from the Valentine Lawford papers at the Churchill Archives Centre, I would like to thank Charles Tilbury.

For permission to quote from the John Colville papers at the Churchill Archives Centre, I would like to thank Rupert Colville.

For permission to quote from Giles Romilly's diaries, letters and papers, I would like to thank Edmund and Lizzie Romilly and Mary Marshall.

For permission to quote from Martin Lindsay's letters and books, I would like to thank Jacynth Fitzalan Howard, Clare Lindsay, Nicoletta Lindsay.

For permission to quote from Irene Ravensdale's papers, I would like to thank Nicholas Mosley.

For permission to quote from Frank Lodge's unpublished diary, I would like to thank Elaine and Rosemary Lodge.

For permission to quote from Geoffrey Shakespeare's papers, I would like to thank James and Tom Shakespeare.

For permission to quote from Henry Morris-Jones's diary, I would like to thank the Flintshire Records Office.

For permission to quote from Nancy Dugdale's letters, I would like to thank James Crathorne.

For permission to quote from Ivan Maisky's diary and for access to unpublished entries, I would like to thank Gabriel Gorodetsky and Yale University Press.

For permission to quote from Evelyn Waugh's *Put out More Flags* and *Men at Arms*, and from his diaries, I would like to thank Alexander Waugh.

I would like to express my gratitude to the following:

Clarissa Avon, Justin and Jane Byam Shaw, Frances Campbell-Preston, Arthur Chamberlain, Francis and Mary Chamberlain, Gay Charteris, Christopher Clement-Davies, Jonathan and Zara Colchester, James Crathorne, Julie Crocker, David Dilks, Martyn Downer, Davina Eastwood, David Faber, Tom Fowler, Gabriel Gorodetsky, Simon Green, Kate Grimond, Duff Hart-Davis, John Hatt, John Hegarty, Patrick Higgins, Diana Holderness, Jacynth Fitzalan Howard, Julian Jackson, François Kersaudy, Herry Lawford, Elaine Lodge, Angela Maclean, Christopher MacLehose, Daisy McNally, Mary Marshall, Julian Metcalfe, Gaye Morgan, Jane Moyle, John Julius Norwich, Avner Offer, Allen Packwood, Julian Paget, Michael Peake, Mary Pearson, Henry Porter, Nicholas and Verity Ravensdale, Graham Rhys-Jones, Andrew Roberts, David Robson, Nicholas Rodger, Edmund and Lizzie Romilly, Dan Rootham, Holly Ross, Arthur Rucker, James Shakespeare, Claire Simpson, Nick Smart, Emma Soames, Keith Thomas, Richard Thorpe, Charles Tilbury, Rick Trainor, Hugo Vickers, John Vickers, Gwendolen Webster, Meredith Whitford, Philip Ziegler, Richard Zimler.

In Norway: Per and Wenche Fahsing, Geirr Haarr, William Hakvaag, Martin Hargensen, Kjell Olav Huage, Kristian Helgesen, Gunnar Hojem, Paul Kiddell, Ivar Kraglund, Ted Kristiansen, Trond Kristiansen, Storm Levensen, Hjørdis Mikalsen, Ulf Eirik Torgersen, Ivan Vanya, Torlaug Werstad.

I would like to thank Jack Deverell, David Dilks, Geirr Haarr, Paul Kiddell, Robert Lisvane and Nicholas Rodger for reading early drafts and for their comments; my editor Liz Foley for her steady encouragement; Rachel

Cugnoni for her faith; Mikaela Pedlow for her limitless patience; my agents, the late Gillon Aitken and Clare Alexander; and Lesley Thorne and the staff at Aitken Alexander.

I have made every effort to trace copyright holders. I greatly regret any omissions. These will be rectified in future editions.

INDEX